C000246890

STRE

East Kent

Ashford, Canterbury, Dover, Folkestone, Maidstone, Margate

www.philips-maps.co.uk
First published in 1989 by
Philip's, a division of
Octopus Publishing Group Ltd
www.octopusbooks.co.uk
2–4 Heron Quays, London E14 4JP
An Hachette UK Company
www.hachettelivre.co.uk

Fourth edition 2009
First impression 2009
EKTDA

ISBN 978-1-84907-019-5 (pocket)

© Philip's 2009

 Ordnance Survey®

This product includes mapping data licensed from
Ordnance Survey® with the permission of the
Controller of Her Majesty's Stationery Office.
© Crown copyright 2009. All rights reserved.
Licence number 100011710.

Speed camera data provided by
PocketGPSWorld.com Ltd

Post Office is a trade mark of Post Office Ltd in the
UK and other countries.

Printed by Toppan, China

Contents

II Mobile safety cameras

III **Key to map symbols**

IV **Key to map pages**

VI **Route planning**

VIII Major administrative and Postcode boundaries

1 **Street maps** at 2⅔ inches to 1 mile

210 **Index** of towns, villages, streets, hospitals, industrial estates, railway stations, schools, shopping centres, universities and places of interest

Digital Data

The exceptionally high-quality mapping found in this atlas is available as digital data in TIFF format, which is easily convertible to other bitmapped (raster) image formats.

The index is also available in digital form as a standard database table. It contains all the details found in the printed index together with the National Grid reference for the map square in which each entry is named.

For further information and to discuss your requirements, please contact
victoria.dawbarn@philips-maps.co.uk

II

Mobile safety cameras

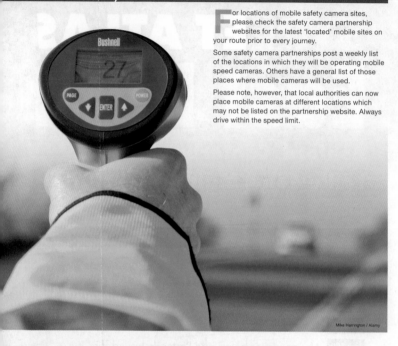

For locations of mobile safety camera sites, please check the safety camera partnership websites for the latest 'located' mobile sites on your route prior to every journey.

Some safety camera partnerships post a weekly list of the locations in which they will be operating mobile speed cameras. Others have a general list of those places where mobile cameras will be used.

Please note, however, that local authorities can now place mobile cameras at different locations which may not be listed on the partnership website. Always drive within the speed limit.

Mike Harrington / Alamy

Useful websites

Kent and Medway Safety Camera Partnership
www.kmscp.org

London Safety Camera Partnership
www.lscp.org.uk

Surrey Safety Camera Partnership
www.surrey-safecam.org

Sussex Safer Roads Partnership
www.sussexsaferroads.gov.uk

Further information
www.dvla.gov.uk
www.thinkroadsafety.gov.uk
www.dft.gov.uk
www.road-safe.org

III

Key to map symbols

Motorway with junction number	
Primary route – dual/single carriageway	
A road – dual/single carriageway	
B road – dual/single carriageway	
Minor road – dual/single carriageway	
Other minor road – dual/single carriageway	
Road under construction	
Tunnel, covered road	
Speed cameras – single, multiple	
Rural track, private road or narrow road in urban area	
Gate or obstruction to traffic – restrictions may not apply at all times or to all vehicles	
Path, bridleway, byway open to all traffic, restricted byway	
Pedestrianised area	
Postcode boundaries	
County or unitary authority boundaries	
Railway with station	
Tunnel	
Railway under construction	
Metro station	
Private railway station	
Miniature railway	
Tramway, tramway under construction	
Tram stop, tram stop under construction	
Bus, coach station	

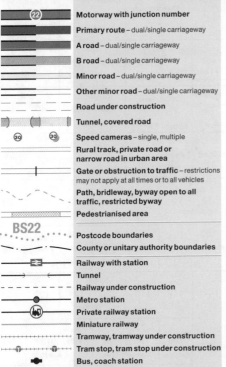

Ambulance station	
Coastguard station	
Fire station	
Police station	
Accident and Emergency entrance to hospital	
Hospital	
Place of worship	
Information centre – open all year	
Shopping centre, parking	
Park and Ride, Post Office	
Camping site, caravan site	
Golf course, picnic site	
Non-Roman antiquity, Roman antiquity	
Important buildings, schools, colleges, universities and hospitals	
Woods, built-up area	
Water name	
River, weir	
Stream	
Canal, lock, tunnel	
Water	
Tidal water	

Adjoining page indicators and overlap bands – the colour of the arrow and band indicates the scale of the adjoining or overlapping page (see scale below)

The dark grey border on the inside edge of some pages indicates that the mapping does not continue onto the adjacent page

The small numbers around the edges of the maps identify the 1-kilometre National Grid lines

Abbreviations

Acad	Academy	Meml	Memorial
Allot Gdns	Allotments	Mon	Monument
Cemy	Cemetery	Mus	Museum
C Ctr	Civic centre	Obsy	Observatory
CH	Club house	Pal	Royal palace
Coll	College	PH	Public house
Crem	Crematorium	Recn Gd	Recreation ground
Ent	Enterprise		
Ex H	Exhibition hall	Resr	Reservoir
Ind Est	Industrial Estate	Ret Pk	Retail park
IRB Sta	Inshore rescue boat station	Sch	School
		Sh Ctr	Shopping centre
Inst	Institute	TH	Town hall / house
Ct	Law court	Trad Est	Trading estate
L Ctr	Leisure centre	Univ	University
LC	Level crossing	W Twr	Water tower
Liby	Library	Wks	Works
Mkt	Market	YH	Youth hostel

The map scale on the pages numbered in blue is 2⅔ inches to 1 mile
4.2 cm to 1 km • 1:23810

0 ¼ mile ½ mile ¾ mile 1 mile
0 250m 500m 750m 1km

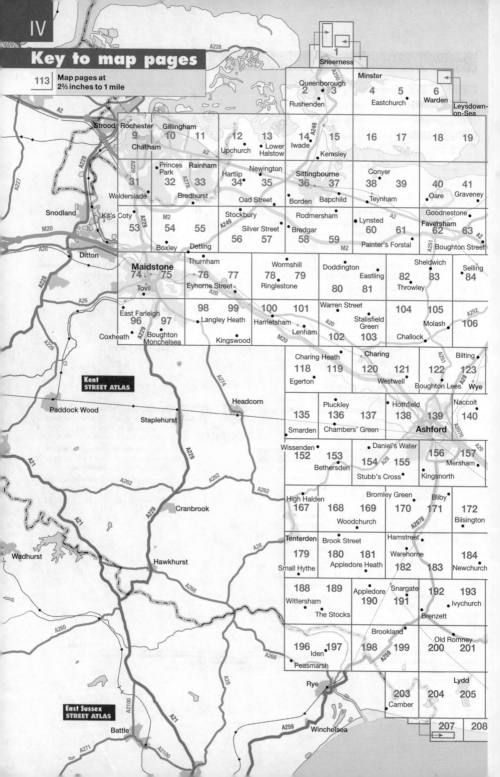

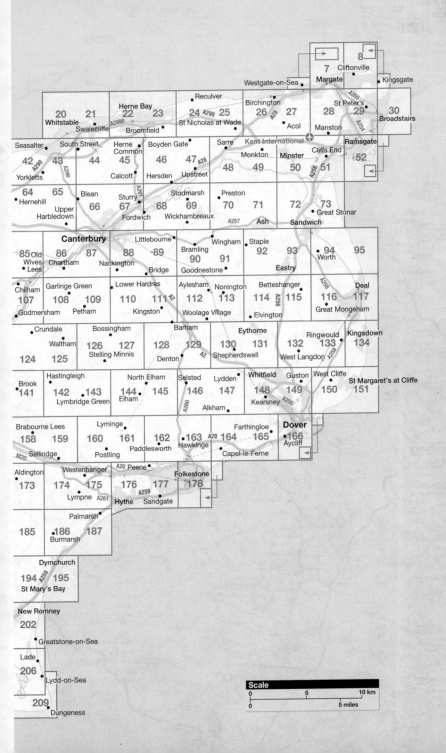

V

7 Cliftonville
Margate
Westgate-on-Sea
Kingsgate

20 Whitstable
21
Herne Bay 22 23
A2990
Reculver
24 A299 25
St Nicholas at Wade
Birchington 26 A28 27
Acol
St Peter's 28 29
Manston
30 Broadstairs

Swalecliffe
Broomfield

Seasalter 42
A299
43
A290
South Street 44
Herne Common 45
Calcott
Boyden Gate 46
Hersden
Sarre 47 A28
Upstreet 48
Kent International 49
Monkton 50
Minster 51
Cliffs End
A258
Ramsgate 52

Yorkletts

64 Hernehill
65
Blean 66
Upper Harbledown
Sturry 67
Fordwich
68
Stodmarsh 69
Wickhambreaux
Preston 70
71
Ash
72
Sandwich
73 Great Stonar
A257

Canterbury

85 Old Wives Lees
86 Chartham
87
Littlebourne 88
Nackington
89 Bridge
Bramling 90
Goodnestone
Wingham 91
Staple 92
93
Eastry
94 Worth
95

Chilham 107
Garlinge Green 108
Godmersham
109
Petham
Lower Hardres 110
Kingston
111 A2
Aylesham 112
Woolage Village
Nonington 113
Elvington
Betteshanger 114 A256 115
116 Great Mongeham
Deal 117

Crundale
Waltham 124
125
Bossingham 126
127
Stelling Minnis
Barham 128
Denton
129 A2
Eythorne 130
Shepherdswell
131 West Langdon
Ringwould 132
133 A258
Kingsdown 134

Brook 141
Hastingleigh 142
143 Lymbridge Green
North Elham 144
Elham
145
Selsted 146
A260
Alkham
Lydden 147
Whitfield 148
Kearsney
Guston 149
West Cliffe 150
St Margaret's at Cliffe 151

Brabourne Lees 158
159
Lyminge 160
Postling
161
Paddlesworth 162
Hawkinge
163 A20
Capel-le-Ferne
164
165
Dover 166 Aycliff

Sellindge
M20

Aldington 173
Westenhanger 174
175
Lympne A261
A20 Peene 176
A259
Hythe
177
Sandgate
Folkestone 178

Palmarsh

185
186
Burmarsh
187

Dymchurch

194 A259 195
St Mary's Bay

New Romney

202

Greatstone-on-Sea

Lade 206

Lydd-on-Sea

209 Dungeness

Scale
0   5   10 km
0   5 miles

Warden
Leysdown-on-Sea

Westgate on Sea **Margate** Cliftonville Kingsgate
Minnis Bay Northdown
Birchington St Peter's **BROADSTAIRS**
Reculver Hillborough St Nicholas
HERNE BAY Beltinge at Wade Acol Northwood
WHITSTABLE Tankerton Swalecliffe Broomfield A28 A299 Manston Dumpton
Greenhill Herne Boyden A253 INTERNATIONAL **Ramsgate**
Seasalter Chestfield Gate Sarre Monkton P-Way Cliffsend
South Hoath Chislet Minster OOSTENDE 4:00
Street Calcott Westbere Pegwell BOULOGNE 1:15
Graveney Yorkletts Hersden West Stourmouth Stour Pegwell
Goodnestone A299 Dargate Honey Broadoak Grove East Stourmouth Bay
Preston Hernhill Hill Tyler Preston Westmarsh Sandwich
Boughton Street Dunkirk Blean Hill Hales Sturry Westbere Stodmarsh Ware Bay
M2 South Street Rough Place Fordwich Wickhambreux Elmstone Hoaden Great Stonar
North Overland Chartham Common **Canterbury** Ickham Ash
Street Selling Hatch Harbledown Littlebourne Wingham Marshborough Woodnesborough **Sandwich**
Shottenden Shalmsford Nackington A2 Bekesbourne Staple Gore Stone Cross
dismere Chilham Street Street End Lower Patrixbourne Goodnestone Knowlton Ham Finglesham Worth
Molash Garlinge Hardres Adisham Eastry Sholden
Green Bishopsbourne Chillenden **DEAL**
Bilting Godmersham Petham Upper Hardres Kingston Snowdown Easole Street Bettshanger Walmer
Sole Street Court Barham Nonington Northbourne THE
Wye Hassell Bossingham Derringstone Womenswold Elvington Great DOWNS
Kennington Street Waltham Woolage Shepherdswell Mongeham Ripple Kingsdown
Hinxhill Brook Stelling Green Denton Coxhill Coldred West East Martin Martin Mill
Brabourne Minnis Windmore Langdon Studdal Ringwould
rough Willesborough Lees Hastingleigh Elmsted Wootton Lydden East Sutton **St Margaret's at Cliffe**
Bodsham Selsted Ewell Langdon **Whitfield** Guston West St Margaret's Bay
Mersham Brabourne Lees Lymbridge Swingfield Minnis Temple Cliffe
Cheeseman's Stowting Green Street Ewell CALAIS 1:30
Green Smeeth Rhodes Ottinge Swingfield Alkham Buckland DUNKERQUE 1:45
Aldington Clap Hill Sellindge Minnis Densole Drellingore West Maxton **DOVER**
Frith Sellinge Lyminge Paddlesworth Hawkinge Houghton Farthingloe Aycliff BOULOGNE 1:45
Bonnington Court-at-Street Postling Etchinghill **CHANNEL** Capel le DIEPPE 4:15
Lympne Beachborough Newington **TUNNEL** Ferne
Bilsington West Hythe Stanford Cheriton East Wear CHANNEL TUNNEL
Newchurch Pedlinge **Folkestone** Bay
Saltwood
HYTHE Sandgate
Palmarsh
Burmarsh A259

St Mary **Dymchurch**
in the Marsh
Ivychurch **St Mary's Bay**

A259 New Littlestone on Sea
Romney
Greatstone on Sea

Lydd Lydd on Sea

Scale
0   5   10km
0   5 miles

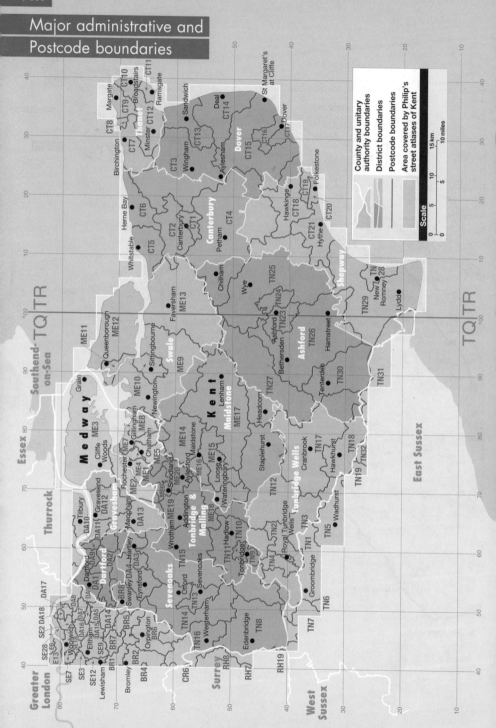

VIII

Major administrative and Postcode boundaries

Scale

County and unitary authority boundaries
District boundaries
Postcode boundaries
Area covered by Philip's street atlases of Kent

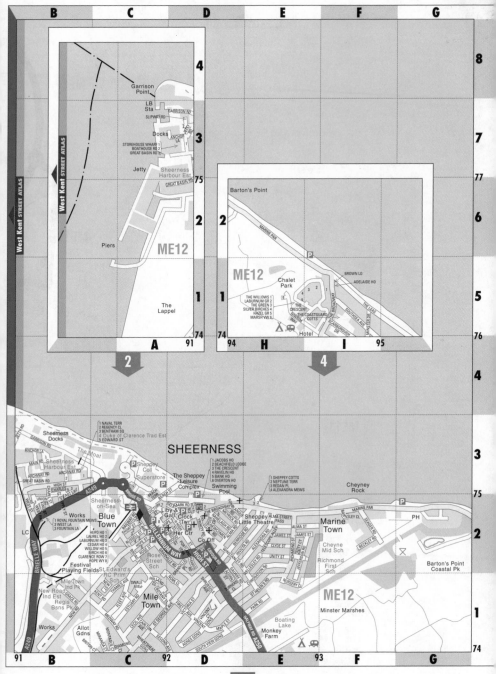

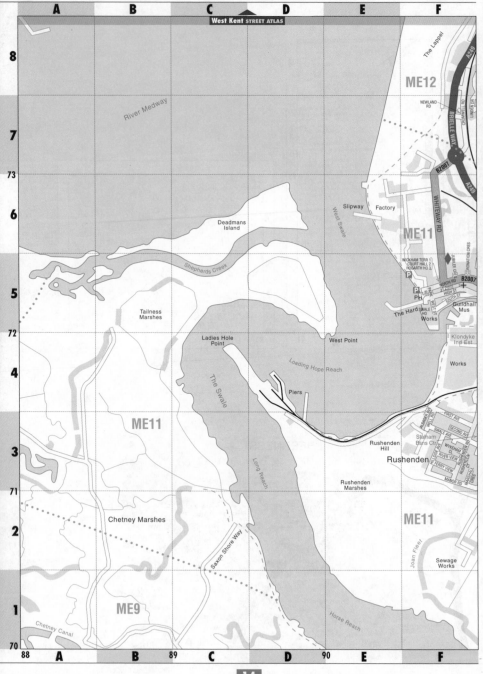

West Kent STREET ATLAS

A   B   C   D   E   F

8

River Medway

7

73

6

Deadmans
Island

Slipway   Factory

West Swale

ME12

NEWLAND
RD

BRIELLE WAY

B2007

WHITEWAY RD

A249

ME11

WICKHAM TERR 1
COURT HALL 2
HOGARTH HO 3

JUBILEE DR

CORONATION CRES

B2007

Shepherds Creek

Tailness
Marshes

5

PH
The Hard

NORTH RD
HIGH ST
WELLS RD
SOUTH RD
WALL HO

Guildhall
Mus

Works

72

Ladies Hole
Point

West Point

Klondyke
Ind Est

Works

4

The Swale

Loading Hope Reach

Piers

FIRST AVE
BRIDGES RD
SWALE AVE
SECOND AVE
WYKEHAM CL
RIVER VIEW
TERRY VIEW
MANOR RD

ME11

3

Long Reach

Rushenden
Hill

Staham
Bsns Ctr

Rushenden

71

Rushenden
Marshes

2

Chetney Marshes

Saxon Shore Way

ME11

Joan Fleet

Sewage
Works

1

ME9

Horse Reach

Chetney Canal

70

88   A   B   89   C   D   90   E   F

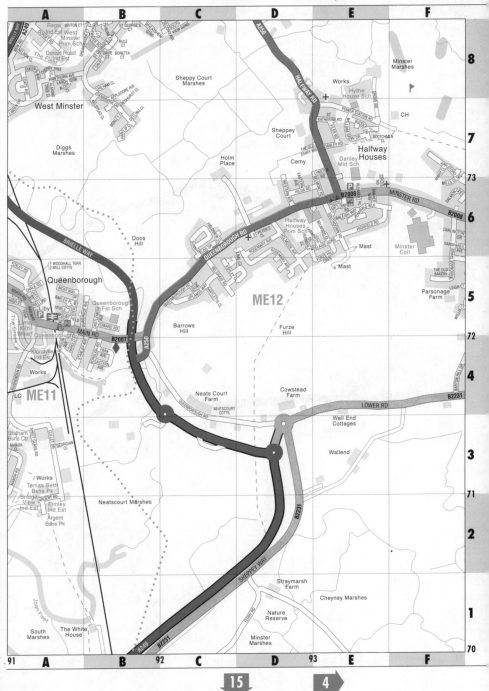

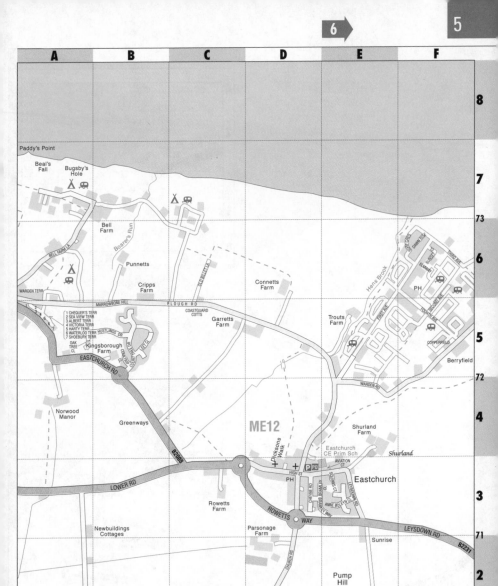

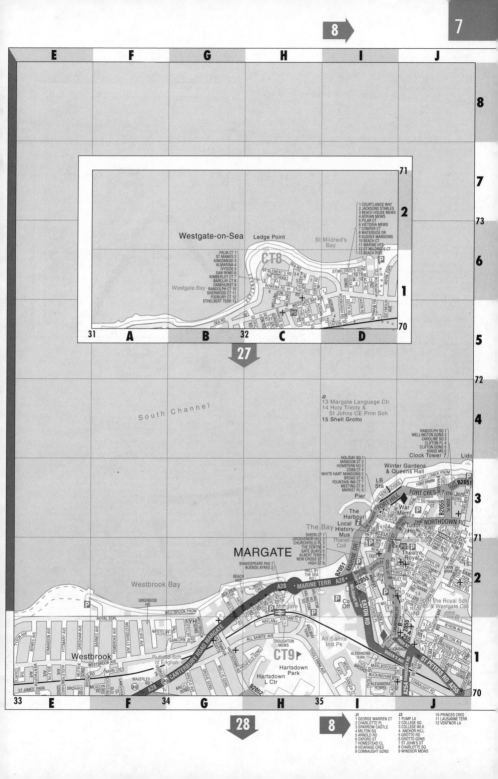

E   F   G   H   I   J

8

7

71

73

2

6

1 COURTLANDS WAY
2 JACKSONS STABLES
3 BEACH HOUSE MEWS
4 ADRIAN MEWS
5 PILAR CT
6 VICTORIA MEWS
7 CONIFER CT
8 WATERSIDE DR
9 SUSSEX MANSIONS
10 BEACH CT
11 MARINE HTS
12 ST MILDREDS CT
13 BEACH RISE

Westgate-on-Sea   Ledge Point   St Mildred's Bay

PALM CT 1
ST MAWES 2
KINGSMEAD 3
ALMARINA 4
IVYSIDE 5
SAN REMO 6
KIMBERLEY CT 7
BARCLAY CT 8
DANEHURST 9
RANDOLPH CT 10
SHERWOOD CT 11
FODBURY CT 12
ETHELBERT TERR 13

CT8

St Mildred's Gdns

Westgate Bay

St Clement's Rd
The School

Rowena Rd

Westgate Bay Ave

1

70

31   A   B   32   C   D

27

5

72

4

South Channel

J2
13 Margate Language Ctr
14 Holy Trinity &
St Johns CE Prim Sch
15 Shell Grotto

RANDOLPH SQ 1
WELLINGTON GDNS 2
CAROLINE SQ 3
CLIFTON PL 4
CLIFTON GDNS 5
KINGS MS 6
Clock Tower 7

Lido

HOLIDAY SQ 1
MANSION ST 2
HOMEFERN HO 3
COBB CT 4
WHITE HART MANSIONS 5
BROAD ST 6
FOUNTAIN INN CT 7
MEETING CT 8
MARKET PL 9

Winter Gardens
& Queens Hall

LB
Sta

FORT CRES

B2051

Pier

The Harbour
Local
History
Mus

FORT HILL
War
Mem

Fort Prom

NORTHDOWN RD

B2055

3

71

SHEEN CT 1
GROSVENOR HILL 2
CHURCHFIELD PL 3
THE CENTRE 4
GATE QUAYS 5
ALBERT TERR 6
NEW CROSS ST 7
HIGH ST 8

The Bay

MARGATE

Thanet
Coll

Theatre
Royal

Tudor
Ho

2

SHAKESPEARE PAS 1
BUENOS AYRES 2

BEACH
RD

Westbrook Bay

GREENSIDE
HO

MARINE TERR

A28

Margate

Co
Off

The Royal Sch
& Westgate Coll

BYRON AV

EATON RD

ST PETERS RD
A255

1

Westbrook

WESTCLIFF

Rutland Sch
of English

CANTERBURY ROAD MARGATE
A28

ALL SAINTS AVE

CT9

Hartsdown
Park

Hartsdown
L Ctr

All Saints
Ind Pk

ALEXANDRA
TERR

MARLBOROUGH

CONNAUGHT RD

70

33   E   F   34   G   H   35   I   J

J1
1 GEORGE WARREN CT
2 CHARLOTTE PL
3 SPARROW CASTLE
4 MILTON SQ
5 ARNOLD RD
6 OXFORD ST
7 HOMESTEAD CL
8 VICARAGE CRES
9 CONNAUGHT GDNS

J2
1 PUMP LA
2 COLLEGE SQ
3 COLLEGE WLK
4 ANCHOR HILL
5 GROTTO RD
6 GROTTO GDNS
7 ST JOHN'S ST
8 CHARLOTTE SQ
9 WINDSOR MEWS

10 PRINCES CRES
11 LAUSANNE TERR
12 VENTNOR LA

| A | B | C | D | E | F |

8

7

73

6

Botany Bay

71

Neptune's Tower

2

Kingsgate Bay

PH

Castle Keep Hotel

KINGSGATE CASTLE

Kingsgate

Hackemdown Point

1

Port Regis

Tower

Joss Bay

WHITENESS RD

JOSS GAP RD

B2052

CONVENT RD

ELMWOOD AVE

B2052

70

CT10

39 G H 40

30

5

72

4

Walpole Bay

Palm Bay

Long Nose Spit

Foreness Point

ETHELBERT TERR 1
SAMUEL CT 2
CLIFTONVILLE CT 3
CLEVELAND CT 4
QUEENS PAR 5
HATHERLEY CT 6
CARLTON MANSIONS 7
GODWIN COTTS 8
SANDOWN COTTS 9
ATHENA CT 10

MARGATE

CLIFTONVILLE CT 1
QUEENS LODGE 2
FLORENCE CT 3
LYNTON COURT MANSIONS
MAURICE CT 5
SANDBACH HO 6
QUEEN'S PROM.
LEWIS CRES

1 MARLBOROUGH HO
2 BLENHEIM HO
3 NORTHUMBERLAND CT

Miniature Golf Course

PRINCE'S WLK

THE RIDINGS

NEWGATE LOWER PROM.
NEWGATE PROM.

1 ROBINA CT
2 LEICESTER CT

3 EASTERN ESPL

PALM BAY AVE

B2051 ETHELBERT CRES

PERCY RD

STANLEY RD

ST PAUL'S RD

GOODWIN BGLWS

ALBION RD

BERESFORD GDNS

WELLINGTON HO

GOODWIN CT

Palm Bay CP Sch

SPRINGFIELD RD

KNOCKHALL RD

71

TURNER ST

OLIVE CT

Cliftonville

MAGNOLIA AVE

Anglian Sch of English

CT9

CORNWALL GDNS

RUTLAND AVE

CHURCHFIELD

SALTWOOD GDNS

2

1 BROCKLEY RD
2 FAIRVIEW CL
3 NIGHTINGALE A
4 CRESCENT HO
5 DANE PARK VILLAS

Cliftonville Prim Sch

Laleham CP Sch

PRINCESS MARGARET AVE

NORTHDOWN RD

FITZROY AVE

Dane Park

1 INVICTA HO
2 APPLEDORE CL

NORTHDOWN RD

Liby P

WALTHAM CL 1
ROSEACRE CT 2

1

VICTORIA AVE

NORTHDOWN PARK RD

QUEEN ELIZABETH AVE

PARK CT

WEST PARK RD

Northdown Park

Northdown

NURSERY GDNS

GEORGE HILL RD

GREYFRIARS CL

B2052

COLLEGE RD

ST ANTHONY'S WAY
ADRIAM WAY
DENTON WAY
ELHAM CL
LYMN... WAY

St Anthony's Sch

70

B2052

Drapers Windmill

LALEHAM WLK 1
WINDSOR CT 2
MEADOW CT 3
UPPER DANE CT 4

MILLMEAD RD

B2052

Northdown Prim Sch

ST MICHAELS AVE

B2052

B2053

CT10

Nursery

HILL RD

36 A B 37 C D 38 E F

A1
1 THE AVENUE
2 ST PETERS FOOTPATH

B2
1 ADAM CT.
2 JAMES CT.
3 RUTLAND HO
4 WESTMOUNT HO
5 HIGHFIELD CT
6 REBECCA CT
7 RICHARD CT
8 LEONA CT

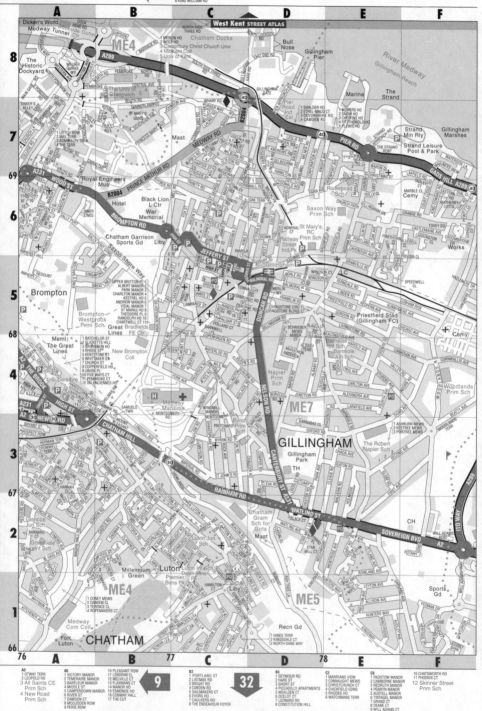

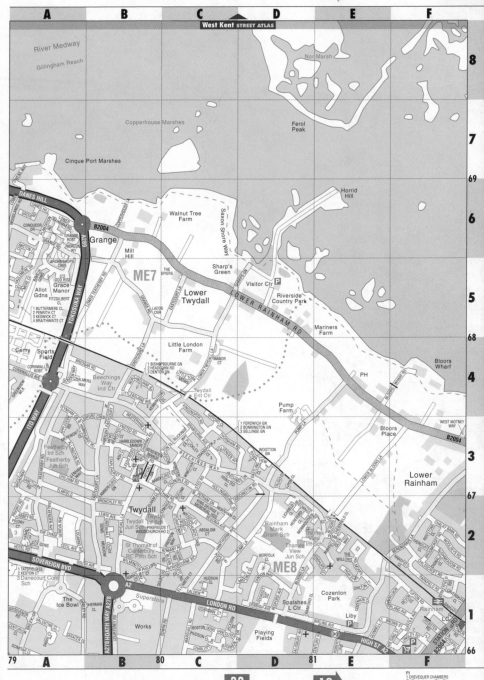

West Kent STREET ATLAS

F1
1 CREVEQUER CHAMBERS
2 Rainham Sh Ctr
3 GRESHAM CL
4 HARRISON CT
5 MAPLINS CL
6 SIGNAL CT
7 SUFFOLK CT

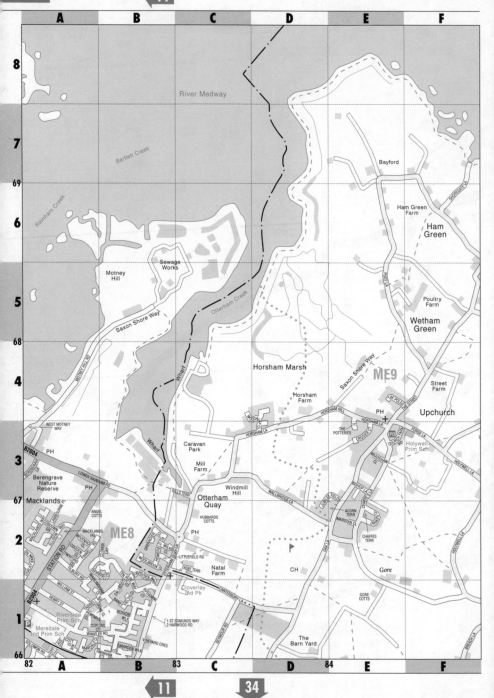

A B C D E F

8

Greenborough
Marshes

Millfordhope Creek

Slaughterhouse
Point

The Shade

Stangate Creek

Millfordhope
Marsh

7

Twinney Creek

69

Barksore
Marshes

River Medway

6

Callows
House

Halstow Creek

Funton Creek

5

Twinney
Wharf

68

Twinney
Acre

FROG FARM
COTTS

Saxon Shore Way

Frog
Farm

Funton
Brick Works

4

Sewage
Works

RASPBERRY HILL LA

Funton

Saxon Shore Way

Great Barksore

+

GREENWAYS

Stray Farm

Little
Barksore

Tiptree Hill

3

BELL
COTTS

THE STREET

PH

THE
CRESCENT

BASSER HILL

WESTMOR

VICARAGE
COTTS

Holywell

Green
Farm

BURNTWICK DR

**Lower
Halstow**

SEA VIEW
COTTS

SCHOOL LA

CUMBERLAND DR

ME9

Tiptree

67

LAMBERT RD

Elm
Farm

WESTFIELD
COTTS

Lower Halstow
Prim Sch

Callum
Hill

STICKFAST LA

2

BERENGRAVE LA

The
Laurels

WARDWELL LA

HIGH OAK HILL

Boxted
Farm

Great
Norwood

1

BEACON HILL

Hawes Wood

66

85 **A** **B** 86 **C** **D** 87 **E** **F**

13
2

A B C D E F

8

Chetney
Hill

The Shade

Horse Reach

Ferry Marshes

Saxon Shore Way

7

Funton Reach

Saxon Shore Way

69

River Medway

Chetney
Cottages

Marshbank

Belt Ferry Rd

Ridham Fleet

6

Bedlams
Bottom

Raspberry
Hill

RASPBERRY HILL LA

Willow
Cottages

Willow Bank
Ind Est

Sheppey Way

A249

5

Raspberry Hill
Park

68

Saxon Shore Way

SHOOTERS CH
STANGATE
DR
UPPER FMS

ME9

Iwade
Prim Sch

PH

THE STREET

CHURCH

SCHOOL MS
PLANTATION
CT

4

SEW

ROOKERY
VW

THE
SALTINGS

SCHOOL LA

EVERGREEN
CT

MEADOW VW

LINDEN WAY

SPRINGDALE

WOODPECKER DR

TURNSTONE CL

SHELDUCK
CL

Iwade

COLESHALL
COTTS

MASEFIELD DR

GERSTONE

HELEN THOMPSON CL

WINDRUSH CL

COMPRAY

SANDPIPER
LA

3

Moat Farm
Cottages

Culnell's
Cottages

Coleshall
Farm

COLSON DR

TERN WAY

PINTAIL DR

WIGEON
RD

GREENSHANKS

Coleshall

Orchard
Farm

Reservoir

67

ME10

FEATHERBED LA

B2005

LC

2

Culnells

GROVEHURST RD

Great
Grovehurst

1 OSTEND CT
2 BRUGES CT
3 MELLOR ROW
4 MONARCH DR
5 PREMIER WAY
6 EDWARD DR
7 MARTIN CT
8 ARCHER CT

Corbiere

SHEPPEY WAY

PO

Kemsley

1

STICKFAST LA

Cambray
Farm

Pheasants
Farmhouse

A249

Kemsley

NEW RIDHAM AVE

FLANDERS

GOLDHARBOUR LA

CASTLE ROUGH HELM SCH

GLOVER CL

BENSTEDE LA

Cambray
Cottages

WOODSIDE
COTTS

LAYFIELD
COTTS

BRAMBLEFIELD LA

Kemsley
SANDSTONE
DR

B2005

66

88 A B 89 C D 90 E F

13
36

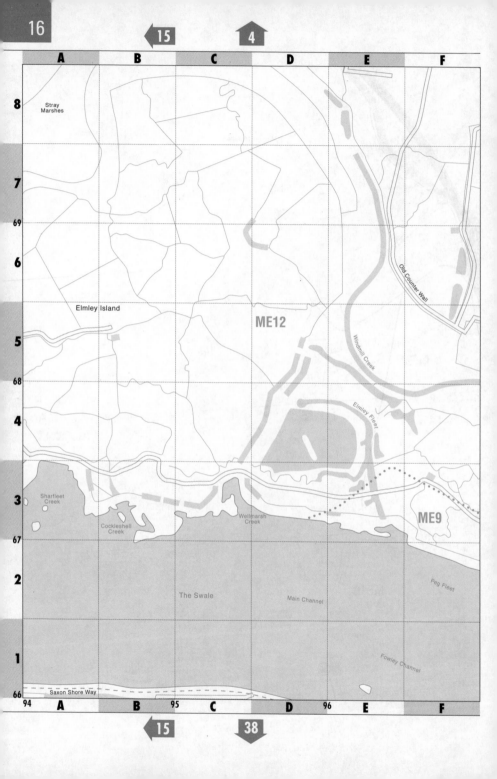

15
4

8
Stray
Marshes

7

69

6

Elmley Island

5

68

4

ME12

Old Counter Wall

Windmill Creek

Elmley Fleet

3
Sharfleet
Creek

Cockleshell
Creek

Wellmarsh
Creek

ME9

67

2

The Swale

Main Channel

Peg Fleet

1

Fowley Channel

66
Saxon Shore Way

94   A   B   95   C   D   96   E   F

15
38

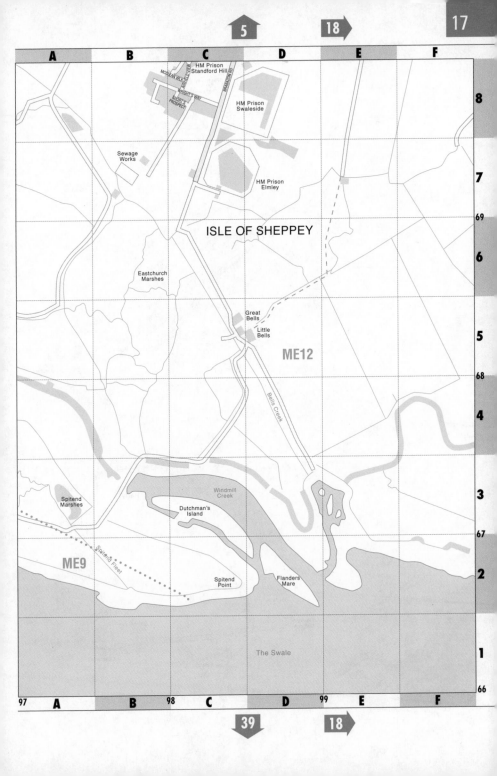

A   B   C   D   E   F

8

HM Prison
Standford Hill

MCLEAN WORLD VIEW
WRIGHT'S WAY
SHORT'S
PROSPECT

HM Prison
Swaleside

Sewage
Works

7

HM Prison
Elmley

69

ISLE OF SHEPPEY

6

Eastchurch
Marshes

Great
Bells

Little
Bells

5

ME12

68

Bells Creek

4

Windmill
Creek

3

Spitend
Marshes

Dutchman's
Island

67

Spitend Fleet

ME9

Spitend
Point

Flanders
Mare

2

The Swale

1

66

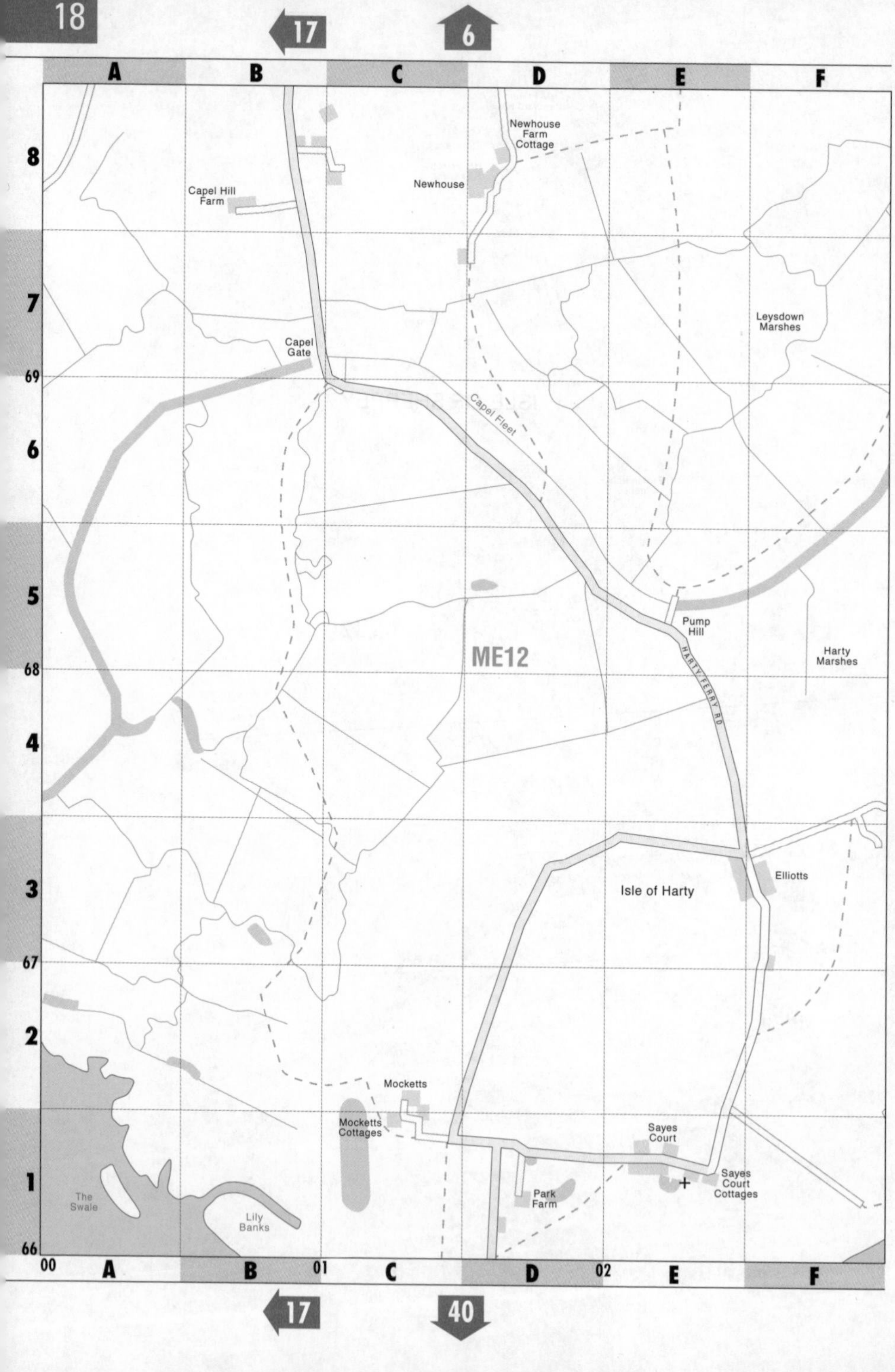

17
6

	A	B	C	D	E	F

8

Newhouse
Farm
Cottage

Capel Hill
Farm

Newhouse

7

Leysdown
Marshes

69

Capel
Gate

Capel Fleet

6

5

Pump
Hill

Harty
Marshes

68

ME12

HARTY FERRY RD

4

3

Isle of Harty

Elliotts

67

2

Mocketts

Mocketts
Cottages

Sayes
Court

1

The
Swale

Park
Farm

Sayes
Court
Cottages

Lily
Banks

66

00	A		B	01	C		D	02	E		F

17
40

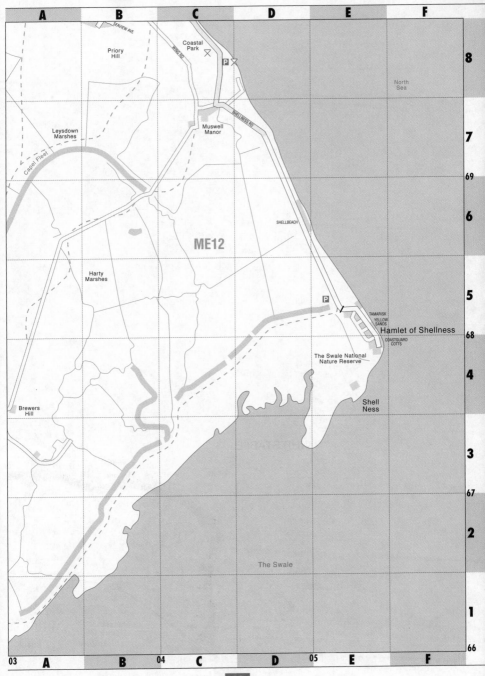

WHITSTABLE

Tankerton Bay

Kingsdown Park

WYNN ELLIS HO 1
THE BARGES 2
MARINERS LEE 3
SOUTH LODGE 4
SOUTH LODGE CL 5
THE EXCHANGE 6
TANKERTON HTS 7

1 CASTLE HO
2 MARINE HO
3 MARINE CT
4 GRAND PAVILION

Swimming
Pool

Harbour

Castle

MARINE PAR

TANKERTON

B2205

EAST QUAY

Saxon Shore
Way

TOWER PAR

TANKERTON RD

IRB
Sta

Reeves
Beach

St Marys RC
Prim Sch

NORTHWOOD RD

STRANGFORD RD

D2
1 STARVATION CNR
2 NEW ST
3 FOUNTAIN ST
4 THE OLD POLICE STA
5 ST PETERS COTTS
6 HARTS LA
7 VICTORIA HO
8 THE OLD HALLS
9 ALBERT CT
10 LEGGETT'S LA
11 RED LION LA
12 WHITEPOST
13 CUSHINGS WALK
14 SQUEEZE GUT ALLEY
15 BEACH ALLEY
16 THE SALTINGS
17 HAYES ALLEY
18 EVELINGS ALLEY
19 BONNERS ALLEY
20 KNIGHTS ALLEY
21 SALT MARSH LA

GLOUCESTER RD

QUEEN'S RD

CLEWER
LO CLOISTERS

PETTMANS
MEWS

SHIPWRIGHTS
LEE

White Marsh
CT

Whitstable

THE BRIDGE APP

SUMMERFIELD AVE

MARINE TERR
COASTGUARD ALLEY

WAVE
CREST

SEAWAY
COTTS
VICTORIA ST

Thurston
Park

CT5
Church
Street

Lower
Island

Liby

INVICTA
RD

09   A   B   10   C   D   11   E   F

43

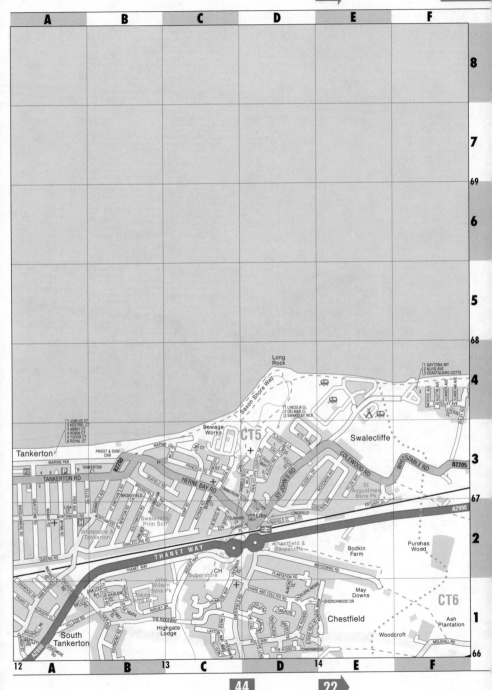

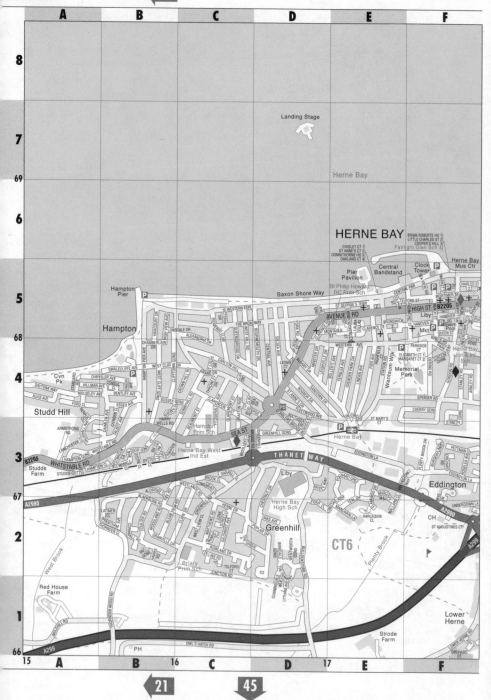

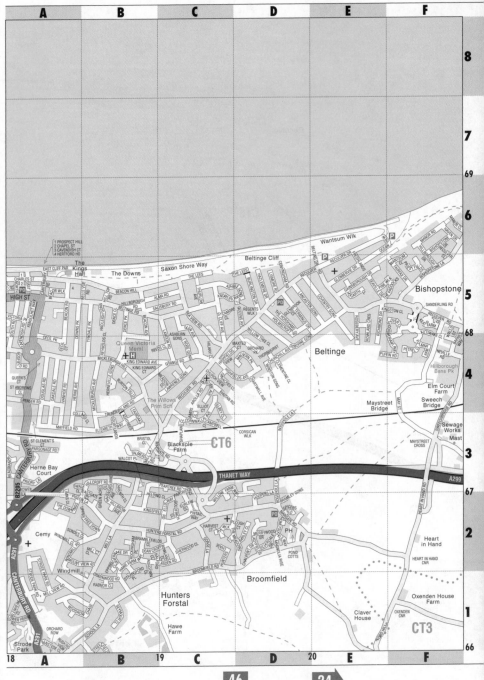

23

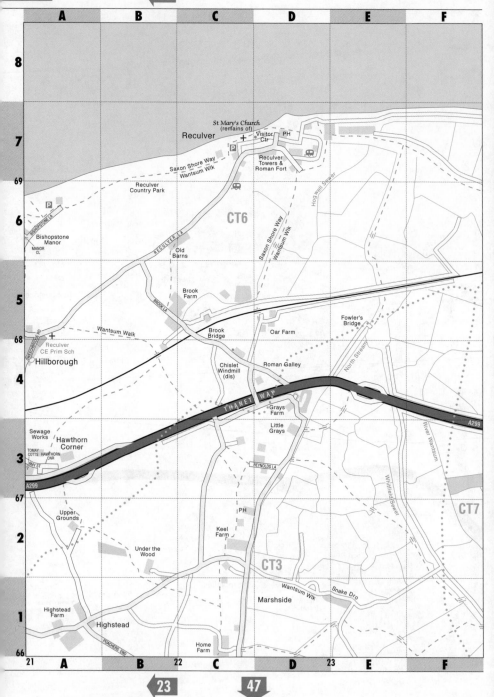

23

47

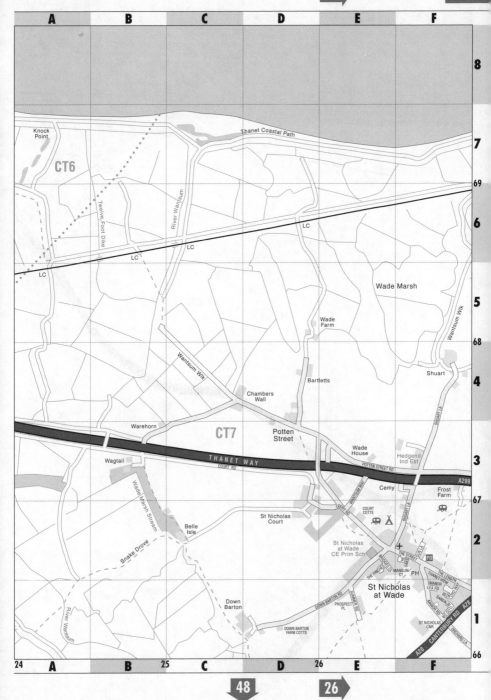

25

F8
1 DALLINGER RD
2 CARMEL CT
3 SANDPIPER CT
4 GAINSBORO RD
5 LYELL CT
6 HOMEBIRCH HO

7 BERESFORD CT

A   B   C   D   E   F

8

LARKESCLIFF CT 1
SEA VIEW HTS 2
APRIL RISE 3
BAY VIEW HTS 4
MCKINLAY CT 5
RINGSLOE CT 6
SHORE CL 7
FERNDOWN 8
FORELAND CT 9
HAZEL CT 10
COASTGUARD COTTS 11

Minnis
Bay

ANNA

SPENCER RD

Groynes

Wantsum Wlk
Thanet Coastal Path

DARYNGTON AVE
DANE RD
HORSA RD

Gore End
Farm

Birchington-on-Sea

7

Plumpudding
Island

LC

LC

BIERCE CT 1
BIERCE CT COTTS 2
ROSSETTI 3
UPPER MALTINGS PL 4
THE MALTHOUSES 5
SANDLE'S RD 6

WALNUT
MEWS

CLAIRE

Birchington

69

LC

LC

6

Brooksend Stream

FLINT COTTS 1
RANSOME WAY 2

Wade
Marsh

Reservoirs

5

CT7

Great
Brooksend
Farm

CANTERBURY ROAD BIRCHINGTON

68

Upper
Hale

Brooks
End

College
Farm

4

Hale

Nether
Hale
Farm

CRISPE RD

Coney
Close

Monkton Road
Farm

3

NETHERHALE FARM RD

A299

POTTEN STREET RD

THANET WAY

67

St NICHOLAS
RDBT

SEAMARK RD

2

CANTERBURY RD

A28

PLUMBTOME RD

1

A28

A28

ORCHARD

CT12

66

27   A   28   B   C   28   D   29   E   F

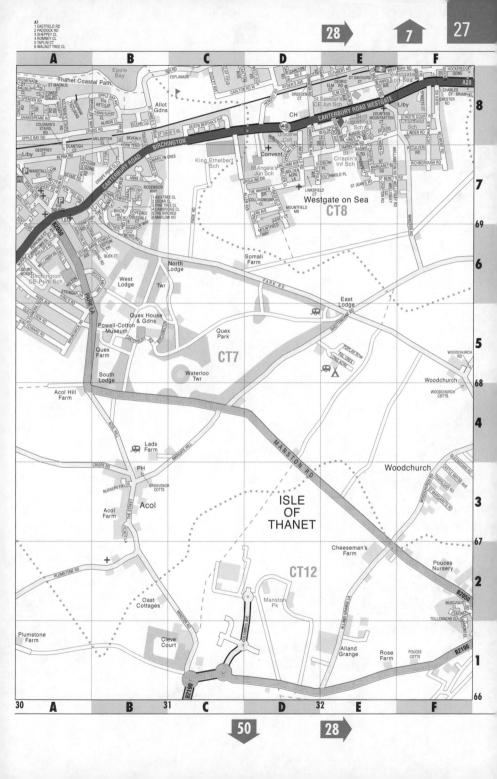

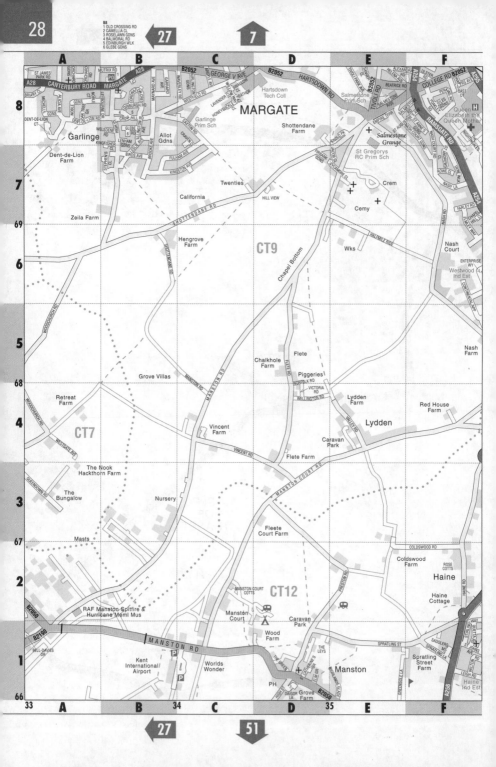

B6
1 OLD CROSSING RD
2 CAMELLIA CL
3 ROSELAWN GDNS
4 BALMORAL RD
5 EDINBURGH WLK
6 GLEBE GDNS

A B C D E F

MATRIX RD

St James' Park Rd

ORCHARD

CANTERBURY ROAD   MARGATE   A28

B2052   GEORGE V AVE   B2052   HARTSDOWN RD   B2052

College Rd   B2052

Hartsdown Tech Coll

MARGATE

8

Salmestone Prim Sch

Queen Elizabeth the Queen Mother   H

Garlinge   Allot Gdns   Garlinge Prim Sch   Shottendane Farm

Salmestone Grange

Dent-de-Lion Farm

St Gregorys RC Prim Sch

7   Twenties   California   HILL VIEW   Crem   Cemy   Nash Court

Zeila Farm

69   Hengrove Farm   **CT9**   Wks   ENTERPRISE WY   Westwood Ind Est

SHOTTENDANE RD

Chapel Bottom

6   Nash Farm

5   Chalkhole Farm   Flete   Piggeries   FLETE RD   VICTORIA RD   WELLINGTON RD   Lydden Farm   Red House Farm

68   Grove Villas   MANSTON RD   NORFOLK RD   Lydden

Retreat Farm   WOODCHURCH RD   Vincent Farm   Caravan Park

4   **CT7**   WESTGATE AVE   VINCENT RD   Flete Farm   **Lydden**

The Nook   Hackthorn Farm   MANSTON COURT RD

3   QUEENDOWN RD   The Bungalow   Nursery   Coldswood Farm   Haine

67   Masts   Fleete Court Farm   COLDSWOOD RD   Rose Cotts

PRESTON RD

2   MANSTON COURT COTTS   **CT12**   Caravan Park   Haine Cottage   Haine Ind Est

RAF Manston Spitfire & Hurricane Meml Mus   Manston Court   Wood Farm   THE LEYS   SPRATLING ST   SPRATLING LA   Spratling Street Farm

B2050   B2190   MANSTON RD

BELL DAVIES RD

1   Kent International Airport   P   Worlds Wonder   THE GREEN   PH   **Manston**   B2050   A256   Haine Ind Est

66   DAGOR GROVE LA

33   A   B   34   C   D   35   E   F

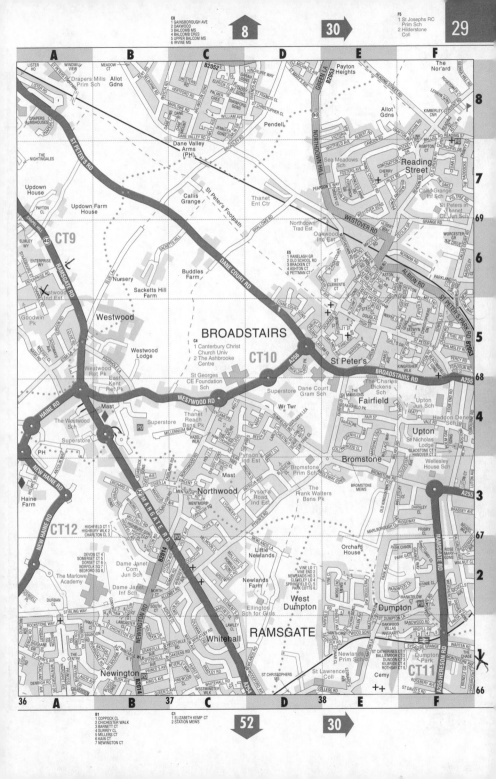

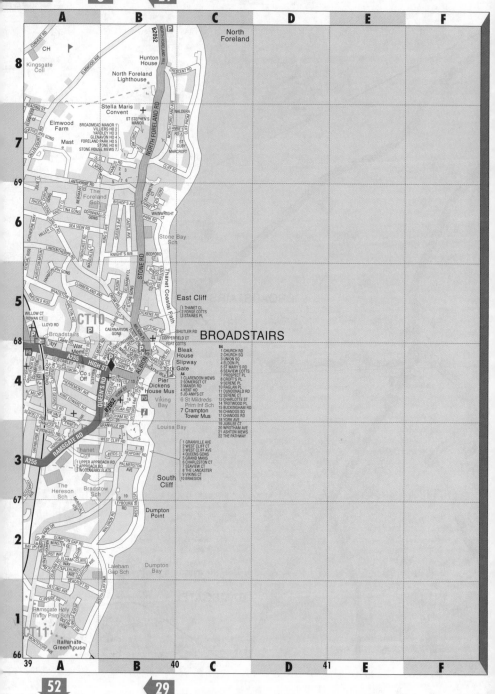

North Foreland

North Foreland Lighthouse

Hunton House

Kingsgate Coll

CH

Stella Maris Convent

Elmwood Farm

Mast

BROADMEAD MANOR 1
VILLIERS HO 2
YARDLEY HO 3
GLENAVON HO 4
FORELAND PARK HO 5
STONE HO 6
STONE HOUSE MEWS 7

ST STEPHEN'S MANOR

NALDERA

ST CUBY MARCROFT

The Foreland Sch

Stone Bay Sch

East Cliff

1 THANET CL
2 FORGE COTTS
3 STAINES PL

BROADSTAIRS

CT10

Broadstairs

War Mem'l

Bleak House

Slipway

Gate

Pier

Dickens House Mus

6 St Mildreds Prim Inf Sch

7 Crampton Tower Mus

Viking Bay

Louisa Bay

B4
1 CHURCH RD
2 CHURCH SQ
3 UNION SQ
4 ELDON PL
5 ST MARY'S RD
6 SEAVIEW COTTS
7 PROSPECT PL
8 CROFT'S PL
9 SERENE PL
10 RAGLAN PL
11 DUNDONALD RD
12 SERENE CT
13 CHARLOTTE ST
14 TROTWOOD CL
15 BUCKINGHAM RD
16 CHANDOS SQ
17 CHANDOS RD
18 YORK AVE
19 JUBILEE CT
20 WROTHAM AVE
21 ASHTON MEWS
22 THE PATHWAY

A4
1 CLARENDON MEWS
2 SOMERSET CT
3 MANOR RD
4 KENT HO
5 JO-ANN'S CT

South Cliff

1 UPPER APPROACH RD
2 APPROACH RD
3 WOODBERRY FLATS

1 GRANVILLE AVE
2 WEST CLIFF CT
3 WEST CLIFF AVE
4 QUEENS GDNS
5 GRAND MANS
6 CHARLESTON CT
7 SEAVIEW CT
8 THE LANCASTER
9 VIKING CT
10 BRAESIDE

Thanet Coll

The Hereson Sch

Bradstow Sch

Dumpton Point

Dumpton Bay

Laleham Gap Sch

Ramsgate Holy Trinity Prim Sch

Italianate Greenhouse

CT11

ROCHESTER

CHATHAM

ME1 ME4 ME5

Nashenden Farm
HM Prison
Nine Acre Wood
Little Monk Wood
Well Wood
Barn Wood
Gorse Wood
Upper Nashenden Farm
Monk Wood
Syle Wood
Bridge Woods
Middlehill Wood
Middle Hill
Buckmore Park International Kart Circuit
Burham Hill Farm
Burham Common
North Downs Way
Lord Leas
Blue Bell Hill
Impton Wood
Crem
Walderslade
Rochester Airport
Rochester Airport Ind Est
Horsted Ret Pk
Hotel
Superstore
Superstores
Factories
MidKent Coll
Horsted Farm
Fort Horsted
Ridge Meadow Prim Sch
Oaklands Inf & Jun Sch
Greenacre Sch
Chatham Gram Sch for Boys
Chatham South Sch
Thorndike Ho
Tunbury Prim Sch

E4	F4	F5
1 LAVENDER CL	1 MALLOW WAY	1 SAFFRON WAY
2 ASPEN WAY	2 JASMINE CL	2 WILLOW HO
3 HONEYSUCKLE CL	3 HAREBELL CL	3 PINE HO
4 GENTIAN CL	4 ROSEMARY CL	4 ROWAN HO
	5 LINDEN HO	5 HAWTHORN HO
	6 OAK HO	6 BLEAKWOOD RD
		7 Walderslade Girls Sch

West Kent STREET ATLAS

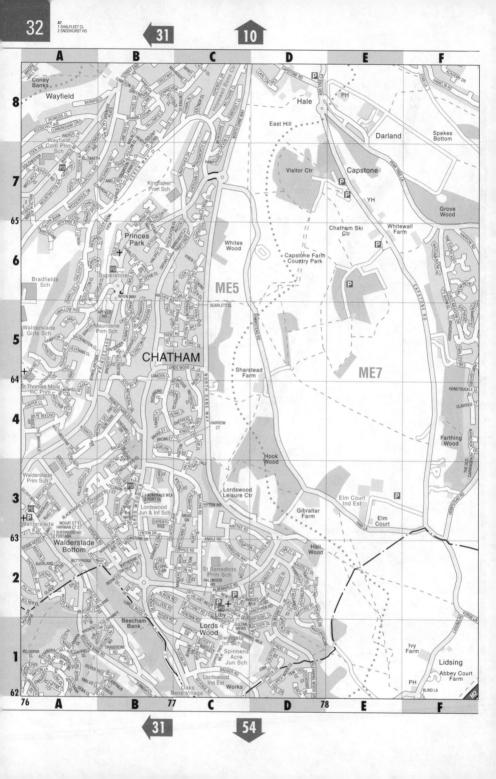

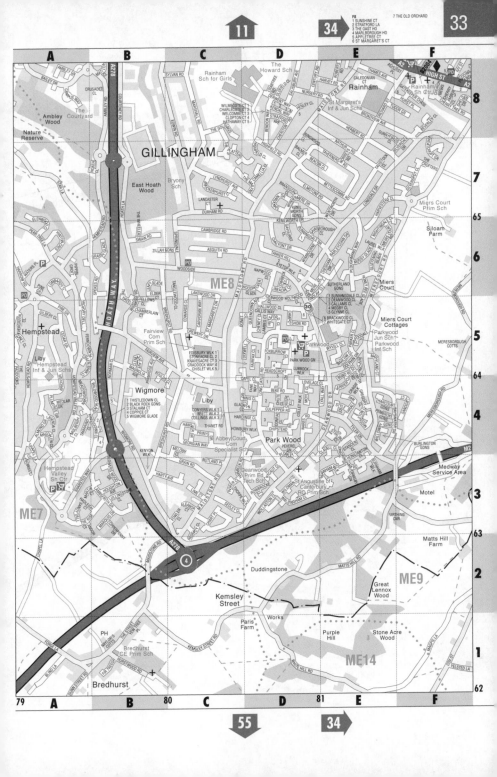

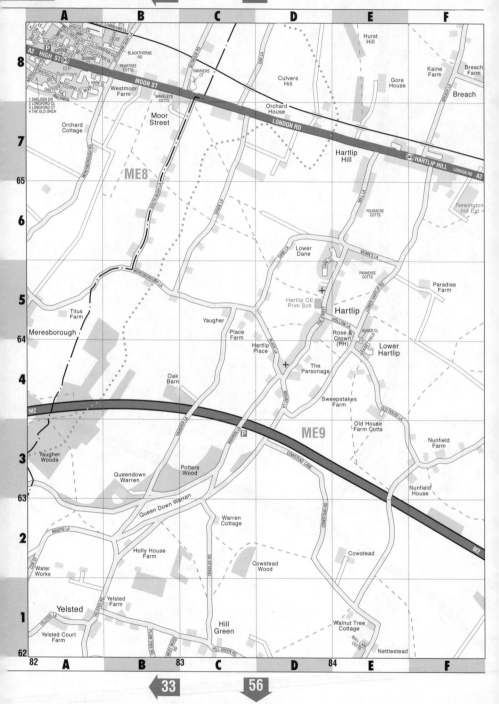

A · B · C · D · E · F

8

1 SHELDEN DR
2 LONGFORD CL
3 LONGFORD CT
4 THE OLD ORCH

Winchester
FARNHAM CL
BUTLER WAY
SUNDERLAND CL
OXFORD
GLOUCESTER CL
QUEENS
A2 **HIGH ST**
P
ISP
Rainham
OASTVIEW
MERSCROFT RD
MIDDLEFIELDS WY
PARK CL
THE SALTINGS

Blackthorne
RD
PEARTREE
COTTS
Westmoor
Farm
WAKELEYS
COTTS
FARRIERS
CT

MOOR ST
Moor Street

Orchard
Cottage

7

ME8

65

6

5

64

4

3

63

2

1

62

Titus
Farm

Meresborough

SOUTH BUSH LA

MERESBROUGH LA

Yaugher
Woods

Queendown
Warren

Queen Down Warren

MAGPIE LA

Water
Works

Holly House
Farm

Yelsted

OAK LA

YELSTED LA

Yelsted
Farm

Yelsted Court
Farm

PLUM TREE RD

LINKS WOOD RD

Oak
Barn

Yaugher

Place
Farm

Hartlip
Place

YAUGHER LA

Potters
Wood

CRADLES RD

Hill Green

HILL GREEN RD

Culvers
Hill

Orchard
House

DANE LA

BOXER RD

MILL LA

Lower
Dane

DANE LA

Hartlip CE
Prim Sch

THE STREET

PLACE LA

WARREN LA

P

The
Parsonage

MUNS LA

Warren
Cottage

COWSTEAD LANE

COWSTEAD RD

Cowstead
Wood

LONDON RD

Hartlip
Hill

Hurst
Hill

Gore
House

Kaine
Farm

Breach
Farm

Breach

HARTLIP HILL

LONDON RD A2

FOURACRE
COTTS

MILL LA

MUNN'S LA

Hartlip

PARADISE
COTTS

Paradise
Farm

HOLLOW LA

LOWER HARTLIP RD

SPRING FIELD RD

Rose &
Crown
(PH)

AUGER CL

Lower
Hartlip

Sweepstakes
Farm

OLD HOUSE LA

Old House
Farm Cotts

ME9

Nunfield
Farm

Nunfield
House

Cowstead

Walnut Tree
Cottage

BULL LANE
COTTS

Nettlestead

Newington
Ind Est

M2

M2

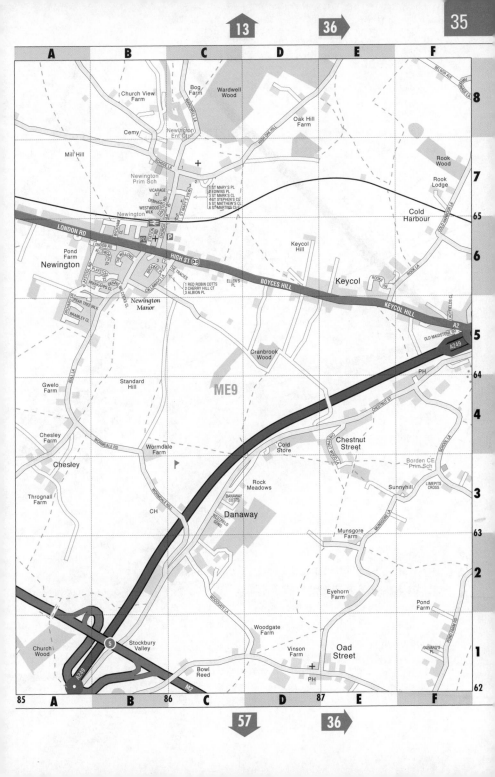

35
14

D6
1 MOONSTONE SQ
2 RUBY CL
3 AMETHYST DR
4 REALGAR CT
5 RAITE GN
6 FIRE OPAL WY
7 TRONA CT
8 PIPPIN CL

SITTINGBOURNE

ME9

Howt Green
Stickfast Farm
Upper Toes
Nether Toes
PH

Parsonage Farm
Parsonage La

Church Farm
Quinton Farm House

1 SUNSTONE DR
2 SAPPHIRE CL
3 JADE CL
4 OLIVINE CL

Bobbing Prim Sch

Bobbing

Bobbing Court

Bobbing Hill

Grove Dairy Farm

Motel

Grove Park CP Sch

Milton Regis

Staplehurst Lodge Ind Est
LC

1 NORWOOD WLK E
2 WENTWORTH HO

DEHAM HO 1
ROENTIEN HO 2
PINCOS HO 3

Regis Manor Com Prim Sch

ALBION TERR 1
OYSTER CL 2
CROSS LA 3
BRAMBLING RISE 4

Recn Gd

Milton Court Prim Sch

Superstore
Trinity Trad Est

Blue Houses
Cricketers Cl
Beauvoir Dr

MILL WAY

Works

ALLENBY WLK 1
NELSON WLK 2
COLLINGWOOD WLK 3
NORWOOD WLK W 4
ANDREWS WLK 5
GAINSBOROUGH CL 6

Key Street
A2
KEY ST

Cherry Fields
Grove Park

London Rd

CHALKWELL
LONDON RD
Cryalls Basns Est

The Westlands Sch
Playing Field

Cryalls

London Road Trad Est

Woodgrove Prim Sch

Sittingbourne Retail Pk

Sittingbourne Ind Pk

Sittingbourne

ME10
WAY B2006

EUROLINK WAY

ST MICHAEL'S RD
WEST ST
DOVER ST

War Memi

Libry
Swallows Ctr
Superstore

The Avenue Theatre
Borden Gram Sch

Hall
Borden Hall

Borden

PH

Street Farm
THE BARN

Pond House

ME9

Harman's Corner

Fernleigh

Meadow Ho 1
Lower Bannister Cotts 2

St Peter's RC Prim Sch
Minterne Jun Sch
The Oaks Int Sch

L Ctr

Cemys

Memorial

Highsted Gram Sch
Fulston Manor Sch

Eden Village

Hearts Delight

Waymarks

35
58
35

E4
1 DOVER ST
2 FOUNTAIN ST
3 FREEMAN CT
4 MOCKETT CT
5 CHURCH ST
6 PIXBURY CT
7 WINGATE CT
8 THE CLOISTERS
9 MIDDLETON CT

10 HAWTHORN HO
11 The ISP Sch

E5
1 ALEXANDER CT
2 PEAR TREE ALLEY
3 PERIWINKLE CT
4 BISHOP CT
5 TANNERY CT
6 RIGDEN'S CT
7 GILES-YOUNG CT

F4
1 CRESCENT ST
2 THE FORUM
3 LION VT
4 DOES ALLEY
5 ST MICHAEL'S CL
6 RIVERBOURNE CT
7 CROWN QUAY LA
8 Bell Sh Ctr

9 The Forum Sh Ctr

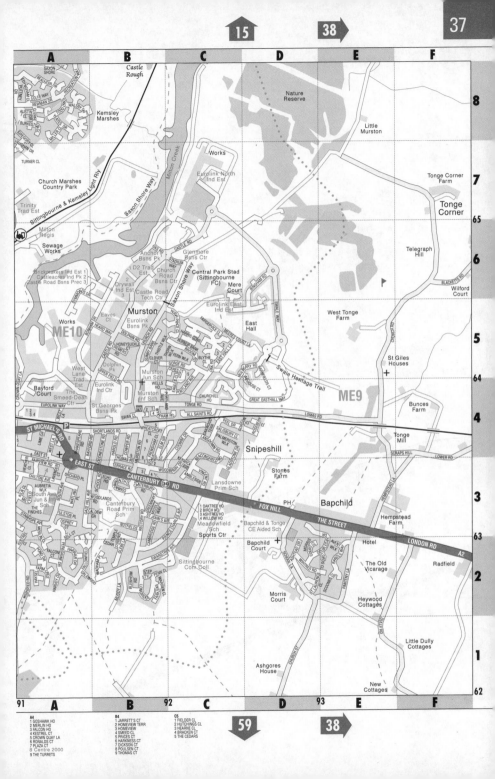

A **B** **C** **D** **E** **F**

8

The Swale

Saxon Shore Way

Wharf

7

Blacketts

Swale Heritage Trail

BLACKETTS
COTTS

Conver Creek

Works

Saxon Shore Way

Rifle Range
(dis)

65

BLACKETTS RD

Wilford Court
Farm

NORTH QUAY

6

Cheke's
Court

QUAY
COTTS

PH

THE QUAY

1 COASTGUARD COTTS
2 BRUNSWICK COTTS

Dock

EASTWOOD
COTTS

THE
MOORINGS

BRUNSWICK FIELD

Conyer

ME9

5

Stone Chimney
Farm

Banks
Farm

64

Teynham
Street

CONYER RD

TEYNHAM ST

New
Cotts

Teynham
Court

4

Bax

Teynham Court
Farm

+

MARSHA LA

Peete
House

LC

Sewage
Works

Fair
View

LOWER RD

LC

Barrow
Green

Osiers
Farm

3

Frognal

CHURCHILL
HO

STATION
ROW

RAILWAY
COTTS

OSIER RD

63

Teynham

FROGNAL LA

LONGHAM VIEW

BAKER CL

ROPER RD

HONEYBALL

PH

THE CRESCENT

BROADOAK

FRENCH ROW

LOWER RD

BELLE FRIDAY CL

2

Radfield

Depot

CLAXFIELD
COTTS

PROGNAL LANE

Teynham Parochial
CE Prim Sch

MELLOR CL

NEW GARDENS

DEURALD MOOR AVE

AGNEL CL

NUTBERRY CT

SANDOWN CL

BEADE LINK

FRENCH ROW

1 ROUNDEL CL
2 TRIGG'S ROW
3 TRIGGS COTTS
4 SELBY CT

Whent's
Farm

Claxfield
Farm

PH

PO

P

Liby

CHEEK NEW GARDENS
RD

LONDON RD

White
Hall

1

+

CLAXFIELD RD

LONGBOLA

VIGO
TERR

PH

CELLAR HILL

CELLAR LA

Sandown
Cotts

MARSHA LA

A2

62

Cellarhill

Cellar Hill
Farm

CAMBRIDGE

Orchard
House

A **B** **C** **D** **E** **F**

94 95 96

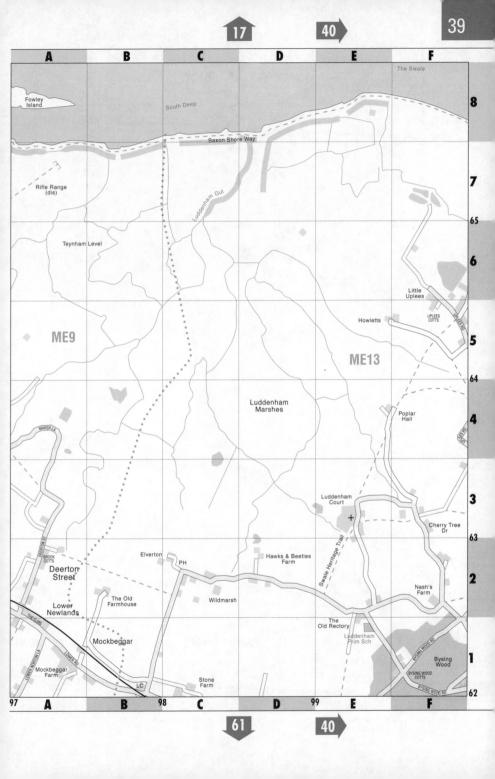

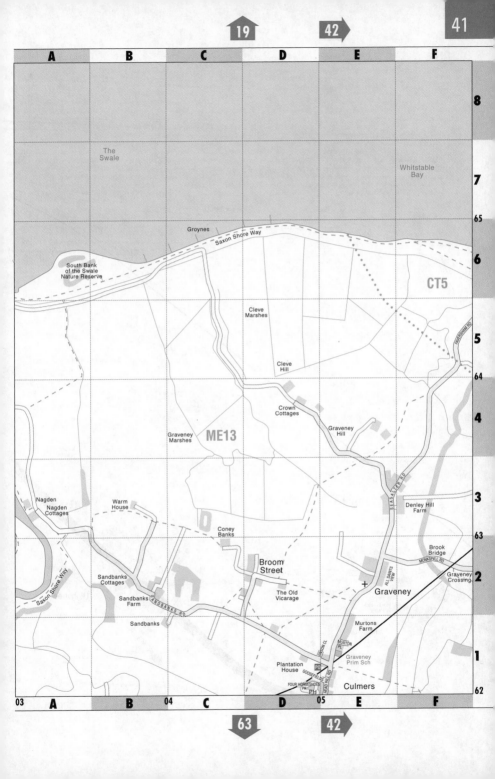

A   B   C   D   E   F

8

The
Swale

Whitstable
Bay

7

65

Groynes
Saxon Shore Way

6

South Bank
of the Swale
Nature Reserve

CT5

Cleve
Marshes

5

Cleve
Hill

64

Crown
Cottages

4

Graveney
Marshes

ME13

Graveney
Hill

SLEASALTER RD

FAVERSHAM RD

Nagden
Nagden
Cottages

Warm
House

Denley Hill
Farm

3

Coney
Banks

Brook
Bridge

MONKSHILL RD

63

Broom
Street

ALL SAINTS VIEW

Graveney
Crossing

2

Saxon Shore Way

Sandbanks
Cottages

The Old
Vicarage

Graveney

Sandbanks
Farm

SANDBANKS RD

Sandbanks

Murtons
Farm

GOSSEFIELD CL

MURTON
PL

HEAD HILL RD

Plantation
House

Graveney
Prim Sch

1

RD

FOUR HORSESHOES
PK

PH

Culmers

62

03   A   B   04   C   D   05   E   F

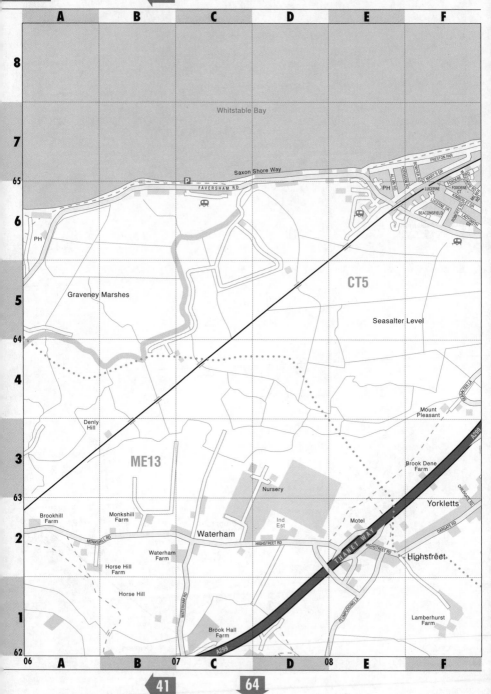

Whitstable Bay

Saxon Shore Way

P

FAVERSHAM RD

PH

CT5

Graveney Marshes

Seasalter Level

Denly
Hill

ME13

Mount
Pleasant

Nursery

Brook Dene
Farm

Yorkletts

Brookhill
Farm

Monkshill
Farm

Ind
Est

Motel

MONKSHILL RD

Waterham

HIGHSTREET RD

HIGHSTREET RD

Highstreet

Waterham
Farm

THANET WAY

DARGATE RD

Horse Hill
Farm

WATERHAM RD

Horse Hill

PLUMPUDDING LA

Brook Hall
Farm

Lamberhurst
Farm

A299

PRESTON PAR

ALBA RD

ST MARY'S GR

LUCERNE
CT

FOXDENE
CT

BEACONSFIELD

LUCERNE DRI

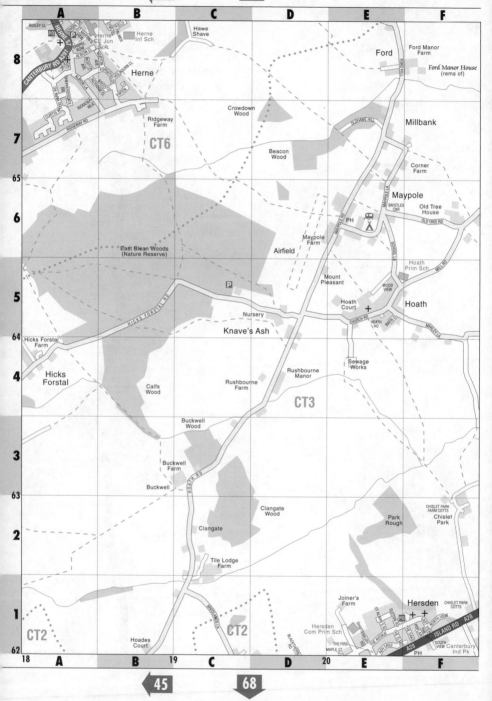

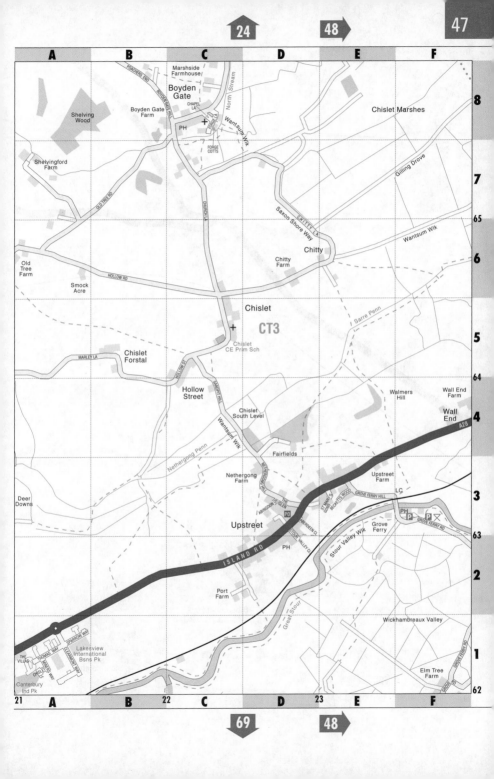

A | B | C | D | E | F

8

Gilling Dro
Wantsum Wlk
Whitfield/Sewer

Chislet
Marshes

7

CT7

Sarre

Bolingbroke
Farm

Wantsum Wlk

The
Peak

CANTERBURY RD

A28

CT12

65

PH

Sarre
Windmill

A253

OLD RD

SARRE CT
THE MANOR
HO

OSTLERS LA

A253

MILL RD

6

Sarre Penn

Sevenscore Dike

Sarre
Bridge

CLEVEN
LODGE

River Wantsum

LC

LC

5

Sarre Wall

ISLAND RD

Riverside
House

Great Stour

Sarre Marshes

64

A28

4

Stourmouth Valley

Stour
Bridge

PH

3

Blood
Point

Little Stour

Saxon Shore Way

CT3

Plucks
Gutter

63

North Court
Farm

Stour Valley Wlk

Stourmouth Stream

2

Red Bridge

DROVE FERRY RD

Russell
Farm

BREWERY SQ

CHURCH LA

SCHOOL LA

Elmstone
Valley

West
Stourmouth

Dean Farm

PH
Stonehall
Farm

THE STREET

1

Blue
Bridge

GROVE RD

Preston
Valley

PRESTON LA

NEWHOUSE
CNR

Newhouse
Farm

BEGGARS
CNR

East
Stourmouth

62

Oast House
Farm

ROOKSTON
CNR

Poulders
Farm

SEATON LA

24 | A | B | 25 | C | D | 26 | E | F

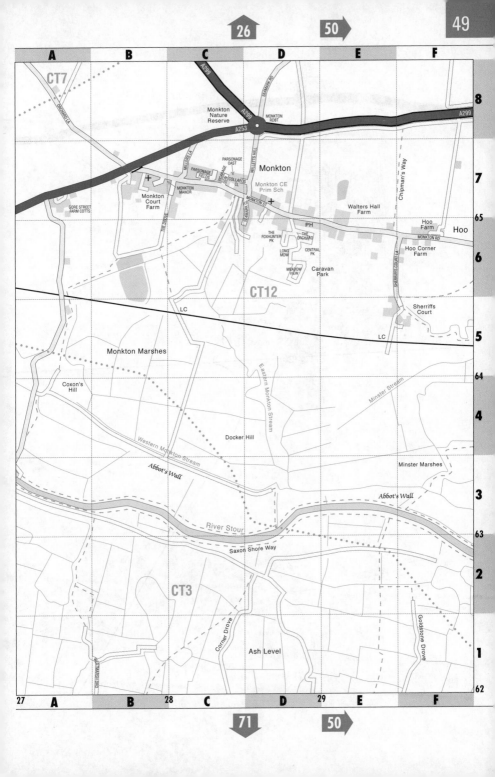

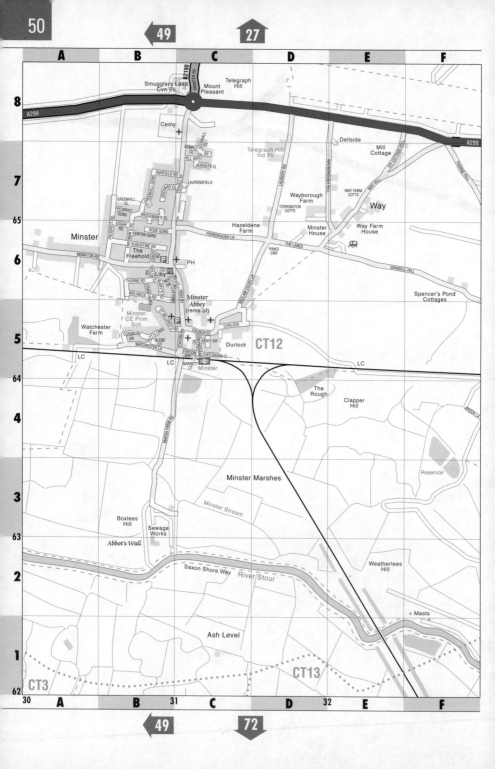

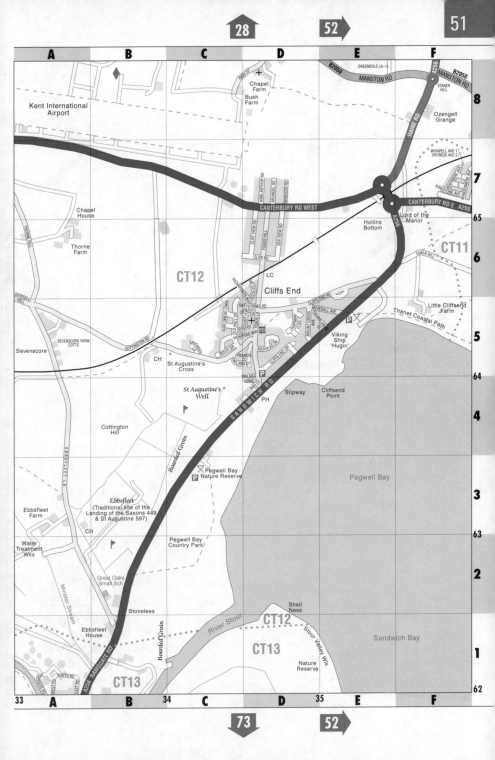

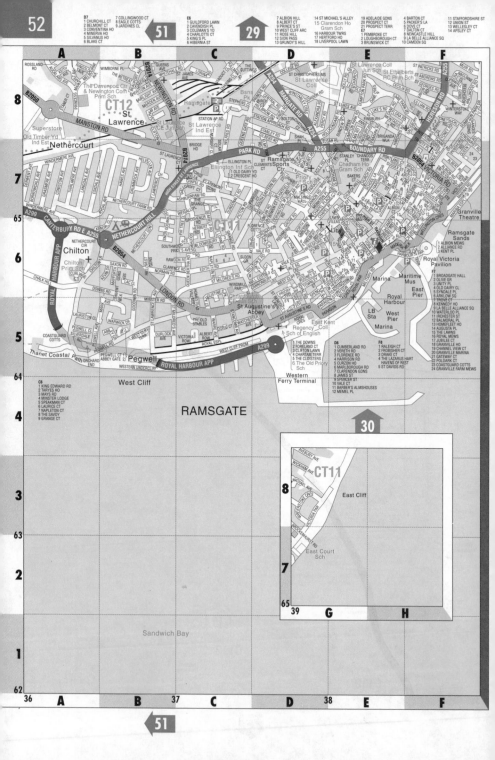

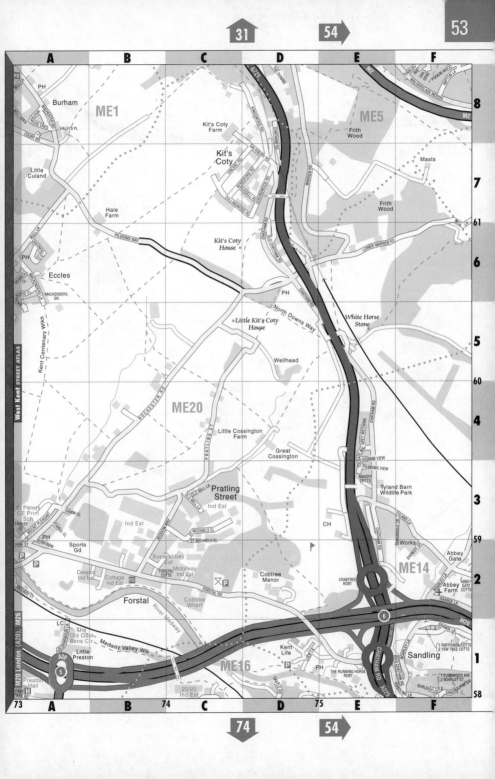

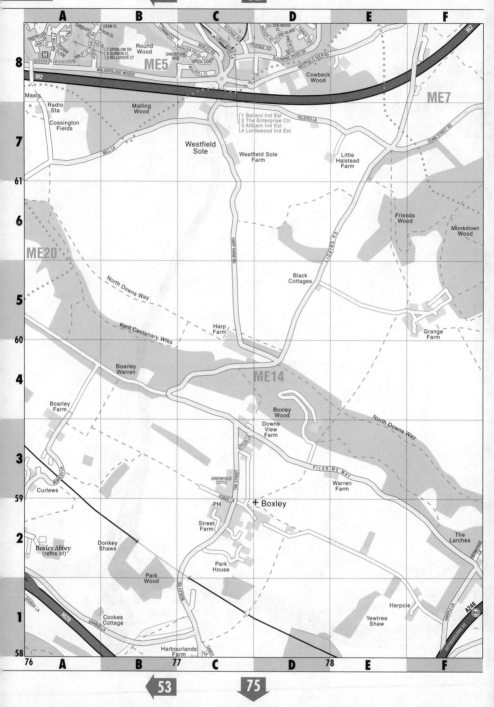

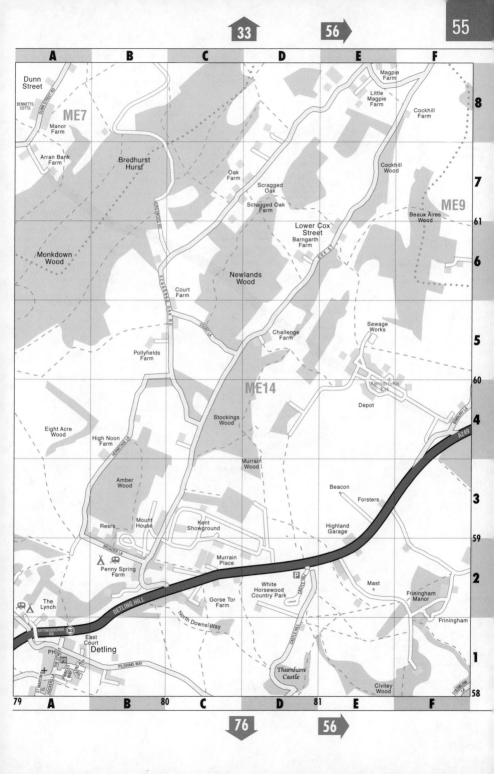

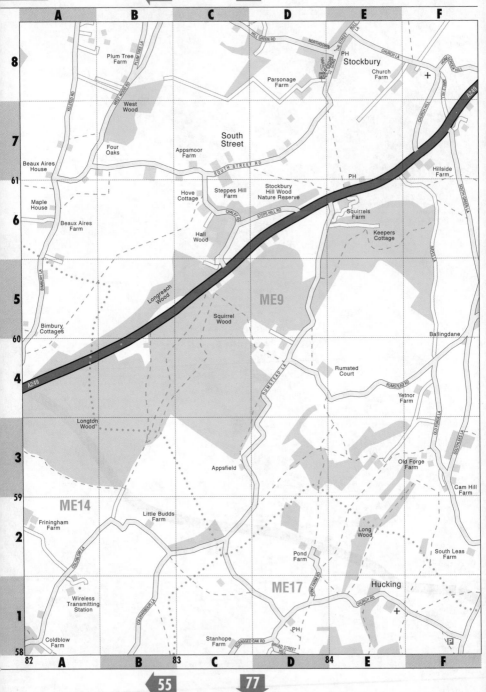

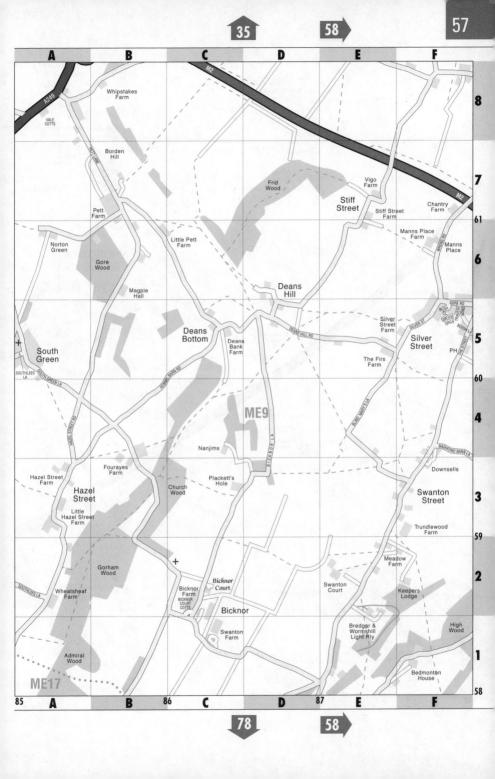

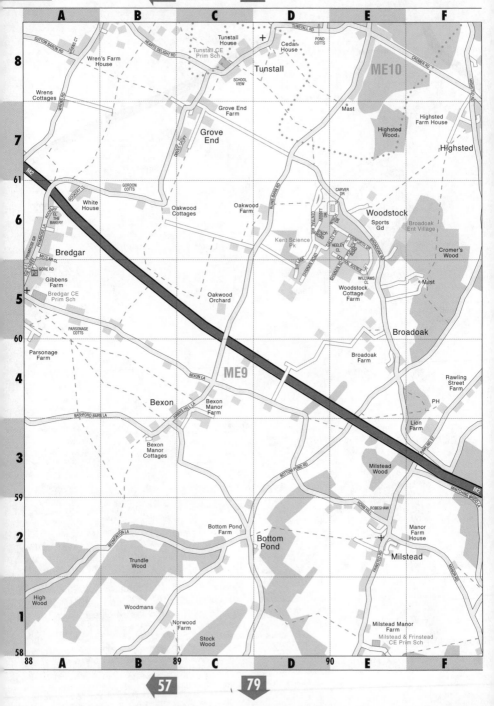

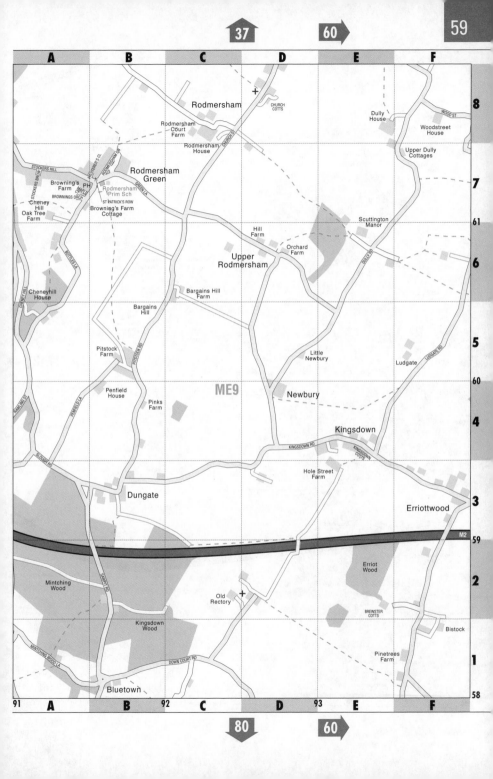

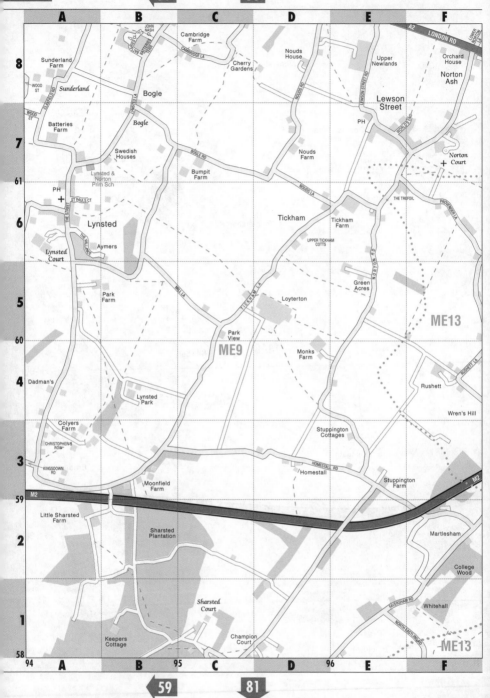

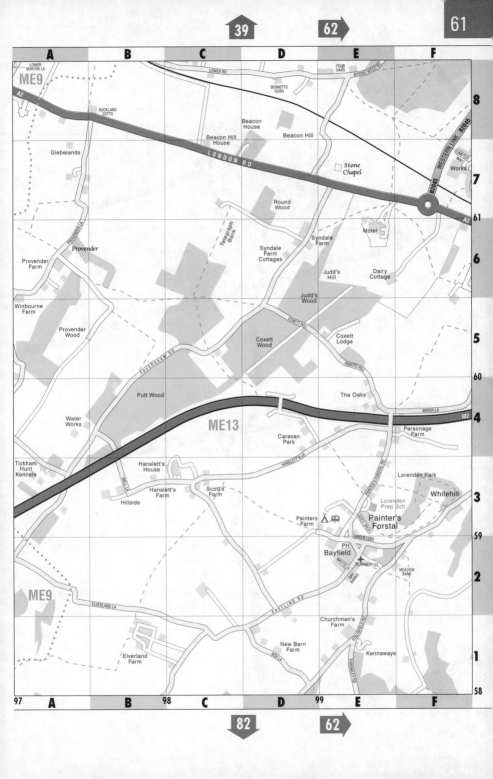

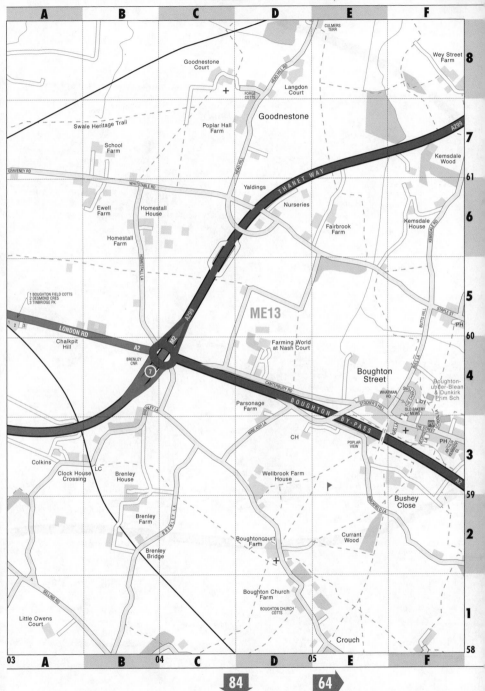

A   B   C   D   E   F

CULMERS TERR

Wey Street Farm **8**

Goodnestone Court

HEAD HILL RD

Langdon Court

FORGE COTTS

Goodnestone

Swale Heritage Trail

A299

THANET WAY **7**

Poplar Hall Farm

Kemsdale Wood

School Farm

GRAVENEY RD

61

WHITSTABLE RD

Yaldings

Nurseries

Kemsdale House **6**

Ewell Farm

Homestall House

Fairbrook Farm

KEMSDALE RD

Homestall Farm

HOMESTALL LA

1 BOUGHTON FIELD COTTS
2 DESMOND CRES
3 TINBRIDGE PK

ME13

STAPLE ST **5**

1 2 3

BUTTS HILL

PH

LONDON RD

A299

M2

60

Chalkpit Hill

A2

Farming World at Nash Court

BELL LA

BRENLEY CNR

⑦

Boughton Street **4**

CANTERBURY RD

Boughton-under-Blean & Dunkirk Prim Sch

WHATMAN HO

SNOUT

THE CROSS

Liby

BRENLEY LA

Parsonage Farm

BOUGHTON

STOCKER'S HILL

OLD BAKERY MEWS

THE STREET

GATE LA

PH

Colkins

NINE ASH LA

BY-PASS

SCHOOL LA

LC

Brenley House

CH

POPLAR VIEW

59

Clock House Crossing

Wellbrook Farm House

A2

Bushey Close

Brenley Farm

BRENLEY LA

BACKFIELD LA

2

Currant Wood

Brenley Bridge

Boughtoncourt Farm

SELLING RD

1

Little Owens Court

Boughton Church Farm

BOUGHTON CHURCH COTTS

Crouch

58

03   A   B   04   C   D   05   E   F

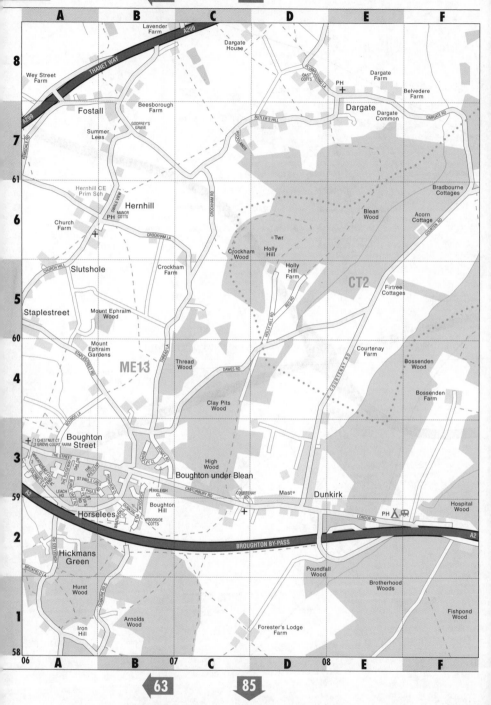

8

Walnut Tree Farm

Well Court

Frog Hall

Amery Court

Timber Wood

Arbele House

Broadlands Ind Est

7

Daw's Wood

The Halt

The Radfall

Honey Wood

Great Hall Wood

THE GAP

LODGE

CHESTNUT AVE

61

A290

BLEAN COMMON

CLOCKTOWER PAR

6

Hothe Court Farm

Church Cottage

Tyler Hill

MOUNT PLEASANT

Blean

Little Hall Wood

Hillside Farm

PH

Luckett's Farm

TILE KILN HILL

5

Woolf Coll

Little Hall Farm

Darwin Coll

60

CT2

Brotherhood Wood

Blean Prim Sch

Park Wood

University of Kent Canterbury

Templeman Liby

GREEN DELL

4

CLOWES CT 1
HOMESTALL CT 3
GRIMSHILL CT 3
THORNDEN CT 4

PURCHAS CT

LYEAT CT

Masts

BISHOPDEN CT

FARTHINGS CT

Rutherford Coll

MOORFIELD

WHITSTABLE RD

ELLENDEN

DENSTEAD

MARLEY CT

TUDOR

Eliot Coll

MOAT LA

OAKS PK

WILLOWS

Brotherwood

Keynes Coll

The Archbishop's Sch

MANWOOD AVE

THE TERRACE

MANWOOD ALMSHOUSE

3

RAVENSCOURT RD

LOVELL RD

FIRTREE CT

Kent College Canterbury

St Edmund's Junior School

CRANBORNE WLK

St Stephen's Jun & Inf Sch

Rough Common

PH

Wtr Twr

St Edmund's Sch

ST THOMAS HILL

Chaucer Coll

THE MANOR

59

STOCKWOOD CHASE

HILLTOP RD

St Stephen's

BEVERLEY HO 1
NEW BEVERLEY HO 2

LC

ST STEPHEN'S LODGE

GARDEN CL

Neal's Place

HACKINGTON TERR

VIKING CT

2

Stock Wood

NURSERY

Recn Ctr

MARKET CL

WHITSTABLE RD

A28/A28

The Grove

Canterbury Christ Church Univ

St Dunstan's

Canterbury West

CALDERWAY

CALDER ROBT

Rec Off

Hall Place

CHANCEL CT 1
JOSEPH CONRAD HO 2
RUNCIE PL 3

Cemy

HANSCOMB RD

DEANS MILL CT

B2248

ST RADIGUNDS

1

A2050

Kent Coll Canterbury Inf & Jun Sch

CHURCH HILL

THE MINT

WHITGIFT

ST DUNSTAN'S ST

QUEEN'S AVE

LC

FAULKNERS LA

HARBLEDOWN

SUMMER HILL

A2050 • RHEIMS WAY

58

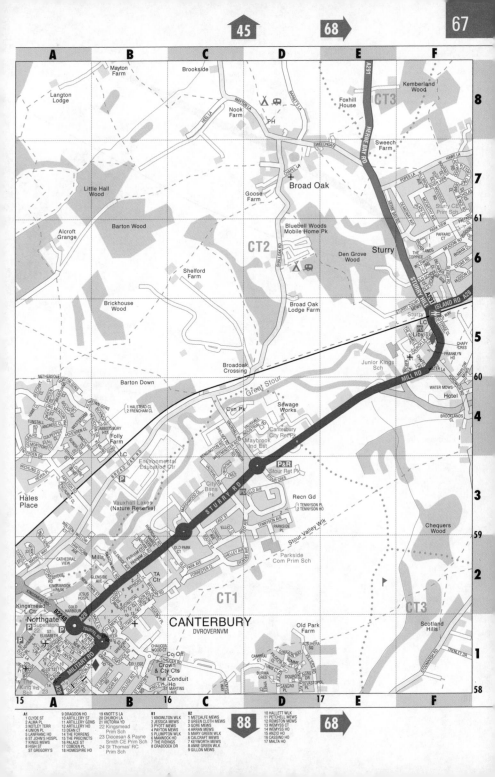

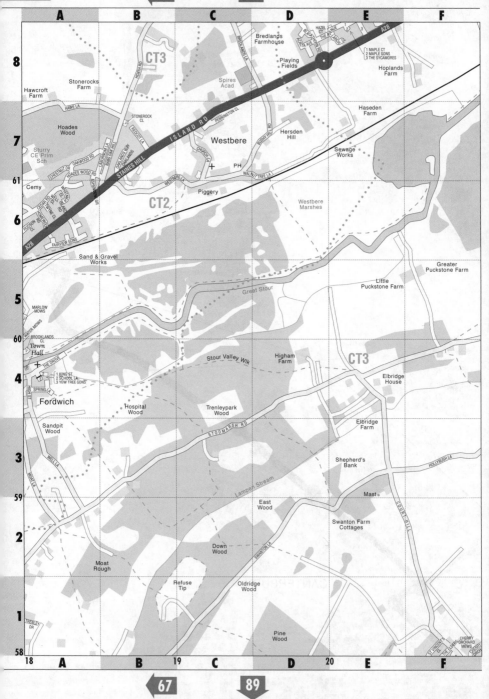

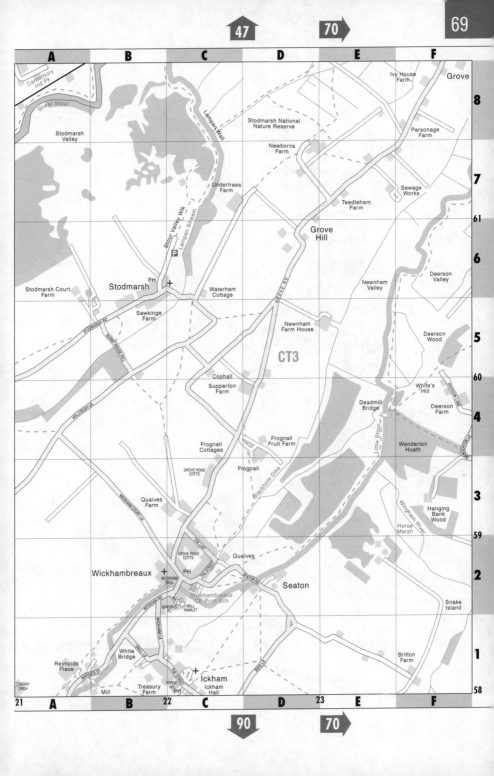

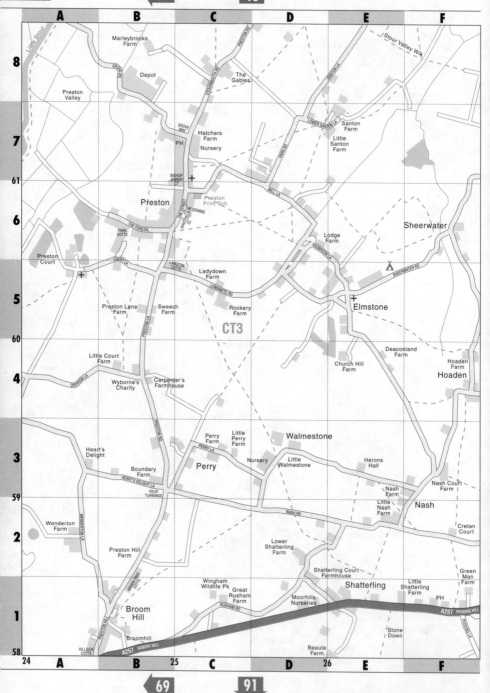

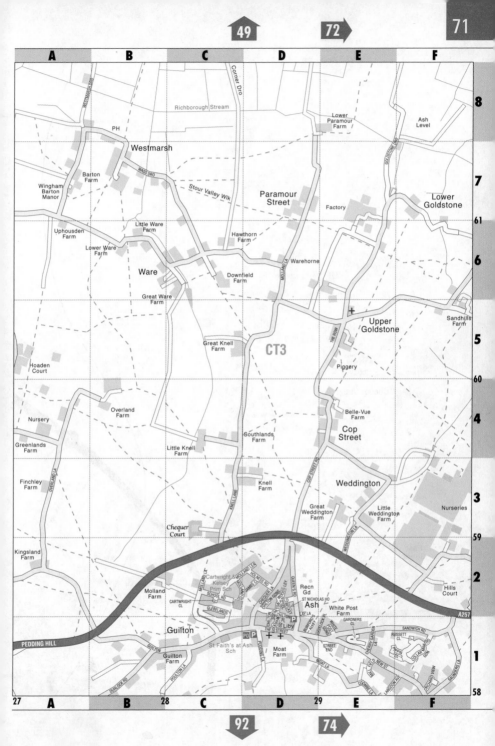

A B C D E F

8

Ash Level

White House

7

Richborough Stream

WHITEHORSE DRO

Bride Farm

Guston Farm

61

RUBERY DRO

Sparrow Castle

Richborough Farm

6

Fleet Farm

Castle Farm

Richborough ROMAN FORT (remains of)

CT3

CT13

CASTLE COTTS

5

Cooper Street Farmhouse

Mus

Swallows Brook Farm

COOPER STREET RD

60

Cooper Street

Sewage Works

RAMSGATE RD A256

Goshall Valley

Roman Amphitheatre

4

Goshall Stream

Stour Valley Wlk

River Stour

The Monks Wall

Brookestreet Farm

3

Pfizer Monk's Wall Nature Reserve

LC

Little East Street Farm

Saxon Shore Way

59

North Poulders Stream

East Street

Gazen Salts Nature Reserve

2

East Street Farm

North Poulders

White Mill Rural Heritage Ctr Ind Est

Goss Hall

A257

A257 SANDWICH RD

THE CAUSEWAY

ASH RD

MILL CL

LC

Sandwich Inf Sch

Each End

A256

South Poulders

Sandwich Guildhall Mus

Each End House

1

THOMAS S HOSPL

LC

Each Manor Farm

Mary-le-bone Hill

WOODNESBOROUGH RD

P

58

30 A 31 B C 32 D E F

F1
1 GUESTLING MILL CT
2 CREIGHTON FLATS
3 CHURCH ST
4 VICARAGE LA
5 GUILDCOUNT LA
6 HARNET ST
7 WANTSUM MEWS
8 STOUR CT
9 LOOP COURT MEWS
10 THE OLD COACHWORKS
11 TANNERY LA
12 ST JOHN'S COTTS
13 WATTS YD
14 WHITEFRIARS WAY
15 WHITEFRIARS MDW

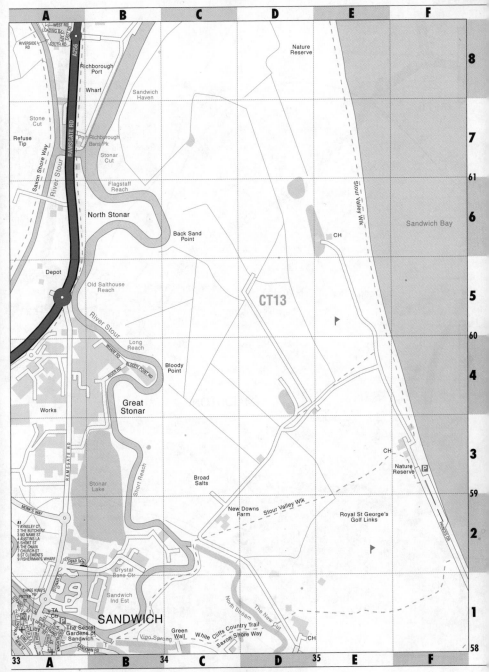

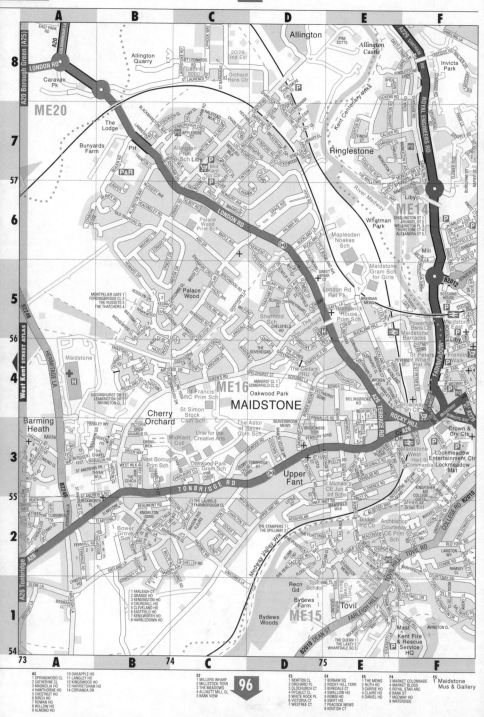

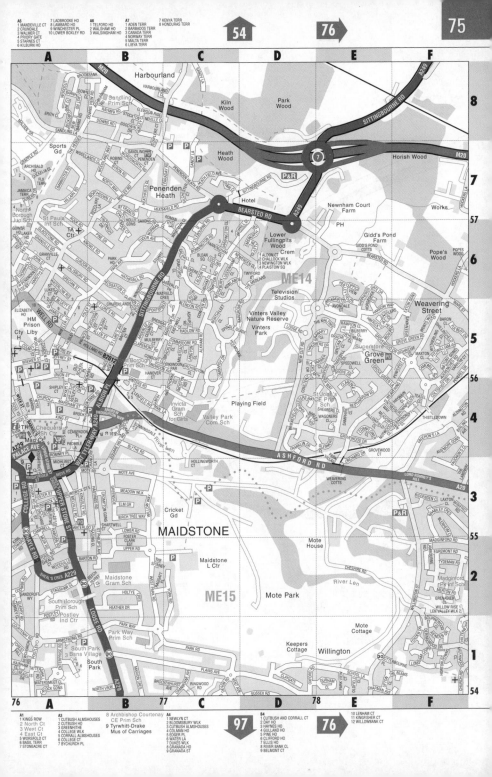

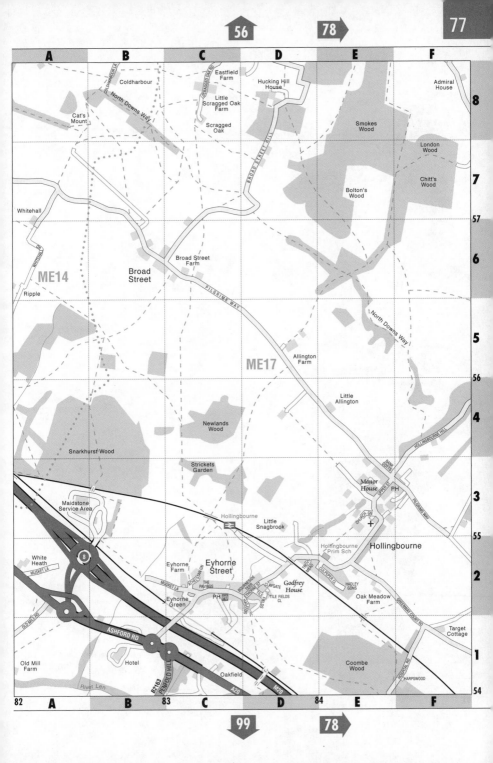

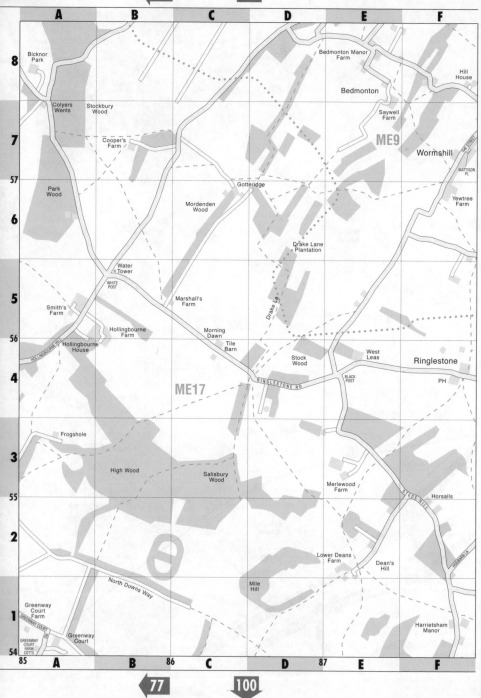

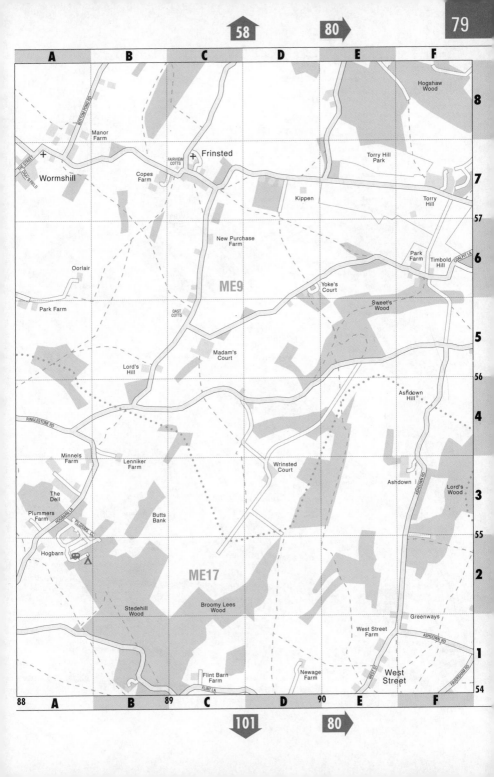

79
59

A **B** **C** **D** **E** **F**

Hollybushes

8

Great
Higham

DOWN COURT RD

Down
Court

PALACE
COTTS

Palace
Farm

Doddington

Home
Farm

7

Lodge

Little
Higham

PH
20

THE STREET

SUNNYSIDE

NORTHDOWN

CHURCH HILL

THE
RETREAT

WEST END
GREEN

WEST END

West
End

57

Ppg Sta

Endings
Wood

Miniature Rly

COALPIT LA

COALPIT LA

Sprats
Hill

Jackson's
Wood

Shulland
Wood

6

Green
Farm

ME9

Temple
Farm

Frangbury

5

Wichling

Solomon's
Cottages

56

Syndale
Bottom

King's
Acre

OXTENHAM RD

FAVERSHAM RD

Filmer Wood

4

Wichling Wood

Takarazuka

Birchwood

ME17

3

Broomhill
Farm

Bank
Farm

The
Manor House

Greet

Wellwood
Farm

55

Lone
Barn
Farm

Rhode
Farm

Wyebanks

2

Maitlands
Farm

ME13

Oakenpole
Wood

Sparks Wood

Centre
Slade
Farm

Slade

1

Forge
Cottage

LONE BARN RD

ME17

PAYDEN ST

Payden
Street

Payden
Street
Farm

Upper
Slade
Farm

SLADE RD

Otterden
Plantation

54

LONE BARN RD

A **B** **C** **D** **E** **F**

91 92 93

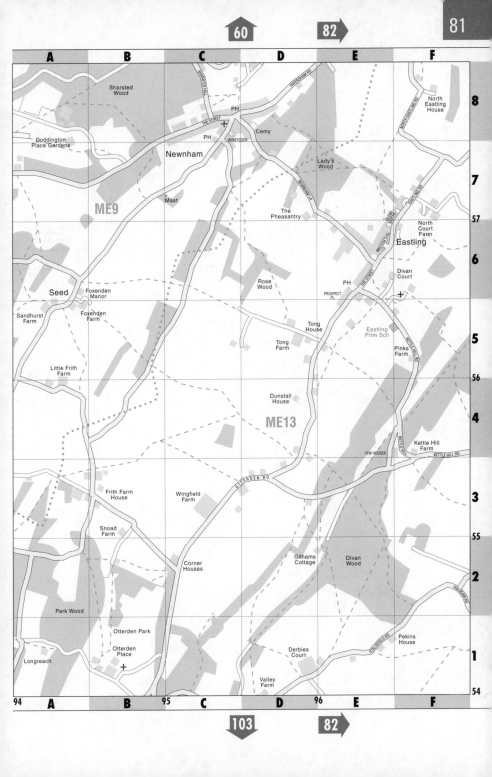

81
61

	A	B	C	D	E	F

8

Rice Wood

Scooks Farm House

Deadman's Wood

Wilderton Wood

7

Mincedane Wood

Pidgeon Cottage

57

STALISFIELD RD

WILGATE GREEN RD

Wilgate Green

CH

6

Belmont Park

Wilgate Green Farm

Barn Wood

Park House

South Wilderton

Pett Dane

Belmont House & Gardens

Belmont

5

New York

THROWLEY RD

Great Bradfield Wood

56

ME13

Town Place

PARSONAGE STOCKS RD

Parsonage Farm

HAYWARD'S HILL

4

Arnold's Oak Farm

Church Farm

✚

Throwley

KETTLE HILL RD

Hockley Hole Farm

3

Hockley

Park Farm

55

Huntingfield

Little Hockley Farm

Valley Farm

STALISFIELD RD

East Wood

2

CHURCH RD

OLD HOCKLEY RD

Park Lane Farm

WORKHOUSE RD

HOLBEAM RD

Throwley Forstal

PARK TERR

BETHEL ROW

1

Helbeam

JUBILEE COTTS

Tong Green Farm

PETTFIELD HILL RD

South Hill Farmhouse

Tong Green

54

81
104

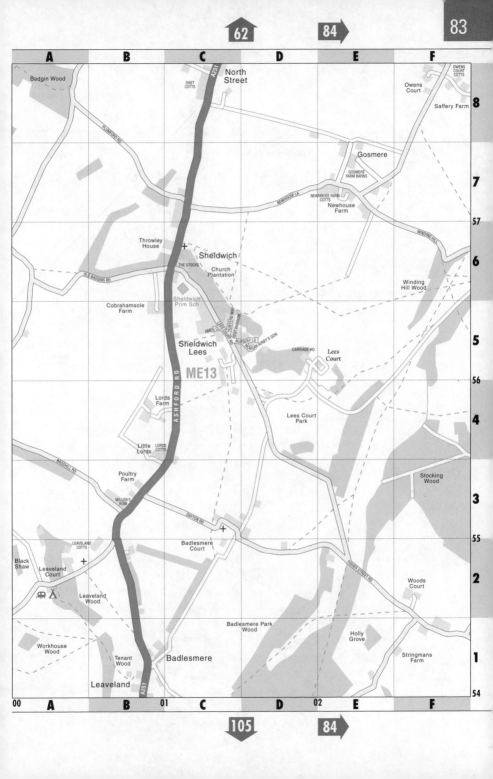

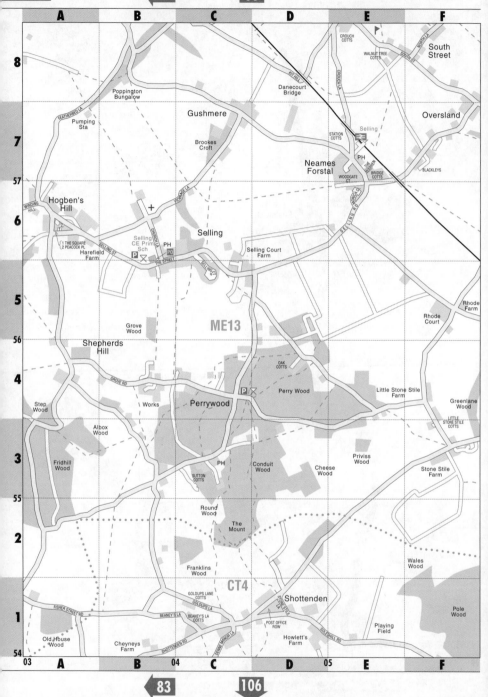

South Street

Poppington Bungalow

8

FEATHERBED LA

Pumping Sta

Gushmere

Danecourt Bridge

CROUCH COTTS

WALNUT TREE COTTS

KIT HILL

SOUTH ST

Oversland

7

Brookes Croft

STATION COTTS

Selling

Neames Forstal

57

Hogben's Hill

WINDING HILL

WOODGATE CT

PH

THE WARREN

BRIDGE COTTS

BLACKLEYS

SELLING RD

NORCLA

6

+

1 THE SQUARE
2 PEACOCK PL

Selling CE Prim Sch

PH

Selling

CHURCH LA

SELLING ST

P

THE STREET

Harefield Farm

SELLING CT

Selling Court Farm

5

Grove Wood

ME13

Rhode Farm

Shepherds Hill

56

Rhode Court

GROVE RD

OAK COTTS

4

Step Wood

Works

Perrywood

P

Perry Wood

Little Stone Stile Farm

Greenlane Wood

LITTLE STONE STILE COTTS

Albox Wood

Priviss Wood

3

Fridhill Wood

PH

SUTTON COTTS

Conduit Wood

Cheese Wood

Stone Stile Farm

55

Round Wood

The Mount

2

Franklins Wood

Wales Wood

CT4

Pole Wood

1

FISHER STREET RD

GOLDUPS LANE COTTS

GOLDUPS LA

BEANEY'S LA

BEANEY'S LA COTTS

Shottenden

STONE STILE RD

POST OFFICE ROW

Howlett's Farm

COLESHILL RD

Playing Field

54

Old House Wood

Cheyneys Farm

SHOTTENDEN RD

DENNE MANOR LA

03

A B 04 C D 05 E F

85
65

8
7
57
6
5
56
4
3
55
2
1
54

A B C D E F

Denstead Cotts
Denstead Oast
Denstead Farm
Poldhurst Farm
CT2
Bigbury Camp
Howfield Wood
Bigbury House
Petty France
North Downs Way
No Man's Orchard Nature Reserve
Bigbury Wood
PRIMROSE HILL
DENSTEAD LA
FALKNERS LA
A2050 A2

Hunstead Wood
Bigberry Farm
Chartham Hatch
Howfield Wood Farm
NIGHTINGALE CL
TOWN LA
BIGBURY RD

Fright Wood
PH
NEW TOWN ST
The Rough
Howfield LA
Howfield Farm
A28

Nickle Farm
Mast
HATCH LA
CT4
Langdane Wood
Stour Valley Ind Est
Stour Valley Works

Dunning Shaw
NICKLE COTTS
Cemy
LC
Stour Valley Ind Est
Horton Cotts
Horton Gdns
LC
Stour Valley Wlk

Great Stour
ASHFORD RD
1 APSLEY COTTS
2 DE L'ANGLE ROW
3 MILL TERR
4 DE L'ANGLE HO
Horton
Sewage Works
A28

The Deanery
RIVERSIDE
LC
Chartham
PARISH RD
LC
CHURCH LA
THE GREEN
3

CARMEL CL
The Hyde
MEWS
ASH SCHOOL LA
BOLAS HILL
Mill
RENTAIN RD
STATION RD
STOUR RD
Chartham
COCKERING RD

PH
BRUNDELL TER
ASHDOWN FIELD
SHALMSFORD ST
SHALMSFORD CT
HANDLEY RD
CRESCENT
HURST LA
LANGTON LA
HATHINGTON ST
LANGS VIEW
1 REDWOOD CL
2 LIME CL
3 CHAPLAINS WLK
4 AINSLEY WAY
5 TOWER VIEW
6 THE CHAPEL
7 CANDLERS WY

Shalmsford Street
Chartham Prim Sch
WOODSIDE AVE
LAWSON CL
POMFRET HO
PH
BEECH AVE
THE CROSS
GARDENERS PL
GODFREY GDNS
CHESTNUT CL

Stour Valley Wlk
THRUSH LA
THE CRESCENT
PH
JASMINE CL
ASH RD
ASPEN RD
THE DOWNS
LITTLE COPSE
MAGNOLIA DR
SYCAMORE CL

Chartham Downs
MYRTLE LA

09 A B 10 C D 11 E F

85
108

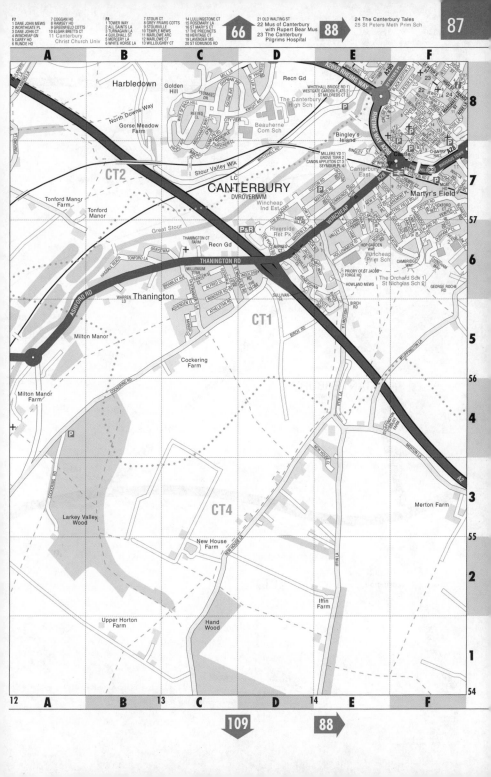

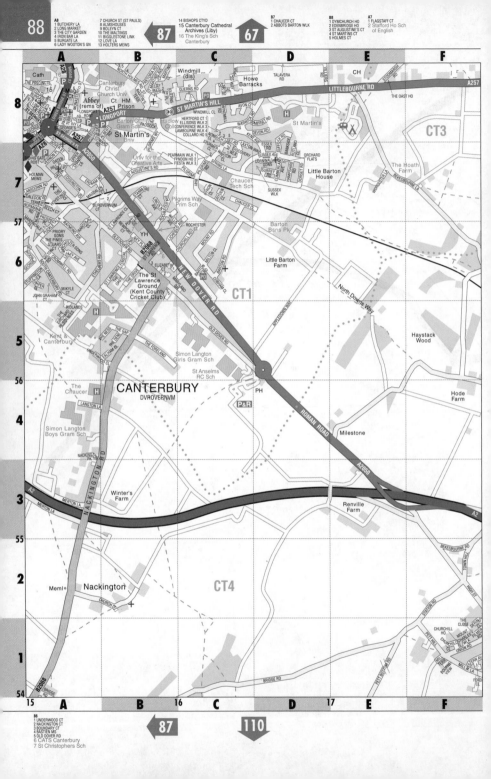

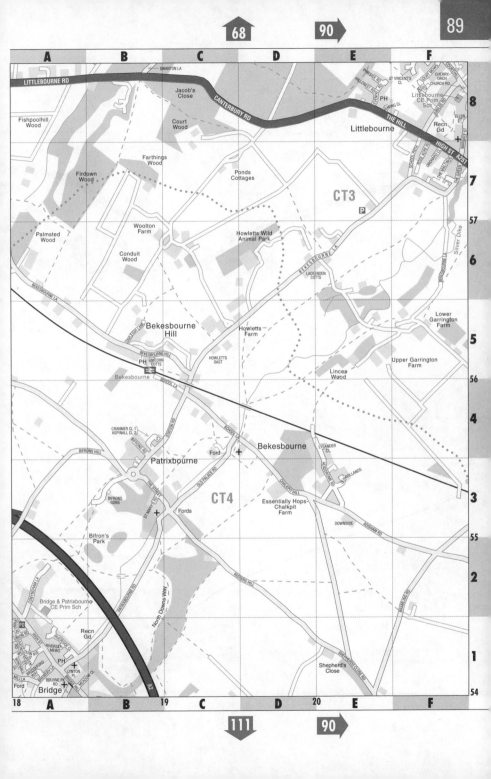

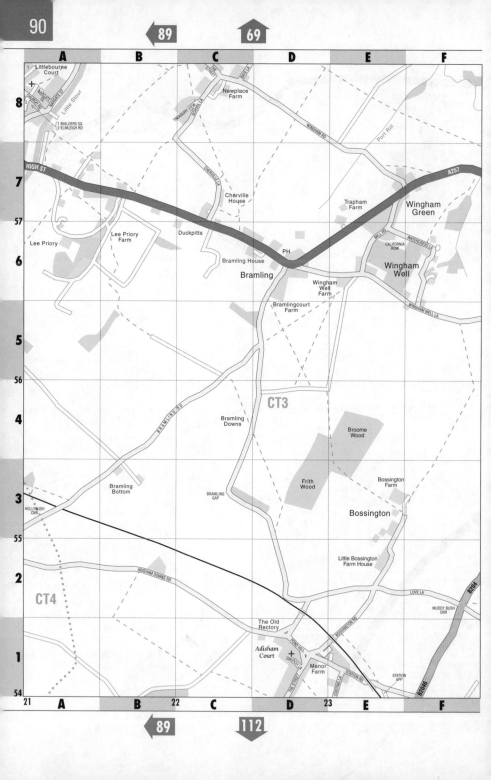

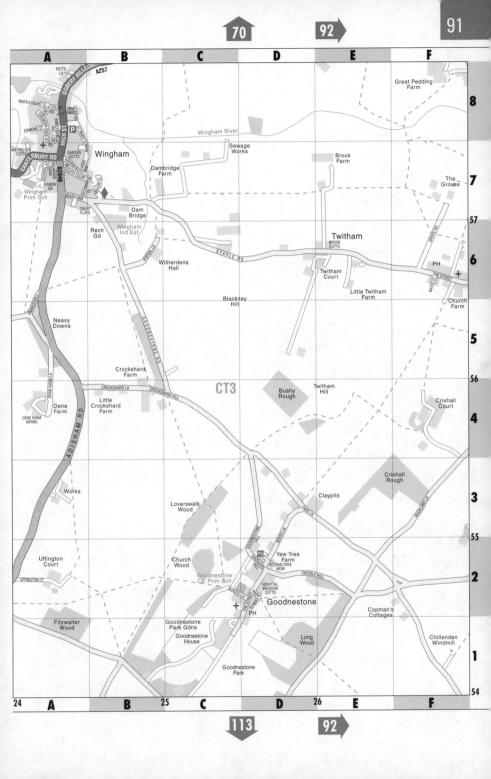

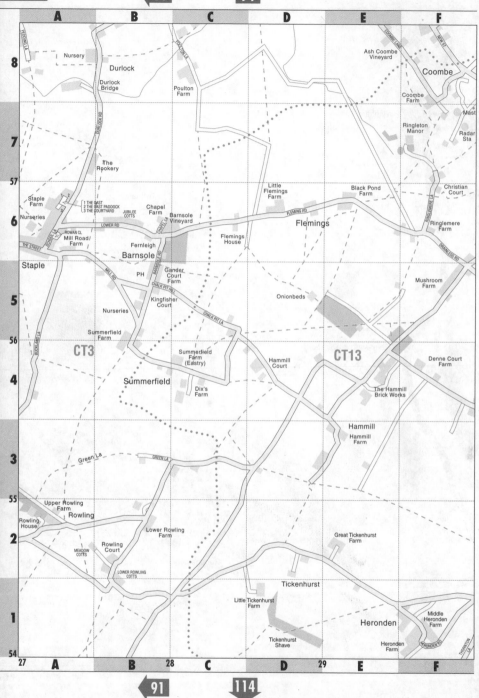

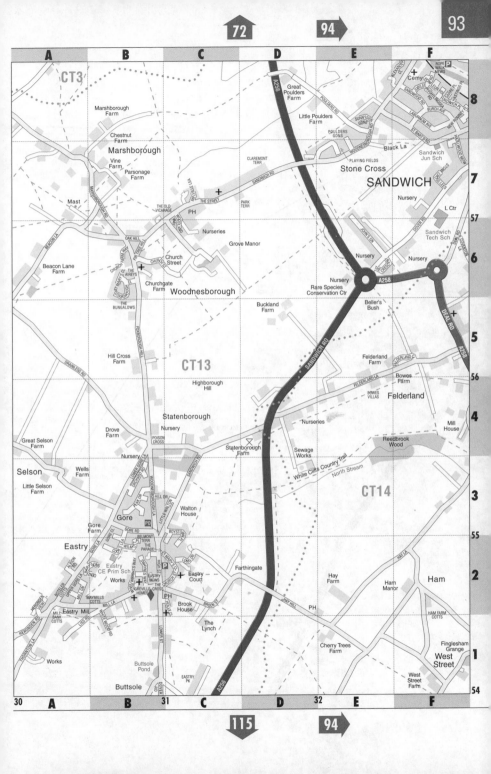

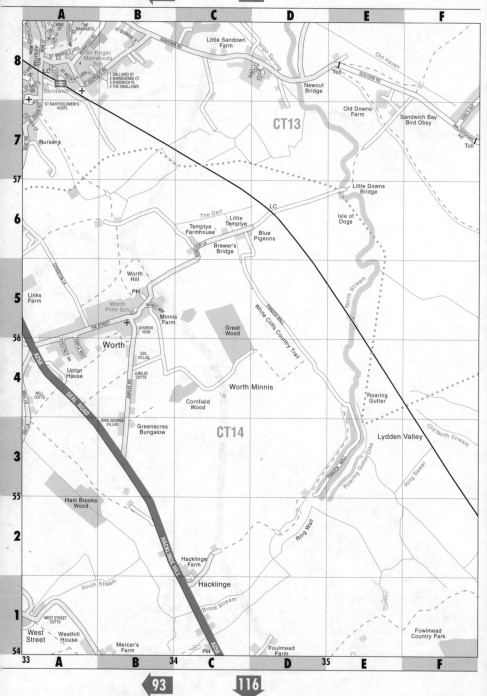

Sandwich Bay

Royal
St George's
Golf Links

KING'S AVE

COASTGUARD
COTTS

Sandwich Bay
Estate

PRINCES DR

NORTH RD

WHITEHALL

WALDERSHARE AVE

FAIRWAY 1
THE SANCTUARY 2
GUILFORD HO 3
THE DUNES 4

SANDOWN AVE

CAMBRIDGE AVE

DICKSON'S
CNR

CT13

Lyddcourt
Stile

Lydden

Mary Bax's
Stone

GREENACRES

Saxon Shore Way
White Cliffs Country Trail

Old North Stream

CT14

Tenants
Hills

Walnut Tree
Farm

Penfield Sewer

REDHOUSE WALL

Redhouse
Farm

CH

GOLF RD

Sandown Castle
(remains of)

1 CASTLE WLK
2 CANUTE WLK

CANUTE RD

SANDOWN RD

ETHELBERT RD

THE MARINA

GODWYN
RD

GOLF CT 1
LINKS CT 2
WALCHEREN CL 3

8

7

57

6

5

56

4

3

55

2

1

54

A   B   37   C   D   38   E   F

36   A   B   C   D   E   F

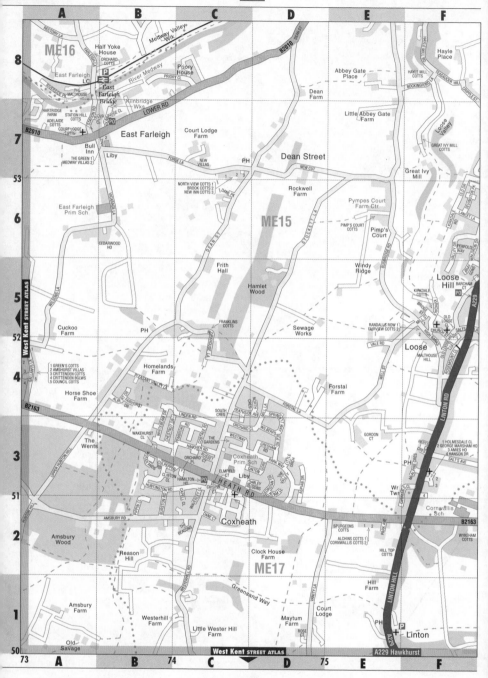

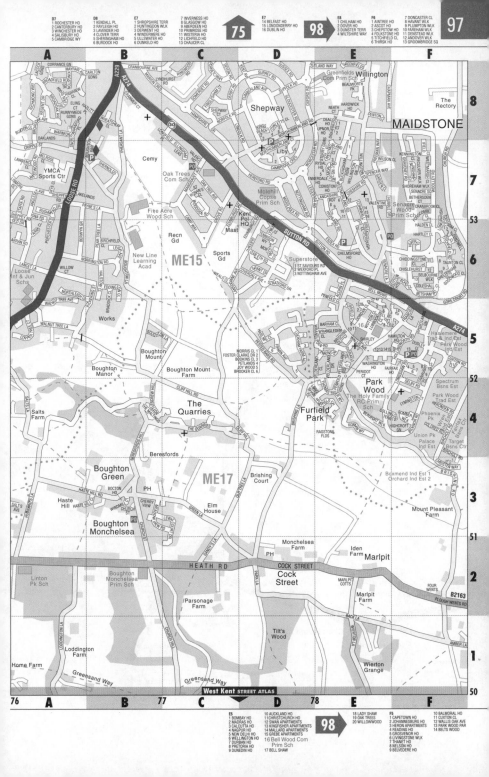

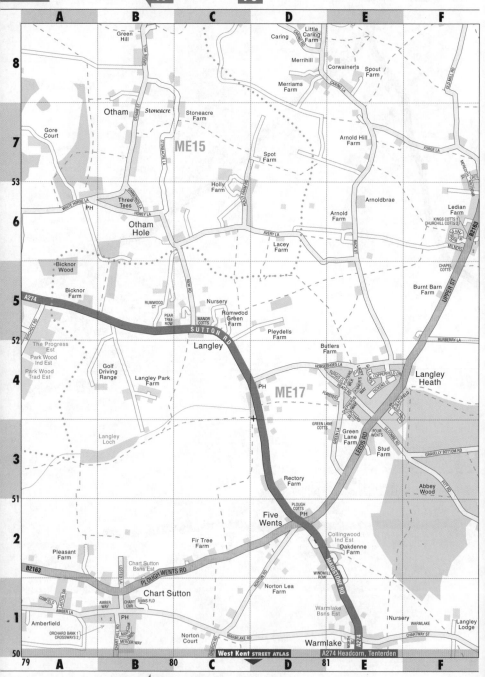

8

Sewage
Works

Leeds &
Broomfield
CE Prim
Sch

Ashbank

ASHBANK
COTTS

Leeds

Battel
Hall

PH

Abbey
Farm

PENFOLD HILL

B2163

P

PH

CH

Warren
Wood

Leeds
Castle

Forge
House

7

GREENWAY COURT RD

GREENWAY LA

A20

M20

ASHFORD RD

M20

53

The
Great
Water

CHEGWORTH
LA

Chegworth

6

River Len

Church
Farm

Broomfield

Roses
Farm

BURBERRY LA

Park Barn
Farm

PARK BARN RD

ME17

Chegworth
Court

CHEGWORTH RD

5

52

Scrub
Wood

BROOMFIELD RD

Glebe
Dene

4

King's
Wood

Apiary
Bsns Pk

The
Apiary

Works

Kingswood
Farm

GRAVELLY BOTTOM RD

PITT RD

CROSS RD

Kingswood

CHARLESFORD AVE

ADHERNO LA

PO

ELDER

THORNEYCROFT
CL

CHESTNUT DR

BELL TREES

COPPERFIELD

Kingswood
Prim Sch

IVY

MEWS

THE
WALK

BELL WAY

WILDWOOD CL

GAYSER

LEBURN RD

3

WATER LA

51

HEATHERWOOD

Greensand
Ridge

College
Farm

2

Cherry
Tree
Farm

BRIDGEFIELD

WORMILL LA

CH

**Chartway
Street**

CHARTWAY ST

CHARLTON LA

Street
Farm

Manor
Farm

MORRY LA

ULCOMBE HILL

1

A   B   C   D   E   F

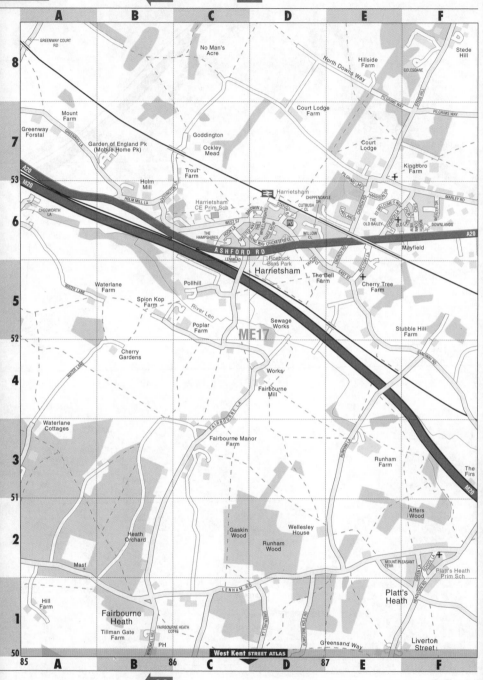

A B C D E F

8 Woodside Green
West Street
Hilltop
Marlow Farm
Marley Court
Lea Farm
Tophill Farm

7 PILGRIMS WAY
Factory
North Downs Way
Highfield
53 Marley Works
LIMETREE TERR

6 A20
Dickley Wood
War Memorial
DICKLEY LA
Westgate House
ASHFORD RD
HILL CRES
Cemy
FROGMORE WLK 1
NAPOLEON WLK 2
RIVERS WLK 3
MORELLA WLK 4
THE CLOISTERS
Swadelands Sch
ROYTON AVE
CHILSTON RD
DOUGLAS ALMSHOUSES
Grove House
ATWATER

5 Boldrewood Farm
Depot
GRANT'S COTTS
Lenham
Lenham Prim Sch
P
PO
Liby
WICKHAM
CHURCH SQ
Northdown Bsns Pk
A20
52 MALTHOUSE CL
CROFT GDNS
ME17
LENHAM HO
Ashmill Bsns Pk
Lenham
Tanyard Farm

4 Kiln Wood
Inkstand Meadow Farm
Nature Reserve
HEADCORN RD
Leadingcross Green
Oxley Wood
Stout Valley Wlk

3 Sandway
Great Stour
PH
Pleasant Farm
Home Farm
Sewage Works
51 M20
LENHAM HEATH RD

2 Ridding Farm
Mount Castle Farm
MOUNT CASTLE LA

1 Lewsome Farm
Chapel Farm
Chilston Park
Chilston Park Hotel
M20
50

88 A B 89 C D 90 E F

	A	B	C	D	E	F

8

LONE BARN RD

Payden Street

Bunker's Hill

PARGES ST

SLADE RD

HURSTWOOD RD

Hurst Farm

7

Birch Wood

Warren Lodge Farm

Stubblefield House

ME13

Bunce Court

BUNCE COURT RD

53

Warren Street

WARREN ST

Blue House Farm

6

Little Pivington Farm

Middleton Farm

PH

Water Tower

Oak Farm

COLD HARBOUR RD

Cold Harbour

Great Pivington Farm

HUBBARDS HILL

Glebe Farm

WATERDITCH LA

Westbury Farm

5

RAYNER HILL COTTS

RAYNERS HILL

HIGHBOURNE PK

Waterditch Farm

Pilgrims' Way

52

A20

ME17

North Downs Way

Fair View

4

ASHFORD RD

3

New Shelve Farm

Old Shelve

Cobham Farm

COUNTRY WAYS

Wheatgratten Farm

Old Shelve Farm

51

2

Acton Farm

TN27

MAIDSTONE RD

Forstal Cotts

Sand Pit

Shepherd's Farm

MOUNT CASTLE LA

THE FORSTAL

Lenham Forstal

Bolton Farm

1

BULL HILL

The Forstal

Lenham Heath

LENHAM FORSTAL RD

CHARING HEATH RD

HEATHFIELD BROWS

ROSE LA

YEW TREE PK

HART HILL

A20

CHARING HEATH RD

50

91	A		B	92	C		D	93	E		F

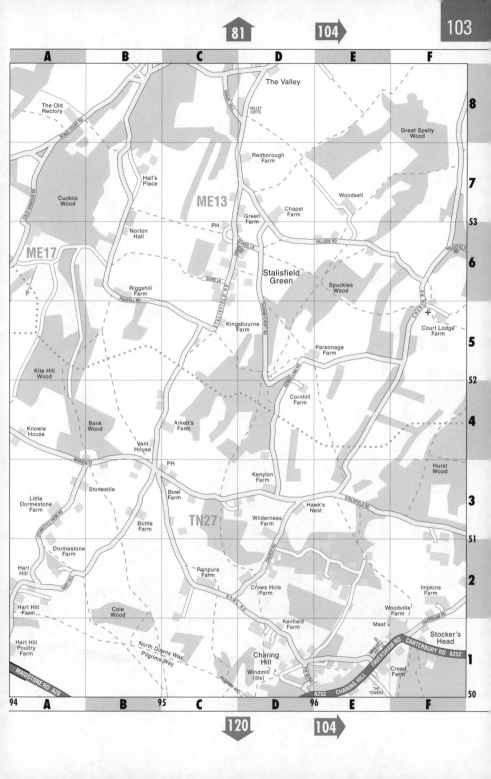

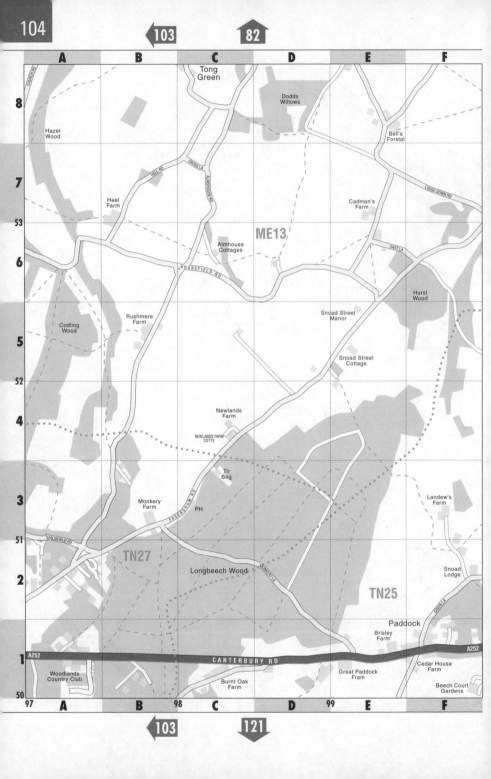

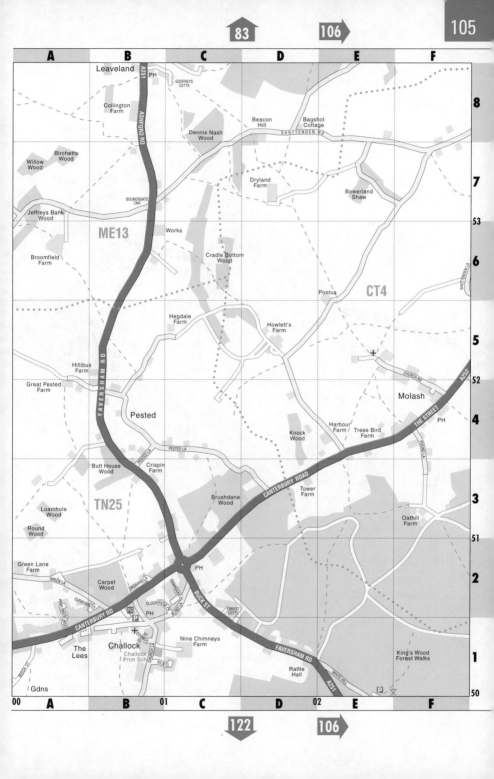

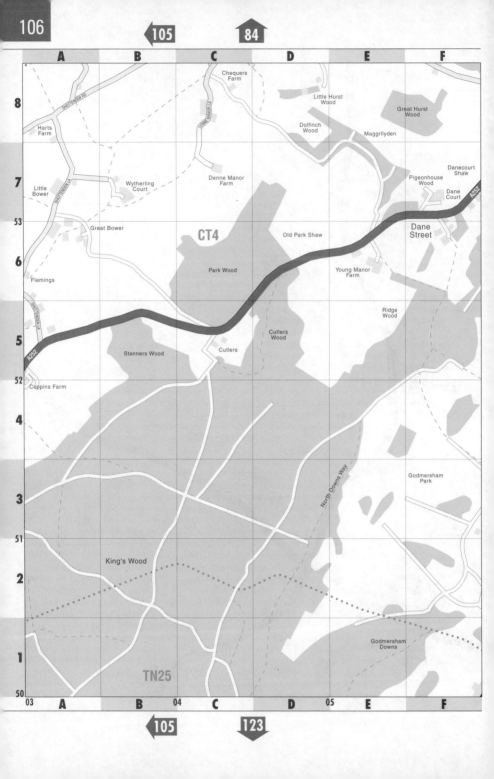

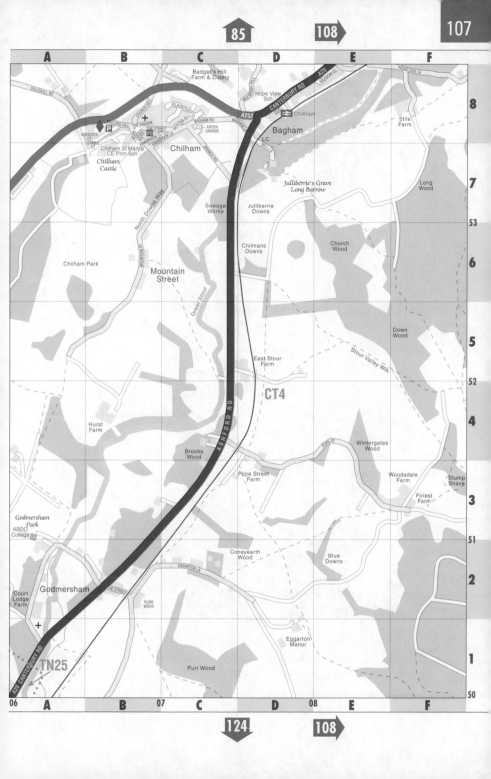

107
86

A   **B**   **C**   **D**   **E**   **F**

FOXENDEN LA

MYSTOLE LA

Stour Valley WLK

MYSTOLE LA

Underdown

2 1

THE DOWNS

UPCHURCH LA

CASTLERS WAY

8

Mystole
House

Mystole
Park

Thruxted

MAGNOLIA DR 1
AINSLEY WAY 2

Perry Hill
Shaw

Canterbury
Steiner Sch

7

Perry Court
Farm

SARLING'S GREEN RD

53

Upper
Mystole Park
Farm

Sappington
Court

Walk
Wood

*Kenfield
Hall*

6

Kenfield
Hall Farm

KENFIELD RD

Garlinge
Green

5

PENNY POT LA

52

Denge Wood

CT4

4

Capel Farm

CAPEL RD

Saw
Mill

Upper Thruxted
Farm

3

Thruxted
Mill

51

Mounts
Wood

Buckholt
Wood

2

P

Eggringe
Wood

Dunstan's
Wood

WALTHAM RD

1

Barton
Wood

Buckholt
Barn

50

107
125

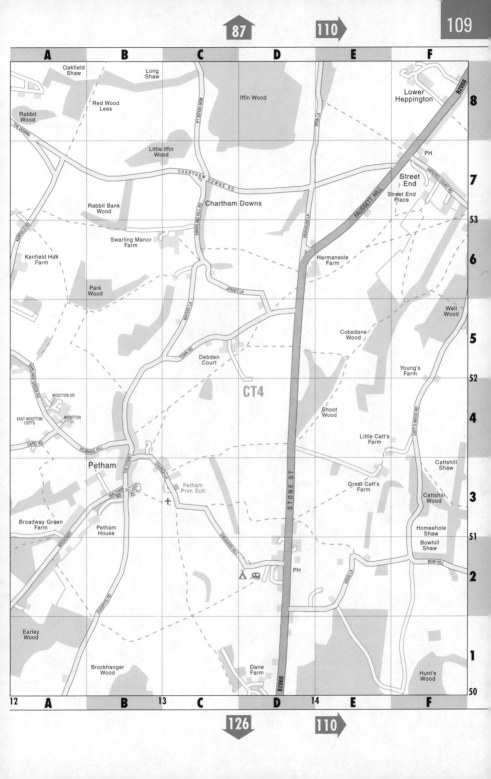

109
88

A **B** **C** **D** **E** **F**

8

Whitehill
Wood

Middle Pett
Farm

7

North Court
Farm

Little Pett
Farm

Warren
Wood

The
Shave

53

Lower
Hardres

Redhill
Wood

BUTTS CT

6

Little
Eaton
Farm

BUTTS
MDW

PH

Lenhall
Farm

SCHOOL LA

PETT BOTTOM RD

Stockfield
Wood

Avenue
Wood

5

Pett
Bottom

CT4

52

Cook's
Farm

PH

MAPLES HILL

4

Gorsley
Wood

HARDRES COURT RD

PILOT'S FARM RD

Pilot's
Wood

BROXHALL RD

CROW CAMP RD

Broxhall
Wood

Broxhall
Farm

3

St Andrew's
Wood

Langham
Park
Farm

MOUNTSFIELD

51

Equestrian
Centre

Bursted
Manor

BOW HILL

2

Upper
Hardres
Court

Hardres
Court
Farm

BURSTED HILL

Bursted
Wood

Park
Rough

PHEASANTS HILL RD

Reed
Farm

1

The
Manor
House

WESTWOOD RD

Westwood
Farm

Marley
Wood

50

15   **A**   **B**   16   **C**   **D**   17   **E**   **F**

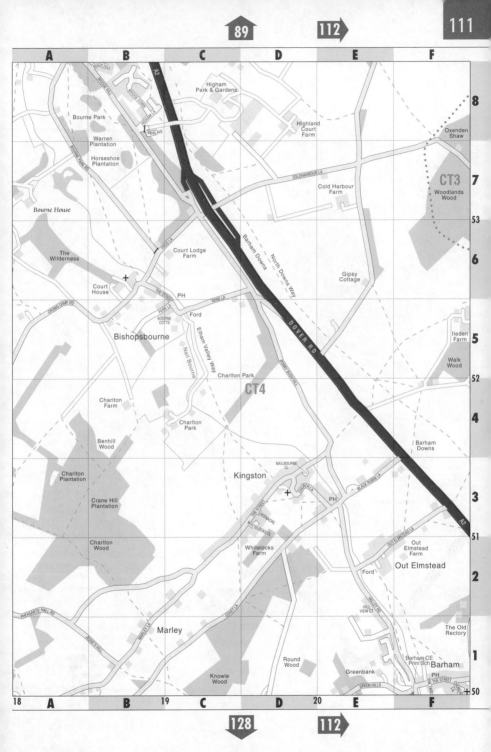

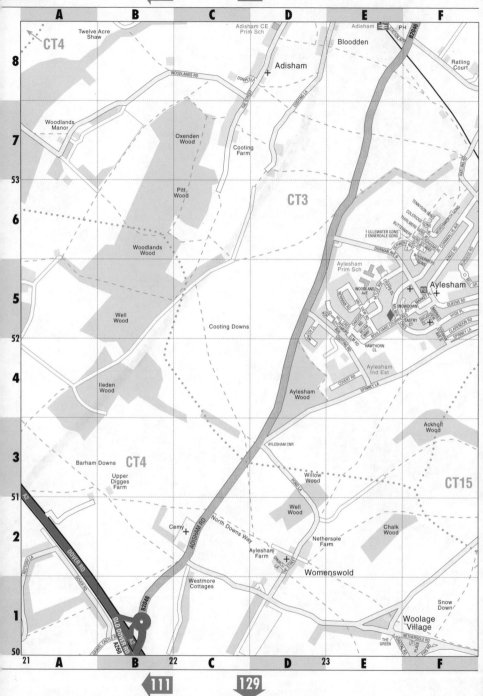

CT4

Twelve Acre Shaw

8

WOODLANDS RD

Woodlands Manor

7

Oxenden Wood

53

Pitt Wood

6

Woodlands Wood

Well Wood

5

52

Cooting Downs

Ileden Wood

4

Barham Downs   CT4

3

51

A2

Upper Digges Farm

Cemy

2

Westmore Cottages

1

50

21   A   22   B   C   23   D   E   F

Adisham CE Prim Sch

Adisham

DONKEY LA

THE STREET

Cooting Farm

COOTING LA

CT3

AYLESHAM CNR

Willow Wood

Well Wood

North Downs Way

ADISHAM RD

Nethersole Farm

Aylesham Farm

Womenswold

THE STREET

Blaodden

Adisham   STATION RD

PH

B2046

Ratling Court

Aylesham Prim Sch

WOODLAND AVE

1 ULLSWATER GDNS
2 ENNERDALE GDNS

DORMAN AVE S

Aylesham

SNOWDOWN

EASTRY CT

HAWTHORN CL

Aylesham Ind Est

SPINNEY LA

Aylesham Wood

COVERT RD

SPINNEY LA

Ackholt Wood

CT15

Chalk Wood

Snow Down

Woolage Village

THE GREEN

DOVER RD

B2046

A2

A260

OLD DOVER RD

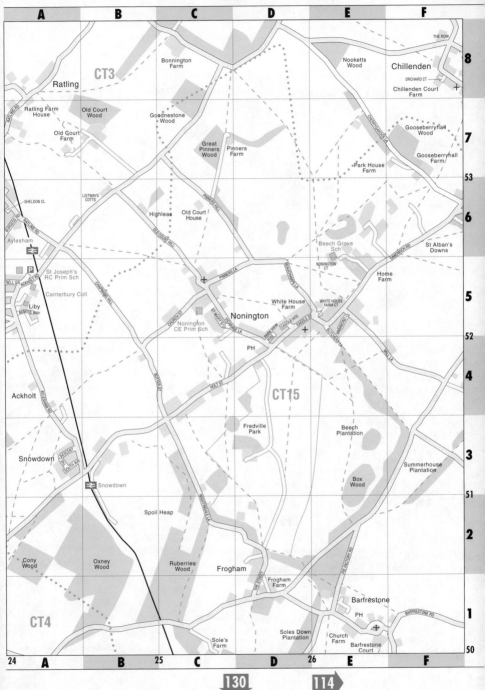

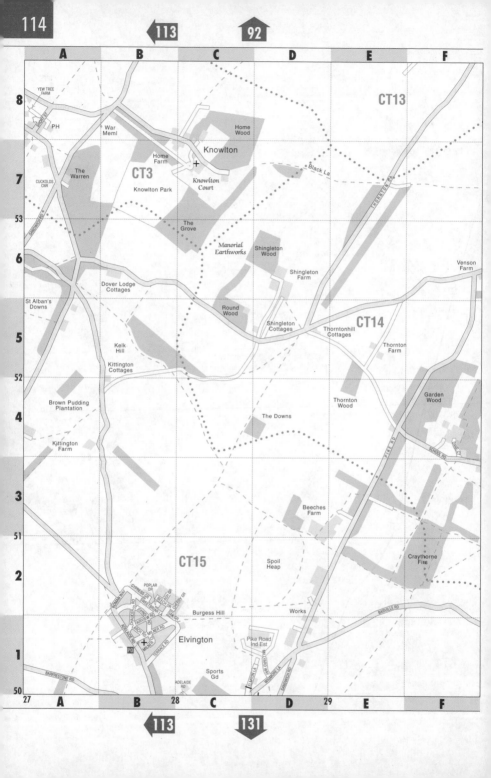

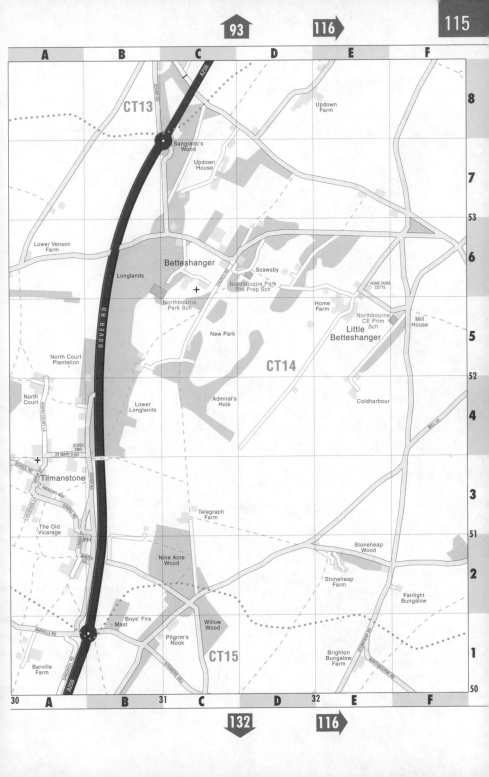

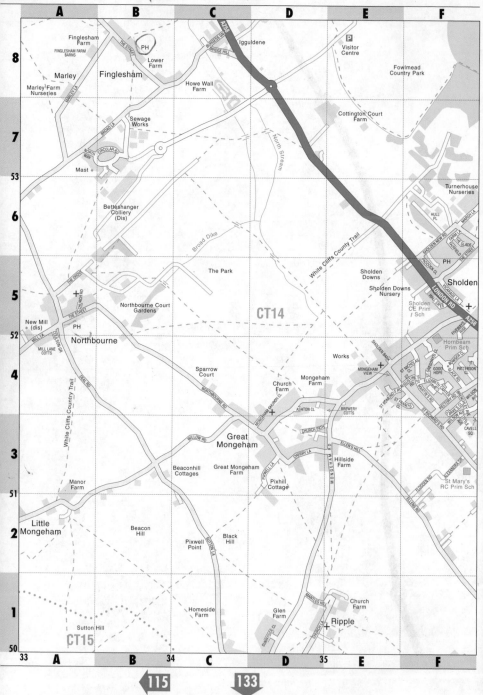

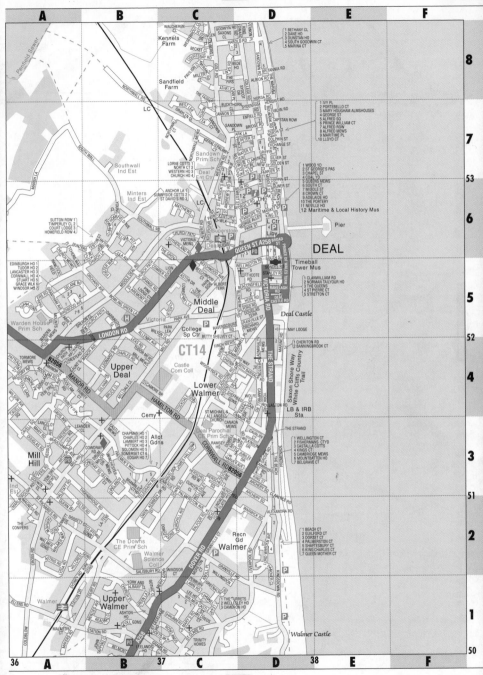

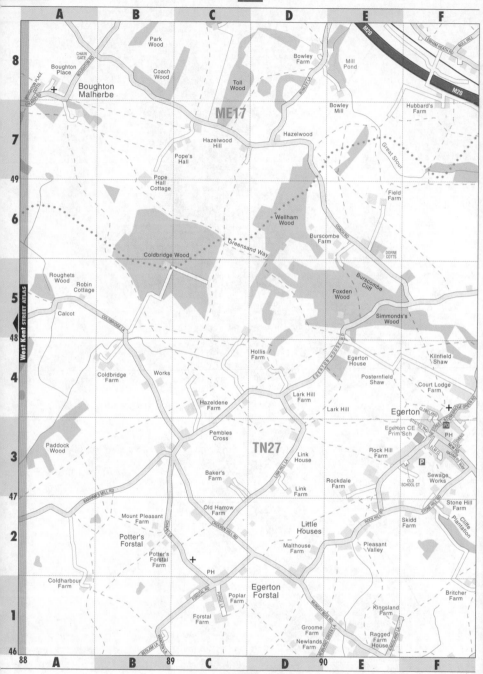

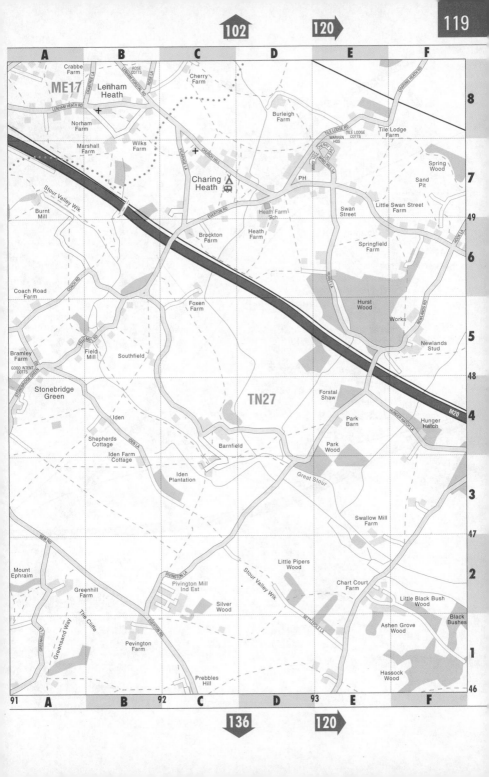

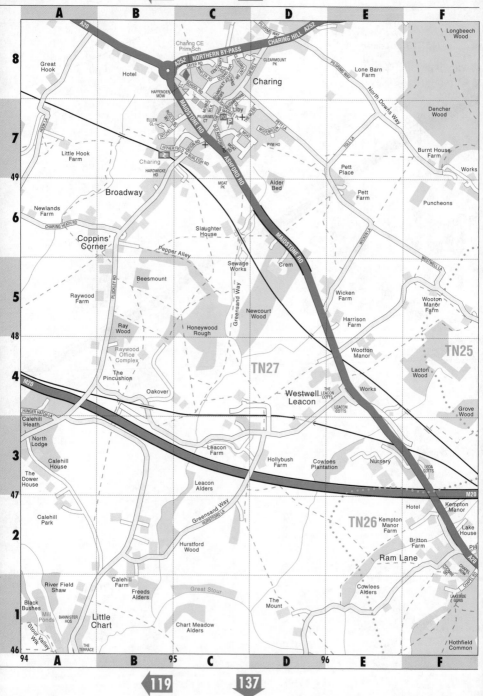

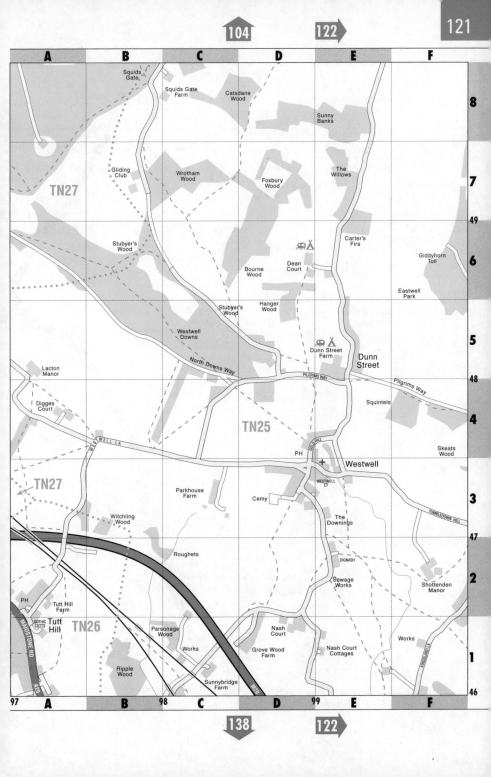

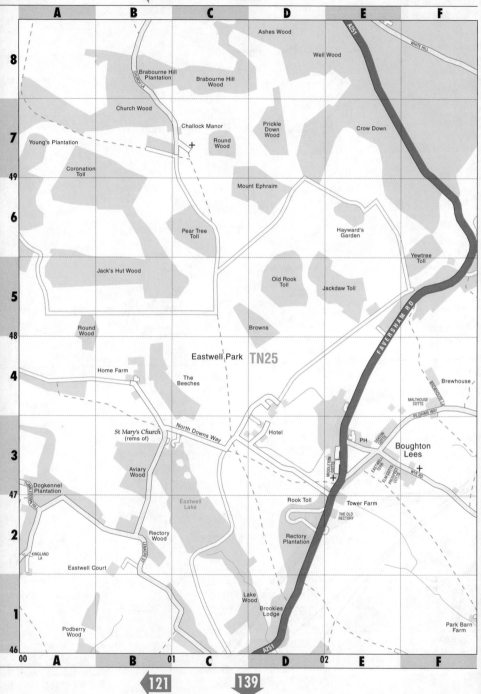

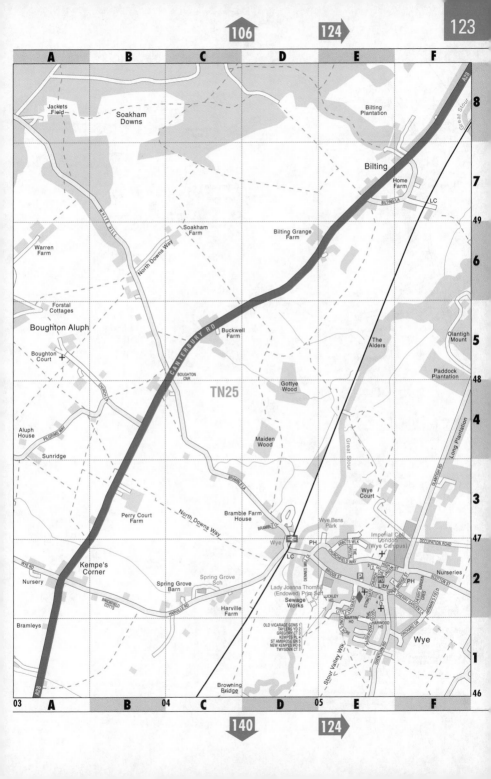

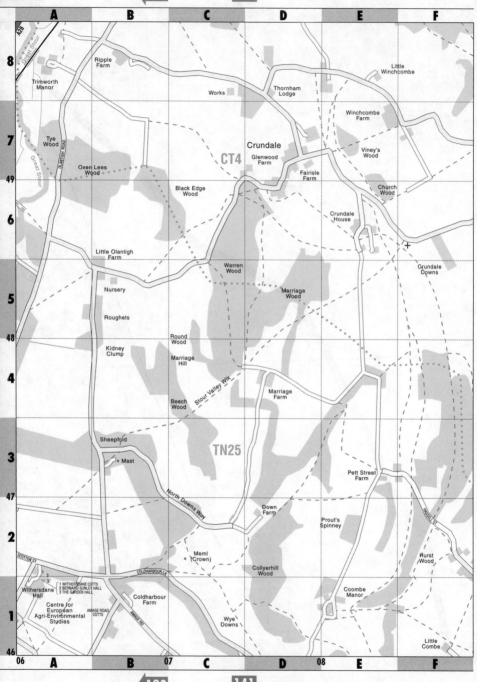

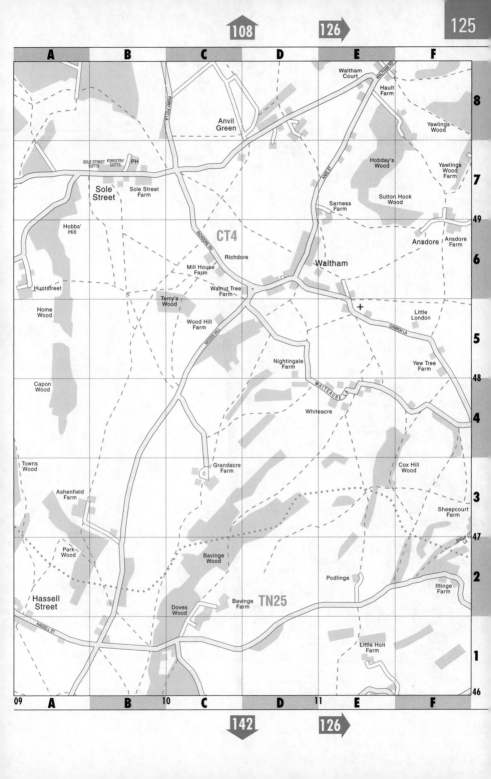

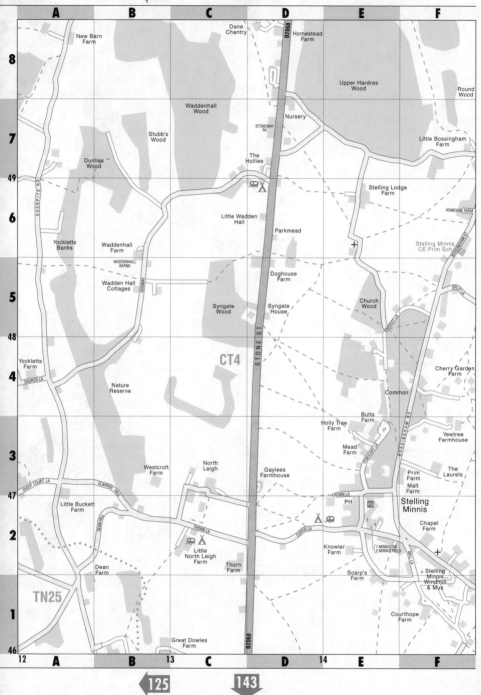

A B C D E F

8

Little Westwood Farm

WESTWOOD RD

Reed's Mill (dis)

Westwood

MARLEY LA

Lynsore Bottom

Quilters Wood

7

Manns Wood

Covet Wood Cottages

Great Bossingham Farm

PETT BOTTOM RD

Kingswood Farm

COVET LA

49

PH

Bossingham

Lynsore Court

6

TERRACE COTTS

MANNS HILL

Covet Wood

Clambercrown

Atchester Wood

SPLIT LA

Great Palmstead Farm

5

CT4

Palmstead

48

Split Lane Farm

Little Palmstead Farm

PEAFIELD WOOD RD

Dane Farm

4

Peafield Wood

High Chimney Farm

Abbotswood

Fryarne Park Wood

Charcoal Farm

Beech Villa

3

South Lodge Farm

47

Fryarne Park

Wildage Farm

Bladbean

Lodge Wood

Stud Farm

2

Farthingsole Farm

Madams Wood

Boormanhatch Farm

Jacques Court

1

PARK GATE

46

15 A 16 B C D 17 E F

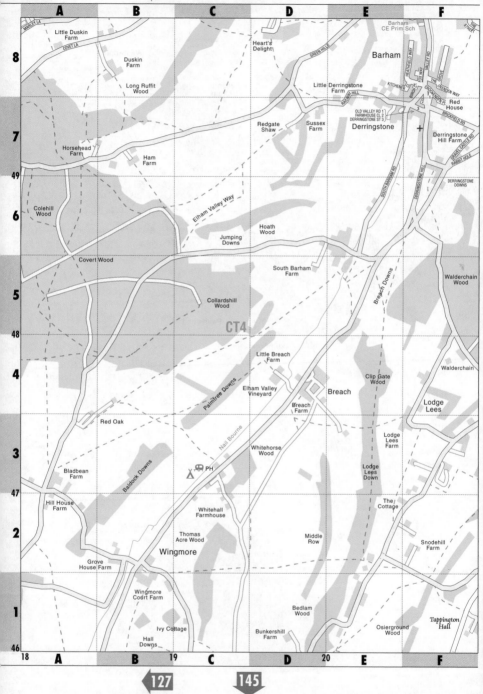

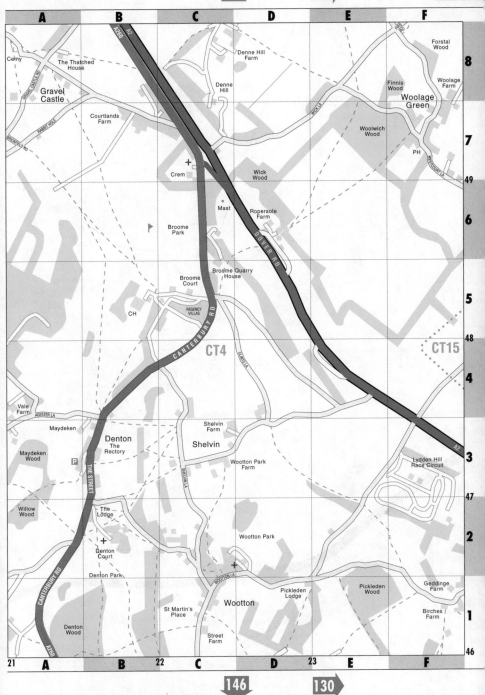

129
113

A **B** **C** **D** **E** **F**

8

Leighgate Bottom

Lower Soles Wood

Three Barrows Down

7

CT4

Long La

Stafflands Wood

49

North Downs Way

LONG LA

Long Lane Farm

Golgotha

SHEPHERDSWELL RD

6

West Court Downs

East Kent Railway

LC

Crossways

CT15

Shepherdswell or Sibertswold

5

WESTCOURT LA

Shepherds Well

STATION RD

MILL LA

48

PH

THE GRANGE

APPROACH RD

Puckland Wood

West Court Farm

THE HAYLEYS

PROSPECT COTTS

CHURCH HILL

PO

MOOR HILL

MILL HILL RD

Botolph Street Farm

P

MOORLAND RD

Sibertswold CE Prim Sch

PH

Upton Court Farm

4

WHITTINGTON

47

Coxhill Farm

Diamond Farm

Halfway Street

3

Hope Wood

COXHILL

COLRED RD

THE CONIFERS

A2

DOVER RD

Claysole Wood

Upton Wood

47

2

CT4

Five Oaks Farm

Mast

Lyddenhill Wood

A2

CHURCH HILL

COLRED HILL

1

LYDDEN HILL

46

24 **A** **B** 25 **C** **D** 26 **E** **F**

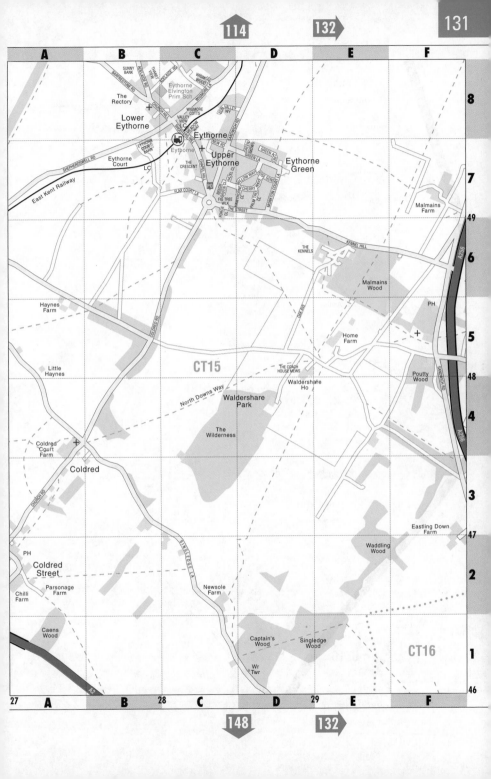

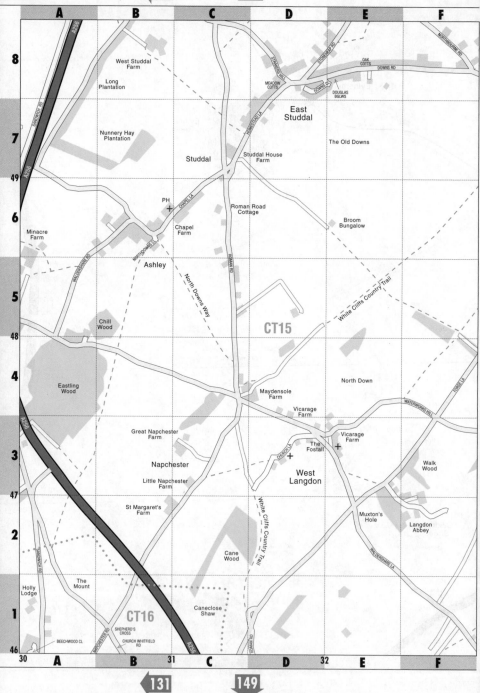

131
115
131
149

A B C D E F

8
West Studdal Farm
Long Plantation

7
Nunnery Hay Plantation

STOKEFREE RD
STONEHEAP RD
MEADOW COTTS
OAK COTTS
DOWNS RD
DOUGLAS BGLWS
DOWNS CL
East Studdal

49
Studdal
Studdal House Farm
The Old Downs

6
PH
CHAPEL LA
Chapel Farm
Roman Road Cottage
Broom Bungalow
Minacre Farm

5
Ashley
NORTHDOWNS CL
WALDERSHIRE RD
North Downs Way
ROMAN RD
White Cliffs Country Trail
CT15

48
Chill Wood

4
Eastling Wood
Maydensole Farm
North Down
WATERWORKS HILL
FOXHILL LA

3
Great Napchester Farm
Vicarage Farm
Vicarage Farm
The Fostall
CHURCH LA
Walk Wood
Napchester
Little Napchester Farm
West Langdon

47
St Margaret's Farm
Muxton's Hole
Langdon Abbey

2
White Cliffs Country Trail
Cane Wood
WALDERSHIRE LA
Holly Lodge
The Mount
SANDWICH RD

1
CT16
Caneclose Shaw
BROCHESTER RD
A258
OLD A256

46
BEECHWOOD CL
SHEPHERD'S CROSS
CHURCH WHITFIELD RD
OLD A256

30 31 32

A B C D E F

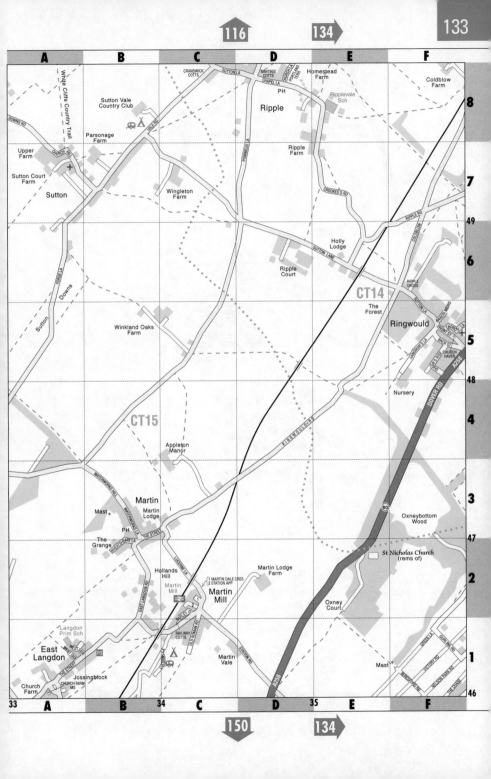

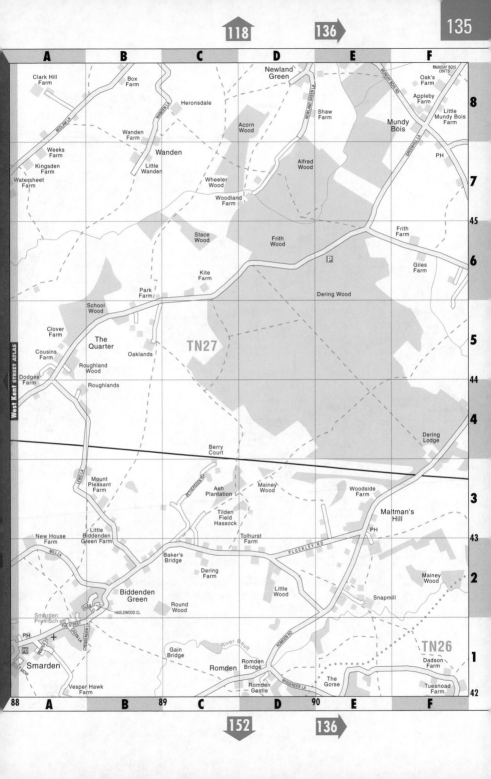

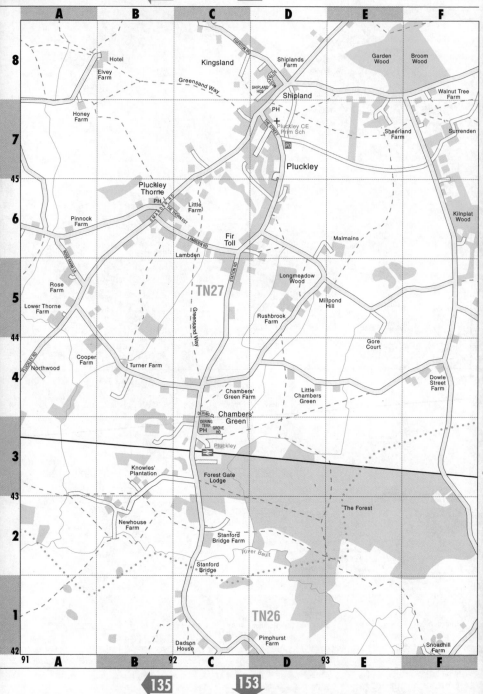

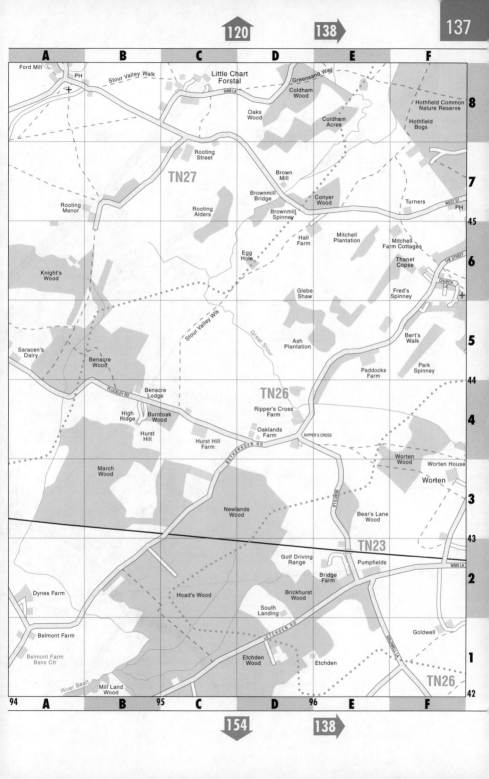

122 140

TN25
TN24
TN23

Tile Lodge Wood
Lenacre Hall Farm
Goat Lees
Alders
Sandyhurst Farm
Ulley Farm
The Towers Sch
Kennington Lees
Golden Ball
Kennington Hall
Wilmington Farm
Downs View Inf Sch
Kennington CE Jun Sch
Kennington
Bockhanger
Bybrook
Bockhanger Liby
Phoenix Com Prim Sch
Eurogate Bsns Pk
Hotels
Eureka L Pk
Cemy
Superstore
Hotel
Warren Ret Pk
Windermere
Spearpoint Cnr
James Haney Dr
Julie Rose Athletics Stadium
Factory
Water Tower
Simone Weil Ave
St Teresas RC Prim Sch
Barrow Hill
Highworth Gram Sch for Girls
Ashford Civic Ceremony Off
Cemy
Copperwood
Hotel
CH
Chart Road Ind Est
Ashford St Mary's CE Prim Sch
Queens Ct
Redington Lower Queens Rd
Works
Ashdown Ct
Mace Ind Est
Riverside Bsns Pk
Henwood Ind Est
Heron Bsns Ctr
Kingfisher Bsns Village
Ashford Art & Design
Highpoint
Henwood Bsns Ctr
Javelin Enterprise Pk
Sewage Works
Ashford Sch
The Norton Knatchbull Sch
Stour Valley Wlk
ASHFORD
Godinton Way Ind Est
Cty & Mag Ct Liby
C Ctr
The Stour Ctr
Ashford
The Ray Clements Skate Pk
The North Sch
Victoria Park
Victoria Road Prim Sch
Fairwood Ind Est
Hillyfields Rise
Chart Rd

Chart Rd
New St
Somerset Rd
Mace La
Hythe Rd
Maidstone Rd
Fougeres Way
Drovers Rdbt
Trinity Rd
Faversham Rd
Canterbury Rd
Willesborough Rd
Nicholas Rd
Station Rd
Elwick Rd

A2042 A251 A28 A2070 A2042 A292 A20 A2070 A292

B2
1 ENGINEERS CT
2 Park Mall
3 ST GEORGE'S SQ
4 GILBERT RD
5 NEW RENTS
6 CASTLE ST
7 KINGS PAR
8 COUNTY SQ
9 TUFTON WLK
10 CHURCH YARD PAS
11 HEMPSTED ST
12 MARKET ST
13 ELWICK LA
14 REGENTS CT
15 Ashford Borough Mus
16 County Square Sh Ctr
17 British MK IV Tank

B3
1 BARROW HILL TERR
2 BARROW HILL PL
3 GRAVEL WLK
4 WOLSELEY PL

C2
1 KNOTTS SQ
2 CHAPEL MEWS
3 MIDDLE ROW
4 CHURCH RD
5 ASHDALE HO
6 COLLEGE CT
7 LESLEY CHALK HO
8 Ashford Sch of Art & Design

156 140

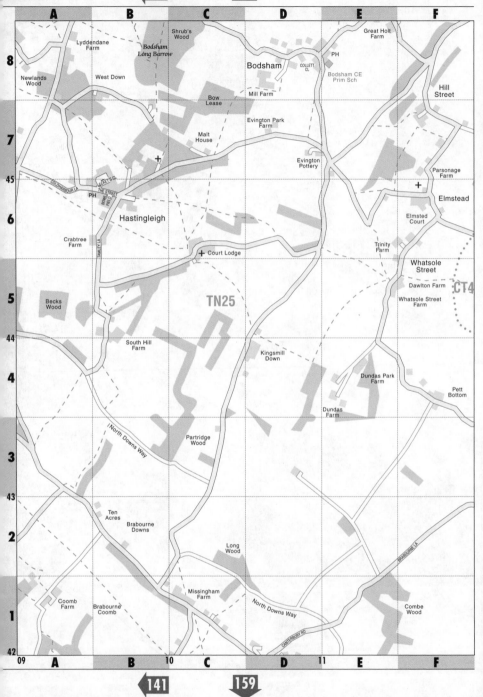

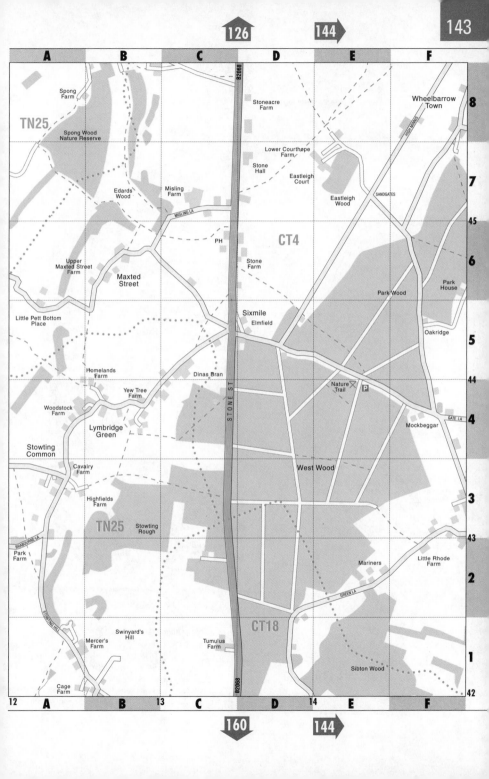

8

Elhampark Wood

Grimsacre Farm

7

Clavertye Wood

Upper Park Gate Farm

Little Gate Farm

Maycroft

Park Gate

45

Hawes Farm

Clavertye Wood

6

Ash Ridge House

Beveridge Bottom Wood

5

Exted Farm

Exted

Elham

CT4

44

Mountbottom

DELLINGS HILL

ST. GENS
LIME
VILLAS
LINDEN
PH
PO

4

GATE LA

PROSPECT TERR 1
MANORFIELD 2
CHURCH WLK 3
ST MARY'S RD 4

STATION MEWS

HUNTER'S MANA

OLD RD

Elham CE Prim Sch

ORMEL LA

Collards Wood

Cemy

Mount Farm

Fir Tree Farm

Collards Wood

COLLARDS LA

Tye

The Laynes

3

Rhodes Minnis

Tye Wood

CANTERBURY RD

Nail Bourne

Elham Valley Way

GREEN LA

WHITE HORSE LA

43

Millhill Farm

2

Wenny Farm

BOYKE LA

Home Farm

Bereforstal Farm

LONGAGE HILL

Ottinge

Mill Down

CT18

1

Ottinge Court Farm

SHUTTLESFIELD LA

CT18

Stonebridge Farm

42

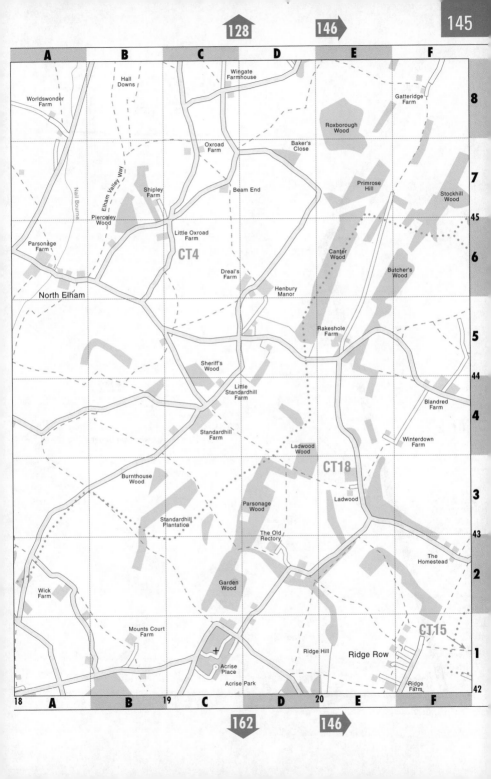

145
129

A   B   C   D   E   F

8

Summer House Wood

Keeper's Lodge

Hill House Farm

Park Wood

CT4

Park Side

7

Biggin Wood

Park Side Farm

WOOTTON LA

West Lees Wood

Park Wood

45

Brenstan

Selsted Farm

6

Selsted CE Prim Sch

Selsted

CANTERBURY RD

5

Stony Lane Wood

Newland's Farm

Stockham

44

Little Smezzel Farm

MANSELL LA

St John's Commandery (rems of)

St Johns Farm

North Court

4

CT18

REGAL LA

CT15

Swingfield Street

Smezzel

North Court Wood

3

Swingfield Minnis

The Butterfly Centre

Hoad Farm

Mast

Beard's Hall Farm

43

HOAD RD

+

Boyington Court

2

Foxholt Cottage

Boyington Wood

Ellinge House

FOXHOLT RD

Little Foxholt

Everden Cottage

1

Red House Farm

A260

Pound Farm

Great Everden Farm

42

CT18

21   A   B   22   C   D   23   E   F

145
163

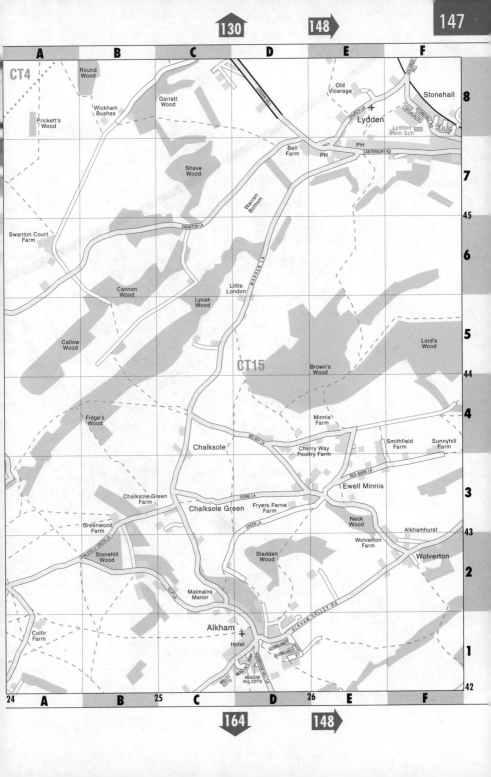

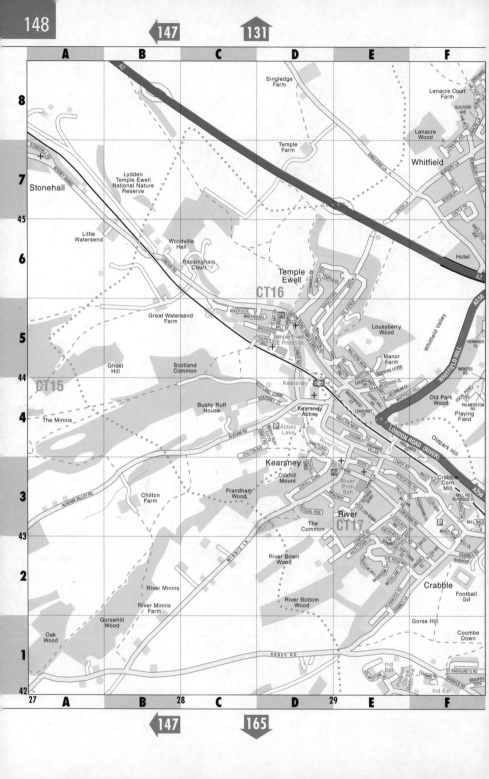

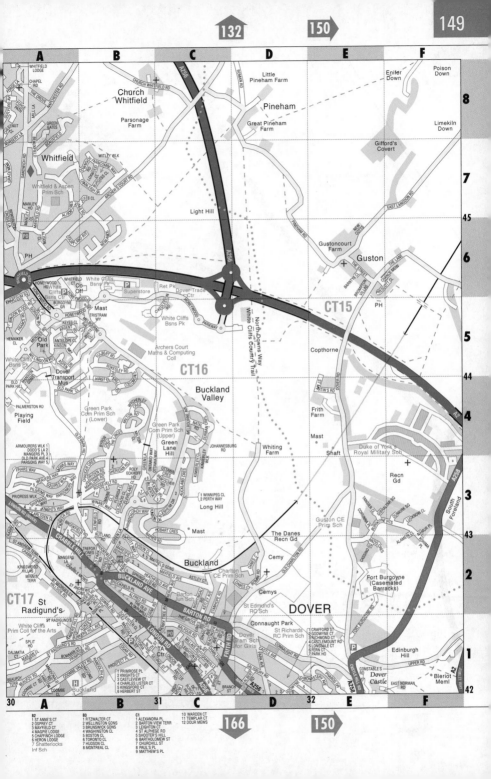

149
133

8
7
45
6
5
44
4
3
43
2
42

A · B · C · D · E · F

THE WALDERSHARE LANE STREET
EAST LANGDON RD
GUSTON RD

White Hill

Solton Close

Famine Down

Solton Manor Farm

Langdon Cross

Mill Hill

GREEN LA
VICTORY RD
NELSON PARK RD
MARCH RD
COLLINGWOOD RD
STATION RD
ST VINCENT RD

Nelson Park

The Old Sch Liby

Townsend Farm

MILFRED LANE
ASH GR

West Cliffe Farm

Wallet's Court

West Cliffe

CLIFFE HO 1
HEATH CT 2

DOVER RD

Cherry Tree Cottage

East Hill

Guston Mill (dis)

THE LANE

Brickfield Cottages

SC

PH

South Foreland

CT15

St Margarets Holiday Park

44

Bere Wood

Reach Court Farm

Bere Farm

A2
A258

Wanstone Farm

South Foreland Lighthouse

JUBILEE WAY

WT Sta

Masts

Memorials

UPPER RD

Bantam Hole

Fan Point

Fan Bay

CT16

Saxon Shore Way

White Cliffs Country Trail

Langdon Hole

Crab Bay

Mast

Fox Hill Down

CLIFFE RD

Langdon Bay

A2

South Foreland

White Cliffs Visitor Ctr

Langdon Cliffs

NORTH CAMBER WAY
SOUTH CAMBER
EASTERN ARM N

Broadlees Bottom

Eastern Docks

UPPER
THE JETTY
EASTERN WAY

33 · A · B · 34 · C · D · 35 · E · F

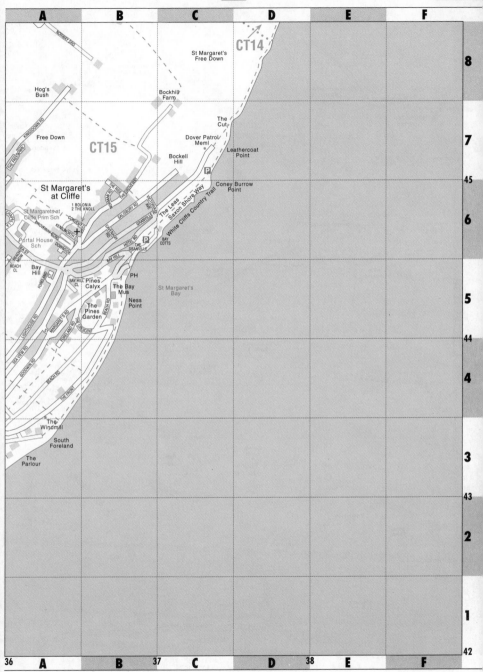

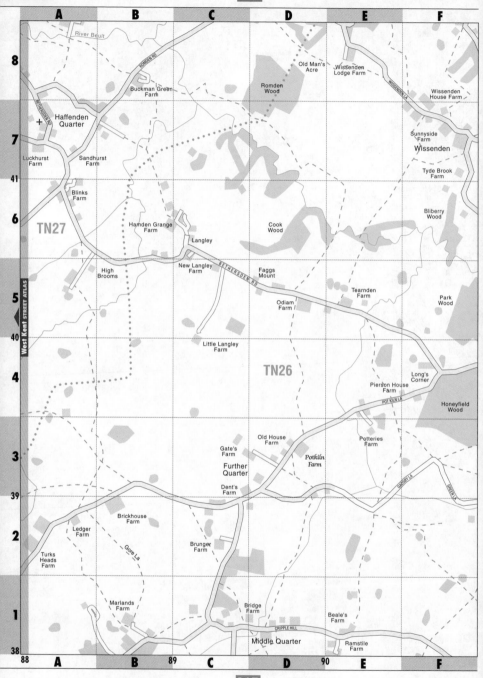

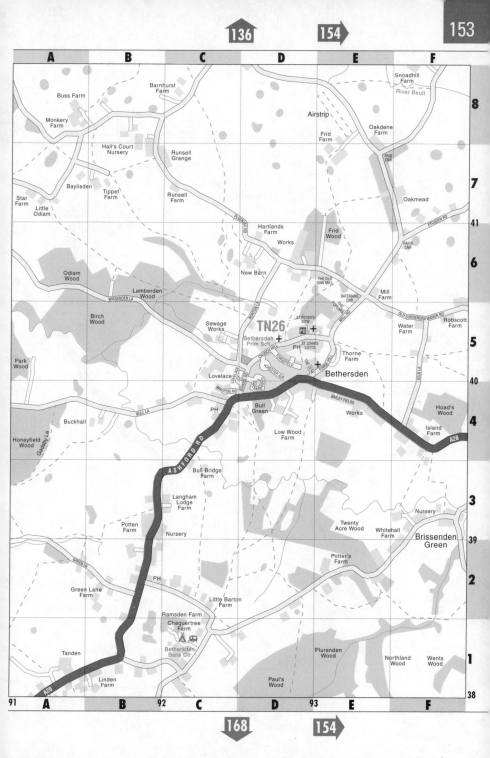

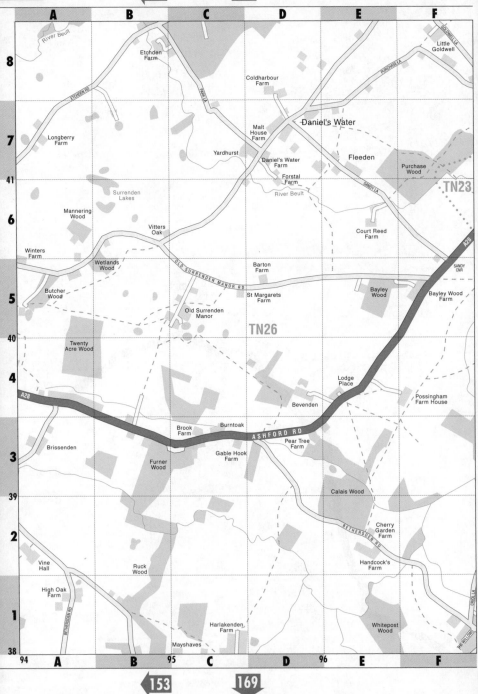

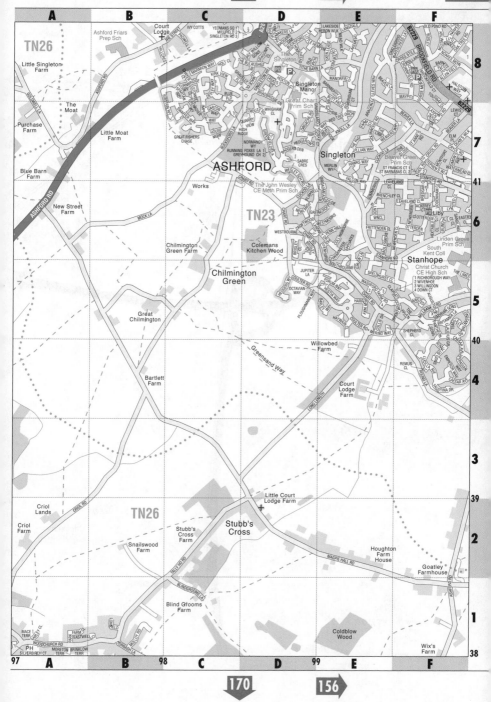

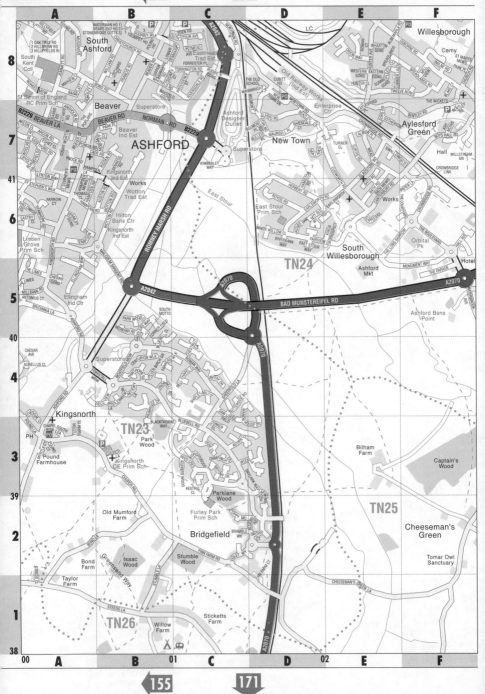

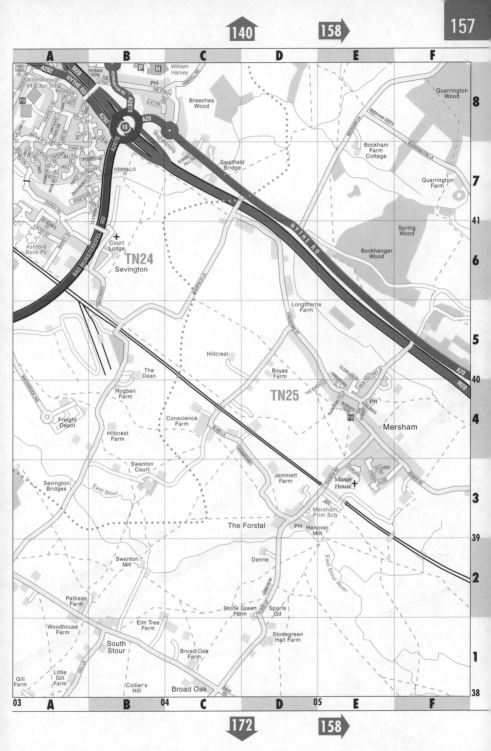

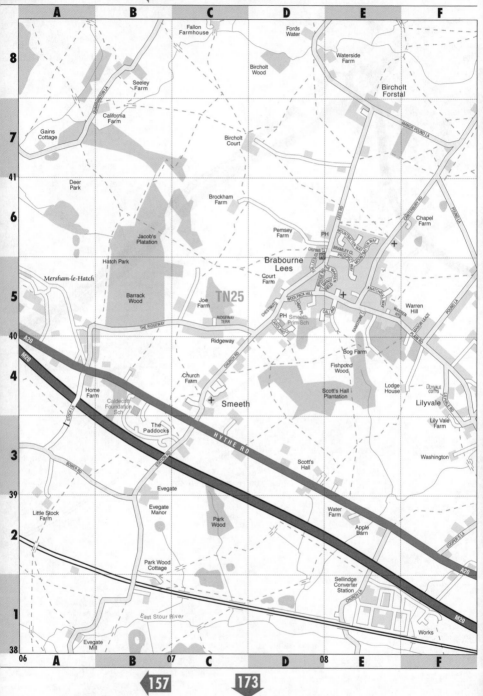

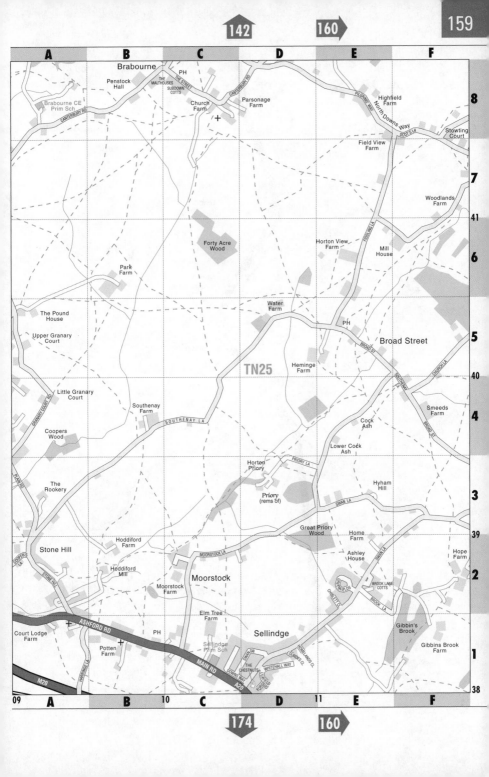

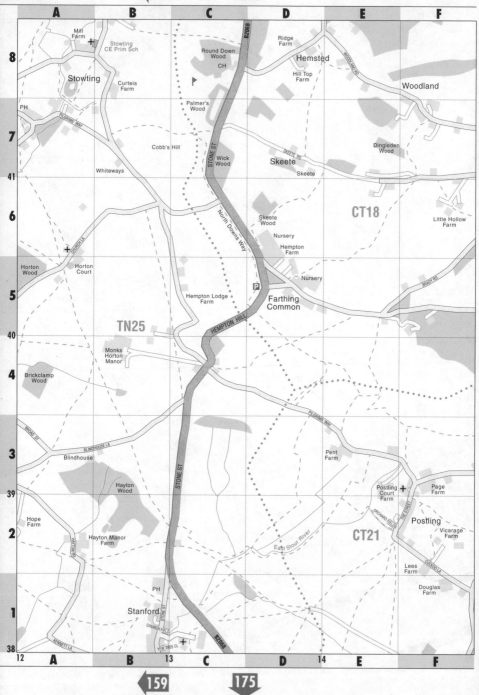

Mill Farm
Stowting CE Prim Sch
Curteis Farm
Stowting
Ridge Farm
Round Down Wood
CH
Hemsted
Hill Top Farm
Woodland
PH
PILGRIMS WAY
Palmer's Wood
Cobb's Hill
STONE ST
Wick Wood
Skeete
WOODLAND RD
SKEETE RD
Dingleden Wood
Whiteways
Skeete
CT18
North Downs Way
Skeete Wood
Nursery
Hempton Farm
Little Hollow Farm
Horton Wood
CHURCH LA
Horton Court
Nursery
BRADY RD
P
Hempton Lodge Farm
Farthing Common
TN25
HEMPTON HILL
Monks Horton Manor
Brickclamp Wood
BROAD ST
BLINDHOUSE LA
Blindhouse
Pent Farm
Postling Court Farm
Page Farm
STONE ST
Hayton Wood
ORCHARD FIELDS
THE STREET
Postling
Hope Farm
Hayton Manor Farm
CT21
East Stour River
Vicarage Farm
COCKERY LA
Lees Farm
PH
Douglas Farm
Stanford
CHURCH FIELD
STONE ST
YEW TREE CL
B2068
KENNETT LA

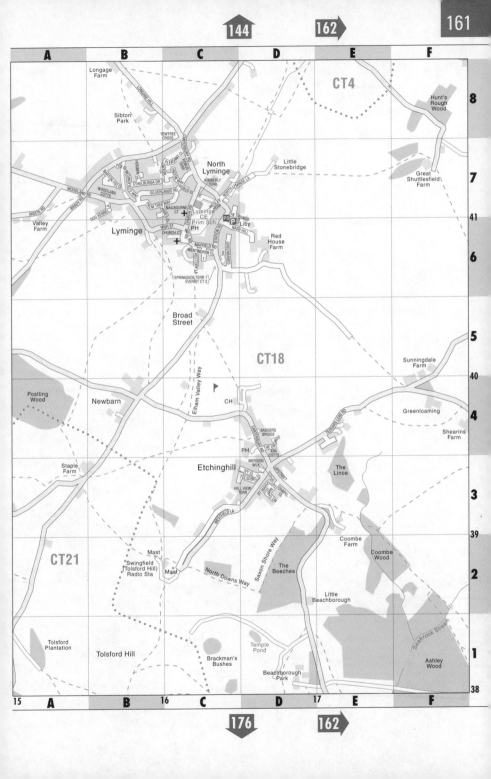

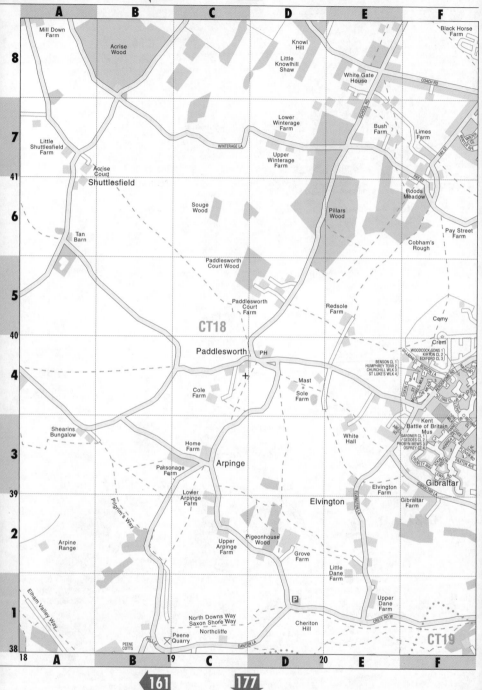

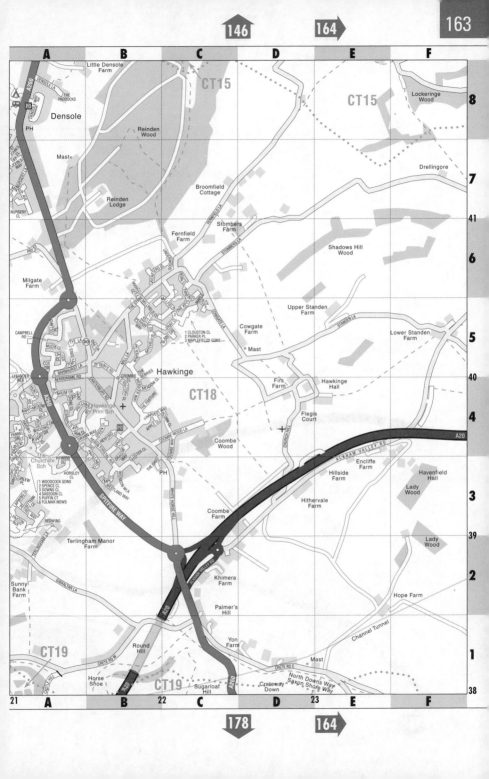

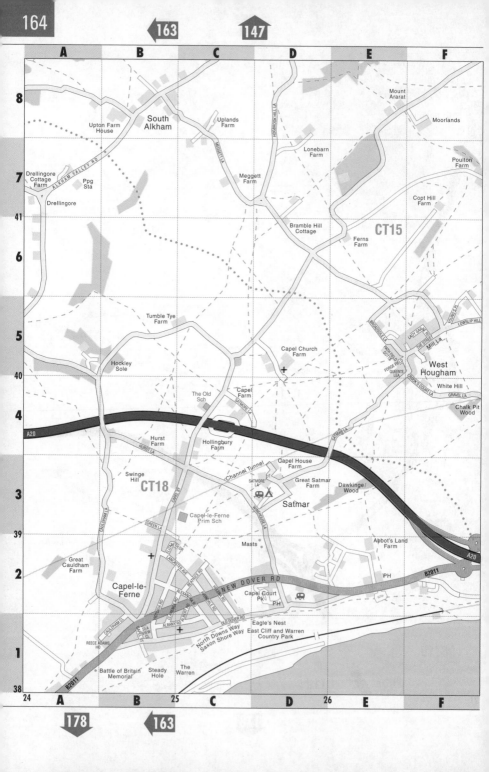

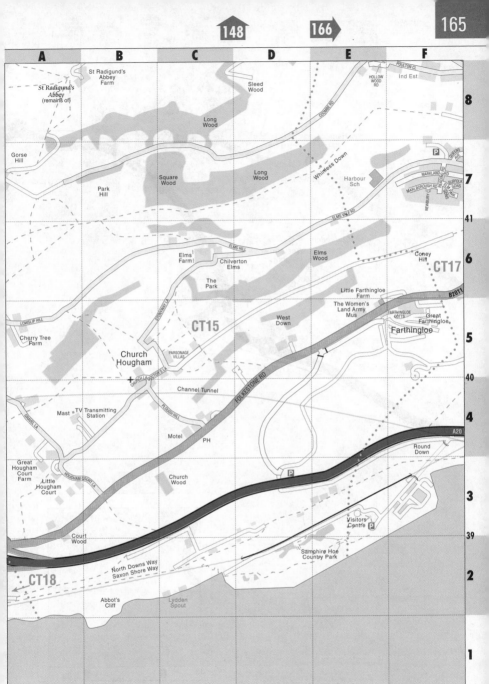

St Radigund's
Abbey Farm

Sleed
Wood

*St Radigund's
Abbey*
(remains of)

Long
Wood

HOLLOW
WOOD
RD

Ind Est

POULTON CL

Gorse
Hill

Square
Wood

Long
Wood

Whitness Down

Harbour
Sch

P

QUEENS AVE

MARKLAND

MARLBOROUGH RD

SUFFOLK
RD GDNS

SANDLING RD

Park
Hill

NEWBURY

8

7

41

COOMBE RD

ELMS VALE RD

Elms
Farm

Chilverton
Elms

ELMS HILL

Elms
Wood

Coney
Hill

CT17

6

The
Park

Little Farthingloe
Farm

B2011

LOWSLIP HILL

Cherry Tree
Farm

CT15

STOMBAY LA

West
Down

The Women's
Land Army
Mus

FARTHINGLOE
COTTS

Great
Farthingloe

Farthingloe

5

Church
Hougham

PARSONAGE
VILLAS

CHURCH HOUGHAM LA

Channel Tunnel

FOLKESTONE RD

40

Mast

TV Transmitting
Station

PLOUGH HILL

Motel

PH

A20

Round
Down

4

BRAVEL LA

Great
Hougham
Court
Farm

Little
Hougham
Court

HOUGHAM COURT LA

Church
Wood

P

3

Court
Wood

Visitors
Centre

P

39

CT18

North Downs Way
Saxon Shore Way

Samphire Hoe
Country Park

2

Abbot's
Cliff

Lydden
Spout

1

38

A B C D E F

A B C D E F

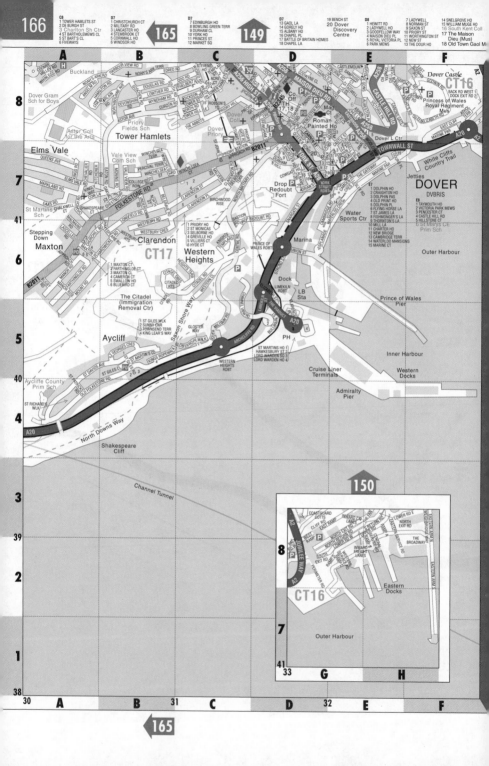

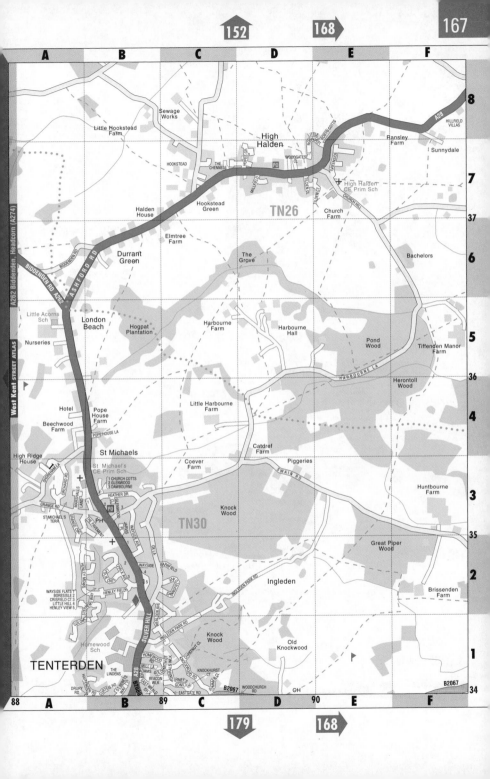

167
153

A   B   C   D   E   F

ASHFORD RD
A28
THE MARTINS

8 Brickyard Farm

Marten Farm

Mace View Farm

Plurenden Manor

Lyndhurst Farm

PLURENDEN MANOR FARM COTTS

7 Oaktree Farm

CUCKOLD'S CNR

PLURENDEN RD

37

Brook Wood

Coomb Wood

6 Little Tiffenden Farm

Grove Farm

Trottingale Wood

Jarvis Farm

SHIRKOAK PK

TN26

REDBROOK ST

5 May Wood

Church Elms Farm

King Farm

36 Appleberry Farm

Butlers Farm

4 Great Doney Wood

Maywood Farm

Barn Wood

Boldshaves Cottage

Boldshaves

3 Godfrey Wood

Ghyll Wood Farm

BRICKWALL TERR. WEST END

Brickwall Farm

SUSAN'S HILL

35 Susan's Hill Farm

SWAIN RD

Robhurst

Ruffets Wood

2 Swain Farm

Great Robhurst Farm

Little Robhurst

1 **TN30**

Haycross Wood

Haycross Farm

Maiden Wood

Cherry Gardens

34 B2067
WOODCHURCH RD   BROOK ST   B2067

91   A   B   92   C   D   93   E   F

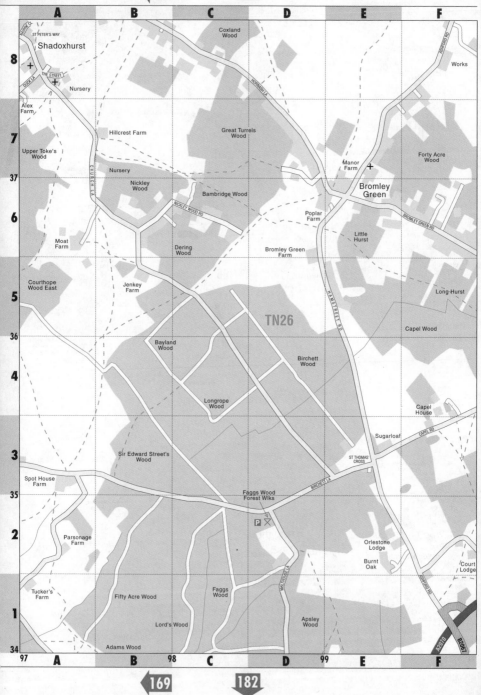

A   **B**   **C**   **D**   **E**   **F**

MEAD CL
ST PETER'S WAY
Shadoxhurst

THE STREET
BUCK LA

Nursery

Alex
Farm

Hillcrest Farm

Coxland
Wood

Great Turrels
Wood

HORNASH LA

Works
ASHFORD RD

8

Upper Toke's
Wood

Nursery

CHURCH LA

Nickley
Wood

Bambridge Wood

NICKLEY WOOD RD

Manor
Farm

Forty Acre
Wood

**Bromley
Green**

7

37

Moat
Farm

Dering
Wood

Poplar
Farm

Little
Hurst

Bromley Green
Farm

BROMLEY GREEN RD

6

Courthope
Wood East

Jenkey
Farm

TN26

HAVET STREET RD

Long Hurst

Capel Wood

5

36

Bayland
Wood

Birchett
Wood

4

Longrope
Wood

Capel
House

Sir Edward Street's
Wood

Sugarloaf

CAPEL RD

St Thomas
Cross

BIRCHETT LA

3

Spot House
Farm

35

Parsonage
Farm

Faggs Wood
Forest Wlks

P ✕

Orlestone
Lodge

Burnt
Oak

Court
Lodge

2

Tucker's
Farm

Fifty Acre Wood

Faggs
Wood

M. TUCKER LA

Apsley
Wood

A2070
B2067

1

Lord's Wood

Adams Wood

34

97   **A**   **B**   98   **C**   **D**   99   **E**   **F**

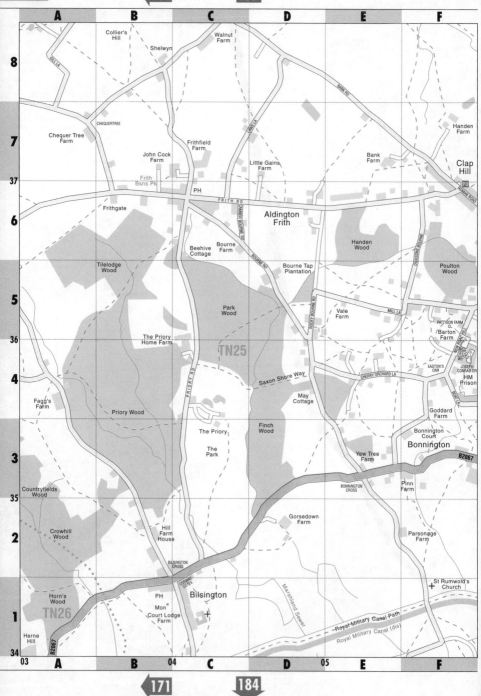

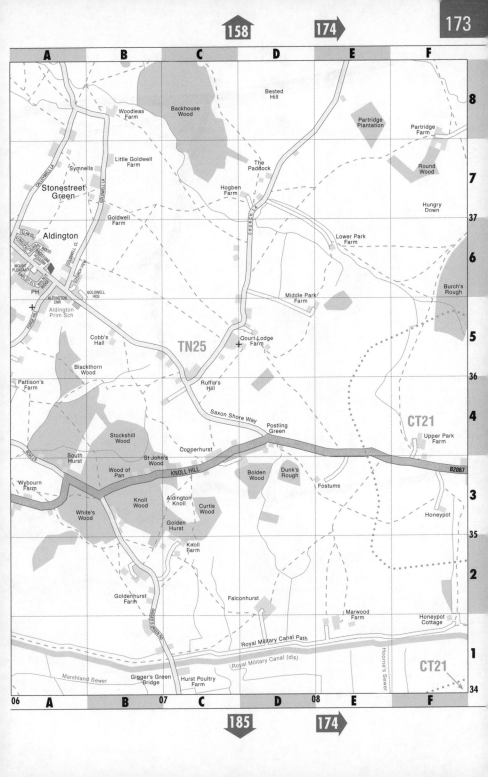

173
159

	A	B	C	D	E	F

8

M20

Harringe Bridge

Rotherwood Farm

SOMERFIELD BARN CT

ASHFORD RD

PO

A20

Brook Farm

M20

Rabbit's Wood

East Stour River

GROVE BRIDGE

Grove Bridge

THE CEDARS

MEADOW DR

Barrowhill

7

BARROW HILL RISE

BARROW HILL

Barrow Hill Farm

Park Wood

OAK COTTS

37

Harringe Court

TN25

HARRINGE LA

Springfield Wood

B2067

Rose Cott

6

Otterpool Manor

Works

ASHFORD RD

A20

Red House Farm

Benham Bans Pk

Benham Water Farm

Harringe Brooks Wood

Upper Otterpool

5

OTTERPOOL LA

36

4

Coldharbour Cott

Danehurst Wood

Court-at-Street

B2067

Lympne Ind Est

BELCAIRE CL

AVE

3

Ashden House

P

Danehurst

ALDINGTON RD

CT21

Rowland Cotts

TOURNEY CL

ACON WAY

THE STREET

35

Port Lympne Wild Animal Park

Lympne Place

BEACH RD

PH

2

Aldergate Wood

Hill Hurst Wood

French Ho

Coombe Farm

CASTLE CL

Lympne Castle

P

TN25

Royal Military Canal Path

Saxon Shore Way

Stutfall Castle (rems of)

1

ALDERGATE LA

Aldergate Bridge

Royal Military Canal (dis)

34

09

| A | B | 10 | C | D | 11 | E | F |

173
186

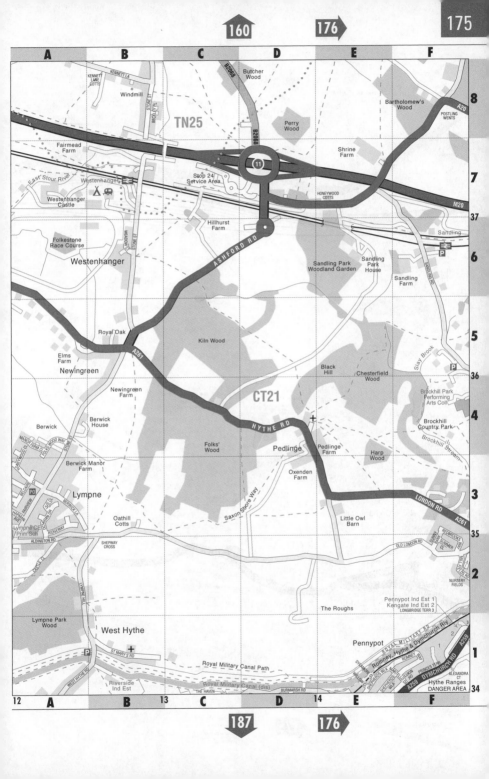

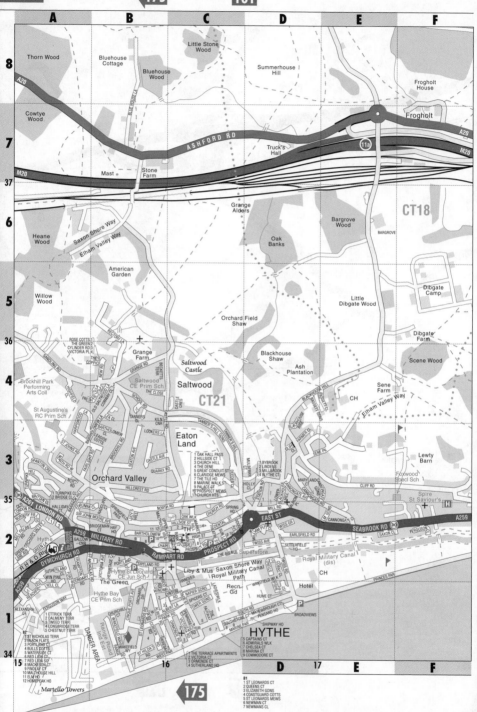

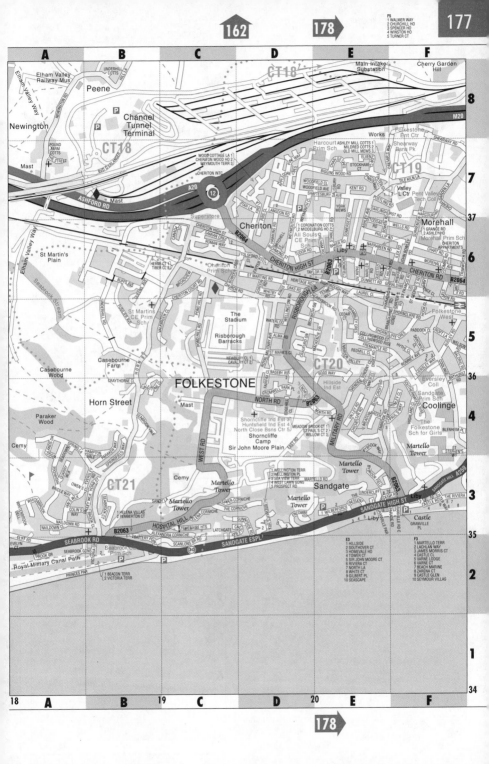

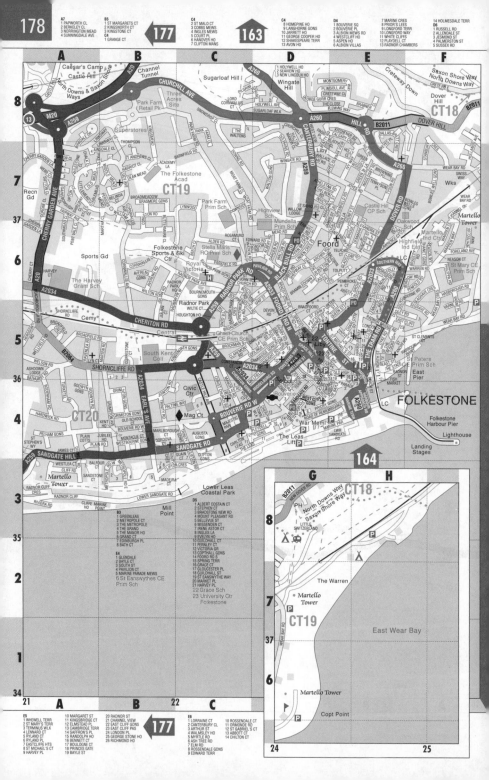

179
168

	A	B	C	D	E	F

The Dandy

Bourne Farm

B2067

Willow Cott Farm

Bower Farm

Berridge Farm

Oakhurst Farm

Ditton Farm

8

B R O O K   S T

B2067

Diamond House

Orange Farm

Brook Street

Malt House Farm

7

33

Glover Farm

6

M O O R   L A

Highbank Farm

B2080

Shirley Farm

TN26

New Bridge

Nurseries

Frenchay Wood

5

S h i r l e y   M o o r

32

Frenchay Farm

Tenterden Sewer

A P P L E D O R E   R D

Fleet Petty Sewer

4

Finchbourne Wood

TN30

3

Barrack Farm

The Century Farm

31

Ramsden

2

Willow Farm

+ Reading Street

R E A D I N G   S T

Nurseries

Chapel Bank Farm

Reading Sewer

T E N T E R D E N   R D

1

Rother Levels

Redhill Bridge

Red Hill

Barrowsland Farm

B2080

30

91	A	B	92	C	D	93	E	F

179
189

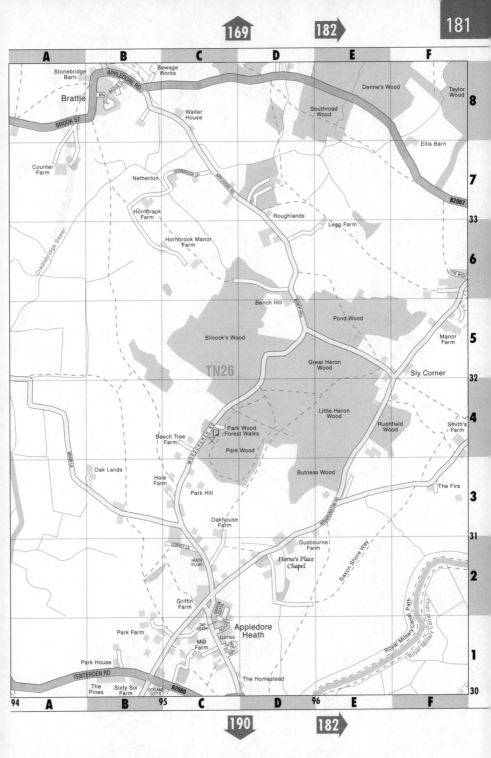

Stonebridge Barn
APPLEDORE RD
Sewage Works
Brattle
BROOK ST
Walter House
Denne's Wood
Southroad Wood
Taylor Wood
Ellis Barn

Counter Farm
Netherton
HORNBROOK LA
APPLEDORE RD
B2067

Hornbrook Farm
Roughlands
Legg Farm
33

Hornbrook Manor Farm

THE WISH
Bench Hill
BENCH HILL
Pond Wood

Silcock's Wood
TN26
Great Heron Wood
Manor Farm
Sly Corner
32

Little Heron Wood
Smith's Farm

Beech Tree Farm
P
Park Wood Forest Walks
Rushfield Wood

Oak Lands
Hole Farm
Park Wood
Butness Wood
The Firs

MORY LA
Park Hill
KENCHURCH RD

Oakhouse Farm
31

DONKEY LA
Gusbourne Farm
Saxon Shore Way

HEATH VILLAS
Horne's Place Chapel

Griffin Farm
GRIFFIN COTTS
Royal Military Canal Path
Royal Military Canal (dis)

Park Farm
THE HEATH
HEATH
Appledore Heath

Park House
Mill Farm
ELMTREE
TENTERDEN RD
B2080
The Homestead

The Pines
Sixty Six Farm
COXLAND COTTS
30

94   95   96

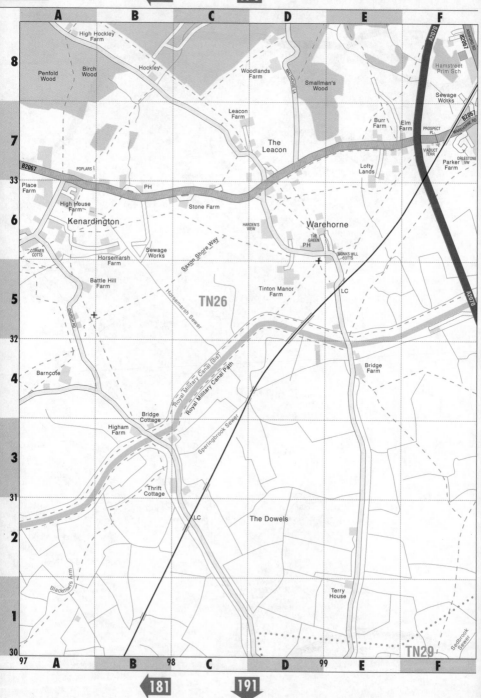

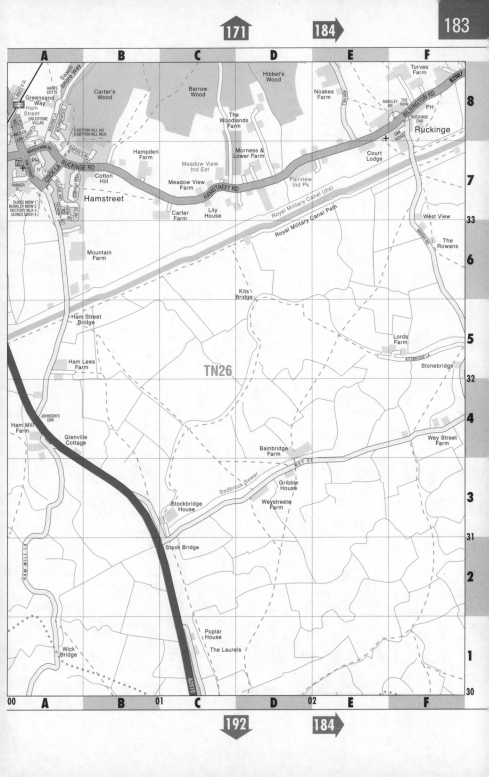

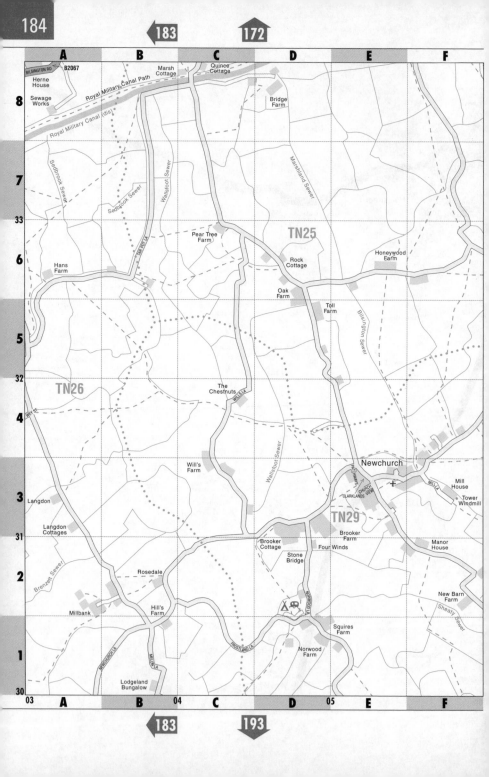

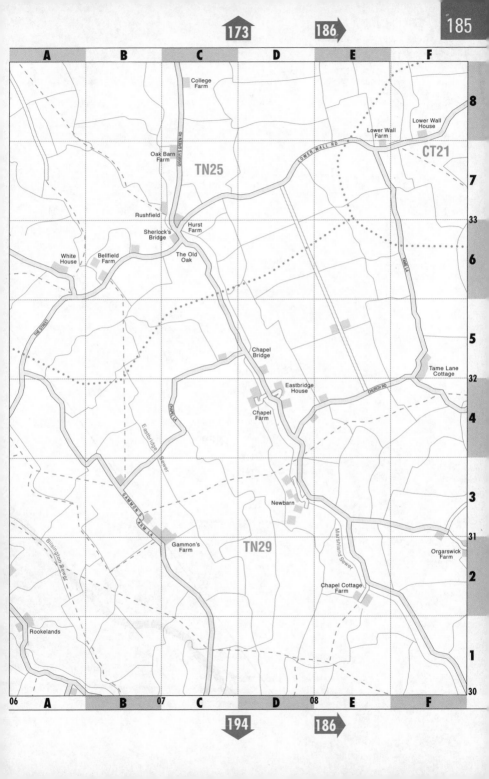

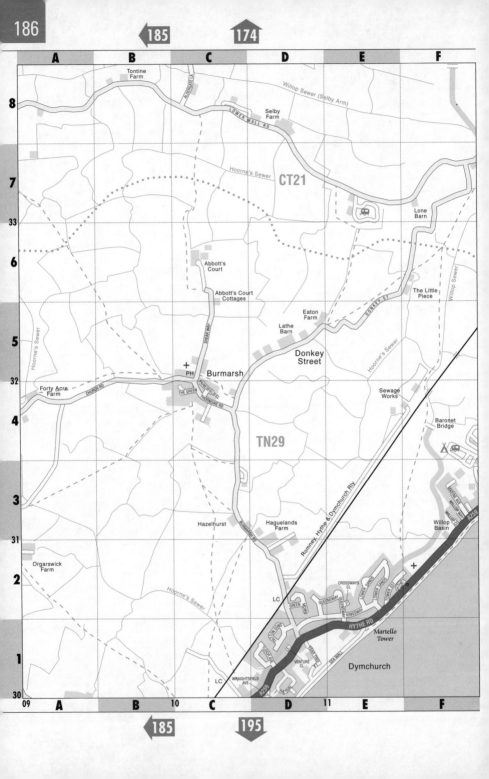

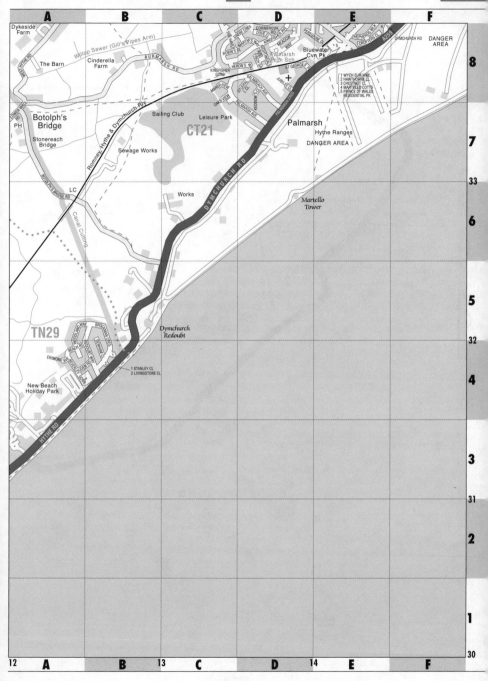

CT21

Palmarsh

Hythe Ranges
DANGER AREA

Botolph's
Bridge

Stonereach
Bridge

Sailing Club

Leisure Park

Sewage Works

Works

Martello
Tower

Dymchurch
Redoubt

TN29

New Beach
Holiday Park

1 STANLEY CL
2 LIVINGSTONE CL

Dykeside
Farm

The Barn

Cinderella
Farm

DANGER
AREA

Bluewater
Cvn Pk

Palmarsh
Prim Sch

1 WYCH ELM WAY
2 HAWTHORNE CL
3 CHESTNUT CL
4 MARTELLO COTTS
5 PRINCE OF WALES
  RESIDENTIAL PK

DYMCHURCH RD

Romney, Hythe & Dymchurch Rly

BURMARSH RD

Willop Sewer (Gill's Pipes Arm)

Canal Cutting

HYTHE RD

LC

PH

DYMCHURCH RD

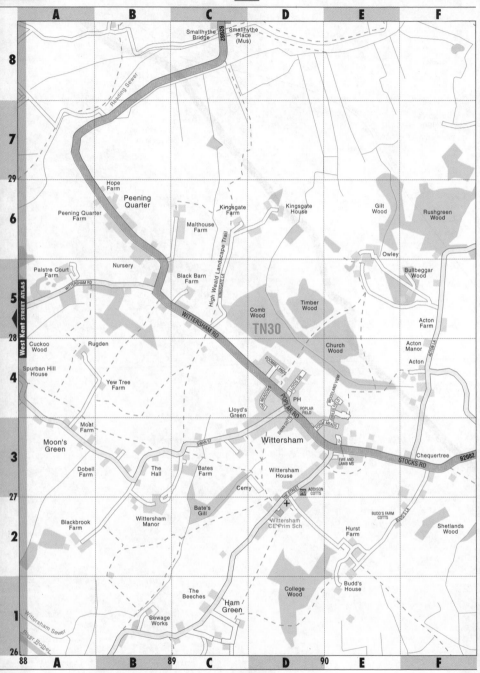

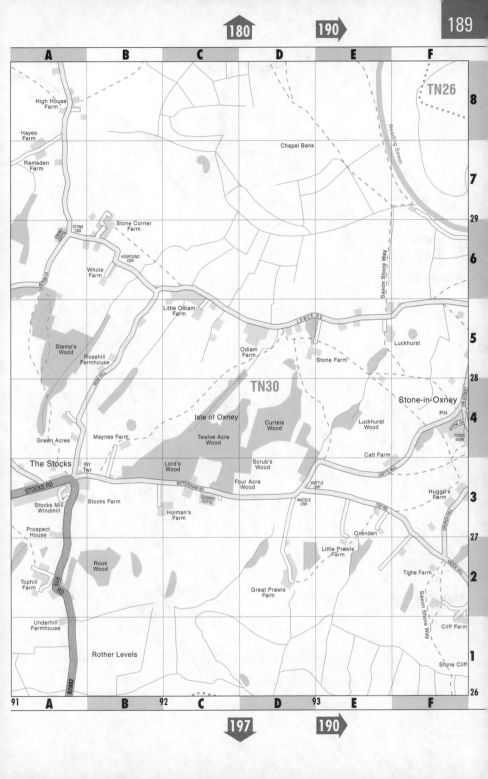

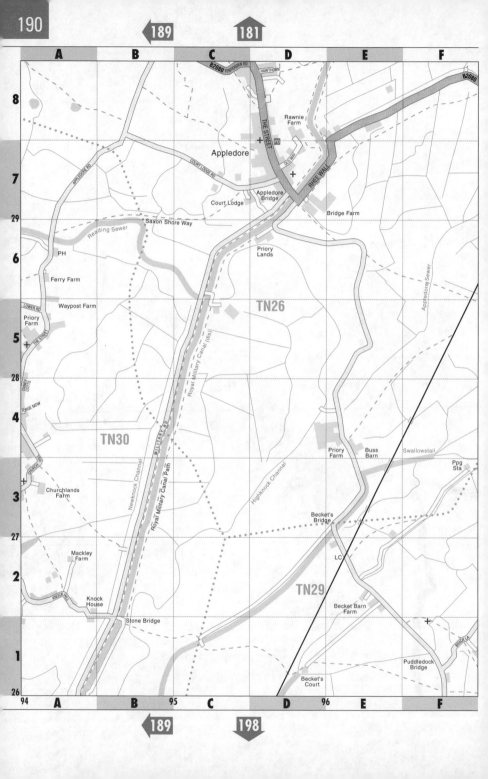

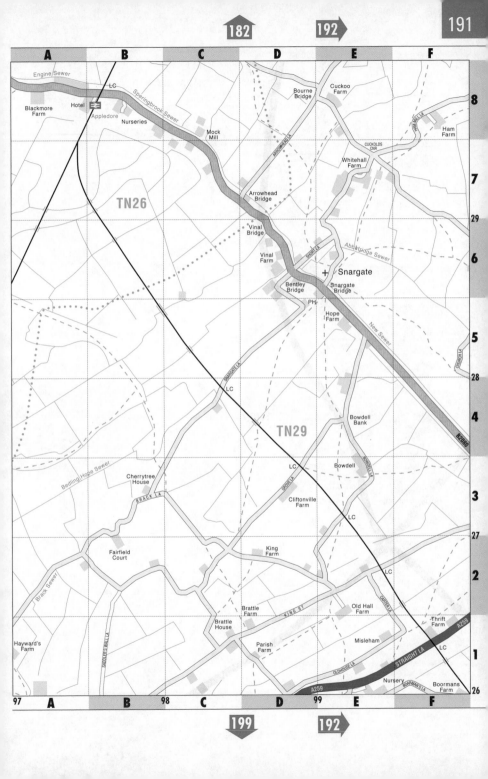

A B C D E F

8

7

29

6

5

28

4

3

27

2

1

26

Engine Sewer
LC
Blackmore Farm
Hotel
Appledore Nurseries
Springbrook Sewer
Mock Mill
Bourne Bridge
Cuckoo Farm
HAM MILL LA
Ham Farm
CUCKOLDS CNR
Whitehall Farm
ARROWHEAD LA
TN26
Arrowhead Bridge
Vinal Bridge
SHORT LA
Abbatbridge Sewer
Vinal Farm
Snargate
Bentley Bridge
Snargate Bridge
New Sewer
PH
Hope Farm
CHURCH LA
Bedling Hope Sewer
SNARGATE LA
LC
TN29
Bowdell Bank
Bowdell
BOWDELL LA
B2080
Black Sewer
Cherrytree House
BRACK LA
Fairfield Court
SPORT LA
LC
Bowdell
LC
Cliftonville Farm
LC
King Farm
LC
Hayward's Farm
SADDLER'S WALL LA
Brattle Farm
Brattle House
KING ST
Old Hall Farm
CARR LA
Thrift Farm
A259
LC
Parish Farm
Misleham
STRAIGHT LA
OLDHOUSE LA
A259
Nursery
BOORMAN'S LA
Boormans Farm

97 A B 98 C D 99 E F

191
183

A B C D E F

8

Snave

TN26

Manor Farm

Court-at-Wick

Abbatridge Sewer

Walnut Tree Farm

Brenzett Sewer

7

Hangman's Toll Bridge

29

Chapel Farm

Poplar Farm

6

Codhall

Brenzett Green

Moat House

NEWCHURCH LA

Springfarm RD

Poplar Farm

5

Hook House

New House Farm

Spring Farm

28

Abbatridge Sewer

MOOR LA

MELON LA

TN29

THE GARDENS

PH

GASTHOUSE FIELD

Marsh's Farm

4

CHURCH LA

Cemy

Brenzett Corner Bridge

Ivychurch

Knowlden Farm

B2080

Brenzett CNR

Brenzett Aeronautical Mus

Brenzett Place

3

MOUNT OF THE KING ST

THE HAVEN

Brenzett

B2080

A2070

HYTHE ROAD

Sumnerhouse Bridge

27

Brenzett District CE Prim Sch

Mast

New Sewer

2

STRAIGHT LA

Blue House Farm

Owen's Bridge

A259

NEWHAM LA

YOAKES LA

A259

Finn Farm

Rhee Wall

Callington Court Farm

Beacon

New Sewer

1

TICKNER LA

TILLERY LA

Rheewall Farm

Yoakes Bridge

26

00 A B 01 C D 02 E F

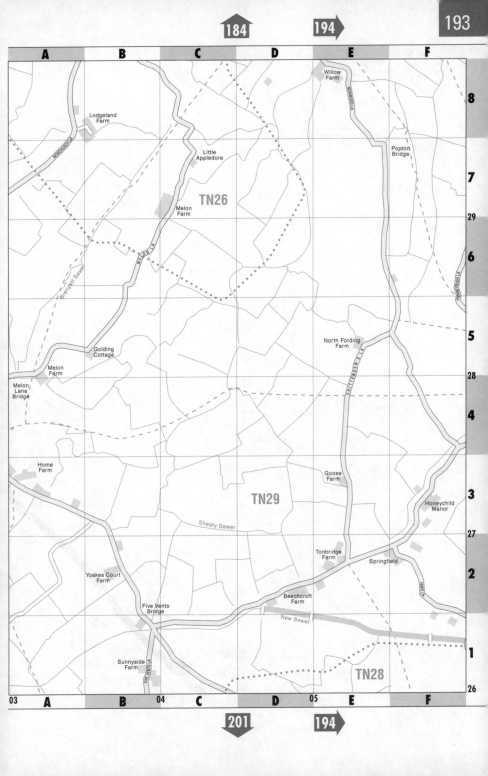

193
185

A B C D E F

8

Oldhouse Bridge

Blue House Farm

Blackmanstone Bridge

GARDEN FARM LA

Eastbridge Sewer

Pickneybush Bridge

7

Pickney Bush Farm

PICKNEY BUSH LA

Sheaty Sewer

Mast

Tatnam Farm

Sellinge Farm

Jefferstone Sewer

Tatnam Bridge

29

Pickney Bush Farm Cotts

Marten Farm

Clobsden Sewer

Swallowtail Bridge

TN29

6

Turngates Bridge

Wild Refuge

5

PICKNEY BUSH LA

Haffenden Farm

ST MARY'S RD

Shingle Hall Farm

Sports Gd

Golden Sands Holiday Centre

28

BECKET RD

WILLIES RD

PH

St Mary in the Marsh

JEFFERSTONE LA

Jesson Court Cvn Pk

St Mary's Bay

JEFFERSTONE LA

LC

4

School Farm

Brodnyx

Jefferstone Sewer

OLD BAKERY CL 1
MULBERRY CL 2

Romney, Hythe & Dymchurch Rly

3

New Sewer

Slinches

MEADS

NEW BRIDGE WAY

ASH TREE CL 1
TURNSTONE CT 2
FULMAR CL 3

CEDAR CRES

27

New Sewer

JENNER WAY

COBBS RD

A259

2

TN28

Winford Bridge

New Sewer

DYMCHURCH RD

The Warren

P

1

Paternosterford Bridge

Romney Warren Country Park

Visitor Centre

Romney Warren Halt

A259

P

26

06 A B 07 C D 08 E F

Brodynex Farm

Marlie Farm

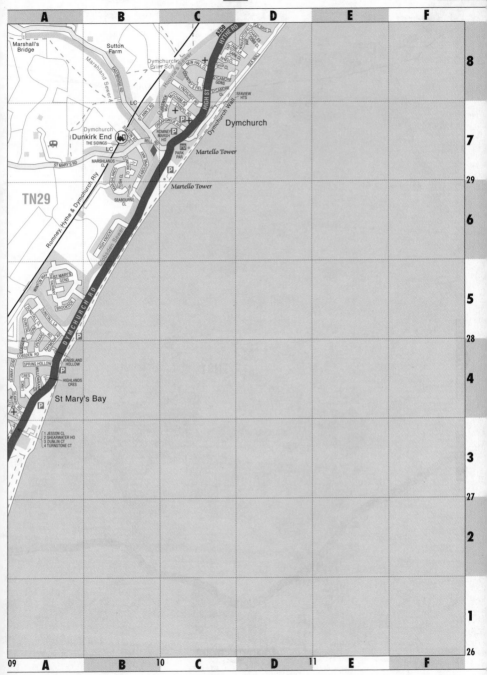

Dymchurch

Martello Tower

Martello Tower

TN29

Romney, Hythe & Dymchurch Rly

St Mary's Bay

1 JESSON CL
2 SHEARWATER HO
3 DUNLIN CT
4 TURNSTONE CT

Marshall's
Bridge

Sutton
Farm

Dymchurch
Dunkirk End
THE SIDINGS

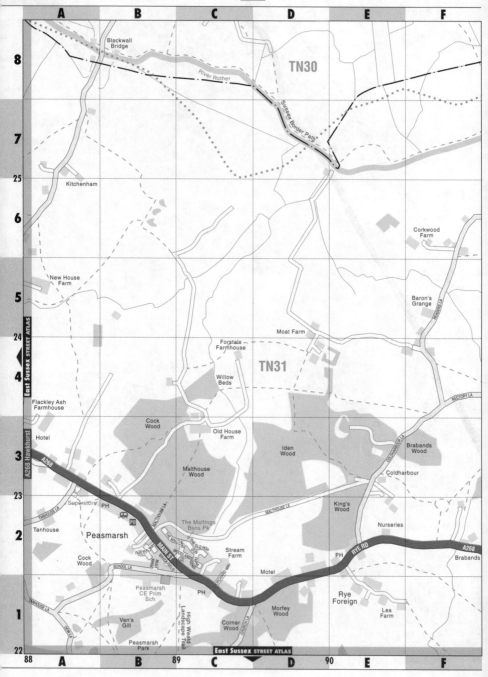

A B C D E F

8

TN30

River Rother

Blackwall Bridge

Sussex Border Path

7

25

Kitchenham

6

Corkwood Farm

5

New House Farm

Baron's Grange

24

Forstals Farmhouse

Moat Farm

TN31

4

Willow Beds

Flackley Ash Farmhouse

Cock Wood

Old House Farm

Iden Wood

Brabands Wood

3

Hotel

Malthouse Wood

Coldharbour

23

Superstore

PH

Malthouse La

King's Wood

2

Tanhouse

PO

The Maltings Bsns Pk

Nurseries

Peasmarsh

Stream Farm

PH

RYE RD

A268

Brabands

Cock Wood

SCHOOL LA

MAIN ST

Motel

3

Peasmarsh CE Prim Sch

PH

Morfey Wood

Rye Foreign

Lea Farm

1

Van's Gill

High Weald Landscape Trail

Corner Wood

22

Peasmarsh Park

88 A B 89 C D 90 E F

East Sussex STREET ATLAS

A268 Hawkhurst

A268

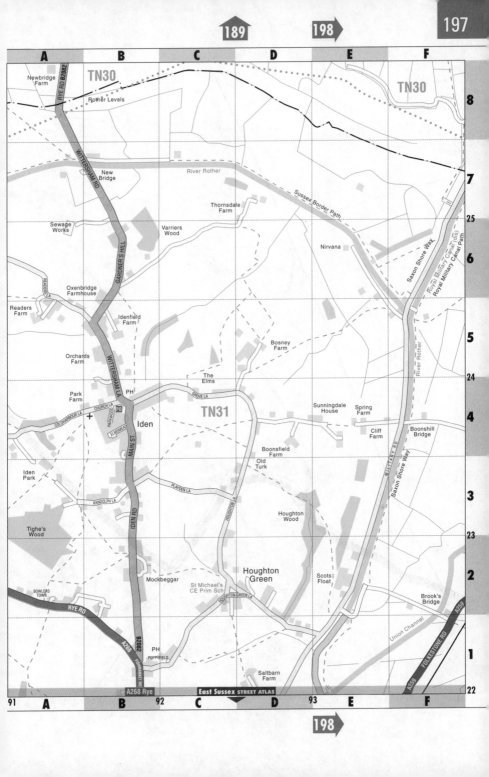

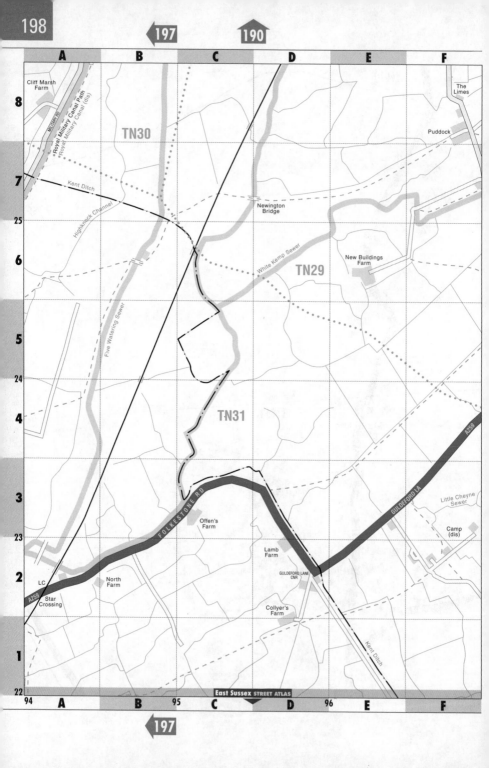

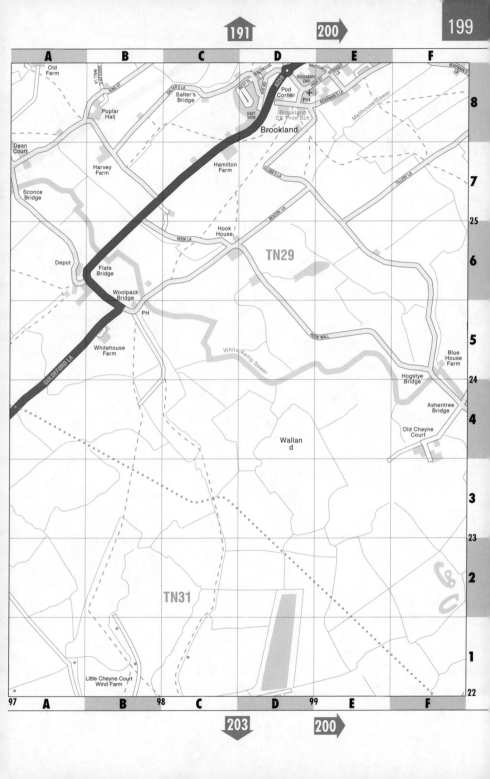

Old Farm

SADDLERS WALL LA

KING ST

SALTER'S LA

Salter's Bridge

WEST RD

EAST HOUSE

RYE RD

A259

WHITEHALL

STRAIGHT

ROSEMARY CNR

HURST ST

BOARMAN'S LA

Poplar Hall

EAST VIEW

Pod Corner

PH

Brookland CE Prim Sch

Brookland

Malthouse Sewer

BOARMAN'S LA

8

Dean Court

Harvey Farm

Hamilton Farm

GLUBB'S LA

TILLERY LA

7

Sconce Bridge

MEADOW LA

25

Depot

HOOK LA

Hook House

TN29

6

Flats Bridge

Woolpack Bridge

PH

HOOK WALL

Blue House Farm

5

Whitehouse Farm

White Kemp Sewer

Hogstye Bridge

24

GUILDEFORD LA

Ashentree Bridge

4

Wallan d

Old Cheyne Court

3

23

2

TN31

Little Cheyne Court Wind Farm

1

22

A B C D E F

8

7

25

6

5

24

4

3

23

2

1

22

LC
TICKNER'S LA
Barnland Farm
BANNINGHOLE LA
TILLERY LA
LC
LC
RANGWELL LA
LC
Mountain La
Coldharbour Farm
St Thomas's Innings
WASHINGTON LA
BIGGARSBUSH LA
Prospect Farm
EIGHTEEN ACRE LA
A259
Bush House Farm
New Sewer
Vine Cottage
Sycamore House
A259
Sycamore Farm
MILLBANK LA
Court Lodge
Coldharbour Bridge
White Kemp Sewer
White's House
LC
COLDHARBOUR LA
Old Romney Bridge
Wheelsgate
TN29
SCULLBEE LA
Cutter's Bridge
Bow Bridge
Baynham Farm
Baynham Petty Sewer
Midley Cottages
LC
HAWTHORN CNR
Scott's Marsh House
Newland Farm
Newland Farm Cottage

00 01 02

A B C D E F

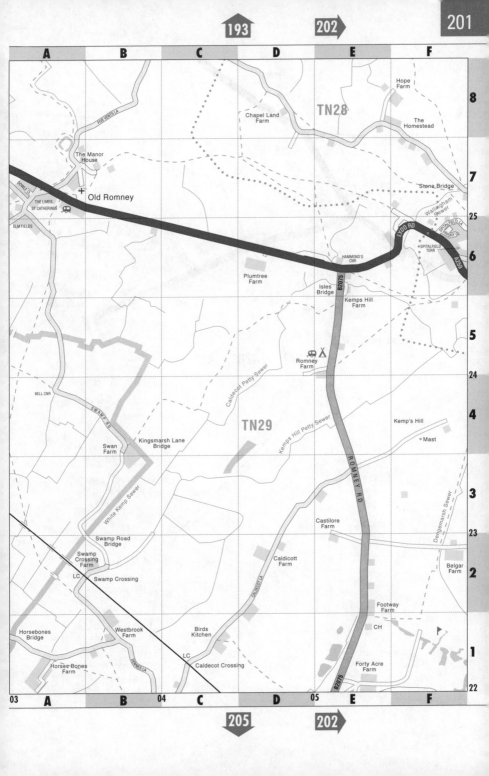

201
194

8

A259

Warren House

LEICESTER MEWS
ELLESMERE MEWS
CLARENDON MEWS

Warren Farm
PH

DYMCHURCH RD

ST EDMUND RD
BRISSENDEN CL

Hotel

7

St Nicholas
CE Prim Sch

OAK LODGE RD

New Romney Main Sewer

Littlestone
Tower

COAST RD

1 MELBURY MEWS
2 PEMBROKE MEWS
3 WINDSOR MEWS
4 RYSWICK MEWS

The Marsh
Academy

COOKREED

WALNUT CL

ROUTE LA

PRESCOTT
HO

25

Liby

B2071

STATION RD

New
Romney
BANK HO

FAIRWAY

ANNE ROVER LA

CH

CH

SANDCROFT

SPITALFIELD

SUSSEX RD

HIGH ST

THE CHURCHLANDS

MOUNTFIELD
RD

BLENHEIM RD

SUNNYSIDE

LINKS WAY

ST ANDREW'S RD

6

ST JOHN'S RD

POST

THE CHURCH

LAURENCE RD

THE MEADOWS

ST NICHOLAS RD

LITTLESTONE RD

BLENHEIM RD

MAPLE RD

A259 LYDD RD

CHURCH LA

Ind Est

CINQUE PORTS
RD

MOUNTFIELD
RD

QUEEN'S RD

NORTH ST

THE RED
HO

CLOVELLY

Cemy

1 GOLDEN SQ
2 MALTHOUSE COTTS
3 ROME HOUSE CNR
4 ROME RD
5 ST LAWRENCE CT
6 VICTORIA ST

SPRINGWOOD CT 1
CHURCHLANDS HO 2
WILES HO 3
DERVILLE HO 4
ASHDOWN CRES 5

COLLINS RD

FISHERS

B2071

Littlestone-on-Sea

5

NEW ROMNEY

Caravan
Pk

VICTORIA RD

DANCY

THE APARTMENTS 1
LITTLESTONE HO 2
GRAND CT 3
LITTLESTONE CT 4
MULBERRY CT 5
PEMBROKE HO 6

VICTORIA RD

HAMILTON CL MEWS

TN28

24

Sewage
Works

CLARK RD

DRAKE LEA

GRAND PDE

4

Romney Salts

ROWE RD

MEEHAN RD

LB Sta

CHANNEL WATCH

3

Romney, Hythe & Dymchurch Rly

TUNEL RD

ALFRED RD

MEEHAN RD S

23

TN29

2

PO

PH

P

DERITT RD

1

Dengemarsh Sewer

Mockmill Sewer

Greatstone
Prim Sch

BALDWIN RD

LC

THE PARADE

ROBERTS RD

BALLARD RD

Greatstone-on-Sea

Northlade

SEAVIEW RD

LC

22

201
206

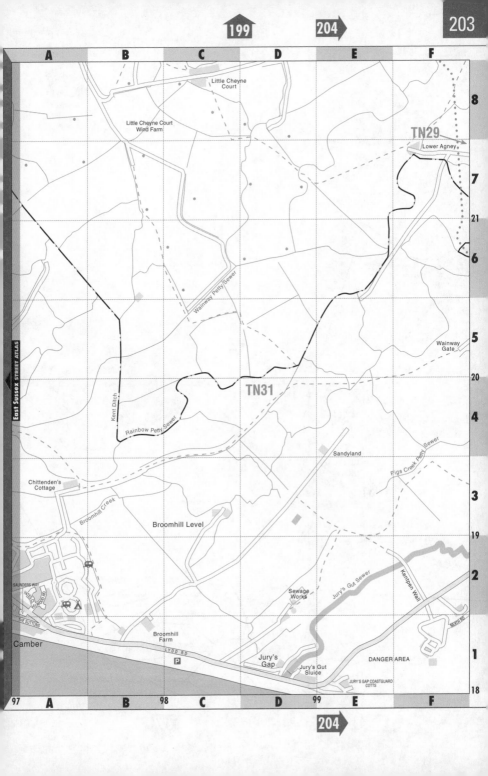

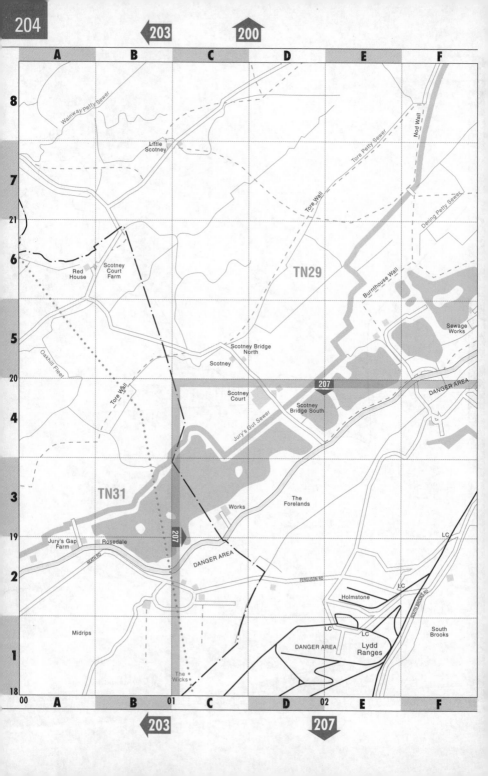

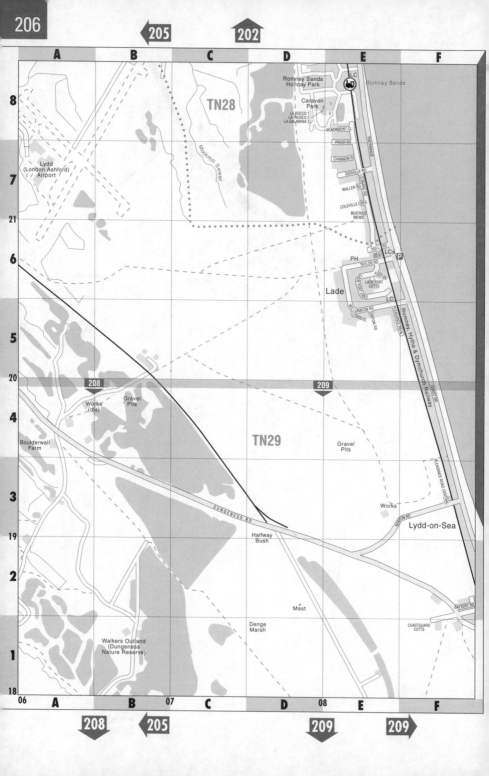

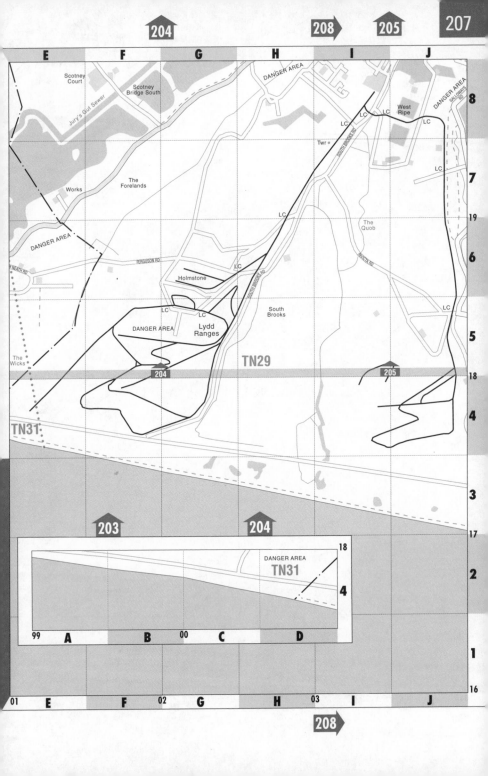

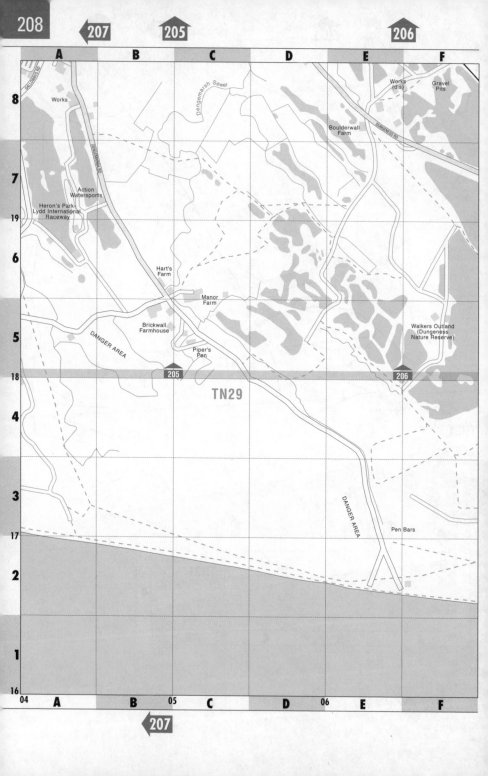

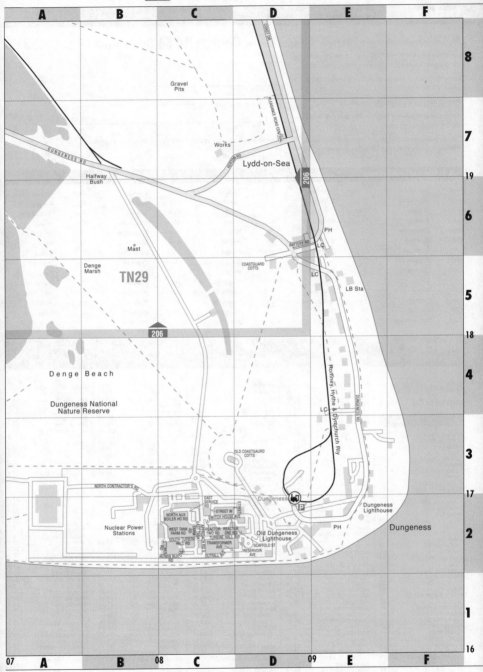

Gravel
Pits

Works

DUNGENESS RD

PLEASANCE ROAD CENTRAL

COAST DR

Lydd-on-Sea

206

Halfway
Bush

19

PH

LC

BATTERY RD

Mast

Denge
Marsh

TN29

COASTGUARD
COTTS

LC

LB Sta

18

5

Denge Beach

Dungeness National
Nature Reserve

Romney, Hythe & Dymchurch Rly

LC

DUNGENESS RD

4

3

OLD COASTGAURD
COTTS

NORTH CONTRACTOR'S RD

17

EAST
SERVICE
RD

STREET W

SWITCH HOUSE AVE

STREET E

Dungeness

P

Dungeness
Lighthouse

Dungeness
Lighthouse

Dungeness

NORTH AUX
BOILER HO RD

Nuclear Power
Stations

WEST TANK
FARM RD

REACTOR
TWO RD

REACTOR
ONE RD

TURBINE HALL AVE

PRODUCTS RD

EASTERN RD

SOUTH TURBINE
HALL RD

TRANSFORMER
AVE

SCAFFOLD ST

RESERVOIR
AVE

ADMIN BLDG

OUTFALL

Old Dungeness
Lighthouse

PH

2

1

07   **A**   08   **C**   **D**   09   **E**   **F**

16

Index

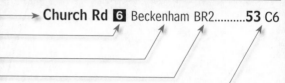

Church Rd 6 Beckenham BR2..........53 C6

- **Place name** May be abbreviated on the map
- **Location number** Present when a number indicates the place's position in a crowded area of mapping
- **Locality, town or village** Shown when more than one place has the same name
- **Postcode district** District for the indexed place
- **Page and grid square** Page number and grid reference for the standard mapping

Cities, towns and villages are listed in CAPITAL LETTERS **Public and commercial buildings** are highlighted in magenta
Places of interest are highlighted in blue with a star★

Abbreviations used in the index

Acad	Academy	Comm	Common	Gd	Ground	L	Leisure	Prom	Promenade
App	Approach	Cott	Cottage	Gdn	Garden	La	Lane	Rd	Road
Arc	Arcade	Cres	Crescent	Gn	Green	Liby	Library	Recn	Recreation
Ave	Avenue	Cswy	Causeway	Gr	Grove	Mdw	Meadow	Ret	Retail
Bglw	Bungalow	Ct	Court	H	Hall	Meml	Memorial	Sh	Shopping
Bldg	Building	Ctr	Centre	Ho	House	Mkt	Market	Sq	Square
Bsns, Bus	Business	Ctry	Country	Hospl	Hospital	Mus	Museum	St	Street
Bvd	Boulevard	Cty	County	HQ	Headquarters	Orch	Orchard	Sta	Station
Cath	Cathedral	Dr	Drive	Hts	Heights	Pal	Palace	Terr	Terrace
Cir	Circus	Dro	Drove	Ind	Industrial	Par	Parade	TH	Town Hall
Cl	Close	Ed	Education	Inst	Institute	Pas	Passage	Univ	University
Cnr	Corner	Emb	Embankment	Int	International	Pk	Park	Wk, Wlk	Walk
Coll	College	Est	Estate	Intc	Interchange	Pl	Place	Wr	Water
Com	Community	Ex	Exhibition	Junc	Junction	Prec	Precinct	Yd	Yard

Index of towns, villages, streets, hospitals, industrial estates, railway stations, schools, shopping centres, universities and places of interest

20/–Ald

20/20 Ind Est ME16 .... 74 C8

A

Abberley Pk ME14 .... 75 C6
Abbeville Ho ME1 .... 9 C4
Abbey Cl
  Deal CT14 .... 117 A5
  Minster (Sheppey) ME12 .... 4 D6
Abbey Ct
  Westgate on Sea CT8 .... 27 D7
  Whitstable CT5 .... 21 A3
Abbey Fields ME13 .... 62 E7
Abbey Fields Ct ME13 .... 62 E7
Abbey Gate CT11 .... 52 B5
Abbey Gate Cotts ME14 .... 53 F2
Abbey Gdns CT2 .... 67 A2
Abbey Gr
  Minster (Thanet) CT12 .... 50 C5
  Ramsgate CT11 .... 52 B5
Abbey Pl ME13 .... 62 D8
Abbey Rd
  Faversham ME13 .... 62 D8
  Gillingham ME8 .... 11 A2
  Kearsney CT16 .... 148 D4
  River CT15, CT17 .... 148 D1
Abbey Sch The ME13 .... 62 C5
Abbey St ME13 .... 62 D8
Abbeyview Dr ME12 .... 4 B6
Abbey Way TN24 .... 140 A1
Abbots Barton Wlk 2 CT1 .... 88 B7
Abbotsbury Hts CT2 .... 67 B4
Abbots Field ME16 .... 74 B2
Abbots Hill ME13 .... 61 E5
Abbot's Hill CT11 .... 52 E6
Abbots Pl CT1 .... 66 F1
Abbots Rd ME13 .... 62 F7
Abbots The CT17 .... 166 C8
Abbots Wlk TN25 .... 123 E2
Abbott Ct 13 CT20 .... 178 E6
Abbott Dr ME9 .... 58 D6
Abbott Rd CT20 .... 178 E6
Abbotts Cl ME1 .... 9 B3
Abbott Way TN30 .... 179 C7
ABDO Coll CT4 .... 107 A3
Aberdeen Cl CT3 .... 47 D3
Aberdeen Ho 9 ME15 .... 97 E7
Abigail Cres ME5 .... 32 A1
Abingdon Gr CT3 .... 47 D3
Abinger Dr ME5 .... 32 D2
Absalom Ct ME8 .... 11 C2
Acacia Ave CT3 .... 68 D8
Acacia Terr ME10 .... 36 C4
Academy Dr ME7 .... 10 F1
Academy La CT19 .... 178 B7
Achilles Rd ME5 .... 32 C2
Ackerey Ct TN23 .... 155 F6
ACKHOLT 113 A4
Ackholt Rd CT3 .... 113 A5
ACOL 27 B3
Acol Hill CT7 .... 27 B4
Acorn Cl
  Hawkinge CT18 .... 163 C4
  Kingsnorth TN23 .... 156 C3
Acorn Pl ME15 .... 97 E6
Acorn Rd ME7 .... 10 F4
Acorn St ME12 .... 1 D1
Acorn Terr ME9 .... 12 E2
Acorn Wharf Rd ME1 .... 9 C6
Acre Cl ME1 .... 9 E1
Acre Ct CT17 .... 166 C8
Acre The CT16 .... 148 F8
Action Watersports TN29 .... 205 D3
Acton La TN30 .... 188 F4
Acton Rd CT5 .... 20 D2
Adam Cl ME17 .... 96 D3
Adam Ct 1 CT9 .... 8 B2
Adams Cl TN30 .... 167 B1
Ada Rd CT1 .... 87 D6
Adbert Dr ME15 .... 96 B4
Addelam Cl CT14 .... 117 A4
Addelam Rd CT14 .... 117 A4
Addington Pl CT11 .... 52 E6
Addington Rd
  Margate CT9 .... 7 J2
  Sittingbourne ME10 .... 36 E3
Addington Sq CT9 .... 7 J2
Addington St
  Margate CT9 .... 7 J2
  Ramsgate CT11 .... 52 D6
Addiscombe Gdns CT9 .... 7 J1
Addiscombe Rd CT9 .... 8 A1
Addison Cotts TN30 .... 188 D3
Adelaide Dr ME10 .... 36 C4
Adelaide Gdns
  Halfway Houses ME12 .... 3 E6
  19 Ramsgate CT11 .... 52 E6
Adelaide Ho
  Deal CT14 .... 117 D6
  Sheerness ME12 .... 1 I1
Adelaide Pl CT1 .... 87 F8
Adelaide Rd
  Elvington CT15 .... 114 B1
  Gillingham ME7 .... 10 C4
Aden Terr 1 ME14 .... 75 A7
Adie Rd TN28 .... 202 D3
ADISHAM 112 D8
Adisham CE Prim Sch CT3 .... 112 D8
Adisham Downs Rd CT3, CT4 .... 90 B2
Adisham Dr ME16 .... 74 B7
Adisham Gdns 1 TN23 .... 155 F6
Adisham Gn ME10 .... 36 F8
Adisham Rd
  Bekesbourne CT4 .... 89 E3
  Wingham CT3 .... 91 A4
  Womenswold CT4, CT3 .... 112 C2
Adisham Sta CT3 .... 112 E8
Adisham Way CT9 .... 8 C1
Admin Building Rd TN29 .... 209 C2
Admiral Ct ME7 .... 10 D6
Admirals Wlk
  Chatham ME5 .... 32 B3
  Halfway Houses ME12 .... 3 E6
  Hythe CT21 .... 176 C1
  Tenterden TN30 .... 167 C1
Admiral's Wlk ME4 .... 9 F7
Admiralty Cl ME13 .... 62 B8
Admiralty Mews CT14 .... 117 D4
Admiralty Terr ME7 .... 10 A7
Admiralty Wlk CT5 .... 43 A7
Adrian Mews CT8 .... 7 D1
Adrian Sq CT8 .... 7 D1
Adrian St CT17 .... 166 D7
Aerodrome Est ME14 .... 55 E4
Aerodrome Rd
  Bekesbourne CT4 .... 89 E3
  Hawkinge CT18 .... 163 A4
Afghan Rd
  Broadstairs CT10 .... 29 F8
  Chatham ME4 .... 9 E4
Agate Ct ME10 .... 36 D6
Agester La CT4 .... 129 A4
Agricultural Mus Brook★ TN25 .... 141 B5
Ainsdale Cl CT19 .... 178 B7
Ainsley Way CT4 .... 108 F8
Aintree Ho 1 ME15 .... 97 F6
Aintree Rd ME5 .... 32 C3
Airedale Cl CT9 .... 8 A1
Aireys The CT13 .... 93 B6
Airfield View ME12 .... 17 C8
Aisne Dr CT1 .... 67 D1
Ajax Rd ME1 .... 31 C8
Alamein Ave ME5 .... 31 F7
Alamein Cl CT15 .... 149 F3
Alaseun Terr ME12 .... 4 A5
Albany Dr CT6 .... 22 D4
Albany Ho 15 CT17 .... 166 D7
Albany Pl CT17 .... 166 D7
Albany Rd
  Capel-le-Ferne CT18 .... 164 C1
  Chatham ME4 .... 10 B2
  Gillingham ME7 .... 10 D4
  Rochester ME1 .... 9 C4
  Sittingbourne ME10 .... 36 E3
Albany St ME14 .... 75 B5
Albany Terr
  Chatham ME4 .... 9 E4
  Gillingham ME7 .... 10 D4
Albemarle Rd
  Ashford TN24 .... 139 F1
  Chatham ME5 .... 32 C2
Alberta Cl CT16 .... 149 B3
Albert Costain Ct 1 CT20 .... 178 D5
Albert Ct
  8 Ramsgate CT12 .... 52 E6
  9 Whitstable CT5 .... 20 D2
Albert La CT21 .... 176 C1
Albert Manor ME7 .... 10 B5
Albert Pl ME2 .... 9 B7
Albert Rd
  Ashford TN24 .... 139 B3
  Broadstairs CT10 .... 29 E8
  Canterbury CT1 .... 88 B8
  Capel-le-Ferne CT18 .... 164 C2
  Chatham ME4 .... 10 A3
  Deal CT14 .... 117 C6
  Dover CT16 .... 149 D1
  Folkestone CT19 .... 178 D6
  Gillingham ME7 .... 10 C4
  Hythe CT21 .... 176 B1
  Margate CT9 .... 7 H2
  Ramsgate CT11 .... 52 F7
  Rochester ME1 .... 9 C3
Albert Reed Gdns ME15 .... 74 E2
Albert Row CT11 .... 52 C5
Albert St
  Maidstone ME14 .... 74 F6
  Ramsgate CT11 .... 52 E6
  Whitstable CT5 .... 20 D2
Albert Terr
  Deal CT14 .... 117 C5
  Margate CT9 .... 7 I2
Albert Terr *continued*
  Minster (Sheppey) ME12 .... 5 A5
Albion Cl CT6 .... 46 A8
Albion Ct CT11 .... 52 E6
Albion Hill 7 CT11 .... 52 E6
Albion La CT6 .... 46 A8
Albion Mews CT11 .... 52 F6
Albion Mews Rd 3 CT20 .... 178 D4
Albion Pl
  Ashford TN24 .... 156 E7
  Canterbury CT1 .... 67 A1
  Faversham ME13 .... 62 C7
  Hythe CT21 .... 176 D2
  Maidstone ME14 .... 75 B4
  Newington ME9 .... 35 B6
  Ramsgate CT11 .... 52 E6
Albion Rd
  Birchington CT7 .... 27 A7
  Broadstairs CT10 .... 29 F6
  Chatham ME5 .... 32 B2
  Deal CT14 .... 117 D8
  Eastry CT13 .... 93 A2
  Folkestone CT19 .... 178 D6
  Margate CT9 .... 8 B3
  Ramsgate CT11 .... 52 F7
Albion St CT10 .... 30 B4
Albion Terr ME10 .... 36 E6
Albion Villas 6 CT20 .... 178 D4
Albuhera Sq CT1 .... 67 D1
Albury Cl ME5 .... 32 D2
Alchins Cotts ME17 .... 96 E2
Alder Cl ME12 .... 3 A8
Aldergate La CT21 .... 174 C1
Alder Ho TN23 .... 138 F1
Alderney Gdns CT10 .... 29 E5
Alderney Way TN24 .... 139 C7
Alder Rd CT19 .... 178 C6
Aldershot Rd ME5 .... 32 A7
ALDINGTON 173 A6
Aldington Cl ME5 .... 32 B5
Aldington Cnr TN25 .... 173 A6
ALDINGTON FRITH 172 D6
Aldington La ME14 .... 76 D8
Aldington Prim Sch TN25 .... 173 A5
Aldington Rd
  Lympne CT21 .... 174 E3
  Maidstone ME14 .... 75 F4
Aldon Cl ME14 .... 75 C6
Aldon Ct ME14 .... 75 C6
Aldred Rd ME13 .... 62 C6
Aldridge Cl CT6 .... 22 B3

Alec Pemble CI TN24 . . . . . .**139** E5
Alefe Way ME9 . . . .**14** D3
Alexander CI CT13 . . . .**93** F8
Alexander Ct
 1 Rochester ME2 . . . .**9** B8
 1 Sittingbourne ME10 . . . . . .**36** E5
Alexander La ME15 . . . .**62** B7
Alexandra Ave ME7 . . . .**10** E4
Alexandra CI ME10 . . . .**36** E7
Alexandra Corniche
 CT21 . . . .**177** C3
Alexandra Ct CT21 . . . .**176** A1
Alexandra Dr CT14 . . . .**116** F3
Alexandra Gdns CT20 . . . . . .**178** D4
Alexandra Glen ME5 . . . .**32** A1
Alexandra Homes CT9 . . . . .**7** J1
Alexandra Mews CT14 . . . . . .**1** E2
Alexandra PI **1** CT17 . . . . .**149** C1
Alexandra Rd
 Birchington CT7 . . . .**27** A5
 Broadstairs CT10 . . . .**30** B4
 Capel-le-Ferne CT18 . . . . . .**164** C2
 Chatham ME4 . . . .**10** B2
 Deal CT14 . . . .**117** D2
 Kingsdown CT14 . . . .**134** C5
 Margate CT9 . . . .**28** E8
 Ramsgate CT11 . . . .**52** D8
 Sheerness ME12 . . . .**1** E2
 Whitstable CT5 . . . .**43** C8
Alexandra St
 Folkestone CT19 . . . .**178** E6
 Maidstone ME14 . . . .**74** F6
Alexandra Terr CT9 . . . .**7** J1
Alexandra Dr CT6 . . . .**22** C5
Alford CI
 Canterbury CT1 . . . .**87** C6
 Chatham ME4 . . . .**10** B2
Alfred Mews CT14 . . . .**117** D7
Alfred Rd
 Ashford TN24 . . . .**156** D7
 Birchington CT7 . . . .**27** A5
 Canterbury CT1 . . . .**87** C6
 Dover CT15 . . . .**149** B5
 Greatstone-on-Sea TN28 . . .**202** D3
 Margate CT9 . . . .**8** B1
Alfred Row CT14 . . . .**117** D7
Alfred Sq CT14 . . . .**117** D7
Alicia Ave CT9 . . . .**28** A8
Alison CI
 Birchington CT7 . . . .**27** B8
 Whitfield CT16 . . . .**149** A6
Alison Cres CT16 . . . .**149** A7
ALKHAM **147** C1
Alkham CI CT9 . . . .**8** F2
Alkham Rd
 Maidstone ME14 . . . .**75** C5
 Temple Ewell CT15, CT16 . .**148** C4
Alkham Valley Rd
 Alkham CT15 . . . .**147** E1
 Hawkinge CT18, CT15 . . . . .**163** E4
Alland Grange La CT12 . . . . .**27** F2
Allan Rd CT5 . . . .**42** E6
Allen Ave CT8 . . . .**27** D7
Allenby Ave CT14 . . . .**117** B5
Allenby Rd CT12 . . . .**29** C2
Allenby Wlk ME10 . . . .**36** B5
Allen CI ME5 . . . .**32** C6
Allen CI ME12 . . . .**4** A5
Allendale St **2** CT19 . . . . .**178** D6
Allen Field TN23 . . . .**155** F8
Allen St ME14 . . . .**75** B5
All Faiths Childrens Com Sch
 6 ME2 . . . .**9** B7
Alliance Rd CT11 . . . .**52** F6
ALLINGTON **74** D8
Allington Prim Sch ME16 . . .**74** C7
Allington Rd ME8 . . . .**11** A3
Allington Way ME16 . . . .**74** B6
Allison Ave ME7 . . . .**7** H1
Allnutt Mill CI **4** ME15 . . . .**74** E2
All Saints CE Prim Sch 3
 ME4 . . . .**10** A3
All Saints' CI CT5 . . . .**20** F1
All Saints Ind Pk CT9 . . . .**7** J1
All Saints La **2** CT1 . . . .**87** F8
All Saints Rd ME10 . . . .**37** C4
All Saints View ME13 . . . .**41** E2
All Souls CE Prim Sch
 CT19 . . . .**177** E6
Allsworth CI ME9 . . . .**35** B6
Alma PI
 2 Canterbury CT1 . . . .**67** A1
 Ramsgate CT11 . . . .**52** E7
 Rochester ME2 . . . .**9** A7
Alma Rd
 Folkestone CT20 . . . .**177** D5
 Herne Bay CT6 . . . .**23** C5
 Margate CT9 . . . .**7** F2
 Ramsgate CT11 . . . .**52** E8
 Sheerness ME12 . . . .**1** D2
Almarina CT8 . . . .**7** C1
Alma St
 Canterbury CT1 . . . .**67** A1
 Sheerness ME12 . . . .**1** E2
Alma Street Pas ME12 . . . . . .**1** E2
Almond CI
 Ashford TN23 . . . .**138** D5
 Broadstairs CT10 . . . .**29** C4
 Whitstable CT5 . . . .**21** D1
Almond Ct CT14 . . . .**96** B5
Almond Gr ME7 . . . .**33** A4
Almond Ho **3** ME14 . . . .**74** A3
Almonds The ME14 . . . .**76** A4
Almond Tree CI ME12 . . . .**3** A8
Almon PI ME1 . . . .**9** D5
Almshouse Rd ME13 . . . . . .**104** C7
Almshouses **6** CT1 . . . .**88** A8

Alpha Rd
 Birchington CT7 . . . .**27** A7
 Ramsgate CT11 . . . .**52** D6
Alsager Ave ME11 . . . .**2** F3
Alsops Rd TN24 . . . .**156** E7
Alston CI ME12 . . . .**4** C7
Altbarn Ind Est ME5 . . . .**54** C8
Alvis Ave CT6 . . . .**22** A4
Amage Rd TN25 . . . .**141** C8
Amage Road Cotts TN25 . .**124** B1
Amanda CI ME5 . . . .**31** F3
Amber CI ME9 . . . .**38** D2
Amber Ct ME7 . . . .**10** D5
Amber La ME17 . . . .**98** A1
Amber Rise ME10 . . . .**36** C7
Amber Way ME17 . . . .**98** B1
Ambleside
 Faversham ME13 . . . .**62** E6
 Sittingbourne ME10 . . . .**37** C3
Ambley Gn ME8 . . . .**33** A8
Ambley Rd ME8 . . . .**33** B8
Ambley Wood Nature
 Reserve* ME7, ME8 . . . . .**33** A8
Ambrose Hill ME5 . . . .**10** C2
Amels Hill ME8 . . . .**56** F8
Ames Ave ME14 . . . .**76** A4
Amethyst Ave ME5 . . . .**31** E6
Amethyst Dr ME10 . . . .**36** D6
Amherst CI
 Maidstone ME16 . . . .**74** D4
 Margate CT9 . . . .**8** C1
Amherst Hill ME7 . . . .**9** F6
Amherst Rd ME15 . . . .**90** D3
Amherst Redoubt ME4 . . . . .**10** A5
Amies Ho ME15 . . . .**96** F3
Amos CI
 Herne Bay CT6 . . . .**23** C3
 Sheldwich ME13 . . . .**83** C5
Amsbury Rd ME15, ME17 . . .**96** B2
Amshurst Villas ME15 . . . . . .**96** A4
Anatase CI ME10 . . . .**36** C7
Anchor Bsns Pk ME10 . . . . . .**37** B2
Anchor Hill **4** CT9 . . . .**7** J2
Anchor Ho ME1 . . . .**9** B4
Anchor La
 Deal CT14 . . . .**117** C6
 Sheerness ME12 . . . .**1** B3
Ancress Ct CT12 . . . .**67** A4
Andover Wlk **2** ME15 . . . . .**97** F6
Andrew Broughton Way
 ME14 . . . .**75** B4
Andrew Manor ME7 . . . .**10** C5
Andrews Wlk ME10 . . . .**36** B5
Anemone Way CT6 . . . .**45** E7
Anerley Ho ME16 . . . .**74** D7
Angel Cotts ME8 . . . .**12** A2
Angel Hts CT18 . . . .**162** C3
Anglesey Ave **4** ME15 . . . . .**97** A7
Anglian Sch of English CT9 **8** B2
Angus Dr TN24 . . . .**139** C7
Anna Pk CT9 . . . .**26** F8
Anne CI CT7 . . . .**27** B7
Anne Boleyn CI ME12 . . . .**5** E3
Anne Green Wlk **8** CT1 . . . .**67** B2
Anne Roper CI TN28 . . . . . .**202** E6
Anne's Rd CT10 . . . .**30** C7
Anns Rd CT1 . . . .**52** E8
Annvera Ho **2** ME14 . . . . . .**10** C7
Ansell Ave
 5 Margate CT9 . . . .**7** J1
Ansell Ave ME4 . . . .**10** A1
Anselm CI ME10 . . . .**36** E4
Anselm Rd CT17 . . . .**166** A8
Anson CI
 Broadstairs CT10 . . . .**29** D3
 Chatham ME5 . . . .**32** C6
Anstee Rd CT17 . . . .**149** C1
Antelope CI CT16 . . . .**149** A5
Anthony Cres CT5 . . . .**43** B6
Anthonys Way ME7 . . . .**9** E8
Antolin Way CT10, CT12 . . . .**29** A3
Antonius Ct TN23 . . . .**156** A5
Anvil CI CT7 . . . .**27** B8
Anzio Cres CT15 . . . .**149** E2
Anzio Ho **15** CT1 . . . .**67** B2
Apartments The ME8 . . . .**202** E5
Apollo Ho ME5 . . . .**32** A6
Appleby CI ME1 . . . .**31** D7
Appleby Rd TN24 . . . .**139** D2
Apple CI CT18 . . . .**163** B4
Apple Craft Ctr* ME13 . . . . .**42** E5
Applecross CI ME1 . . . .**9** B4
APPLEDORE **190** C2
Appledore Ave ME12 . . . .**3** B8
Appledore CI CT9 . . . .**8** C1
Appledore Cres CT19 . . . . . .**177** D2
Appledore Rd ME16 . . . .**74** C7
APPLEDORE HEATH **181** C1
Appledore Rd
 Appledore TN26, TN30 . . . .**190** A7
 Brattle TN26 . . . .**181** C7
 Gillingham ME8 . . . .**11** A3
 Tenterden TN30 . . . .**179** E2
Appledore Sta TN26 . . . . . .**191** B8
Appledown Way CT1 . . . .**88** D5
Appleford Dr ME12 . . . .**3** F7
Applegarth Pk CT5 . . . .**43** A6
Applegate Ct **5** ME8 . . . . . .**33** F8
Approach Rd
 Broadstairs CT10 . . . .**30** A4
 Dover CT17 . . . .**166** A6
 Margate CT9 . . . .**8** A2
 Shepherdswell CT15 . . . . . .**130** D5
Approach Road S TN29 . . . .**209** C2

April Rise
 Birchington CT7 . . . .**26** D8
 Whitstable CT5 . . . .**43** B7
Apsley Gdns CT14 . . . .**86** D3
Apsley St TN23 . . . .**139** B2
Aragon CI TN23 . . . .**155** E7
Archbishop Courtenay CE
 Prim Sch (Tovil Site)
 ME15 . . . .**74** D2
Archbishop Courtenay CE
 Prim Sch (Town Site) 8
 ME15 . . . .**55** A3
Archbishops Cres ME7 . . . . .**11** A5
Archbishop's Sch The
 CT2 . . . .**66** E3
Archcliffe Rd CT17 . . . .**166** C5
Archer Ct ME10 . . . .**14** F2
Archer Rd
 Chatham ME5 . . . .**32** B6
 Folkestone CT19 . . . .**178** D6
Archers Court Maths &
 Computing Coll CT17 . . .**149** B5
Archer's Court Rd CT15,
 CT16 . . . .**149** B7
Archery Sq CT14 . . . .**117** D7
Archibald Ho ME14 . . . .**75** A7
Archway Ct **4** ME2 . . . .**9** B8
Archway Rd
 Ramsgate CT11 . . . .**52** E6
 Sheerness ME12 . . . .**1** E2
Arcon CI TN23 . . . .**156** A7
Arcon Rd TN23 . . . .**156** A7
Arden Bsns Ctr ME2 . . . .**9** E7
Arden Dr CT4 . . . .**139** C3
Arden Grange CT4 . . . .**107** C8
Ardenlee Dr ME14 . . . .**75** B5
Arden Rd
 Faversham ME13 . . . .**62** B3
 Herne Bay CT6 . . . .**23** C2
Arden St ME7 . . . .**10** C6
Ardent Ave CT14 . . . .**117** C4
Ardent Rd CT5 . . . .**149** A5
Arethusa Rd ME1 . . . .**31** C3
Argent Bsns Pk ME11 . . . .**3** A2
Argent Rd ME11 . . . .**3** A2
Argent Way ME10 . . . .**36** C6
Argyle Ave CT9 . . . .**7** G1
Argyle CI ME1 . . . .**31** E8
Argyle Gdns CT9 . . . .**7** G1
Argyle Rd CT5 . . . .**20** D1
Argyll Dr CT11 . . . .**29** F1
Ark Cotts CT18 . . . .**161** D4
Ark La CT14 . . . .**117** D7
Arkley Rd CT6 . . . .**22** A4
Arklow Sq **6** CT1 . . . .**52** F7
Arlington TN23 . . . .**155** F8
Arlington Gdns CT9 . . . .**29** C8
Arlington Ho CT19 . . . .**7** H2
Arlington Sq CT9 . . . .**7** H2
Arlott CI ME1 . . . .**31** C4
Armada CI ME4 . . . .**9** E1
Armada Ct ME4 . . . .**9** E1
Armadale CT10 . . . .**8** F1
Armada Way ME4 . . . .**9** E1
Armourers Wlk CT16 . . . . . .**149** A3
Armstrong Rd ME15 . . . .**75** A1
Armstrong Sq CT6 . . . .**22** A3
Arnhem Dr ME5 . . . .**31** F7
Arnold Rd
 Chartham CT4 . . . .**86** C2
 5 Margate CT9 . . . .**7** J1
Arolla Rd CT6 . . . .**23** C4
ARPINGE **162** C3
Arran Mews **4** CT1 . . . .**67** B2
Arran Rd ME15 . . . .**97** A6
Arrowhead La TN26,
 TN29 . . . .**191** D7
Arthur Kennedy CI ME13 . . .**63** F3
Arthur Rd
 Birchington CT7 . . . .**26** D8
 Deal CT14 . . . .**117** A3
 Gillingham ME8 . . . .**33** E7
 Hythe CT21 . . . .**176** C1
 Margate CT9 . . . .**8** B2
 Rochester ME1 . . . .**9** D3
Arthur Salmon CI ME13 . . . . .**62** B7
Arthur St
 3 Folkestone CT19 . . . . . .**178** E6
 Sittingbourne ME10 . . . .**36** E4
Artillery Gdns **11** CT1 . . . . .**67** A1
Artillery Ho **12** CT1 . . . .**67** A1
Artillery Rd **2** CT1 . . . .**52** F7
Artillery St **10** CT1 . . . .**67** A1
Arundel Ave ME5 . . . .**32** D1
Arundel CI ME5 . . . .**32** D1
Arundel Rd
 Cliffs End CT12 . . . .**51** D7
 Margate CT9 . . . .**8** B2
Arundel Sq ME14 . . . .**74** F6
Ascot CI ME5 . . . .**32** C2
Ascot Gdns CT9 . . . .**28** C7
Ascot Ho **2** ME15 . . . .**97** F6
ASH **71** D2
ASHBANK **99** B2
Ashbank Cotts ME17 . . . .**99** B2
Ashbee Gdns CT6 . . . .**23** C5
Ashbrooke Ctr The 2
 CT10 . . . .**29** C4
Ashburn Gdns CT6 . . . .**23** C5
Ashburnham Rd
 Maidstone ME14 . . . .**75** B8
 Ramsgate CT11 . . . .**52** C7
Ashburn Mews ME7 . . . .**10** E3
Ashburton CI TN24 . . . .**139** E2

Ash CI
 Ashford TN23 . . . .**138** E3
 Broadstairs CT10 . . . .**29** C4
 Chatham ME5 . . . .**10** C1
 Crabble CT17 . . . .**148** E3
 Gillingham ME8 . . . .**11** B3
 Herne Bay CT6 . . . .**22** F1
Ash Cres CT3 . . . .**46** E1
Ash Ct CT12 . . . .**51** D4
Ashdale Ho **5** TN23 . . . . . .**139** C2
Ashdown CI
 Herne Bay CT6 . . . .**23** B2
 Maidstone ME16 . . . .**74** D3
Ashdown Cres TN28 . . . . . .**202** B6
Ashdown Ct TN24 . . . .**139** C3
Ashdown Field CT4 . . . .**86** B2
Ashdown Lodge CT20 . . . . .**178** A5
Ashdown Rd ME17, ME9 . . . .**79** F3
Ashenden CI CT1 . . . .**87** C5
Ashendene Gr CT2 . . . .**68** A6
Ashen Tree Cotts CT3 . . . . . .**70** B1
Ashentree La TN24 . . . .**200** A5
Ashen Tree La CT16 . . . .**166** A8
ASHFORD **139** A2
Ashford Borough Mus*
 TN23 . . . .**139** B2
Ashford Bsns Pk TN24 . . . .**157** A6
Ashford Bsns Point TN24 . .**157** A6
Ashford Designer Outlet
 TN24 . . . .**156** C7
Ashford Dr ME17 . . . .**99** B3
Ashford Friars Prep Sch
 TN23 . . . .**155** B8
Ashford Int Sta TN24 . . . . . .**139** C1
Ashford Mkt TN24 . . . .**156** C5
Ashford Oaks Com Prim Sch
 TN23 . . . .**155** F8
Ashford St Mary's CE Prim
 Sch TN23 . . . .**139** A3
Ashford Sch of Art & Design
 8 TN23 . . . .**139** C2
Ashford Sch of Art & Design
 (Henwood Campus)
 TN25 . . . .**139** D3
Ashford Sch of Art & Design
 (Tufton Campus) TN25 . .**139** C1
Ashford Sta TN24 . . . .**139** C1
Ash Gr
 Elvington CT15 . . . .**114** B2
 Lydd TN29 . . . .**205** D7
 Maidstone ME14 . . . .**76** A4
St Margaret's at Cliffe
 CT15 . . . .**150** F6
Ashgrove TN23 . . . .**138** F5
Ashington CI ME10 . . . .**36** C5
Ashleigh Gdns ME5 . . . .**31** D1
ASHLEY **132** B5
Ashley Ave CT19 . . . .**177** E6
Ashley CI
 Halfway Houses ME12 . . . . . .**3** C5
 Ramsgate CT12 . . . .**29** B2
Ashley Dr CT5 . . . .**43** A7
Ashley Mill Cotts CT19 . . . .**177** E6
Ashley Rd ME8 . . . .**11** C2
Ash Mdws ME7 . . . .**156** F7
Ashmead CI ME5 . . . .**32** C3
Ashmill Bsns Pk ME17 . . . . .**101** F6
Ash Rd
 Aylesham CT3 . . . .**112** C5
 Gillingham ME7 . . . .**10** E3
 Sandwich CT13 . . . .**72** E2
Ashtead Dr ME9 . . . .**37** D2
Ashton CI CT14 . . . .**116** D4
Ashton Ct **4** CT10 . . . .**29** E5
Ashton Ho CT14 . . . .**117** B1
Ash Tree CI
 Birchington CT7 . . . .**27** B7
 St Mary's Bay TN29 . . . . . .**194** F3
Ashtree Ho ME10 . . . .**37** B3
Ash Tree La ME5 . . . .**10** D1
Ash Tree Rd **6** CT19 . . . . . .**178** E6
Ashtrees CT6 . . . .**23** B3
Ashurst Ave CT5 . . . .**43** C6
Ashurst Gdns CT9 . . . .**8** E3
Ashurst PI ME8 . . . .**33** E8
Ashurst Rd ME14 . . . .**75** C5
Askes Ct TN23 . . . .**155** D8
Aspen CI TN29 . . . .**194** F3
Aspen Dr
 Ashford TN23 . . . .**138** D3
 Dover CT16 . . . .**149** A5
Aspen Ho **5** CT20 . . . .**178** D4
Aspen Way
 Chartham CT4 . . . .**86** E1
 Herne CT6 . . . .**45** E7
Aspen Way **2** ME5 . . . .**31** E4

Aspian Dr ME17 . . . .**96** D3
Aspinall CI CT4 . . . .**89** B4
Asquith Rd ME8 . . . .**33** C6
Association Wlk ME1 . . . . .**31** C7
Aster Rd ME12 . . . .**4** B4
Astley Ave CT16 . . . .**149** C2
Astley Ct CT16 . . . .**149** C2
Astley St ME14 . . . .**75** A4
Aston CI ME5 . . . .**32** A2
Aston PI CT10 . . . .**29** D2
Astor Ave CT17 . . . .**166** E8
Astor Coll for the Arts
 CT17 . . . .**166** A8
Astor Dr CT14 . . . .**117** C5
Astor of Hever Com Sch The
 ME16 . . . .**74** C3
Astor Rd CT10 . . . .**29** F8
Astrid Rd CT14 . . . .**117** A2
Astwater CI ME17 . . . .**77** C2
Athelstan Rd CT14 . . . .**117** C8
Athelstan Rd
 Canterbury CT1 . . . .**87** C5
 Chatham ME4 . . . .**9** F2
 Faversham ME13 . . . .**62** C6
 Folkestone CT19 . . . .**178** D7
 Margate CT9 . . . .**8** A3
Athena CI CT9 . . . .**8** A3
Athol PI ME13 . . . .**62** A8
Athol Rd
 Ashford TN23 . . . .**155** F7
 Whitstable CT5 . . . .**20** F2
Athol Terr CT16 . . . .**166** F8
Atkinson Rd CT18 . . . .**162** F3
Atkinson Wlk TN24 . . . .**139** F5
Atlanta Ct ME4 . . . .**9** D3
Attlee Ave CT3 . . . .**112** C5
Attlee Way ME10 . . . .**36** E8
Atwater Ct ME17 . . . .**101** D5
Aubretia Wlk ME10 . . . .**37** A3
Auckland Ave CT12 . . . .**52** A8
Auckland Cres CT13 . . . .**149** C3
Auckland Dr ME10 . . . .**36** C3
Auckland Ho **10** ME15 . . . . .**97** E5
Audley Ave
 Gillingham ME7 . . . .**10** E1
 Margate CT9 . . . .**7** E1
Audley CI ME16 . . . .**74** B5
Audley Rd CT20 . . . .**177** F5
Auger CI ME9 . . . .**34** E5
Augusta CI **1** ME7 . . . .**10** C7
Augusta Gdns CT20 . . . .**178** C4
Augusta PI **14** CT11 . . . .**52** F7
Augusta Rd CT11 . . . .**52** F7
Augustine Rd
 Minster (Sheppey) ME12 . . . .**4** B8
 Minster (Thanet) CT12 . . . . .**50** B6
Augustus Wlk TN23 . . . .**155** F5
Aurelie Way CT5 . . . .**43** F7
Aurellus CI TN23 . . . .**156** A4
Austell Manor **5** ME7 . . . . .**10** C6
Austens Orch **13** TN30 . . . .**179** A7
Austin Ave CT6 . . . .**21** F4
Austin CI
 Gillingham ME5 . . . .**10** E2
 Sittingbourne ME10 . . . .**37** A8
Austin Rd TN23 . . . .**156** B6
Austins La **4** CT13 . . . .**73** A1
Autumn Glade ME5 . . . .**54** D8
Avebury Ave CT11 . . . .**52** G8
Aveling Ct **2** ME2 . . . .**9** B7
Avent Wlk ME1 . . . .**37** E2
Avenue Gdns CT9 . . . .**8** C3
Avenue of Remembrance
 ME10 . . . .**36** F3
Avenue Rd
 Dover CT16 . . . .**149** C1
 Herne Bay CT6 . . . .**22** E5
 Ramsgate CT11 . . . .**52** F7
Avenue The
 Deal CT14 . . . .**117** C7
 Hersden CT3 . . . .**46** E1
 Hythe CT21 . . . .**176** C2
 Kingsdown CT14 . . . .**134** D4
 1 Margate CT9 . . . .**8** A1
 St Margaret's at Cliffe
 CT15 . . . .**150** F6
 Temple Ewell CT15 . . . .**148** E5
Avenue Theatre The*
 ME10 . . . .**36** F3
Averenches Rd ME14 . . . .**75** F5
Avereng Gdns CT19 . . . .**178** B6
Avereng Rd CT19 . . . .**178** B6
Avery CI ME15 . . . .**74** F1
Avery La ME15, ME17 . . . . . .**98** D6
Aviation St **5** E3
Aviemore Gdns ME14 . . . . . .**75** F4
Avington CI ME15 . . . .**74** F4
Avocet Wlk ME5 . . . .**32** D2
Avon CI CT11 . . . .**88** C8
Avondale CI CT14 . . . .**44** A8
Avondale CI ME14 . . . .**75** E5
Avondale Rd
 Capel-le-Ferne CT18 . . . . . .**164** C2
 Gillingham ME7 . . . .**10** D5
Avon Ho **13** CT20 . . . .**178** C4
Avon Rd ME14 . . . .**34** A8
AYCLIFFE **166** B5
Aycliffe City Prim Sch
 CT17 . . . .**166** A4
Aylesbury Rd TN25 . . . .**139** B7
Aylesford Cres ME8 . . . .**11** B4
AYLESFORD GREEN **156** F7
Aylesford Rd TN24 . . . .**156** E7
AYLESHAM **112** F5
Aylesham Cnr CT3 . . . .**112** D3

Aylesham Ind Est CT3....112 E4
Aylesham Prim Sch CT3...112 E5
Aylesham Rd CT15, CT3...113 A4
Aylesham Sta CT3........113 A6
Aylewyn Gn ME10.........36 F8
Aynsley Ct █ CT13........73 A1
Ayrshire Cl TN24.........139 C7
Ayton Rd CT11...........52 C6

B

Babs Oak Hill CT2........68 B7
Backfields ME1...........9 B4
Back La
  ⬛ Faversham ME13.....62 D7
  Maidstone ME14.........97 E1
  Minster (Sheppey) ME12..4 D6
Back Road W CT16........166 G8
Back St
  Leeds ME17............98 E6
  Ringwould CT14........133 F5
Baddlesmere Rd CT5......21 A2
Baden Rd ME7............10 D7
Bader Cres ME5..........32 A7
Badger Rd ME5...........32 C1
Badgers Bridge CT18....161 D4
Badgers Cl CT2..........66 A7
Badgers Den TN23.......155 D7
Badger's Hill Farm &
  Cidery* CT4...........107 C3
Badgers Oak TN23.......155 D8
Badgers Rise
  Deal CT14.............134 C8
  Kearsney CT17.........148 D3
BADLESMERE.............83 C1
Badlesmere Cl TN23.....155 E8
Bad Munstereifel Rd TN23,
  TN24................156 D5
Baffin Cl ME4............9 F2
BAGHAM.................107 D8
Bagham La CT4..........107 D8
Bagham Rd CT4..........107 C8
Bagshill Rd ME13........83 A3
Bailey Dr ME7...........11 A1
Bailey Fields TN26......153 E4
Baileys Field TN23......138 F1
Baird's Hill CT10........29 F6
Bairdsley Cl CT10........29 F6
Bakenham Ho █ ME1.....9 C1
Baker Cl ME9............38 C2
Baker Rd CT19..........177 E6
Bakers Cl CT2............87 C7
Bakers Ct CT11..........52 F7
Baker's La CT4...........86 D2
Baker St ME1............9 C3
Baker's Wlk ME1.........9 C5
Bakery Cotts ME14......53 E3
Bakery The ME9.........58 A6
Balas Rd ME10..........36 C7
Balcomb Cres
  ⬛ Margate CT9.........29 C8
Margate CT9............29 C8
Balcomb Mews ❸ CT9....29 C8
Baldric Rd CT20.........177 F5
Baldwin Rd
  Greatstone-on-Sea TN28..202 D1
  Minster (Sheppey) ME12...4 D7
Baldwin's Pl ME17.......100 D6
Baldwin Terr ME10......178 D6
Balfour Ct CT20.........178 B3
Balfour Inf Sch ME1......9 E1
Balfour Jun Sch ME4......9 E2
Balfour Rd
  Chatham ME4...........9 E1
  Chatham ME4...........9 E2
  Deal CT14.............117 C2
  Dover CT16............149 C1
Baliol Rd CT5............20 E2
Ballard Inf Est ME5.....54 C8
Ballard Rd TN28.........202 D1
Ballens Rd ME5..........32 C3
Balliemoor Ct CT11......29 F1
Balliol Rd CT10..........29 F8
Ball La TN24.............139 F7
Balmer Cl ME8...........33 D7
Balmoral Ho █ CT11......95 F5
Balmoral Pl █ CT11......52 F7
Balmoral Rd
  Gillingham ME7.........10 D5
  ⬛ Kingsdown CT9.......134 C6
  Margate CT9...........29 B8
Balmoral Terr ME10......36 D4
Bambridge Ct ME14......74 F6
Bamford Way CT14.......117 C4
Bank Cotts ME17.........77 E3

Bank View █ ME15........74 E2
Banky Fields Cl ME8......12 B1
Banner Way ME12........3 E6
Banningbrook Cl CT14...117 D4
Banning St ME2...........9 B8
Bannister Hill ME9........36 B2
Bannister Hos TN26......120 A1
Bannister Rd ME14.......75 A7
BAPCHILD...............37 E3
Bapchild & Tonge CE Aided
  Sch ME9...............37 D3
Barbados Terr ❷ ME14...75 A7
Barberry Ave ME5........31 E5
Barber's Almshouses █
  CT11.................52 D6
Barcham Ct ME15........96 F5
Barclay Ct CT8...........7 C1
Bardell Terr ME1.........9 D5
Barden Ct ME14..........75 B5
Barfleur Manor ❸ ME7....10 A6
Barfreston CT15.........113 C1
Barfreston Rd CT15.....114 A1
Bargates TN23..........155 E6
Barges The CT5..........20 E3
Barge Way ME10........115 B2
Bargrove CT18.........176 E6
Bargrove Rd ME14.......75 C5
Barge's Point Coastal Pk*
  ....1 G2
Barham ME14............75 A4
BARHAM
  111 F1
  128 E8
Barham CE Prim Sch
  CT4.................128 F8
Barham Cl ME15..........97 E5
Barham's Mill Rd TN27..118 B3
Barker Rd ME16..........74 F3
Barkers Ct ME10.........36 D4
Barkis Cl ME1...........31 D7
Barler Pl ME11...........3 A5
Barley Cl
  Herne Bay CT6.........23 D2
  Martin Mill CT15.......133 C2
Barleycorn Dr ME8.......33 E6
Barley Fields ME14......75 D4
Barleymow Cl ME5.......32 C7
Barley Way TN23.......155 E5
Barling Cl ME5...........33 E5
Barlow Cl ME8...........33 E5
BARMING HEATH.........74 A3
Barnaby Terr ME1........9 D2
Barnard Ct ME4..........10 A2
Barnberry Cl TN23......155 E8
Barn Cl
  Borden ME9............36 A2
  Hoath CT3.............46 E5
  Yorkletts CT5..........43 A3
Barn Cres CT9...........7 F1
Barncroft Cl ME14.......75 D4
Barncroft Dr ME7........32 F4
Barnes Ave CT9..........7 F1
Barnes Cl ME13..........62 B8
Barnes Ct CT17..........87 D6
Barnesende Ct CT13.....94 A8
Barnes Cl ME13..........62 B8
Barnet's La CT2..........67 D8
Barnett Ct
  Minster (Thanet) CT12...50 C5
  ❸ Ramsgate CT12......29 B1
Barnett Field TN23.....155 F8
Barnfield
  Chatham ME5..........32 A8
  Herne Bay CT6.........22 C2
  Tenterden TN30.......167 C2
Barnfield Rd
  Faversham ME13.......62 C8
  Folkestone CT19.......178 C2
Barnfields ME10.........37 D5
Barnhouse La ME17.....200 A8
Barnhurst La CT18......163 A5
Barnhurst Rd ME14......75 A8
Barn Platt TN25........156 C6
Barnsley Cl ME12........1 F2
BARNSOLE..............92 B6
Barnsole Inf Sch ME7....10 E4
Barnsole Jun Sch ME7...10 E4
Barnsole Rd
  Gillingham ME7.........10 E3
  Staple CT3............92 B5
Barnsole Vineyard*
  Barnsole CT3..........92 C6
  Sandwich CT3..........92 B6
Barn The ME9...........36 A2
Barntye Cl CT15........149 E6
Barn Tye Cl CT15.......149 E6
Barnwell Pl ME7.........10 C5
Barnwood CT14.........11 B8
Barn Yard The* ME9.....12 D1
Baron Cl
  Gillingham ME7.........10 E7
  Maidstone ME14........75 F5
Barrack Hill CT21.......176 A2
Barrack Rd ME4.........10 B8
Barrier Rd ME4..........9 F5
Barrington Cl ME5.......31 F5
Barrington Cres CT7.....27 B7
Barrowfields ME5........32 D1
Barrow Gr ME10.........10 B7
BARROWHILL............174 D7
BARROW HILL...........139 A3
Barrow Hill
  Ashford TN23..........139 B2
  Barrowhill TN25.......174 D7
Barrow Hill Cotts TN23..139 B3
Barrow Hill Pl ❷ TN23..139 B3
Barrow Hill Rise TN25..174 D7

Barrow Hill Terr █
  TN23.................139 B3
Barrows Cl CT7..........27 A6
Bartholomew Cl CT21...176 B3
Bartholomew La CT21...176 B3
Bartholomew St
  ⬛ Dover CT16.........149 C1
  Hythe CT21...........176 B2
Bartlett Cl ME5..........32 C1
Bartlett Dr CT5.........21 A1
Bartletts Cl ME13........3 C5
Barton Bsns Pk CT1......88 D6
Barton Court Gram Sch
  CT1..................88 B8
Barton Ct ❹ CT11.......52 E7
Barton Field CT18.....161 B7
Barton Hill Dr ME12.....4 A5
Barton Mill La CT1.....149 C2
Barton Mill Ct ❷ CT2....66 F1
Barton Mill Rd CT1......67 B2
Barton Rd
  Canterbury CT1........88 C6
  Dover CT16...........149 C2
  Maidstone ME15........75 A2
  Rochester ME2.........9 A7
Barton's Point Coastal Pk*
  ....1 G2
Barton View Terr ❷
  CT17.................149 C1
Barville Rd CT15.......114 E2
Barwick Rd CT17.......148 C7
Bashford Barn La ME9...58 A4
Basil Terr ❻ ME15.......75 A1
Basing Ct ME15..........75 B3
Baskerville TN24.......139 B3
Basmere Cl ME14........75 C6
Basser Hill ME9.........13 E3
Bassett Cl CT21.......176 E4
Bassett Gdns CT21.....176 D4
Bassett Rd ME10........36 D4
Bastien Mews ❹ CT1....88 B6
Bastion Rd CT17........166 C6
Batchelor St ME4........10 A4
Bateman Cnr TN26.....153 E6
Bates Cl CT3............91 F6
Bath Ct ❽ CT20.........178 B3
Bath Hard ME1..........9 D5
Bath Mews CT24.......156 E6
Bath Pl CT9.............7 J2
Bath Rd
  Ashford TN24.........156 E6
  Margate CT9...........7 J2
Bathurst Cl CT12.......29 B1
Bathurst Rd CT20......178 A5
Batteries Cl ME9........60 B8
Batteries Terr ME9......60 B8
Battery Point CT21.....177 B2
Battery Rd TN29........156 E6
Battle of Britain Homes ❼
  CT17.................156 A7
Battle of Britain Meml*
  CT18.................164 A1
Bawden Cl CT2..........67 A4
Baxendale Ct TN24.....156 D7
Bay Cotts CT15.........151 E2
Baye La CT3............69 D1
Bayeux Gdns ME7........11 A5
Bay Hill CT15...........151 B6
Bay Hill Cl CT15........151 A5
Bayle Ct ❷ CT20.......178 E4
Bayle St ❶❾ CT20......178 E5
Bayle The CT20........178 E4
Bay Mus The* CT15....151 B5
Bayswater Dr ME8......33 E4
BAY VIEW..............6 D2
Bay View Gdns ME12.....6 D1
Bay View Hts CT7.......26 D8
Bayview Rd
  Kingsdown CT14.......134 C4
  Whitstable CT5........43 D7
Beach App ME12.........6 E3
Beach Ave CT7.........26 F8
Beachborough Rd CT19,
  CT20.................178 A5
Beach Ct
  Deal CT14............117 D2
  Westgate on Sea CT8...7 D1
Beachfield Lodge ME12...1 D2
Beach Flats ❷ CT21....176 B2
Beach Hos CT5.........43 C7
Beach House Mews CT8...7 D1
Beach Marine ❼ CT20..177 F3
Beachmont CT28......206 B8
Beach Rd
  Dymchurch TN29......187 A4
  St Margaret's at Cliffe
    CT15...............151 B5
  Westgate on Sea CT8...7 D1
Beach Rise CT8.........7 D1
Beach St
  Folkestone CT20......178 E4
  Herne Bay CT6.........22 F5
  Sheerness ME12........1 C2
Beach The CT14.........117 D3
Beach Wlk CT5..........20 E3
Beacon Cl ME8..........33 D7
Beacon Hill
  Gillingham ME7........10 D2
  Herne Bay CT6.........23 B5

Beacon La
  Brookland TN29.......199 D7
  Woodnesborough CT13...93 A6
Beacon Oak Rd TN30...179 B8
Beacon Rd
  Broadstairs CT10......29 F7
  Chatham ME5..........10 C2
  Herne Bay CT6.........23 A5
  Lenham ME17.........101 C5
Beaconsfield CT5........42 F6
Beaconsfield Ave
  Dover CT16...........149 C1
  Gillingham ME7........10 D5
Beaconsfield Gdns CT10..29 F5
Beaconsfield Rd
  Canterbury CT2........66 F2
  Chatham ME4..........9 F3
  Deal CT14............117 D5
  Dover CT16...........131 C7
  Maidstone ME15........74 E2
  Sittingbourne ME10....37 C4
Beacons The ME7........96 C2
Beacon Terr CT21......177 B2
Beacon Way CT21......174 F3
Beacon Wlk
  Herne Bay CT6........23 A5
  Tenterden TN30......167 B1
Bean Cl TN23...........138 C1
Beaney's La CT4.........84 C1
Beaney's La Cotts CT4...84 C1
Bears End Ho TN23....156 B8
Bear's La TN23, TN26...137 E3
Beary Ave ME8..........11 C2
Beatrice Hills Cl TN24..139 E5
Beatrice Mews TN28...206 E7
Beatrice Rd
  Folkestone CT19......178 D8
  Rochester ME1........31 D8
Beauchamp Ave CT17..117 A3
Beauchamp Cl TN24...139 E5
Beauchamps La CT15...113 D5
Beaufort Ave CT12.....52 B8
Beaufort Ct ME2........9 F2
Beaufort Wlk ME15......97 E4
Beaufoy Rd CT17.......149 A1
Beaufoy Terr CT17.....148 F1
Beauherne Com Sch CT2..87 D8
Beaulieu Rise ME9.......9 D1
Beaulieu Wlk ME16......74 C7
Beaumanor CT6.........23 A3
Beaumont Davy Cl ME13..62 C5
Beaumont Rd ME16......74 B2
Beaumont St CT2........22 C4
Beaumont Terr ME13....62 D6
Beauvoir Dr ME10.......37 A8
Beauworth Pk ME15.....97 E8
Beauxfield CT14........149 A7
BEAVER.................156 B7
Beaverbrook Mews ME6..74 D3
Beaver Ct TN23, TN24...156 A7
Beaver Green Prim Sch
  TN23.................155 E7
Beaver Ind Est TN23...156 B7
Beaver La
  Ashford, Beaver TN23..156 A7
  Ashford, Singleton TN23..155 F7
  Ashford TN23..........138 C1
Beaver Rd
  Ashford TN23.........156 B8
  Maidstone ME16........74 B7
Beazley Ct TN24.......156 D7
Beckenham Dr ME6......74 D7
Becket Ave CT2.........66 D1
Becket Cl
  Ash CT3...............71 D2
  Deal CT14............117 C8
  Whitstable CT5........21 B1
Becket Mews CT2.......66 F1
Becket's Cl TN25.......142 B6
Beckett St ❹ ME13.....62 C7
Becketts Wood CT3.....47 E3
Beckley Mews ME5.......31 F5
Beckley Pl TN25.......175 B8
Beckley Rd ME12.........1 F2
Becksbourne Cl ME14....75 A8
Beckwith Gn CT20......177 E5
Beckworth Pl ME16......74 B2
Beddow Way ME20......53 B3
Bede Ho CT14..........117 D8
Bedford Ave ME8........11 D1
Bedford Ct CT10.........30 B6
Bedford Rd ME16........74 E4
Bedford Sq CT12........29 B2
Bedford Way CT7........25 F1
Bedgebury Cl
  Maidstone ME14........75 C6
  Rochester ME1........31 D8
Bedingfield Way CT18..161 B7
Bedlam Court La CT12...50 C6
BEDMONTON............78 E8
Bedmonton La ME9.....58 B2
Bedson Wlk ME8.........12 B1
Bedwin Cl ME4..........31 D7
Beech Ave CT4..........86 E1

Beech Cl
  Faversham ME13.......62 B7
  Folkestone CT19......178 C6
Beech Court Gdns*
  TN25.................104 F1
Beechcroft CT5.........21 D1
Beechcroft Gdns CT11...52 F8
Beech Ct CT11...........88 A7
Beech Dr
  Broadstairs CT10......29 D4
  Elvington CT15........114 B2
  Hothfield TN26........138 A7
  Maidstone ME16........74 C5
Beechen Bank Rd ME5...32 A1
Beeches The
  Chatham ME5..........32 A4
  Lydd TN29............205 D7
Beech Gr CT12..........51 C5
Beech Green CT15......131 C7
Beech Grove Sch CT15..131 E6
Beech Hill CT4.........111 B8
Beech Hurst Cl ME15....75 B2
Beeching Rd ME5........32 B3
Beechings Gn ME8......11 C3
Beechings Way ME8.....11 C3
Beechings Way Ind Ctr
  ME8.................11 B4
Beecholme Dr TN23.....32 A2
Beecholme Dr TN24....139 C5
Beechwood Ave
  Deal CT14............117 C5
  Gillingham ME5........10 D2
  Sittingbourne ME10....36 E6
Beechwood Cl
  St Mary's Bay TN29...194 F3
  Whitfield CT16........132 A1
Beechwood Ct
  Deal CT14............117 C5
  Temple Ewell CT16...148 E4
Beecroft Cl CT2.........67 A4
Beer Cart La CT1........87 F8
Beggarsbush La TN29...200 D7
Beggars Cnr CT3........48 D1
Begonia Ave ME8.......11 C2
Beke Rd ME8............33 D4
BEKESBOURNE..........89 D4
BEKESBOURNE HILL.....89 B5
Bekesbourne La
  Bekesbourne CT3, CT4..89 E6
  Canterbury CT3........88 F7
  Littlebourne CT3.......88 F7
Bekesbourne Rd CT4....88 F7
Bekesbourne Sta CT4...89 B5
Belcaire Cl CT15.......175 A3
Belfast Ho █ ME15.......97 E7
Belgrave Cl CT11........52 C3
Belgrave Ct CT14......117 D3
Belgrave Rd
  Dover CT17...........166 B7
  Halfway Houses ME12...3 C5
  Margate CT9...........7 I2
Belinda Ct CT19.......178 B7
Bell Chapel Cl TN23....156 C4
Bell Cnr TN29..........201 A4
Bell Cotts ME9.........13 B3
Bell Cres ME1...........53 A8
Bell-Davies Dr CT12....28 A1
Belle Friday Cl ME9......38 C7
Bellevue Ave CT11......52 F7
Bellevue Rd
  Minster (Sheppey) ME12...4 C6
  Ramsgate CT11........52 F7
  Whitstable CT5........43 F8
Belle Vue Rd CT6.......23 B5
Bellevue St ❺ CT20...178 D5
Bell Farm La ME12.......5 A6
Bellflower Ave ME12.....4 A4
Bell Gr CT3............113 A5
Bellgrove Ct ME5.......54 A8
Bell La
  Burham ME1...........53 A8
  Chatham ME1..........31 C8
  Maidstone ME14........76 A5
  Sandwich CT13.........73 A1
Bell Mdw ME15..........97 E6
Bell Rd
  Maidstone ME10.......97 E5
  ⬛ Sittingbourne ME10...36 F3
Bell's Cl TN30.........179 A7
Bell Sh Ctr █ ME10......36 F4
Bell Shaw ❶❼ ME15....97 E5
Bells La ❽ TN30.......179 A7
Bell Way ME17..........99 E2
Bell Wood Prim Sch ❶❻
  ME15.................97 E4
Belmont Ct CT14.......117 B1
Belmont Ct
  ❸ Maidstone ME15.....75 B4
  ❷ Ramsgate CT11......52 C6
Belmont Farm Bsns Ctr
  TN26.................137 A3
Belmont House & Gdns*
  ME13.................82 D5
Belmont Pl TN14.......156 D7
Belmont Rd
  Ashford TN24.........139 D6
  Broadstairs CT10......30 A4
  Faversham ME13.......62 C6
  Gillingham ME7........10 C4
  Halfway Houses ME12...3 E6
  Ramsgate CT11........52 D7
  Sittingbourne ME10....36 E3
  Westgate on Sea CT8...7 D7
  Whitstable CT5........21 C1
Belmont St CT11........52 E7
Belmont Terr TN14......93 B3
Belmont Yd ❽ CT5......20 D1

Belmore Pk TN24 . . . . .139 B3
Belnor Ave ME7 . . . . .13 F1
Belsey La CT15 . . . . .147 D4
Belting Dr CT6 . . . . .23 E5
BELTINGE 23 E4
Beltinge Rd CT6 . . . . .23 B5
Belton Cl CT5 . . . . .43 E8
Belts Wood 14 ME15 . . . . . . .97 F5
Belvedere Cl ME13 . . . . .62 D8
Belvedere Ho 9 ME15 . . . . . .97 D8
Belvedere Rd
Broadstairs CT10 . . . . .30 B4
Faversham ME13 . . . . .62 D8
Benacre Rd CT5 . . . . .43 D6
Bench Hill TN26 . . . . .181 D5
Bench St 10 CT16 . . . . .166 D7
Bendon Way ME8 . . . . .33 D8
Benenden Manor ME8 . . . . . .11 B3
Bengal Rd TN24 . . . . .29 A1
Benham Bsns Pk CT21 . .174 F5
Bennells Ave CT5 . . . . .21 B3
Bennett Cl 10 CT20 . . . . . .178 E5
Bennetts Cotts ME7 . . . . .55 A8
Bennetts Gdns CT1 . . . . .61 D8
Bennetts Mews 12 TN30 . .179 A7
Benson Cl CT18 . . . . .162 F4
Benson La CT18 . . . . .162 F4
Bensted TN23 . . . . .155 F5
Bensted Cl CT6 . . . . .23 A1
Bensted Gr ME13 . . . . .62 A7
Bentham Sq ME12 . . . . .1 B3
Bentley Ave CT6 . . . . .22 B4
Bentley Cl ME5 . . . . .32 C2
Bentley Rd TN24 . . . . .156 F7
Bentlif Cl ME16 . . . . .74 D5
Berber Rd ME9 . . . . .9 B8
Berengrave La ME8 . . . . .11 D3
Berengrave Nature Reserve*
ME8 . . . . .12 A3
Beresford Ave ME1 . . . . .9 E2
Beresford Ct 11 CT7 . . . . . . .26 F8
Beresford Gap CT7 . . . . .26 F8
Beresford Gdns CT9 . . . . .8 C3
Beresford Rd
Gillingham ME7 . . . . .10 D4
Kit's Coty ME20 . . . . .53 D7
Ramsgate CT11 . . . . .52 D6
River CT17 . . . . .148 E3
St Margaret's at Cliffe
CT15 . . . . .133 F1
Whitstable CT5 . . . . .20 D2
Beresfords Hill ME17 . . . . . .97 B4
Bergamot Cl ME10 . . . . .36 F2
Bergland Pk ME2 . . . . .9 D8
Berkeley Cl
Boughton Street ME13 . . . . .64 B3
2 Folkestone CT19 . . . . . .178 A7
Rochester ME1 . . . . .31 D8
Berkeley Ct ME10 . . . . .36 D3
Berkeley Mount 8 ME4 . . . . . .9 F4
Berkeley Rd CT7 . . . . .26 F8
Berkshire Cl ME5 . . . . .32 C8
Bernards Gdns CT15 . . . . . .130 E5
Bernard Sunley Hall
TN25 . . . . .124 A2
Berridge Rd ME12 . . . . .1 C2
Berries The CT18 . . . . .163 B5
Berry St ME10 . . . . .36 A4
Berwick La CT21 . . . . .175 A3
Berwyn Gr ME15 . . . . .97 A6
Best La CT1 . . . . .87 F8
Best St ME4 . . . . .9 F4
Bethany Cl CT14 . . . . .117 C8
Bethel Row ME13 . . . . .83 F8
BETHERSDEN 153 E5
Bethersden Bsns Ctr
TN26 . . . . .153 C1
Bethersden Ct ME15 . . . . . . .97 F7
Bethersden Prim Sch
TN26 . . . . .153 E5
Bethersden Rd
Hothfield TN26 . . . . .137 D4
Shadoxhurst TN26 . . . . . . .154 E2
Smarden TN27 . . . . .135 C3
Smarden TN27 . . . . .152 C5
Woodchurch TN26 . . . . . . .169 A6
Betony Gdns ME14 . . . . .75 F5
Betsham Rd ME15 . . . . .97 F6
Betteridge Cl ME1 . . . . .32 A2
Bettescombe Rd ME8 . . . . . . .33 E7
Betty Shelvey Ct CT14 . . . .117 D4
Beult Mdw TN27 . . . . .135 A1
Bevan Way CT3 . . . . .112 F5
Beverley Cl ME8 . . . . .33 F8
Beverley Gdns TN29 . . . . . .187 A4
Beverley Ho CT2 . . . . .66 F2
Beverley Rd CT2 . . . . .66 E2
Beverley Way CT12 . . . . .29 C1
Beverly Cl CT7 . . . . .27 B8
Bewsbury Cres CT16 . . . . . .148 F7
Bewsbury Cross La CT16 . .148 E8
Bexley St CT5 . . . . .20 D2
BEXON 58 B4
Bexon La ME9 . . . . .58 C4
Bhutan Rd CT6 . . . . .23 C4
BICKNOR 57 C2
Bicknor Cl CT2 . . . . .67 B4
Bicknor Court Cotts ME9 . . . . .57 C2
Bicknor Rd ME14 . . . . .57 D3
Bicknor Rd ME15 . . . . .97 F4
Biddenden Cl
Maidstone ME15 . . . . .75 F3
Margate CT9 . . . . .8 C1
BIDDENDEN GREEN 135 B2
Bierce Court Cotts CT7 . . . . . . .26 F7
Bierce Ct CT7 . . . . .26 F7
Bifrons Gdns CT4 . . . . .89 B3

Bifrons Hill CT4 . . . . .89 B4
Bifrons Rd CT4 . . . . .89 B4
Bigbury Rd CT2, CT4 . . . . . . .86 E7
Biggin St 1 CT16 . . . . .166 D8
Biggins Wood Rd CT19 . . . .177 E7
Biggleswade Link 11 CT1 . . .88 A8
Bilberry Cl ME14 . . . . .75 E5
Bill Deedes Way TN25 . . . . .172 F4
Bilsington Gdns TN24 . . . . .155 E8
Bill Street Rd 1 ME2 . . . . .9 C8
BILSINGTON 172 C1
Bilsington Cl ME5 . . . . .32 B5
Bilsington Cross TN25 . . . . .172 C2
BILTING 123 E7
Bilting La TN25 . . . . .123 E7
Bimbury La ME14 . . . . .74 A4
Bindon Blood Rd CT16 . . . .149 A5
Bingham Rd ME10 . . . . .37 D6
Bingley Cl CT1 . . . . .87 E7
Bingley Rd 1 ME1 . . . . .9 E4
Binland Gr ME5 . . . . .31 D5
Binnacle Rd ME1 . . . . .31 C8
Birch Cl CT10 . . . . .29 F2
Birch Cl
Ashford TN24 . . . . .139 F2
Broadstairs CT10 . . . . .29 C3
Birch Ho
Barham CT4 . . . . .128 F8
Ramsgate CT11 . . . . .52 D8
Birch Dr ME5 . . . . .32 D1
Birches The CT7 . . . . .27 B7
Birchett Rd 2 TN23 . . . . . . .138 E1
Birchett La CT4 . . . . .170 D3
Birchfield Cl ME15 . . . . .97 B6
Birchfields ME5 . . . . .32 A3
Birch Rd ME4 . . . . .33 A4
Birch Hill Ct CT7 . . . . .27 B7
Birch Row
6 Maidstone ME16 . . . . .74 A3
Sheerness ME12 . . . . .1 D2
Sittingbourne ME10 . . . . . . .37 B3
BIRCHINGTON 26 E7
Birchington CE Prim Sch
CT7 . . . . .27 A6
Birchington Ct ME14 . . . . . . .75 C5
Birchington-on-Sea Sta
CT7 . . . . .26 F7
BIRCHOLT FORSTAL 158 E8
Bircholt Forstal TN25 . . . . .158 E7
Bircholt Rd ME15 . . . . .97 F4
Birch Rd
Canterbury CT1 . . . . .87 E6
Whitstable CT5 . . . . .44 A8
Birch Tree Way ME15 . . . . . .75 B3
Birchwood Rd ME16 . . . . . . .74 C5
Birchwood Rise CT17 . . . . .166 C7
Birchwood Wlk CT2 . . . . . . .56 B8
Birdswood Ave CT14 . . . . . .117 A5
Birkdale Cl CT5 . . . . .44 D8
Birkdale 3 ME16 . . . . .74 E4
Birkdale Dr CT19 . . . . .178 A8
Birkdale Gdns CT6 . . . . .22 D2
Birkhall Cl ME5 . . . . .32 A5
Bir La ME9 . . . . .58 D5
Birling Ave
Gillingham ME8 . . . . .11 E1
Maidstone ME14 . . . . .76 A4
Birling Cl ME14 . . . . .76 A4
Birling Rd TN24 . . . . .139 D1
Birnam Sq 1 ME16 . . . . .74 E4
Bishopbourne Gn ME8 . . . . .11 B4
Bishop Ct
4 Sittingbourne ME10 . . . . .36 E5
Whitstable CT5 . . . . .20 E6
Bishopden Ct CT2 . . . . .66 C4
Bishop Jenner Ct CT7 . . . . . .70 C7
Bishop La ME9 . . . . .12 E3
Bishop's Ave CT10 . . . . .30 B6
Bishop's Ct CT17 . . . . .166 D5
Bishops Ctyd 10 CT1 . . . . . .88 A8
Bishops Gn TN23 . . . . .155 E7
BISHOPSTONE 23 F5
Bishopstone Dr CT6 . . . . . . .23 F6
Bishopstone La CT6 . . . . . . .23 F5
Bishops Way
Canterbury CT1 . . . . .66 D1
Maidstone ME15 . . . . .74 F4
Bishops Wlk ME1 . . . . .9 C5
Bishopswood TN23 . . . . . . .156 C3
Bismuth Rd ME10 . . . . .36 D6
Bittern Cl CT18 . . . . .163 A3
Blackberry Way CT5 . . . . . . .44 B8
Black Bull Rd CT19 . . . . . . .178 D6
Blackburn Rd CT6 . . . . .22 B2
Blackdown Dr TN24 . . . . . . .139 B4
Blacketts Cotts ME9 . . . . . . .38 B7
Blacketts Rd ME9 . . . . .38 A6
Blackfriars St 18 CT1 . . . . . .66 F1
Black Griffin La CT1 . . . . . . .87 F8
Blackhouse Hill CT18,
CT21 . . . . .176 D4
Blackhouse Rise CT21 . . . . .176 D3
Blackleys ME13 . . . . .84 F7
Black Lion L Ctr ME4 . . . . . .10 B6
Blackmanstone Way
ME16 . . . . .74 B7
Black Post ME17 . . . . .78 E4
Black Robin La CT4 . . . . . . .111 E3
Black Rock Gdns ME7 . . . . . .10 E6
Blacksmith Dr ME14 . . . . . . .75 D5
Blackstable Ct CT5 . . . . .43 D8
Blackthorn Ave ME15 . . . . . .32 A3
Blackthorne Rd ME8 . . . . . . .34 B8
Blackthorn Way TN23 . . . . .156 A7
Blackthorn Rd CT3 . . . . .68 C8
Blackwall Rd N TN24 . . . . . .140 A2
Blackwall Road N TN24 . . . .140 A2

Blackwall Road S TN24 . . . .140 A2
BLADBEAN 127 F2
Blake Cl CT14 . . . . .134 C8
Blake Ct
Ashford TN24 . . . . .156 F8
6 Ramsgate CT11 . . . . .52 D7
Blakeney Cl ME14 . . . . .76 B4
Blaker Ave ME1 . . . . .9 E1
Bland Dr CT18 . . . . .163 C5
Blandford Gdns ME10 . . . . . .36 E1
Blatcher Cl ME12 . . . . .4 B6
Blaxland Cl ME13 . . . . .62 B8
Bleak Ho* CT10 . . . . .30 B4
Bleak House CT10 . . . . .30 B4
Bleak Rd TN29 . . . . .205 C6
Bleakwood Rd 8 ME5 . . . . . .31 F5
BLEAN 66 A6
Blean Comm CT2 . . . . .66 A6
Blean Ct ME14 . . . . .11 C2
Blean Sq ME14 . . . . .75 C6
Blean View Rd CT6 . . . . .22 B2
Blean Woods Nature
Reserve* CT2 . . . . .65 F4
Blendon Rd ME14 . . . . .75 C5
Blenheim Ave
Canterbury CT1 . . . . .67 D1
Chatham ME4 . . . . .9 E2
Faversham ME13 . . . . .62 E5
Blenheim Cl
Broadstairs CT10 . . . . .29 D3
Herne Bay CT6 . . . . .23 A1
Maidstone ME15 . . . . .75 F3
Blenheim Ct ME4 . . . . .9 E3
Blenheim Dr
Dover CT16 . . . . .149 C3
Hawkinge CT18 . . . . .163 A4
Blenheim Ho CT9 . . . . .8 C3
Blenheim Pl 2 CT20 . . . . . .177 F4
Blenheim Rd
Deal CT14 . . . . .117 D5
Littlestone-on-Sea TN28 . .202 D6
Sittingbourne ME10 . . . . . . .37 B2
Bleriot Meml* CT16 . . . . . . .149 F1
BLIBY 171 F8
Bliby Bsns Ctr TN25 . . . . . .171 F7
Bliby Cnr TN25 . . . . .171 F8
Blindhouse La TN26 . . . . . . .155 C1
Blindhouse La TN23 . . . . . . .160 B3
Blind La
Bredhurst ME7 . . . . .33 A1
Challock TN25 . . . . .105 C2
Gillingham ME7 . . . . .32 F1
Mersham TN25 . . . . .157 C4
Blind Mary's La ME9 . . . . . . .57 E4
Blockmakers Ct ME4 . . . . . . .10 B1
BLODDEN 112 E8
Bloody Point Rd CT13 . . . . . .73 B4
Bloomsbury Rd CT11 . . . . . . .52 C6
Bloomsbury Way TN24 . . . .139 B7
Bloomsbury Wlk 2 ME15 . .74 E4
Bloors La ME8 . . . . .11 D1
Bloors Wharf Rd ME7 . . . . . .11 F4
Blossom La TN25 . . . . .138 E5
Blowers Wood Gr ME7 . . . . .33 B3
Bluebell Cl
Gillingham ME7 . . . . .10 F6
Kingsnorth TN23 . . . . .156 B4
Bluebell Dr ME10 . . . . .36 F1
BLUE BELL HILL 31 D5
Bluebell Rd TN23 . . . . .156 D2
Bluebell Woods Mobile
Home Pk CT2 . . . . .67 D6
Blue Bear La ME1 . . . . .9 D5
Blue Field TN29 . . . . .155 C8
Bluefield Mews CT5 . . . . .43 C6
Blue House La CT17 . . . . . .176 B8
Blue Line La TN24 . . . . .139 B3
Blue Skies St 17 ME1 . . . . . . .9 D4
BLUETOWN 59 B1
Bluett St ME14 . . . . .75 A5
Bluewater Crn Pk CT17 . . . .187 E8
Blythe Cl ME10 . . . . .37 C5
Blythe Rd ME14 . . . . .75 B4
Boarley Cl ME14 . . . . .53 F1
Boarley La ME14 . . . . .53 F2
Boarman's La TN29 . . . . . . .199 E8
Boat La TN25 . . . . .173 A4
Bob Amor Cl ME13 . . . . .62 E7
BOBBING 36 A7
Bobbing Hill ME9 . . . . .36 A6
Bobbing Prim Sch ME9 . . . . .36 B7
Bobbin Lodge Hill ME14 . . . .74 B2
Bockham Cotts TN25 . . . . . .157 B8
Bockham La
Ashford TN25 . . . . .141 A1
Mersham TN25 . . . . .157 B8
BOCKHANGER 139 C6
Bockhanger Ct TN24 . . . . . .139 D5
Bockhanger La TN24 . . . . . .139 C6
Bockingford La ME15 . . . . . . .96 F8
Bocton Ho ME17 . . . . .97 B3
Bodenham Rd CT20 . . . . . . .178 A4
Bodiam Cl ME8 . . . . .11 C3
Bodiam Ct ME16 . . . . .74 F3
Bodkins Cl ME17 . . . . .97 D5
BODSHAM 142 D8
Bodsham CE Prim Sch
TN25 . . . . .142 E8
Bodsham Cres ME15 . . . . . . .76 B3
BOGLE 60 B8
Bogle Rd ME9 . . . . .60 C7
Bognor Dr CT6 . . . . .22 D4

Bogshole La
Herne Bay CT6 . . . . .23 D3
Whitstable CT5 . . . . .43 E4
Boley Hill ME1 . . . . .9 C6
Boleyn Ave CT9 . . . . .7 E1
Bolingo Ct 17 CT15 . . . . . . .88 A8
Bolingbroke Ho ME16 . . . . . .74 E3
Bolner Cl ME5 . . . . .31 F2
Bolonia ME15 . . . . .151 A6
Bolton Cl CT19 . . . . .178 D6
Bolton St CT11 . . . . .52 D8
Bombay Ho 1 ME15 . . . . . . .97 E5
Bond La TN23 . . . . .156 A2
Bond Rd
Ashford TN23 . . . . .156 B8
Gillingham ME8 . . . . .33 C5
Bonetta Cl ME12 . . . . .3 B7
Bonham Dr ME10 . . . . .37 B5
Bonners Alley 19 CT5 . . . . . .20 D2
BONNINGTON 172 F3
Bonnington Cross TN25 . . . .172 E3
Bonnington Gn ME8 . . . . . . .11 C3
Bonnington Rd ME14 . . . . . . .75 C6
Bonny Bush Hill CT4 . . . . . .111 D5
Bonsor Rd CT19 . . . . .178 D6
Boorman Way CT5 . . . . .43 B6
Booth Cl
Gillingham ME7 . . . . .10 D4
Queenborough ME11 . . . . . . .3 B4
Borrowdale Ave CT11 . . . . . .52 B4
Booth Pl ME7 . . . . .7 J3
Booth Rd ME4 . . . . .9 F4
BORDEN 36 B2
Borden CE Prim Sch ME9 . . .35 F3
Borden Gram Sch ME10 . . . .36 F3
Borden La ME10, ME9 . . . . . .36 E2
Boresisle TN30 . . . . .167 B2
Bornefields TN23 . . . . .156 A7
Borough CT1 . . . . .67 A1
Borough Rd
Gillingham ME7 . . . . .10 D4
Queenborough ME11 . . . . . . .3 B4
Borrowdale Ave CT11 . . . . . .52 B4
BORSTAL 9 B2
Borstal Ave CT5 . . . . .43 D6
Borstal Hill CT5 . . . . .43 D7
Borstal Mews ME1 . . . . .9 A2
Borstal Rd ME1 . . . . .9 B3
Borstal St ME1 . . . . .9 B3
Boscombe Rd CT19 . . . . . . .178 C6
Bosman Ct ME5 . . . . .74 A1
Bosney Banks CT15 . . . . . . .148 A7
Bosman Cl ME5 . . . . .32 C5
BOSSINGHAM 127 A6
Bossingham Rd CT4 . . . . . . .126 F3
Bossingham St CT4 . . . . . . .126 E6
BOSSINGTON 90 E1
Bossington Rd CT3 . . . . .90 E1
Boston Cl 5 CT16 . . . . .149 B3
Boston Gdns ME8 . . . . .11 C1
Boston Rd ME5 . . . . .32 C2
Botany Cl ME12 . . . . .1 C1
Botany Rd CT10 . . . . .8 F2
Boteler Cotts CT13 . . . . .93 A2
BOTOLPH'S BRIDGE 187 A7
Botolph's Bridge Rd
CT21 . . . . .187 A6
Bottlescrew Hill ME17 . . . . . .97 B4
Bottles La ME9 . . . . .59 A6
BOTTOM POND 59 D2
Bottom Pond Rd ME9 . . . . . .58 D3
Boughton Aluph CT4 . . . . . .123 A5
Boughton Ave CT10 . . . . .30 A2
Boughton Church Cotts
ME13 . . . . .63 D5
Boughton Cl ME8 . . . . .11 B3
Boughton Cnr TN25 . . . . . . .123 C5
Boughton Field Cotts
ME13 . . . . .63 A5
BOUGHTON GREEN 97 B3
Boughton Hill ME13 . . . . . . .64 C3
Boughton La ME15 . . . . .97 B6
BOUGHTON LEES 122 F4
BOUGHTON MALHERBE . .118 A8
BOUGHTON
MONCHELSEA 97 B3
Boughton Monchelsea Prim
Sch ME17 . . . . .97 B2
Boughton Par ME15 . . . . .97 A7
Boughton Place Cotts
ME17 . . . . .118 A8
Boughton Rd ME17 . . . . . . .101 B2
BOUGHTON STREET 64 C3
BOUGHTON UNDER
BLEAN 64 C3
Boughton-under-Blean &
Dunkirk Prim Sch ME13 . . .63 F3
Boulevard Courrieres
CT3 .112 E5
Boulevard d'Erlanger
CT18 . . . . .177 B7
Boulevard The CT6 . . . . .156 F6
Boulogne Ct 17 CT20 . . . . .178 E5
Boundary Chase CT5 . . . . . .44 E8
Boundary Cl ME12 . . . . .4 E6
Boundary Ct 3 CT1 . . . . .88 B7
Boundary Rd
Chatham ME4 . . . . .9 E3
Deal CT14 . . . . .134 C6
Hythe CT21 . . . . .176 A2
Ramsgate CT11 . . . . .52 E7
Boundary The CT7 . . . . .87 D2
Boundsgate Cnr ME17 . . . . .105 B7
Bounds La ME17 . . . . .64 A3
Bourne Cotts CT4 . . . . .111 C5
Bourne Gr ME10 . . . . .9 D5
Bourne Gr ME10 . . . . .9 D5
Bourne La TN26 . . . . .183 A8
Bourne Lodge Cl CT2 . . . . . .66 A7
Bournemouth Dr CT6 . . . . . . .22 D4
Bournemouth Gdns
CT19 . . . . .178 C6

Bournemouth Rd CT19 . . . .178 C5
Bourne Park Rd CT4 . . . . . .111 A7
Bourne Rd CT4 . . . . .89 A1
Bourne Rd TN25 . . . . .172 D5
Bournes Cl CT2 . . . . .67 F7
Bourneside Terr ME17 . . . . . .77 D2
Bournes Pl TN26 . . . . .169 A2
Bourne View CT4 . . . . .88 F1
Bournewood TN26 . . . . .183 A8
Bournewood Cl ME15 . . . . . .75 F1
Bournville Ave ME4 . . . . .9 F1
Bouverie Pl 2 CT20 . . . . . . .178 D4
Bouverie Road W CT20 . . . .178 C4
Bouverie Sh Ctr CT20 . . . . .178 D4
Bouverie Sq 1 CT20 . . . . . .178 D4
Bowdell La TN29 . . . . .191 E3
Bowden Cres CT20 . . . . .177 C6
Bowen Cl CT1 . . . . .52 D7
Bowen Rd CT19 . . . . .177 E6
Bowens Field TN23 . . . . . . .139 B1
Bower Cl ME16 . . . . .74 E4
Bower Gn ME5 . . . . .32 C1
Bower Grove Sch ME16 . . . .74 B2
Bower La ME16 . . . . .74 F4
Bowerland La
Chilham CT4 . . . . .85 E1
Old Wives Lees CT4 . . . . . . .85 C2
Bower Mount Rd ME16 . . . . .74 F4
Bower Pl ME16 . . . . .74 F3
Bower Rd TN25 . . . . .158 A3
Bowers Ho ME7 . . . . .10 E7
Bower St ME14 . . . . .74 E4
Bower Terr ME16 . . . . .74 E4
Bowes Ave ME15 . . . . .7 E1
Bowes La CT6 . . . . .23 A3
Bowes Rd ME2 . . . . .9 B8
Bowes Villas CT14 . . . . .93 E4
Bow Hill CT4 . . . . .109 F2
Bowland Cl CT6 . . . . .23 C2
Bowlers Town TN31 . . . . . . .197 A2
Bowles Well Gdns CT19 . . .178 F7
Bowley La ME17 . . . . .118 D8
Bowl Field TN25 . . . . .142 B6
Bowling Green La CT14 . . . .117 B5
Bowling Green Terr 8
CT17 . . . . .166 D7
Bowling St CT13 . . . . .72 F1
Bowman Rd TN27 . . . . .103 D2
Bowman Cl ME5 . . . . .32 C5
Bowman Ct CT17 . . . . .149 A1
Bowser Cl CT14 . . . . .116 F4
Bowyer Rd CT5 . . . . .42 F7
Box La ME13 . . . . .61 D1
BOXLEY 54 D2
Boxley Cl
Maidstone ME14 . . . . .75 B8
West Minst ME17 . . . . .3 B7
Boxley Rd
Chatham ME5 . . . . .32 B2
Maidstone ME14 . . . . .75 B7
Boxmend Ind Est ME15 . . . . .97 F3
Boxted La ME1 . . . . .13 A1
Boyces Hill ME9 . . . . .35 C6
BOYDEN GATE 47 C8
Boyden Gate Hill CT3 . . . . . .47 B8
Boyes La CT3 . . . . .91 D3
Boyke La CT4 . . . . .144 C2
Boyland Rd ME15 . . . . .134 A1
Boyne Rd CT15 . . . . .134 A1
Boys Hall Rd TN24 . . . . .156 F7
Boystown Pl CT13 . . . . .93 C3
Brabazon Rd ME12 . . . . .5 C1
Brabner Ct CT19 . . . . .178 E8
BRABOURNE 159 B8
Brabourne Ave ME8 . . . . .11 C3
Brabourne CE Prim Sch
TN25 . . . . .159 A8
Brabourne Cl CT2 . . . . .67 A4
Brabourne Gdns CT20 . . . . .177 C5
Brabourne Ho TN25 . . . . . . .142 F2
BRABOURNE LEES 158 D5
Brabourne Rd TN25 . . . . . . .141 D6
Bracken Cl TN24 . . . . .139 C6
Bracken Ct
3 Broadstairs CT10 . . . . . . .29 C5
4 Sittingbourne ME10 . . . . .37 C5
Bracken Hill ME5 . . . . .32 A1
Bracken Lea ME5 . . . . .10 C1
Bracken La TN23 . . . . .191 B3
Brackley Cl ME14 . . . . .75 D5
Brackwood Cl ME8 . . . . .33 D5
Bradbridge Gn TN23 . . . . . .155 D8
Braddick Cl ME15 . . . . .97 B6
Bradfield Ave ME9 . . . . .38 D2
Bradfield Rd TN24 . . . . .139 B5
Bradfields Ave ME5 . . . . .31 F5
Bradfields Avenue W ME5 . .31 E5
Bradfields Further Education
Ctr ME7 . . . . .10 B5
Bradfields Sch ME5 . . . . .32 A6
Bradford Ct CT20 . . . . .178 D5
Bradley Dr ME15 . . . . .36 E2
Bradley Rd
Folkestone CT19 . . . . .178 F6
Ramsgate CT12 . . . . .29 C1
Bradstone Ave ME17 . . . . . . .12 E3
Bradstone Cl CT19 . . . . .178 D5
Bradstone New Rd 3
CT20 . . . . .178 D5
Bradstone Rd CT20 . . . . . . .178 D5
Bradstow Sch CT10 . . . . .30 A3
Bradstow Way CT10 . . . . . . .30 A5
Brady Rd CT18 . . . . .161 A2
Braeside CT10 . . . . .30 B3
Braggs La CT6 . . . . .45 E6

Braithwaite Ct ME7 . . . . .11 A5
Brake Ave ME5 . . . . .31 E5
Bramble Cl
  Maidstone ME16 . . . . .74 B3
  Wye TN25 . . . . .123 D3
Brambledown
  Chatham ME5 . . . . .32 B8
  Folkestone CT19 . . . . .178 D6
Bramblefield La ME10,
  ME9 . . . . .14 E1
Bramblefields Cl CT6 . . . . .22 E1
Bramblehill Rd ME13 . . . . .62 C8
Bramble La TN25 . . . . .123 C3
Brambles Cl ME4 . . . . .4 A5
Brambles Clyd CT14 . . . . .117 B3
Bramble Wlk TN23 . . . . .156 C2
Bramley Cres CT17 . . . . .177 E5
Brambling Rise ME10 . . . . .36 E6
Bramley Ave
  Canterbury CT1 . . . . .87 C6
  Faversham ME13 . . . . .62 A4
Bramley Cl
  Brabourne Lees TN25 . . . . . .158 E6
  Eastchurch ME12 . . . . .5 D3
  Gillingham ME8 . . . . .34 B8
  Newington ME9 . . . . .35 A5
Bramley Cres ME15 . . . . .75 F3
Bramley Gdns
  Ashford TN23 . . . . .156 A6
  Coxheath ME17 . . . . .96 C3
  Herne Bay CT6 . . . . .23 D2
Bramley Way ME12 . . . . .5 B3
BRAMLING 90 C6
Bramling Gap CT3 . . . . .90 C3
Bramling Rd CT3, CT4 . . . . .90 B4
Bramshaw Rd CT12 . . . . .66 E2
Bramshott Cl ME16 . . . . .74 C6
Bramston Rd ME12 . . . . .4 C6
Branchley Mews TN27 . . . . . . .120 C8
Branch Ct CT4 . . . . .107 C7
Branch St CT16 . . . . .149 C1
Brandon Rd CT12 . . . . .29 A1
Brandon Way CT7 . . . . .27 B6
Bransgore Cl ME8 . . . . .33 D7
Brasenose Rd ME7 . . . . .10 E4
Brasier Ct ME2 . . . . .4 A3
Brassey Ave CT10 . . . . .29 F3
BRATTLE 181 A8
Brattle TN26 . . . . .181 B8
Braunstone Dr ME16 . . . . .74 D7
Bray Gdns ME15 . . . . .96 F5
BREACH
  Derringstone 128 C4
  Newington 34 F8
Breach La ME9 . . . . .13 A2
Breadlands Cl TN24 . . . . .156 E8
Breadlands Rd TN24 . . . . .156 E8
Brecon Chase ME12 . . . . .4 C7
Brecon Rise TN24 . . . . .139 B4
Brecon Sq CT12 . . . . .29 A1
BREDGAR 58 A6
Bredgar CE Prim Sch
  ME9 . . . . .58 A5
Bredgar Cl
  Ashford TN23 . . . . .155 F6
  Maidstone ME14 . . . . .75 A6
Bredgar Rd ME8 . . . . .11 B4
Bredgar & Wormshill Light
  Rly* ME9 . . . . .57 E1
BREDHURST 33 B1
Bredhurst CE Prim Sch
  ME7 . . . . .33 B1
Bredhurst Rd ME12 . . . . .3 B7
Bredhurst Rd ME8 . . . . .33 B4
Bredlands La CT3, CT2 . . . . . . .46 C1
Brenchley Ave CT14 . . . . .116 F4
Brenchley Cl
  Ashford TN23 . . . . .155 E6
  Rochester ME1 . . . . .9 D2
Brenchley Rd
  Gillingham ME8 . . . . .11 B2
  Maidstone ME15 . . . . .74 F2
  Sittingbourne ME10 . . . . .36 F2
Brendon Ave ME5 . . . . .32 A3
Brendon Dr TN24 . . . . .139 B3
Brenley Cnr ME13 . . . . .63 B4
Brenley La ME13 . . . . .63 C2
Brennan Ct ME7 . . . . .10 D6
Brennan Mews ME5 . . . . .31 E5
Brent Cl ME5 . . . . .31 E5
Brent Hill ME13 . . . . .62 C8
Brent Rd ME13 . . . . .62 C8
Brents Inst Est ME13 . . . . .40 D1
Brentwood TN23 . . . . .155 F6
BRENZETT 192 A3
Brenzett Aeronautical Mus*
  TN29 .192 A3
Brenzett Cl ME8 . . . . .32 B5
Brenzett Cnr TN29 . . . . .192 A3
Brenzett District CE Prim
  Sch TN29 . . . . .192 A3
BRENZETT GREEN 192 C6
Breton Rd ME1 . . . . .9 C2
Brett Wlk ME8 . . . . .33 D4
Brewer's Hill CT20 . . . . .177 D3
Brewer St
  Deal CT14 . . . . .117 D6
  Maidstone ME14 . . . . .75 A5
Brewery Cotts CT14 . . . . .116 E4
Brewery La CT14 . . . . .89 A1
Brewery Rd ME10 . . . . .36 E6
Brewery Sq CT3 . . . . .48 D2
Brewhouse La TN25 . . . . .122 F4
Brewster Cotts ME9 . . . . .59 E2
Brian Roberts Ho CT6 . . . . .22 F5

Briar Cl
  Ashford TN24 . . . . .139 C6
  Aylesham CT3 . . . . .112 F5
Briar Fields ME14 . . . . .75 E5
Briars TN29 . . . . .194 F3
Briars The CT5 . . . . .43 C6
Briars Wlk CT10 . . . . .29 F3
Briary Cl CT9 . . . . .28 A8
Briary Prim Sch CT6 . . . . .22 C2
Brice Ave CT4 . . . . .86 C1
Brickfield TN31 . . . . .196 B2
Brickfield Cotts ME13 . . . . .84 E7
Brickfield La ME13 . . . . .63 E2
Brickfield Rd CT14 . . . . .128 F7
Brickmakers Ind Est
  ME10 .37 B6
Bricknall Terr TN26 . . . . .168 F3
Bridewell La TN30 . . . . .179 A7
Bridewell Pk CT5 . . . . .21 A1
BRIDGE 89 A1
Bridge App The CT5 . . . . .20 F1
Bridge Cl
  Hythe CT21 . . . . .176 A2
  Woodchurch TN26 . . . . .181 B8
Bridge Cotts ME13 . . . . .84 E7
Bridge Down CT4 . . . . .111 A3
BRIDGEFIELD 156 C2
Bridgefield ME17 . . . . .99 B1
Bridgefield Ct CT5 . . . . .21 B3
Bridgefield Rd CT5 . . . . .21 B3
Bridgeford Way CT4 . . . . .89 A1
Bridge Hill
  Bridge CT4 . . . . .111 B8
  Finglesham CT14 . . . . .116 C8
Bridge Ho
  Ramsgate CT11 . . . . .52 C7
  Rochester ME1 . . . . .9 B4
Bridge Home Pk TN29 . . . . . . .205 D6
Bridge Ind Ctr ME15 . . . . .74 E2
Bridgeman Ct CT21 . . . . .176 B2
Bridge Mill Way ME15 . . . . .74 D2
Bridge & Patrixbourne CE
  Prim Sch CT4 . . . . .89 A2
Bridge Rd
  Ashford TN23 . . . . .138 F2
  Brabourne Lees TN25 . . . . . .158 D5
  Bridge CT4 . . . . .88 D1
  Deal CT14 . . . . .117 D7
  Faversham ME13 . . . . .62 D4
  Gillingham ME7 . . . . .10 C7
  Margate CT9 . . . . .9 E2
  Sheerness ME12 . . . . .1 C2
Bridge Rd Ind Ctr TN23 . . . . . .138 F2
Bridges Cl CT7 . . . . .25 E2
Bridgeside CT14 . . . . .117 C6
Bridgeside Mews ME15 . . . . . . .74 E2
Bridge St
  Dover CT16 . . . . .149 C1
  Folkestone CT19 . . . . .178 E6
  Maidstone ME15 . . . . .96 F5
  Wye TN25 . . . . .123 E2
Bridge View Ind Est ME11 . . . .3 A2
Bridgewater Rd ME12 . . . . .3 B8
Bridgeway CT5 . . . . .20 F2
Bridle Way
  Herne Bay CT6 . . . . .22 D3
  Hythe CT21 . . . . .177 A3
Bridleway Gdns CT10 . . . . .29 E3
Bridleway La TN23 . . . . .156 B4
Brielle Way
  Queenborough ME11, ME12 . .3 A6
  Sheerness ME12 . . . . .1 B2
Brier Rd ME10 . . . . .36 B4
Brier Rd ME10 . . . . .36 B4
Brigadier Gdns TN23 . . . . .138 F4
Brigania Wlk CT11 . . . . .52 E8
Brightlingsea Rd CT13 . . . . .93 F8
Bright Rd ME4 . . . . .10 B2
Brights Pl CT11 . . . . .52 F7
Brindle Cl CT11 . . . . .29 F1
Brindle Way ME5 . . . . .32 C1
Brinklow Terr TN26 . . . . .155 A1
Brisbane Ave ME10 . . . . .36 C4
Brisbane Dr CT12 . . . . .29 A1
Brisbane Rd ME4 . . . . .10 A3
Brishing Cl ME15 . . . . .97 E5
Brishing La ME17 . . . . .97 D4
Brishing Rd ME15, ME17 . . . . . .97 F3
Brisley Cl TN23 . . . . .155 D6
Brisley Ct TN23 . . . . .155 D6
Brisley La TN26 . . . . .171 D6
Brissenden Cl TN28 . . . . .202 B8
BRISSENDEN GREEN 153 F3
Bristles Cnr CT3 . . . . .46 E6
Bristol Cl CT6 . . . . .23 B3
Bristol Pl CT11 . . . . .52 D7
Bristol Rd CT11 . . . . .87 F6
Britannia Ave CT5 . . . . .43 B7
Britannia Cl ME10 . . . . .36 E7
Britannia La TN23 . . . . .155 F5
Britannia Rd CT14 . . . . .117 D3
British MK IV Tank* **15**
Broadacre
  Lydden CT15 . . . . .147 F8
  Teynham ME9 . . . . .38 D2
Broader La ME14 . . . . .55 B2
Broadfield Cres CT20 . . . . .178 A5
Broadfield Rd
  Folkestone CT20 . . . . .178 A5
  Loose ME15 . . . . .97 A8
Broadgate Hall **1** ME11 . . . . .52 F7

Briar Cl
  Ashford TN24 . . . . .139 D7
Broad La CT14 . . . . .116 B7
Broadlands CT2 . . . . .67 F6
Broadlands Ave ME8 . . . . .202 B8
Broadlands Cres TN28 . . . . . . .202 B8
Broadlands Ind Est ME8 . . . . . .32 B4
Broadlands Ind Est CT2 . . . . . .66 A7
Bradley Rd CT10, CT9 . . . . .29 C7
Broadmead TN23 . . . . .155 E6
Broadmead Manor CT10 . . . . . .30 B7
Broadmead CT19 . . . . .178 B7
Broadmead Rd CT19 . . . . .178 C5
Broadmere Terr ME16 . . . . .74 D3
BROADOAK 58 E5
BROAD OAK
  Ashford 157 C1
  Sturry .46 D5
Broadoak Ave ME15 . . . . .97 A8
Broadoak Ent Village ME9 . . . . .58 F6
Broadoak La ME9 . . . . .58 E6
Broad Oak Rd CT2 . . . . .67 B3
Broadsole La CT15 . . . . .164 E5
Broad St
  Canterbury CT1 . . . . .67 A1
  Deal CT14 . . . . .117 D6
  Margate CT9 . . . . .7 H2
  Ramsgate CT11 . . . . .52 E7
  Sellindge TN25 . . . . .159 E5
  Sheerness ME12 . . . . .1 C2
BROADSTAIRS 30 C5
Broadstairs Rd CT10 . . . . .29 E5
Broadstairs Sta CT10 . . . . .30 A4
BROAD STREET
  Lyminge 161 C5
  Maidstone 77 B6
  Sellindge 159 F5
Broad Street Hill ME17 . . . . . . .77 D7
BROAD TENTERDEN 179 B4
Broadview CT20 . . . . .177 C6
Broadview Ave ME8 . . . . .33 E8
Broadwaters CT21 . . . . .176 D1
BROADWAY 120 B6
Broadway
  Gillingham ME8 . . . . .11 A3
  Maidstone ME14 . . . . .74 F4
  Petham CT4 . . . . .109 A2
Broadway Sh Ctr ME14 . . . . . . .74 F4
Broadway The
  Broadstairs CT10 . . . . .30 A4
  Dover CT16 . . . . .166 H8
  Herne Bay CT6 . . . . .22 C5
  Minster (Sheppey) ME12 . . . . .4 B7
  Sheerness ME12 . . . . .1 J2
Brockbank Cl ME5 . . . . .32 A1
Brockenhurst Ave ME15 . . . . . . .75 C1
Brockenhurst Cl
  Canterbury CT2 . . . . .66 E2
  Gillingham ME8 . . . . .33 C7
Brockenhurst Rd CT11 . . . . .52 G8
Brockhill Ctry Pk* CT21 . . . . .175 F4
Brockhill Park Performing
  Arts Coll CT21 . . . . .175 F4
Brockley Rd CT9 . . . . .8 A2
Brockman Cres TN29 . . . . .187 B4
Brockman Rd CT20 . . . . .178 C5
Brockman's Cl CT12 . . . . .50 B7
Brogdale Farm Cotts
  ME13 .62 A3
Brogdale Farm National Fruit
  Collection* ME13 . . . . .62 B4
Brogdale Rd ME13 . . . . .62 B5
Brogden Cres ME17 . . . . .98 F7
Bromley Cl ME5 . . . . .32 B4
BROMLEY GREEN 170 E6
Bromley Green Rd TN26 . . . . .171 A5
BROMPTON 10 A5
Brompton Hill ME4 . . . . .9 F6
Brompton La ME2 . . . . .9 A8
Brompton Rd ME7 . . . . .10 B6
Brompton Villas CT5 . . . . .149 A6
Brompton Westbrook Prim
  Sch ME7 . . . . .10 A5
BROMSTONE 29 E3
Bromstone Mews CT10 . . . . . . .29 E3
Bromstone Prim Sch
  CT10 .29 D3
Bromstone Rd CT10 . . . . .29 E3
Bronington Cl ME5 . . . . .32 A5
BROOK 141 B5
Brookbank
  Brook TN25 . . . . .141 A5
  Maidstone ME14 . . . . .75 A8
Brook Cl
  Herne Bay CT6 . . . . .22 C3
  Hythe CT21 . . . . .177 B3
Brook Com Prim Sch
  TN25 .141 A4
Brook Cotts
  East Farleigh ME15 . . . . .96 C7
  Staple CT3 . . . . .91 E6
  Teynham ME9 . . . . .39 A2
Brooke Ave CT9 . . . . .28 B7
Brooker Cl ME17 . . . . .97 D5
Brooke Rd TN24 . . . . .139 B3
Brookes Pl ME9 . . . . .35 B6
Brookfield Ave CT16 . . . . .149 B2
Brookfield Ct TN23 . . . . .155 F8
Brookfield Ind Pk TN23 . . . . . .138 F1
Brookfield Pl CT16 . . . . .149 B2
Brookfield Rd
  Ashford TN23 . . . . .155 F8
  Dover CT16 . . . . .149 A3
Brook La
  Cliffs End CT12 . . . . .50 F4
  Reculver CT6 . . . . .24 B5

Brook La continued
  Sellindge TN25 . . . . .159 E2
BROOKLAND 199 D8
Brookland CE Prim Sch
  TN29 .199 D8
Brooklands Cl TN25 . . . . .156 D6
Brooklands Ct CT2 . . . . .67 F4
Brook Lane Cotts TN25 . . . . . .159 E2
Brooklyn Paddock ME7 . . . . . . .10 D6
Brook Rd
  Faversham ME13 . . . . .40 D1
  Whitstable CT5 . . . . .21 C3
BROOKS END 26 E4
Brookside
  St Mary's Bay TN29 . . . . .195 A5
  Temple Ewell CT16 . . . . .148 D5
Brooks Pl ME14 . . . . .75 A4
Brook St
  Eastry CT13 . . . . .93 C2
  Woodchurch TN26 . . . . .180 C8
BROOK STREET 180 E8
Brooks Way TN29 . . . . .205 C5
Brook The ME4 . . . . .10 A4
Brook Theatre* ME4 . . . . .9 F5
Broomcroft Rd ME8 . . . . .11 F2
BROOMFIELD
  Herne Bay 23 D1
  Kingswood 99 D5
Broomfield Cres CT9 . . . . .8 F2
Broomfield Gate CT5 . . . . .44 D5
Broomfield Rd
  Faversham ME13 . . . . .62 C8
  Folkestone CT19 . . . . .177 E6
  Herne Bay CT6 . . . . .23 C2
  Kingswood ME17 . . . . .99 D4
BROOM HILL 70 B1
Broom Rd ME10 . . . . .37 C5
BROOM STREET 41 D2
Brotherhood Cl CT2 . . . . .66 D4
Broughton By-Pass ME13 . . . .64 C2
Broughton Ct TN23 . . . . .138 E1
Brownelow Copse ME5 . . . . . . .32 B1
Brownhill Cl ME5 . . . . .32 A4
Browning Pl CT19 . . . . .178 D4
Browning Orch ME9 . . . . .59 A7
Brown Lo ME12 . . . . .1 L1
Brown St ME8 . . . . .11 F1
Broxhall Rd CT4 . . . . .110 B3
Bruce Cl CT14 . . . . .117 B4
Bruges Ct ME10 . . . . .14 F1
Brundell Terr CT4 . . . . .86 B2
Brunell Cl ME6 . . . . .74 D5
Brunel Way ME4 . . . . .10 A5
Brunswick Cotts ME9 . . . . .38 E6
Brunswick Cl **5** CT11 . . . . .52 E7
Brunswick Field ME15 . . . . .38 E6
Brunswick Gdns **3** CT11 . . . . .149 B3
Brunswick House Prim Sch
  ME16 .74 E5
Brunswick Ind Ctr TN23 . . . . .138 F2
Brunswick Rd
  Ashford TN23 . . . . .138 F2
  Birchington CT7 . . . . .27 A5
Brunswick Sq CT6 . . . . .22 E5
Brunswick St
  Maidstone ME15 . . . . .75 A3
  Ramsgate CT11 . . . . .52 E7
Brunswick Street E ME15 . . . . .75 A3
Bryant Rd ME2 . . . . .9 A7
Bryant St ME4 . . . . .10 A3
Bryces Alley CT5 . . . . .20 D2
Brymore Cl CT1 . . . . .67 B2
Brymore Rd CT1 . . . . .67 B2
Bryony Dr TN23 . . . . .156 C3
Bryony Sch ME8 . . . . .33 C7
Buckhurst Dr CT9 . . . . .8 F2
Buckingham Rd
  15 Broadstairs CT10 . . . . . . .30 B4
  Gillingham ME7 . . . . .10 D5
  Margate CT9 . . . . .7 I1
  Whitstable CT5 . . . . .21 B2
Buckingham Row ME15 . . . . . . .97 E7
BUCKLAND 149 C2
Buckland Ave CT16 . . . . .149 B2
Buckland Cl ME5 . . . . .32 A2
Buckland Cotts ME13 . . . . .61 B8
Buckland Hill ME16 . . . . .74 E5
Buckland Hospl CT17 . . . . .149 A1
Buckland La
  Maidstone ME16 . . . . .74 D6
  Staple CT3 . . . . .92 A4
Buckland Pl ME16 . . . . .74 E4
Buckland Rd ME16 . . . . .74 E4
BUCKLAND VALLEY 149 C4
Bucklers Cl ME12 . . . . .6 E4
Bucksford La TN23 . . . . .155 C7
Buck St TN25 . . . . .105 C2
Buckthorn Cl CT14 . . . . .117 C7
Buckthorne Ho ME12 . . . . .4 A4
Buckthorne Rd ME12 . . . . .4 A4
Buddle Dr ME12 . . . . .3 E7
Budd's Farm Cotts TN30 . . . .188 E2
Budd's La TN30 . . . . .188 F2
Buenos Ayres CT9 . . . . .7 H2
Buffs Ave CT20 . . . . .177 B6
Builders Sq CT13 . . . . .90 A8
Bulldog Rd ME5 . . . . .32 B2
Bulleid Pl TN24 . . . . .156 D7
Buller Rd ME4 . . . . .9 F2
Buller's Ave CT6 . . . . .22 E4
Bull Hill
  Lenham Heath ME17 . . . . . . .102 A1
  Lenham ME17 . . . . .118 F8
Bull La
  Bethersden TN26 . . . . .153 B4
  Boughton Street ME13 . . . . . .63 F4
  Eccles ME20 . . . . .53 A6

Bull La continued
  Yelsted ME9 . . . . .34 E2
Bull Lane Cotts ME9 . . . . .34 E1
BULLOCKSTONE 45 D8
Bullockstone Rd CT6 . . . . .45 E7
Bulls Cotts **4** CT21 . . . . .176 B2
Bulltown Cnr TN25 . . . . .141 F3
Bullwark St CT17 . . . . .166 D5
Bulrush Cl ME5 . . . . .31 F3
Bulrush Rd TN23 . . . . .155 D8
Bulwark Rd CT14 . . . . .117 D7
Bumbles Cl ME1 . . . . .31 D7
Bunce Court Rd ME13,
  ME17 . . . . .102 E7
Bungalows The
  Faversham ME13 . . . . .62 A4
  Tenterden TN30 . . . . .179 D7
  Woodnesborough CT13 . . . . .93 B5
Bunker's Hill CT17 . . . . .149 B2
Bunkers Hill Ave CT17 . . . . . . .149 A1
Bunkers Hill CT17 . . . . .149 A1
Bunkley Mdw TN26 . . . . .183 A7
Burberry La ME17 . . . . .99 B5
Burch Ave CT13 . . . . .93 F8
Burdock Ct ME16 . . . . .74 A3
Burdock Ho **6** ME16 . . . . .97 D8
Burford's Alley CT13 . . . . .71 D1
Burgate CT1 . . . . .88 A8
Burgate La **5** CT1 . . . . .88 A8
Burgate Terr TN25 . . . . .157 E4
Burgess Ct
  Minster (Thanet) CT12 . . . . . .50 C7
  Whitfield CT16 . . . . .149 B7
Burgess Gn CT14 . . . . .116 C8
Burgess Hall Dr ME17 . . . . .98 F6
Burgess Row **9** TN30 . . . . . . .179 A7
Burghclere Dr ME16 . . . . .74 B2
Burgoyne Ct ME14 . . . . .74 F7
Burgoyne Gr CT16 . . . . .149 A5
Burgoyne Hts CT15 . . . . .149 E3
BURHAM 53 A8
Burial Ground La ME15 . . . . . . .74 E5
Burkeston Cl ME10 . . . . .37 A8
Burleigh Dr ME14 . . . . .53 F1
Burleigh Rd TN27 . . . . .120 C7
Burley Rd ME10 . . . . .36 E4
Burlington Dr CT6 . . . . .23 D5
Burlington Gdns
  Gillingham ME8 . . . . .33 E4
  Margate CT9 . . . . .28 C8
Burma Cres CT1 . . . . .67 D2
BURMARSH 186 C5
Burmarsh Cl ME5 . . . . .32 B5
Burmarsh Rd
  Burmarsh TN29 . . . . .186 C3
  Hythe CT21 . . . . .187 C8
Burma Way ME5 . . . . .31 F6
Burnan Ct CT5 . . . . .21 C2
Burnan Rd CT5 . . . . .21 C2
Burnham Cl ME10 . . . . .36 E8
Burnham Wlk ME8 . . . . .33 E3
Burns Rd ME16 . . . . .74 C2
Burn's Rd ME7 . . . . .10 C7
Burnt House Hill CT3 . . . . .69 B5
Burnt Oak Prim Sch **1**
  ME7 . . . . .10 D6
Burnt Oak Terr ME7 . . . . .10 D6
Burnt Oast Rd ME13 . . . . .64 A3
Burntwick Dr ME9 . . . . .13 B3
Burnup Bank ME10 . . . . .37 C5
Burritt Mews ME1 . . . . .9 C2
Burrow Rd CT19 . . . . .178 F6
Burrs The ME10 . . . . .36 F3
Burstock Way ME8 . . . . .12 B3
Bursill Cres CT12 . . . . .29 B1
Burstead Hill CT4 . . . . .110 B2
Burston Rd ME17 . . . . .96 B2
Burton Ct CT19 . . . . .178 A7
Burton Fields CT6 . . . . .23 B4
Burton Rd TN24 . . . . .139 E6
Bus Bridge Rd ME15 . . . . .96 E6
Bush Ave CT12 . . . . .29 B1
Bush Cl ME9 . . . . .57 F5
Bushey Cl ME13 . . . . .63 F3
Bushyfields Rd CT6 . . . . .45 F6
Bushmeadow Rd ME8 . . . . .11 F2
Bush Row ME20 . . . . .53 A3
Bushy Hill Rd CT2 . . . . .68 D7
Bushy Royds TN24 . . . . .156 D6
Bushy Ruff Cotts CT16 . . . . . .148 C4
Butchers La CT15 . . . . .113 E5
Butchery La **1** CT1 . . . . .88 A8
Butchery The **2** CT13 . . . . .73 A1
Butler's Hill ME13 . . . . .64 F7
Butterfly Centre The*
  CT15 .146 B3
Buttermere ME13 . . . . .62 E6
Buttermere Cl CT19 . . . . .178 B6
Buttermere Gdns CT13 . . . . . .112 G6
Butternut Copse TN23 . . . . . . .138 D3
Butterside Rd TN23 . . . . .156 C4
Butter St CT15 . . . . .113 C2
Butt Field Rd TN23 . . . . .155 E7
Button La ME15 . . . . .76 B2
Butts Cl CT4 . . . . .110 A6
Butts Hill ME13 . . . . .63 F5
Butts Mdw CT4 . . . . .110 A6
BUTTSOLE 93 B1
Butts The
  Sandwich CT13 . . . . .72 F1
  Sittingbourne ME10 . . . . .36 F4
Buxton Cl
  Chatham ME5 . . . . .32 D1
  Loose ME15 . . . . .97 A8

Buxton Rd CT12	29 B2
BYBROOK	139 D5
Bybrook CT21	176 D3
Bybrook Ct TN24	139 C4
Bybrook Field CT20	177 E3
Bybrook Rd TN24	139 C5
Bybrook Way CT20	177 E4
Bychurch Pl **7** ME15	75 A3
Byllan Rd CT17	148 E3
Byron Ave CT9	7 J1
Byron Cl CT1	88 C7
Byron Cres CT16	149 B4
Byron Rd	
Gillingham ME7	10 C3
Maidstone ME14	75 A3
Bysing Wood Cotts ME13	39 F1
Bysing Wood Prim Sch ME13	62 A8
Bysing Wood Rd ME13	62 A8
Bythorne Ct ME8	12 B1

C

Cabin The TN24	139 D7
Cade Rd TN23	156 B7
Cades Orch ME13	61 E3
Cadnam Cl CT2	66 E3
Caernarvon Dr ME15	75 A3
Caernarvon Gdns CT10	30 B5
Caesar Ave TN23	156 A5
Caesar's Way CT19	177 E2
Calais Hill CT2	66 E6
CALCOTT	45 E2
Calcraft Mews **6** CT1	67 B2
Calcutta Ho **3** ME15	97 E5
Caldecote Cl ME8	12 B1
Caldecott La TN29	201 D2
Caldecott Foundation Sch TN25	158 B4
Calder Rd ME14	74 E2
Caldew Ave ME8	11 C1
Caldew Gr ME10	37 A3
Caledonian Ct ME8	33 E8
Caledon Terr CT1	88 A7
Calehill Cl ME14	75 C6
Calgary Cres CT19	178 E8
California Row CT3	90 E6
Callams Cl ME8	33 D6
Calland TN25	158 E5
Callaways La ME9	35 B6
Calleywell La TN25	173 A7
Callis Court Rd CT10	29 F7
Callis Grange Inf Sch CT10	29 F7
Callisto Cl ME16	74 D3
Callis Way ME8	33 D5
Calverden Rd CT12	29 A1
CAMBER	203 A1
Camber Bourne Rd TN25	172 C6
Camborne Manor **2** ME7	10 C8
Cambourne Ave CT8	27 D8
Cambrai Ct CT1	67 D1
Cambridge Ave CT13	95 B7
Cambridge Cl CT17	87 B7
Cambridge Cres ME15	97 D7
Cambridge Gdns CT20	178 E5
Cambridge La ME9	60 C8
Cambridge Mews CT14	117 D3
Cambridge Rd	
Canterbury CT1	87 F6
Deal CT14	117 D3
Dover CT17	166 E7
Faversham ME13	62 B6
Gillingham ME8	33 C6
Rochester ME2	9 A8
Sittingbourne ME10	37 B3
Cambridge Terr	
1 Chatham ME4	9 F4
5 Dover CT17	166 E7
6 Folkestone CT20	178 E5
Margate CT9	8 B1
Cambridge Way	
Canterbury CT1	87 F6
5 Maidstone ME15	97 D7
Camden Cl ME5	32 B5
Camden Cres CT16	166 E7
Camden Rd	
Broadstairs CT10	29 E7
Gillingham ME7	10 D7
Ramsgate CT11	52 E2
Camden Sq **10** CT11	52 E7
Camden St ME14	75 A5
Camden Terr TN24	139 E1
Camellia Cl	
Gillingham ME8	33 D7
2 Margate CT9	28 B8
Cameron Cl ME5	32 B8
Cameron Ho CT14	166 A6
Cameron Rd CT14	117 C1
Camomile Dr ME14	75 F5
Campbell Cl CT6	23 C3
Campbell Rd	
Deal CT14	117 D4
Hawkinge CT18	163 A5
Maidstone ME15	97 C6
Camperdown Manor **5** ME7	10 A6
Campion Cl ME13	62 A8
Campleshon Rd ME8	33 D5
Campus Way ME8	33 A8
Camp Way ME15	97 C6
Canada Cl CT19	177 C6
Canada Mews CT14	117 C3
Canada Rd CT14	117 C3
Canada Terr **3** ME14	75 A7

Canadian Ave ME7	10 F4
Canal Rd ME2	9 C7
Canberra Gdns ME10	36 C4
Candlers Way CT4	108 F8
Canning St ME14	75 A6
Cannonbury Rd CT11	52 D6
Cannongate Ave CT21	176 D3
Cannongate Cl CT21	176 E2
Cannongate Gdns CT21	176 E3
Cannongate Rd CT21	176 D3
Cannon Rd CT11	52 D7
Cannon St	
Deal CT14	117 C7
Dover CT16	166 D8
Lydd TN29	205 C6
New Romney TN28	202 B7
Canon Appleton Ct CT1	87 E7
Canon Cl ME1	9 B2
Canon Gn CT3	91 A7
Canons Gate Rd CT14	166 E8
Canon Woods Way TN24	139 F6
CANTERBURY	87 C7
Canterbury Cathedral* CT1	88 A8
Canterbury Cathedral Archives* **15** CT1	88 A8
Canterbury Centre The (Mus)* CT1	66 F1
Canterbury Christ Church Univ (Augustine House Campus) **1** CT1	87 F7
Canterbury Christ Church Univ (Broadstairs Campus) **1** CT10	29 C4
Canterbury Christ Church Univ (Hall Place Enterprise Ctre) CT1	66 B1
Canterbury Christ Church Univ (Medway Campus) ME4	10 B8
Canterbury Christ Church Univ (North Holmes Campus) CT1	88 B8
Canterbury City Ret Pk CT1	67 D4
Canterbury Cl	
Broadstairs CT10	29 D5
1 Folkestone CT19	178 E6
Canterbury Coll CT3	113 A5
Canterbury Ct TN24	139 D2
Canterbury East Sta CT1	87 F7
Canterbury Environmental Education Ctr CT2	67 B3
Canterbury High Sch CT2	87 D8
Canterbury Ho **2** ME15	97 D7
Canterbury Ind Pk CT3	69 A8
Canterbury La	
Canterbury CT1	88 A8
Gillingham ME8, ME9	12 C1
Canterbury Pilgrims Hospl The* CT1	87 F8
Canterbury Rd	
Ashford, Kennington TN24	139 E5
Ashford TN24	156 E6
Barham CT4	129 C5
Boughton Aluph TN25	123 C5
Boughton Street ME13	63 D4
Brabourne Lees TN25	158 A4
Brabourne TN25	159 C8
Challock TN25, TN27	140 C3
Chilham CT4	85 F1
Denton CT4	129 A1
Dunkirk ME13	64 C3
Elham CT4	144 E3
Etchinghill CT18	161 D4
Faversham ME13	62 E5
Folkestone CT19	178 D7
Folkestone, Foord CT19	178 E6
Hawkinge CT18, CT19, CT20, CT4	163 B4
Herne Bay CT6	23 A3
Herne CT3, CT6	45 E5
Littlebourne CT3	89 C8
Lydden CT15	147 E2
Lyminge CT18	161 C7
Sarre CT7	48 C7
Sittingbourne ME10	37 B3
Whitstable CT5	43 D2
Wingham CT3	91 A7
Canterbury Rd Birchington CT7	27 B5
Canterbury Road Birchington CT7	27 B7
Canterbury Road E CT11, CT12	52 A6
Canterbury Road Margate CT9	7 G1
Canterbury Road Prim Sch ME10	37 B3
Canterbury Road W CT12	51 D7
Canterbury Road Westgate CT8, CT9	27 E8
Canterbury St ME7	10 C4
Canterbury Steiner Sch CT4	108 E7
Canterbury Tales The* **24** CT1	87 F8
Canterbury West Sta CT2	66 F1
Capel Cl	
Ashford TN23	138 F1

Capel Cl continued	
Broadstairs CT10	8 F1
Gillingham ME8	33 D4
Capel Court Pk CT18	164 D2
Capel Cl ME17	96 C3
CAPEL-LE-FERNE	164 B2
Capel-le-Ferne Prim Sch CT18	164 C3
Capel Rd	
Bromley Green TN26	171 B4
Faversham ME13	62 B7
Petham CT4	127 A3
Capel St CT18	164 B3
Capetown Ho **1** ME15	97 F5
Capstan Row CT14	117 D7
CAPSTONE	32 E7
Capstone Farm Ctry Pk* ME7	32 D5
Capstone Rd	
Chatham ME5	10 D1
Gillingham ME7	32 F6
Captains Ct CT14	117 D7
Cardinal Cl ME12	4 D7
Cardine Cl ME10	36 E7
Carey Cl TN28	202 B6
Carey Ho **5** CT1	87 F7
Caring La ME14, ME17	76 E1
Caring Rd ME15, ME17	76 C1
Carisbrooke Dr ME16	74 D4
Carlsden CT17	149 A3
Carlton Ave	
Broadstairs CT10	30 A5
Gillingham ME7	10 E4
Ramsgate CT11	52 D6
Sheerness ME12	1 C1
Carlton Cres ME5	32 D8
Carlton Gdns ME15	97 B8
Carlton Hill CT6	22 C4
Carlton Leas CT20	178 C4
Carlton Mans CT9	8 A3
Carlton Rd	
Ashford TN23	139 A2
Kingsdown CT14	134 C6
Whitstable CT5	43 D2
Carlton Rise CT8	27 D8
Carlton Road E CT8	27 D8
Carlton Road W CT8	27 D8
Carman's Cl ME15	96 F3
Carmel Cl CT4	86 B2
Carmel Ct **2** CT7	26 F8
Carn Brae CT7	7 J2
Carnoustie Cl CT5	44 E8
Caroland Cl TN25	158 D5
Caroline Cl CT5	43 B6
Caroline Cres	
Broadstairs CT10	29 E6
Maidstone ME16	74 D7
Caroline Sq CT9	7 J3
Carpeaux Cl ME4	10 A4
Carpenters Cl ME1	9 E2
Carpinus Cl ME5	32 B1
Carriage Ho ME13	83 D5
Carriage Mews CT2	66 F1
Carrie Ho **6** ME16	74 E5
Carrington Cl ME7	10 F6
Carroway's Pl CT9	7 J2
Carter Cl CT18	163 A5
Carter La CT29	191 E2
Carter's Rd CT20	177 F5
Carter's Wood TN26	183 B7
Carton Cl ME1	9 E2
Cartwright Cl CT3	71 C2
Cartwright & Kelsey Prim Sch CT3	71 C2
Carver Dr ME9	58 E6
Carvoran Way ME5	33 C5
Caslocke St **2** ME13	62 C7
Cassino Ho **16** CT1	67 B2
Cassino Sq CT14	149 E2
Castalla Cotts CT14	117 D3
Castellan Ind Pk ME10	37 B6
Castle Ave	
Broadstairs CT10	30 B6
Dover CT16	149 D1
Hythe CT21	176 B3
Rochester ME1	9 C4
Castle Bay CT20	177 D3
Castle Cl	
4 Folkestone CT20	177 F3
Lympne CT21	174 F2
Castle Com Coll CT14	117 C4
Castle Cotts CT13	72 E5
Castle Cres CT14	74 E8
Castle Dene ME14	74 F8
Castle Dr CT16	148 F7
Castle Glen **8** CT20	177 F3
Castle Hill	
Folkestone CT19, CT18	178 A8
Rochester ME1	9 C6
Thurnham ME14	55 D1
Castle Hill Ave CT20	178 C4
Castle Hill CP Sch CT18	178 E7
Castle Hill Cl ME1	9 C6
Castle Hill Rd **4** CT16	166 E8
Castle Ho CT5	20 F3
Castlemaine Ave ME7	10 F6
Castle Mayne Ave CT7	26 C7
Castlemere Ave ME1	3 B5
Castle Mews CT14	117 A4
Castlemount Ct CT16	166 E8
Castlemount Rd CT16	149 D1
Castle Rd	
Chatham ME4	10 B4
Folkestone CT20	177 F3
Hythe CT21	176 B4
Maidstone ME16	74 D7
Sittingbourne ME10	37 B5

Castle Rd continued	
Whitstable CT5	20 F2
Castle Road Bsns Prec ME10	37 B6
Castle Road Tech Ctr ME10	37 B6
Castle Rough La ME10	14 F1
Castle Row CT1	87 F7
Castle St	
8 Ashford TN23	139 E3
Canterbury CT1	87 F8
Dover CT16	166 E8
Queenborough ME11	3 A5
Castle View Bsns Ctr ME1	9 C6
Castleview Ct CT17	149 B1
Castle View Mews ME1	9 C6
Castle View Rd ME1	9 A7
Castle Wlk CT14	95 D1
Cathedral View	67 A2
Catherine Ct **2** ME16	74 A3
Catherine St ME1	9 D3
Catherine Way CT10	30 A6
Catkin Cl ME5	31 F1
CATS Canterbury **6** CT1	88 B6
Catsole Hill CT3	91 D2
Catterick Rd ME5	32 D2
Cattle Market CT13	72 F1
Catt's Wood Rd CT4	109 F4
Cauldham Cl CT18	164 B1
Cauldham La CT18	164 B3
Caulkers Ho **7** ME4	10 B2
Causeway The	
Canterbury CT1	66 F1
Sandwich CT13	72 F3
Cavalry Cl	
Deal CT14	117 D3
Folkestone CT20	177 D5
Cave Hill ME15	74 F1
Cave La CT3	91 D3
Cavell Sq CT14	117 A3
Cavell Way ME10	36 E5
Cavenagh Rd CT15	151 B6
Cavendish Ave ME7	10 E6
Cavendish Ct CT16	166 A7
Cavendish Dr CT10	23 A5
Cavendish Pl **2** CT11	52 E6
Cavendish Rd	
Herne Bay CT6	23 A5
Rochester ME1	9 D3
Cavendish St CT11	52 E8
Cavendish Way ME15	76 B3
Caversham Cl ME8	11 F1
Cavour Rd	
Faversham ME13	62 C7
Sheerness ME12	1 C5
Caxton Ho TN24	139 C3
Caxton Rd CT9	28 C8
Cayser Dr ME17	99 E2
Cazeneuve St ME1	9 C5
Cecil Ave	
Gillingham ME8	11 A2
Rochester ME2	9 B8
Cecil Rd	
Kingsdown CT14	134 D7
Rochester ME1	9 C3
Cecil Sq CT9	7 I2
Cecil St CT9	7 I2
Cedar Cl	
Ashford TN23	138 D3
Birchington CT8	27 B7
Broadstairs CT10	29 D5
Margate CT9	8 B1
Sittingbourne ME10	37 B1
Cedar Cres CT6	23 A4
Cedar Ct	
Folkestone CT20	177 E5
Maidstone ME14	75 B5
11 Tenterden TN30	179 A7
Cedar Gdns ME9	56 E8
Cedar Gr ME7	33 A5
Cedar Ho ME12	1 C2
Cedars PRU The ME14	76 D4
Cedars Rd CT5	43 A4
Cedars The	
Barrowhill TN25	174 D8
5 Sittingbourne ME10	37 C5
Cedar Terr ME13	62 A4
Cedarview CT2	66 C1
Cedarwood Ho ME15	96 B6
Cedric Rd CT8	27 C8
Celak CT1	94 B4
Celak Ct TN25	173 A6
Celestine Cl ME5	32 A1
CELLARHILL	38 C1
Celt Cl ME10	36 E8
Celtic Ho CT14	117 A2
Cemetery La TN24	139 C4
Centenary Ct TN27	120 C8
Centenary Gdns ME13	93 A2
Central Ave	
Chatham ME4	10 B8
Herne Bay CT6	22 E9
Sittingbourne ME10	37 B1
Woodstock ME9	58 D6
Central Bsns Pk ME2	9 E7
Central Par	
Herne Bay CT6	22 E9
Rochester ME1	9 D2
Central Park Gdns ME4	9 E2
Central Park Stad ME10	102 C6

Bux–Cha 215

Central Pk CT12	49 D6
Central Rd	
Ramsgate CT11	52 D8
Rochester ME2	9 A7
Central Service Rd CT16	166 H8
Central Theatre The* **10** ME4	9 F4
Centre 2000	
Maidstone ME16	74 C8
3 Sittingbourne ME10	37 A4
Centre Ct ME2	9 E7
Centre Rd CT17	166 C6
Centre The	
Margate CT9	7 I2
Ramsgate CT12	29 A1
Centurion Cl ME8	10 F1
Centurion Wlk TN23	156 B4
Century Ct ME1	9 C5
Century Rd	
Faversham ME13	62 E7
Gillingham ME8	33 D8
Century Wlk CT14	117 C6
Ceres Ct ME10	37 C5
Chada Ave ME7	10 E3
Chaffe's La ME9	12 E3
Chaffes Terr ME9	12 E2
Chaffinch Cl ME5	32 A7
Chaffinch Dr TN23	156 C3
Chaffinch Lodge **5** CT16	149 B2
Chafy Cres CT2	67 F5
Chain Gate ME17	118 A8
Chain The **6** CT13	73 A1
Chalcroft Rd CT20	177 E4
Chalfont Dr	
Gillingham ME8	33 D6
Herne Bay CT6	23 D2
Chalk Ave TN30	167 B2
Chalk Cl CT19	178 A7
Chalkenden Ave ME5	11 A2
Chalkers Way ME8	11 B4
Chalk Hill CT11, CT12	51 F6
Chalk Hill Rd CT11	134 C5
Chalkpit Hill CT4	89 D3
Chalk Pit Hill	
Chatham ME4	10 A3
Staple CT3	92 B5
Chalk Pit La CT13, CT14	92 C5
Chalk Rd ME11	3 A5
CHALKSOLE	147 C4
CHALKSOLE GREEN	147 C3
Chalksole Green La CT15	147 B5
CHALKWELL	36 D4
Chalkwell Ct CT17	166 A7
Chalkwell Rd ME10	36 D5
Chalky Bank Rd ME8	11 F2
Chalky Rd ME9	56 C6
Challenger Cl ME10	36 E7
CHALLOCK	105 B1
Challock Ct CT9	8 F2
Challock Prim Sch TN25	105 B1
Challock Wlk ME14	75 C6
Chalmers Way ME8	11 B4
Chamberlain Ave ME16	74 C8
Chamberlain Ct ME8	33 B5
Chamberlain Dr CT6	22 B4
Chamberlain Rd	
Chatham ME4	10 B2
Dover CT17	166 B8
CHAMBERS' GREEN	136 C4
Chambers Wharf La ME13	62 E8
Chancel Ct	66 D1
Chance Mdw CT15	149 E6
Chancery La ME15	75 B3
Chanctonbury Chase CT5	43 A6
Chandlers Wharf ME1	9 B5
Chandos Rd **7** CT10	30 B4
Chandos Sq **8** CT10	30 B4
Chandos Terr	52 E7
Channel Cl CT19	178 F7
Channel Lea CT14	117 C1
Channel Rd CT9	29 A6
CHANNEL TUNNEL TERMINAL	177 B8
Channel View **1** CT19	178 E5
Channel View Ct **9** CT11	52 F7
Channel View Rd CT17	166 C5
Channel Watch TN28	202 E4
Channon Rd TN28	206 E7
Chantry Ct **18** CT1	66 F1
Chantry Hall CT1	87 F7
Chantry Pk CT7	48 D7
Chapel Cl CT18	161 D3
Chapel Cotts ME17	98 F5
Chapel Hill	
Eythorne CT15	131 C7
Margate CT9	29 A6
Chapel Hill Cl CT9	28 F7
Chapel La	
Blean CT2	66 A7
Boyden Gate CT3	47 C8
Bredhurst ME7	33 A2
Broad Oak CT2	67 D7
8 Dover CT16	166 D7
East Studdal CT15	132 C6
Egerton Forstal TN27	118 C2
Gillingham ME7	33 A4
Maidstone ME14	76 A5
Newchurch TN29	185 C4
Rhodes Minnis CT4	144 B4
Ripple CT14	133 D8
Staple CT3	92 B6
St Margaret's at Cliffe CT15	150 F6

Chapel La continued
Sturry CT2 . . . . .67 F5
Chapel Mews 2 TN23 . . . .139 C2
Chapel Pl
10 Dover CT17 . . . . .166 D7
Ramsgate CT11 . . . . .52 D7
Chapel Place La CT11 . . . .52 D7
Chapel Rd
Dymchurch TN29 . . . . .195 C7
Ram Lane TN26 . . . . .120 F1
Ramsgate CT11 . . . . .52 C7
Tilmanstone CT14 . . . . .115 A3
Whitfield CT16 . . . . .149 A8
Chapel Row
Herne CT6 . . . . .46 A8
Kingsnorth TN23 . . . . .156 A3
Lydd TN29 . . . . .205 C6
Ram Lane TN26 . . . . .120 F2
Chapel St
Deal CT14 . . . . .117 D6
Faversham ME13 . . . . .62 D6
Herne Bay CT6. . . . . .23 A5
Hythe CT21 . . . . .176 B2
Minster (Sheppey) ME12 . . . .4 D6
Sheerness ME12 . . . . .1 B2
Chapel The
Chartham CT4 . . . . .86 F1
Maidstone ME16 . . . . .74 B3
Chaplains Wlk CT4 . . . . . .86 E1
Chapman Ave ME15 . . . . .97 E8
Chapman Fields CT12 . . . .51 D5
Chapman Ho CT14 . . . . . .117 B3
Chapmans Cl TN25 . . . . . .105 C2
Chapmans Hill CT15, CT3 .113 B5
Chappell Way ME10 . . . . .36 E6
CHARING 120 D8
Charing CE Prim Sch
TN27 . . . . .120 C8
Charing Cl CT12 . . . . .52 C8
Charing Cres CT8 . . . . . . .27 D7
CHARING HEATH 119 C6
Charing Heath Rd
Charing Heath TN27 . . . . . .119 F8
Charing TN27 . . . . .120 A6
CHARING HILL 103 D1
Charing Hill TN27 . . . . .103 E1
Charing Rd ME8 . . . . .11 B3
Charing Sta TN27 . . . . .120 B7
Charlbury CT4 ME16 . . . . .74 C3
Charlecote Ct ME8 . . . . . . .33 D8
Charles Cobb Cl TN29 . .195 D8
Charles Cres CT19 . . . . . .177 E7
Charles Ct CT8 . . . . .27 F8
Charles Dickens Sch The
CT10 . . . . .29 E4
Charles Drayson Ct ME13 .62 E7
Charlesford Ave ME17 . . . .99 D3
Charles Ho CT14 . . . . .117 B3
Charles Lister Ct CT17 . . .149 B1
Charles Rd
Deal CT14 . . . . .117 B4
Ramsgate CT11 . . . . .52 E8
Charles St
Chatham ME4. . . . . .9 E3
Herne Bay CT6 . . . . .23 A5
Maidstone ME16 . . . . .74 B3
Rochester ME2 . . . . .9 A7
Sheerness ME12 . . . . .1 B3
Charleston Ct CT10 . . . . . .30 B3
Charlesworth Dr CT7 . . . . .27 B7
Charlock Cl ME16 . . . . .74 D8
Charlock Dr ME12 . . . . .4 A4
Charlton St ME16 . . . . .74 C2
Charltons The ME13 . . . . . .63 F4
Charminster TN23 . . . . . . .155 E6
Charnwood CT5 . . . . .21 D1
Charnwood Rd CT6 . . . . . .23 B1
Charolais Cl CT12 . . . . .67 A2
Chartam Terr CT11 . . . . . . .52 D5
Chart Cl ME13 . . . . .62 B7
Chart Cnr ME17 . . . . .98 B1
Charter Ho 11 CT16 . . . . .166 D7
Charter St
Chatham ME4. . . . . .9 F2
Gillingham ME7 . . . . .10 C7
Chartfield Sch CT8 . . . . . . .27 F8
Chart Gunpowder Mill☆
ME13 . . . . .62 E7
CHARTHAM 86 E2
CHARTHAM DOWNS 86 D1
Chartham Downs Rd
CT4 .109 C7
CHARTHAM HATCH 86 D6
Chartham Prim Sch CT4 . . .86 C2
Chartham Sta CT4 . . . . .86 D3

Chart Hill Rd ME17 . . . . . . .98 B1
Chart Pl ME8 . . . . .33 C3
Chart Rd
Ashford, Godinton Park
TN23 . . . . .138 F2
Ashford, Great Chart TN23 138 D1
Ashford, Stanhope TN23 . .155 D6
Folkestone CT19 . . . . .177 F6
Chart Road Ind Est TN23 139 A3
CHART SUTTON 98 B1
Chart Sutton Bsns Est
ME17 . . . . .98 B2
Chartway St ME17 . . . . . . .99 C1
CHARTWAY STREET 99 C1
Chartwell Ave CT6 . . . . . . .23 D4
Chartwell Cl
Chatham ME4. . . . . .9 E4
Maidstone ME15 . . . . .75 B3
Chartwell Dr ME16 . . . . . . .74 B4
Chartwell Dr ME10 . . . . . . .36 C3
Chase The
Chatham ME4. . . . . .9 D2
Gillingham ME8 . . . . .11 A2
Ramsgate CT11 . . . . .29 F1
St Margaret's at Cliffe
CT15 . . . . .133 F1
Whitstable CT5 . . . . .43 C8
Chater Cl
Ashford TN23 . . . . .155 C8
Deal CT14 . . . . .117 C4
Chatham ☆ 9 E5
Chatham Ct CT11 . . . . .52 D8
Chatham Gr ME4 . . . . .9 F1
Chatham Gram Sch for Boys
ME4 .31 F8
Chatham Gram Sch for Girls
ME5 . . . . .10 C2
Chatham Hill ME4 . . . . . . .10 B3
Chatham House Gram Sch
CT11 . . . . .52 E7
Chatham Rd
Kit's Coty ME20 . . . . .53 D6
Maidstone ME14 . . . . .53 E1
Sandling ME14 . . . . .53 E1
Whitstable CT5 . . . . .44 C8
Chatham Ski Ctr ME7 . . . . .32 E6
Chatham South Sch ME4 . .31 F8
Chatham St CT11 . . . . .52 E7
Chatham Sta ME4 . . . . .9 E4
Chatsworth Dr ME10 . . . . .36 B5
Chatsworth Rd 10 ME7 . . .10 C5
Chattenden Ct ME14 . . . . .75 B6
Chatwell Ct ME7 . . . . .10 C5
Chaucer Ave CT5 . . . . .21 B1
Chaucer Cl
Canterbury CT1 . . . . .88 C7
13 Maidstone ME15 . . . . . .97 E7
Rochester ME2 . . . . .9 E8
Chaucer Coll CT2 . . . . .66 D3
Chaucer Cres CT14 . . . . . .149 B3
Chaucer Ct 1 CT1 . . . . . . .88 B7
Chaucer Hospl The CT4 . . .88 A4
Chaucer Mews CT2 . . . . . .65 E1
Chaucer Rd
Broadstairs CT10 . . . . .30 A3
Canterbury CT1 . . . . .67 C1
Elvington CT15 . . . . .114 B2
Gillingham ME7 . . . . .10 D3
Sittingbourne ME10. . . . . . .36 D3
Chaucer Tech Sch CT1 . . . .88 C7
Chaucer Wood Ct CT1 . . . .67 B1
Cheddar Cl TN24 . . . . .139 B4
CHEESEMAN'S GREEN . . .156 F2
Cheeseman's Green La TN23/
TN25 . . . . .156 E1
Cheesmans Cl CT12 . . . . . .50 C5
Cheffins Ho ME7 . . . . .10 E7
Chegwell Dr ME5 . . . . .32 B4
Chegworth Gdns ME10 . . . .36 E1
Chegworth La ME17 . . . . .100 A6
Chegworth Rd ME17 . . . . . .99 F5
Chelmar Rd ME7 . . . . .10 B4
Chelmsford Ho ME15 . . . . .97 E6
Chelsea Cl CT21 . . . . .176 C1
Chelsea Rd CT1 . . . . .67 C4
Chelsfield Ho ME16 . . . . . .74 D5
Cheltenham Cl ME15 . . . . .97 F6
Cheney Cl ME8 . . . . .33 D8
Cheney Hill ME9 . . . . .59 A5
Cheney Rd ME13 . . . . .62 F7
Channels The TN26 . . . . . .167 C2
Chepstow Rd 3 ME15 . . . .97 F6
Chequer La CT3 . . . . .71 D2
Chequers Cl ME5 . . . . .54 A8
Chequers Hill CT4 . . . . . .109 C2
Chequers Pk TN25 . . . . . .123 E1
Chequers Rd ME12 . . . . . . .4 E6
Chequers Sh Ctr ME15 . . . .75 A4
Chequer's Terr TN25 . . . . . .5 A5
Chequertree CT25 . . . . . . .172 B7
Cherbourg Cres ME5 . . . . .31 F7
CHERITON 177 D6
Cheriton Apartments
CT19 . . . . .177 F6
Cheriton Ave CT12 . . . . . . .52 B8
Cheriton Court Rd CT20 .177 C6
Cheriton Gdns CT20 . . . . .178 C4
Cheriton High St CT19 . . .177 D6
Cheriton Intc CT20 . . . . . .177 C7
Cheriton Pl
Deal CT14 . . . . .117 D4

Cheriton Rd continued
Folkestone CT19, CT20 . . . .178 B5
Folkestone, Morehall CT19 .177 F6
Ramsgate CT11 . . . . .52 B8
Cheriton Way ME16 . . . . . .74 C7
Cheriton Wood Ho CT19 .177 D7
Cherries The ME10 . . . . . . .36 E6
Cherry Amber Cl ME8 . . . . .33 F8
Cherry Ave CT2 . . . . .66 D2
Cherrybrook Rd CT20 . . . .177 D6
Cherry Cl
Lenham ME17 . . . . .101 C5
Sittingbourne ME10. . . . . . .36 D6
Cherry Ct
Ashford TN23 . . . . .139 B1
Broadstairs CT10 . . . . .29 E7
Folkestone CT19 . . . . .178 A6
Cherry Dr CT2 . . . . .66 D2
Cherry Fields ME10 . . . . . .36 A5
Cherry Garden Ave CT19 .178 A4
Cherry Garden Cres
TN25 . . . . .123 F2
Cherrygarden La CT15,
CT3 . . . . .113 E7
Cherry Garden La
Ash CT3 . . . . .71 E1
Folkestone CT19 . . . . .177 F7
Wye TN25 . . . . .123 F2
Cherry Garden Rd CT2 . . . .66 D2
Cherry Gdns
Ashford TN23 . . . . .156 A5
Broadstairs CT10 . . . . .29 C3
Elham CT4 . . . . .144 F5
Herne Bay CT6. . . . . .22 F4
Littlestone-on-Sea TN28 . .202 D6
Teynham ME9 . . . . .38 C2
Cherry Glebe TN25 . . . . . .157 E3
Cherry Gr TN25 . . . . .157 D3
Cherry Hill Ct ME9 . . . . . . .35 B6
Cherry La CT14 . . . . .116 D3
Cherry Orch
Littlebourne CT3 . . . . .68 F1
Old Wives Lees CT4 . . . . . . .85 C2
Tenterden TN30 . . . . .179 A6
Whitstable CT5 . . . . .44 C8
Woodchurch TN26 . . . . . . .169 A3
CHERRY ORCHARD 74 B3
Cherry Orchard La TN25 . .172 E4
Cherry Orchard Mews
CT3 .68 F1
Cherry Orchard Way
ME16 . . . . .74 B3
Cherry Tree Ave CT16 . . . .149 C1
Cherry Tree Cl
Teynham ME9 . . . . .38 D2
West Minst ME12 . . . . .3 A8
Cherry Tree Gdns CT21 . .29 B3
Cherry Tree Rd
Charing Heath TN27 . . . . . .119 F8
Gillingham ME8 . . . . .33 F8
Cherry View ME17 . . . . . . .97 B3
Cherry Waye CT15 . . . . . .131 D7
Cherrywood Rise TN25 . . .138 F4
Cherville La CT3 . . . . .90 C7
Chervilles ME16 . . . . .74 A2
Chesham Dr ME8 . . . . .33 E6
Cheshire Rd
Maidstone ME15 . . . . .97 E7
Maidstone, Willington ME15 .75 E2
CHESLEY 35 A3
Chessenden La TN27 . . . .135 A1
Chester Ave TN26 . . . . . . .153 D5
Chester Rd
Gillingham ME7 . . . . .10 D2
Westgate on Sea CT8 . . . . . .27 F8
CHESTFIELD 21 E1
Chestfield Cl ME8 . . . . .11 E2
Chestfield Rd CT5 . . . . .44 C7
Chestfield & Swalecliffe Sta
CT5. . . . . .21 D2
Chestnut Ave
Blean CT2 . . . . .66 A7
Chatham ME5. . . . . .31 F3
Chestnut Cl
Ashford TN23 . . . . .138 E3
Chartham CT4 . . . . .86 F1
Hythe CT21 . . . . .187 E8
Tenterden TN30 . . . . .167 C1
Whitfield CT16 . . . . .149 A8
Chestnut Ct ME13 . . . . .64 A3
Chestnut Dr
Broadstairs CT10 . . . . .29 C4
Coxheath ME17 . . . . .96 B3
Herne Bay CT6. . . . . .22 D3
Kingswood ME17 . . . . .99 D2
Sturry CT2 . . . . .68 A7
Worth CT14 . . . . .94 A4
Chestnut La
Bearsted TN25 . . . . .156 C4
Boughton Aluph TN25 . . . .156 C4
Coxheath ME17 . . . . .166 B7
Sturry CT2 . . . . .68 A7
Wye TN25 . . . . .98 F6
Chestnuts The
Brabourne Lees TN25 . . . .158 D5
Sellindge TN25 . . . . .159 D1
CHESTNUT STREET 35 E4
Chestnut Terr TN25 . . . . . .176 A1
Chestnut Wood La ME9 . . .35 E3
Chetney View ME9 . . . . . . .14 D4
Chevalier Rd CT17 . . . . . . .166 B7
Chevening CT5 . . . . .32 A5
Cheviot Ct CT10 . . . . .30 B5
Cheviot Gdns ME15 . . . . . .76 A1
Cheviot Way TN24 . . . . . . .139 C4
Cheyne Cl ME10 . . . . .36 F8
Cheyne Mid Sch ME12 . . . .1 E2
Cheyne Rd ME12 . . . . .5 D3
Chicago Ave ME7 . . . . .10 F5

Chichester Cl
Ashford TN23 . . . . .139 B1
Gillingham ME8 . . . . .34 A8
Chichester Rd
Folkestone CT20 . . . . .177 E4
Ramsgate CT12 . . . . .29 B1
Chichester Wlk 2 CT12 . . .29 B1
Chickfield Gdns 4 ME5 . . .10 C2
Chiddingfold CT17 . . . . .4 D6
Chiddingstone Cl ME15 . . .97 F6
Childgate Rd CT5 . . . . .42 F2
Childscroft Rd ME8 . . . . . . .11 F2
CHILHAM 107 C7
Chilham Ave CT8 . . . . .27 D7
Chilham Cl
Chatham ME4. . . . . .9 E3
West Minst ME12 . . . . .3 B8
Chilham Ho 1 ME15 . . . . .97 E8
Chilham Rd
Folkestone CT19 . . . . .177 E6
Gillingham ME8 . . . . .11 A3
Maidstone ME16 . . . . .74 C7
Chilham St Mary's CE Prim
Sch CT4 . . . . .107 D8
Chilham Sta CT4 . . . . .107 D8
CHILLENDEN 113 F8
Chillenden Windmill☆
CT3 .91 F1
Chillington St ME14 . . . . . .74 F6
CHILMINGTON GREEN . . .155 C5
Chilston Rd ME17 . . . . . . .101 D5
Chiltern Cl ME15 . . . . .75 F1
Chiltern End TN24 . . . . . . .139 B3
CHILTON 52 A6
Chilton Ave
Sittingbourne ME10. . . . . . .37 A3
Temple Ewell CT16 . . . . . . .148 C4
Chilton Ct
14 Folkestone CT20. . . . . .178 E6
Gillingham ME8 . . . . .11 E1
Chilton Field CT3 . . . . .71 D2
Chilton Gdns CT3 . . . . .71 D2
Chilton La CT11 . . . . .52 A6
Chilton Pl CT3 . . . . .71 D2
Chilton Prim Sch CT11 . . . .52 A6
Chilton Sq CT3 . . . . .71 D2
Chilton Way CT17 . . . . . . .148 D3
Chimes The
Ashford TN24. . . . . .139 C3
Maidstone ME14 . . . . .76 A5
Rochester ME1 . . . . .9 C5
Chineham Way CT1 . . . . . . .87 F6
Chippendale Cl ME5 . . . . . .31 F1
Chippendayle Dr ME17 . .100 D6
Chippie's Way CT13 . . . . . .72 F1
Chipstead Cl ME16 . . . . . . .74 D6
Chipstead Rd ME8 . . . . . . .33 D4
Chislehurst Cl ME15 . . . . . .97 F6
CHISLET 69 A4
Chislet CE Prim Sch CT3 . . .47 C5
Chislet Cl CT3 . . . . .47 A1
Chislet Ct CT6 . . . . .22 C5
CHISLET FORSTAL 47 B5
Chislet Park Cotts CT3 . . . .46 F1
Chislet Park Farm Cotts
CT3. .46 F2
Chislet Cl TN25 . . . . .159 E2
Chislet Wlk ME8 . . . . .33 D5
Chisnall Rd CT17 . . . . .148 E4
Chittenden's La TN29 . . . .193 E5
CHITTY 47 D6
Chitty La CT3 . . . . .47 D6
Christ Church CE High Sch
TN23 . . . . .155 F5
Christ Church CE Jun Sch
CT11. . . . . .52 C6
Christ Church CE Prim Sch
CT20. . . . . .178 C5
Christchurch Ct
3 Chatham ME5. . . . . .10 C2
1 Dover CT16. . . . . .166 D7
Christchurch Ho 11 ME15 .97 E5
Christchurch Rd TN23 . . . .156 B8
Christ Church Rd CT20 . . .178 C4
Christchurch Way CT16 . .149 B3
Christen Way ME15, ME17 .97 F3
Christian Ct 3 ME2. . . . . . .9 C8
Christie Cl ME5 . . . . .32 B6
Christmas St ME7 . . . . .10 E7
Christopher Bushell Way
TN24 . . . . .139 E4
Christopher's Row ME9 . . .60 A3
Chrysler Ave CT6 . . . . .22 B4
Church App TN28 . . . . .202 A6
Church Cl TN25 . . . . .157 E3
Church Cliff CT14 . . . . .134 C6
Church Cotts
Rodmersham ME9 . . . . .59 D8
Tenterden TN30 . . . . .167 B3
Church Court Gr CT10. . . . . .29 E6
Church Cres ME17 . . . . . . .100 F6
Church Ct CT18 . . . . .161 C6
Churcham Mews CT15 . . .133 A1
Church Farm Rd ME9 . . . . .12 E3
Church Farm Way CT13 . . .93 B6
Church Field TN25 . . . . . . .160 B1
Churchfield Pl CT9 . . . . .7 I2
Churchfields
Broadstairs CT10 . . . . .29 C7
Dover CT9 . . . . .7 J1
Churchfields Terr ME9 . . . . .9 B4
Churchfield Way TN25 . . .123 E2
Church Gn
Hollingbourne ME17 . . . . . .77 E3
Rochester ME2 . . . . .9 C8
Church Haven CT14 . . . . . .133 F5
Church Hill
Bethersden TN26 . . . . .153 D5

Church Hill continued
Boughton Street ME13 . . . .64 A5
Canterbury CT2 . . . . .66 C1
Charing Heath ME17,
TN27. . . . . .119 C7
Chatham ME5. . . . . .10 C2
Chilham CT4. . . . . .107 B8
Doddington ME9 . . . . .80 F8
Eythorne CT15 . . . . .131 C8
Hawkinge CT18 . . . . .163 D4
High Halden TN26 . . . . . . .167 E7
Hythe CT21 . . . . .176 C2
Kingsnorth TN23 . . . . .156 B3
Loose ME17 . . . . .97 C1
Ramsgate CT11 . . . . .52 E7
Shepherdswell CT15 . . . . . .130 D4
Stockbury ME9 . . . . .56 F7
Stone in Oxney TN30 . . . . .189 F3
Sutton CT15 . . . . .133 A7
Temple Ewell CT16 . . . . . . .148 D5
Church Ho CT14 . . . . .117 C7
CHURCH HOUGHAM 165 B5
Church Hts CT1 . . . . .176 C2
Churchill Ave
Chatham ME5. . . . . .32 A7
Deal CT14 . . . . .117 C2
Folkestone CT19 . . . . .178 C8
Herne Bay CT6. . . . . .23 D4
Churchill Cl
Bridge CT4. . . . . .88 F1
Folkestone CT19 . . . . .178 D8
St Margaret's at Cliffe
CT15. . . . . .150 F5
Churchill Cotts ME17 . . . . . .98 F6
Churchill Ct
Hythe CT21 . . . . .176 B1
1 Ramsgate CT11 . . . . .52 D7
Churchill Ho
Bridge CT4. . . . . .88 F1
2 Folkestone CT20. . . . . . .177 F5
Maidstone ME16 . . . . .74 B2
Sittingbourne ME10. . . . . . .37 C4
Teynham ME9 . . . . .38 C3
Churchill Rd
Canterbury CT1 . . . . .88 C6
Dover CT17 . . . . .166 A6
Minster (Sheppey) ME12 . . . .4 D4
Churchill Sch The CT18 . . .163 A4
Churchill St 7 CT16 . . . . .149 C1
Churchill Way ME13 . . . . . .40 B1
Churchill Wlk CT18 . . . . . .162 F4
Church La
Adisham CT3 . . . . .90 D1
Aldington TN25 . . . . .173 D7
Barham CT4. . . . . .111 F1
Boughton Aluph TN25 . . . .123 B4
Boyden Gate CT3. . . . . .47 C7
Brenzett TN29 . . . . .191 F5
Canterbury CT1. . . . . .87 F8
20 Canterbury, Northgate
CT1 .67 A1
Challock TN25 . . . . .122 B8
Chartham CT4 . . . . .86 D3
Chatham ME4. . . . . .9 F6
Church Hougham CT15 . . .165 B5
Deal CT14 . . . . .117 B6
Harrietsham ME17. . . . . . . .100 E6
Hothfield TN26 . . . . .137 F6
Iden TN31 . . . . .197 B4
Kingsnorth TN23 . . . . .156 B3
Kingston CT4 . . . . .111 D3
Lower Hardres CT4 . . . . .88 B2
Lydden CT15 . . . . .147 E8
Maidstone, Bearsted ME14 .76 C4
Newington ME9 . . . . .35 B6
New Romney TN28 . . . . . . .202 B5
Peasmarsh TN31 . . . . .196 C1
Petham CT4 . . . . .109 C3
Ringwould CT14 . . . . .133 F5
Ripple CT14 . . . . .116 B1
Selling ME13 . . . . .84 B6
Shadoxhurst TN26 . . . . . . .170 A7
Stockbury ME9 . . . . .56 E8
Stourmouth CT3 . . . . .48 C2
Stowting TN25 . . . . .160 A6
Sturry CT2 . . . . .67 F5
Waltham CT4. . . . . .125 F5
Westbere CT2 . . . . .68 C7
West Langdon CT15 . . . . . .132 D3
Whitstable CT5 . . . . .43 A6
Womenswold CT4 . . . . .112 D2
Churchlands ME14 . . . . . . .75 B5
Churchlands Ho TN28 . . . .202 B6
Churchlands The TN28 . . .202 B6
Church Marshes Ctry Pk☆
ME10. . . . . .37 A7
Church Mews
Gillingham ME8 . . . . .33 F8
Iwade ME9 . . . . .14 E4
Church Path
Deal CT14 . . . . .117 B5
Gillingham ME7 . . . . .10 E6
Great Mongeham CT14 . . .116 D3
Church Rd
Ashford, Aylesford Green
TN24 . . . . .157 A8
Ashford, Kennington TN24. .139 C2
Ashford, Willesborough
TN24. . . . . .157 A8
1 Broadstairs CT10 . . . . . . .30 A4
Burmarsh TN29 . . . . .185 E4
Charing TN27 . . . . .103 D2
Chart Sutton ME17 . . . . . . .98 C1
Coldred CT15 . . . . .131 A3
Dover CT17 . . . . .166 A7
Eastchurch ME12. . . . . .5 D2

Church Rd continued
Eastling ME13 . . . . 82 B2
Faversham ME13 . . . . 62 D7
Faversham, Oare ME13 . . . . . 40 B3
Faversham, The Brents
ME13 . . . . 62 D8
Folkestone CT20 . . . . 177 C6
Harrietsham ME17 . . . . 100 E6
Hoath CT3 . . . . 46 E5
Hucking ME17 . . . . 56 E1
Hythe CT21 . . . . 176 C2
Kenardington TN26 . . . . 182 A5
Littlebourne CT3 . . . . 90 A8
Lydd TN29 . . . . 205 C6
Lyminge CT18 . . . . 161 C7
Maidstone ME15 . . . . 97 F7
Maidstone, Tovil ME15 . . . . . 74 E2
Margate CT9 . . . . 7 J1
Mersham TN25 . . . . 157 E3
Molash CT4 . . . . 105 F5
New Romney TN28 . . . . 202 A6
Northbourne, Betteshanger
CT14 . . . . 115 C6
Northourne CT14 . . . . 116 A5
Ramsgate CT11 . . . . 52 E7
Sevington TN24 . . . . 157 B6
Sittingbourne ME9 . . . . 37 E5
Sittingbourne, Murston
ME10 . . . . 37 B5
Smeeth TN25 . . . . 158 C4
Stalisfield Green ME13 . . . . 103 F5
Tenterden TN30 . . . . 179 A7
Church Road Bsns Ctr
ME10 . . . . 37 A4
Church St (St Pauls) [7]
CT1 . . . . 88 A8
Church Sq
[2] Broadstairs CT10 . . . . . . 30 B4
Lenham ME17 . . . . 101 D5
Church St
Broadstairs CT10 . . . . 29 E6
Canterbury CT2 . . . . 66 E1
Chatham ME4 . . . . 10 A4
Deal CT14 . . . . 117 D8
Dover CT16 . . . . 166 D7
Eastry CT13 . . . . 93 C2
Faversham ME13 . . . . 62 D8
Folkestone CT20 . . . . 178 D4
Gillingham ME7 . . . . 10 E6
Maidstone, Boughton
Monchelsea ME17 . . . . 97 B2
Maidstone, Loose ME15 . . . 96 F5
Maidstone ME14 . . . . 75 A4
Maidstone, Tovil ME15 . . . . . 74 E2
Margate CT9 . . . . 7 J1
Minster (Thanet) CT12 . . . . . 50 C5
Nonington CT15 . . . . 113 C5
Rochester ME1 . . . . 9 C4
Rodmersham ME9 . . . . 59 C8
[7] Sandwich CT13 . . . . 73 A1
[3] Sandwich, The Butts
CT13 . . . . 72 F1
[5] Sittingbourne ME10 . . . . 36 E4
Sittingbourne ME10 . . . . 36 E5
Whitstable CT5 . . . . 20 F1
Woodnesborough CT13 . . . . 93 A4
Wye TN25 . . . . 123 F2
CHURCH STREET 20 F1
Church Terr
Chatham ME4 . . . . 10 C2
Minster (Sheppey) ME12 . . . 4 C7
Church View
Aldington TN25 . . . . 173 A6
Herne Bay CT6 . . . . 23 C4
Newchurch TN29 . . . . 184 E3
Worth CT14 . . . . 94 B5
Church Way CT5 . . . . 21 D3
CHURCH WHITFIELD. . . 149 B6
Church Whitfield Rd
CT16 . . . . 149 B8
Church Wlk CT14 . . . . 144 F4
Church Wood Cl CT2 . . . . 66 B2
Churchwood Dr CT5 . . . . . 21 D1
Church Yard Pas [10]
TN23 . . . . 139 B2
Church Yd [4] TN23 . . . . . 139 C2
Chute Cl ME8 . . . . 33 D4
Cinder Path CT10 . . . . 30 A4
Cinnabar Cl ME5 . . . . 32 A1
Cinnabar Dr ME10 . . . . . . 36 C6
Cinnamon Gr ME16 . . . . . 74 A3
Cinque Ports Ave CT21 . 176 B1
Cinque Ports Rd TN28 . . 202 C5
Circular Rd
Dover CT15 . . . . 150 B1
Finglesham CT14 . . . . 116 A3
Circus The CT6 . . . . 22 E4
Citadel Cres CT17 . . . . 166 B6
Citadel Hts CT17 . . . . 166 B6
Citadel Rd CT17 . . . . 166 B6
**Citadel The (Immigration
Removal Ctr)** CT17 . . . . . 166 B5
Citroen Cl CT6 . . . . 22 B4
City Bsns Pk CT1 . . . . 67 C3
City Garden The [3] CT1 . . 88 A8
City View CT2 . . . . 87 C8
City Way ME1 . . . . 9 C3
Claire Ct
Birchington CT7 . . . . 26 F7
Broadstairs CT10 . . . . 30 B5
Claire Ho [4] ME4 . . . . 10 A4
Clandon Rd ME5 . . . . 32 D2
Clanwilliam Rd CT14 . . . . 117 D5
Clare Dr CT6 . . . . 22 C4

Claremont Cl CT14 . . . . . . 134 C6
Claremont Gdns CT11 . . . 52 C7
Claremont Pl CT1 . . . . 87 F7
Claremont Rd
Deal CT14 . . . . 117 B5
Folkestone CT20 . . . . 178 C5
Kingsdown CT14 . . . . 134 C6
Maidstone ME14 . . . . 75 B5
Claremont St CT6 . . . . 22 C4
Claremont Terr CT13 . . . . . 93 D7
Claremont Way [2] ME4 . . . 9 F3
Clarence Ave
Margate CT9 . . . . 8 D2
Rochester ME1 . . . . 9 C4
Clarence Ct ME14 . . . . 75 E4
Clarence Gdns ME12 . . . . . 6 E3
Clarence Pl
Deal CT14 . . . . 117 D7
Dover CT17 . . . . 166 D5
Clarence Rd
Capel-le-Ferne CT18 . . . . . 164 B2
Chatham ME4 . . . . 10 B2
Deal CT14 . . . . 117 D3
Herne Bay CT6 . . . . 22 D5
Ramsgate CT11 . . . . 52 C6
Clarence Row
Folkestone CT20 . . . . 178 D5
Herne Bay CT6 . . . . 22 C5
Clarence St
Folkestone CT20 . . . . 178 D5
Herne Bay CT6 . . . . 22 C5
CLARENDON 166 B6
Clarendon Cl
Maidstone ME14 . . . . 76 A4
Sittingbourne ME10 . . . . 36 F1
Clarendon Gdns [7] CT11 . 52 D6
Clarendon House Gram Sch
[15] CT11 . . . . 52 E6
Clarendon Mews
[1] Broadstairs CT10 . . . . . . 30 A4
New Romney TN28 . . . . 202 C8
Clarendon Pl
Dover CT17 . . . . 166 C7
Maidstone ME14 . . . . 75 A4
Clarendon Rd
Aylesham CT3 . . . . 112 F5
Broadstairs CT10 . . . . 30 A4
Dover CT17 . . . . 166 C7
Margate CT9 . . . . 8 A2
Clarendon St
Dover CT17 . . . . 166 C7
Herne Bay CT6 . . . . 22 C4
Clare Rd CT5 . . . . 20 E2
Claridge Ct ME7 . . . . 32 F4
Claridge Mews CT21 . . . . 176 C2
Clare Cres TN24 . . . . 139 F4
Clarke's Cl CT14 . . . . 116 F4
Clarklands TN29 . . . . 186 A3
Claris Rd TN23 . . . . 202 E4
Claudius Dr ME13 . . . . 155 F5
Clavell Cl ME8 . . . . 33 E4
Claxfield Cotts ME9 . . . . . . 38 A3
Claxfield Rd ME9 . . . . 60 A8
Claygate
Ashford TN23 . . . . 155 F5
Eyhorne Street ME17 . . . . . . 77 D2
Clearmont Way CT3 . . . . . 47 A1
Clearmont Dr TN27 . . . . . 120 C8
Clearmont Pk TN27 . . . . . 120 D8
Cleave Rd ME7 . . . . 10 E1
Cleaver La CT11 . . . . 52 E7
Clematis Ave ME8 . . . . 33 B5
Clement Cl
Canterbury CT1 . . . . 67 B1
Sittingbourne ME10 . . . . 36 E8
Clement St ME4 . . . . 74 D5
Clementine Cl CT6 . . . . 23 D4
Clement's Rd CT12 . . . . . . 29 C2
Clerke Dr ME10 . . . . 37 A8
Clermont Cl ME7 . . . . 33 A4
Clevedon Cl TN25 . . . . 105 B2
Cleveland Cl CT16 . . . . 149 B3
Cleveland Ct CT9 . . . . 8 A1
Cleveland Ho ME16 . . . . . . 74 B2
Cleveland Rd ME7 . . . . 10 D6
Cleveley Lo CT11 . . . . 29 E2
Cleven Lodge CT7 . . . . 48 D6
Cleves Way TN23 . . . . 155 E8
Clewson Rise ME14 . . . . . . 75 B8
Cliff Ave CT6 . . . . 23 C5
Cliff Cl CT21 . . . . 176 D3
Cliff Dr
Herne Bay CT6 . . . . 22 C4
Warden ME12 . . . . 6 E4
Cliffe Ave CT9 . . . . 7 F1
Cliffe Ho
Folkestone CT20 . . . . 178 A3
St Margaret's at Cliffe
CT15 . . . . 150 F6
Cliffe Rd
Deal CT14 . . . . 134 C6
Rochester ME1 . . . . 9 B8
Cliffestone Ct CT20 . . . . . 178 B5
Cliff Field CT8 . . . . 27 C8
Cliff Gdns ME12 . . . . 4 E7
Cliff Hill ME17 . . . . 97 D4
Cliff Hill Rd ME17 . . . . 97 C4
Cliffjoit La ME17 . . . . 92 D5
Clifford Gdns CT14 . . . . . 117 B2
Clifford Ho [6] ME14 . . . . . 76 B8
Clifford Rd CT5 . . . . 43 F8
Clifford Way ME15 . . . . 74 E2
Cliff Prom CT10 . . . . 30 C7
Cliff Rd
Birchington CT7 . . . . 26 F8
Broadstairs CT10 . . . . 30 B7
Dover CT15, CT16 . . . . 150 C1
Folkestone CT20 . . . . 178 A3
Hythe CT21 . . . . 176 D3

Cliff Rd continued
Whitstable CT5 . . . . 20 F3
Cliff Sea Gr CT6 . . . . 22 C4
CLIFFS END 51 D6
Cliffs End Gr CT12 . . . . 51 D5
Cliffs End Rd CT12 . . . . 51 E5
Cliffside Dr CT10 . . . . 30 A1
Cliff St CT11 . . . . 52 E6
Cliff Terr CT9 . . . . 7 J3
Clifftown Gdns CT6 . . . . . . 22 B4
Cliff View Gdns
Leysdown-on-Sea ME12 . . . 6 D1
Warden ME12 . . . . 6 E4
Cliff View Rd CT12 . . . . 51 D6
Clifton Ct CT11 . . . . 75 B5
Clifton Cres CT20 . . . . 178 B3
Clifton Gdns
Canterbury CT2 . . . . 66 D2
Folkestone CT20 . . . . 178 A3
Margate CT9 . . . . 7 J3
Whitstable CT5 . . . . 43 D8
Clifton Lawn CT11 . . . . 52 D6
Clifton Mans [1] CT20 . . . 178 C4
Clifton Pl CT9 . . . . 8 A3
Clifton Rd
Folkestone CT20 . . . . 178 C4
Gillingham ME7 . . . . 10 C7
Margate CT9 . . . . 8 A2
Ramsgate CT11 . . . . 52 B8
Whitstable CT5 . . . . 43 D8
Clifton St CT9 . . . . 7 J3
CLIFTONVILLE 8 C1
Cliftonville Ave
Margate CT9 . . . . 8 A2
Ramsgate CT12 . . . . 29 B1
Cliftonville Ct CT9 . . . . 8 B3
Margate, Cliftonville CT9 . . . 8 B3
Cliftonville Prim Sch CT9 . 8 C2
Clim Down CT4 . . . . 134 D6
Clinton Cl ME7 . . . . 96 B3
Clints La CT4 . . . . 129 D4
Clipper Cl ME2 . . . . 9 E7
Clipper Ho ME2 . . . . 9 E7
Clive Ct CT9 . . . . 8 A1
Cliveden Cl ME16 . . . . 74 D7
Clive Dennis Ct TN24 . . . 139 E1
Clive Rd
Margate CT9 . . . . 29 A5
Rochester ME1 . . . . 9 C3
Sittingbourne ME10 . . . . 36 B5
Clockhouse TN23 . . . . 138 F1
Clockhouse Pk TN25 . . . . 105 C2
Clock House Rise ME17 . . 96 C2
Clock Tower [3] CT2 . . . . . 66 A6
Clocktower Par CT2 . . . . . . 66 A6
Cloisterham Rd ME1 . . . . . 31 D7
Cloisters The
[18] Canterbury CT1 . . . . . . 66 F1
Lenham ME17 . . . . 101 C5
Ramsgate CT11 . . . . 52 D5
[6] Sittingbourne ME10 . . . . 36 E4
Whitstable CT5 . . . . 20 F2
Clopton Cl ME8 . . . . 33 D8
Close The
Ashford TN23 . . . . 155 F7
Bridge CT4 . . . . 88 F1
Canterbury CT1 . . . . 87 D6
Canterbury, Hales Place CT2 66 C3
Canterbury, St Dunstan's
CT2 . . . . 66 C3
Faversham ME13 . . . . 62 C6
Folkestone CT19 . . . . 178 E8
Hythe CT21 . . . . 176 B4
Lydden CT15 . . . . 147 F8
Rochester ME1 . . . . 9 C4
Wye TN25 . . . . 123 F2
Cloudberry Cl ME16 . . . . . . 74 D6
Cloudesley Cl ME1 . . . . 9 B1
Clouston Cl CT18 . . . . 163 B5
Clovelly TN28 . . . . 202 E6
Clovelly Cl ME12 . . . . 4 B8
Clovelly Dr ME12 . . . . 4 B8
Clovelly Rd CT5 . . . . 43 D7
Clover Bank View ME5 . . . 32 B6
Clover Cl ME12 . . . . 4 A5
Clover Ct ME10 . . . . 37 B5
Clover Lay ME8 . . . . 12 B2
Cloverlay Ind Pk ME8 . . . . 12 C1
Clover Rise CT5 . . . . 21 B1
Clover St [3] ME4 . . . . 9 F4
Clover Terr [3] ME15 . . . . . 97 D8
Clowes Ct CT2 . . . . 66 C4
Clubb's La TN29 . . . . 199 D7
Cluny Rd ME13 . . . . 62 F7
Clyde St
[1] Canterbury CT1 . . . . 67 A1
Sheerness ME12 . . . . 1 E2
Clynton Way TN23 . . . . . . 156 A7
Coach Dr TN26 . . . . 158 A7
Coach House Mews The
CT15 . . . . 131 D5
Coach Rd
Charing Heath TN27 . . . . . . 119 A6
Densole CT18 . . . . 162 F8
Egerton ME17, TN27 . . . . . 118 E6
Coach Yd The [6] ME16 . . 74 B3
Coachman's La ME9 . . . . . 80 A6
Coast Dr
Greatstone-on-Sea TN28 . . 202 E6
Lydd-on-Sea TN29 . . . . 209 D8
St Mary's Bay TN29 . . . . . . 194 F2
Coastguard Alley CT5 . . . . 20 C1
Coastguard Cotts
Birchington CT7 . . . . 26 D8
Conyer ME9 . . . . 38 E6
Dover CT15 . . . . 166 G8
Herne Bay CT6 . . . . 21 F4

Coastguard Cotts continued
[4] Hythe CT21 . . . . 176 B1
Kingsdown CT14 . . . . 134 D4
Leysdown-on-Sea ME12 . . 19 E4
Lyddon-Sea TN29 . . . . 209 D5
Minster (Sheppey) ME12 . . . 5 C5
[22] Ramsgate, East Cliff
CT11 . . . . 52 F7
Ramsgate, Pegwell CT11 . . 52 A1
Sandwich CT13 . . . . 95 A8
Coastguard Cotts The
ME12 . . . . 1 I1
Coastguard Hos CT12 . . . . 6 C5
Coast Rd TN28 . . . . 202 F7
Coats Ave ME12 . . . . 3 A8
Cobay Cl CT21 . . . . 176 D2
Cobb Ct CT9 . . . . 7 I3
Cobblers Bridge Rd CT6 . 22 D3
Cobblestones ME7 . . . . 32 F5
Cobbs Hill CT4 . . . . 85 C2
Cobbs Mews [3] CT20 . . . 178 C4
Cobbs Pl CT9 . . . . 7 I3
Cobbs Wood Ind Est
TN23 . . . . 138 F2
Cobb Wlk ME13 . . . . 62 B8
Cobden Pl [17] CT1 . . . . . . 67 A1
Cobden Rd
[4] Chatham ME4 . . . . 10 B2
Hythe CT21 . . . . 176 B1
Cobdown Gr ME18 . . . . 12 A2
Cobfield ME17 . . . . 98 A1
Cobham Ave ME10 . . . . 36 E1
Cobham Chase ME13 . . . . . 62 B8
Cobham Cl
Canterbury CT1 . . . . 88 C6
Maidstone ME16 . . . . 74 E4
Cobham Rise ME7 . . . . 10 F5
Cobsden Cl TN29 . . . . 195 A4
Cobsden Rd TN29 . . . . 195 A4
Cobtree Cl ME5 . . . . 32 C8
Cobtree Rd ME17 . . . . 96 C2
Cobtree Wharf ME20 . . . . . 53 C2
Cobweb Cnr CT2 . . . . 66 B4
Cockering Rd
Canterbury CT1, CT4 . . . . . . 87 B4
Chartham CT4 . . . . 86 E2
Cock La
Elham CT4 . . . . 144 F4
Hamstreet TN26 . . . . 183 A4
Leaveland TN28 . . . . 202 B7
Cock St ME17 . . . . 97 D1
COCK STREET 97 D1
Codrington Rd CT11 . . . . . . 52 D7
Cogans Terr CT1 . . . . 87 E6
Cogan Ho [4] CT1 . . . . 87 F7
Coburn Rd CT14 . . . . 30 A2
Colchester Cl ME5 . . . . 32 A7
Coldblow CT14 . . . . 117 A1
Coldblow La
Hucking ME14 . . . . 56 A2
Woodchurch TN26 . . . . 169 D4
Coldbridge La TN27 . . . . . 118 B5
COLD HARBOUR
Lenham 102 F6
Sittingbourne 35 F7
Cold Harbour Cl 67 A2
Coldharbour La
Bridge CT4, CT3 . . . . 111 D7
Forstal ME20 . . . . 53 C1
Hucking ME14, ME9 . . . . 56 B1
Old Romney TN29 . . . . 200 C5
Peasmarsh TN31 . . . . 196 E3
Sittingbourne ME9 . . . . 14 F1
Sittingbourne ME10 . . . . 15 A1
Wye TN25 . . . . 124 B2
Cold Harbour La ME9 . . . . . 35 F6
Cold Harbour Rd ME13 . . 103 A7
COLDRED 131 A3
Coldred Hill CT15 . . . . 130 F1
Coldred Rd
Coldred CT15 . . . . 131 B5
Maidstone ME15 . . . . 97 F4
Shepherdswell CT15 . . . . . . 130 E3
COLDRED STREET 131 A2
Coldswood Rd CT12 . . . . . . 28 F2
Colegate Dr ME14 . . . . 76 C4
Colegates Ct ME13 . . . . 40 B2
Colegates Rd ME13 . . . . . . 40 B2
Coleman Cres ME13 . . . . . . 40 B2
Coleman Cres CT9 . . . . 29 C1
Coleman Dr ME10 . . . . 14 F1
Colemans Rd TN29 . . . . . . 205 D2
Coleman's Stairs Rd CT7 . 27 A8
Coleman's Yd [3] CT11 . . . 52 E6
Cole Rd ME13 . . . . 62 E7
Coleridge Gdns CT3 . . . . . 112 F6
Colesdane ME17 . . . . 100 E8
Coleshall Cotts ME9 . . . . . . 14 C3
Cole Terr ME17 . . . . 101 C4
Colette Cl CT10 . . . . 8 G2
Coleville Cres TN28 . . . . . . 202 D6
Colewood Rd CT5 . . . . 21 E3
Colfe Way ME10 . . . . 37 A8
Colin's Way CT21 . . . . 177 A3
Collard Cl CT6 . . . . 23 A4
Collard Ho CT1 . . . . 88 C8
Collard Pl CT18 . . . . 163 A5
Collard Rd TN24 . . . . 157 A8
Collards Cl CT12 . . . . 49 C7
Collards La CT4 . . . . 144 E3
Collar Makers Gn CT3 . . . . 71 F1
College Ave
Gillingham ME7 . . . . 10 B4
Maidstone ME15 . . . . 74 F7
College Cotts ME16 . . . . . . 74 F3
College Ct
[6] Ashford TN23 . . . . 139 C2

Chu–Con 217

College Ct continued
Canterbury CT1 . . . . 67 B1
[6] Maidstone ME15 . . . . . . 75 A3
College Gdns CT8 . . . . 27 E8
College Rd
Canterbury CT1 . . . . 67 B1
Chatham ME4 . . . . 10 A7
Deal CT14 . . . . 117 D8
Maidstone ME15 . . . . 74 F2
Margate CT9 . . . . 8 A1
Ramsgate CT11 . . . . 29 E1
Sittingbourne ME10 . . . . 36 D3
College Row CT17 . . . . 166 B7
College Sq [2] CT9 . . . . 7 J2
College Square Sh Ctr CT9 . 7 J2
College Way CT12 . . . . 91 A7
College Wlk
[6] Maidstone ME15 . . . . . . 75 A3
[3] Margate CT9 . . . . 7 J2
College Yd ME1 . . . . 9 C6
Collett CT1 TN25 . . . . 142 D8
Collett Wlk ME8 . . . . 33 D4
Collie Dr CT3 . . . . 155 E5
Collingborne TN23 . . . . . . 155 C6
Collings Wlk ME8 . . . . 33 D4
Collington Terr ME15 . . . . . 97 E4
Collingwood Cl
Broadstairs CT10 . . . . 29 E4
Westgate on Sea CT8 . . . . . . 27 D7
Collingwood Ct
Folkestone CT20 . . . . 177 E5
[7] Ramsgate CT11 . . . . 52 D7
Collingwood Ind Est
ME17 . . . . 98 E2
Collingwood Rd
Kit's Coty ME20 . . . . 53 C7
St Margaret's at Cliffe
CT15 . . . . 150 F8
Whitstable CT5 . . . . 20 C1
Collingwood Rise CT20 . . 177 E5
Collingwood Wlk ME10 . . . 36 B5
Collins Rd
Herne Bay CT6 . . . . 22 C2
Nelson PI TN30 . . . . 179 D7
Rochester ME2 . . . . 9 A8
Colman Ho [4] ME14 . . . . . 75 A4
Colombo Sq CT12 . . . . 29 A1
Colonel's La CT13 . . . . 73 A1
**Colonel Stephens Rly Mus*
TN30 . . . . 179 A8
Colonel Stephens Way
TN30 . . . . 167 B2
Colorado Cl CT16 . . . . 149 B3
Colson Dr ME9 . . . . 14 E3
Colton Cres CT16 . . . . 149 B4
Coltsfoot Dr ME14 . . . . 75 F4
Columbia Ave CT5 . . . . 43 B7
Columbine Cl [4] CT5 . . . . 43 C6
Colvanley Rd CT5 . . . . 43 D8
Com Coll Whitstable CT5 . 43 F8
Command Rd ME14 . . . . . . 74 F8
Commercial Rd ME2 . . . . . . 9 B7
Commissioners Ct ME4 . . . 9 F7
Commissioner's Rd ME2 . . 9 C8
Commodore Ct CT21 . . . . 176 C1
Commodore Rd ME14 . . . . 75 C5
Common La CT17 . . . . 148 E3
Common Rd ME13 . . . . 81 B1
Common The ME1 . . . . 9 C6
Common Way TN26 . . . . . 138 A7
Commonwealth CE ME10 . 37 B3
Compass Cl ME1 . . . . 9 C5
Compass Ctr ME4 . . . . 10 A8
Compton Ct ME5 . . . . 32 D2
Concord Ave ME5 . . . . 31 E5
Condor Ct ME4 . . . . 10 A8
Conduit Ho The* CT1 . . . . . . 67 B1
Conduit St ME13 . . . . 62 D8
Coney Mews ME14 . . . . 10 A1
Conference Wlk CT1 . . . . . 88 C8
Conifer Cl CT8 . . . . 7 D1
Conifer Dr ME5 . . . . 32 D1
Conifers The
Deal CT14 . . . . 117 A2
Shepherdswell CT15 . . . . . . 130 F2
Coniston Ave CT11 . . . . 52 A7
Coniston Dr CT3 . . . . 112 F6
Coniston Ho ME15 . . . . 97 E7
Coniston Rd CT19 . . . . 178 B1
Conker Cl TN23 . . . . 156 C3
Connaught Cl ME15 . . . . . . 97 E4
Connaught Gdns [9] CT9 . . 7 J1
Connaught Mews [2] ME4 . 10 C2
Connaught Pk* CT16 . . . . . 149 D1
Connaught Rd
Chatham ME4 . . . . 10 C2
Dover CT16 . . . . 149 D1
Folkestone CT20 . . . . 178 D5
Gillingham ME7 . . . . 10 D5
Margate CT9 . . . . 7 J1
Sittingbourne ME10 . . . . 36 D3
Conqueror Dr ME7 . . . . 11 A6
Conquest Ind Est ME2 . . . . 9 A5
Conrad Ave CT1 . . . . 67 C3
Conrad Cl ME8 . . . . 33 D4
Consort Cl ME14 . . . . 75 B5
Constable Rd CT7 . . . . 27 A8
Constable's Rd CT16 . . . . 166 E8
Constancia Ct CT20 . . . . . 178 C5
Constantine Ct TN23 . . . . 155 F5
Constitution Hill [8] ME5 . . 10 B2
Constitution Rd ME5 . . . . . 10 B2
Consul Cl CT6 . . . . 22 B4

Continental App CT9. . . . . .28 F6
Convent CI CT15. . . . . .151 B6
Conventina Ho **3** CT11 . . .52 D7
Convent Rd CT10. . . . . .8 G1
Convent Wlk CT11 . . . . . . .52 B5
CONYER. 33 F5
Conyer Rd ME9. . . . . .38 F4
Conyers Wlk ME8. . . . . .33 D4
Conyngham CI CT4. . . . . .89 A2
Conyngham La CT4 . . . . . . .89 A2
Conyngham Rd
  Herne Bay CT6. . . . . .23 D5
  Minster (Thanet) CT12. . . .50 C5
Cooden CI ME4. . . . . .32 C6
Cook CI ME5. . . . . .32 C6
Cookham Hill ME1. . . . . .9 A2
Cookham Wood Rd ME1. .31 B8
Cooks La ME10 . . . . .36 C6
Cook's Lea CT13. . . . . .93 B2
Cooks Wharf ME1. . . . . .9 B4
Cooling CI ME14. . . . . .75 C6
COOLINGE. 177 F4
Coolinge La CT20. . . . . . . .177 F4
Coolinge Rd CT20. . . . . . . .178 D5
COOMBE. 92 F8
Coombe CI
  Chatham ME5. . . . . .32 B3
  Dover CT17. . . . . .149 A1
Coombe Ct CT17. . . . . .149 A1
Coombe Dr
  Shepherdswell CT15. . . . .130 E5
  Sittingbourne ME10. . . . . .37 C4
Coombe Gr TN26. . . . . .120 F2
Coombe La
  Ash CT13, CT3. . . . . .92 E8
  Tenterden TN30 . . . . .179 A7
Coombe Lands TN30 . . . . .188 D4
Coombe Rd
  Crabble CT17. . . . . .148 F1
  Dover CT15, CT17. . . . . . .165 E8
  Folkestone CT19 . . . . .177 F6
  Maidstone ME15. . . . . .74 F2
Coombe Valley Rd CT17 .149 A1
Coombe Way CT18. . . . . . .163 C4
Coombe Wlk CT5 . . . . .43 A2
Coombe Wood La CT18 .163 C4
Cooper Rd ME5. . . . . .32 B3
Cooper's Hill CT6. . . . . .22 F5
Coopers La CT1. . . . . .87 E7
Cooper's La TN25 . . . . .158 F2
Cooper Street Dr 72 B4
Cooper Street Drove CT3.72 B4
Cooting La CT3. . . . . .112 D8
Cooting Rd CT3. . . . . .112 C4
Copenhagen Rd ME7. . . . . .10 C4
Copinger CI CT2. . . . . .67 A4
Copland Ave ME12. . . . . .4 C6
Copperfield ME12. . . . . .5 F5
Copperfield CI
  Ashford TN24. . . . . .139 C6
  Kingswood ME17. . . . . . . .99 D2
Copperfield Ct CT10 . . . . . .30 B5
Copperfield Dr ME17. . . . . .98 E4
Copperfield Ho **6** ME4. . . .9 F4
Copperfield Rd ME1. . . . . . .9 C2
Copperfields TN29 . . . . . . .205 B6
Copperfields The ME1. . . . . .9 B4
Coppergate
  Canterbury CT2. . . . . .66 F2
  Gillingham ME7. . . . . .32 F5
Copperhouse La ME7. . . . . .11 B6
Copperhurst Wlk CT9 . . . . . .8 F2
Copperpenny Dr ME7. . . . . .33 B3
Copper Tree Ct ME15. . . . . .97 A5
Copper Tree Wlk ME5. . . . .32 C1
Copperwood TN24 . . . . . . .139 C4
Coppice Ct ME7. . . . . .33 B4
Coppice Rd ME5. . . . . .32 C2
Coppice The
  Hythe CT21. . . . . .176 B4
  Sturry CT2. . . . . .67 E6
Copse CI ME1. . . . . .9 E1
Copse The TN23. . . . . .138 D3
Copsewood Way ME4. . . . . .76 A3
COP STREET 71 E4
Cop Street Rd CT3. . . . . . . .71 D3
Copt CI CT2. . . . . .67 F7
Copthall Gdns **4** CT20 .178 D5
Coral Pk ME14. . . . . .75 B5
Coral Rd ME12. . . . . .4 B5
Corben CI ME16 . . . . .74 B6
Cordelia Cres ME1 . . . . .9 A2
Cordingham Rd CT5. . . . . . .43 A6
Cordova Ct CT20. . . . . .178 B4
Corianda Dr **14** ME16. . . . .74 A3
Corkwell St ME14. . . . . .9 E3
Cormorant Rd ME9 . . . . . . .14 E3
Cormorant Way CT6 . . . . . .23 F4
Cornbrook Rd CT21 . . . . .187 D8
Cornelis Dr CT12 . . . . .50 B5
Corner Cotts TN26 . . . . . . .182 A6
Corner Field TN23 . . . . . . .156 B5
Cornes CT24 . . . . .140 A1
Cornflower La ME14. . . . . . .75 E4

Cornford Rd CT7. . . . . .27 A7
Cornforth Dr ME9. . . . . .58 E6
Corniche The CT20. . . . . . .177 C3
Cornwall Ave CT11. . . . . . . .52 F8
Cornwall CI ME15. . . . . .97 E7
Cornwall Gdns
  Canterbury CT1. . . . . .88 D7
  Margate CT9 . . . . .8 B3
Cornwall Ho
  Deal CT14 . . . . .117 A5
  5 Dover CT17. . . . . . . .166 D7
Cornwallis Ave
  Aylesham CT3 . . . . .112 F6
  Chatham ME4. . . . . .9 A1
  Gillingham ME8 . . . . .11 A4
  Herne Bay CT6. . . . . .23 C3
Cornwallis Circ CT5. . . . . . .20 D1
Cornwallis CI
  Ashford TN24. . . . . .157 B7
  Folkestone CT19 . . . . .178 B6
Cornwallis Cotts ME17. .96 E2
Cornwallis Gdns CT10. . . . .30 A6
Cornwallis Rd ME16. . . . . . .74 D4
Cornwallis Rdbt ME8. . . . . .11 A4
Cornwallis Sch ME15. . . . . .96 F1
Cornwall Rd
  Deal CT14 . . . . .117 C3
  Gillingham ME7. . . . . .10 D6
  Herne Bay CT6. . . . . .22 B2
  Rochester ME1 . . . . .9 C3
Coronation CI CT10 . . . . . . .29 E7
Coronation Cotts
  Coronation Cres
  Margate CT9 . . . . .28 B8
  Queenborough ME11. . . . . .2 F5
Coronation Dr
  Ashford TN23. . . . . .138 C1
  Leysdown-on-Sea ME12. . . .6 D2
Coronation Flats ME4 . . . .9 F3
Coronation Rd
  Chatham ME5. . . . . .10 C2
  Ramsgate CT11. . . . . .52 D6
  Sheerness ME12. . . . . .1 E1
Coronation Sq TN29. . . . .205 C6
Corone CI CT19 . . . . .178 A7
Corporation Rd ME7. . . . . . . .10 D7
Corporation St ME1. . . . . . . .9 C6
Corral CI ME5. . . . . .32 C1
Corral Almshouses **5**
  ME15. . . . . .75 A3
Corrance Gn ME15. . . . . . . .97 A8
Corsican Wlk CT5 . . . . .23 C3
Cortanore ME10 . . . . .36 E2
Cortland CI ME10 . . . . .36 E6
Cortland Mews ME10. . . . . .36 E6
Corunna CI CT21. . . . . .176 A2
Corunna PI CT15. . . . . .149 E3
Corylus Dr CT5 . . . . .43 A7
Cory's Rd ME1. . . . . .9 D6
Cossack St ME1. . . . . .9 D3
Cossington Rd
  Canterbury CT1. . . . . .88 A7
  Chatham ME5. . . . . .32 B1
Cosway Cotts TN25. . . . . .172 C1
Cotswold Cl TN24. . . . . . . .139 B4
Cotswold Gdns ME15. . . . .76 A2
Cottage Ind Est ME20. . . . .53 B2
Cottage Rd
  Chatham ME4. . . . . .9 F6
  Ramsgate CT11. . . . . .52 E6
Cottage Row ME4. . . . . .9 F2
Cottall Ave ME4. . . . . .9 F2
Cottington Rd CT12. . . . . . .51 B5
Cotton Hill Ho TN26. . . . . .183 A7
Cotton Hill Wlk TN26. . . . .183 A7
Cotton Rd CT11. . . . . .87 E7
Coulman St ME7. . . . . .10 D5
Coulson Gr CT14. . . . . .116 A5
Coulter Rd
  Ashford TN23. . . . . .155 D5
  Herne Bay CT6. . . . . .22 B2
Coulters CI ME14. . . . . .75 D5
Coultrip CI ME12. . . . . .5 B5
Council Cotts ME15. . . . . . .96 F4
Countess Mountbatten Ct
  CT8. . . . . .27 E8
Country's Field TN29 . . .195 C8
Country Ways ME17. . . . . .102 D3
County Rd ME14. . . . . .75 A5
County Sq **8** TN23. . . . .139 B2
County Square Sh Ctr **16**
  TN25 . . . . .139 B2
COURT-AT-STREET 174 A4
Court Cotts
  St Nicholas at Wade CT7. . .25 E2
  Wingham CT3 . . . . .91 A7
Court Dr ME16. . . . . .74 D4
Courtenay Ho ME13. . . . . . .64 C3
Courtenay Rd
  Boughton Street CT2,
  ME13. . . . . .64 E5
  Deal CT14 . . . . .117 C8
  Maidstone ME15. . . . . .74 F2
Courteney Rd ME8. . . . . . . .33 B8
Courten Rd CT12. . . . . .64 F6
Courtfield Ave ME5. . . . . . . .32 B3
Court Flats CT3. . . . . .91 A7
Court Hill ME1 . . . . .2 F5
Court Hill CT12. . . . . .68 C2
Court Hill Ho CT16. . . . . . .148 E4
Court La
  Detling ME14. . . . . .55 C5
  Preston CT3. . . . . .70 B6
Courtland Ave CT16. . . . . .149 A6
Courtland Dr CT16. . . . . . .148 E4
Courtlands
  Deal CT14 . . . . .134 C6

Courtlands continued
  Herne Bay CT6. . . . . .23 B3
Courtlands CI CT12. . . . . . . .51 E5
Courtlands Way CT8 . . . . . . .7 D1
Court Lodge CT14. . . . . . . .117 B6
Court Lodge Cotts ME15 . .96 A7
Court Lodge Rd
  Appledore TN26. . . . . . . .190 C2
  Gillingham ME7. . . . . .10 F6
Court Mdw ME8 . . . . .11 B2
Court Mdws CT3. . . . . .89 F8
Court Mews CT3. . . . . .89 F8
Court Mount CT7. . . . . .27 A6
Court PI **5** CT20. . . . . . .178 C4
Court Rd
  Burham ME1. . . . . .53 A8
  Deal CT14 . . . . .117 B1
  Sittingbourne ME10. . . . . . .36 F7
  St Nicholas at Wade CT7 . .25 E2
Court St ME13. . . . . .62 D7
Courts The CT9. . . . . .7 E1
Court Wurtin TN23. . . . . . .156 A7
Courtyard The TN24. . . . . .156 F6
Courtyard The ME8 . . . . . . .33 A8
Courtyard The CT3. . . . . . . .89 A2
Coventon La CT14 . . . . .94 A5
Coventry Gdns CT6 . . . . . . .23 E5
Coverdale Ave ME15 . . . . . .97 D6
Coverdale CI ME5. . . . . .32 B7
Covert TN23. . . . . .138 C1
Covert Rd CT3. . . . . .112 E4
Covert The ME5. . . . . .32 B1
Covet La CT4 . . . . .111 C2
Cowbeck CI ME8. . . . . .33 D6
Cowden Rd ME14. . . . . .75 C5
Cowdray Rd CT14 . . . . .117 A3
Cowdray Sq CT14 . . . . .117 A3
Cowdrey CI
  Ashford TN24. . . . . .157 A7
  Maidstone ME16. . . . . .74 B2
  Rochester ME1 . . . . .9 E3
Cowdrey PI CT1. . . . . .88 B6
Cowgate Hill CT17. . . . . . .166 D7
Cowgate La CT18. . . . . .163 C5
Cow La
  Canterbury CT1. . . . . .87 D7
  Dover CT17. . . . . .166 A7
Cowley Rise CT9. . . . . .29 C8
Cowper CI CT5 . . . . .21 D3
Cowper Rd
  Crabble CT17. . . . . .148 E3
  Deal CT14 . . . . .117 C5
  Gillingham ME7. . . . . .10 D3
  Margate CT9 . . . . .7 J1
  Sittingbourne ME10. . . . . . .37 B4
Cowstead La ME9. . . . . .34 D3
Cowstead Rd ME9. . . . . .34 D2
Cox Dr CT18. . . . . .163 A5
Coxes Ave CT12. . . . . .29 B3
Coxes La CT12. . . . . .29 B3
Coxett Hill ME13. . . . . .61 D5
Cox Gdns ME8. . . . . .11 A2
Cox St ME14. . . . . .55 E6
Cozenton CI ME8. . . . . .11 E1
CRABBLE. 148 F2
Crabble Ave CT17. . . . . . . .149 A2
Crabble CI CT17. . . . . .148 F2
Crabble Corn Mill*
  . . . . .148 F3
Crabble Hill CT16, CT17. .149 A2
Crabble La CT17. . . . . .148 E2
Crabble Mdws CT17. . . . . .149 A2
Crabble Rd CT17. . . . . .149 A3
Crabtree La ME17. . . . . . . .119 B8
Crabtree Rd ME8. . . . . .33 D8
Crabtree Rdbt ME14. . . . . . .53 E2
Craddock Dr **8** CT1. . . . . .67 B1
Craddock Ho CT1. . . . . .67 B1
Craddock Rd CT1. . . . . .67 B1
Craddock Way ME8. . . . . . . .33 D5
Cradle Bridge Dr TN24. . .139 F2
Cradles Rd ME9. . . . . .34 C2
Crafford St CT16. . . . . .149 D1
Cragie Wlk ME8 . . . . .33 E4
Craig Ho ME1. . . . . .9 E1
Craighton Ho **2** CT16 .166 E7
Crampton Ct CT14 . . . . .30 A4
Crampton Tower Mus* **7**
  CT10. . . . . .30 A4
Cranborne Ave ME15. . . . . .75 C1
Cranborne Wlk CT16 . . . . . .66 E3
Cranbourne Ave ME15. . . . .97 B8
Cranbourne CI CT11 . . . . . .52 F8
Cranbrook CI
  Gillingham ME8 . . . . .11 C3
  Maidstone ME15. . . . . .97 F7
  Margate CT9 . . . . .8 E1
Cranbrook Dr ME10. . . . . . .36 D1
Cranbrooks TN25. . . . . . . .157 D4
Cranford CI ME8. . . . . .11 D1
Cranleigh Ct CT13. . . . . .43 E8
Cranleigh Dr CT16. . . . . . .149 B7
Cranleigh Gdns
  Chatham ME4. . . . . .9 D3
  Maidstone ME14. . . . . .74 C7
  Whitstable CT5. . . . . .43 E8
Cranmer CI CT4 . . . . .89 B4
Cranmer CI ME5. . . . . .97 B8
Cranmere Ct ME7. . . . . .32 F6
Cranmer Ho **6** CT2. . . . . .66 E1
Cranswick Cotts CT14. . . .133 C8
Craufurd Gn CT20. . . . . . . .177 D5

Craven CI CT9 . . . . .28 C8
Crawford Gdns CT9. . . . . . . .8 B2
Crawford Rd CT9 . . . . .29 F5
Crayford CI ME14 . . . . .75 C6
Craythorne TN30. . . . . .179 B8
Craythorne CI
  Hythe CT21. . . . . .177 B4
  New Romney TN28. . . . . .202 B8
Craythorne Ho TN30 . . . . .179 B8
Craythorne La TN28. . . . . .202 B7
Creighton Flats **2** CT13. .72 F1
Creine Mill Lane N CT1. . . .87 E8
Cremer CI CT4. . . . . .86 C2
Cremer PI ME13. . . . . .62 A8
Cremers Rd ME10. . . . . .37 B5
Crescent Ho
  Margate CT9 . . . . .8 A2
  Ramsgate CT12. . . . . .52 C7
  Rochester ME2 . . . . .9 C7
Crescent Rd
  Birchington CT7. . . . . .27 A7
  Broadstairs CT10. . . . . . . .30 C8
  Faversham ME13. . . . . .62 D7
  Margate CT9 . . . . .7 H2
  Ramsgate CT11. . . . . .52 D7
Crescent St **8** ME10 . . . . .36 F4
Crescent The
  Aylesham CT15 . . . . .113 A3
  Boughton Street ME13 . . . .64 A3
  Canterbury CT2. . . . . .66 F4
  Chartham CT4 . . . . .86 D1
  Chatham ME4. . . . . .9 B8
  Eythorne CT15 . . . . .131 C2
  Folkestone CT20 . . . . .177 E3
  Halfway Houses ME12. . . . . .3 E6
  Lower Halstow ME9. . . . . . .13 C3
  Maidstone ME14. . . . . .74 F8
  Sandwich CT13 . . . . .93 E6
  Sheerness ME13. . . . . .1 D2
  Sheerness ME12. . . . . .1 H1
  Sittingbourne ME10. . . . . . .15 A1
  St Margaret's at Cliffe
  CT15. . . . . .151 A5
  Teynham ME9. . . . . .38 D3
Crescent Way ME5. . . . . .31 D5
Cressey Ct **7** ME4 . . . . . . .9 E4
Cressfield TN23. . . . . .139 A3
Cress Way TN23 . . . . .62 A7
Cresta CI CT6. . . . . .21 F4
Crest Rd ME1. . . . . .31 C5
Crestway ME5. . . . . .32 B8
Crete Road E CT18, CT19 .163 D1
Crete Road W CT18. . . . . .163 B1
Creteway CI CT19 . . . . .178 E8
Creve Coeur CI ME14. . . . . .76 A5
Crevequer Chambers **1**
  ME8 . . . . .11 F1
Cricketers CI
  Harrietsham ME17. . . . . .100 D6
  Hawkinge CT18 . . . . .163 B6
  Sittingbourne ME10. . . . . . .37 A8
Crimond Ave TN29 . . . . . .187 A4
Criol Rd TN26. . . . . .155 A2
Cripple Hill TN26. . . . . .152 D1
Cripple St ME15. . . . . .97 A7
Cripps Ct CT13. . . . . .112 E5
Cripps' La CT15. . . . . .150 F6
Crisfield Ct TN30. . . . . .167 B2
Crismill La ME14. . . . . .76 F4
Crispe CI ME8 . . . . .33 D4
Crispe Park CI CT7. . . . . . . .27 B7
Crispe Rd CT7. . . . . .27 B7
Crispin Ct ME13. . . . . .62 D8
Crispin Ct ME17 . . . . .96 C3
Crittenden Bglws ME15. . . .96 A4
Crittenden Cotts ME15. . . .96 A4
Crocken Hill Rd TN27. . . . .118 C2
Crockham La ME13. . . . . . . .64 B6
Crockham Rd ME13. . . . . . . .64 C6
Crockshard Hill CT3. . . . . . .91 B4
Crockshard La CT3. . . . . . . .91 B4
Crocus Dr ME9/ME10. . . . .36 F2
Croft CI ME5. . . . . .32 C1
Crofters CI CT21. . . . . .187 E8
Crofters The ME8 . . . . .33 F4
Croft Gdns ME17. . . . . .101 C4
Croft La CT20. . . . . .177 F5
Crofton CI TN24. . . . . .139 C6
Crofton Rd CT8. . . . . .27 E7
Croft Rd TN24 . . . . .139 D2
Croft The TN30. . . . . .179 B7
Croftwood TN23. . . . . .155 D6
Croidene Ct ME12. . . . . .4 A6
Crombie CI CT18. . . . . .163 B5
Cromer Rd
  Rochester ME2 . . . . .9 B8
  Sittingbourne ME9, ME10. . .58 F8
Crompton Gdns ME15. . . . .75 B3
Cromwell Park PI CT20. . .177 D4
Cromwell Rd
  Canterbury CT1. . . . . .88 A6
  Maidstone ME14. . . . . .75 B5
  West Minst ME11 . . . . .2 F3
  Whitstable CT5. . . . . .20 E1
Cromwell Terr ME14 . . . . . .10 A3
Crooked South Rd CT14. .133 C7
Crookenden PI CT14 . . . . .128 F8
Crook's Court La CT15 . . .164 F4
Croombridge Dr ME7 . . . .10 F6
Crosier CI ME9 . . . . .12 E3
Crosley Rd ME7. . . . . .10 D3
Cross Dr ME17. . . . . .99 B1
Cross Keys ME5. . . . . .76 C4
Cross La
  7 Faversham ME13. . . . .62 D7
  Sittingbourne ME10. . . . . . .36 E6
  Throwley Forstal ME13 . . .104 C7

Crossley Ave CT6 . . . . .21 F4
Cross Rd
  Birchington CT7. . . . . .27 B8
  Deal CT14 . . . . .117 A2
Cross St
  2 Canterbury CT2 . . . . . .66 E1
  Chatham ME4. . . . . .10 C6
  Gillingham ME7. . . . . .10 C6
  Herne Bay CT6. . . . . .22 D3
  Maidstone ME14. . . . . .75 A6
  Rochester ME2 . . . . .9 B8
Cross Stile TN23. . . . . .155 F8
Cross The CT13 . . . . .93 B2
Crossway ME5 . . . . .31 E6
Cross Way ME1 . . . . .9 C3
Crossways
  Canterbury CT2. . . . . .66 F4
  Chart Sutton ME17 . . . . . .98 B1
  Sittingbourne ME10. . . . . . .36 F1
Crossways Ave CT9 . . . . . . .29 A5
Crossways CI TN29. . . . . . .186 E2
Crouch Cotts ME13 . . . . . . .84 E8
Crouch Hill Ct ME9 . . . . . . .13 C3
Crouch La ME13. . . . . .84 E8
Crowbridge Link TN24. . . .156 F7
Crowbridge Rd TN24 . . . . .156 F6
Crow Cnr
  Brabourne TN25. . . . . .141 E4
  Rochester ME1 . . . . .9 C5
Crow Hill CT10. . . . . .30 B5
Crow Hill Rd CT9 . . . . .28 B8
Crow La ME1 . . . . .9 C5
Crow The CT14. . . . . .117 D6
Crownfield Rd TN23. . . . . .155 F8
Crownfields ME14. . . . . .75 E4
Crown Gdns CT2. . . . . .66 E1
Crown Hill Rd CT6 . . . . .22 C4
Crown Ho ME1. . . . . .9 B4
Crown La CT4. . . . . .126 E3
Crown Quay La **5** ME10. .37 A4
Crown Rd ME10. . . . . .36 E6
Crows Camp Rd CT14 . . . .111 A5
Croydon CI ME5. . . . . .32 C4
Cruise Liner Terminals
  CT17. . . . . .166 C5
CRUNDALE. 124 D7
Crundale **2** ME14 . . . . . . .75 A5
Crundale CI TN23. . . . . .155 F6
Crundale Rd ME8 . . . . .11 C3
Crundale Way CT9. . . . . .8 E1
Crusader CI ME8. . . . . .33 J8
Cryalls Bsns Est ME10. . . . .36 C4
Cryalls La ME10, ME9 . . . . .36 C3
Cryol Rd TN23. . . . . .156 A2
Crystal Bsns Ctr CT13. . . . .73 B2
Ctr for European Agri-
  Environmental Studies
  TN25 . . . . .124 A1
Cubitt Ho CT19 . . . . .178 D6
Cuckolds Cnr
  Chillenden CT3. . . . . .114 A7
  Snargate TN29. . . . . .191 E7
Cuckold's Cnr TN26. . . . . .168 B7
Cuckoo La
  Ashford, Singleton TN23 . .155 E7
  Ashford TN23. . . . . .155 D6
  Posting CT21. . . . . .160 F2
Cuckoowood Ave ME14. . .53 F1
Cudham CT4 . . . . .75 C6
Cudham Gdns CT9. . . . . . . .30 C8
Cudworth Rd TN24. . . . . . .156 E7
Cullens Hill CT4 . . . . .144 F4
Cullet Dr ME1. . . . . .3 A3
Culling's Hill CT4. . . . . .144 F4
Culmers CT15. . . . . .41 E1
Culmers Terr ME13. . . . . . . .63 E8
Culpeper CI
  Hollingbourne ME17. . . . . .77 E2
  Rochester ME2 . . . . .9 C6
Culpeper Ct CT2. . . . . .67 A4
Culpeper Rd
  Coxheath ME17 . . . . .96 B3
  Gillingham ME8. . . . . .33 D4
Culter Field TN23. . . . . .155 E8
Culver's La TN29. . . . . .205 D5
Cumberland Ave
  Broadstairs CT10. . . . . . . .30 A5
  Canterbury CT1. . . . . .88 D7
  Maidstone ME15. . . . . .97 D8
Cumberland Dr ME9 . . . . . .13 C3
Cumberland Rd
  Chatham ME4, ME7. . . . . . .10 B7
  Gillingham ME7. . . . . .10 D7
  Margate CT9 . . . . .8 B3
  1 Ramsgate CT11. . . . . .52 D6
Cundishall CI CT15. . . . . . . .43 C8
Cunningham Cres
  Birchington CT7. . . . . .26 E7
  Chatham ME5. . . . . .32 A8
Cunningham Ho ME1 . . . . . .9 B4
Curlew Ave ME9 . . . . .14 E3
Curlew CI CT6 . . . . .23 C2
Curlew PI CT18 . . . . .163 A3
Curlinge Ct CT11 . . . . .52 A6
Curteis Rd TN30 . . . . .167 B1
Curtis La CT4. . . . . .126 D2
Curtis Rd TN24. . . . . .156 E7
Curtis Way
  1 Faversham ME13. . . . .62 C7
  Rochester ME1 . . . . .9 E3
Curtis Wood Park Rd CT6. .46 A7
Curtis Wood Pk Rd CT6. . .45 E7
Curtis Wood Rd CT6. . . . . .45 F7
Curzon CI CT14. . . . . .117 C3
Curzon Ho **5** CT11 . . . . . .52 D6
Curzon Rd
  Chatham ME4. . . . . .9 F3

Curzon Rd continued
Dover CT17 . . . . .166 B8
Maidstone ME14 . . . . .75 A6
Cushings Wlk 13 CT5 . . . .20 D2
Cushman Rd CT1 . . . . .87 E7
Cutbush Almshouses
  3 Maidstone ME14 . . . . .75 A4
  3 Maidstone ME15 . . . . .75 A3
Cutbush CI ME17 . . . . .100 D6
Cutbush & Corrall Ct 1
  ME14 . . . . .75 B4
Cutbush Ho 2 ME15 . . . . .75 A3
Cuthbert Rd CT8 . . . . .27 E8
Cut The 17 ME4/ME7 . . . . .10 A6
Cuttings The CT12 . . . . . . .52 C8
Cuxton CI 11 ME15 . . . . . . .97 F5
Curzon Rd
Maidstone ME15 . . . . .97 F5
Rochester ME2 . . . . .9 A7
Cygnet Rd ME5 . . . . .32 C2
Cygnet Way TN23 . . . . . . .138 F2
Cylinder Rd CT21 . . . . .176 B4
Cypress Ave TN23 . . . . . . .138 E2
Cypress CI CT5 . . . . .43 C2
Cypress Ct ME7 . . . . .10 F6
Cypress Gr CT15 . . . . .114 B2
Cyprus CI ME13 . . . . .62 E7
Cyprus Rd ME13 . . . . .62 E7

D

D2 Trad Est ME10 . . . . .37 B6
Daglish CI TN28 . . . . .202 B6
Dagmar Rd ME4 . . . . .10 B2
Daigor La CT12 . . . . .28 D1
Daimler Ave CT6 . . . . .22 B3
Dajen Bsns Pk ME4 . . . . . . .10 C1
Dalby CT9 . . . . .8 A3
Dalby Sq CT9 . . . . .8 A3
Daleacres Cvn Pk CT21 . .186 E7
Dale CI ME5 . . . . .32 A2
Dale Rd ME1 . . . . .9 C3
Dale St ME4 . . . . .9 E2
Dale Wlk TN24 . . . . .139 C7
Dalewood ME10 . . . . .37 A2
Dallas-Brett Cres CT19 . .178 E8
Dallinger Rd 1 CT7 . . . . . .26 F8
Dalmatia Ct CT17 . . . . . . .149 A1
Dalmeny Ave CT9 . . . . .8 D1
Dalmeny Terr CT21 . . . . . .176 A1
Dalton CI 7 CT11 . . . . .52 E7
Dalton St ME7 . . . . .10 C6
Dame Janet Com Jun Sch
  CT12 . . . . .29 B2
Dame Janet Inf Sch CT12 .29 B2
Damerham CI CT2 . . . . .66 E3
Damien CI ME4 . . . . .10 A2
DANAWAY 35 C3
Danaway Cotts ME9 . . . . . .35 C3
Dan Dr ME13 . . . . .62 A8
Dane CI
Chatham ME5 . . . . .32 C2
Hartlip ME9 . . . . .34 D6
Danecourt Com Sch ME8 .11 A2
Dane Court Gram Sch
  CT14 . . . . .29 E4
Dane Court Rd CT10 . . . . .29 C6
Dane Cres CT11 . . . . .52 E8
Dane Ct
Coxheath ME17 . . . . .96 C2
Tilmanstone CT14 . . . . . .114 F4
Danedale Ave ME12 . . . . . .4 F6
Dane End Rd CT3 . . . . .27 D8
Danefield Ct ME14 . . . . . . .76 B4
Dane Gdns CT9 . . . . .29 B8
Dane Hill CT9 . . . . .7 J3
Dane Hill Gr CT9 . . . . .7 J2
Dane Hill Row CT9 . . . . . . .7 J2
Dane Ho CT17 . . . . .117 D8
Danehurst CT8 . . . . .7 C1
Dane John CI 3 CT1 . . . . .87 F7
Dane John Mews 11 CT1 .87 F7
Dane Johns CT1 . . . . .87 F7
Dane La ME9 . . . . .34 D6
Danemore TN30 . . . . .179 B8
Dane Mount CT9 . . . . .29 C8
Dane Park Rd
Margate CT9 . . . . .7 J2
Ramsgate CT11 . . . . .52 E8
Dane Park Villas CT9 . . . . .8 A2
Dane Pk ME15 . . . . .96 C6
Dane Rd
Birchington CT7 . . . . .26 D7
Margate CT9 . . . . .8 A2
Ramsgate CT11 . . . . .52 E8
Dane Rise CT9 . . . . .29 C8
Danes Ct CT16 . . . . .149 D2
Danes Dr ME12 . . . . .6 D2
Danes Hill ME7 . . . . .11 A6
Danes Mead ME10 . . . . . . .14 F1
Danesmead Terr CT9 . . . . .7 J2
DANE STREET 106 F6
Dane Valley Rd CT10 . . . . .29 C8
Daniel Ho 5 ME16 . . . . . . .74 E5
Daniels CI CT5 . . . . .20 C1
DANIEL'S WATER 154 D7
Danley Mid Sch ME12 . . . . .3 E7
Danley Rd ME12 . . . . .3 E7
Danson Way ME11 . . . . . . .11 D2
Danton La CT18 . . . . .162 C1
Darby PI CT20 . . . . .178 D5
Darby Rd CT20 . . . . .178 D5
Darcy Sq TN28 . . . . .202 E5
Darenth Ct CT6 . . . . .23 B3
Darenth Rise ME5 . . . . .32 B3
DARGATE 64 E7

Dargate CI ME16 . . . . . . .74 D7
Dargate Rd
Dargate CT2, ME13 . . . . . .64 F7
Yorkletts CT5 . . . . .43 A3
Dargets Rd ME5 . . . . .32 A3
Dark Hill ME13 . . . . .62 C8
DARLAND 32 E8
Darland Ave ME7 . . . . .10 E1
Darlinghurst Rd CT19 . . .177 E7
Darlington Dr ME12 . . . . . .4 A6
Darlington St CT20 . . . . . .178 D5
Darnley CI
Broadstairs CT10 . . . . .29 F3
Folkestone CT20 . . . . .177 F4
Darnley Rd ME2 . . . . .9 A6
Darracott Ct CT14 . . . . . .117 B5
Darrell CI CT6 . . . . .22 C3
Darren Gdns CT10 . . . . . . .29 F2
Darwin Coll CT2 . . . . .66 E5
Darwin Ct ME1 . . . . .9 C5
Darwin Rd
Birchington CT7 . . . . .26 F8
Canterbury CT2 . . . . .66 E5
Daryngton Ave CT7 . . . . . .26 C7
Davenport Ave ME17 . . . . .10 E7
Davey CI ME1 . . . . .9 C5
David Ave CT9 . . . . .8 D2
Davids CI CT10 . . . . .30 B3
Davidson Rd CT2 . . . . .66 D1
Davie CI ME12 . . . . .3 B8
Davie CI ME14 . . . . .3 B8
DAVINGTON 62 A8
Davington Hill ME13 . . . . .62 C8
Davington Prim Sch
  ME13 . . . . .62 C8
Davis Ave CT14 . . . . .117 A4
Dawbourne TN30 . . . . . . .167 B3
Dawes Rd CT2, ME13 . . . . .64 F4
Dawes St ME7 . . . . .10 C5
Dawn Rise ME12 . . . . .5 F6
Dawson Ct 7 ME7 . . . . . .10 A6
Dawson Rd CT9 . . . . .178 D6
Dawson's Row ME13 . . . . .62 A6
Day Ho 2 ME14 . . . . .75 B4
Daytona Way CT6 . . . . .22 A4
Dayton Rd ME13 . . . . .83 C3
Deacon Ind Est ME20 . . . .53 A2
Deacon Trad Ctr ME2 . . . . .9 B4
DEAL 117 E6
Deal Castle* CT14 . . . . . .117 E5
Deal Castle Rd CT14 . . . .117 D5
Deal Ent Ctr CT14 . . . . . .117 C7
Deal Ho ME15 . . . . .97 E8
Deal Maritime & Local
  History Mus* 12 CT14 .117 D6
Deal Parochial CE Prim Sch
  CT14 . . . . .117 C3
Deal Rd
Northbourne CT14 . . . . . .116 A4
Sandwich CT13, CT14 . . . .93 F5
Deal Sta CT14 . . . . .117 C6
Dean Croft CT6 . . . . .23 B2
Dean Ct 13 CT1 . . . . .67 A1
Deane CI CT5 . . . . .43 E7
Deane Ct 8 ME7 . . . . .10 C6
Dean Hill CT4, TN25 . . . . .126 B2
Dean Mead CT19 . . . . . . .178 B7
Dean Rd ME10 . . . . .36 E6
DEANS BOTTOM 57 C5
DEANS HILL 57 D6
Deans Hill Rd ME9 . . . . . . .57 D5
Deans Mill Ct CT1 . . . . . . .66 F1
Dean St ME15 . . . . .96 C1
DEAN STREET 96 D7
Deansway Ave CT2 . . . . . . .67 F7
Dean's Wlk TN23 . . . . . . .155 F7
Deanwood CI ME8 . . . . . . .33 D6
Deanwood Dr ME8 . . . . . . .33 E4
**Deanwood Prim Education
  Tech Sch** ME8 . . . . .33 D3
Deanwood Rd CT17 . . . . .148 E2
Deborah CI CT5 . . . . .43 F7
De Burgh Hill CT17 . . . . .149 C1
De Burgh St 2 CT17 . . . .166 C8
Deedes CI CT21 . . . . .176 C3
Deerhurst Gdns ME16 . . . .74 D4
Deerson La CT3 . . . . .70 A4
Deerton St ME9 . . . . .39 A2
DEERTON STREET 39 A2
Defiant CI ME5 . . . . .32 B6
Defoe CI ME5 . . . . .32 B6
Deham Ho ME10 . . . . .10 F6
De Havillands CI CT18 . . .163 B4
De Havillands CT4 . . . . . . .89 E3
Delacourt CI CT12 . . . . . . .51 D5
Delamark Rd ME12 . . . . . . .1 D2
Delane Rd CT14 . . . . .117 A5
De l'Angle Ho CT4 . . . . . . .86 D3
De l'Angle Row CT4 . . . . . .86 D3
Delaware CI CT7 . . . . .67 F6
Delce Jun & Inf Schs ME1 . .9 D2
Delce Rd ME1 . . . . .9 D4
Delfside CT13 . . . . .94 A8
Delf St CT13 . . . . .72 F1
Delmaney CI CT10 . . . . . . .30 B5
Delmar CI CT5 . . . . .21 D3
De Mere CI ME8 . . . . .33 D6
Demozay CI CT18 . . . . . . .163 A4
Denbigh Ave ME8 . . . . .11 D1
Denbigh CI ME10 . . . . .36 E7
Denbigh Rd ME12 . . . . .29 A1
Dence CI CT6 . . . . .23 B5
Dence Pk CT6 . . . . .23 B4
Dencorra Way TN23 . . . . .139 A1
Dene Farm Barns CT3 . . . .91 A4
Dene Farm La CT3 . . . . . . .91 A4
Dene The
Bethersden TN26 . . . . . . .153 D5

Dene The continued
Canterbury CT1 . . . . .88 B5
Hythe CT21 . . . . .176 C2
Dene Wlk CT9 . . . . .28 F7
Dengemarsh Rd TN29 . . .208 A7
Denham CT7 . . . . .187 B4
Denham Rd ME9 . . . . .35 B7
Denmark CI CT11 . . . . .52 E8
Denmark St CT19 . . . . . . .178 E6
Denne CI CT2 . . . . .67 F7
Denne Manor La CT4 . . . .106 C8
Dennes Mill CI TN25 . . . .123 D2
Denness Rd TN23 . . . . . . .156 B7
Denning CI ME16 . . . . .74 B4
Dennis Way CT19 . . . . . . .177 E7
Dennis Wilcocks CI ME7 . .35 B6
DENSOLE 163 A8
Densole La CT18 . . . . .163 A8
Densole Way CT18 . . . . . .163 A8
Denstead Cotts CT4 . . . . . .86 B8
Denstead Ct CT2 . . . . .66 F5
Denstead La CT4, ME13 . . .86 C7
Denstead Oast CT4 . . . . . .86 B8
Denstead Wlk 11 ME15 . . .97 F8
DENSTROUDE 65 C8
Denstroude La CT2 . . . . . .65 D8
Dental CI ME10 . . . . .36 A5
Dental Ct ME7 . . . . .10 C6
Dent CI ME13 . . . . .176 C2
Dent-de-Lion Ct CT9 . . . . .28 A8
Dent-de-Lion Rd
Margate CT9 . . . . .28 A8
Westgate on Sea CT8 . . . . .7 C1
DENTON 129 B3
Denton CI ME15 . . . . .97 E8
Denton Gn ME8 . . . . .11 B4
Denton Way CT9 . . . . .8 C1
Derby CI ME10 . . . . .36 D6
Derby Rd
Gillingham ME8 . . . . .10 E2
Maidstone ME15 . . . . .97 C8
Dering CI
Bridge CT4 . . . . .88 F1
Pluckley TN27 . . . . .136 C4
Derings The TN29 . . . . . . .205 B6
Dering Terr TN27 . . . . .36 C3
Deringwood Dr ME15 . . . .75 F7
DERRINGSTONE 128 E7
Derringstone Downs
  CT4 . . . . .128 F6
Derringstone Hill CT4 . . .128 E6
Derringstone St CT4 . . . .128 F7
Derville Ho TN28 . . . . . . .202 B6
Derville Rd TN29 . . . . .206 F7
Derwent Ave CT11 . . . . . . .52 A7
Derwent Ho 3 ME15 . . . . .97 E7
Derwent Way
Aylesham CT3 . . . . .112 F6
Gillingham ME8 . . . . .33 D8
Desmond Cres ME13 . . . . .63 A5
D'Este Rd CT11 . . . . .52 F7
Detling CI ME8 . . . . .33 D5
Detling Ave CT10 . . . . .30 A1
Detling CI
Gillingham ME8 . . . . .11 C2
West Minst ME12 . . . . .3 B7
Detling Hill ME14 . . . . .55 B2
Devon Ave CT14 . . . . .117 C3
Devon CI
Chatham ME5 . . . . .32 C7
Gillingham ME8 . . . . .11 F1
Gillingham CT7 . . . . .29 B2
Devon Gdns CT7 . . . . .26 F7
Devon Rd
Canterbury CT1 . . . . .88 D3
Folkestone CT19 . . . . .178 D5
Maidstone ME15 . . . . .97 C8
Devonshire Gdns CT9 . . . . .8 C3
Devonshire Rd
Dover CT16 . . . . .166 B8
Gillingham ME7 . . . . .10 D7
Devonshire Terr CT10 . . . .30 B5
Dew La TN31 . . . . .196 A1
Dexter CI TN25 . . . . .139 C8
Deyley Way TN23 . . . . . . .155 C8
Dhekelia CI ME14 . . . . .75 A7
Dial CI ME7 . . . . .10 F6
Dial Rd ME7 . . . . .10 F6
Diamond Ct ME12 . . . . .1 C2
Diamond Rd CT5 . . . . .20 E2
Diana Gdns CT14 . . . . . . .117 A5
Diana Rd ME4 . . . . .10 A2
Dibdin Rd CT14 . . . . .117 D7
Dickens Ave CT1 . . . . .67 D2
Dickens CI ME17 . . . . .98 E4
Dickens CI ME2 . . . . .9 D8
Dickens House Mus*
  CT10 . . . . .30 B4
Dickens Rd
Broadstairs CT10 . . . . .30 B5
Maidstone ME14 . . . . .74 E8
Rochester ME1 . . . . .9 C2
Dickens Wlk CT10 . . . . . . .30 B4
Dickens World* ME4 . . . . .10 A8
Dickley La ME17 . . . . .101 A6
Dickson CI 2 ME10 . . . . . .37 B8
Dickson Rd CT17 . . . . . . .166 C8
Dicksons Bourne TN25 . .172 F6
Dickson's Cnr CT13 . . . . . .95 A4
Dieu Stone La CT16 . . . . .166 E8
Digby Rd CT20 . . . . .177 E5
Dignals CI ME8 . . . . .11 F2
Dignash TN25 . . . . .121 E2
Diligent Dr ME10 . . . . .36 F7

Dilnot La CT7 . . . . .27 B3
**Diocesan & Payne Smith CE
  Prim Sch** 22 CT1 . . . . . .67 A1
Discovery Rd ME15 . . . . . .76 B2
Discovery Wlk CT1 . . . . . . .88 C7
Disraeli CI ME15 . . . . .97 E5
Dixon CI ME15 . . . . .74 F2
Dixwell CI ME8 . . . . .33 D5
Dixwell Rd CT20 . . . . .178 A4
Dobbie CI ME10 . . . . .36 E6
Dock Exit Rd CT16 . . . . . .166 F8
Dock Head CT4 . . . . .10 A8
Dock Rd ME4 . . . . .9 F6
Dockside Outlet Ctr ME4 . .10 A8
Doctor's La CT15 . . . . .165 B5
DODDINGTON 80 E7
Doddington Ct ME16 . . . . .74 E5
Doddington Place Gdns*
  ME9 . . . . .81 A7
Doddington Rd ME8 . . . . . .11 D3
Dodd's La CT15 . . . . .149 A3
Does Alley 4 ME10 . . . . . .36 E5
Doggerel Acre CT5 . . . . . . .43 F7
Dog Kennel La CT18 . . . . .161 B7
Dogwood CI ME5 . . . . .32 D1
Dola Ave CT14 . . . . .117 B6
Dolphin CI CT10 . . . . .8 G3
Dolphin Dr ME8 . . . . .33 E5
Dolphin Ho
  1 Dover CT16 . . . . .166 E7
  2 .9 E5
Dolphin La CT16 . . . . .166 E7
Dolphin Pas 8 CT16 . . . . .166 E7
Dolphin PI 5 CT16 . . . . . .166 E7
Dolphin Rd
Lydd TN29 . . . . .205 C6
Sittingbourne ME10 . . . . . .37 B5
Dolphins Rd CT19 . . . . . . .178 D7
Dolphin St
Deal CT14 . . . . .117 D7
Herne Bay CT6 . . . . .22 E5
Dombey CI ME1 . . . . .9 C3
Domneva Rd
Minster (Thanet) CT12 . . . .50 B6
Westgate on Sea CT8 . . . . .27 D8
Donald Moor Ave ME9 . . . .38 C2
Donald Troup Ho ME1 . . . . .9 C4
Donatello CI 2 ME15 . . . . .97 F6
Donegal Rd CT1 . . . . .88 C8
Donemowe Dr ME8 . . . . . .36 F8
Donet CI ME8 . . . . .33 C5
Dongola Rd ME2 . . . . .9 B8
Donkey La
Adisham CT3 . . . . .112 C8
Appledore Heath TN26 . .181 C2
Donkey St CT21, TN29 . . .186 D5
DONKEY STREET 186 D5
Donnahay Rd CT12 . . . . . .29 C3
Donnithorne Ho CT6 . . . . .22 E5
Dorcas Gdns CT10 . . . . . . .30 A6
Doric Ct CT11 . . . . .52 C5
Dorman Avenue N CT3 . . .112 E6
Dorman Avenue S CT3 . . .112 F5
Dornden Gdns ME5 . . . . . .32 B2
Dorne Cotts TN27 . . . . . . .118 E6
Dorothy Dr CT12 . . . . .29 C2
Dorrit Way ME1 . . . . .9 D2
Dorset CI
Deal CT14 . . . . .117 D2
Ramsgate CT12 . . . . .29 B2
Dorset Gdns
Birchington CT7 . . . . .26 F7
Deal CT14 . . . . .117 C2
Dorset PI ME13 . . . . .62 C7
Dorset Rd
Canterbury CT1 . . . . .88 D3
West Minst ME12 . . . . .3 A8
Dorset Road Ind Est ME12 .3 A8
Dorset Sq ME8 . . . . .11 D1
Dorset Way ME15 . . . . .97 C8
Dossett Ct CT14 . . . . .117 A2
Dotterel CI ME5 . . . . .32 D2
Doubleday Dr ME9 . . . . . . .37 E2
Douglas Almshouses
  ME7 . . . . .101 C5
Douglas Ave
Hythe CT21 . . . . .176 C2
Whitstable CT5 . . . . .20 E1
Douglas Bglws CT15 . . . . .132 E8
Douglas CI CT10 . . . . .29 E5
Douglas Rd
Deal CT14 . . . . .117 D2
Dover CT17 . . . . .166 B8
Herne Bay CT6 . . . . .23 A4
Lenham ME17 . . . . .101 D5
Maidstone ME16 . . . . .74 E3
Douglas Terr CT14 . . . . . .117 D6
Dour Ho CT16 . . . . .166 D8
Dour Mews 12 CT16 . . . . .166 D8
Douro CI CT1 . . . . .67 D1
Douro PI CT16 . . . . .166 E7
Dour Side CT17 . . . . .148 F3
Dour St CT16 . . . . .166 D8
Doust Way ME1 . . . . .9 D5
Dove CI
Chatham ME5 . . . . .32 B6
Hythe CT21 . . . . .187 D8
Kingsnorth TN23 . . . . . . .156 C3
Whitstable CT5 . . . . .43 C7
Dovecote CT4 . . . . .107 B8
Dove Ct 6 CT11 . . . . .52 E7
Dovedale CT7 . . . . .27 B7
Dovedale Ct
Ashford TN24 . . . . .139 B4
Birchington CT7 . . . . .27 B7
Dove Lea Gdns CT17 . . . .148 E3

DOVER 166 F7
**Dover Castle & Princess of
  Wales Regiment Mus***
  CT16 . . . . .166 F8
Dover Coll CT17 . . . . .166 C8
Dover Discovery Ctr* 20
  CT16 . . . . .166 D7
Dover Gram Sch for Boys
  CT17 . . . . .166 A8
Dover Gram Sch for Girls
  CT16 . . . . .149 C1
Dover Hill CT19 . . . . .178 F8
Dover Ho 2 ME15 . . . . . . .97 E8
Dover L Ctr CT17 . . . . . . .166 E8
Dover Mus* CT16 . . . . . . .166 D7
Dover Patrol Meml*
  CT15 . . . . .151 C2
Dover PI TN23 . . . . .139 C1
Dover Priory Sta CT17 . . .166 C8
Dover Rd
Barham CT4 . . . . .112 A1
Bishopsbourne CT4 . . . . .111 D5
Dover CT15 . . . . .149 C4
Folkestone CT19, CT20 . .178 E7
Ringwould CT14 . . . . .134 A6
Sandwich CT13 . . . . .93 F5
St Margaret's at Cliffe
  CT15 . . . . .150 D6
Tilmanstone CT13, CT14 . .115 B5
Woolage Green CT4 . . . . .129 D6
Dover St
Canterbury CT1 . . . . .88 A7
  1 Maidstone ME16 . . . . .74 C2
  1 Sittingbourne ME10 . . .36 E4
Dover Trade CT13 . . . . . . .94 A5
Dover Transport Mus*
  CT16 . . . . .149 A5
Doves Cnr CT14 . . . . .115 A4
Doves Croft ME9 . . . . .58 C7
Dowell Mews CT14 . . . . . .117 C3
Dowle CI TN29 . . . . .201 A7
Dowle The
Deal CT14 . . . . .134 B8
Harrietsham ME17 . . . . . .100 F6
Downland Wlk ME15 . . . . .32 A5
Downs Ave CT15 . . . . .2 B1
Downs CE Prim Sch CT14
  .117 B2
Downs Ct
Charing TN27 . . . . .120 C8
East Studdal CT15 . . . . . .132 D8
Hawkinge CT18 . . . . .163 A4
Maidstone ME14 . . . . .75 B8
Sittingbourne ME10 . . . . . .36 D2
Downside
Bekesbourne CT4 . . . . . . .89 E3
Folkestone CT19 . . . . .178 C7
Rochester ME2 . . . . .9 A7
St Margaret's at Cliffe
  CT15 . . . . .151 A6
Downside Rd CT16 . . . . . .149 C8
Downs Pk CT6 . . . . .23 A5
Downs Rd
Canterbury CT2 . . . . .66 F5
Deal CT14 . . . . .117 C3
East Studdal CT15 . . . . . .132 E8
Folkestone CT19 . . . . .178 C7
Maidstone ME14 . . . . .75 B8
Ramsgate CT11 . . . . .52 B6
Downs The
Chartham CT4 . . . . .86 E1
Chatham ME5 . . . . .31 D1
Preston CT3 . . . . .70 C6
Ramsgate CT11 . . . . .52 D5
Downsview ME5 . . . . .32 C8
Downs View Inf Sch
  TN24 . . . . .139 E7
Downs View Rd ME14 . . . .75 B8
Downs Way
Charing TN27 . . . . .120 C8
Sellindge TN25 . . . . .159 C1
Dragonfly CI TN23 . . . . . .155 D8
Dragonfly Way CT18 . . . .163 B4
Dragoon Ho 9 CT11 . . . . .67 A1
Drainless Rd CT13 . . . . . . .93 A5
Drake Ave ME12 . . . . .4 D5
Drake Ct 3 CT11 . . . . .52 F8
Drake Rd TN24 . . . . .157 B7
Drakes CI ME9 . . . . .12 C2
Drakes Lee TN28 . . . . . . .202 E5
Drapers Almshouses CT9 . .29 A8
Drapers Ave CT9 . . . . .28 F8
Drapers CI CT9 . . . . .29 A8
Drapers Mills Prim Sch
  CT9 . . . . .29 A8
Drapers Windmill* CT9 . . .8 A1
Dray's Field ME9 . . . . .79 A7
Dreadnought Ave ME12 . . .4 A6
Dresden Ct CT8 . . . . .27 D8
Drewery Dr ME8 . . . . .33 C5
Drew La CT14 . . . . .117 C4
Drill La CT3 . . . . .69 B1
Drive The
Broadstairs CT10 . . . . .29 F6
Canterbury CT1 . . . . .88 B6

Drive The continued
Deal CT14 . . . . 117 C5
Whitstable CT5 . . . . .44 D8
Drop Redoubt Fort★
CT17 . . . . 166 D7
Drop Redoubt Rd CT17 . .166 D7
Drove Rd ME12 . . . . 3 E6
Drovers Rdbt TN24 . . . . . . 139 A4
Drove The
Fordwich CT2 . . . . .68 A4
Monkton CT12 . . . . .49 B6
Northbourne CT14 . . . . 116 A5
Whitfield CT16 . . . . 149 A8
Whitstable CT5 . . . . .44 D6
Droveway Gdns CT15 . . . 151 A6
Droveway The CT15 . . . . . 151 B6
Druidstone Pk★ CT2 . . . . . .65 F7
Drum La TN23 . . . . 139 B2
Drum Major Dr CT14 . . . . 117 B3
Drury Rd TN30 . . . . 167 B1
Drybeck Ave CT11 . . . . 51 F7
Dryden Cl CT11 . . . . .88 C7
Dryden Rd CT16 . . . . 149 B3
Drywall Ind Est ME10 . . . . .37 B6
Dublin Ho 10 ME15 . . . . . . .97 E6
Duchess of Kent Dr ME5 . .32 B3
Duck La
Canterbury CT1 . . . . .67 A1
Shadoxhurst TN26 . . . . 169 F7
Duck St CT4 . . . . 144 F4
Duckworth CT14 . . . . 157 B7
Dudley Ave CT8 . . . . .27 C8
Dudley Cl ME15 . . . . 97 F5
Dudley Rd
Ashford TN24 . . . . 139 C5
Folkestone CT19 . . . . 178 E6
Duke of Clarence Trad Est
The ME12 . . . . 1 B3
Duke of York's Royal Military
Sch CT15 . . . . 149 F4
Dukes Mdw TN26 . . . . 183 A7
Dukes Meadow Dr ME7 . . 32 F6
Duke St
Deal CT14 . . . . 117 C5
Margate CT9 . . . . 7 I3
Dukes Wlk 7 ME15 . . . . . . .75 A4
Dukeswood CT5 . . . . .44 D6
Dully Rd
Lynsted ME9 . . . . 59 E6
Sittingbourne ME9 . . . . 37 E1
Dumbourne La TN30 . . . . 179 D2
Dumergue Ave ME11 . . . . . . 3 B5
DUMPTON 29 E2
Dumpton Gap Rd CT10 . . .30 A2
Dumpton La CT11 . . . . 29 E1
Dumpton Park Dr CT10,
CT11 . . . . .30 A2
Dumpton Park Rd CT11 . . 29 F1
Dumpton Park Sta CT11 . .29 F1
Duncan Cl CT5 . . . . 43 D7
Duncan Dr CT7 . . . . .26 E8
Duncan Rd
Gillingham ME7 . . . . 10 D5
Ramsgate CT11 . . . . 52 D7
Whitstable CT5 . . . . .44 E8
Dundonald Rd
11 Broadstairs CT10 . . . . . . .30 B4
Ramsgate CT11 . . . . 52 C7
Dunedin Cl ME10 . . . . .36 C3
Dunedin Dr CT16 . . . . 149 B3
Dunedin Ho 9 ME15 . . . . . 97 E5
Dunedin Rd CT12 . . . . .29 A1
Dunera Dr ME14 . . . . .75 A7
Dunes Rd ME9 . . . . 202 D3
Dunes The CT13 . . . . .95 A7
DUNGATE 59 B3
DUNGENESS 209 F2
Dungeness National Nature
Reserve★ TN29 . . . . 209 A4
Dungeness Nature Reserve★
TN29 . . . . 208 F5
Dungeness Rd TN29 . . . . . 209 A2
Dungeness Sta★ TN29 . . 209 D2
Dunkeld Ho 6 ME15 . . . . . .97 E7
Dunkery Ho TN24 . . . . 139 B4
DUNKIRK 64 D3
Dunkirk Cl TN29 . . . . 195 B7
Dunkirk Dr ME5 . . . . .31 F6
DUNKIRK END 195 B7
Dunkirk Road N ME13 . . . . 64 B2
Dunkirk Road S ME13 . . . . .64 B1
Dunkirk Sq CT15 . . . . 149 F3
Dunlin Ct TN29 . . . . 195 A3
Dunnett Rd CT19 . . . . 177 E6
Dunning's La ME1 . . . . 9 C4
Dunnings The ME16 . . . . . . 74 A2
Dunnock Rd TN25 . . . . 139 B7
DUNN STREET
Gillingham 55 A8
Westwell 121 C5
Dunn Street Rd ME7 . . . . . .55 A8
Dunoon Ct CT11 . . . . .29 F1
Dunstall Cl TN29 . . . . 195 A5
Dunstall Gdns TN29 . . . . . 195 A5
Dunstall La TN29 . . . . 195 A5
Dunstan Ave CT8 . . . . .27 D7
Dunstan Ho CT14 . . . . 117 C4
Dunster Terr 3 ME15 . . . . .97 E8
Durban Cl CT12 . . . . 29 A2
Durban Cres CT16 . . . . 149 C4
Durban Ho 7 ME15 . . . . . . .97 E5
Durban Rd CT9 . . . . 8 A1
Durham Cl
Canterbury CT1 . . . . .87 F6

Durham Cl continued
9 Dover CT17 . . . . 166 D7
Maidstone ME15 . . . . .75 C1
Durham Hill CT17 . . . . 166 D7
Durham Rd ME8 . . . . .33 C7
Durling Ct ME8 . . . . 12 A1
DURLOCK 92 B8
Durlock Cl CT12 . . . . 50 C5
Durlock Ave CT11 . . . . .52 B5
Durlock Rd CT3 . . . . 92 B7
Durlocks The CT19 . . . . . . 178 E5
Durnford Cl CT2 . . . . .66 E2
Durovernum Ct CT1 . . . . . . .88 A7
DURRANT GREEN 167 B6
Durrell Gdns ME5 . . . . 10 C1
Duval Dr ME1 . . . . .31 E8
Duvard's Pl ME9 . . . . 35 F1
Dyke Rd CT9 . . . . 178 E5
DYMCHURCH 195 C7
Dymchurch Ho 1 CT4 . . . . .88 B8
Dymchurch Martello Tower★
TN29 . . . . 195 C2
Dymchurch Prim Sch
TN29 . . . . 195 C8
Dymchurch Rd
Hythe CT21, TN29 . . . . 187 C6
St Mary's Bay TN29, TN28 . 195 A5
Dymchurch Sta★ TN29 . . 195 B7
Dyngley Ct ME10 . . . . .36 C6

E

EACH END ME10 . . . . 72 B1
Eadred Way ME10 . . . . 15 A1
Eagle Cotts 8 CT11 . . . . . . .52 D7
Eagle Hill CT11 . . . . .52 D7
Eagles Cl ME10 . . . . .37 C4
Ealham Cl
Ashford TN24 . . . . 157 A8
Canterbury CT4 . . . . .88 B5
Ealing Cl ME5 . . . . .32 C4
Earl Cl ME5 . . . . .32 B4
Earls Ave ME14 . . . . 139 F1
Earl's Ave CT20 . . . . 178 B4
Earlsfield TN25 . . . . 173 A6
Earlsfield Rd CT21 . . . . 176 D2
Earlsmead Cres CT12 . . . . .51 C5
Earl St ME14 . . . . .74 F4
Earlsworth Ct TN24 . . . . . . 156 E6
Earlsworth Rd TN24 . . . . . 156 D6
Easole Hts CT3 . . . . 113 D5
Easole St CT15 . . . . 113 D5
East Blean Woods (Nature
Reserve)★ CT6, CT4 . . . . . .46 B6
East Borough Prim Sch
ME14 . . . . 75 B5
Eastbridge Rd TN29 . . . . . 195 B8
Eastbrook Pl CT16 . . . . 166 E8
EASTCHURCH 5 E3
Eastchurch CE Prim Sch
ME12 . . . . 5 E3
Eastchurch Rd
Margate CT9 . . . . 8 E3
Minster (Sheppey) ME12 . . . 5 B5
East Cliff
Dover CT16 . . . . 166 F8
Folkestone CT19 . . . . 178 E5
Eastcliffe Hts 7 CT20 . . . . 178 E6
East Cliff Gdns 22 CT19 . .178 E5
East Cliff Parc CT5 . . . . 23 A5
East Cliff Pas 8 CT19 . . . . 178 E5
East Cliff & Warren Ctry Pk★
CT18 . . . . 164 D1
Eastcourt Gn ME8 . . . . .11 B4
Eastcourt La
Gillingham, Lower Twydal ME7,
ME8 . . . . 11 C5
Gillingham ME8 . . . . 11 B3
East Court Sch CT11 . . . . . . 52 G7
East Cross TN30 . . . . 179 B3
East Ct 44 ME15 . . . . 75 A1
East End Rd ME4, ME7 . . . .10 D8
Eastern Arm N CT16 . . . . . 166 D8
Eastern Arm S CT16 . . . . . 166 H8
Eastern Ave
Ashford TN23 . . . . 139 A2
Halfway Houses ME12 . . . . . . 3 D6
Margate CT9 . . . . 8 B3
Eastern Esp
Broadstairs CT10 . . . . 30 B5
Margate CT9 . . . . 8 B3
Eastern Gdns TN24 . . . . . . 156 E8
Eastern Rd
Gillingham ME7 . . . . 10 F6
Leysdown-on-Sea ME12 . . . . 6 G2
Lydd TN29 . . . . 205 D7
Eastern Service Rd CT16 166 H8
EAST FARLEIGH 96 B7
East Farleigh Prim Sch
ME15 . . . . .96 B8
East Farleigh Sta ME16 . . .96 B8
Eastfield Ho ME16 . . . . .74 B2
Eastfield Rd 1 CT7 . . . . 27 A7
Eastfields CT19 . . . . 178 D6
Eastgate ME1 . . . . 9 C5
Eastgate Cl CT6 . . . . 23 B3
Eastgate Ct ME1 . . . . 9 C5
Eastgate Rd TN30 . . . . 179 C8
Eastgate Terr ME1 . . . . 9 C5
East Gn ME10 . . . . 15 A1
East Hall La ME10 . . . . .37 C5
East Hill
Ashford TN24 . . . . 139 C2
Tenterden TN30 . . . . 179 B8
East Kent Coll CT11 . . . . 52 E5
East Kent Ret Pk CT10 . . . . 29 A4
East Kent Rly★ CT15 . . . . . 131 A7

East La ME12 . . . . 1 B2
EAST LANGDON 133 A1
East Langdon Rd
Guston CT15 . . . . 149 F7
Martin Mill CT15 . . . . 133 B2
EASTLING 81 F6
Eastling Cl ME8 . . . . .11 D3
Eastling Prim Sch ME13 . . .81 F5
Eastling Rd
Eastling ME13 . . . . .81 F7
Painters Forstal ME13 . . . . . .61 D2
East Lodge Rd TN23 . . . . . 138 F3
Eastmead Ave TN23 . . . . . 156 C8
Eastmead Trad Est TN23 . 156 C8
East Mountain La TN24 . . 139 F7
East Norman Rd CT16 . . . . 149 E1
East Northdown Cl CT9 . . . . 8 E1
East Quay CT5 . . . . .20 D3
East Ramp CT16 . . . . 166 G8
East Rd
Chatham ME4 . . . . .10 A7
Folkestone CT20 . . . . 177 D4
Sandwich CT13 . . . . .73 A8
East Row ME1 . . . . 9 C5
Eastry Cl
Ashford TN23 . . . . 156 A6
Maidstone ME16 . . . . .74 C7
Eastry Ct CT3 . . . . 112 F5
Eastry Mews CT13 . . . . .93 B2
Eastry Pk CT13 . . . . 93 C1
East Service Rd CT9 . . . . . 209 C2
East St
Ashford TN23 . . . . 139 B2
Canterbury CT1 . . . . .67 C3
Chatham ME4 . . . . .10 A3
Dover CT17 . . . . 166 C8
Faversham ME13 . . . . .62 D7
Folkestone CT19 . . . . 178 E5
Gillingham ME7 . . . . 10 D6
Harrietsham ME17 . . . . 100 E5
Herne Bay CT6 . . . . .23 A3
Hythe CT21 . . . . 176 D2
Sittingbourne ME10 . . . . 37 A4
East Stour Ct TN24 . . . . . . 139 D1
EAST STOURMOUTH 48 E1
East Stour Prim Sch
TN24 . . . . 156 D6
East Stour Way TN24 . . . . 156 D6
EAST STREET 72 A2
EAST STUDDAL 132 D7
East Tank Farm Rd TN29 . 209 C2
East View
Brookland TN29 . . . . 199 D8
Hersden CT3 . . . . 46 F1
East Weald Dr TN30 . . . . . 167 B1
Eastwell 5 TN30 . . . . 179 A7
Eastwell Barn Mews
TN30 . . . . 179 A8
Eastwell Cl
Maidstone ME14 . . . . .75 C5
Shadoxhurst TN26 . . . . 155 B1
Eastwell Mdws TN30 . . . . 179 A8
Eastwell Terr TN25 . . . . . . 122 E3
Eastwood Cotts ME5 . . . . . 38 E6
Eastwood Rd ME10 . . . . 36 D5
East Wootton Cotts CT4 . 109 A4
Eaton Hill CT9 . . . . 7 I2
EATON LANDS 176 C3
Eaton Rd
Dover CT17 . . . . 166 B7
Margate CT9 . . . . 7 I1
Eaves Ct ME10 . . . . .37 B5
Eaves Rd CT17 . . . . 166 A7
Ebbsfleet La CT12 . . . . .51 A3
Ebony Cotts TN30 . . . . 189 A6
Ebony Wlk ME16 . . . . .74 B3
ECCLES 53 A6
Eccleston Rd ME15 . . . . . . .74 F2
Echo Cl ME5 . . . . .97 F6
Echo Ho ME10 . . . . .37 B3
Echo Wlk ME12 . . . . 4 D6
Eckford Cl CT18 . . . . 162 F4
Eclipse Dr ME10 . . . . .36 E8
Eddie Willet Rd CT6 . . . . . . 22 B3
EDDINGTON 22 F3
Eddington La CT6 . . . . 22 F3
Eddington Way CT6 . . . . 22 E3
Edelin Rd ME14 . . . . .76 A5
Eden Ave ME5 . . . . 32 A7
Edenbridge Dr ME10 . . . . . . 3 B8
Edenbridge Ho 2 CT1 . . . . .88 B8
Edenfield CT7 . . . . .27 B7
Eden Ho TN23 . . . . 156 C6
Eden Rd CT5 . . . . 43 A7
EDEN VILLAGE 36 F1
Edgar Cl CT5 . . . . 21 D3
Edgar Ho CT14 . . . . 117 B3
Edgar Rd
Canterbury CT1 . . . . .67 B1
Dover CT17 . . . . 149 B1
Minster (Thanet) CT12 . . . . .50 B6
Edge End Rd CT10 . . . . .29 F4
Edgehill Cl CT20 . . . . 177 D4
Edger Pl 8 ME15 . . . . .75 A4
Edinburgh Ho
Deal CT14 . . . . 117 A5
7 Dover CT17 . . . . 166 D7
Edinburgh Pl 7 CT20 . . . . 178 B3
Edinburgh Rd
Ashford TN24 . . . . 139 B2
Chatham ME4 . . . . .10 C2
Gillingham ME7 . . . . 10 D5

Edinburgh Rd continued
Margate CT9 . . . . .28 B8
Edinburgh Sq ME15 . . . . . . .97 C7
Edinburgh Wlk 5 CT9 . . . . .28 B8
Edisbury Wlk ME8 . . . . 33 D5
Edith Rd
Faversham ME13 . . . . .62 C6
Ramsgate CT11 . . . . 52 C6
Westgate on Sea CT8 . . . . . . 7 D1
Edmanson Ave CT9 . . . . 7 E1
Edmund Cl ME16 . . . . .74 A3
Edmund St CT13 . . . . 91 A8
Edna Rd ME14 . . . . .74 F8
Edred Rd CT17 . . . . 166 B8
Edward Ct ME5 . . . . 10 C1
Edward Dr
Birchington CT7 . . . . .27 B7
Sittingbourne ME10 . . . . 14 F1
Edward Rd
Canterbury CT1 . . . . .88 A8
Folkestone CT19 . . . . 178 D6
Kingsdown CT14 . . . . 134 C6
Queenborough ME11 . . . . 3 B5
Edwards Cl ME8 . . . . .33 C5
Edwards Rd CT16 . . . . 166 D8
Edward St
Chatham ME4 . . . . .10 A3
Margate CT9 . . . . .28 B8
Sheerness ME12 . . . . 1 B3
Edward Terr 9 CT20 . . . . . 178 E6
Edward Vinson Dr ME13 . . 62 E7
Edwina Ave ME12 . . . . 4 A7
Edwin Rd ME8 . . . . .33 C8
Edwins Pl ME9 . . . . .35 C7
Edyngham Cl ME10 . . . . 37 A8
Effingham Cres CT17 . . . . 166 D8
Effingham St
Dover CT17 . . . . 166 D8
Ramsgate CT11 . . . . 52 E6
Egbert Rd
Birchington CT7 . . . . .26 D8
Faversham ME13 . . . . .62 C6
Minster (Thanet) CT12 . . . . .50 B6
Westgate on Sea CT8 . . . . . . 7 C1
EGERTON 118 F4
Egerton CE Prim Sch
TN27 . . . . 118 F3
Egerton Dr CT9 . . . . 8 E2
EGERTON FORSTAL 118 D1
Egerton House Rd TN27 . . 118 F4
Egerton Rd
Charing Heath TN27 . . . . . . 119 C3
Maidstone ME14 . . . . .74 E7
Pluckley TN27 . . . . 119 B1
Temple Ewell CT16 . . . . 148 E5
Eggarton La CT4 . . . . 107 A8
Eggringe TN23 . . . . 138 E1
Egremont Rd ME15 . . . . . . .75 F2
Eider Cl CT6 . . . . .22 C7
Eighteen Acre La TN29 . . 200 D8
Elder Cl ME17 . . . . 99 D2
Elder Ct ME8 . . . . 33 B6
Elders The CT3 . . . . .68 F1
Eldon Gr CT11 . . . . .52 D6
Eldon Ho 4 CT10 . . . . 30 B4
Eldon St ME14 . . . . .10 A4
Eleanor Cl ME8 . . . . .33 C3
Eleanor Dr ME10 . . . . 36 C8
Elfrida Cl CT9 . . . . .29 C8
Elgar Bretts Ct 10 CT1 . . . .87 F7
Elgar Pl CT11 . . . . .52 D7
ELHAM 144 F5
Elham CE Prim Sch CT4 . 144 F4
Elham Cl
Gillingham ME8 . . . . 11 B3
Margate CT9 . . . . 8 C1
Elham Ct CT1 . . . . .87 E6
Elham Valley Railway Mus★
CT18 . . . . 177 A8
Elham Valley Vineyard★
CT4 . . . . 128 D4
Elham Way CT10 . . . . 30 A2
Eling Ct ME15 . . . . 97 A8
Eliot Coll CT2 . . . . .66 E4
Elizabethan Ct TN27 . . . . . 120 C7
Elizabeth Carter Ave
CT14 . . . . 116 F4
Elizabeth Ct
Broadstairs CT10 . . . . 30 B6
Canterbury CT1 . . . . .88 B6
Chatham ME5 . . . . .32 A7
Gillingham ME8 . . . . 11 C1
Herne Bay CT6 . . . . .22 F5
Elizabeth Dr CT18 . . . . 164 B2
Elizabeth Gdns 3 CT21 . . 176 B1
Elizabeth Ho
Maidstone ME14 . . . . .75 A6
Rochester ME1 . . . . 9 C4
Elizabeth Kemp Ct 1
CT12 . . . . .29 C1
Elizabeth St CT17 . . . . 166 D6
Elizabeth Way CT6 . . . . .23 B3
Ellen Ave CT11 . . . . .29 E2
Ellen Cl TN27 . . . . 120 B7
Ellen Cl CT3 . . . . .89 F8
Ellen Ct CT1 . . . . .66 C4
Ellen's Hill CT14 . . . . 116 E3
Ellen's Pl ME9 . . . . .35 C6
Ellens Rd CT14 . . . . 116 F2
Ellenswood Cl ME15 . . . . . .76 A1
Ellesmere Mews TN28 . . . 202 C8
Ellingham Ind Ctr TN23 . . 156 A5
Ellingham Leas ME15 . . . . .97 C7
Ellingham Way TN23 . . . . . 156 A5
Ellington Ave CT9 . . . . .28 B8
Ellington Inf Sch CT11 . . . .52 C7
Ellington Pl CT11 . . . . .52 C7

Ellington Rd CT11 . . . . .52 D7
Ellington Sch for Girls
CT11 . . . . 29 D2
Elliot Cl CT11 . . . . .67 C3
Elliot Ct CT6 . . . . .23 C4
Elliots Pl ME13 . . . . 62 D7
Elliott Park Sch ME12 . . . . . 4 A7
Ellis Dr TN28 . . . . 202 C8
Ellis Ho 7 ME8 . . . . .75 B4
Ellison Cl CT5 . . . . 21 C1
Ellison Ct ME13 . . . . .62 D8
Ellisons Wlk CT1 . . . . .88 C8
Ellison Way ME8 . . . . .12 A2
Ellis Rd CT5 . . . . 21 A3
Ellis Way CT6 . . . . .23 C2
Elm Ave ME4 . . . . 9 E1
Elm Cl TN27 . . . . 118 F3
Elm Cotts TN25 . . . . 122 E3
Elm Court Ind Est ME7 . . . .32 E3
Elm Ct CT18 . . . . .27 E8
Elmfield
Gillingham ME8 . . . . 11 A3
Tenterden TN30 . . . . 179 B8
Elmfield Ct
Coxheath ME17 . . . . .96 C3
Tenterden TN30 . . . . 179 B8
Elm Fields TN29 . . . . 201 A6
Elm Gdns CT21 . . . . 176 E2
Elm Gr
Maidstone ME15 . . . . .75 B3
Manston CT12 . . . . 28 D1
Sittingbourne ME10 . . . . 37 B4
Westgate on Sea CT8 . . . . . .27 E8
Elm Ho 11 CT21 . . . . 176 B2
Elmhurst Cl TN25 . . . . 138 F4
Elmhurst Gdns ME4 . . . . 9 E3
Elm La ME12 . . . . 4 E5
Elmleigh Rd CT13 . . . . .90 A8
Elmley Ind Est ME11 . . . . . . 3 A2
Elmley Marshes Nature
Reserve★ ME12 . . . . .15 F4
Elmley Rd ME12 . . . . 4 D3
Elmley Way CT9 . . . . .28 F6
Elm Park Gdns CT17 . . . . . 165 F7
Elm Pk TN23 . . . . 155 F7
Elm Rd
Aylesham CT3 . . . . 112 E5
7 Folkestone CT19 . . . . 178 E6
Gillingham ME7 . . . . 10 E6
St Mary's Bay TN29 . . . . . . 194 F3
Elms Ave CT11 . . . . .52 D6
Elms Hill CT15 . . . . 165 D6
Elmsmead TN31 . . . . 197 B4
ELMSTEAD 142 F6
Elms The
Hersden CT3 . . . . 46 E1
Teynham ME9 . . . . 39 A2
ELMSTONE 70 E5
Elmstone Cl ME16 . . . . .74 B2
Elmstone Gdns ME8 . . . . . . 8 E2
Elmstone Hole Rd ME17 . 100 D1
Elmstone La ME16 . . . . .74 B2
Elmstone Rd
Gillingham ME8 . . . . 33 D7
Ramsgate CT11 . . . . 52 D7
ELMS VALE 166 A7
Elms Vale Rd CT15, CT17 . 165 F7
Elmton La CT15 . . . . 114 C1
Elmtree TN26 . . . . 181 C1
Elm Tree Ave ME9 . . . . 14 D4
Elm Tree Dr ME1 . . . . 9 A2
Elmway ME12 . . . . 4 A6
Elmwood Ave CT10 . . . . 30 A8
Elmwood Cl CT10 . . . . 30 A7
Elm Wood Cl CT5 . . . . 21 C2
Elm Wood Way CT5 . . . . 21 C2
Elswick Sq TN25 . . . . 139 B2
Elventon Cl CT19 . . . . 177 E7
Elverland La ME13, ME9 . . . 61 B2
ELVINGTON
Eythorne 114 C1
Hawkinge 162 E2
Elvington Cl ME16 . . . . 74 D5
Elvington La CT18 . . . . 162 E2
Elwick La 12 TN23 . . . . 139 B2
Elwick Rd TN23 . . . . 139 B2
Ely Cl ME8 . . . . 11 E2
Embassy Cl ME7 . . . . 10 F1
Emelina Way CT5 . . . . 43 B6
Emerald Cl ME1 . . . . .31 D7
Emerald Cres ME10 . . . . . . .36 C6
Emerald View ME12 . . . . 6 E4
Emily Rd ME5 . . . . .32 B6
Emmerson Gdns CT5 . . . . . 21 D3
Emperor Way TN23 . . . . . . 155 F4
Empire Terr CT9 . . . . 28 E8
Empress Gdns ME12 . . . . . . 6 D4
Emsworth Gr ME14 . . . . 75 D6
Enbrook Rd CT20 . . . . 177 E4
Enbrook Valley CT20 . . . . . 177 E5
Encombe CT20 . . . . 177 D3
Endeavour Foyer The 8
ME4 . . . . 10 B2
Enfield Rd CT14 . . . . 117 D7
Engineers Ct 1 TN23 . . . . 139 B2
English Martyrs RC Prim Sch
ME1 . . . . 9 B8
Ennerdale Rd 1 . . . . .62 E6
Ennerdale Gdns CT3 . . . . . 112 F6
Ennerdale Ho ME15 . . . . . . .97 E7
Enterprise Bsns Est ME2 . . 9 E7
Enterprise Cl ME2 . . . . 9 D8
Enterprise Ctr TN23 . . . . . . 156 A6
Enterprise Ctr The ME5 . . . 54 C8
Enterprise Rd
Maidstone ME15 . . . . .75 A1
Margate CT9 . . . . .29 A6

Enterprise Way CT9....29 A6
Enticott CI CT5....21 A1
Epaul La ME1....9 C6
Eppe CI **2** ME2....9 B8
Epping CI CT6....23 B2
Epple Bay Ave CT7....27 B8
Epple Bay Rd CT7....27 A8
Epple Rd CT7....27 B8
Epps Rd ME10....36 E3
Epsom CI ME15....97 F6
Eric Rd CT17....149 B2
Erith CI ME14....75 A8
Erith St CT17....149 B1
Ernest Dr ME16....10 A3
Ernest Rd ME4....10 A3
Ernwell Rd CT19....178 D6
ERRIOTWOOD....59 F3
Ersham Rd CT1....88 A7
Eshet CI TN23....156 A7
Eskdale Ave CT11....52 A7
Esmonde Dr CT12....27 F2
Esmonde Ho **15** ME7....10 A6
Esplanade
 Dover CT17....166 D6
 Rochester ME1....9 B5
 Westgate on Sea CT8....7 C1
Essella Pk TN24....139 E1
Essella Rd TN24....139 E1
Essentially Hops* CT4....89 D3
Essetford Rd TN23....156 A7
Essex Ave CT7....22 B4
Essex Gdns CT7....26 F6
Essex Rd
 Canterbury CT1....88 D7
 Maidstone ME15....97 E6
 Westgate on Sea CT8....27 F8
Essex St CT5....43 D8
Estelle CI ME1....31 D7
Esther CI ME10....36 E8
Estuary CI CT5....21 E2
Estuary Rd ME12....1 C1
Estuary Reach ME4....9 F6
Etchden Rd TN26....154 A8
ETCHINGHILL....161 C3
Ethelbert Cres CT9....8 A3
Ethelbert Gdns CT9....7 J3
Ethelbert Rd
 Birchington CT7....26 D8
 Canterbury CT1....88 B6
 Deal CT14....95 C1
 Dover CT17....166 C8
 Faversham ME13....62 C6
 Folkestone CT19....178 D7
 Margate CT9....7 J3
 Ramsgate CT11....52 D6
 Rochester ME1....9 C4
Ethelbert Road Inf Sch ME13....62 C6
Ethelbert Sq CT8....7 C1
Ethelbert Terr
 Margate CT9....8 A3
 Westgate on Sea CT8....7 C1
Ethelburga Dr CT18....161 B7
Ethel-Maud Ct ME7....10 D7
Ethel Rd CT3....29 F5
Ethelred Ct ME13....62 C6
Ethelred Rd CT5....7 C1
Eton CI ME5....31 F4
Ettrick Terr CT21....176 A2
Eureka Leisure Pk TN24....139 B5
Eurogate Bsns Pk TN24....139 B5
Eurolink Bsns Pk ME10....37 B5
Eurolink E ME10....37 C5
Eurolink N ME10....37 C7
Eurolink Way ME10....36 F4
Evans Rd CT14....157 A7
Eva Rd ME7....10 D3
Evelings Alley **18** CT5....20 D2
Evelyn CI ME2....9 C8
Evelyn Ct CT21....177 A2
Evelyn Ho
 9 Folkestone CT20....178 D5
 5 Rochester ME2....9 C8
Evelyn Rd ME16....74 B2
Evenhill Rd CT3....89 E8
Everard Way ME14....62 B8
Everglades The ME7....32 F6
Evergreen CI
 Gillingham ME7....33 A5
 Iwade ME9....14 D4
Evergreen Way TN23....138 E3
Everist Ct CT18....161 C6
Eversleigh Rise CT5....43 F7
Eversley CI ME16....74 C6
Eversley Coll CT20....177 F4
Eversley Rd CT21....177 B3
Eversley Way CT20....177 F5
Evington Pottery* TN25....142 D7
Evison CI CT16....149 B2
Evorg Ho **6** ME4....10 B2
Ewart Rd ME4....9 E1
Ewe & Lamb Mews TN30....188 E3
EWELL MINNIS....147 E3
Exchange St CT14....117 D7
Exchange The CT5....20 E3
Exeter CI CT19....177 D6
Exeter Wlk ME1....31 C7
Exmoor Rise TN24....139 B4
Exmouth Rd ME7....10 C7
EXTED....142 E5
Exton CI ME5....32 C2
Exton Gdns ME7....75 F5
Eye The ME4....9 F5
Eyhorne St ME17....77 D2
EYHORNE STREET....77 C2
Eylesden Ct ME14....76 C4
Eynsford CI CT9....8 F2
Eynsford Rd ME16....74 D7

Eythorn Court Barn CT15....131 B7
EYTHORNE....131 C8
Eythorne CI TN24....139 D5
Eythorne Elvington Prim Sch CT15....131 C8
EYTHORNE GREEN....131 D7
Eythorne Rd CT15....130 E6
Eythorne Sta* CT15....131 C8

F

Faggs Wood Forest Wlks* TN26....170 D2
Fagus CI ME5....32 B1
Fairacre CT10....29 E4
Fairacres CT16....23 C4
FAIRBOURNE HEATH....100 B1
Fairbourne Heath Cotts ME17....100 B1
Fairbourne La ME17....100 C4
Fairborne Bsns Ctr ME15....97 F4
Fairfax CI
 Folkestone CT20....177 D5
 Gillingham ME8....33 D5
Fairfax Dr CT6....23 F5
Fairfax Ho ME15....97 F5
Fairfield
 Deal CT14....116 F6
 Elham CT4....144 F5
Fairfield CI TN28....202 B7
Fairfield Pk CT10....29 E4
Fairfield Rd
 Broadstairs CT10....29 E4
 Minster (Thanet) CT12....50 B7
 New Romney TN28....202 B7
 Ramsgate CT12....29 E2
Fairfield Terr TN26....183 A7
Fairhurst Dr ME15....96 B4
Fairings The TN30....179 B8
Fairlawn CT5....21 D1
Fairlawn Rd CT12....29 B3
Fairlead Rd ME1....9 C6
Fairleas ME10....37 B2
Fairlight Ave CT12....51 B6
Fairlight Cotts **8** ME13....62 C7
Fairlight Glen Sch CT6....22 F5
Fairlight Rd CT21....176 A3
Fairmeadow ME14....74 F4
Fairoaks CT6....23 B3
Fairservice CI ME10....37 C5
Fair St CT10....29 E4
Fairview CT21....175 A3
Fairview Ave ME8....33 B5
Fairview CI CT9....8 A2
Fairview Com Prim Sch ME8....33 C5
Fairview Cotts
 Maidstone ME15....96 F5
 Wormshill ME9....79 C5
Fairview Dr TN24....156 D6
Fairview Gdns
 Deal CT14....117 A2
 Sturry CT2....68 A6
Fairview Ind Pk TN26....183 F7
Fairview Rd
 Elvington CT15....114 B1
 Sittingbourne ME10....37 A3
Fairway CT13....95 A3
Fairway Ave CT19....178 A7
Fairway CI
 Rochester ME1....9 C1
 St Mary's Bay TN29....194 F3
Fairway Cres CT5....43 A7
Fairways The ME13....62 A6
Fairway The
 Deal CT14....117 C8
 Herne Bay CT6....22 D7
 Hythe CT21....176 C1
 Littlestone-on-Sea TN28....202 D6
 Rochester ME1....9 C1
 Sittingbourne ME10....36 E1
 St Mary's Bay TN29....195 A5
Fairwood Ind Est TN23....139 A1
Fairwood Ind Pk TN23....138 F2
Falcon CI CT14....45 F7
Falcon Ct ME10....37 C6
Falcon Gdns ME12....4 D7
Falcon Ho **3** ME10....37 A4
Falcon Way TN23....155 E7
Falkland Pl ME15....31 E1
Fallowfield
 Chatham ME5....32 B8
 Sittingbourne ME10....37 A3
Fallowfield CT14....75 E4
Fanconi Rd ME5....32 B3
Fancy Row ME14....76 C5
Fane Way ME8....33 D4
Fan The CT16....166 H8
Fant La ME16....74 B2
Faraday Ho ME1....9 D5
Faraday Rd ME14....75 C7
Fareham Wlk **10** ME15....97 F6
Farington CI ME16....74 B4
Farleigh CI ME16....74 B4
Farleigh Hill ME15....74 C3
Farleigh Hill Ret Pk ME15....74 E1
Farleigh La ME16....74 A1
Farleigh Rd ME15....67 A3
Farleigh Trad Est ME15....74 E1
Farley CI
 Chatham ME5....32 D2
 Shadoxhurst TN26....155 A1
Farley Rd CT9....28 F7
Farleys Way TN31....196 B2
Farm CI TN23....155 E7

Farm Cres ME10....37 A2
Farm CI
 Hythe CT21....176 D3
 Leeds ME17....99 A6
Farm Gdns TN31....196 C2
Farmhouse CI CT14....128 F7
Farm House CT14....43 F8
Farming World at Nash
 Court* ME13....63 D4
Farm La CT14....116 F6
Farm Rd
 Chatham ME5....31 E3
 Hamstreet TN26....183 A7
Farnborough CI ME16....74 C2
Farncombe Way TN23....149 B7
Farne CI ME15....97 A6
Farnham CI ME8....12 B1
Farningham CI ME14....75 C6
Farraday CI ME14....31 D8
Farrar Rd CT7....27 A6
Farrers Wlk TN23....156 B4
Farrier CI
 Ashford TN23....138 F5
 Maidstone ME14....75 E5
Farriers Ct ME8....34 C8
Farrier St CT14....117 D7
Farrow Ct TN23....156 A6
Farthing Cnr ME9....33 E3
FARTHING COMMON....160 D5
FARTHINGLOE....165 F5
Farthingloe Cotts CT15....165 F5
Farthingloe Ct CT17....166 A6
Farthingloe Rd CT17....166 A6
Farthings Cotts ME14....53 F1
Farthings Ct CT2....66 C4
Fauchon's La ME14....75 F3
Fauchon's La ME14....75 F4
Faulkners La CT17....109 E7
Faussett Hill CT4....109 E7
Faustina Dr TN23....155 F4
FAVERSHAM....62 A5
Faversham Cottage Hospl
 ME13....62 C7
Faversham Ind Est ME13....62 F7
Faversham Miniature Rly*
 ME13....61 E7
Faversham Reach ME13....62 D8
Faversham Sta ME13....62 D6
Faversham Stone Chapel*
 ME13....61 E7
Fawley Rd CT5....43 B6
Fawkham Rd CT5....74 E7
Fay CI ME7....9 B3
Featherbed La
 Iwade ME9....14 E2
 Selling ME13....84 A7
Featherby Cotts ME7....10 F6
Featherby Inf Sch ME8....11 A3
Featherby Jun Sch ME8....11 A3
Featherby Rd ME8....11 A3
Felborough CI CT4....107 C8
FELDERLAND....93 F4
Felderland CI
 Maidstone ME17....97 E5
 Sandwich CT14....93 F5
Felderland Dr ME17....97 E5
Felderland La CT14....93 E4
Felderland Rd ME17....97 E5
Feldspar CI
 Chatham ME5....32 A1
 Sittingbourne ME10....36 D6
Fellows CI ME8....11 B3
Fennel CI ME16....9 B3
Fennel Ct ME10....177 E4
Fenner CI CT20....177 E4
Fenoulhet Way CT6....23 A5
Fenton Ct CT14....117 B6
Ferdi Lethert Ho TN24....175 A3
Ferguson CI CT21....176 F2
Ferguson Rd TN29....207 F6
Fern Bank Cres CT19....178 D6
Fernbank CI ME5....31 F2
Fern CI
 Hawkinge CT18....163 C6
 Whitstable CT5....21 C1
Fern Ct
 Broadstairs CT10....30 B5
 Dover CT16....149 D1
Ferndale CI ME12....2 E7
Ferndale Ct CT7....27 A6
Ferndale Rd CT7....27 A6
Ferndown CI ME5....26 D8
Ferndown Ct ME7....33 A5
Ferne La CT15....147 D3
Ferne Way CT20....177 E6
Fernfield CT18....163 C6
Fernfield La CT17....163 C7
Fernhill Rd ME16....74 A2
Fernlea Ave CT6....22 E4
FERNLEIGH....64 B3
Fernleigh ME13....64 B3
Fernley CI **11** CT20....178 D5
Fern Wlk ME10....37 C5
Ferrier CI ME8....33 E4
Ferry Rd
 Iwade ME9....14 E4
 Queenborough ME11, ME12....3 D1

Ferry View ME11....159 E6
Fiddling La TN25....159 E6
Field Ave CT1....67 D3
Field CI ME5....31 E6
Field End TN24....140 A1
Field End PI ME13....64 A3
Fielder CI **1** ME10....37 C5
Fielding St ME13....62 C7
Fieldings The ME10....36 E2
Field Mill Rd TN27....119 B5
Field View
 Kingsnorth TN23....156 B4
 Whitstable CT5....43 B7
Fieldview CI ME14....3 C6
Field Way CT2....67 F5
Fieldworks Rd ME7....10 A7
Fiesta Wlk CT1....88 C7
Fife Rd CT6....22 B3
Fifth Ave CT9....8 B3
Fig Tree Rd CT10....29 F7
Fig Tree Wlk CT15....131 C7
Fig Terr ME14....75 A7
Filer Rd ME13....3 E7
Filmer Rd CT4....88 F1
Finch CI ME13....62 D6
Finch Mews ME14....74 E7
Finches The
 Sittingbourne ME7....36 F3
 St Nicholas at Wade CT7....25 E2
Finch Gr CT2....187 D8
Finch Mews CT4....117 C4
Findlay CI ME8....33 D6
Findlay CI **9** CT21....176 B2
FINGLESHAM....116 B8
Finglesham Ct ME15....97 C8
Finglesham Farm Barns
 CT14....116 A8
Finlay CI ME13....62 B7
Finn Farm Ct TN23....156 D1
Finn Farm Rd TN23....156 C2
Finsbury Ct CT11....52 E8
Finsbury Rd CT11....52 E8
Fintonagh Dr ME14....75 B6
Finwell Rd ME8....12 A2
Firbank Gdns CT9....28 D7
Firbanks CT5....43 A8
Fir CI TN24....139 F1
Fire Opal Way **6** ME10....36 D6
Firethorn CI ME7....10 E6
Firmin Ave ME7....97 D5
Firs CI CT19....177 D7
Firs La CT19....177 D7
Firs Rd CT4....112 F1
First Ave
 Broadstairs CT10....8 F2
 Chatham ME4....10 C2
 Eastchurch ME12....5 E5
 Gillingham ME7....10 E3
 Margate CT9....8 B3
 Rushenden ME11....2 F3
 Sheerness ME12....1 C1
Firs The
 Deal CT14....117 C8
 Hersden CT3....46 E1
First La ME17....76 E2
FIR TOLL....136 C6
Firtree CI CT2....66 B3
Fir Tree CI CT11....52 C6
Fir Tree Gr
 Bredhurst ME7....33 B1
 Chatham ME5....32 D1
Fir Tree Hill CT13....93 B6
Fisher CI CT21....176 D1
Fishermans Ctyd CT14....117 D7
Fisherman's Wharf **9**
 CT13....73 A1
Fisher Rd
 Canterbury CT2....66 D1
 Chatham ME5....32 B7
Fishers TN28....202 E5
Fisher St
 Maidstone ME14....75 A4
 Sandwich CT13....73 A1
Fisher Street Rd ME13....83 E2
Fish Market CT19....178 E5
Fishmarket Rd TN31....197 E3
Fishmonger's La **8** CT16....166 E7
Fitzgerald Ave CT15....22 C4
Fitzgilbert CI ME7....11 A5
Fitzmary Ave CT9....7 E1
Fitzroy Ave
 Broadstairs CT10....8 G2
 Margate CT9....8 B1
 Ramsgate CT12....29 B2
Fitzroy Rd CT5....20 F2
Fitzthorold Ho ME7....10 E7
Fitzwalter Ct **1** CT16....149 B3
Fitzwalters Mdw CT3....91 D2
Fitzwilliam Rd ME14....75 F5
Five Acre Wood Sch
 ME15....97 B7
Five Bells La **5** ME1....9 D4
Five Vents La TN29....201 B8
Fiveways **6** CT17....166 C8
Five Ways St ME4....10 A4
Fiveways Rise CT14....116 F5
FIVE WENTS....98 C2
Flagstaff Ct **1** CT1....88 A7
Flamingo CI CT6....22 E3
Flamingo Dr CT6....22 E3
Flanders CI ME10....14 F1
Flanders Field TN25....157 E4
Flax Court La CT15....131 C7
Flaxman Ct **13** ME7....10 A6
Flaxman Dr ME16....74 C6
Flaxpond Rd TN23....155 F7
FLEEDEN....154 C7
Fleet Ave ME12....1 C1

Fleet Rd
 Rochester ME1....9 D1
 St Margaret's at Cliffe
 CT15....134 A1
Fleets La CT2....66 D7
Fleet Villas TN24....139 D7
Fleetwood Ave CT6....22 D4
Fleetwood CI ME12....4 B6
Fleming Rd CT13, CT3....92 D6
FLEMINGS....92 D6
Fleming Way CT1....178 E8
Fletcher Rd CT5....21 B1
Fletchers Way CT14....117 A5
Flete Rd CT9....28 D5
Fleur de Lis Heritage Ctr*
 7 ME13....62 D7
Flimwell CT11....36 E8
Flint CI ME14....26 F6
Flint Cotts CT7....26 F6
Flint Gn ME5....32 C3
Flint Gr CT10....29 E5
Flint Ho CT9....7 J3
Flint La
 Lenham ME17....79 C1
 Woodside Green ME17....101 C8
Flodden Rd CT14....116 F3
Flood Hatch ME15....74 D2
Flood La ME13....62 C8
Flood St TN25....157 D2
Flora Rd CT11....52 E8
Florence Ave CT5....43 B7
Florence Cotts CT11....52 D6
Florence Ct CT19....178 A4
Florence Rd
 Maidstone ME16....74 E3
 8 Ramsgate CT11....52 D6
Florence St **3** ME2....9 B8
Florida CI CT16....149 B3
Florin Dr ME1....9 B4
Flower Rise ME14....74 F7
Flume End ME15....74 D2
Flying Horse La **6** CT16....166 E7
Foads Hill CT12....51 D6
Foads La CT12....51 D5
Focal Point Rd CT16....148 F4
Fodbury Ct CT8....7 C1
Foley CI TN24....157 A7
Foley St ME14....75 A5
FOLKESTONE....178 B7
Folkestone Acad CT19....178 B7
Folkestone Central CT19....178 C5
Folkestone Ent Ctr CT19....177 F8
Folkestone Martello Tower*
 CT19....178 G6
Folkestone Race Course
 CT21....175 A6
Folkestone Rd
 Brookland TN31....198 B3
 Church Hougham CT15....165 D4
 Dover CT17, CT15....166 B7
Folkestone Sch for Girls The
 CT20....177 F4
Folkestone Sports & Ski Ctr
 CT19....178 B6
Folkestone West Sta
 CT20....177 F5
Folkstone Ho **4** ME5....97 F6
Folkstone, St Martins CE
 Prim Sch CT18....177 B5
Folks Wood Way CT21....175 E4
Folly Rd CT20....178 E6
FOLLY TOWN....141 F7
Fonblanque Rd ME12....1 D2
Fontana ME5....32 A3
Fontwell CI ME15....97 F6
FOORD....178 D6
Foord Almshouses ME1....9 B3
Foord CI ME15....101 D5
Foord Road N CT19, CT20....178 D5
Foord Road S CT20....178 D5
Foord St ME1....9 D4
Forbes Rd ME13....62 C6
FORD....46 E8
Ford CI
 Bridge CT4....88 F1
 Herne Bay CT6....22 A4
Fordcombe CI ME15....97 F7
Ford Hill CT3, CT6....46 E8
Fordingbridge CI ME16....74 B5
Fordoun Rd CT10....29 F5
Ford Way TN23....138 F1
FORDWICH....68 A4
Fordwich CI ME16....74 B7
Fordwich Gn ME8....11 C3
Fordwich Gr CT10....29 E7
Fordwich Pl CT13....93 F8
Fordwich Rd CT2....67 F4
Ford Wlk CT5....43 A3
Foreland Ave
 Folkestone CT19....178 F6
 Margate CT9....7 J4
Foreland Ct
 Birchington CT7....26 D8
 Ramsgate CT11....52 D5
 St Margaret's at Cliffe
 CT15....151 A5
Foreland Hts CT10....30 B7
Foreland Park Ho CT10....30 B7
Foreland Rd CT15....151 A4
Foreland Sch The CT10....30 A6
Forelands Sq CT10....30 B7
Foreman Ct CT5....88 B5
Foreness Ct CT10....8 G3
Forestall Mdw TN23....156 B4
Forest Ave TN25....138 E4

Forest Cotts TN25......... 105 C2
Forestdale Rd ME5.........54 A8
Forest Dr ME5..............31 F2
Foresters CI ME5..........31 F2
Foresters Way CT20...178 D5
Forest Hill ME15..........74 C1
Forestry Cotts CT4...125 B7
Forge CI
  Eythorne CT15.........131 C7
  Sellindge TN25.........159 D1
  Sturry CT2...............67 F5
Forge Cotts
  Boyden Gate CT3.......47 C8
  Broadstairs CT10.......30 B5
  Faversham ME13.......63 D8
Forgefield TN26.........153 D5
Forge Field CT15......164 E5
Forgefields CT6..........46 B8
Forge Hill
  Aldington TN25.........173 A5
  Bethersden TN26.....153 E5
Forge Ho
  Canterbury CT1.........87 E6
  Ickham CT3..............69 C1
Forge La
  Ashford TN23...........139 B2
  Boxley ME14............54 C2
  Boyden Gate CT3.......47 C8
  Bredhurst ME7..........33 A1
  East Farleigh ME15....96 C7
  Egerton Forstal TN27..118 C1
  Gillingham ME7..........10 E7
  Leeds ME17..............98 F7
  Maidstone ME14.......76 C4
  Ramsgate CT11.........52 C7
  Sutton CT15.............133 A6
  Upchurch ME9..........12 F3
  Whitfield CT16.........149 A8
  Whitstable CT5.........43 D8
Forge Mdw
  Harrietsham ME17.....100 D6
  Stone in Oxney TN30...190 A4
Forge Meads TN30.....188 B3
Forge Path CT16.......149 A8
Forge Rd ME10.........36 E6
Forrens The [14] CT1....67 A1
Forrester CI CT1.........67 C2
Forson CT TN30.........179 B8
FORSTAL.................53 B2
Forstal Cotts
  Forstal ME20...........53 B2
  Lenham Heath ME17..102 A1
Forstal La ME17.........96 D4
Forstal Rd
  Egerton Forstal TN27..118 C1
  Forstal ME20...........53 C2
  Woolage Village CT4..112 E1
Forstal The
  Lenham Heath ME17...102 A1
  Preston CT3.............70 B6
  Wye TN25................123 E2
Forsters ME17...........98 E4
Forsyth Ct [7] ME7......10 C7
Fort Amherst *
  (Caisemated
  Barracks) CT15.......149 E2
Fort Burgoyne Rd CT16..149 F1
Fort CI TN29............206 E6
Fort Cotts CT10.........30 B4
Fort Cres CT9...........7 J3
Fort Hill CT9............7 J3
Fort Lower Prom CT9....7 J3
Fort Luton * ME4.......10 A1
Fort Paragon CT9.......7 J3
Fort Pitt Gram Sch ME4...9 E4
Fort Pitt Hill ME4, ME4...9 E4
Fort Pitt St ME4........9 E3
Fort Prom CT9..........7 J3
Fort Rd
  Broadstairs CT10.......30 B4
  Hythe CT21...........176 A2
Fort St ME5.............9 D4
Fortuna Ct CT11........52 D7
Forty Acres Rd ME14....4 C4
Forty Acres Rd CT2....66 C2
Forum Sh Ctr The [9]
  ME10....................36 F4
Forum The [2] ME10...36 F4
Forum Way TN23.......155 E5
Forward Way ME1......31 C6
FOSTALL..................64 A7
Fostall Gn TN23.........155 F7
Fostall Rd ME13........40 C1
Foster CI CT19.........177 E7
Foster Clarke Dr ME17..97 D5
Foster Clark Est ME15..75 B2
Foster Rd TN24.........157 A6
Foster's Ave CT10......29 E7
Foster's Ct CT13.......94 A7
Foster St ME15.........75 A3
Foster Way CT14......117 B5
Fostington Way ME5....31 F1
Fougeres Way TN24....139 A4
Foulds CI ME8..........33 B5
Foundry Wharf ME1.....9 E4
Fountain Inn Ct CT9....7 I3
Fountain La
  Maidstone ME14.......74 A2
  Sheerness ME12........1 B2
Fountains CI TN24.....140 A1
Fountain St
  [2] Sittingbourne ME10..36 E4
  [3] Whitstable ME5.....20 D2
Fouracre Cotts ME9....34 E6

Four Horseshoes Pk
  ME13...................41 D1
Four Oaks ME13........61 E8
Fourth Ave
  Eastchurch ME12......5 F5
  Gillingham ME7........10 E4
Four Turnings CT3.....70 B3
Four Wents
  Langley Heath ME17....98 E3
  Maidstone ME17.......97 F2
Fowey CI ME5...........32 C5
Fowler CI ME8..........33 C3
Fowlmead Cntry Pk*
  CT14..................116 E8
Foxborough CI CT13....93 B6
Foxborough Hill CT13...93 B5
Foxborough La CT12...50 C6
Foxburrow CI ME8......33 D5
Fox CI CT18.............161 B7
Foxden Dr ME15.........75 F1
Foxdene Ct CT5.........42 F6
Foxdene Rd CT5.........42 F6
Foxdown CI CT2.........66 E2
Foxglove Cres ME5......31 E4
Foxglove Gn TN24....139 E7
Foxglove Rd ME15......97 E8
Foxglove Rise ME14....74 E7
Foxgrove La ME14.......36 E7
Foxgrove Rd CT5........21 A1
Fox Hill ME10, ME9.....37 D3
Fox Holt Rd CT15.....146 B2
Foxhunter Pk The CT12..49 D6
Forley Rd ME11.........3 A5
Fox's Cross CT5.........43 A3
Fox's Cross Hill CT5....43 A3
Fox's Cross Rd CT5.....43 C3
Fox St ME7..............10 C5
Fox Way CT4...........128 F8
Foxwood Specl Sch
  CT21...................176 F3
Frampton Rd CT21....176 A2
France Rd CT16........149 A5
Frances Gdns CT11.....52 F8
Francis CI CT12.........51 D5
Francis Dr ME5.........32 A2
Francis La ME15.........97 F5
Francis Rd
  Ashford TN23...........156 B8
  Broadstairs CT10.......30 B7
Frankapps CI ME9......35 B6
Frank Edinger Ct ME14..139 D4
Franklin Dr ME14.......75 F2
Franklin Rd ME7........10 D5
Franklins Cotts ME15...96 C5
Franklyn Ho CT7.......67 F5
Franklyn Rd CT7........87 C8
Franks Ct ME8...........11 B2
Frank Walters Bsns Pk The
  CT10....................29 D3
Freathy La TN25......139 C8
Freda CI CT10..........29 F1
Frederick Rd
  Deal CT14..............117 A3
  Gillingham ME7........10 C4
Frederick St ME10......36 E4
Freedown The CT15....151 A4
Freeman CI ME8........36 E4
Freeman Gdns ME4.....9 F2
Freeman's Cl CT5.......43 A6
Freeman's Rd CT12.....50 B6
Freeman Way ME15.....97 E7
Freeman's Way CT14...117 B3
Freesia CI ME7..........10 F6
Fremantle Rd CT20...177 E5
Fremlins Rd ME14......76 C4
Fremlin Walk Sh Ctr
  ME14...................74 F4
Frencham Ct CT2.......67 A4
French's Row ME9......38 D2
Frensham Cl ME10......37 B4
Frensham Wlk ME5......31 F1
Freshfield La CT21.....176 B4
Freshland Rd ME16.....74 B4
Freshlands CT6.........23 E5
Freshwater Ct CT6......22 B3
Freshwater Rd ME5.....32 B2
Friars Ave ME5..........31 F2
Friars CI CT5............21 A1
Friars The CT1..........66 F1
Friars Way CT16........149 A3
Friary PI [3] ME2......9 B7
Friary Prec ME2.........9 B7
Friary Way CT2.........66 D2
Frid Cnr TN26.........153 E7
Friendly CI CT9.........8 D1
Friends Ave CT12.......29 D8
Friesian Way TN24....139 C8
FRINDSBURY.............9 C8
Frindsbury Rd ME2.....9 B8
Frinstead Wlk ME16....74 B7
FRINSTED.................79 C7
Frinsted CI ME8........11 C3
Frinsted Rd ME9........58 E2
Friston Way ME1........31 D8
Frith Bsns Pk TN25...172 B6
Frith Rd
  Aldington Frith TN25..172 C6
  Dover CT16............149 C1
Frithwood CI ME15.....75 F1
Frittenden CI TN23....155 E6
Frobisher CI ME10......36 E7
Frobisher Ct [2] CT11...52 F8
Frobisher Gdns ME11...9 C2
Frog Farm Cotts ME9...13 A4
FROGHAM................113 C2
FROGHOLT................176 F7
Frog La CT4.............111 C6
Frogmore Wlk ME17...101 C5

Frognal CI ME9..........38 B2
Frognal Gdns ME9......38 C2
Frognal La ME9.........38 B2
Front Brents ME13......62 D8
Front Rd TN26..........169 A1
Front St CT14...........133 F5
Front The CT15.........151 A4
Frost Cres ME5..........32 A7
Frostland La TN26, TN29..184 C1
Froyle CI ME15.........74 C6
Fruiterer's CI ME9......59 B7
Fulbert Dr ME14........75 F5
Fulbert Rd CT16......149 B5
Fulham Ave CT9.........28 C7
Fullers CI ME14.........74 A4
Fullers Yd CT9..........7 J2
Fulmar CI TN29.........194 F3
Fulmar Mews CT18....163 A3
Fulmar Way CT6.........23 F4
Fulsam PI CT9............7 H1
Fulston Manor Sch ME10..36 F2
Fulston PI ME10........37 A3
Furfield Chase ME15...97 E4
Furfield CI ME17.........97 E5
FURFIELD PARK........97 D4
Furley Park Prim Sch
  TN23...................156 C2
Furrell's Rd ME1.........9 D5
FURTHER QUARTER...152 C3
Furze Hill Cres ME12...3 E6
Fusilier Ave CT20.....177 B5
Fyndon Ho CT1..........88 C7

G

Gabriel's Hill ME15.....75 A4
Gadby Rd ME10.........36 C5
Gadsby La TN26.......152 F3
Gads Hill ME7............10 F6
Gagetown Terr [1] ME14..74 F7
Gainsboro Rd [4] CT2....8 B2
Gainsborough Ave [1] CT9..29 C8
Gainsborough CI
  Folkestone CT20......178 A7
  Gillingham ME8........33 D6
  Sittingbourne ME10...36 B5
Gainsborough Dr
  Herne Bay CT6.........23 C5
  Maidstone ME16........74 B4
Gainsborough Ho ME1...9 D5
Galena CI
  Chatham ME5...........32 A1
  Sittingbourne ME10...36 C6
Gallants La ME15........96 A2
Galleon CI ME1..........31 C8
Galley Dr ME9...........38 E6
Galliard St CT13.........94 A8
Galloway Dr TN25......139 C8
Galloways Rd TN29.....205 C5
Gallow's Cnr CT21......176 A2
Galwey Ave CT7.........26 E7
Galway Rd ME12........1 D1
Gammon's Farm La
  TN29...................185 B3
Gammons Yd [6] CT2...66 F1
Gandy's La ME17........97 C2
Gange Mews [3] ME13..62 D7
Gann Rd CT5............66 B2
Gaol La [13] CT14.....166 D7
Gap The
  Blean CT2...............66 A7
  Canterbury CT1.........88 B5
Garden CI
  Maidstone ME15.......97 E3
  Rough Common CT2....66 A3
Garden Cotts CT3.......91 A7
Gardeners PI CT14......86 F1
Garden Hall The ME15..124 A1
Garden of England Pk
  (Mobile Home Pk)
  ME17...................100 B7
Garden PI TN24.........139 E6
Garden Rd CT19........178 D6
Gardens The
  Coxheath ME17........96 C5
  Dryhurch TN29.......192 F6
Gardiner's Hill TN31...197 B6
Gardiner St ME7........10 C6
Gardner Ct CT17.......162 F3
Gardners Ct CT13.......71 E1
Garfield PI [4] ME4.....62 D7
Garfield Rd
  Gillingham ME7........10 D6
  Margate CT9............7 H2
GARLINGE................28 A8
GARLINGE GREEN.....108 E5
Garlinge Green Rd CT4...108 E6
Garlinge Prim Sch CT9..28 B8
Garrard Ave CT9.........28 B8
Garrington CT14.........75 C6
Garrison Rd ME12.......1 B3
Garton Way TN23......155 C7
Gascoyne CI ME15......76 B2
Gas House Rd ME1......9 C6
Gaskin Rd ME13.........62 E7
Gas La ME13.............63 F3
Gas Rd
  Sittingbourne ME10...37 A3
  Sittingbourne, Murston..37 B6
Gas St CT1..............87 F2
Gasworks La TN23......139 B2
Gatcombe CI
  Chatham ME5...........32 A5
  Maidstone ME16.......74 B5
Gateacre Rd CT5........43 A6

Gatefield La [9] ME13...62 D7
Gatekeeper Chase ME8..33 F8
Gate La CT4.............144 A4
Gate Quays CT9.........7 I2
Gateway CI [21] CT11...52 F7
Gateway The CT16....166 E2
Gatland La ME16.......74 B2
Gault CI ME15...........76 A2
Gaunt's CI CT14........117 A4
Gault Wade ME8........33 D6
Gayhurst CI ME8.........33 D6
Gayhurst Dr ME8........33 D6
Gazedown TN29.......194 F3
Gaze Hill Ave ME10.....37 A3
Gazen Salts Nature Reserve *
  CT13....................72 F2
Gean CI ME5.............54 A8
Geddes CI CT18........162 F3
Genesta Ave CT5.......43 B7
Genesta CI ME10........36 E7
Geneva Ave ME8........11 A2
Gentian CI
  [4] Chatham ME5......31 E4
  Maidstone ME14.......75 E5
Geoffrey Ct CT7.........27 A7
George Alley CT14......117 C6
George Cooper Ho [11]
  CT20...................178 C4
George Gurr Cres CT9..178 D8
George Hill Rd CT10, CT9...8 E1
George La
  Boughton Street ME13..63 F3
  Folkestone CT20......178 D4
  Leeds ME17...............99 B7
  New Romney TN28....202 B7
  Rochester ME1.........52 E7
George Marsham Ho
  ME15...................96 F3
George Parris Ct ME12...4 C6
George Pk CT9...........7 F1
George Roche Rd CT1...88 A6
George's Ave CT5........43 A7
George St
  Ashford TN23...........139 B1
  Dover CT17.............117 D2
  Maidstone ME15........75 A3
  Ramsgate CT11........52 E7
  Sittingbourne ME10...37 B4
George Stone Ho [25]
  CT20...................178 E5
George Summers CI ME2...9 E8
George V Ave CT9.......28 C8
George Warren Ct [1] ME7..9 F2
George Williams Way
  TN24...................139 E5
George Wood St TN29...205 C6
Georgian CI ME11........9 A3
Georgian Dr ME17........96 D3
Georgian Way ME8.....33 C4
Gerald Ave ME4...........9 F2
Geraldine Rd CT19......177 F6
Gerald Palmbly Ct CT14..117 C7
Gerhic Ho TN24.........139 E6
Gerrard Ave ME4.........31 E8
Gerrards Dr ME10........36 F2
Gibbons Rd ME10........36 B5
Gibraltar Ave ME7......10 B7
Gibraltar Hill ME4.......9 F4
Gibraltar La
  Hawkinge CT18........163 A2
  Maidstone ME14.......74 F8
Gibraltar Sq CT15......149 E3
Gibson St ME10..........36 E4
Gidd's Pond Cotts ME14..75 E6
Giddyhorn La ME16.....74 C5
Gifford CI ME8...........11 C3
Gigger's Green Rd TN25..185 C7
Gilbert CI ME7...........33 A5
Gilbert PI [9] CT20.....177 E3
Gilbert Rd
  [4] Ashford TN24......139 B2
  Ramsgate CT11........52 D8
Gilbert Terr [2] ME14...74 F7
Gilbert Way CT1.........87 E6
Gilchrist Ave CT6........22 C2
Giles Gdns CT9..........28 F8
Giles La CT2.............66 A4
Giles-Young Ct [7] ME8..36 E5
Gilford Rd CT14........117 D5
Gilham Gr CT14........117 A4
Gillett Rd TN29.........205 D7
GILLINGHAM.............10 D3
Gillingham Gate ME7...10 C8
Gillingham Gate Rd ME7..10 C8
Gillingham Rd ME7......10 E6
Gillingham Rd ME7.....10 D5
Gillingham Sta ME7......10 D5
Gill La
  Aldington Frith TN25..172 A6
  Ruckinge TN26........171 C2
Gilman CI CT18........162 F4
Gillon Mews [9] CT15...67 B2
Gills Terr ME13..........12 C3
Ginsbury CI ME7.........10 F6
Giraud Dr ME13..........62 B8
Glack Rd CT14..........116 F4

Glade The
  Chatham ME5...........32 A2
  Deal CT14...............116 F6
Gladstone Ct CT10......29 F4
Gladstone Dr ME10......37 C4
Gladstone Rd
  Ashford TN24...........156 E7
  Broadstairs CT10.......29 F4
  Chatham ME4............9 E2
  Deal CT14...............117 C4
  Folkestone CT20......178 E6

Gladstone Rd *continued*
  Maidstone ME14.......75 A6
  Margate CT9............7 I1
  Whitstable CT5........20 D2
Gladwyn CI ME8.........33 D8
Glamis CI ME5...........32 A5
Glanville Rd
  Gillingham ME7........10 D5
  Rochester ME2.........9 A8
Glasgow Ho [8] ME5...97 E7
Glayton Gdns ME5......31 F4
Gleaming Wood Dr ME5..54 D8
Gleaners CI ME14.......75 E4
Gleanings Mews [9] CT9..9 C5
Glebe CI
  Smarden TN27........135 B2
  St Margaret's at Cliffe
    CT15..................150 F6
Glebe Cotts ME13......81 E7
Glebe Ct CT12...........50 B5
Glebe Gdns
  Lenham ME17..........101 C5
  [4] Margate CT9.......28 B8
Glebe La
  Maidstone ME16........74 A1
  Sittingbourne ME10....37 B2
Glebeland TN27.........118 F4
Glebelands
  Alkham CT15..........147 D1
  Ash CT3................71 C2
  Mersham TN25.........157 E4
Glebe Rd
  Gillingham ME7........10 E3
  Margate CT9............28 B8
Glebe The TN27........120 D7
Glebe Way
  Ashford TN24..........139 D6
  Whitstable CT5.........43 D8
Glemsford Cotts CT2....65 C1
Glen Ave CT6............23 C5
Glenavon Ho CT10......30 B7
Glenbervie Dr CT6.......23 E5
Glenbrook CI CT6........23 D5
Glenbrook Rd ME10.....36 E7
Glencoe Rd
  Chatham ME4...........10 A2
  Margate CT9............8 A1
Glendale [1] CT20......178 E4
Glendale Rd ME12.......4 B7
Gleneagles CI ME5......31 F2
Gleneagles Dr ME8......75 A1
Glenfield Rd CT16.....149 B3
Glen Gr CT17...........166 B7
Glen Iris Ave CT2........66 C2
Glen Iris CI CT2..........66 C2
Glenmore Ctr ME10.....37 C6
Glen Rd CT14...........134 C6
Glenside CT5............44 A8
Glenside Ave CT1........67 B2
Glen The
  Minster (Sheppey) ME12..4 B7
  Shepherdswell CT15..130 D5
  Upstreet CT3............47 D5
Glen Wlk CT5............43 A3
Glenwood TN30.........167 B3
Glenwood CI
  Chatham ME5...........10 C1
  Gillingham ME7........33 A7
  Maidstone ME16.......74 C5
  Tenterden TN30........167 B3
Glenwood Dr ME12......4 B7
Glistening Glade ME8...33 E6
Globe La ME4............9 F5
Gloster CI CT18.........163 B3
Gloster Ropewalk CT17..166 C5
Gloster Way CT17.......166 C5
Gloucester Ave
  Broadstairs CT10.......29 F3
  Chatham ME5............10 C1
Gloucester CI ME8......34 A8
Gloucester Mews CT9..202 C8
Gloucester PI [17] CT20..178 D5
Gloucester Rd
  Maidstone ME16........97 D8
  Whitstable CT5.........20 F2
Glover CI ME10..........14 F1
Glover Rd TN24..........139 E1
Glovers Cres ME10......36 F3
Glovers Mill ME4........9 F2
Glynne CI ME8...........33 D6
Goad Ave ME5...........32 B3
GOAT LEES................139 C8
Goat Lees La TN25.....139 D8
Gobery Hill CT3..........70 B1
Godden Rd CT2...........67 A4
Godden Way ME17.......9 A3
Goddings Dr ME1........52 A6
Goddington La ME17...100 B6
Goddington Rd ME2.....9 B8
Godfrey Gdns CT4.......86 F1
Godfrey Ho CT5..........43 E8
Godfreys Cotts ME15...105 C8
Godfrey's Grave ME13...64 B7
Godfrey Wlk TN23......156 B8
GODINGTON PARK....138 E2
Godinton House & Gdns *
  TN23...................138 C4
Godinton La TN23, TN26..138 D5
Godinton Prim Sch
  TN23...................138 D3
Godinton Rd TN23......139 A2
Godinton Way TN23....139 A2
Godinton Way Ind Est
  TN23...................139 B2
GODMERSHAM..........107 A2
Godwin Bglws CT9........8 B3

Godwin Cl
  Deal CT14 . . . . 117 A3
  Sittingbourne ME10 . . . . . . .14 F1
Godwin Cotts CT9 . . . . .8 A3
Godwin Rd
  Canterbury CT1 . . . . .87 C6
  Dover CT16 . . . . .166 F8
Margate CT9 . . . . .8 A3
Godwyne Ct CT16 . . . . . . .166 D8
Godwyne Rd CT16 . . . . . . .149 D1
Godwyne Rd CT16 . . . . . . .149 D1
Godwyn Gdns CT20 . . . . . .178 A4
Godwyn Rd
  Deal CT14 . . . . 117 C8
  Folkestone CT20 . . . . .178 A4
Gogway CT14 . . . . .126 B5
Goldcrest Wlk CT5. . . . . . . .43 B6
Golden Acre La CT8. . . . . . .27 D7
Golden Cl CT8 . . . . .27 D7
Golden Hill CT5. . . . . .43 F6
Golden Sq
  New Romney TN28. . . . . . .202 A6
  Tenterden TN30 . . . . .179 B8
Golden St CT14 . . . . .117 D5
Golden Wood Cl ME5 . . . . . .54 D8
Goldfinch Cl
  Faversham ME13 . . . . .40 C1
  Herne Bay CT6. . . . . .23 C2
Gold Hill ME1. . . . . .9 E1
Goldings The ME8. . . . . .33 C8
Goldsmith St TN30. . . . . . .167 B1
Goodall Cl NR8 . . . . .33 E5
Goodban Sq CT3. . . . . .71 D1
Goodcheap La TN25. . . . . . .140 C2
Goodfellow Way **3**
  CT16. . . . . .166 D8
Good Hope CT16 . . . . .116 F4
Good Intent Cotts TN27 . .119 A5
GOODNESTONE
  Faversham. 63 D7
  Wingham. 91 D2
Goodnestone CE Prim Sch
  CT3. . . . . .91 C2
Goodnestone Hill CT3. . . . . .91 D2
Good Shepherd Prim Sch
  The ME4 . . . . .9 E1
Goodwin Ave CT5 . . . . .21 E2
Goodwin Ct CT9 . . . . .8 D3
Goodwin Dr ME14. . . . . .75 B8
Goodwin Pk CT9. . . . . .29 A5
Goodwin Rd
  Ramsgate CT11 . . . . .52 B5
  St Margaret's at Cliffe
    CT15. . . . . .151 A4
Goodwood Cl ME15 . . . . . . .97 F6
Goose Cl ME5 . . . . .32 A7
Goose Farm CT2 . . . . .67 D7
Goosefields ME13. . . . . .41 E1
Gordon Ave ME11. . . . . .3 A4
Gordon Cl
  Ashford TN24. . . . . .139 D2
  Sittingbourne ME10. . . . . . .37 C4
Gordon Cotts ME9 . . . . .58 B6
Gordon Ct ME17 . . . . .96 E3
Gordon Gr CT8 . . . . .7 C1
Gordon Inf Sch ME2 . . . . . . .9 A8
Gordon Jun Sch ME2 . . . . . . .9 A8
Gordon Rd
  Canterbury CT1 . . . . .87 F7
  Chatham, Luton ME4 . . . . . .10 B2
  Chatham ME4 . . . . .10 A6
  Dover CT16 . . . . .149 A5
  Faversham ME13 . . . . .62 E8
  Folkestone CT20 . . . . .177 D6
  Gillingham ME7 . . . . .10 E5
  Herne Bay CT6. . . . . .22 F4
  Margate CT9 . . . . .8 A3
  Margate, Westwood CT9 . . . .29 A5
  Ramsgate CT11 . . . . .52 D8
  Rochester ME2 . . . . .9 A8
  Whitstable CT5 . . . . .43 D8
Gordon Sq
  Birchington CT7. . . . . .26 F7
  Faversham ME13 . . . . .62 E7
Gordon Terr
  Lydd TN29 . . . . .205 C5
  Rochester ME1 . . . . .9 C4
GORE. 93 B3
Gore Cl CT13 . . . . .93 B3
Gore Cotts ME9. . . . . .12 E1
Gore Court Rd
  Maidstone ME15 . . . . .97 F5
  Sittingbourne ME10. . . . . . .36 E2
Gore Ct TN24 . . . . .139 C3

Gore End Cl CT7. . . . . .26 F7
Gore Farm CT13 . . . . .93 B3
Gore La CT13 . . . . .93 B2
Gorely Ho **14** CT17. . . . . . .166 D7
Gore Mews **3** CT11. . . . . . .67 B2
Gore Rd
  Eastry CT13 . . . . .93 B3
  Silver Street ME9. . . . . .57 F5
Gore Street Farm Cotts
  CT12. . . . . .49 A7
Gore Terr CT13 . . . . .93 B3
Goretop La CT14. . . . . .94 C6
Gorham Dr ME15 . . . . .76 A1
Gorrell Rd CT5. . . . . .20 F3
Gorse Ave ME5 . . . . .31 F5
Gorse La CT6 . . . . .23 C2
Gorse Mead TN23 . . . . .155 F8
Gorse Rd ME10 . . . . .37 C5
Gorst St ME7 . . . . .10 C5
Goschen Rd CT17 . . . . .166 B8
Gosfield Rd CT6 . . . . .23 A4
Goshawk Ho **1** ME10. . . . . .37 A4
GOSMERE. 83 E7
Gosmere Farm Barns
  Doddington ME13 . . . . .80 E7
  Sheldwich ME13 . . . . .83 E7
Gosselin St CT5. . . . . .43 E8
Goss Hall La CT3 . . . . .72 A2
Goteley Mere TN24. . . . . . .139 C7
Gothic Cl CT14. . . . . .117 B1
Gothic Cotts TN26. . . . . . . .121 A1
Goudhurst Cl
  Canterbury CT2 . . . . .67 A4
  Maidstone ME16 . . . . .74 E4
Goudhurst Rd ME8. . . . . . . .11 B3
Gough Rd CT20 . . . . .177 E3
Gould Rd ME5 . . . . .32 B3
Gower Ho ME14 . . . . .75 A6
Grace Ave ME16 . . . . .74 D6
Grace Ct **16** CT20 . . . . . . .178 D5
Grace Hill CT20 . . . . .178 D5
Grace Mdw CT16 . . . . .149 A7
Grace Rd
  Faversham ME13 . . . . .62 F7
  Maidstone ME15 . . . . .97 F7
Grace Sch **22** CT20. . . . . . .178 D5
Grace Wlk CT14 . . . . .117 A5
Grafton Ave ME1. . . . . .31 E8
Grafton Rd
  Broadstairs CT10. . . . . .29 F8
  Sittingbourne ME10. . . . . . .36 F4
Grafton Rise CT6 . . . . .22 C4
Graham Cl ME4 . . . . .9 E2
Grainey Field ME9 . . . . .34 E4
Grain Rd ME8. . . . . .33 C3
Grampian Way ME15 . . . . . .76 A1
Grampion Cl TN24 . . . . . . .139 C4
Grams Rd CT14 . . . . .134 C8
Granada Ho **8** ME15 . . . . . .75 A4
Granada St **9** ME15 . . . . . .75 A4
Granary Cl
  Gillingham ME8 . . . . .11 F1
  Maidstone ME14 . . . . .75 F7
Granary Court Rd TN25. . .159 A4
Granary Pl CT5 . . . . .43 D8
Grand Ct
  6 Folkestone CT20. . . . . .178 B3
  7 Gillingham ME7 . . . . . . .10 C6
Grand-on-Sea TN28. . . . . . .202 E15
Grand Dr CT14. . . . . .30 B3
Grand Mans CT20 . . . . .178 B3
Grand Par TN28. . . . . .202 E5
Grand Pavilion CT5 . . . . . . .20 F3
Grand The* CT20 . . . . .178 B3
GRANGE. 11 B6
Grange Cres TN30. . . . . . . .167 A3
Grange Ct
  7 Folkestone CT20. . . . . .178 C4
  8 Ramsgate CT11 . . . . . . .52 C6
Grange Hill ME5 . . . . .10 B3
Grange Ho 74 A2
Grange La ME14 . . . . .54 A1
Grange Rd
  Broadstairs CT10. . . . . .29 F6
  Deal CT14 . . . . .117 B5
  Folkestone CT19 . . . . .177 E4
  Gillingham ME7 . . . . .11 A6
  Herne Bay CT6. . . . . .23 C4
  Hythe CT21 . . . . .176 B4
  Ramsgate CT11 . . . . .52 C6
  Rochester ME2 . . . . .9 B7
Grange Rdbt ME7 . . . . .11 A6
Grange The
  Ramsgate CT11 . . . . .52 C7
  Shepherdswell CT15 . . . . . .130 D5
  Whitstable CT5 . . . . .43 A6
Grange Way
  Broadstairs CT10. . . . . .29 F2
  Rochester ME1 . . . . .9 E5
Grant Cl CT10 . . . . .29 E6
Grant Dr ME15. . . . . .97 D6
Grantham Ave CT14 . . . . . .117 A5
Grantham Ct TN23. . . . . . .156 A8
Grant's Cotts ME17 . . . . . .101 B5
Granville Ave
  Broadstairs CT10. . . . . .30 B3
  Ramsgate CT12 . . . . .29 B1
Granville Cl ME13. . . . . .62 C7
Granville Ct
  Deal CT14 . . . . .117 C2
  Maidstone ME14 . . . . .75 A6
Granville Dr CT16. . . . . . . .149 B3
Granville Farm Mews **24**
  CT11. . . . . .52 F7
Granville Pl
  Folkestone CT20 . . . . .177 F3
  Sheerness ME20 . . . . .1 F3

Granville Rd
  Broadstairs CT10. . . . . .30 B3
  Deal CT14 . . . . .117 C2
  Gillingham ME7 . . . . .10 E5
  Kingsdown CT14 . . . . .134 D3
  Maidstone ME14 . . . . .75 A6
  Sheerness ME12 . . . . .1 D2
  St Margaret's at Cliffe
    CT15. . . . . .151 B6
Granville Road E CT20 . . . .177 F3
Granville St
  Deal CT14 . . . . .117 D5
  Dover CT14 . . . . .149 C1
Granville The CT15. . . . . . .151 B6
Granville Theatre* **25**
  CT11. . . . . .52 F7
Grapple Rd ME14 . . . . .75 A7
Grasmere Ave CT11 . . . . . . .52 A7
Grasmere Gdns CT19 . . . . .178 B2
Grasmere Pk CT5 . . . . .44 B8
Grasmere Rd
  Ashford TN24. . . . . .139 C6
  Whitstable CT5 . . . . .44 B8
Grasmere Way CT3 . . . . . . .112 F6
Grasslands
  Ashford TN23 . . . . .155 D7
  Langley Heath ME17 . . . . . .98 E4
Grassmere TN29 . . . . .194 E3
Grassy Glade ME7 . . . . .33 B6
GRAVEL CASTLE. 129 A8
Gravel Castle Rd CT14 . . . .129 A8
Gravel Hill ME13 . . . . .103 C8
Gravel La CT15 . . . . .165 A4
Gravelly Bottom Rd ME17 .99 B2
Gravelly Field TN23 . . . . . .155 C8
Gravelly Fields TN23 . . . . .155 C8
Gravel Wlk
  3 Ashford TN23 . . . . . . .139 B3
  Rochester ME1 . . . . .9 D5
GRAVENEY. 41 E2
Graveney Prim Sch ME13. .41 E1
Graveney Rd
  Faversham ME13 . . . . .62 F7
  Maidstone ME15 . . . . .97 F7
Gray Cl CT18 . . . . .163 C5
Graylen Cl CT14 . . . . .117 C7
Graylings Cl ME10 . . . . .36 C2
Graylings The ME1. . . . . .9 E1
Graystone Rd CT21 . . . . . . .21 A2
Grays Way CT1 . . . . .87 B6
Great Basin Rd ME12 . . . . . .1 B3
Great Burton Ho TN24. . . .139 E5
GREAT CHART. 138 C1
Great Chart Prim Sch
  TN23 . . . . .155 D8
Great Conduit St CT21 . . . .176 C2
Great Easthall Way ME10. . .37 D4
Great Fishers TN23 . . . . . . .155 C7
Great Ivy Mill Cotts ME17 .96 F7
Great Lines ME7 . . . . .10 B5
GREAT MONGEHAM 116 C3
Great Oaks Small Sch
  CT12. . . . . .51 B2
Great South Ave ME4. . . . . .10 A1
GREAT STONAR 73 B4
GREATSTONE-ON-SEA. . . .202 E1
Greatstone Prim Sch
  TN28 . . . . .202 D2
Great Stour Pl CT1 . . . . .87 F8
Grebe Apartments **13**
  ME15 . . . . .97 E5
Grebe Cl CT18 . . . . .163 A4
Grebe Cres CT21. . . . . .187 C8
Grecian St ME14 . . . . .75 A6
Greenacre CT1 . . . . .111 D3
Greenacre CT15. . . . . .32 A5
Greenacre Dr CT14. . . . . . .117 C1
Greenacres CT14. . . . . .95 B4
Greenacre Sch ME5. . . . . . . .31 F5
Green Acres CT15. . . . . . . .131 D7
Green Acres ME5. . . . . .23 B3
Greenbank
  Ashford TN24. . . . . .139 D6
  Chatham ME5. . . . . .32 B8
Green Bank Cl ME7 . . . . .33 A5
Greenbanks CT18 . . . . .161 C6
Greenborough Cl ME15. . . .97 E6
Green Cl
  Hawkinge CT18 . . . . .163 B4
  Rochester ME1 . . . . .9 D2
Green Cloth Mews **7**
  CT3. . . . . .67 B2
Greencroft TN23 . . . . .155 E6
Green Ct
  Bridge CT4. . . . . .89 A1
  Whitstable CT5 . . . . .44 C3
Green Dell ME7 . . . . .64 F4
Greenfield Cl ME20 . . . . . . .53 A6
Greenfield Cotts
  Boxley ME14 . . . . .54 C3
  1 Canterbury CT1 . . . . . . .87 F7
Greenfield Rd
  Folkestone CT19 . . . . .178 E2
  Gillingham ME7 . . . . .10 D6
  Ramsgate CT12 . . . . .29 C2
Greenfields
  Maidstone ME15 . . . . .97 E8
  Sellindge TN25. . . . . .159 E2
Greenfields Com Prim Sch
  ME15 . . . . .97 E8
Green Fields La TN23 . . . . .155 C7
Greenfinches ME7 . . . . .32 F6
Green Gates CT15. . . . . . . .149 A8
Green Hedges TN30. . . . . . .179 B8
GREENHILL. 22 D2
Green Hill ME15 . . . . .76 B1
Greenhill Bridge Rd CT6 . . .22 D3
Greenhill La CT12. . . . . .50 B7

Greenhill Gdns
  Herne Bay CT6. . . . . .22 D3
  Minster (Thanet) CT12. . . . . .50 B7
Greenhill La TN27 . . . . .135 F7
Green Hill La ME17 . . . . . . .100 D1
Greenhill Rd CT6 . . . . .22 D3
Green Hills CT5 . . . . .128 D8
Greenhithe **3** ME15 . . . . . .75 A3
Greenhouse La CT2 . . . . . . .66 E2
Green La
  Alkham CT15 . . . . .147 D3
  Ashford TN23 . . . . .155 E5
  Bethersden TN26 . . . . .153 A2
  Broadstairs CT10. . . . . .29 E5
  Capel-le-Ferne CT18 . . . . . .164 B3
  Challock TN25 . . . . .105 A2
  Deal CT14 . . . . .117 B5
  Dover CT16 . . . . .149 B3
  Eythorne CT15 . . . . .131 D7
  Folkestone CT19 . . . . .178 E7
  Goodnestone CT3 . . . . .92 B3
  High Halden TN26 . . . . . . .152 F3
  Hythe CT21 . . . . .176 A2
  Langley Heath ME17 . . . . . .98 E3
  Maidstone ME17 . . . . .97 C3
  Margate CT9 . . . . .29 E8
  Old Wives Lees CT4 . . . . . . .85 C2
  Platt's Heath ME17 . . . . . .100 C7
  Rhodes Minnis CT4, CT18 . .143 E2
  Rodmersham ME9 . . . . .59 B7
  St Margaret's at Cliffe
    CT15. . . . . .133 F1
  Temple Ewell CT16 . . . . . . .148 E6
  Whitfield CT16. . . . . .148 E7
  Whitstable CT5 . . . . .43 D8
Green Lane Ave CT21 . . . . .176 A2
Green Lane Cotts ME17 . . . .98 E3
Greenlea **8** CT20 . . . . .178 B3
Green Leas CT5. . . . . .21 D1
Green Lees ME12 . . . . .61 E2
Greenlees Cl ME10 . . . . .36 B5
Greenly Way TN28 . . . . . . .202 C6
Green Mdws
  Dymchurch TN29 . . . . .186 D2
  Eythorne CT15 . . . . .131 D7
Green Porch Cl ME10 . . . . .36 F7
Green Rd
  Birchington CT7. . . . . .26 F8
  Stalisfield Green ME13 . . . .103 C6
Greensand Rd ME15. . . . . . .76 A1
Greensand Ridge ME17. . . . .99 E2
Green Sands ME5. . . . . .54 C8
Green's Cotts ME15 . . . . . . .96 A4
Greenshanks ME9. . . . . .14 E3
Greenside
  High Halden TN26 . . . . . . .167 E7
  Maidstone ME15 . . . . .75 B3
Greenside Ho CT9 . . . . .7 F1
Greensole La CT12. . . . . . . .28 E1
Green St ME7. . . . . .10 C5
Green The
  Blean CT2 . . . . .66 A6
  Burmarsh TN29 . . . . .186 C4
  Chartham TN29 . . . . .86 D3
  East Farleigh ME15 . . . . . . .96 B7
  Harbledown CT2. . . . . .65 C1
  Hythe CT21 . . . . .176 B4
  Littlebourne CT3 . . . . .69 F7
  Lower Halstow ME9. . . . . . .13 B3
  Lydd TN29 . . . . .205 B5
  Manston CT12 . . . . .28 D1
  Sheerness ME12 . . . . .1 D1
  Warehorne TN26 . . . . .182 D6
  Woodchurch TN26 . . . . . . .169 A2
  Woolage Village CT4 . . . . . .112 E1
  Wye TN25. . . . . .123 E2
Greenvale Gdns ME8 . . . . . .11 B2
Greenvale Inf Sch ME4 . . . . .10 A2
Greenview Wlk ME8. . . . . . .11 A4
Greenway
  Chatham ME5. . . . . .31 D6
  Faversham ME13 . . . . .62 B8
Green Way
  Lydd TN29 . . . . .205 C5
  Maidstone ME14 . . . . .75 F5
  Sittingbourne ME10. . . . . . .37 B3
Greenways
  Lower Halstow ME9. . . . . . .13 B3
  Maidstone ME14 . . . . .75 F5
  Sittingbourne ME10. . . . . . .37 B3
Greenwich Cl
  Chatham ME5. . . . . .32 B4
  Maidstone ME16 . . . . .74 D4
GREET. 80 D3
Gregory Cl
  Gillingham ME8 . . . . .33 E4
  Sittingbourne ME10. . . . . . .37 A8
Gregory Ct TN25. . . . . .123 E2
Grenadier Cl
  Gillingham ME8 . . . . .12 B2
  Maidstone ME15 . . . . .75 F2
Grenadier Way TN23 . . . . .155 C8
Grenham Bay Ave CT7 . . . . .26 E8
Grenham Rd CT7 . . . . .26 F8
Grenville Gdns CT17 . . . . . .26 E8
Grenville Way CT10 . . . . . . .29 E4
Gresham Ave CT9 . . . . .7 F1
Gresham Cl **3** ME8 . . . . . . .11 F1
Gresham Rd ME7 . . . . .96 D3
Greville Ho CT17. . . . . .166 C7

Greville Homes CT13 . . . . . .93 B2
Greyfriars Cl ME16. . . . . . . .74 D5
Grey Friars Court **8** CT1 . .87 F8
Greyfriars Ct CT10 . . . . .8 F2
Greyhound Chase TN23. . . .155 C7
Greystones Rd
  Cliffs End CT12 . . . . .51 D5
  Maidstone ME15 . . . . .76 A2
Grey Wethers ME14 . . . . . . .53 C4
Grey Willow Gdns TN23. . .155 D8
Grice Cl CT18 . . . . .162 F3
Grieveson Ho ME4 . . . . .10 A4
Griffin Cotts TN26. . . . . . . .181 C2
Griffin's Cnr CT7. . . . . .140 F7
Griffin St CT14 . . . . .117 D7
Grimshill Ct CT2. . . . . .66 C4
Grimshill Rd CT5 . . . . .43 E8
Grimston Ave CT20. . . . . . .178 B4
Grimston Gdns CT20 . . . . .178 B4
Grimthorpe Ave CT5. . . . . . .43 C7
Grinsell Hill CT12. . . . . .50 E6
Grisbrook Farm CT TN29. . .205 D6
Grisbrook Rd TN29. . . . . . .205 D6
Grizedale Cl ME15 . . . . .97 C8
Groombridge Sq **13** ME15 .97 F6
Groom Way ME17. . . . . . . .101 E6
Grosvenor Ave ME4 . . . . .9 E3
Grosvenor Cotts CT7 . . . . . .27 B3
Grosvenor Gdns CT9 . . . . . . .7 I1
Grosvenor Ho CT9 . . . . .7 I2
Grosvenor Ho **5** ME15 . . . .97 F5
Grosvenor Pl CT9 . . . . .7 I2
Grosvenor Rd
  Ashford TN24. . . . . .139 D7
  Broadstairs CT10. . . . . .30 A4
  Gillingham ME7 . . . . .11 A1
  Ramsgate CT12 . . . . .52 C7
  Whitstable CT5 . . . . .43 D7
Grotto Gdns **6** CT9 . . . . . . .7 J2
Grotto Hill CT9 . . . . .7 J2
Grotto Rd **5** CT9 . . . . .7 J2
GROVE. 69 F8
Grove Ave ME12 . . . . .6 G2
Grove Bridge TN25 . . . . . . .174 D8
Grove Cl ME13 . . . . .62 A6
Grove Cotts TN30 . . . . .179 B6
Grove Court Farm ME13 . . .64 A3
Grove Ct **4** ME2. . . . . .9 A4
Grove Dairy Farm ME9 . . . . .36 A6
GROVE END. 58 C7
Grove Ferry Hill CT3 . . . . . .47 E3
Grove Ferry Rd CT3. . . . . . .48 A2
Grove Gdns CT9 . . . . .7 G1
GROVE GREEN. 75 E5
Grove Green La ME14 . . . . . .75 E5
Grove Green Rd ME14. . . . . .75 E5
GROVE HILL. 69 D6
Grove Ho TN27. . . . . .136 C3
Grovehurst Ave ME10 . . . . .14 F1
Grovehurst Rd ME10, ME9 . .14 E2
Grove La
  Brookland TN29 . . . . .191 D3
  Iden TN31 . . . . .197 C4
Grovelands ME17 . . . . .101 E5
Grove Park Ave ME10 . . . . . .36 B4
Grove Park CP Sch ME10. . .36 B4
Grove Pl ME13 . . . . .62 A6
Grove Rd
  Chatham ME4. . . . . .10 B2
  Deal CT14 . . . . .117 D3
  Folkestone CT20 . . . . .178 E6
  Gillingham ME7 . . . . .10 E5
  Maidstone ME15 . . . . .97 C2
  Preston CT3. . . . . .70 B8
  Ramsgate CT11 . . . . .52 C6
  Rochester ME7 . . . . .9 B8
  Selling ME13 . . . . .84 B4
  Staple CT3 . . . . .91 F6
  Wickhambreaux CT3 . . . . . .69 D6
Grove Road Cotts
  Wickhambreaux CT3 . . . . . .69 C2
  Wickhambreaux, Frognall
    CT3. . . . . .69 C3
Grove Terr CT1. . . . . .87 E7
Grove The
  Ashford TN24. . . . . .139 E6
  Barham CT4 . . . . .128 F8
  Deal CT14 . . . . .117 C6
  Dover CT16 . . . . .149 C1
  Herne Bay CT6. . . . . .23 A2
  Maidstone ME14 . . . . .76 A3
  Westgate on Sea CT8 . . . . . .27 F8
Groveway 6 F2
Grove Way CT3 . . . . .70 C7
Grovewood Ct ME14 . . . . . .75 E4
Grovewood Dr ME14 . . . . . .75 E4
Grummock Ave CT11. . . . . . .52 B7
Grundy's Hill **13** CT11. . . . .52 E6
Guardian Ct ME8 . . . . .11 C1
Guernsey Way TN24 . . . . . .139 C7
Guestling Mill Ct **11** CT13 .72 F1
Guildcourt La **5** CT13 . . . . .72 F1
Guildford Lawn **4** CT11. . . .52 E6
Guildford Rd CT17. . . . . . . .87 F6
Guildhall Cl CT20 . . . . .178 D5
Guildhall Mus*
  Queenborough ME11. . . . . . .2 F5
  Rochester ME1 . . . . .9 C6
Guildhall St
  4 Canterbury CT1 . . . . . . .87 F8
  6 Folkestone CT20. . . . . .178 D5
Guildhall Street N CT19,
  CT20. . . . . .178 D5
Guilford Ave CT16 . . . . . . .149 A8

Guilford Ct CT14........117 D2
Guilford Ho CT13.......95 A7
Guilford Rd CT13........94 E8
Guilton CT3................71 C1
Guilton CT3................71 E1
Guldeford La TN29, TN31..198 F3
Guldeford Lane Cnr
TN31...........................198 D2
Gulland Ho **4** ME14....75 B4
Gullands ME17.............98 E4
Gundulph Rd ME1........9 E4
Gundulph Sq ME1........9 C4
Gun La ME2..................9 B7
Gun Lane Bsns Est **5** ME2..9 B7
Gunnis Cl ME8...............33 D4
Gun Tower Mews ME1......5 B4
Gurling Rd CT15..........133 F1
GUSHMERE....................84 C7
GUSTON........................149 E6
Guston CE Prim Sch
CT15............................149 E3
Guston Rd
East Langdon CT15.....150 A8
Maidstone ME14..........75 C6
Guthrie Gdns CT17........148 E3
Guy Cl CT10.................30 A7
Gwyn Rd CT12..............29 C5
Gypsy Cnr CT5.............44 D3

H

Hackfield TN23..............138 F1
Hackington Cl CT2.........66 E4
Hackington Pl CT2.........66 E7
Hackington Rd CT2........66 E7
Hackington Terr CT2......66 F2
HACKLINGE....................94 C1
Hacklinge Hill CT14.......94 B2
Hackney Rd ME16.........74 C2
Haddon Dene Sch CT10...29 F4
Hadleigh Cl ME7...........33 A3
Hadleigh Gdns CT6........23 B5
Hadley Gdns ME17........77 E2
Hadlow Coll CT11..........88 B8
Hadlow Dr CT9..............8 E2
Hadlow Rd ME14..........75 C5
Hadrian Gdns TN23.......155 F5
Haffenden Mdw TN27....122 C8
HAFFENDEN QUARTER....152 A7
Haffenden Rd TN30........167 B1
Haig Ave
Chatham, Luton ME4.....10 A2
Chatham ME1...............9 D1
HAINE..........................28 F2
Haine Ind Est CT12.......28 E1
Haine Rd CT12, CT10.....28 E2
Halden Cl ME15............97 F6
HALE
Birchington..................26 B4
Chatham.......................32 D8
Hales Cl TN30.............179 B8
Hales Dr CT2...............179 B8
Hales Dr CT2...............66 D3
HALES PLACE...............67 A3
Hales Rd ME10.............36 D1
Haleys Pl ME1.............53 A8
Halfmile Ride CT9..........28 E6
Halford Cl CT6..............23 B2
Halfpenny Cl ME16.......74 A2
Halfway Houses Prim Sch
ME12............................3 D6
Halfway Rd ME12...........3 D8
HALFWAY STREET.......130 D4
Halifax Cl ME5.............32 B6
Hall Ave TN24..............156 F6
Hall Cl ME10................36 E6
Hall Cres CT14...........116 F5
Hallcroft Ct CT11..........52 C7
Hallett Wlk **10** CT11....67 B2
Halliday Ct CT21..........176 A2
Halliday Dr CT14..........117 D3
Hall Rd ME5................32 C3
Hallsfield Rd ME5.........31 D2
Hallwood Cl ME8..........33 D5
Hallwood Ho ME5..........32 C2
Halstatt Rd CT14.........117 E3
Halstead Cl CT2............67 B4
Halstead Gdns CT9.......8 E3
Halstead Wlk ME16......74 C7
Halstow Cl ME15..........97 B6
Halstow Way TN23.......155 F8
Halt The
Elham CT4...................144 F4
Whitstable CT5............44 A7
HAM..............................93 F2
Hambledon Ct ME16......74 B3
Hambrook Cl CT4..........107 B8
Hambrook La CT4..........107 C8
Hambrook Wlk ME10.....36 F8
Hamele The CT2...........67 F5
Hamelin Rd ME7...........32 B8
Ham Farm Cotts CT14...93 F2
HAM GREEN
Upchurch....................12 F6
Wittersham.................188 C1
Hamill Terr CT1............67 B2
Hamilton Cl
Littlebourne-on-Sea TN28...202 E5
Ramsgate CT11............29 B1
Hamilton Cres ME10......36 C3

Hamilton Ct
Chatham ME5...............10 C1
Rochester ME1.............9 B4
Hamilton Ho
Coxheath ME17............96 C3
Maidstone ME15..........97 F5
Hamilton Rd
Ashford TN24..............156 D6
Deal CT14...................117 C4
Dover CT17.................166 B8
Gillingham ME7............10 D7
Lydd TN29...................205 C6
Whitstable CT5............20 D1
Ham La
Gillingham ME7............32 E3
Lenham ME17..............101 C5
HAMLET OF SHELLNESS...19 E5
HAMMILL......................92 E3
Ham Mill La TN26, TN29..183 A2
Hammond Cl CT15........113 E5
Hammond's Cnr TN29...201 E6
Hammond's Rd CT20....177 E5
Hamond Hill **6** ME4.....9 E4
Hampden La TN23.........156 A7
Hampden Pl TN23.........156 A7
Hampden Rd TN23........156 A6
Hampshire Cl ME5.........31 F3
Hampshire Dr ME15......97 C8
Hampshire Rd CT1........88 D7
Hampshires The CT1.....100 C6
Hampson Way ME14......76 A4
HAMPTON......................22 B5
Hampton Cl
Chatham ME5...............32 A5
Herne Bay CT6.............22 A3
Hampton Gdns CT6.......22 A3
Hampton La TN25.........141 C3
Hampton Pier Ave CT6...22 B4
Hampton Rd ME14........75 C6
Hampton Vale CT21.......177 B4
Ham Rd ME13...............40 C1
Ham St St Woods National
Nature Reserve* TN26..171 B2
Ham Shades La CT5......21 A1
HAMSTREET..................183 B7
Hamstreet Prim Sch
TN26...........................182 F8
Hamstreet Rd
Bromley Green TN26......170 E5
Hamstreet TN26...........183 C7
Ham Street Sta TN26....183 A8
Hamwick Gn ME5..........32 C1
Hancocks Field CT14.....117 A5
Hangman's La CT14......133 F5
Hannah Cl ME4.............10 A3
Hanover Cl
Ashford TN23...............138 F2
Deal CT14...................117 D2
Margate CT9.................8 E2
Sittingbourne ME10.......36 E2
Hanover Ct
Broadstairs CT10..........29 F4
Faversham ME13..........62 B8
Hythe CT21.................176 C1
Maidstone ME14..........75 B5
Hanover Dr ME8...........33 C4
Hanover Ho **8** CT20....178 C4
Hanover Pl CT2............66 E7
Hanover Rd ME17.........96 C3
Hanover Sq CT6...........22 F5
Hanover St CT6............22 F5
Hanscomb Ho CT2........66 E2
Hansletts' La ME13.......61 D3
Hanson Dr CT11...........96 F3
Hanway ME8................11 A2
HARBLEDOWN.................87 B8
Harbledown Gdns CT9...8 E3
Harbledown Ho ME16....74 B2
Harbledown Manor ME8..11 B3
Harbledown Pk CT2......66 C1
Harbour Approach Rd
CT20............................178 E4
HARBOURLAND..............75 B8
Harbourne La TN26, TN30..162 E5
Harbour Par CT11..........52 E6
Harbour Point CT11.......178 F5
Harbour Sch CT15.........165 E7
Harbour St
Broadstairs CT10..........30 B4
Folkestone CT20..........178 E5
Ramsgate CT11............52 E6
Whitstable CT5............20 D2
Harbour Twrs **8** CT11...52 E6
Harbour View Rd CT17...166 B8
Harbour Way CT20.........178 E5
Harcourt Dr
Canterbury CT2............66 D2
Herne Bay CT6.............22 B5
Harcourt Gdns ME8........33 E4
Harcourt Prim Sch CT19..177 E7
Harcourt Rd CT19.........177 F7
Harden Rd TN29...........205 D7
Harden's View TN26......182 D6
Hardinge Cl ME8...........33 D4
Hardinge Rd TN24........139 C3
Hardres Court Rd CT4....110 A3
Hardres St CT11...........52 E8
Hardres St CT11...........52 E7
Hardstown ME14..........75 A5
Hardwicke Ho TN27.......120 B7
Hardwicke Rd CT17.......166 B6
Hardwick Rd CT20.........178 A4
Hardy Cl
Ashford TN24..............157 A2
Canterbury CT2............66 C1

Hardy Cl continued
Chatham ME5...............32 B6
Hardy Lodge ME1..........9 B4
Hardy Rd
Greatstone-on-Sea TN28...202 D3
St Margaret's at Cliffe
CT15............................150 E8
Hardy St ME14.............75 A6
Harebell Cl
8 Chatham ME5........31 F4
Maidstone ME14..........75 E5
Minster (Sheppey) ME12...4 A4
Harebrook CT11............29 F1
Haredale Cl ME14.........31 D7
Hare St **2** ME4..........10 B3
Harkness Cl **6** ME10...37 B4
Harkness Dr CT2...........66 E2
Harlequin Cl CT6..........22 E2
Harling Cl ME17............97 D5
Harman Ave CT11........174 F3
Harman Cl ME5.............32 B3
HARMAN'S CORNER.......36 B2
Harmers Way TN27......118 F3
Harmony Cl ME10.........36 D3
Harmsworth Gdns CT10..30 A5
Harnet St **4** CT13.......72 F1
Harold Ave
Gillingham ME7.............10 E4
Westgate on Sea CT8....27 E8
Harold Ct ME13.............62 C6
Harold Rd
Birchington CT7............26 E8
Deal CT14...................117 D8
Margate CT9.................8 B3
Sittingbourne ME10......37 B4
Harold's Rd CT16.........166 E8
Harold St
Dover CT16.................166 D8
Queenborough ME11......3 A4
Harper Rd TN23...........155 F8
Harp Farm Rd ME14.....54 C6
Harple La ME14............54 F1
Harps Ave ME12...........4 C6
Harpswood ME17..........77 F1
Harpswood La CT21......176 A4
Harptree Dr ME5..........31 F5
Harrier Dr ME10...........37 A2
Harriestsham Sta ME17..100 D6
Harriet Dr ME1.............9 B3
Harriets Cnr CT5...........43 B5
HARRIETSHAM...............100 D5
Harrietsham CE Prim Sch
ME17............................100 C6
Harrietsham Ho ME16....74 A3
Harrietsham Rd ME13....33 C3
Harringe La CT21, TN25..174 A6
Harriot Cl CT19...........178 E7
Harris Gdns ME10.........37 C5
Harrison Cl **4** ME8......11 F1
Harrison Dr ME7...........100 E6
Harrison Rd **4** CT11....52 D6
Harrison Terr ME13........40 A2
Harris Pl ME15..............74 E1
Harris's Alley ME2.........1 D2
Harrow Ct
Chatham ME5...............32 C4
Stockbury ME9..............56 D8
Harrow Dene CT10........29 E6
Harrow Rd ME7.............32 F6
Harrow Way
Ashford TN23...............155 F5
Maidstone ME14..........75 C8
Harry Pay Cl TN24.......139 D4
Harrys Rd ME9.............38 D3
Harry Wells Rd CT6......22 B3
Hart Cl CT18.................163 A4
Hart Hill TN27..............103 A2
Hartington St ME4........10 A3
Hartley Cl ME15...........97 F6
Hartley Mews ME8........11 B3
HARTLIP.......................34 E5
Hartlip Cl ME12............3 B7
Hartlip Endowed CE Prim
Sch ME9.......................34 D5
Hartlip Hill ME9............34 F7
Hartnup St ME16...........74 C2
Hartpiece Cl ME8..........11 F1
Hartridge Farm ME15....96 A7
Harts Cotts TN26.........183 A8
Hartsdown L Ctr CT9.....7 H1
Hartsdown Rd CT9........8 D8
Hartsdown Tech Coll CT9..8 D8
Harts La **5** CT5.........20 D2
Hart St ME16...............74 F3
Hart Street Commercial Ctr
ME16............................74 F3
Harty Ave ME8.............33 B3
Harty Ferry Cotts ME13..40 C5
Harty Ferry Rd ME12....18 E4
Harty Ferry View CT5....43 C6
Harty Terr ME12.............5 A5
Harvest Ct CT6............23 A2
Harvesters Cl ME8........33 E7
Harvesters Way ME14...75 D4
Harvest La CT14...........126 E5
Harvest Way
Ashford TN23...............155 D7
Hawkinge CT18............163 B4
Harvey Ave CT14.........117 C3
Harvey Ct CT19...........178 A6
Harvey Dr
Sittingbourne ME10.......37 A2
Whitstable CT5.............21 B1
Harvey Gram Sch The
CT19............................178 A6
Harvey Pl
21 Folkestone CT20...178 D5
9 Folkestone CT20...178 E5

Harvey Rd
Ashford TN24..............139 F1
Gillingham ME8............33 E8
Harvey St CT20...........178 E5
Harville Rd TN25.........123 C2
Harwich St CT5.............43 D8
Harwick Dr TN28.........202 C8
Harwood Ho TN25........123 E1
Harwood Rd ME8..........12 B1
Haslard Cl CT14..........178 F4
Haslard Cl CT14..........162 F4
Haslemere Trad & Ind Est
ME15............................99 A1
Haslewood Cl TN27......135 B2
Hassall Reach CT1........87 B6
Hassell St TN25............124 F2
HASSELL STREET.........125 A2
Haste Hill Rd ME17........35 B7
Hasteds ME17..............77 D2
Haste Hill Cl ME17........97 B3
Haste Hill Rd ME17.......97 B3
HASTINGLEIGH............142 B6
Hastings Ave CT9...........8 A1
Hastings Pl CT13..........93 F8
Hastings Rd ME15.........75 B3
Hatch La CT4................86 C5
Hatch Rd ME17............101 C5
Hatch St **3** ME13.......62 C7
Hatfield Rd
Margate CT9.................7 G2
Ramsgate CT11............52 D7
Rochester ME2.............9 A8
Hathaway Ct
Gillingham ME8............33 D8
Rochester ME1.............9 B5
Hatherall Rd ME14........75 B6
Hatherley Ct CT19.........8 A3
Hatton Rd ME5.............32 C3
Havant Wlk **8** ME15....97 F6
Havelock Cl CT18..........71 E1
Havelock Pl CT13..........71 E1
Havelock St CT11..........67 A1
Haven Cl ME1...............9 C2
Haven Dr
Hawkinge CT18............163 A4
Herne Bay CT6.............23 F6
Haven The
Ashford TN23...............155 F5
Brenzett TN29.............192 A3
Hythe CT21.................187 C8
Haventhorpe ME14.......139 C3
Havisham Cl ME1...........9 C2
Havock La **1** ME14.....74 F4
Hawbeck Rd ME8..........33 C3
Hawe Cl CT2................67 A4
Hawe Farm Way CT6.....23 B2
Hawe La CT2................68 A2
Hawes Ave CT11..........52 B7
Hawk Cl CT5................43 C7
Hawkesbury St CT17.....166 D5
Hawkhurst Cl CT7.........27 B8
Hawkhurst Rd ME8.......11 C3
Hawkhurst Way CT10....30 A2
HAWKINGE...................163 C5
Hawkinge Prim Sch
CT18............................163 B4
Hawkins Ct
Chatham ME7...............10 A6
Sittingbourne ME10......36 E7
Hawkins Rd CT19.........177 D6
HAWKSDOWN................134 B8
Hawksdown CT14.........134 B8
Hawksdown Rd CT14....134 C8
Hawks Hill La ME9.........58 C4
Hawkshill Rd CT14........134 D8
Hawk's La CT1..............87 F8
Hawks Rd CT6..............22 B2
Hawks Way TN23.........155 E7
Hawkwood ME16...........74 B5
Hawkwood Cl ME1.........9 D5
Hawley Cl ME16............74 E4
Hawley Sq CT9.............7 J2
Hawley St CT9..............7 I2
Hawser Rd ME1.............9 C1
Hawthorn Ho ME16......190 D8
Hawthorn Ave
Canterbury CT2............67 A2
West Minster ME12........3 A8
Hawthorn Cl
Aylesham CT3..............112 E4
Crabble CT17................148 E2
Hythe CT21.................187 E8
Ramsgate CT11............29 E1
St Mary's Bay TN29.....194 F3
Hawthorn Cnr
Herne Bay CT6.............24 A3
Old Romney TN29.........200 E3
HAWTHORN CORNER.....24 A3
Hawthorne Ave ME8.....11 C2
Hawthorne Cl CT15......131 D7
Hawthorne Rd **4** ME16..74 A3
Hawthorn Ho
5 Chatham ME5.......31 F5
10 Sittingbourne ME10..36 E4
Hawthorn Rd
Kingsnorth TN23...........156 B4
Sittingbourne ME10.......36 E4
Hawthorns ME15...........31 F1
Hawthorns The
Broadstairs CT10..........29 C4
Chatham ME5...............31 F6
Haydon Cl ME16...........74 B4
Hayes Alley **8** CT5.....20 D2
Hayes La ME9...............56 F6
Hayfields ME5..............32 D2
Haygate Ho ME1...........9 C4
Hay Hill CT13, CT14......93 D2
Hay Ho CT21...............176 B2

Hay La CT14.................93 F2
Hayle Mill Cotts ME15...96 F8
Hayle Mill Rd ME15.......96 F8
Hayle Rd ME15...............75 A3
Haymakers La TN23......155 C8
Haymen St ME4..............9 E3
Haynes Ho **3** ME14....75 B4
Hayrick Cl ME14...........75 E5
Haysel ME10................37 A2
Hayton Rd TN25...........160 A2
Haywain Cl
Ashford TN23...............155 E5
Maidstone ME14..........75 F4
Hayward Ave ME2.........9 B8
Hayward Cl
Ashford TN24..............157 A8
Deal CT14...................117 A4
Hayward's Cl TN28.......202 B6
Hayward's Hill ME13......82 C4
Hayward's Ho ME1.........9 C4
Hazebrouck Rd ME13....62 A7
Hazel Ave ME16............74 C5
Hazel Cl CT15..............131 C7
Hazel Ct
Birchington CT7............26 B8
Hersden CT3................68 D8
Hazeldown Cl CT17.......148 E2
Hazel Gr
Chatham ME5...............32 B8
Sheerness ME12............1 H1
Hazel Hts TN25............138 E5
Hazels The ME8............33 B5
HAZEL STREET..............57 A3
Hazel Street Rd ME9.....57 A4
Hazel Wlk CT10............29 C4
Hazelwood Dr ME16......74 B4
Hazelwood Mdw CT13....93 F7
Hazlemere Dr
Gillingham ME7.............11 A3
Herne Bay CT6.............23 D5
Hazlemere Rd CT5.........43 A7
Hazling Dane CT15.......130 F5
Hazlitt Dr ME15............74 D5
Hazlitt Pl ME15.............97 B8
Headcorn Dr CT2...........67 B4
Headcorn Rd
Gillingham ME8.............11 A4
Platt's Heath ME17.......100 F1
Head Hill ME13..............63 D7
Head Hill Rd ME13.........63 D8
Headingley Rd ME16......74 B6
Head Race The ME15.....74 D2
Heard Way ME10...........37 B5
Hearne Cl ME10............37 B5
Hearne CI ME10............37 C5
Heart in Hand Cnr CT6...23 F2
Heart in Hand Rd CT6....23 F2
HEARTS DELIGHT..........36 B1
Hearts Delight ME9........36 B1
Heart's Delight La CT3...70 B3
Hearts Delight Rd ME9...36 B1
Heartwood Dr TN23......138 E3
Heath Cl CT12...............67 F7
Heath Ct CT5...............150 F6
Heather Cl
Chatham ME5...............31 F4
Margate CT9.................28 C8
Sittingbourne ME10......37 A3
Heather Dr
Maidstone ME15..........75 B2
Tenterden TN30...........167 B3
Heatherwood Cl ME17....99 E2
Heath Farm Sch TN27...119 C2
Heathfield ME17............98 E4
Heathfield Ave
Dover CT16.................149 B2
Maidstone ME14..........75 C7
Heathfield Bglws ME17..102 B3
Heathfield Cl
Chatham ME5...............32 B7
Maidstone ME14..........75 B7
Heathfield Rd
Ashford TN24..............139 C3
Maidstone ME14..........75 C7
Hazel Gr.......................128 E5
Heath Gr ME16.............74 A2
Heath Rd ME3..............46 E5
Heath St ME14.............75 B5
Heath Rd
Coxheath ME17...........96 C3
Langley Heath ME17......98 E4
Maidstone, Cock Street
ME17............................97 C2
Heathside TN26............181 C1
Heathside Ave ME17.....96 C4
Heath The
Appledore Heath TN26..181 C1
Whitstable CT5.............21 B1
Heath Villas TN26.........181 C2
Heathwood Dr CT11......29 E1
Heaton Rd CT1..............87 F6
Hedgend Ind Est CT7....25 F3
Hedgerows TN23..........155 D7
Hedgerow The ME14.....75 E5
Hedgers Way TN23.......155 D5
Hedges The ME14..........75 D5
Hedley St ME14............75 A5
Heeley Cl ME9...............58 E6
Heel La CT2..................67 C8
Heel Rd ME13...............104 B7
Heights Terr CT17.........166 C6
Heights The CT5...........43 C6
Helding Cl CT6...............23 B2
Helena Ave CT9.............28 E8
Helena Cnr CT9.............28 E8
Helena Corniche CT17...177 C3
Helena Rd CT18............164 C2
Helena Villas CT21.......177 B3

Helen Thompson Cl ME9 ..14 E4
Hellyar Ct ME1 .... 9 C4
Helmdon Cl CT12 ....29 C2
Helvellyn Ave CT11 ......52 B7
HEMPSTEAD 33 A5
Hempstead Inf Sch ME7 ...33 A5
Hempstead Jun Sch ME7 ..33 A5
Hempstead La ME9 ....37 E3
Hempstead Rd ME7, ME8 ..33 A5
Hempstead Valley Dr
  ME7 ....33 A4
Hempstead Valley Sh Ctr
  ME7 ....33 A4
Hempton Hill TN25 ....160 C5
HEMSTED 160 D8
Henbane Cl ME14 ....75 E5
Hengist Ave CT9 .... 8 B1
Hengist Rd
  Birchington CT7 ....26 C7
  Deal CT14 ....117 D7
  Westgate on Sea CT8 ...27 D8
Henley Bsns Pk ME2 .... 9 D7
Henley Cl
  Chatham ME5 ....32 A6
  Gillingham ME8 ....33 D8
Henley Fields
  Maidstone ME14 ....75 E6
  Tenterden TN30 ....167 B2
Henley Mdws TN30 ......167 A2
Henley View TN30 ....167 B2
Henniker Ct CT16 ....149 A3
Henry Ct CT1 ....87 F7
Henry St
  Chatham ME4 ....10 B3
  Gillingham ME8 ....12 A1
Henwood TN24 ....139 D2
Henwood Bsns Ctr TN24 .139 D2
Henwood Ind Est TN24 ..139 D2
Herbert Dane Ct ME6 ...62 D7
Herbert Rd
  Ashford TN24. ....156 D6
  Chatham ME4. ....10 A3
  Gillingham ME8 ....33 E8
  Ramsgate CT11 ....52 C6
Herbert St CT17 ....149 B1
Herdson Rd CT20 ....178 A5
Hereford Cl
  Ashford TN24. ....139 C7
  Gillingham ME8 ....11 D2
Hereford Gdns CT11 .....52 B8
Hereford Rd ME15 ....97 D7
Hereson Rd CT11 ....52 E8
Hereson Sch The CT10 ...30 A3
Hereward Ave CT6 ....26 E8
Heritage Cl CT5 ....43 A6
Heritage Ct ME7. ....87 F8
Heritage Dr ME7. ....10 F1
Heritage Est CT16. ......166 E8
Heritage Rd
  Chatham ME5. ....32 A6
  Folkestone CT20 ....177 D6
Herlun Way ME1 ....11 A6
Herman Terr ME4 ....10 A3
Hermitage Cl CT21 ......176 B2
Hermitage La
  Boxley ME14 ....54 F2
  Detling ME14 ....55 B4
HERNE 46 B8
Herne Ave CT6. ....23 A4
Herne Bay Sta CT6. .....22 E6
Herne Bay Inf Sch CT6. ..22 F3
Herne Bay Jun Sch CT6. ..22 F4
Herne Bay Mus Ctr* CT6. .22 F5
Herne Bay Mus & Gall*
  CT6. ....22 F5
Herne Bay Rd
  Sturry CT2. ....45 E2
  Whitstable CT5. ....21 C3
Herne Bay Sta CT6. .....22 E6
Herne Bay West Ind Est
  CT6. ....22 C3
Herne CE Jun Sch CT6. ..46 A8
HERNE COMMON 45 F6
Herne Ct CT19 ....177 C6
Herne Dr CT6. ....22 C2
Herne Inf Sch CT6. ......46 B8
Herne Rd ME8 ....11 C2
Herne St CT6. ....46 A8
Herneville Gdns CT6 ....23 B4
Herne Windmill* CT6. ...23 B2
HERNHILL 64 B6
Hernhill CE Prim Sch
  ME13 ....64 B6
Heron Ho ME12 .... 1 C2
Heron Apartments 3
  ME15 ....97 F5
Herons Bsns Ctr TN24. ..13 B3
Heron Cl ME9 ....13 B3
HERONDEN 92 E1
Heronden Rd
  Eastry CT13 ....92 F1
  Maidstone ME15 ....97 F4
Heronden View CT13 ....93 A2
Heron Dr ME12 .... 4 B5
Heron Forestall Ave
  CT18 ....163 B4
Heron Ho TN23 ....138 F1
Heron Lodge 6 CT16 ...149 B2
Heron's Brook TN25 ....140 E6
Herons Cl CT14. ....107 C8
Herons Park – Lydd Int
  Raceway TN29 ....205 C3
Herons Swimming Pool
  CT6. ....22 F5
Heron's Way CT21 ....187 D8
Heron Way ME5. ....32 B7

Heron Wlk TN23 ....155 E8
Hero Wlk ME1 ....31 C7
Herschell Rd CT7 ....26 F8
Herschell Road E CT14. .117 C3
Herschell Road W CT14. .117 C3
Herschell Sq CT14 ....117 C3
HERSDEN 46 F1
Hersden Com Prim Sch
  CT3. ....46 E1
Hertford Cl CT1 ....88 C8
Hertford Ho
  Herne Bay CT6. ....23 A5
  17 Ramsgate CT11 .....52 E6
Hertford Pl CT11. ....52 E6
Hertford Rd CT9 ....29 C8
Hertford St CT1 ....52 E6
Herts Cres ME15 ....96 F3
Hestia Way TN23 ....155 E5
Hever Cl ME15. ....97 F6
Hever Gdns ME16 ....74 E3
Hever Mews ME1 .... 9 C3
Hever Pl
  Canterbury CT2 ....67 A3
  Sittingbourne ME10 ....36 D3
Hewitt Cl
  Gillingham ME7 ....10 F6
  Maidstone ME16 ....74 D7
Hewitt Rd 1 CT16 ....166 D8
Hewitts ME1 TN24. ....139 F1
Hextable Cl
  Ashford TN23. ....155 F6
  Maidstone ME16 ....74 D7
Heyford Cl ST18 ....163 B4
Hibernia St 6 CT11. ....52 E6
HICKMANS GREEN 64 A2
Hickory Dell ME7 ....33 A5
HICKS FORSTAL 46 A4
Hicks Forstal Rd CT3. .....46 B5
Higgins' La ME4 .... 9 F4
Higham Cl ME15 ....74 E2
Higham Ct ME4 ....111 B8
Higham View ME14. ......53 E4
High Bank ME1 .... 9 D2
High Banks ME15 ....96 F5
Highbury Gdns CT12 .....29 B3
Highbury La TN30. ....179 A7
Highbury Wlk CT12 ....29 B2
Highcroft ME15. ....97 F4
High Dewar Rd ME8 ......34 A8
High Elms ME1 ....11 E1
Highfield Cl
  Gillingham ME8 ....33 D7
  Hythe CT21 ....176 A4
  Ramsgate CT12 ....29 B3
  Rough Common CT2 ...66 B3
Highfield Ct
  Herne Bay CT6. ....22 E4
  5 Margate CT9 .... 8 B2
  Ramsgate CT12 ....29 B2
Highfield Gdns CT9 .... 7 F1
Highfield Ind Est CT13 ..178 F6
Highfield La TN24, TN25. .157 C6
Highfield Rd
  Ashford TN24. ....157 A8
  Gillingham ME8 ....33 D7
  Halfway Houses ME12. .. 3 E6
  Ramsgate CT12 ....29 B3
Highfields Ave CT6. ....23 C4
Highfields View CT6. .....23 C4
Highgate Rd CT5. ....21 B1
Highgrove Rd ME5. ....32 A5
HIGH HALDEN 167 D7
High Halden CE Prim Sch
  TN26 ....167 E7
High Knocke TN29 ....195 B6
Highland CT20 ....177 F4
Highland Rd
  Chartham CT4 ....86 D1
  Maidstone ME15 ....97 F6
Highlands Cres TN29 ....195 A4
Highlands Glade CT12 ...28 E1
High Mdw CT7 ....149 C1
High Minnis CT4 ....143 F8
High Oak Hill ME9 ....35 D8
Highpoint TN24 ....139 D3
Highpoint Bsns Village
  TN25 ....139 D3
Highridge
  Gillingham ME7 ....10 F1
  Hythe CT21 ....177 A3
High Ridge TN23 ....155 C7
Highridge Cl ME14 ....74 F5
High St The TN27 ....120 C7
High Snoad Wood TN25 .105 A1
High St
  Ashford TN24. ....139 C2
  Bridge CT4. ....89 A1
  Broadstairs CT10. ....30 A4
  Broadstairs, St Peter's CT10 .29 E5
  Brookland TN29 ....199 E8
  Canterbury CT1. ....87 F8
  Chatham ME4. ....10 A6
  Deal CT14 ....117 D6
  Dover CT16 ....166 C8
  Dymchurch ME12 ....195 C8
  Eastchurch ME12. .... 5 D3
  Eastry CT13 ....93 B2
  Elham CT4. ....144 F5
  Fordwich CT2. ....68 A4
  Forstal ME20. ....53 A3
  Gillingham ME7 ....10 C5
  Gillingham, Rainham ME8 .33 F8
  Herne Bay CT6. ....22 F5
  Hythe CT21 ....176 C2
  Lenham ME17 ....101 D5
  Littlebourne CT3 ....89 F7
  Lydd TN29 ....205 C6

High St continued
  Lyminge CT18 ....161 C2
  Maidstone ME14 ....74 F4
  Manston CT12 ....51 D8
  Margate CT9 .... 7 I2
  Margate, Garlinge CT9 ..28 B7
  Minster (Sheppey) ME12. ..4 B7
  Minster (Thanet) CT12. .50 C6
  Newington ME9 ....35 C6
  New Romney TN28. ....202 B6
  Queenborough ME11... 2 F5
  Ramsgate CT11 ....52 E7
  Rochester ME1 .... 9 C6
  Rochester, Strood ME2 .9 B7
  Sandwich CT13 ....73 A1
  Sheerness, Blue Town ME1 .1 B3
  Sheerness ME12 .... 1 C5
  Sittingbourne ME10 ....36 F4
  Sittingbourne, Milton Regis
    ME10. ....36 C6
  St Margaret's at Cliffe
    CT15 ....150 F6
  Sturry CT2 ....67 F5
  Temple Ewell CT16 ....148 D5
  Tenterden TN30. ....179 A7
  Whitstable CT5. ....21 A1
  Wingham CT3. ....91 A8
  Wye TN25. ....123 C2
HIGHSTEAD 24 A1
HIGHSTED 58 F7
Highsted Gram Sch ME10 .36 F2
Highsted Rd ME9, ME10. .36 F1
HIGHSTREET 42 F2
Highstreet Rd
  Waterham ME13 ....42 D2
  Yorkletts CT5, ME13 ....42 B2
High Street St Gregory's 8
  CT1. ....67 A1
High Street St Lawrence
  CT11. ....52 B7
High Trees Cl TN24 ......157 A8
High View Ave CT9 ....28 B7
Highview Cl
  Boughton Street ME13. ..64 B3
  Loose ME15. ....97 A8
Highview Dr ME5 ....31 D5
Highview Rd ME5. .... 4 C7
Highview Sch CT19 ......178 D6
Highworth Gram Sch for
  Girls TN24. ....139 A3
Hilary Cl CT6. ....23 C4
Hilda Rd
  Chatham ME4. ....10 A3
  Halfway Houses ME12. .. 3 D6
Hildenborough Cres
  ME16 ....74 C7
Hildersham Cl CT10 .....29 E5
Hilderstone Coll 2 CT20. .29 F5
Hillary Rd CT2 .... 1 A5
Hill Ave CT15 ....130 E5
HILLBOROUGH 24 A4
Hillborough Bsns Pk CT6. .23 F4
Hillborough Dr CT6. ......23 F5
Hillborough Gr CT6. ......32 A3
Hillborough Rd CT6. .....23 B5
Hill Brow
  Maidstone ME14 ....76 A5
  Sittingbourne ME10. ...36 D2
Hillbrow Ave
  Herne Bay CT6. ....23 B2
  Sturry CT2 ....67 F7
Hillbrow La TN23 ....138 F1
Hillbrow Rd
  Ashford TN24. ....139 A1
  Ramsgate CT11 ....52 D8
Hill Cres
  Aylesham CT3 ....112 E5
  Lenham ME17 ....101 D5
Hillcrest TN23 ....155 B8
Hillcrest Cl TN24 ....139 E6
Hillcrest Gdns
  Deal CT14 ....117 A2
  Ramsgate CT11 ....52 B6
Hillcrest Rd
  Chatham ME4. .... 9 F2
  Hythe CT21 ....176 B3
  Kingsdown CT14 ....134 D4
  Littlebourne CT3 ....89 E8
Hillcroft Rd CT6 ....23 B3
Hill Ct TN27 ....103 E1
Hillden Shaw ME15 ......97 A8
Hill Dr CT13 ....93 B3
Hillier Cl CT10. ....30 B5
Hillfield Villas TN26 ....167 F8
HILL GREEN 34 C1
Hill Green Rd ME9 ....56 D8
Hill House Dr CT12 ......50 C7
Hill La CT18 ....162 B1
Hillman Ave CT6. ....22 A4
Hill Rd
  Burham ME1 ....31 A3
  Folkestone CT19 ....178 E8
  Folkestone, Foord CT19. .178 E7
  Rochester ME1 .... 9 A2
Hill Rise TN25 ....138 C5
Hillside
  1 Folkestone CT20. ...177 E3
  Rochester ME1 .... 9 A2
Hillside Ave
  Canterbury CT1 ....66 C2
  Gillingham ME8 .... 9 B8
  Rushenden ME11. .... 2 F3
Hillside Cotts CT3 ....70 A1
Hillside Ct
  Hythe CT21 ....176 C2
  2 Rochester ME1 .... 9 A7
Hillside Ind Est CT20. ...177 E4

Hillside Rd
  Chatham ME4. ....10 A4
  Dover CT17 ....149 A2
  Minster (Sheppey) ME12. ..4 B7
  Stalisfield Green ME13 .103 E6
  Whitstable CT5. ....21 A1
Hillside St CT21. ....176 C2
Hillstone Cl 6 CT16 ....166 E8
HILL STREET 142 F8
Hill Terr ME14 .... 9 F3
Hill The
  Charing TN27 ....120 D8
  Littlebourne CT3 ....89 F8
Hilltop CT5. ....43 D7
Hill Top Cotts ME17 .....96 E2
Hilltop Rd CT2. ....66 B2
Hilltop Rd ME14 .... 4 A5
Hill Top Rd CT6 ....23 B5
Hill View
  Ashford TN24. ....139 C3
  Margate CT9 ....28 D7
Hill View Ct CT4 ....111 E2
Hillview Rd
  Canterbury CT2 ....66 C2
  Whitstable CT5 ....43 D8
Hill View Terr CT18. .....161 D3
Hill View Way ME5. ......31 E5
Hillyfield Rd TN23. ......156 A8
Hillyfields Rise TN23 ....139 A1
Hilton Bsns Ctr TN23 ...156 B6
Hilton Cl ME13. ....62 D6
Hilton Dr ME10 ....36 B6
Hinchliffe Way CT9 ....29 D8
Hind Cl TN29 ....195 C8
Hinde Cl ME10. ....36 F7
Hinde Ho ME10 ....36 E6
Hines Terr ME5 ....10 C1
Hinton Cres ME7. ....33 A6
HINXHILL 140 D1
Hinxhill Rd TN24, TN25. .140 D1
Hirst Cl CT16 ....149 B4
Historic Dockyard The*
  ME4 .... 10 A8
Hither Field TN27 ....120 C7
HOADEN 70 F4
Hoades Wood Rd CT2 ....68 A7
Hoad Rd CT15, CT18 ....146 A2
Hoads Wood Gdns TN25. .138 E6
HOATH 47 F3
Hoath Cl ME8. ....33 B7
Hoath Farm The CT3 .....88 F7
Hoath La ME8 ....33 B7
Hoath Prim Sch CT3 .....46 C5
Hoath Rd CT3 ....46 C3
Hoath Way ME7, ME8 ...33 B5
Hobart Cres CT16 ....149 C3
Hobart Gdns ME10 ....36 C4
Hobart Rd CT12. ....29 A1
Hockeredge Gdns CT8 ...27 F8
Hockers Cl ME14 ....76 A8
Hockers La ME14 ....76 A8
Hockley 82 C3
Hodge's Gap CT9 .... 8 C3
Hodgson Rd CT5. ....42 F6
Hogarth Cl CT6. ....23 E5
Hogarth Ho ME11. .... 2 F5
Hogbarn La ME17 ....79 A3
Hogben Cl CT18 ....161 B7
Hogben's Hill ME13 ......84 A6
HOGBEN'S HILL 84 A6
Hogbrook Hill La CT15 .164 D8
Hogg La CT4 ....109 C3
Hog Gn CT4 ....144 F4
Hogg La ME14 ....76 B5
Hoggound Cnr TN30 .....139 B6
Holbeam Rd ME13 ....82 A1
Holborn La ME4 .... 9 F5
Holbourn CT12 ....29 B1
Holbrook Dr CT12. ....29 B1
Holcombe Rd
  Chatham ME4. .... 9 F2
  Rochester ME1 .... 9 C3
Holdenhurst TN23 ....155 E6
Holdenby Cl ME15 ....32 C6
Holding St ME8. ....11 F1
Holiday Sq CT8. .... 8 B2
Holland Cl
  Broadstairs CT10. ...... 8 G2
  Sheerness ME12 .... 1 C1
Holland Ho ME1. .... 9 D5
Holland Rd
  Chatham ME4. ....31 E4
  Maidstone ME14 ....75 B5
Hollands Ave CT14 ......178 F7
Hollicondane Rd CT11 ...52 E8
HOLLINGBOURNE 77 E2
Hollingbourne Prim Sch
  ME17 ....77 C2
Hollingbourne Rd ME8 ..11 B4
Hollingbourne Stn ME17 .77 C3
Hollington Pl TN24. ....139 B3
Hollingworth Cl ME14 ...75 C3
Hollingworth Rd ME15 ..97 F5
Hollow La
  Canterbury CT1 ....87 E5
  Hartlip ME9 ....34 E5
Hollowmede CT1 ....87 E6
Hollow Rd CT3. ....47 B6
Hollow St CT3 ....47 C5
HOLLOW STREET 47 C4
Hollow Wood Rd CT17 ..165 E8
Hollybank Hill ME3 ....36 D4
Hollybush Cnr CT18 ......90 A3
HOLLYBUSHES 80 A8
Hollybush La CT3. ....69 A4

Hel–Hon 225

Holly Cl
  Broadstairs CT10. ....29 C4
  Chatham ME5. ....32 C8
  Eastry CT13 ....93 B2
  Folkestone CT19 ....178 E7
  Gillingham ME7 ....10 E6
  Hythe CT21 ....176 D3
Holly Dr ME12 .... 4 B4
Holly Farm Rd ME15 ....98 C6
Holly Gdns
  Maidstone ME14 ....75 B7
  Margate CT9 .... 8 C2
Holly Hill Rd ME13 ....64 D5
Holly La CT9 .... 8 C2
Holly Mdws TN23 ....138 D3
Holly Rd
  Ramsgate CT11 ....52 E8
  St Mary's Bay TN29 ...194 F4
Holly Tree Cl ME17 ....99 E2
Holman Mews CT1. ....88 A7
Holme Oak Cl CT1. ....87 F6
Holmes Ct 5 CT1. ....88 B8
Holmesdale Cl ME15. ....96 F3
Holmesdale Terr 14
  CT20. ....178 D4
Holmestone Rd CT17. ...148 E1
Holmes Way CT12. ....29 A3
Holmlea Cl TN24 ....139 E1
Holm Mill La ME17. .....100 B6
Holm Oak Gdns CT10 ...29 F4
Holmoaks
  Gillingham ME8 ....11 E2
  Maidstone ME14 ....75 C5
Holmscroft Rd CT6. ......23 D5
Holmside ME7 .... 10 E3
Holmside Ave ME12. ..... 3 D6
Holmwood Rd TN23 ....155 E2
Holness Rd CT3. ....71 D2
Holt Cl TN23 ....155 C8
Holters Mews CT1. ....88 A8
Holters Mill CT1. ....66 F2
Holton Cl CT7 ....27 A6
Holt St CT15 ....113 C4
Holtwood Cl ME4 ....33 D6
Holtye Cres ME15. ....75 B2
Holy Family RC Prim Sch The
  CT1. ....97 F4
Holyrood Dr ME12 .... 4 A8
Holy Trinity & St Johns CE
  Prim Sch 14 CT9 .... 7 J2
Holywell Ave CT19 ......178 D8
Holywell Ho CT19 ....178 D8
Holywell La ME9. ....12 F3
Holywell Prim Sch ME9 ..12 F3
Homebirch Ho CT7. ......26 F8
Home Farm Cotts CT14 .115 E6
Homefern Ho CT9. .... 7 I3
Homefield Ave CT14 .....117 B6
Homefield Dr ME8 ....12 B2
Homefield Row CT14 ....117 B6
Homefleet Ho 13 CT11 ..52 F7
Homelands Cl TN25 .....159 D1
Homeleigh Rd CT12. .....29 B3
Homepeak Ho 12 CT21. .176 B2
Homersham CT1. ....87 D6
Homeside Farm CT14 ...126 F6
Homespire Ho 10 CT1. ...67 A1
Homestall Ct CT2. ....66 C4
Homestall La ME13 ....63 B5
Homestall Rd ME9 ....60 D3
Homestead TN23. ....155 D8
Homestead Ct 7 CT19 ... 7 J1
Homestead Ct CT14 .....117 A4
Homestead La CT15. ....132 C7
Homestead View ME15. .132 C7
Homevale Ho 3 CT20. ..177 E3
Homeview 3 ME10 ....77 B4
Homeview Terr 2 ME10 ..37 B4
Homewood Ave ME10 ...36 D3
Homewood Rd
  Sturry CT2 ....68 A6
  Tenterden TN30 ....167 B1
Homewood Sch TN30 ...167 B1
Honduras Terr 8 ME14. .75 A7
Hone St ME2 .... 9 B8
Honesty Rd ME9/ME10. .36 F1
Honeyball Wlk ME9 ......10 C1
Honey Bee Glade ME8 ...33 E6
Honey Cl ME7 ....33 A5
Honeycrock Hill ME5. ....56 F8
Honeyfield TN23 ....138 E1
HONEY HILL 65 C8
Honey Hill CT2, CT5. .....65 F8
Honey La ME15 ....98 B6
Honeypot Cl ME2 .... 9 B8
Honeysuckle Cl
  3 Chatham ME5. ....31 E4
  Gillingham ME7 ....32 F4
  Margate CT9 ....28 C8
Honeysuckle Ct CT10. ...37 B5
Honeysuckle Rd CT11. ...52 B8
Honeysuckle Way CT6. ..23 D2
Honeywood Cl
  Canterbury CT1 ....67 B2
  Dover CT16 ....149 A6
Honeywood Parkway
  CT16. ....149 B5
Honeywood Rd CT16 ....149 A5
Honfleur Rd CT13. ....93 B3
Honner Cl CT18. ....162 F3
Honywood Rd ME17. ....101 C4

HOO...................................49 F6
Hoo Farm CT12..............49 F6
Hook Cl
  Chatham ME5..............31 E5
  Folkestone CT20.........177 F5
Hook La
  Brookland TN29..........199 C6
  Charing TN27.............120 A7
  Harrietsham ME17........100 C6
Hookstead TN26............167 C7
Hoopers La CT6...........23 D3
Hooper's Pl ME1............9 C4
Hooper's Rd ME1...........9 C4
Hope La
  New Romney TN28.......202 A8
  St Mary in the Marsh TN29 193 F2
Hope Rd CT14.............117 D5
Hopes Gr TN26............167 D7
Hope's La CT12............29 C3
Hope St
  Chatham ME4.............10 A3
  Maidstone ME14..........74 F6
  Sheerness ME12............1 C2
Hope View Sch CT4........107 D8
Hope Villas CT1...........87 B2
Hopeville Ave CT10........29 E6
Hope Way ME12..............1 C2
Hopewell Bsns Ctr ME5...32 C8
Hopewell Dr ME5...........32 C8
Hop Garden Way CT1........87 E6
Hop Gdn TN26.............181 C1
Hoppers Way TN23........155 D8
Hopsons Pl ME12............4 C5
Horatio Pl ME1.............9 B4
Hornash La TN26...........170 D8
Hornbeam Ave ME5.........32 B2
Hornbeam CT4.............138 F3
Hornbeam Prim Sch
  CT4.....................116 F4
Hornbrook La TN26........181 C7
Horne's Place Chapel*
  TN26....................181 D2
Hornet Cl CT10............29 D3
Horn Hill ME9..............58 C2
Horn St CT19, CT20, CT21..177 B4
HORN STREET...............177 B4
Horsa Rd
  Birchington CT7..........26 D7
  Deal CT14...............117 D8
Horsebridge Rd CT5........20 D2
HORSELEES.................64 A2
Horselees Rd ME13.........64 A2
Horseshoe Cl
  Gillingham ME7...........32 F5
  Maidstone ME14..........75 E5
Horseshoes La ME17.......98 E4
Horse Wash La ME1..........9 C6
Horsford Wlk ME13.........62 A8
Horsham Hill ME9..........12 E4
Horsham La ME8, ME9.......12 D3
Horshams The CT6..........23 D5
Horsley Cl CT18...........163 B4
Horsley Rd ME1.............9 B4
Horsted Ave ME4............9 E1
Horsted Inf Sch ME4.......31 D5
Horsted Jun Sch ME4.......31 D5
Horsted Ret Pk ME5........31 D5
Horsted Way ME1...........86 F3
HORTON....................86 F3
Horton Cotts CT4...........86 E4
Horton Downs ME15.........75 F1
Horton Gdns CT4...........86 E4
Horwood Cl ME1............31 B8
Hoser Gdns CT7............27 A7
Hospital Hill CT20, CT21..177 C3
Hospital La
  Canterbury CT1...........87 F8
  Chatham ME1..............9 E4
Hospital Meadow Cotts
  CT3.....................91 D2
Hospital Rd ME9............99 E8
Hotel Rd
  Gillingham ME8...........11 A2
  St Margaret's at Cliffe
  CT15...................151 B6
HOTHFIELD................138 A7
Hothfield Common Nature
  Reserve* TN26..........137 F8
Hothfield Rd ME8..........11 F1
Hougham Court La CT15....165 A3
Houghton Ave ME7.........33 B3
HOUGHTON GREEN..........197 D2
Houghton Green La
  TN31....................197 C2
Houghton Ho CT19.........178 C5
Houghton La TN31.........197 C3
Househeld Inf Sch TN24..139 F2
Househeld Rd ME13.......104 C6
House Mdw TN23...........155 C7
Hovenden Cl CT2............67 A4
Howard Ave
  Rochester ME1.............9 D3
  Sittingbourne ME10.......36 D6
Howard Cl ME12.............4 C7
Howard Dr ME16............74 A3
Howard Rd CT10............30 A3
Howard Sch The ME8........33 D8
Howbury Wlk ME8...........33 D4
Howfield La CT4............86 E5
Howland Mews CT1.........87 E6
Howletts Oast CT4.........89 C5
Howletts Wild Animal Pk*
  CT4.....................89 D6
Hoxton Cl TN23...........155 D8

Hoystings Cl The CT1......88 A7
Hubbards Cotts ME8.......12 C2
Hubbards Hill ME17.......102 B6
Hubbard's La ME15.........97 A3
Hubble Dr ME15............97 E7
Hubert Way CT10...........29 E6
HUCKING....................56 E1
Huckleberry Cl ME5........32 B3
Hudson Cl
  Dover CT17..............149 B3
  Gillingham ME8...........11 C1
  Sturry CT2...............67 F6
Hudson Rd CT1.............67 B2
Hugh Pl ME13...............62 D7
Hugh Price Cl ME8..........37 C5
Hugin Ave CT10............29 E7
Hulkes La ME1..............9 E4
Hull Pl CT14.............116 F6
Hull Rd TN29.............206 E6
Humber Ave CT6............21 F4
Hume Ct CT21.............176 D1
Humphrey Terr CT18......162 F4
Hundreds CT8..............27 D7
Hunger Hatch La TN27....119 F7
Hunstanton Cl ME8.........33 E3
Hunt Cl CT18............163 A4
Hunter Ave TN24..........156 E8
Hunter Rd TN24...........139 E1
Hunters Bank CT4.........144 F4
Hunters Chase
  Herne Bay CT6............23 C2
  Whitstable CT5...........43 E7
Hunters Cl ME4.............10 C7
Huntersfield Cl ME5........32 C1
HUNTERS FORSTAL...........23 C2
Hunters Forstal Rd CT6....23 C2
Hunters Way
  Gillingham ME7...........10 E1
  Sheldwich ME13...........83 D5
Hunters Way W ME5.........10 E1
Hunters Wlk CT14.........117 B6
Huntingdon Wlk [2] ME15..97 E2
Hunting Gate CT7..........26 F8
Huntington Rd ME17........96 B3
Hunton Gdns CT2...........67 A4
Hunton Hill ME5...........96 A2
Huntsfield Ind Est CT20..177 D4
Huntsman La ME14..........75 B4
Huntsmans Cl ME1..........9 E1
Huntsman's Cnr ME4........31 D8
Huntswood TN23...........138 E1
Hurst Cl ME5..............31 E6
Hurstford La TN26, TN27..120 C2
Hurst Gr CT12.............29 C1
Hurst Hill ME5............31 E2
Hurstings The ME15........74 D2
Hurst La
  Capel-le-Ferne CT18.....164 B4
  Charing Heath TN27......119 E6
  Sittingbourne ME10.......14 F1
Hurst Pl ME8..............33 F8
Hurst Rd TN24............139 C7
Hurstwood ME5.............31 E4
Hurstwood Rd
  Bredhurst ME7............33 B1
  Warren Street ME13......103 E8
Hussar Ho ME1..............9 C3
Hustlings Dr ME12..........5 B5
Hutchings Cl [2] ME10......37 C5
Hutsford CT3...............33 D5
Huxley Ct [3] ME1...........9 D1
Hybrid Cl ME1..............9 D1
Hyde Cl CT17.............166 C7
Hyde Pl CT3.............112 F5
Hyde Rd ME8...............74 D6
Hyde The CT4..............86 B2
Hylands Cotts TN26.......169 A2
Hythe La CT1...............88 A8
Ivy Mews ME17..............99 E2
HYTHE....................176 D1
Hythe Bay CE Prim Sch
  CT21....................176 B1
Hythe House Sch ME12.......3 B7
Hythe Pl CT13..............94 A8
Hythe Rd
  Ashford TN24............139 E1
  Dymchurch TN29.........186 E1
  Lympne CT21............175 D4
  Sittingbourne ME10.......36 D5
  Smeeth TN25.............158 C3
Hythe St Leonard's CE Jun
  Sch CT21................176 B2
Hythe Sta* CT21.........176 A2
Hyton Dr CT14...........117 B6

I

Ian's Wlk CT21...........177 A3
Ibis Cl CT5...............43 B6
Ice Bowl The* ME8.........11 A1
ICKHAM....................69 C1
Ickham Court Farm CT3....69 C1
IDEN.....................197 B4
Iden La TN27.............119 B4
Iden Rd TN31............197 B3
Idenwood Cl ME8...........33 D4
Iffin La
  Canterbury CT1...........87 E4
  Canterbury CT4...........87 F7
Ifield Cl ME15............97 F7
Ilex Rd CT19.............177 F6
Illustrious Cl ME5........32 A6
Imbert Cl TN28...........202 C6
Imperial Ave ME12..........4 D7
Imperial Dr CT7............6 E4

Imperial Rd ME7...........10 C3
Imperial Way TN23........155 C8
Impton La ME5.............32 A1
Ince Rd CT14..............67 F7
Ingle Cl CT7..............27 B7
Ingleden CT18............162 F4
Ingleden Park Rd TN30...167 C1
Ingle Rd ME4.............10 B6
Ingles La [3] CT21........178 D5
Ingles Mews [4] CT20.....178 C4
Ingles Rd CT20...........178 C4
Ingoldsby Rd
  Birchington CT7..........26 C7
  Canterbury CT1...........87 D6
  Folkestone CT19.........178 E7
Ingram Ct CT18..........162 F3
Ingram Rd ME7............10 E6
Inner Lines ME7...........10 A6
Institute Rd
  Chatham ME4.............10 A4
  Faversham ME13..........62 D7
Intelligence Wlk TN25...138 F4
Inverary Ct CT11..........29 E1
Inverness Ho [7] ME15....97 E7
Inverness Terr CT19.......30 A3
Invicta Ct ME10...........36 E2
Invicta Gram Sch for Girls
  ME14.....................75 C4
Invicta Ho
  Folkestone CT19.........178 D7
  Lydd TN29...............207 I6
  Margate CT9..............29 B8
  Sheerness ME12............1 D2
  Whitstable CT5...........43 F8
Invicta Rd ME14...........76 C4
Invicta Villas ME14.......76 C4
Inward Car Lanes CT16...166 D5
Inward Freight Lanes
  CT16....................166 G3
Iona Cl ME5...............32 D1
Iona Rd ME15..............97 A7
Irchester St [11] CT11....52 F7
Ireland Ct TN24..........139 D2
Irene Astor Ct [7] CT20..178 D5
Iris Cl ME5...............54 A8
Iron Bar La [4] CT1.......88 A8
Irvine Cl ME8.............32 A8
Irvine Dr CT9.............29 C8
Irvine Mews [6] CT9.......29 C8
Isis Cl CT21.............175 A3
Island Rd
  Upstreet CT3, CT7........47 D2
  Westbere CT2, CT3........68 C7
Island Wall CT5...........20 C1
ISP Sch The [12] ME10.....36 E4
Italianate Greenhouse*
  CT3.....................30 A1
Ito Way ME10..............11 A3
Ivanhoe Rd
  Herne Bay CT6............23 A4
  Westgate on Sea CT8......7 C1
Ivans Field ME17..........98 B1
Ivens Way ME17...........100 D6
Iversgate Cl ME8..........11 F2
Ivory Cl ME13.............40 A1
Ivy Cl ME5................32 B3
Ivy Cottage Hill CT12.....50 E7
Ivy Cotts TN23...........155 C8
Ivy Ct CT2................66 C6
Ivy House Rd CT5..........65 F4
Ivy La CT1................88 A8
Ivy Mews ME17.............99 E2
Ivy Pl
  Canterbury CT1...........87 C7
  Deal CT14...............117 D7
  Rochester ME1.............9 A2
Ivyside CT8................7 C1
Ivy St ME8................33 F8
Ivy Way CT19.............178 E7
IWADE.....................14 D4
Iwade Prim Sch ME9.......14 D4

J

Jaarlen Rd TN29.........205 B6
Jacinth Dr ME10...........36 C6
Jacklin Cl CT13...........31 F2
Jackson Ave ME1..........31 E8
Jackson Cl ME8............11 C1
Jackson Rd CT1............87 E7
Jacksons Stables CT8.......7 D1
Jacob Cl CT9..............28 E7
Jacobs Ho ME12.............1 D2
Jacobs Oak TN24..........156 D6
Jacob Yd [3] ME13.........62 D7
Jade Cl ME10..............36 C7
Jaffa Ct [1] CT5..........43 D8
Jamaica Terr ME14.........75 A7
James Allchin Gdns
  ME14....................139 F4
James Cl
  Ash CT3..................71 D2
  Lyminge CT18............161 C7
James Ct
  Folkestone CT20.........178 A4
  [2] Margate CT9...........8 B2
James Hall Gdns CT14....117 C3
James Haney Dr TN24.....139 F5
James Morris Ct [3]
  CT20....................177 F3

James St
  Ashford TN23............139 A2
  [5] Chatham ME4...........9 F4
  Folkestone CT19.........178 D6
  Gillingham ME7...........10 C6
  Maidstone ME14...........75 B4
  [8] Ramsgate CT11........52 D6
  Rochester ME1.............9 C4
  Sheerness ME12............1 E2
James Whatman Way
  ME14.....................74 F5
Japonica Cl ME5...........32 C2
Jardines Cl [3] CT11......52 D7
Jarman's Field TN25.....123 F2
Jarrett Ho [10] CT20.....178 C4
Jarrett's Ct [1] ME10.....37 B4
Jarvis Dr TN24...........157 A7
Jarvis Pl TN30...........167 B3
Jarvist Pl CT14..........134 D6
Jasmine Cl
  Chartham CT4.............86 E1
  [2] Chatham ME5..........31 F4
Jasper Ave ME1.............9 D2
Javelin Ent Pk TN25.....139 E3
Javelin Way TN24.........139 E3
Jayne Wlk CT5.............43 B6
Jefferson Cl TN23........138 F1
Jefferson Dr ME8..........11 C1
Jefferson Rd ME12..........1 E2
Jefferstone Gdns TN29...194 E4
Jefferstone La TN29.....194 E4
Jeffery St ME7............10 C6
Jeffrey St ME14...........75 A5
Jellicoe Cl TN24.........157 A7
Jemmett Rd TN23.........156 A8
Jenkins' Dale ME4.........9 F3
Jenkins Dr ME15...........97 E5
Jenner Rd ME4.............9 C4
Jenner's Way TN29.......194 E3
Jennifer Gdns CT9.........29 C8
Jersey Ct TN24...........139 C8
Jersey La CT14...........109 C6
Jersey Rd ME2.............9 A8
Jesmond St [3] CT19.....178 D6
Jesse's Hill CT14........111 B1
Jessica Mews
  [2] Canterbury CT1.......67 B1
  Sittingbourne ME10.......36 E7
Jesson Cl TN29...........195 A4
Jesson Court Cvn Pk
  TN29....................194 F4
Jesuit Cl CT2.............67 A4
Jesus Hospl CT1...........67 A1
Jetty Rd
  Sheerness ME12............1 B3
  Warden ME12..............6 E4
Jewry La CT1..............87 F8
Jeyes Rd ME1.............10 D3
Jezreels Rd ME7..........10 D3
Jillian Way TN23.........155 E7
Jiniwin Rd ME1...........31 D7
Jo-Ann's Ct [5] CT10.....30 A4
Johannesburg Ho [2]
  ME15....................97 F5
Johannesburg Rd CT16...149 C4
John Anderson Ct [11]
  ME13....................62 D7
John Badger Cl TN24.....139 E5
John Bowley Ho CT4......177 F6
John Dutton Way TN24....139 E4
John Graham Ct CT1.......88 A6
John Hall Cl ME13.........40 B2
John Nash Cl ME8..........60 B8
John Newington Cl TN24..139 F5
John's Gn CT13............93 E6
Johnson Ave ME7..........10 C7
Johnson Cl TN24..........157 A7
Johnson Ct ME13..........40 B1
Johnson Ho ME10..........36 D4
Johnson Rd ME10..........36 D4
Johnson's Cnr TN26......183 A4
Johnson Way ME12..........4 A7
John St
  Broadstairs ME10.........30 B4
  Maidstone ME14...........75 A6
  Rochester ME1.............9 C4
John Tapping Cl CT14....117 B1
John Wesley CE/Methodist
  Prim Sch The TN23......155 D7
John Wilson Bsns Pk CT5..21 B1
Joiners ME14..............10 B2
Jointon Rd CT20..........178 B4
Jordan Cl ME15............97 E5
Joseph Conrad Dr TN25..172 F4
Joseph Conrad Rd CT2.....66 D1
Joseph Wilson Ind Est
  CT5......................44 A7
Joss Gap Rd CT10..........8 H1
Joyes Cl
  Folkestone CT19.........178 E7
  Whitfield CT16..........149 B7
Joyes Rd
  Folkestone CT19.........178 E7
  Whitfield CT16..........149 B7
Joy La CT5................43 B8
Joy Lane Prim Sch CT5....43 C7
Joy Wood ME17............97 D5
Jubilee Cl CT21..........187 D8
Jubilee Cotts
  Staple CT3...............92 B6
  Throwley ME13............82 D1
  Worth CT14...............94 B4
Jubilee Cres ME1...........2 F5
Jubilee Ct CT14..........117 D3

Jubilee Field TN30.......188 E4
Jubilee Fields ME4........12 C2
Jubilee Ho CT20.........178 B4
Jubilee Rd
  Littlebourne CT3.........89 F8
  Sandwich CT13............93 F8
  Worth CT14...............94 B4
Jubilee Sch ME16..........36 E5
Jubilee Terr ME7..........10 C6
Jubilee Way
  Dover CT15, CT16........150 A2
  Faversham ME13...........62 E6
Judd Rd ME13..............62 A7
Judkins Cl ME5............32 C6
Julian Cl CT19...........178 B5
Julian Rd CT19...........178 B5
Julie Cl CT10.............30 A7
Julien Pl TN24...........157 A8
Julie Rose Athletic Stadium
  TN24....................139 F4
Junction Rd
  Gillingham ME7...........10 C4
  Herne Bay CT6............22 C2
Junior Kings Sch CT2......67 E5
Juniper Cl
  Ashford TN23............138 E2
  Canterbury CT1...........88 A6
  Chatham ME5..............32 A4
  Maidstone ME16...........74 B6
  Whitstable CT5...........20 F1
Jupiter La TN23..........155 E5
JURY'S GAP................203 D1
Jury's Gap Coastguard Cotts
  TN31....................203 E1
Jury's Gap Rd TN29......205 A5

K

Kain Ct [6] CT12..........29 B1
Kake St CT4..............125 E7
Katherine Ct ME5.........32 B2
KEARSNEY.................148 D3
Kearsney Abbey* CT16....148 D4
Kearsney Ave CT16.......148 D4
Kearsney Ct CT16........148 D4
Kearsney Sta CT16.......148 D4
Keat Farm Cl CT6..........23 F5
Keating Cl ME1.............9 A3
Keddow's Cl CT21........187 D8
Kedleston Rd CT16.......149 C5
Keefe Cl ME5..............31 D1
Keel Ct ME2...............9 D8
Keeley Mews ME7..........10 E3
Keeper's Hill CT4.........89 D2
Keith Ave CT12............52 A8
Kellaway Rd ME5...........32 A2
Kelly Dr ME7.............10 C7
Kelly Ho ME1.............31 C7
Kelvedon Rd CT4.........117 C2
Kemp Alley [2] CT5.......20 D1
Kemp Cl ME5..............31 E4
KEMPE'S CORNER..........123 A2
Kempes Pl TN23..........123 E2
Kemp Rd CT5..............21 C2
Kempton Cl ME5...........32 C2
Kemsdale Rd ME13.........63 F6
Kemsing Gdns CT2.........67 B4
KEMSLEY..................11 E1
Kemsley Down Sta*
  ME10....................15 C1
Kemsley Rd ME10.........14 F1
Kemsley Sta ME10........14 F1
KEMSLEY STREET...........33 C2
Kemsley Street Rd ME7....33 C1
KENARDINGTON...........182 A6
Kenardington Rd TN26....181 E3
Kenbrook TN24...........139 C7
Kendal Cl CT11............52 B6
Kendall Pl [1] ME15......97 D8
Kendal Mdw CT5...........21 E1
Kendal Rise CT10.........30 A5
Kendal Way ME8...........11 F1
Kendon Bsns Pk ME2........9 D8
Kenfield Rd CT4.........109 A6
Kengate Ind Est CT21....175 F1
Kenilworth Cl CT15......151 A6
Kenilworth Ct CT16.......36 C5
Kenilworth Dr ME8........33 D4
Kenilworth Gdns ME8......33 D4
Kenilworth Ho ME16.......74 B2
Kennedy Cl ME13..........62 D8
Kennedy Dr CT14.........117 B2
Kennedy Ho [8] CT1.......52 F7
Kennel Barn Rd ME7.......57 C5
Kennel Hill CT13.........131 E6
Kennelling Rd ME13,
  TN27....................103 D5
Kennels The CT15.........131 E6
Kennet Ct CT14..........117 A2
Kennett La TN25.........175 B8
Kennett Lane Cotts
  TN25....................175 B8
KENNINGTON..............139 E6
Kennington CE Jun Sch
  TN24....................139 E7
Kennington Cl
  Gillingham ME8...........11 A4
  Maidstone ME15..........97 F7
KENNINGTON LEES.........139 D8
Kennington Pl TN24......139 D7
Kennington Rd TN24......140 A1
Kensington Ho ME16.......74 A2
Kensington Rd CT7........67 C4
Kent Ave
  Ashford TN24............139 B3
  Canterbury CT1...........88 D3
  Maidstone ME15...........75 C1

Kent Ave continued
Minster (Sheppey) ME12. . . . . .4 B6
Sittingbourne ME10. . . . . .36 D3
Kent Battle of Britain Mus*
CT18. . . . . .162 F4
Kent & Canterbury Hospl
CT1. . . . . .88 A5
Kent Cl ME1. . . . . .31 C8
Kent College Canterbury
CT2. . . . . .66 C3
Kent College Canterbury Inf
& Jun Sch CT2. . . . . .66 A1
Kent & East Sussex Rly*
TN30. . . . . .179 A8
Kent Gdns CT7. . . . . .26 F7
Kent Ho
  4 Broadstairs CT10. . . . . . . .30 A4
Folkestone CT20. . . . . .178 B4
Kent International Airport
CT12. .28 B1
Kentish Ct 8 ME16. . . . . .74 E4
Kent Life* ME14. . . . . .53 D1
Kent Masonic Liby & Mus*
  22 CT1. . . . . .66 F1
Kent Masonic Mus* CT1. . . . .66 F1
Kentmere Ave CT11. . . . . .53 F7
Kent Music Sch 25 CT1. . . . . .66 F1
Kenton Gdns CT12. . . . . .50 B6
Kent Pl CT11. . . . . .52 F6
Kent Rd
Folkestone CT19. . . . . .177 E7
Margate CT9. . . . . .29 B8
Sheerness ME12. . . . . .1 C1
Kent Science Pk ME9. . . . . . . .58 D6
Kent Showground ME14. . . . . .55 C3
Kent St CT5. . . . . .43 D8
Kentstone St ME4. . . . . .9 C2
Kent Terr
Gillingham ME8. . . . . .12 C2
Ramsgate CT11. . . . . .52 F6
Kent View Dr ME12. . . . . .5 D1
Kenward Rd ME14. . . . . .74 C5
Kenwood Ave ME5. . . . . .32 A4
Kenya Terr ME4. . . . . .75 A7
Kenyon Wlk ME4. . . . . .33 B3
Kerry Hill Way ME14. . . . . . . .74 E6
Kerton Rd TN29. . . . . .209 D7
Keston Ct ME8. . . . . .11 A2
Kestrel Cl
Kingsnorth TN23. . . . . .156 C3
Sittingbourne ME10. . . . . . . .37 A2
Kestrel Ct
  4 Sittingbourne ME10. . . . . .37 A4
Whitstable CT5. . . . . .21 A3
Kestrel Ho ME7. . . . . .10 B6
Kestrel Rd ME5. . . . . .32 C2
Keswick Ave ME15. . . . . .37 C3
Keswick Ct ME7. . . . . .11 A5
Keswick Dr ME16. . . . . .74 B5
Keswick The CT18. . . . . .163 B5
Kettle Dr CT18. . . . . .81 F4
Kettle Hill Rd
Eastling ME13. . . . . .81 F5
Throwley ME13. . . . . .82 A4
Kevin Cl CT11. . . . . .52 B6
Kewlands ME14. . . . . .75 C6
KEYCOL. 35 E6
Keycol Hill ME9. . . . . .35 F5
Keyes Ave ME4. . . . . .9 F2
Keyes Cl CT18. . . . . .149 A5
Keyes Pl CT19. . . . . .178 E7
Keynes Coll CT2. . . . . .66 D4
Key St ME10. . . . . .36 A5
Keyes The CT18. . . . . .163 C5
Keyworth Mews 7 CT1. . . . . .67 B2
Khartoum Rd ME7. . . . . .10 A6
Khartoum Sq CT16. . . . . . . .149 A6
Khyber Rd ME4, ME7. . . . . . . .10 B7
Kilbride Ct CT11. . . . . .29 F1
Kilburn Ho 6 ME14. . . . . .75 A5
Kilnbridge Cl ME15. . . . . .96 B7
Kilnbridge Wks ME15. . . . . . .96 B7
Kiln Cl
Challock TN25. . . . . .105 B1
Sittingbourne ME10. . . . . . . .37 A3
Kiln Cnr CT21. . . . . .176 B4
Kilndown Cl
Ashford TN23. . . . . .155 E6
Maidstone ME16. . . . . .74 C7
Kilndown Gdns
Canterbury CT2. . . . . .67 A4
Margate CT9. . . . . .8 E2
Kiln Field TN23. . . . . .179 C7
Kiln La TN26. . . . . .153 F5
Kimberley Cl CT16. . . . . .149 C3
Kimberley Cnr CT10. . . . . . . .29 F8
Kimberley Ct CT8. . . . . .7 C1
Kimberley Gr CT5. . . . . .42 F6
Kimberley Rd
Gillingham ME7. . . . . .10 D3
Ramsgate CT12. . . . . .29 A1
Kimberley Way TN24. . . . . . .156 C7
Kimberley Terr CT18. . . . . . .161 C7
King Arthur Ct ME10. . . . . . . .36 E3
King Arthur Rd CT12. . . . . . . .51 D7
King Charles Ct CT14. . . . . . .117 D2
King Edward Rd
Birchington CT7. . . . . .27 A5
Chatham ME4. . . . . .9 F2
Deal CT14. . . . . .117 D8
Gillingham ME7. . . . . .10 F6
Maidstone ME15. . . . . .74 F2
  11 Ramsgate CT11. . . . . .52 C6

King Edward Rd continued
Minster (Sheppey) ME12. . . . . .9 C5
King Edward St CT5. . . . . .20 D1
King Ethelbert Sch CT7. . . . . .27 C7
Kingfisher Apartments 13
CT6. . . . . .22 D3
Kingfisher Ave CT21. . . . . . .187 D8
Kingfisher Bsns Pk
TN24. . . . . .139 D3
Kingfisher Cl
Ashford TN24. . . . . .157 A7
Iwade ME9. . . . . .14 E4
Margate CT9. . . . . .28 B8
Whitstable CT5. . . . . .43 C7
Kingfisher Ct
Herne Bay CT6. . . . . .22 D3
  11 Maidstone ME15. . . . . . . .75 B4
Kingfisher Dr ME5. . . . . .32 C7
Kingfisher Gdns CT21. . . . . .187 C8
Kingfisher Ho TN23. . . . . . . .138 F1
Kingfisher Mdw ME16. . . . . . .74 F3
Kingfisher Prim Sch ME5. . .32 B7
Kingfisher Wlk CT10. . . . . . . .29 F5
King George Rd ME5. . . . . . . .31 E4
King George Villas CT14. . . . .94 B3
King George V Meml Houses
ME8. .11 C2
King Lear's Way CT17. . . . . .166 B5
Kingly Way CT17. . . . . .166 A7
Kings Acre ME15. . . . . .76 A1
Kings Ave
Ashford TN23. . . . . .139 A2
Birchington CT7. . . . . .26 D7
Broadstairs CT10. . . . . .30 B6
Rochester ME1. . . . . .9 C3
Sandwich CT13. . . . . .95 A8
Whitstable CT5. . . . . .20 E1
King's Bastion ME7. . . . . .10 A5
Kingsbridge Ct 11 CT20. . . .178 E5
Kingsbrook Pk CT1. . . . . .67 A2
Kings Chase TN24. . . . . .140 A2
King's Cl CT14. . . . . .134 D6
Kings Cotts ME17. . . . . .98 F6
Kings Ct CT14. . . . . .117 D3
Kingsdale Ct ME5. . . . . .10 C1
KINGSDOWN
Deal. 134 D5
Lynsted. 59 E4
Kingsdown Cl
Gillingham ME7. . . . . .33 B4
Maidstone ME16. . . . . .74 E4
Kingsdown Cotts ME9. . . . . . .59 E4
Kingsdown Hill CT14. . . . . . .134 D4
Kingsdown Rd
Kingsdown CT14. . . . . .134 D7
Lynsted ME9. . . . . .59 D4
St Margaret's at Cliffe
CT15. . . . . .151 A7
Kingsdown & Ringwould CE
Prim Sch CT14. . . . . .134 C5
Kingsfield Rd CT6. . . . . .23 B2
Kingsford Cl TN25. . . . . .157 E4
Kingsford Ct CT17. . . . . .149 B1
Kingsford St CT25. . . . . .157 D5
KINGSGATE. 8 G1
Kingsgate Ave CT10. . . . . .8 F1
Kingsgate Bay Rd CT10. . . . . .8 H2
Kingsgate Castle CT10. . . . . . .8 H2
Kingsgate Cl ME16. . . . . .74 C4
Kingsgate Coll CT10. . . . . . . .30 A8
Kingsgate La TN30. . . . . . . .188 C5
Kings Hall The* CT6. . . . . . . .23 A5
KINGSLAND. 136 C8
Kingsland Gdns CT14. . . . . .134 B8
Kingsland Hollow TN29. . . . .195 A4
Kingsland La
Egerton Forstal TN27. . . . . .118 C1
Westwell TN25. . . . . .121 F1
Kingsley Rd
Maidstone ME15. . . . . .75 A3
Whitstable CT5. . . . . .43 E8
Kingsmarsh La TN29. . . . . . .201 C5
Kings Mdw TN24. . . . . .139 E7
Kingsmead
Folkestone CT19. . . . . .178 B8
Westgate on Sea CT8. . . . . . . .7 C1
Kingsmead L Ctr CT2. . . . . . .67 A2
Kingsmead Prim Sch 22
CT1. . . . . .67 A1
Kingsmead Rd CT1, CT2. . . . .67 A2
Kings Mews
  7 Canterbury CT1. . . . . .67 A1
Margate CT9. . . . . .7 J3
Kings Mill ME10. . . . . .36 E5
KINGSNORTH. 156 A4
Kingsnorth CE Prim Sch
TN23. . . . . .156 B3
Kingsnorth Ct 2 CT20. . . . .178 B5
Kingsnorth Gdns CT20. . . . .178 C5
Kingsnorth Ind Est TN23. . . .156 B6
Kingsnorth Rd
Ashford TN23. . . . . .156 A6
Faversham ME13. . . . . .62 C6
Gillingham ME8. . . . . .11 C4
Kings Oak Mews ME5. . . . . . .31 F4
King's Orch ME9. . . . . .9 C5
Kings Par 7 TN24. . . . . .139 B2
King's Pk CT1. . . . . .67 B1
Kings Pl 8 CT11. . . . . .52 C6
Kings Prep Sch ME1. . . . . .9 C5
Kings Prospect TN24. . . . . . .156 C6
Kings Rd
Aylesham CT3. . . . . .112 F6
Dover CT17. . . . . .166 A7
Folkestone CT20. . . . . .177 D6

Kings Rd continued
Minster (Sheppey) ME12. . . . . .4 D7
Ramsgate CT11. . . . . .52 D8
King's Rd
Birchington CT7. . . . . .27 A6
Chatham ME5. . . . . .10 C1
Faversham ME13. . . . . .62 C7
Sandwich CT13. . . . . .73 A1
Kings Reach ME15. . . . . .97 D8
Kings Ropewalk CT7. . . . . . .166 B5
Kings Row
  1 Maidstone ME15. . . . . .75 A1
Rochester ME1. . . . . .9 B4
King's Sch ME1. . . . . .9 C5
King's Sch Canterbury The
CT1. . . . . .67 A1
King's Sch Recn Ctr The
CT1. . . . . .66 F2
Kings Sch The 11 CT1. . . . . . .88 A8
King St
Brookland TN29. . . . . .191 D2
Canterbury CT1. . . . . .66 A1
Chatham ME4. . . . . .10 A4
Deal CT14. . . . . .117 D6
Deal, Walmer CT14. . . . . . . .117 D3
Dover CT16. . . . . .166 D7
Fordwich CT2. . . . . .68 A4
Gillingham ME7. . . . . .10 C6
Maidstone ME15. . . . . .75 A4
Margate CT9. . . . . .7 J3
Ramsgate CT11. . . . . .52 E7
Rochester ME1. . . . . .9 C4
Sandwich CT13. . . . . .73 A1
Sheerness ME12. . . . . .1 D3
Sittingbourne ME10. . . . . . . .36 E5
KINGSTON. 111 D3
Kingston Ave CT9. . . . . .28 C7
Kingston Cl
Crabble CT18. . . . . .148 F3
Herne Bay CT6. . . . . .23 F5
Ramsgate CT12. . . . . .29 B2
Kingston Cres ME5. . . . . .32 A4
Kingston Dr ME15. . . . . .97 A8
Kingstone Ct 3 CT20. . . . . .178 B5
Kingsway
Chatham ME5. . . . . .10 D1
Dymchurch TN29. . . . . .186 E2
Gillingham ME10. . . . . .10 E1
Kingswear Gdns ME2. . . . . . . .9 C7
Kings Wlk ME14. . . . . .75 B5
KINGSWOOD. 99 E3
Kingswood Ave ME4. . . . . .9 F2
Kingswood Ct TN24. . . . . . . .139 D5
King's Wood Forest Wlks*
TN25. . . . . .105 F1
Kingswood Ho ME16. . . . . . . .74 A3
Kingswood Prim Sch
ME17. . . . . .99 E2
Kingswood Rd
Gillingham ME7. . . . . .10 D6
Kit's Coty ME20. . . . . .53 D8
Kingswood Villas CT17. . . . .149 A2
King William Rd 6 ME7. . . . . .10 C7
Kinross Cl ME1. . . . . .32 B7
Kinson Way CT10. . . . . .149 A5
Kipling Rd TN23. . . . . .139 A3
Kipping Cl CT18. . . . . .163 A4
Kirby's Hts 8 CT2. . . . . .66 F1
Kirby's La CT2. . . . . .66 F1
Kirkdale ME15. . . . . .96 F5
Kirkdale Cl ME5. . . . . .32 D1
Kirkdale Cotts ME5. . . . . .96 F5
Kirkdale Rd ME15. . . . . .96 F6
Kirk Gdns CT14. . . . . .117 B2
Kirkstone Ave CT11. . . . . .51 F7
Kirk View TN23. . . . . .155 C8
Kirkwood Ave TN26. . . . . . . .169 A1
Kirton Cl CT18. . . . . .162 F4
Kitchener Ave ME4. . . . . .10 A1
Kitchener Ct CT4. . . . . .128 E8
Kitchener Rd
Dover CT17. . . . . .166 A7
Rochester ME2. . . . . .9 A8
Kitchener Sq CT19. . . . . .178 E8
Kite Farm CT5. . . . . .21 D3
Kitewell La TN29. . . . . .205 D8
Kither Rd TN23. . . . . .156 A7
Kit Hill ME13. . . . . .84 D8
Kit Hill Ave ME5. . . . . .31 E3
Kitsbridge La TN26. . . . . . . .183 F5
KIT'S COTY. 53 C7
Kit's Coty Ho* ME20. . . . . . . .53 C6
Kittiwake Cl CT18. . . . . .23 F5
Klondyke Ind Est ME11. . . . . . .2 F4
Knatchbull Way ME25. . . . . .158 E5
Knavesacre Ct ME8. . . . . .33 D5
KNAVE'S ASH. 46 C5
Knell La CT3. . . . . .71 C3
Knight Ave
Canterbury CT2. . . . . .87 D8
Gillingham ME7. . . . . .10 D7
Knight Rd ME2. . . . . .9 A6
Knightrider St
Maidstone ME15. . . . . .75 A3
Sandwich CT13. . . . . .73 A1
Knights Alley 20 CT5. . . . . . .20 D2
Knight's Ave CT10. . . . . .30 B6
Knights Ct
Dover CT17. . . . . .149 B1
Sittingbourne ME10. . . . . . . .36 E3
Knightsfield Rd ME10. . . . . . .36 D7
Knights Park and Est ME2. . . .9 A6
Knight's Rd CT16. . . . . .166 B8
Knights Templars CT17. . . . . .166 A8
Knights Way CT16. . . . . .149 A3
Knock Hill TN30. . . . . .190 A2
Knockholt Rd CT9. . . . . .8 F3

Knockhurst Ct TN30. . . . . . .167 C1
Knock Rd TN23. . . . . .156 A7
Knockwood Rd TN30. . . . . . .167 C1
Knold Pk CT9. . . . . .28 E8
Knole Pk ME5. . . . . .32 C3
Knole The ME13. . . . . .62 B7
Knoll Cl CT20. . . . . .178 C4
Knoll Hill TN25. . . . . .173 C3
Knoll La TN23. . . . . .155 E7
Knoll Pl CT14. . . . . .117 C2
Knoll The CT15. . . . . .151 A6
Knoll Way ME12. . . . . .6 D4
Knott Cres TN24. . . . . .157 A7
Knott Ct ME14. . . . . .74 F6
Knotts La CT15. . . . . .150 F6
Knott's La 19 CT1. . . . . .67 A1
Knotts Sq 1 TN23. . . . . .139 C2
Knowle Rd ME14. . . . . .75 B6
Knowler Way CT6. . . . . .23 C5
KNOWLTON. 114 C2
Knowlton Gdns ME16. . . . . . .74 B2
Knowlton Wlk 1 CT1. . . . . . . .67 B1
Kohima Pl CT17. . . . . .149 F2
Kyetop Wlk ME8. . . . . .33 D6

L

La Belle Alliance Sq 9
CT11. .52 E7
Laburnum Ave CT13. . . . . . . .93 F8
Laburnum Cl CT16. . . . . .148 E4
Laburnum Gr ME12. . . . . .1 I1
Laburnum Ho ME12. . . . . .1 C2
Laburnum La CT2. . . . . .68 B7
Laburnum Pl ME10. . . . . .36 E4
Labworth Cl ME12. . . . . .3 E6
Lacey Cl ME17. . . . . .98 F4
Lachlan Way 2 CT20. . . . . . .177 F3
Lackenden Cotts CT3. . . . . . . .89 D6
Lacock Gdns
Loose ME15. . . . . .97 A8
Maidstone ME15. . . . . .75 A1
Lacton Oast TN24. . . . . .157 B8
Lacton Way TN24. . . . . .157 A8
Lacy Cl ME15. . . . . .74 D7
Ladbrooke Ho 7 ME14. . . . . .75 A5
Ladds Cnr ME7. . . . . .11 B5
LADE. 206 C6
Lade Fort Cotts TN29. . . . . .206 C6
Lade Fort Cres TN29. . . . . . .206 C6
Ladies Wlk CT21. . . . . .176 C1
Ladyfields
Chatham ME5. . . . . .32 D2
Herne Bay CT6. . . . . .23 D2
Ladyfields ME14. . . . . .35 F5
Lady Garne Rd CT15. . . . . . .164 F5
Lady Joanna Thornhill
(Endowed) Prim Sch
TN25. . . . . .123 E2
Lady Share 18 ME15. . . . . . . .97 E5
Ladysmith Gr CT5. . . . . .42 F6
Ladywell 2 CT16. . . . . .166 D8
Ladywell ME7. . . . . .22 A7
Lady Wootton's Gn 6
CT1. . . . . .88 A8
La Galamina TN28. . . . . .206 E8
Lagos Ave CT12. . . . . .29 A1
Lakelands
Harrietsham ME17. . . . . .100 C6
Loose ME15. . . . . .97 A7
Lakemead TN23. . . . . .155 E8
Laker Ho ME14. . . . . .75 A6
Laker Rd ME1. . . . . .31 C6
Lakeside TN23. . . . . .155 E8
Lakeside Gdns TN26. . . . . . .169 F1
Lakeside Pk ME2. . . . . .9 E7
Lakesview International Bsns
Pk CT3. . . . . .47 A1
Lakewood Dr ME8. . . . . .33 C6
Laking Ave CT10. . . . . .30 B7
Laleham Gap Sch CT10. . . . . .30 B2
Laleham Rd CT9. . . . . .8 B1
Laleham Sch CT9. . . . . .8 B1
Laleham Wlk CT9. . . . . .8 B1
Lambard Ho 8 ME14. . . . . . . .75 A5
Lambden Rd TN27. . . . . .136 C6
Lamberhurst Farm ME13. . . . .42 F1
Lamberhurst Rd ME8. . . . . . . .11 B3
Lamberhurst Rd ME16. . . . . . .74 B7
Lamberhurst Way CT9. . . . . . .8 E3
Lambert Ho CT14. . . . . .117 B3
Lambes Cl ME8. . . . . .33 D5
Lambeth Cl ME5. . . . . .32 B4
Lambeth Rd CT1. . . . . .67 C4
Lambourne Pl ME8. . . . . .12 A2
Lambourne Wlk CT1. . . . . . . .88 C8
Lambourn Way ME5. . . . . .32 C2
Lambsfrith Gr ME7. . . . . .33 B3
Lamb's Wlk CT5. . . . . .43 C6
Lambton Rd CT17. . . . . .149 A1
Laming Rd CT7. . . . . .27 A6
Lammas Dr ME10. . . . . .36 E6
Lammas Gate ME13. . . . . .62 D8
Lamplighters CT ME7. . . . . . . .32 F5
Lancashire Rd ME15. . . . . . . .97 E7
Lancaster Ave CT18. . . . . . . .164 C2
Lancaster Cl
Hamstreet TN26. . . . . .183 A8
Ramsgate CT12. . . . . .29 B1
Lancaster Ct ME8. . . . . .33 C7
Lancaster Gdns
Birchington CT7. . . . . .26 F6
Herne Bay CT6. . . . . .23 D5

Lancaster Ho
Deal CT14. . . . . .117 A5
  3 Dover CT17. . . . . .166 D7
Lancaster Rd
Canterbury CT1. . . . . .87 F6
Dover CT17. . . . . .166 D7
Lancaster The CT10. . . . . .30 B3
Lancaster Way TN23. . . . . . .138 F4
Lance Cl ME10. . . . . .36 F8
Lancelot Ct CT14. . . . . .117 A3
Lancer Ho ME1. . . . . .9 C3
Lancet La ME15. . . . . .97 A6
Lanchester Cl CT6. . . . . .22 A3
Landbury Wlk TN23. . . . . . . .138 F4
Landon Rd CT6. . . . . .23 C4
Landon Ct ME7. . . . . .33 A3
Landrail Rd ME9. . . . . .13 B3
Landway The ME14. . . . . .76 A4
Lane End CT6. . . . . .22 D5
Lanes The CT12. . . . . .50 D6
Lane's Wlk CT5. . . . . .20 E2
Lane The CT15. . . . . .149 F6
Lanfranc Gdns CT2. . . . . .66 C1
Lanfranc Ho 5 CT1. . . . . .67 A1
Lanfranc Rd CT14. . . . . .117 C8
Lang Ct CT5. . . . . .21 C3
Langdale TN23. . . . . .155 E8
Langdale Ave CT11. . . . . .52 A7
Langdale Cl ME8. . . . . .11 D1
Langdale Rise ME16. . . . . .74 C5
Langdon Ave CT3. . . . . .71 F1
Langdon Cl CT15. . . . . .150 F5
Langdon Cross CT15. . . . . . .150 C7
Langdon Prim Sch CT15. . .133 A1
Langdon Rd
Folkestone CT19. . . . . .177 D7
Rochester ME1. . . . . .9 C4
Langham Cl CT9. . . . . .7 F1
Langham Gr ME16. . . . . .74 C4
Langholm Rd TN23. . . . . . . .156 A7
Langhorne Gdns 9
CT20. . . . . .178 C4
LANGLEY. 98 C4
Langley Gdns CT9. . . . . .8 E3
LANGLEY HEATH. 98 F4
Langley Ho 11 ME10. . . . . . . .74 A3
Langley Rd ME10. . . . . .36 F7
Langney Dr TN23. . . . . .155 E6
Langport Rd TN28. . . . . .202 C6
Langton Cl ME14. . . . . .75 C5
Langton Cotts CT3. . . . . .70 B5
Langton La CT14. . . . . .88 A4
Langton Way ME15. . . . . .74 F2
Lankester Parker Rd ME1. . . .31 C6
Lansdowne Ave ME15. . . . . . .97 C6
Lansdowne Ct 8 ME4. . . . . . . .9 F4
Lansdowne Prim Sch
ME10. . . . . .37 C3
Lansdowne Rd ME4. . . . . .9 E2
Lansdown Rd
Canterbury CT1. . . . . .88 A7
Sittingbourne ME10. . . . . . . .37 C4
Lanthorne Rd CT10. . . . . .30 A6
La Providence ME7. . . . . .9 C5
Lapwing Cl
Hawkinge CT18. . . . . .163 A3
Minster (Sheppey) ME12. . . . .4 B5
Lapwing Dr
Ashford TN23. . . . . .156 D3
Lower Halstow ME9. . . . . .13 B3
Larch Cl
Broadstairs CT10. . . . . .29 D4
Hersden CT3. . . . . .68 E8
Larchcroft ME5. . . . . .32 A4
Larches The
Faversham ME13. . . . . .62 A8
Whitstable CT5. . . . . .43 C8
Larch Rd CT15. . . . . .114 B1
Larch Terr ME12. . . . . .3 A8
Larch Wlk TN24. . . . . .139 C6
Larkey View CT4. . . . . .86 E1
Larkfield Ave
Gillingham ME7. . . . . .10 E4
Sittingbourne ME10. . . . . . . .36 E6
Larking Dr ME16. . . . . .74 D7
Larkscliff Ct CT7. . . . . .26 D8
Larksfield Rd ME13. . . . . .40 C1
Larkspur Rd ME5. . . . . .31 E4
La Rocco TN28. . . . . .206 E8
Lascelles Rd CT17. . . . . .166 A6
Laser Quay ME2. . . . . .9 D6
La Tausco TN28. . . . . .206 D8
Latchgate CT20. . . . . .177 C3
Lathe Barn* TN29. . . . . .186 D5
Latimer Cl CT12. . . . . .22 B2
Latimer Pl 4 ME7. . . . . .10 C7
Launder Way ME15. . . . . .74 E2
Laundry Rd CT12. . . . . .50 D7
Laura Pl ME1. . . . . .9 A2
Laura Villas CT12. . . . . .22 E5
Laureate Cl CT9. . . . . .8 B2
Laurel Ave TN29. . . . . .194 F4
Laurel Cl ME17. . . . . .177 E6
Laurel Gr ME17. . . . . .99 D2
Laurel Ho ME1. . . . . .1 C2
Laurel Rd ME7. . . . . .10 C8
Laurels The ME12. . . . . .74 C2
Laurel Way CT4. . . . . .86 E1
Laurel Wlk ME8. . . . . .33 E6
Laurensfield CT12. . . . . .50 C7
Laureston Pl CT16. . . . . .166 E8
Laurice Ct 6 CT11. . . . . .52 C6
Laurie Gray Ave ME5. . . . . . . .31 D1

Lauriston Cl CT11	52 A5
Lauriston Mount CT10	30 A5
Lausanne Rd CT9	7 J2
Lausanne Terr 11 CT9	7 J2
Lavenda Cl ME7	33 A4
Lavender Cl	
1 Chatham ME5	31 E4
Margate CT9	28 C8
Whitstable CT5	
Lavender Ct ME10	37 A3
Lavender Ho 3 ME15	97 D8
Lavender La CT12	51 C5
Lavender Mews 15 CT1	87 F8
Laverstoke Rd ME16	74 C8
Law Cl CT7	87 C8
Lawley Cl CT12	29 C1
Lawn Cl ME4	10 B2
Lawn Rd	
Broadstairs CT10	30 A4
Deal CT14	117 C1
Lawns The 15 CT11	52 F7
Lawn Villas CT5	52 E6
Lawrence Cl	
Folkestone CT19	177 F6
Loose ME15	97 A7
Lawrence Ct CT19	178 E6
Lawrence Gdns CT16	23 C4
Lawrence St ME7	10 C5
Laws La TN25	172 D7
Lawson Cl CT4	86 D2
Laxey The ME15	74 E1
Laxton Cl ME5	75 F3
Laxton Dr ME17	98 A1
Laxton Way	
Canterbury CT1	88 C7
Faversham ME13	62 E5
Sittingbourne ME10	36 D6
Whitstable CT5	21 C1
Layfield Cotts ME9	14 D1
Layfield Rd ME7	10 F7
Lay La CT3	71 D2
Laylam Cl CT10	29 D5
Lazarus Hart Havens of Rest	
The 4 CT11	52 F8
Leach Ho ME13	64 A3
Lea Cl CT21	176 B4
Leacon Cotts TN27	120 E4
Leacon Cotts The TN27	120 E4
Leacon Rd TN23	138 F2
Lea Ct ME4	9 C1
LEADINGCROSS GREEN	101 C3
Leafield TN25	159 D1
Leafy Glade ME8	33 B6
Leafy La ME16	74 E5
Leahurst Ct CT16	148 E4
Leake Ho 2 ME1	9 C1
Leamington Dr ME16	74 B4
Leander Cl CT14	117 A3
Leander Rd ME1	31 C7
Learoyd Rd TN28	202 C6
Leas Gn CT10	29 D4
Leaside Cotts CT21	176 B3
Leas Lift The* CT20	178 D4
Leas Rd CT14	117 B4
Leas The	
Faversham ME13	62 B8
Folkestone CT20	178 C4
Kingsdown CT14	134 D3
Minster (Sheppey) ME12	4 C8
Sheerness ME12	1 11
Whitstable CT5	21 D1
Leatt Cl CT10	29 F4
LEAVELAND	83 B1
Leaveland Cl TN23	155 F6
Leaveland Cotts ME13	83 B2
Leda Cotts TN25	120 F3
Leech Ho ME1	9 D5
LEEDS	99 A7
Leeds & Broomfield CE Prim	
Sch ME17	99 A7
Leeds Castle* ME17	99 D7
Leeds Rd ME17	98 E3
Leeds Sq ME8	11 B3
Lee Ho CT14	117 C1
Leelands Ho CT14	117 B1
Lees Cl The TN25	158 D5
Lees Court Rd ME13	83 C5
Lees Rd	
Ashford TN24	140 A1
Brabourne Lees TN25	158 E6
Lees Terr CT5	85 C2
Lees The CT6	23 C5
Leeswood TN24	140 B1
Leet Cl	
Gillingham ME7	10 E6
Minster (Sheppey) ME12	5 B5
Leeward Rd ME1	9 C1
Leggett's La 10 CT5	20 D2
Leicester Ave CT9	8 C2
Leicester Ct CT9	8 D3
Leicester Gdns ME12	6 E3
Leicester Rd ME15	97 D7
Leigh Ave ME15	97 B6
Leigh Ct ME12	3 F5
LEIGH GREEN	179 F6
Leigh Green Ind Est	
TN30	179 E6
Leigh Rd CT11	28 F1
Leighton Ct 3 ME4	149 C1
Leighton Rd CT16	149 C1
Leighville Dr CT6	22 D4
Leitch Row ME7	10 A7
Leivers Rd CT14	117 A3
Lenacre Ave CT16	148 F7
Lenacre La CT16	148 F8
Lenacre St TN25	122 B2
Lendrim Cl 11 ME7	10 A6
Lenfield Ave ME14	75 B4
Length The CT7	25 F2
LENHAM	101 D5
Lenham Cl CT10	30 A2
Lenham Ct 10 ME15	75 B4
LENHAM FORSTAL	102 B1
Lenham Forstal Rd	
ME17	119 B8
Lenham Gdns CT9	28 B8
LENHAM HEATH	119 B8
Lenham Heath Rd ME17	101 C2
Lenham Ho ME17	101 C5
Lenham Prim Sch ME17	101 C5
Lenham Rd ME17	100 C1
Lenham Sta ME17	101 C4
Lenham Way ME8	11 A3
Lenmead ME17	100 C6
Lennard Ct 4 CT20	178 E5
Lennard Rd CT20	178 E5
Lenside Dr ME15	75 F4
Len Valley Wlk ME15	75 F1
Leona Ct 8 CT9	8 B2
Leonard Cl ME16	74 B6
Leonard Rd	
4 Chatham ME4	10 B3
Greatstone-on-Sea TN28	206 F7
Leonard's Ave CT11	29 E1
Leonie Ct CT6	22 D4
Leopold Rd	
2 Chatham ME4	10 A3
Ramsgate CT11	52 E8
Leopold St CT11	52 E6
Le Roux Cl CT18	162 F4
Lerryn Gdns CT10	29 F8
Lesley Ave CT1	88 A6
Lesley Chalk Ho 7 ME13	139 C2
Lesley Pl ME16	74 E5
Leslie Ave CT9	28 B8
Leslie Cres TN30	167 B2
Leslie Rd	
Birchington CT7	27 A8
Gillingham ME7	10 D1
Leslie Smith Dr ME13	62 C7
Les Spickett Cl ME13	62 E6
Lested La ME17	98 B3
Lester Rd ME4	10 A3
Letchworth Ave ME4	9 F1
Leviathan Way ME4	10 A8
Lewd La TN27	135 A3
Lewis Ave ME8	11 B2
Lewis Cl ME13	62 A7
Lewis Court Dr ME17	97 C3
Lewis Cres CT9	8 B3
Lewis Ct TN23	155 F7
Lewisham Rd CT17	148 E3
Lewis Rd CT16	162 F3
LEWSON STREET	60 E7
Lewson Street Rd ME9	60 E8
Leybourne Cl ME5	32 A2
Leybourne Dr CT9	28 B8
Leybourn Rd CT10	30 B2
Leyburne Rd CT16	166 D8
Leycroft Cl CT12	66 E3
LEYSDOWN-ON-SEA	6 H2
Leysdown Rd	
Eastchurch ME12	5 E3
Leysdown-on-Sea ME12	6 C1
Leysdown View 1 CT5	43 C6
Leys The CT12	28 D1
Leyton Ave ME7	10 E1
Library Rd CT12	66 D4
Libya Terr 9 ME14	75 A7
Lichfield Ave CT1	88 B6
Lichfield Cl ME8	11 D2
Lichfield Ho 12 ME15	97 E7
LIDSING	32 F1
Lidsing Rd ME14	54 E6
Liege Cl ME10	14 F1
Lighthouse Rd CT15	151 A5
Lilac Cl TN23	138 E3
Lilac Rd ME12	4 B5
Lilk Hill ME14	76 C3
Lillian Rd CT11	52 F8
LILYVALE	158 F4
Lilyvale Cotts TN23	158 F4
Lilyvale Rd TN25	158 F4
Lime Cl	
Ashford TN23	138 F3
Chartham CT4	86 E1
Lime Ct ME8	33 C3
Lime Gr	
Halfway Houses ME12	3 D5
Sittingbourne ME10	37 D5
Limehouse Ct ME10	37 D5
Lime Kiln Rd CT1	87 F6
Limekiln Bglit CT17	166 D6
Limekiln St CT17	166 D5
Lime Kiln Wharf ME11	3 A5
Limepits Cross ME9	35 F3
Limes Cl TN30	179 C8
Limes Pl 18 ME13	62 D7
Limes The	
Dover CT16	149 C1
Folkestone CT19	177 F6
Limes The	
Ashford TN23	156 A5
Lenham ME17	101 D5
Old Romney TN29	201 A7
Limetree Cl ME5	32 B8
Limetree Terr ME17	101 E6
Lime Villas CT14	144 F5
Linces The CT5	149 B4
Lincoln Ave CT1	88 B7
Lincoln Cl CT5	21 D3
Lincoln Gdns CT7	26 F7
Lincoln Rd ME15	97 D8
Lincol n Rd ME7	10 D7
Lindale Flats CT14	117 C2
Linden Ave	
Broadstairs CT10	30 B5
Herne Bay CT6	22 E4
Whitstable CT5	20 F1
Linden Chase CT2	66 E1
Linden Cl	
Sittingbourne ME10	36 D3
Westgate on Sea CT8	27 E7
Linden Cres CT19	178 D6
Linden Dr	
Elham CT4	144 F5
West Minst ME12	3 A7
Linden Gr 2 CT17	66 E1
Linden Grove Prim Sch	
TN23	155 F6
Linden Ho 5 ME5	31 F4
Linden Rd	
Ashford TN24	139 D1
Chatham CT4	86 E1
Coxheath ME17	96 C4
Gillingham ME7	10 E5
Westgate on Sea CT8	27 F8
Lindens CT21	176 D2
Lindens The TN30	167 B1
Lindenthorpe Rd CT10	30 A6
Lindfield Cotts ME13	62 A6
Lindisfarne Gdns ME16	74 B2
Lindridge Cl CT6	46 A8
Lineacre Cl ME8	33 D6
Linen Ct CT14	87 F8
Lines Terr ME4	10 A4
Linington Rd CT7	27 A6
Link Hill La TN27	118 D3
Link La CT1	88 A8
Link Rd	
Broadstairs CT10	29 F7
Tyler Hill CT2	66 E6
Links Cl CT6	23 A3
Links Ct CT14	95 C1
Linksfield Cl CT8	27 D7
Linksfield Rd CT8	27 D7
Linksway CT19	178 B8
Links Rd CT14	117 C8
Links The ME5	32 B8
Linksway CT19	178 B8
Links Way TN28	202 D6
Linkway ME9	14 D4
Link The CT23	155 C7
Linley Rd CT10	29 E7
Linnet Ave CT5	43 B6
LINTON	96 F1
Linton Gore ME17	96 D3
Linton Park Sch ME17	97 A2
Linton Rd ME15	96 F4
Lionard Ho 3 CT2	66 E1
Lion Ct CT14	117 C5
Lion Field ME13	62 B7
Lion's Rd TN28	202 A6
Lion Yd	
Faversham ME13	62 A6
8 Sittingbourne ME10	36 F4
Liphook Way ME16	74 C8
Lisa Ct CT5	21 A2
Lismore Cl ME15	97 A7
Lismore Rd	
Herne Bay CT6	23 D5
Whitstable CT5	44 B8
Liss Rd CT13	93 A1
Lister Cl	
Deal CT14	117 C5
Dover CT17	149 B1
Lister Ho CT19	29 A8
Lister Rd CT9	29 A8
Lister Way CT20	177 F3
Listmas Rd ME4	10 B3
List Mdws CT3	89 F8
List The CT3	69 C2
Listways Cotts CT3	113 B6
Little Acorns Sch ME10	167 A5
Little Acres TN25	171 E7
Little Ave CT14	116 F3
Little Betteshanger	115 C5
LITTLEBOURNE	89 B8
Littlebourne Ave ME8	11 B4
Littlebourne CE Prim Sch	
CT3	89 F8
Littlebourne Rd	
Canterbury CT1, CT3	88 E8
Maidstone ME14	75 C6
Littlebrook CT13	139 A3
Little Brook Rd CT13	139 A3
Little Buckland Ave ME16	74 D6
Little Charlton St CT6	22 F5
LITTLE CHART	120 A1
LITTLE CHART	
FORSTAL	137 C8
Little Chequers TN25	123 E2
Little Copse CT4	86 E1
Little Ct ME16	74 D2
Littlefield Rd ME8	12 B2
Little Glovers ME10	36 F3
Little Hempen TN23	155 D8
Little Hill TN30	167 B2
LITTLE HOUSES	118 D2
Little John Ave ME5	31 F2
Little Kit's Coty Ho*	
ME20	53 C5
Little Knoll TN23	155 F8
Little Mdw CT7	65 E1
Littlemead CT19	178 A7
LITTLE MONGEHAM	116 A2
Little Orch ME17	96 D3
Little Paddocks CT7	44 D7
Little Robhurst TN26	167 D8
Littlestone Ct TN28	202 E5
Littlestone Ho TN28	202 E5
LITTLESTONE-ON-SEA	202 F5
Littlestone Rd TN28	202 D6
Little Stone Stile Cotts	
ME13	84 F4
Little Walton CT19	178 G8
Little Walton CT13	93 C3
Little York Mdws ME7	11 C4
Liverpool Lawn 18 CT11	52 E6
Liverpool Rd CT14	117 D2
LIVERTON STREET	100 F1
Livingstone Bldgs ME7	10 D5
Livingstone Circ ME7	10 D5
Livingstone Rd TN29	187 B4
Livingstone Rd	
Broadstairs CT10	29 E6
Gillingham ME7	10 E5
Livingstone Wlk 6 ME15	97 F5
Lloyd Ct CT14	117 D7
Lloyd Dr ME10	15 A1
Lloyd Rd CT10	30 A5
Lloyds Gn TN30	188 D4
Loading Bay App CT13	73 A8
Loaland Bsns Ctr ME2	9 D8
Lobelia Cl ME7	10 E6
Locarno Ave ME8	11 A2
Lockham Farm Ave ME17	97 D5
Lockholt Cl TN23	138 E3
Lockington Gr ME1	9 C5
Lock La ME14	53 D1
Lockmeadow Entertainment	
Ctr ME16	74 F3
Locksley Cl ME5	31 E2
Lock St ME7	10 C5
Lockwood Rd ME5	31 E2
Loddington La ME17	97 A1
Loder Cl ME17	101 B5
Lodge Field Rd CT5	21 D1
LODGE LEES	128 F4
Lodge Rd ME14	75 D5
Lodge Wood Dr TN25	138 E5
Lomas Rd ME10, ME9	37 D4
Lombard St ME7	7 I3
Lombardy Cl ME7	33 A6
Lombardy Dr ME14	75 C5
LONDON BEACH	167 B5
Londonderry Ho 15 ME15	97 E7
London Pl 24 CT20	178 E5
London Rd	
Canterbury CT2	66 D1
Deal CT14	117 B5
Dover CT16, CT17	149 B1
Dunkirk ME13	64 E2
Faversham ME13	63 A6
Gillingham ME8	11 C1
Hartlip ME8, ME9	34 D7
Hythe ME9	175 F3
Maidstone ME14	74 C6
Newington ME9	35 A6
Ramsgate CT11	52 B6
Rochester ME2	9 A7
Sittingbourne ME10	36 C4
Temple Ewell CT15, CT16	148 B6
Teynham ME9	38 C1
London Road Ret Pk	
ME16	74 E5
London Road (River) CT16,	
CT17	148 F4
London Road Temple Ewell	
CT16	148 D5
London Road Trad Est	
ME10	36 D4
London St CT20	178 E5
Lone Barn Rd ME17	102 B8
Lonefield TN26	155 B1
Longacre CT5	21 D1
Long Acre CT7	27 E5
Longacre Rd TN23	155 D7
Longage Hill CT18, CT4	144 A1
Long Barrow The TN24	156 E6
Long Beech TN23	138 E3
Longbridge TN24	140 B1
Longbridge Terr TN21	175 F1
Long Catlis Rd ME8	33 D4
Longdown Ho ME5	31 F6
Long Dr CT13	93 C2
Longfellow Rd ME7	10 C3
Longfield TN30	179 A6
Longfield Cl CT5	21 D2
Longfield Ct CT5	21 D2
Longfield Pl ME15	97 C8
Longfields Dr ME14	76 A5
Longford Cl ME8	34 A8
Longford Ct ME8	34 A8
Longford Terr 10 CT20	178 D4
Longford Way 11 CT20	178 D4
Longham Copse ME15	75 F1
Long Hill CT4	85 C1
Longhill Ave ME5	10 B3
Longhurst Dr ME5	31 F2
Long La CT15	130 D7
Long Length TN23	155 D4
Longley Rd	
Gillingham ME8	11 F1
Rochester ME1	9 C4
Long Market 2 CT1	88 A8
Long Mdw CT21	49 D6
Longmead Cl CT6	22 C3
Long Meadow Way CT2	67 A4
Longmete Rd CT3	70 C5
Longmore Dr ME12	5 C1
Longparish CT21	97 F6
Longport CT1	88 A8
Long Reach CT5	43 C6
Longridge ME10	37 B2
Long Rock CT5	21 D3
Long Row TN25	157 D2
Long's Acre TN25	123 E1
Longsfield TN25	173 A6
Long Shaw Cl ME17	97 D4
Longshaw Rd ME15	97 F5
Longtail Rise CT6	22 E2
Longtye Dr CT5	44 C7
Long Wlk TN23	138 E4
Longwood ME5	32 B1
Lonsdale Ave CT9	8 C3
Lonsdale Cl CT16	149 D1
Lonsdale Dr	
Gillingham ME8	33 E7
Herne Bay CT6	22 B5
Sittingbourne ME10	36 C5
Lookers La CT21	176 B3
Loop Court Mews 9 CT13	72 F1
Loop St CT13	72 F1
LOOSE	96 F4
Loose Down Rd ME15	104 F7
LOOSE HILL	96 F5
Loose Inf & Jun Schs	
ME15	97 A6
Loose Rd ME15	97 A6
Lord Cornwallis CT19	178 C8
Lord Romney's Hill ME14	75 F3
Lords Cl ME9	37 E2
Lords Cl ME15	83 C4
LORDS WOOD	32 C1
Lords Wood Cl ME5	32 B2
Lordswood Ind Est ME5	54 C8
Lordswood Inf & Jun Sch	
ME5	32 B3
Lords Wood La ME5	32 B3
Lordswood L Ctr ME5	32 C3
Lord Warden Ave CT14	117 D2
Lord Warden Ho CT17	166 D5
Lord Warden Sq CT17	166 D5
Lorenden Park* ME13	61 F3
Lorenden Prep Sch ME13	61 E3
Lorien Flats TN24	139 D7
Lorimar Ct ME10	36 C7
Lorina Rd CT12	52 C8
Lorne Cotts CT14	117 C7
Lorne Rd	
Dover CT16, CT17	149 B2
Ramsgate CT11	52 C6
Lorraine Cl 1 CT19	178 E6
Loudon Ct TN23	138 E3
Loudon Path TN23	138 E3
Loudon Way TN23	138 E3
Loughborough CT 2 CT11	52 E7
Louisville Ave ME7	10 D4
Lourdes Cl TN25	159 D1
Love La	
Adisham CT3	90 F2
12 Canterbury CT1	88 A8
Faversham ME13	62 F6
Margate CT9	
Minster (Sheppey) ME12	4 D7
Rochester ME1	9 C5
Lovelace Cl ME8	33 D4
Lovelace Ct TN26	153 C5
Lovell Rd	
Minster (Sheppey) ME12	4 A5
Rough Common CT2	66 B3
Love Street CT6	22 C2
Lower Bannister Cotts	
ME9	36 B2
Lower Blackhouse Hill	
CT21	176 D3
Lower Bloors La ME8	11 E3
Lower Boxley Rd 10 ME14	75 A5
Lower Bridge St CT1	88 A8
Lower Buttermere Cl ME7	11 A5
Lower Chantry La CT1	88 A8
Lower Denmark Rd	
TN23	156 C8
Lower Ensden Rd CT4	85 D4
LOWER EYTHORNE	131 B8
Lower Fant Rd ME16	74 D2
Lower Featherby Rd ME7	11 B5
LOWER GOLDSTONE	71 F7
Lower Gore La CT13	93 B3
LOWER HALSTOW	13 C3
Lower Halstow Prim Sch	
ME9	13 B2
LOWER HARDRES	110 A6
LOWER HARTLIP	34 E4
Lower Hartlip Rd ME9	34 E5
LOWER HEPPINGTON	109 F8
LOWER HERNE	22 F1
Lower Herne Rd CT6	45 E8
LOWER ISLAND	20 C1
Lower Lees Rd CT4	85 D2
Lower Mill La CT14	117 C5
LOWER NEWLANDS	39 A2
Lower Northdown Ave CT9	8 B2
Lower Norton La ME9	39 A1
Lower Queens Rd TN24	139 C3
LOWER RAINHAM	11 F3
Lower Rainham Rd	
Gillingham, Lower Rainham	
ME8	12 A3
Gillingham ME7	11 D5
Lower Rd	
Eastchurch ME12	5 B3
East Farleigh ME15	96 B7
Faversham ME13	61 C8
Maidstone ME15	75 B3
Minster (Sheppey) ME12	3 E6
River CT17	148 E2
Staple CT3	92 B6
Stone in Oxney TN30	189 D5
Temple Ewell CT16	148 D5
Teynham, Lower Newlands ME9,	
ME13	38 E2

Lower Rd continued
Teynham ME9. . . . . .38 B3
Woodchurch TN26. . . . . .169 B3
Lower Road E CT16. . . . . .166 H8
Lower Road W CT16. . . . . .166 G8
Lower Rowling Cotts CT3 .92 B2
Lower Sandgate Rd
CT20. .178 B3
Lower Santon TN29. . . . . .186 E2
Lower Santon La CT3 . . .70 D7
Lower St
Eastry CT13. . . . . .93 B1
Leeds ME17. . . . . .99 A7
Tilmanstone CT14. . . . . .115 A2
Lower Stone St ME15. . . . .75 A3
Lower Tovil CT15. . . . . .74 E2
LOWER TWYDALL. 11 C5
Lower Twydall La ME7,
ME8. . . . . .11 C4
Lower Vicarage Rd
TN24. .139 D2
Lower Wall Rd
Burmarsh CT21. . . . . .186 D8
Dymchurch CT21. . . . . .187 A7
LOWER WALMER. 117 C4
Lower Warren Rd ME20 . .53 E4
Lower Woodlands Rd
ME7. . . . . .11 A6
Lowfield Rd ME12. . . . . .3 E6
Lowslip Hill CT15. . . . . . . .165 A5
Lowther Rd CT17. . . . . .166 B8
Loxwood Cl CT16. . . . . .149 B7
Lubbock Cl CT15. . . . . .97 E5
Lubbock Wlk ME8. . . . . .33 D5
Lucerne Ct CT5. . . . . .42 F6
Lucerne Dr CT5. . . . . .42 F6
Lucerne La CT15. . . . . .133 C2
Lucerne St ME14. . . . . .75 A5
Lucilla Ave TN23. . . . . .155 F4
Luckhurst Gdns CT9 . . . . . . .8 E3
Luckhurst Rd
Ashford TN24. . . . . .157 A7
Crabble CT17. . . . . .148 E3
Luckley Ho TN25. . . . . .123 E2
Lucknow CT15. . . . . .149 F3
Lucy Ave CT19. . . . . .178 B7
Lucy's Hill CT21. . . . . .176 B2
Luddenham Cl
Ashford TN23. . . . . .155 F6
Maidstone ME14 . . . . .75 C6
Luddenham Prim Sch
ME13. . . . . .59 E5
Ludgate Rd ME9. . . . . .59 F5
Lukes CT17. . . . . .149 B1
Lukin Ho CT21. . . . . .175 F1
Lullingstone Cl TN23 . . . . .33 B3
Lullingstone Cl CT1. . . . . . .87 F8
Lullingstone Rd ME16. . . . .74 C7
Lumsden Terr ME4 . . . . .9 E4
Lushington Rd ME14. . . . . . .74 E7
LUTON. 10 B2
Luton Ave CT10. . . . . .29 D3
Luton Ct CT10. . . . . .29 D3
Luton High St ME5. . . . . .10 C2
Luton Inf Sch ME5. . . . . .10 C2
Luton Jun Sch ME4 . . . . .10 C2
Luton Rd
Chatham ME4, ME5. . . . . .10 B2
Faversham ME13. . . . . .62 E7
Lyall Way ME8 . . . . .33 E4
Lychfield Dr ME2. . . . . .9 A8
Lydbrook Cl ME10. . . . . .36 D4
LYDD. 205 D6
LYDD CAMP. 205 B5
LYDDEN
Broadstairs. 28 E4
Dover. .147 E8
Lydden Hill CT15. . . . . .130 C1
Lydden Hill Race Circuit
CT4. . . . . .129 F3
Lydden Prim Sch CT15 .147 F8
Lydden Temple Ewell
National Nature Reserve*
CT15. .148 B1
Lydd (London Ashford)
Airport* TN29. . . . . .206 A7
LYDD-ON-SEA. 209 D7
Lydd Prim Sch TN29 . . . .205 C6
Lydd Rd
Chatham ME5. . . . . .32 B5
New Romney TN28, TN29. . .201 F6
Lydd Town Crossing
TN29. .205 D8
Lydd Town Mus* TN29 .205 C6
Lydia Rd CT14. . . . . .117 A2
Lydos Cl TN29. . . . . .206 E5
Lyeat Ct CT2. . . . . .66 C4
Lyell Cl CT21. . . . . .176 A1
Lyell Ct CT7. . . . . .26 F6
Lyell Rd CT7. . . . . .26 F6
Lyle Cl ME2. . . . . .9 B8
Lyle Ct ME16. . . . . .74 C5
LYMBRIDGE GREEN. . . .143 B4
LYMINGE. 161 B6
Lyminge CE Prim Sch
CT18. .161 C2
Lyminge Cl ME8. . . . . .11 C2
Lyminge Way CT9. . . . . .8 C1
Lymington Ct ME15. . . . . . . .97 F4
Lymington Rd CT8. . . . . .27 E7
LYMPNE. 175 A3
Lympne Castle* CT21. . . .174 F2
Lympne CE Prim Sch
CT21. .175 A3
Lympne Ind Est CT21. . . .174 E3
Lynacre CT2. . . . . .66 C1
Lyn Ct CT20. . . . . .178 A5

Lyndhurst Ave
Gillingham ME8. . . . . .33 C7
Margate CT9. . . . . .8 B2
Lyndhurst Cl CT2. . . . . .66 E3
Lyndhurst Gr ME10. . . . . . . .36 E2
Lyndhurst Rd
Broadstairs CT10. . . . . .30 A6
Crabble CT17. . . . . .148 E2
Dymchurch TN29 . . . . .195 C8
Maidstone ME15 . . . . .97 C8
Ramsgate CT11. . . . . .52 F7
Lyndon Way CT18. . . . . . . .161 C7
Lyngate Ct CT9. . . . . .8 D2
Lynley Cl ME15. . . . . .97 D6
Lynmouth Dr ME12. . . . . .4 C7
LYNSORE BOTTOM. 127 D8
Lynstead Ho ME16. . . . . .74 A1
LYNSTED. 60 A6
Lynsted Cl TN23. . . . . .155 F6
Lynsted La ME9. . . . . .60 A6
Lynsted & Norton Prim Sch
ME9. . . . . .60 A7

M

Mabledon Ave TN24. . . . . .139 D3
Mabledon Ho ME8. . . . . . . .202 B6
McAlpine Cres ME15. . . . . .96 F3
McCarthy Ave CT3. . . . . .67 F7
McClean Wlk ME12. . . . . . . .17 C8
McCudden Row ME7. . . . . .10 A6
MacDonald Par CT5. . . . . . .43 A6
MacDonald Rd
Dover CT17. . . . . .149 A1
Gillingham ME7. . . . . .10 D6
Mace Ind Est TN24. . . . . . .139 C2
Mace Terr TN26 . . . . .155 A1
Mackenders Cl ME20. . . . . .53 A6
Mackenders Gn ME20. . . . . .53 A6
Mackenders La ME20. . . . . .53 A6
McKenzie Ct ME4 . . . . .74 F5
Mackenzie Dr CT20. . . . . . .177 E5
Mackenzie Rd ME5. . . . . . . .32 A3
Mackeson Ct CT21. . . . . . . .176 B2
McKinlay Ct CT7. . . . . .26 D8
MACKLANDS. 12 A2
Macklands Ho ME8. . . . . . . .12 A2
Macklands Way ME8. . . . . .12 A2
Madden Ave ME5. . . . . .31 E5
Madeira Ct CT14. . . . . .117 A2
Madeira Rd CT20. . . . . .178 B3
Madeira Wlk CT11. . . . . .52 E6
Madginford Cl ME15. . . . . . .76 A2
Madginford Park Inf Sch
ME15. . . . . .76 A2
Madginford Park Jun Sch
ME15. . . . . .76 A2
Madginford Rd ME15. . . . . . .76 A2
Madhuran Ct ME2. . . . . .9 A7
Madras Ho 2 ME14. . . . . . .97 E5
Mafeking Rd ME5. . . . . .31 F3
Magazine Rd TN24 . . . . . . .139 B3
Magdala Rd
Broadstairs CT10. . . . . .29 E6
Dover CT17. . . . . .149 B1
Magdalen Cl ME7. . . . . .33 A4
Magdalen Rd
Broadstairs CT10. . . . . .30 A6
Canterbury CT1. . . . . .88 B7
Magness Rd CT14. . . . . .117 A2
Magnolia Ave
Gillingham ME7. . . . . .10 E6
Margate CT9. . . . . .8 D2
Magnolia Dr CT4. . . . . .86 E1
Magnolia Ho 3 ME16. . . . . .74 A3
Magnolia Rise CT5. . . . . . . .23 D2
Magpie Hall Rd
Chatham ME4. . . . . .10 A2
Stubb's Cross TN26. . . . . .155 E2
Magpie La
Rhodes Minnis CT4. . . . . .144 B3
Yelsted ME9, ME14. . . . . .33 F1
Magpie Lodge 4 ME14. . .149 B2
Magwitch Cl ME1. . . . . .9 A6
Maida Rd ME4. . . . . .10 B2
Maiden La CT1. . . . . .87 D6
MAIDSTONE. 75 C3
Maidstone Barracks Sta
ME16. . . . . .74 E5
Maidstone East Sta ME14 .74 F5
Maidstone Gram Sch
ME15. . . . . .75 B2
Maidstone Gram Sch for
Girls ME16. . . . . .74 E5
Maidstone Hospl ME15. . . . .96 A5
Maidstone L Ctr ME15. . . . .75 C2
Maidstone Mus & Gallery*
1 ME14. . . . . .75 C3
Maidstone Rd
Bredhurst ME7, ME8 . . . . .33 B2

Maidstone Rd continued
Charing TN25, TN26, TN27 .120 D6
Chatham ME4. . . . . .9 F2
Chatham, Walderslade ME5. .31 D4
Danaway ME9 . . . . .35 A8
Five Wents ME17. . . . . .99 E2
Gillingham ME8 . . . . .33 C6
Lenham ME17. . . . . .101 D5
Potters Corner TN25,
TN26. .138 D7
Rochester ME1. . . . . .9 C3
Maidstone West Sta ME16 .74 F3
Mailyns The ME8. . . . . .33 D7
Maine Cl CT16. . . . . .149 B3
Main Rd
Queenborough ME11, ME12 . .3 B5
Sellindge TN25. . . . . .159 C1
Sheerness ME12. . . . . .1 B3
Main St
Iden TN31. . . . . .197 B4
Peasmarsh TN31. . . . . .196 D8
Maison Des Fleurs ME16 .74 C2
Maison Dieu*
17 Dover CT17. . . . . .166 D8
Faversham ME13. . . . . .62 A6
Maison Dieu Pl 4 CT16 .166 D8
Maison Dieu Rd CT16 . . .166 D8
Maitland Ct ME13. . . . . .40 B1
Majestic Par CT20. . . . . . . .178 C4
Major Cl CT5. . . . . .43 B6
Makenade Ave ME13. . . . . . .62 E6
Mallow The 1 ME5. . . . . . . .31 F4
Mall The CT2. . . . . .62 C6
Malmains Rd CT17. . . . . . . .166 A6
Malmedy Ct CT14. . . . . .117 A1
Malta Ave ME5. . . . . .32 A7
Malta Ho 17 CT1. . . . . .67 B2
Malta Terr ME7. . . . . .75 A7
Malthouse Cl ME7. . . . . .101 D5
Malthouse Cotts
Boughton Lees TN25. . . . . . . .122 F4
New Romney TN28. . . . . .202 A6
Malthouse Hill
10 Hythe CT21. . . . . .176 B2
Maidstone ME15. . . . . .96 F4
Malthouse La
Hamstreet TN26. . . . . .170 D1
Peasmarsh TN31. . . . . .196 D2
Malt House La TN30. . . . . . .179 A7
Malthouse Rd CT2. . . . . .66 F2
Malthouses The
Birchington CT7. . . . . .26 F7
Brabourne TN25. . . . . .159 B8
Maltings Bsns Pk The
TN31. . . . . .196 C2
Maltings Hall The CT1. . . .52 D7
Maltings The
7 Canterbury, St Dunstan's
CT2. . . . . .66 E1
10 Canterbury, St Martin's
CT1. . . . . .88 A8
Deal CT14. . . . . .134 B8
Faversham ME13. . . . . .62 D8
Littlebourne CT3. . . . . .89 F7
Loose ME17. . . . . .97 B4
Peasmarsh TN31. . . . . .196 D8
MALTMAN'S HILL. 135 F3
Malt Mews ME9. . . . . .9 C5
Malus Cl ME5. . . . . .32 B1
Malvern Mdw CT16. . . . . . . .148 E5
Malvern Pk CT6. . . . . .23 D4
Malvern Rd
Ashford TN24. . . . . .139 B4
Dover CT17. . . . . .166 C7
Gillingham ME7. . . . . .10 E3
Temple Ewell CT16. . . . . .148 E5
Mamignot Cl ME14. . . . . .76 A5
Manchester Cl ME5. . . . . . . .32 C6
Manciple Cl CT2. . . . . .87 C8
Mandarin La CT6. . . . . .22 B2
Mandeville Cl 1 ME14. . . . .75 A5
Mandeville Rd CT2. . . . . .66 E2
Mangers La CT16. . . . . .149 A2
Mangers Pl CT16. . . . . .149 A3
Mangravet Ave ME15. . . . . .97 C7
Manktelow Ct CT10. . . . . . . .29 F2
Manley Cl CT15. . . . . .149 A7
Manley Ho CT16. . . . . .149 A7
Mannering Cl CT17. . . . . . . .148 F3
Mannock Ho 6 CT5. . . . . . . .67 B1
Manns Hill CT14. . . . . .127 A6
Manor Ave CT14. . . . . .117 B4
Manor Cl
Canterbury CT1. . . . . .87 C5
Deal CT14. . . . . .117 A4
Herne Bay CT6. . . . . .23 F6
Maidstone ME14. . . . . .76 B3

Manor Cl continued
Rushenden ME11. . . . . .3 A3
Manor Cotts
Hernhill ME13. . . . . .64 B6
Langley ME17. . . . . .98 C5
Manor Ct
Canterbury CT1. . . . . .87 F7
Gillingham ME7. . . . . .11 C5
Maidstone ME14. . . . . .76 B3
Manor Dr CT7. . . . . .26 F6
Manor Farm Cl CT21. . . . .175 A4
Manorfield
Ashford TN23. . . . . .155 E8
Elham CT4. . . . . .144 F4
Manor Gdns
Chatham ME5. . . . . .31 F4
Whitfield CT16. . . . . .149 A8
Manor Gr ME10. . . . . .36 D3
Manor Ho 14 ME7. . . . . .10 A6
Manor Ho The
Canterbury CT2. . . . . .66 F2
5 Folkestone CT20. . . . . .178 B3
Margate CT9. . . . . .48 D6
Manor House Dr
Ashford TN23. . . . . .156 D3
Maidstone ME16. . . . . .74 D3
Manor La ME1. . . . . .9 A2
Manor Lea Rd CT7. . . . . .25 F1
Manor Leaze TN25. . . . . . . .158 F5
Manor Mews
Chatham ME4. . . . . .9 F4
Ringwould CT14. . . . . .133 F5
Manor Pound La CT21. . . .158 F7
Manor Rd
3 Broadstairs CT10. . . . . .30 A4
Chatham ME4. . . . . .9 F4
Deal CT14. . . . . .117 A4
Dover CT17. . . . . .166 A6
Folkestone CT20. . . . . .178 C4
Lydd TN29. . . . . .205 C6
Milstead ME9. . . . . .58 F2
St Nicholas at Wade CT7. . . .25 F1
Whitstable CT5. . . . . .21 A2
Manor Rise
Dover CT17. . . . . .166 A6
Maidstone ME14. . . . . .76 B3
Manor St ME7. . . . . .10 A6
Manor Way
Ashford TN23. . . . . .138 F4
Leysdown-on-Sea ME12. . . . . . .6 H2
Warden ME12. . . . . .6 D6
Manse Field TN25. . . . . .158 E5
Mansel Dr ME1. . . . . .9 A2
Mansell La CT15. . . . . .146 B4
Mansfield Dr ME9. . . . . .14 D3
Mansfield Wlk ME16. . . . . . .74 E2
Mansion Gdns CT16. . . . . .149 A4
Mansion Row ME7. . . . . .10 A6
Mansion St CT9. . . . . .7 I3
Mansions The CT10. . . . . . . .29 E4
MANSTON. 28 E1
Manston Court Cotts
CT12. . . . . .28 C2
Manston Court Rd CT12,
CT9. . . . . .28 D3
Manston Pk CT12. . . . . .27 D7
Manston Rd
Acol CT13. . . . . .27 D4
Margate CT12, CT9. . . . . .28 C4
Ramsgate CT11, CT12, CT9 . .52 A8
Mansum Ct CT7. . . . . .25 F2
Manwood Almshouse CT2 .66 F3
Manwood Cl ME16. . . . . .74 C5
Manwood Rd CT13. . . . . .94 B8
Maple Ave
Gillingham ME7. . . . . .10 E6
Maidstone ME14. . . . . .74 C6
Maple Cl
Ashford TN23. . . . . .138 E3
Broadstairs CT10. . . . . .8 E1
Rough Common CT2. . . . . .66 B3
Maple Ct
Hersden CT3. . . . . .68 C8
Rodmersham ME9. . . . . .59 A7
Maple Dr
Hawkinge CT18. . . . . .163 C5
St Mary's Bay TN29. . . . . .194 F4
Maple Gdns CT18. . . . . .163 C5
Maple Gdns CT5. . . . . .68 E8
Mapleden Noakes Sch
ME16. . . . . .74 E6
Maple St ME12. . . . . .1 D1
Maples The
Broadstairs CT10. . . . . .29 D4
Minster (Sheppey) ME12. . . . . .4 B6
Maplins Cl 6 ME8. . . . . .11 F1
Mara Ct ME4. . . . . .9 E1
Marathon Paddock ME7 . .10 D4
Marble Cl ME7. . . . . .10 F6
Marc Brunel Way ME4 . . . .10 A7
Marconi Way ME1. . . . . .31 D7
Marcroft Ct CT10. . . . . .30 B7
Mardale Pl ME8. . . . . .12 A1
Marden Ave CT12. . . . . .52 B8
Mardol Rd TN24. . . . . .139 C5
Maresfield Cl CT16. . . . . . . .149 B2
Margaret Ct CT6. . . . . .22 F4
Margaret St 10 CT20. . . . . .178 E5
MARGATE. 7 H2
Margate Cl ME7. . . . . .10 E6
Margate Hill CT7. . . . . .27 A6
Margate Language Ctr 19
CT9. . . . . .7 J2

Margate Local History Mus*
CT9. . . . . .7 I3
Margate Rd
Herne Bay, Broomfield
CT6. . . . . .23 D2
Herne Bay CT6. . . . . .23 C3
Ramsgate CT10, CT12, CT11 .29 B3
Margate Sta CT9. . . . . .7 H2
Marian Ave ME12. . . . . .4 A7
Marigold Dr ME10. . . . . .36 F3
Marigold Way ME16. . . . . . . .74 A3
Marilyn Cres CT7. . . . . .27 B7
Marina Ct
Deal CT14. . . . . .117 D8
Hythe CT21. . . . . .176 C1
Marina Dr ME12. . . . . .4 A7
Marina Espl CT11. . . . . .52 F7
Marina Rd CT11. . . . . .52 F7
Marina The CT14. . . . . .117 D8
Marina The TN29. . . . . .186 F3
Marine Cres
7 Folkestone CT20. . . . . .178 D4
Whitstable CT5. . . . . .21 B3
Marine Ct
Dover 15 CT16. . . . . .166 E7
Whitstable CT5. . . . . .20 F3
Marine Dr
Broadstairs CT10. . . . . .8 G3
Margate CT9. . . . . .7 I2
Marine Gap CT5. . . . . .20 C1
Marine Gdns CT9. . . . . .7 I2
Marine Ho CT5. . . . . .20 F3
Marine Hts CT8. . . . . .7 D1
Marine Par
Dover CT16. . . . . .166 E7
Folkestone CT20. . . . . .178 E4
Hythe CT21. . . . . .176 C1
Littlestone-on-Sea TN28 . . .202 E5
Sheerness ME12. . . . . .1 F2
Whitstable CT5. . . . . .21 A3
Marine Parade Mews 5
CT20. . . . . .178 E4
Marine Point CT20. . . . . . . .178 A3
Marine Terr CT14. . . . . .117 D4
Mariners Ct 2 CT5. . . . . .43 D8
Mariners Lea CT10. . . . . .29 D4
Mariners Lee CT5. . . . . .20 E3
Mariners The ME7. . . . . .9 B4
Mariners Way ME7. . . . . .10 F7
Marine Terr
Folkestone CT20. . . . . .178 E4
Margate CT9. . . . . .7 H2
Whitstable CT5. . . . . .20 C1
MARINE TOWN. 1 F2
Marine Walk St CT1. . . . . .176 C2
Marion Cl ME5. . . . . .32 A2
Marion Cres ME15. . . . . .97 B8
Maritime Ave CT6. . . . . .23 C4
Maritime Cl ME2. . . . . .9 D8
Maritime Est ME2. . . . . .9 D8
Maritime Pl CT14. . . . . .117 D7
Maritime Way ME4. . . . . .10 A7
Marjan Cl CT17. . . . . .149 A1
Marjoram Dr ME9. . . . . .36 F2
Mark Ave CT11. . . . . .52 B5
Market Bldgs 4 ME14 . . . .74 F4
Market Colonnade 3
ME14. . . . . .74 F4
Market Hill CT21. . . . . .176 C2
Market La 12 TN23. . . . . . . .139 B2
Market Pl
Aylesham CT3. . . . . .112 F5
Charing TN27. . . . . .120 C7
1 Faversham ME13. . . . . .62 D7
20 Folkestone CT20. . . . . . . .178 D5
Margate CT9. . . . . .7 I3
Market Sq 12 CT16, CT17. 166 D7
Market St
Deal CT14. . . . . .117 D6
Faversham ME13. . . . . .62 D7
Herne Bay CT6. . . . . .22 F5
2 Maidstone ME14. . . . . .74 F4
Margate CT9. . . . . .7 I3
Sandwich CT13. . . . . .73 A1
Market View CT3. . . . . .112 F5
Market Way CT3. . . . . .67 A2
Markland Rd CT17. . . . . .165 F7
Mark St ME4. . . . . .10 A2
Marlborough Cl
Broadstairs CT10. . . . . .29 E3
Littlestone-on-Sea TN28 . . .202 E6
Marlborough Ct
Folkestone CT20. . . . . .178 B4
Hythe CT21. . . . . .176 D1
Marlborough Ho
4 Gillingham ME8. . . . . .33 F8
Margate CT9. . . . . .8 C3
Marlborough Rd
Deal CT14. . . . . .117 A2
Dover CT17. . . . . .165 F7
Gillingham ME7. . . . . .10 B5
Margate CT9. . . . . .7 I1
6 Ramsgate CT11. . . . . .52 A2
Marlborough Road Ind Est
CT14. . . . . .117 A3
Marlborough St CT5. . . . . . . .43 D5
Marlborough Way TN24 .139 F7
Marler Rd CT19. . . . . .177 E6
MARLEY
Barham. 111 B1
Deal. 116 A8
Marley Ct CT2. . . . . .66 C4
Marley La
Chislet CT3. . . . . .47 A5
Finglesham CT14. . . . . .116 A8

Marley La *continued*
Kingston CT4 . . . . 111 B1
Marley Rd ME17 . . . . 100 F6
Marley Way ME1 . . . . 9 C2
Marlow Cl CT5 . . . . 21 B1
Marlow Copse ME5 . . . . 31 F1
Marlowe Arc 11 CT1 . . . . . . 87 F8
Marlowe Ave CT1 . . . . 87 F8
Marlowe Ct 12 CT1 . . . . 87 F8
Marlowe Rd
Ashford TN23 . . . . 139 B2
Dover CT16 . . . . 149 B3
Margate CT9 . . . . 29 C8
Marlow Ho CT7 . . . . 27 B7
Marlow Mdws CT2 . . . . 67 F5
MARLPIT 97 E2
Marlpit Cotts ME17 . . . . 97 E2
Marmion Way TN23 . . . . . . 155 C8
Marquis Dr ME7 . . . . 33 B3
Marr Cl CT1 . . . . 3 F7
Marrians View 1 ME5 . . . . . 10 C2
Marrose Ave CT12 . . . . 29 B3
Marrowbone Hill ME12 . . . . . 5 B5
Marsh Acad TN28 . . . . 202 B7
Marshall Cres
Broadstairs CT10 . . . . 29 E4
Rushenden ME11 . . . . 2 F3
Marshall Rd ME8 . . . . 33 C8
Marshalls Land TN30 . . . . . 167 A3
Marshall St CT19 . . . . 178 E7
Marsham Cres ME17 . . . . . . 98 B1
Marsham St ME14 . . . . 75 A4
MARSHBOROUGH 93 B7
Marshborough Rd CT13 . . . . 93 B7
Marsh Cres TN28 . . . . 202 B6
Marsh Farm Rd CT12 . . . . . . 50 B4
Marsh La
Deal CT14 . . . . 117 A7
Teynham Street ME9 . . . . . . 39 A4
Marshlands TN29 . . . . 195 B7
Marshlands Cl TN29 . . . . . . 195 B7
Marsh Rd TN26 . . . . 183 F6
Marsh Rise ME10 . . . . 15 A1
MARSHSIDE 24 D1
Marsh St ME2 . . . . 9 B7
Marsh View
Hythe CT21 . . . . 187 C8
Sheerness ME12 . . . . 1 H1
Marshwood Cl CT1 . . . . 67 C3
Marstan Cl ME9 . . . . 12 E2
Marston Cl ME5 . . . . 31 E3
Marston Dr ME14 . . . . 75 C5
Marston Wlk ME5 . . . . 31 E3
Martello Cotts CT21 . . . . . . 187 E8
Martello Dr CT21 . . . . 175 F1
Martello Ind Ctr CT19 . . . . 178 B7
MARTIN 133 B3
Martin Cl
Gillingham ME7 . . . . 33 A3
Sittingbourne ME10 . . . . . . 14 F1
Martindale Cl CT1 . . . . 88 A7
Martin Dale Cres CT1 . . . . . 133 C2
Martindown Rd CT5 . . . . . . 43 C7
Martin Ho TN25 . . . . 123 E2
MARTIN MILL 133 C2
Martin Mill Sta CT15 . . . . . 133 C2
Martin Rd ME2 . . . . 9 B8
Martin's Cl CT12 . . . . 29 C2
Martins Cl TN30 . . . . 179 C8
Martin's The TN26 . . . . 168 A8
Martin's Way CT21 . . . . 187 D8
MARTYR'S FIELD 87 F7
Martyrs' Field Rd CT1 . . . . . 87 F7
Mary Ct ME4 . . . . 10 A2
Mary Green Wlk 5 CT1 . . . . 67 B2
Mary Hougham Almshouses
CT14 . . . . 117 D7
Maryland Ct
Gillingham ME8 . . . . 33 E5
Hythe CT21 . . . . 176 D3
Maryland Gr CT1 . . . . 88 C6
Mary Rd CT14 . . . . 117 A3
Masons Rd CT17 . . . . 149 B1
Masons' Rise CT10 . . . . 30 A5
Matfield Cres ME14 . . . . 75 C5
Matilda Cl ME8 . . . . 33 B8
Matthews Cl CT14 . . . . 117 C6
Matthew's Pl 9 CT16 . . . . . 149 C1
Matthews Rd CT6 . . . . 22 C2
Mattison Pl ME9 . . . . 78 F7
Matts Hill Rd ME9 . . . . 33 E2
Maugham Ct CT5 . . . . 43 D8
Maundene Prim Sch ME5 . . 32 B5
Maunders Cl ME5 . . . . 32 C8
Maunsell Pl TN24 . . . . 156 D7
Maurice Ct CT9 . . . . 8 B3
Maxine Gdns CT10 . . . . 29 F5
Maxted Ct CT6 . . . . 23 C4
MAXTED STREET 143 B6
MAXTON 166 A6
Maxton Cl
Dover CT17 . . . . 166 A6
Maidstone ME14 . . . . 75 F5
Maxton Ct CT17 . . . . 166 A6
Maxton Rd CT17 . . . . 166 A6
Maxwell Dr ME16 . . . . 74 B6
Maxwell Pl CT14 . . . . 117 C4
Maxwell Rd ME7 . . . . 10 A6

Marybrook Ind Est CT1 . . . . 67 D4
Maydowns Rd CT5 . . . . 21 D2
Mayers Rd CT14 . . . . 117 A1
Mayfair 2 ME2 . . . . 9 C8
Mayfair Ave ME15 . . . . 97 A8
Mayfield Ave CT16 . . . . 149 C2
Mayfield Cl
Chatham ME5 . . . . 32 A1
Gillingham ME8 . . . . 11 E2
Mayfield Ct 3 CT1 . . . . 149 B2
Mayfield Gdns CT1 . . . . 149 C2
Mayfield Rd
Herne Bay CT6 . . . . 23 A3
Lyminge CT18 . . . . 161 C6
Whitfield CT16 . . . . 149 A7
Mayflower Ho ME1 . . . . 9 B4
Mayfly Dr CT18 . . . . 163 A4
Mayford Rd ME5 . . . . 32 D2
Mayforth Gdns CT1 . . . . 52 B6
Mayhew Cl TN23 . . . . 156 A8
Maylam Gdns ME10 . . . . . . 36 B4
May Lodge CT14 . . . . 117 D5
Maymills Cotts CT13 . . . . . . 93 B2
Maynard Ave CT9 . . . . 28 B8
Maynard Pl ME5 . . . . 10 D2
Maynard Rd CT1 . . . . 87 E7
Maypits TN23 . . . . 155 F8
MAYPOLE 46 F6
Maypole Cl CT18 . . . . 163 B6
Maypole La CT3 . . . . 46 E6
Maypole Rd CT3 . . . . 46 E6
May Rd
Gillingham ME7 . . . . 10 C4
Rochester ME1 . . . . 9 C3
Mays Rd 3 CT11 . . . . 52 C6
May St CT3 . . . . 23 F4
Maystreet Cross CT6 . . . . . . 23 F3
May Terr ME7 . . . . 10 A7
Mayton La CT2 . . . . 45 C1
Maytree Cotts CT14 . . . . . . 133 D8
Mayville Rd CT10 . . . . 29 E6
Maywood Ave ME5 . . . . 31 E4
Meade The CT18 . . . . 162 F4
Mead Gn ME5 . . . . 32 C3
Meadowbank Rd ME4 . . . . . 10 A4
Meadowbrook CT20 . . . . . . 177 E4
Meadowbrook Cl TN24 . . . . 139 D6
Meadow Brook Ct CT20 . . . 177 E4
Meadowbrook Rd TN24 . . . 139 D6
Meadow Cl
Bridge CT4 . . . . 89 A1
Chatham ME5 . . . . 31 F5
Chilham CT4 . . . . 107 C2
Hawkinge CT18 . . . . 163 B4
Herne Bay CT6 . . . . 23 C4
Iwade ME9 . . . . 14 D4
Meadow Cotts
East Studdal CT15 . . . . 132 D8
Goodnestone CT3 . . . . 92 A2
Meadow Ct
Margate CT9 . . . . 29 B8
Westenhanger CT21 . . . . . . 175 B6
Meadowdown ME14 . . . . . . 75 F4
Meadowdown Cl ME7 . . . . . 33 A4
Meadow Dr CT5 . . . . 44 B8
Meadow Gr TN25 . . . . 174 D8
Meadow Hill Cotts CT15 . . . 147 D1
Meadow Ho ME2 . . . . 36 B2
Meadow Rd
Ashford TN23 . . . . 139 A4
Canterbury CT2 . . . . 66 C2
Margate CT9 . . . . 7 F1
Sturry CT2 . . . . 67 F6
Meadow Rise ME9 . . . . 14 D4
Meadows The
Herne Bay CT6 . . . . 23 D2
3 Maidstone ME15 . . . . 74 E2
New Romney TN28 . . . . . . 202 C6
Sittingbourne ME10 . . . . . . 36 F2
Wittersham TN30 . . . . 188 D4
Meadowsweet Ho TN23 . . . 138 F1
Meadow View
Hothfield TN26 . . . . 138 A6
Lydd TN29 . . . . 205 D7
Monkton CT12 . . . . 49 D6
Meadow View Ind Est
TN26 . . . . 183 C7
Meadow View Rd
Maidstone ME16 . . . . 97 B3
Shepherdswell CT15 . . . . . . 130 E3
Meadow Way
Eythorne CT15 . . . . 131 C8
Hythe CT21 . . . . 187 B8
Meadow Wlk
Maidstone ME15 . . . . 75 B3
Whitstable CT5 . . . . 43 C6
Mead Rd
Ashford TN24 . . . . 156 E7
Folkestone CT19 . . . . 178 D6
Meads Ave The ME10 . . . . . 36 D7
Meadside Wlk ME5 . . . . 31 F6
Meads Way TN29 . . . . 194 E3
Meadway CT17 . . . . 148 E3
Mead Wlk TN23 . . . . 155 E8
Medina Ave CT5 . . . . 43 B7
Medlar Cl ME5 . . . . 58 A6
Medlar Gr ME7 . . . . 33 A4
Medlars The ME14 . . . . 75 D6
Medway City Est ME2 . . . . . . 9 D7
Medway Com Coll ME4 . . . . 10 A1
Medway Cl TN23 . . . . 155 A2
Medway Ent Ctr ME2 . . . . . . 9 D8
Medway Gdns ME4 . . . . 9 F7

Medway Ho 7 ME14 . . . . . . 74 F4
Medway Hts 5 ME4 . . . . 9 E4
Medway Maritime Hospl
ME7 . . . . 10 B4
Medway Rd
Gillingham ME7 . . . . 10 C7
Sheerness ME12 . . . . 1 C1
Medway St
Chatham ME4 . . . . 9 F5
Maidstone ME14 . . . . 74 F4
Medway Trad Est ME16 . . . . 74 F2
Medway Villas ME15 . . . . . . 96 B7
Meehan Rd TN28 . . . . 202 E4
Meehan Road S TN28 . . . . 202 E3
Meeres Court La ME10 . . . . 37 C5
Meeson's Cl ME13 . . . . 81 E6
Megabyte Ho ME13 . . . . . . 62 D7
Meggett La CT15 . . . . 164 C7
Megone Cl ME8 . . . . 33 D6
Meirs Court Rd ME8 . . . . . . 33 E6
Melbourne Ave
Dover CT16 . . . . 149 C4
Ramsgate CT12 . . . . 29 B1
Melbourne Rd ME4 . . . . 10 A3
Melbury Mews CT10 . . . . . 202 C8
Melford Dr ME16 . . . . 74 C4
Mellanby Cl CT7 . . . . 27 A6
Mellor Row ME10 . . . . 14 F1
Melody Cl
Gillingham ME8 . . . . 33 C4
Warden ME12 . . . . 6 E4
Melon La TN26, TN29 . . . . 193 B6
Melrose CT15 . . . . 97 A7
Melsetter Cl CT7 . . . . 27 B7
Melville Ct ME4 . . . . 9 F6
Melville Lea CT13 . . . . 93 C7
Melville Rd ME15 . . . . 75 A3
Memel Pl 1 CT11 . . . . 52 D6
Mendfield St 8 ME13 . . . . . 62 E7
Mendip TN24 . . . . 139 B4
Mendip Rise TN24 . . . . 139 B4
Menin Rd ME15 . . . . 14 F1
Mentmore Ho CT12 . . . . . . 29 C3
Mentmore Rd CT12 . . . . . . 29 C3
Menzies Ave CT11 . . . . 117 B1
Menzies Cl ME12 . . . . 4 A5
Menzies Rd CT16 . . . . 149 A5
Mercer Cl ME5 . . . . 31 E1
Mercer Dr ME17 . . . . 100 F6
Mercer Way ME17 . . . . 98 B1
Mercery La 5 CT1 . . . . 87 F8
Merchant Store The 7
CT2 . . . . 66 F1
Merchants Way CT1 . . . . . . 87 C8
Mercury Cl ME1 . . . . 9 A3
Meredale Ind Prim Sch
ME8 . . . . 12 A1
Meredith Cl CT17 . . . . 98 F7
Mere Gate CT9 . . . . 7 I1
MERESBOROUGH 34 A5
Meresborough La ME8,
ME9 . . . . 33 F5
Meresborough Rd ME8 . . . . 34 A7
Mereworth Ct ME8 . . . . 11 A3
Meriden Wlk CT18 . . . . 161 D3
Meridian Ct
Ashford TN23 . . . . 155 E7
Maidstone ME16 . . . . 74 E4
Meridian Pk ME2 . . . . 9 E6
Merino Way TN23 . . . . 155 E5
Merivale Gr ME5 . . . . 32 B4
Merleburgh Dr ME10 . . . . . 36 F8
Merlin Cl ME10 . . . . 37 A3
Merlin Ho
Chatham ME4 . . . . 10 B8
2 Sittingbourne ME10 . . . . . 37 A4
Merlin Way
Ashford TN23 . . . . 155 E7
Gillingham ME7 . . . . 10 D5
Mermaid Cl ME5 . . . . 32 A6
Merritt Rd TN28 . . . . 202 E2
Merrivale Hts CT10 . . . . 30 A2
Merryman's Hill CT13 . . . . . 93 B3
Merrywood ME7 . . . . 87 D8
MERSHAM 157 E4
Mersham Prim Sch
TN25 . . . . 157 E3
Merton Cl ME5 . . . . 32 C5
Merton La CT4 . . . . 87 F4
Merton Rd ME15 . . . . 75 B2
Meryl Gdns CT14 . . . . 117 C1
Metcalfe Mews 1 CT1 . . . . . 67 B2
Meteor Ave CT5 . . . . 43 B7
Meteor Cl ME10 . . . . 36 E8
Michelle Gdns CT9 . . . . 28 A8
Micketts Gdns ME10 . . . . . . 36 B4
Mickleburgh Ave CT6 . . . . . 23 D6
Mickleburgh Hill CT6 . . . . . 23 B4
Middelburg Ho CT19 . . . . . 177 D6
Middelburg Sq CT20 . . . . . 178 D4
Middle Cl TN23 . . . . 138 C1
MIDDLE DEAL 117 C5

Middle Deal Rd CT14 . . . . . 117 B5
Middlefields ME8 . . . . 34 A8
Middle Mead CT19 . . . . 178 B7
MIDDLE QUARTER 152 D1
Middle Row
3 Ashford TN23 . . . . 139 C2
2 Faversham ME13 . . . . 62 D7
Middlesex Rd ME15 . . . . 97 D7
Middle St
Ashford TN23 . . . . 139 B2
4 Chatham ME7 . . . . 10 A6
Deal CT14 . . . . 117 D6
Middleton Cl ME8 . . . . 33 E4
Middleton Cotts TN25 . . . . 122 E3
Middleton Gr ME8 . . . . 11 A3
Middletune Ave ME10 . . . . . 36 E7
Middle Wall CT5 . . . . 20 D2
Midhope Way ME10 . . . . . . 37 B3
Midhurst Ct ME15 . . . . 75 A3
MidKent Coll (Chatham Maritime) ME4 . . . . 10 B8
MidKent Coll (City War Ctr)
ME1 . . . . 9 E4
MidKent Coll (Horsted Ctr)
ME5 . . . . 31 E6
MidKent Coll (Oakwood Park Ctr) ME16 . . . . 74 C3
Mid Kent Sh Ctr
ME16 . . . . 74 C7
Midley Cl ME16 . . . . 74 C7
Midsummer Hill TN24 . . . . 139 D6
Mierscourt Prim Sch
ME8 . . . . 33 F7
Mierscourt Rd ME8 . . . . 33 E6
Mikyle Ct CT1 . . . . 88 A6
Milbourne Gr ME10 . . . . . . 36 E7
Milburn Rd ME7 . . . . 10 C2
Mildred Cotts CT19 . . . . . . 177 F7
Mile Rd CT12 . . . . 48 F6
Miles Cl CT3 . . . . 91 A8
Miles Pl ME12 . . . . 9 D3
Milestone Cl CT19 . . . . 178 A7
Milestone Rd CT14 . . . . 117 B5
Miles Way CT6 . . . . 26 F7
MILE TOWN 1 C1
Mile Town Ind Est ME12 . . . . 1 B1
Milford Cl ME16 . . . . 74 D5
Military Rd
Canterbury CT1 . . . . 67 A1
Chatham ME4 . . . . 9 F5
2 Dover CT17 . . . . 166 D7
Folkestone CT20 . . . . 177 E4
Houghton Green TN31 . . . . 197 E3
Hythe CT21 . . . . 176 B2
Ramsgate CT11 . . . . 52 E6
Stone in Oxney TN26,
TN30 . . . . 190 B4
Millais Rd CT16 . . . . 149 C1
MILLBANK 46 F7
Mill Bank CT13 . . . . 93 A6
Mill Bank Cotts CT13 . . . . . 93 A2
Millbank La TN29 . . . . 200 E7
Millbank Rd TN23 . . . . 155 F5
Mill Bay CT20 . . . . 178 E5
Millbrook Cl ME15 . . . . 74 F1
Millbrook Mdw TN23 . . . . . 138 E1
Mill Cl
Crabble CT17 . . . . 148 F2
Lenham ME17 . . . . 101 C4
Sandwich CT13 . . . . 72 E2
Wickhambreaux CT3 . . . . . . 69 C2
Mill Cotts
Queenborough ME11 . . . . . . 3 A5
Ramsgate CT11 . . . . 52 D6
Worth CT14 . . . . 94 A4
Mill Court Cl CT6 . . . . 23 B2
Mill Cr
Ashford TN24 . . . . 139 D2
Sittingbourne ME10 . . . . . . 37 A3
Milldale Cl CT14 . . . . 117 B4
Millenium Terr CT1 . . . . 87 C6
Millennium Way
Broadstairs CT10 . . . . 29 C4
Sheerness ME12 . . . . 1 C2
Miller Cl
Ashford TN24 . . . . 139 D2
Deal CT14 . . . . 117 C8
Sittingbourne ME10 . . . . . . 37 A8
Wingham CT3 . . . . 91 B7
Miller Cotts TN24 . . . . 139 D2
Miller Ct ME12 . . . . 4 A5
Millers Ct
5 Ramsgate CT12 . . . . 29 B1
Whitstable CT5 . . . . 43 D7
Millers La CT12 . . . . 49 C7
Millers Wharf 1 ME15 . . . . . 74 E2
Millers Yd CT1 . . . . 87 E7
Millfield
Ashford TN23 . . . . 155 D8
Folkestone CT20 . . . . 178 D5
Hawkinge CT18 . . . . 163 C5
High Halden TN26 . . . . 167 D7
Sittingbourne ME10 . . . . . . 37 A3
St Margaret's at Cliffe
CT15 . . . . 150 F7
Mill Field
Ash CT3 . . . . 71 E1
Broadstairs CT10 . . . . 29 E3
Millfield Cl CT18 . . . . 163 B5
Millfield Manor CT5 . . . . 20 E1
Millfield Rd
Faversham ME13 . . . . 62 E7
Ramsgate CT12 . . . . 29 B3

Millfields
Chatham ME5 . . . . 32 D2
Shepherdswell CT15 . . . . . . 130 E4
Mill Fields Rd CT21 . . . . . . 175 F2
Mill Gn CT13 . . . . 93 A2
Mill Hamlet CT3 . . . . 69 C2
MILL HILL 117 A3
Mill Hill CT14 . . . . 117 A3
Mill Ho CT17 . . . . 148 F3
Mill La
Ashford TN24 . . . . 140 A1
Birchington CT7 . . . . 26 F6
Bonnington TN25 . . . . 172 E5
Bridge CT4 . . . . 88 F1
Canterbury CT1 . . . . 66 F1
Canterbury, Harbledown
CT2 . . . . 87 C8
Chatham, Bluebell Hill ME5 . 31 D1
Chatham, Luton ME5 . . . . . 10 C1
Chilham CT4 . . . . 107 D7
Coxheath ME17 . . . . 96 D4
10 Dover CT16 . . . . 166 E7
Eastry CT13 . . . . 93 B2
Hartlip ME9 . . . . 34 E6
Hawkinge CT18 . . . . 163 B5
Herne Bay CT6 . . . . 23 B2
Lydd TN29 . . . . 205 D7
Lynsted ME9 . . . . 60 C5
Maidstone ME14 . . . . 74 F6
Margate CT9 . . . . 7 I2
Newchurch TN29 . . . . 184 F3
Nonington CT15 . . . . 113 F4
Northbourne CT14 . . . . . . 115 F4
Preston CT3 . . . . 70 D6
Shepherdswell CT15 . . . . . . 130 F5
Sholden TN27 . . . . 135 A2
Stelling Minnis CT4 . . . . . . 126 F2
Tenterden TN30 . . . . 167 B1
Whitfield CT16 . . . . 149 A8
Worth CT14 . . . . 94 A4
Mill Lane Cotts CT14 . . . . . 116 A4
Millmead Ave CT9 . . . . 8 D1
Millmead Gdns CT9 . . . . 8 D1
Millmead Rd CT9 . . . . 8 C1
Mill Mews CT14 . . . . 117 D8
Mill Pl ME13 . . . . 62 D8
Millpond Cl ME2 . . . . 9 B8
Mill Race CT17 . . . . 148 F3
Mill Rd
Bethersden TN26 . . . . 153 E5
Bramling CT3 . . . . 90 E6
Deal CT14 . . . . 117 C4
Dymchurch TN29 . . . . 195 B7
Gillingham ME7 . . . . 10 C6
Hoath CT3 . . . . 46 F5
Hythe CT21 . . . . 176 D2
Lydd TN29 . . . . 205 D7
Rochester ME2 . . . . 9 B8
Staple CT3 . . . . 92 B5
Sturry CT2 . . . . 67 F5
Mill Row CT7 . . . . 26 F6
Mills Cl ME12 . . . . 3 F3
Mill St
Maidstone, Loose ME15 . . . 96 F5
Maidstone ME15 . . . . 74 F4
Sittingbourne ME10 . . . . . . 36 E5
Temple Ewell CT16 . . . . . . 148 D5
Mills Terr ME4 . . . . 10 A3
Millstock Terr 2 ME15 . . . . 74 E2
Millstream Cl
Faversham ME13 . . . . 62 C7
Whitstable CT5 . . . . 20 E1
Millstream Cotts CT5 . . . . . 43 E8
Millstream Gn TN24 . . . . . . 156 F7
Millstrood Rd CT5 . . . . 43 E8
Mill Terr
Bridge CT4 . . . . 88 F1
Chartham CT4 . . . . 86 D3
Mill View
Ashford TN24 . . . . 156 F6
Woodchurch TN26 . . . . . . 169 A3
Mill View Rd CT6 . . . . 23 A1
Mill Wall Pl CT13 . . . . 94 A8
Mill Way ME10 . . . . 36 F6
Mill Wlk ME16 . . . . 74 A3
Millwood Ct 4 ME4 . . . . 9 F4
Millyard Way CT15 . . . . . . 114 D1
Milner Cl CT15 . . . . 114 A1
Milner Cres CT15 . . . . 112 E5
Milne Rd TN24 . . . . 156 F8
Milner La CT7 . . . . 67 F5
Milner Rd
Elvington CT15 . . . . 114 B1
Gillingham ME7 . . . . 10 D7
Whitstable CT5 . . . . 43 A6
Meers ME17 . . . . 98 F6
MILSTEAD 58 E2
Milstead Cl
Maidstone ME14 . . . . 75 C5
West Minst ME12 . . . . 3 B7
**Milstead & Frinstead CE
Prim Sch** ME9 . . . . 58 E1
Milsted Rd ME8 . . . . 11 C3
Milton Ave CT9 . . . . 7 J1
Milton Cl
Canterbury CT1 . . . . 88 C6
Dover CT16 . . . . 149 B4
Milton Court Prim Sch
ME10 . . . . 36 E6
Milton Rd
Ashford TN23 . . . . 139 B2
Canterbury CT1 . . . . 88 A6
Dover CT16 . . . . 149 B4
Gillingham ME7 . . . . 10 C3
Sittingbourne ME10 . . . . . . 36 C6
MILTON REGIS 36 C6
Milton Regis Halt* ME10 . . 37 A6
Milton Sq 4 CT9 . . . . 7 J1

Milton St ME16 . . . . . 74 C2
Mincers Cl ME5. . . . . 32 C2
Miners Way
  Aylesham CT3 . . . . . 113 A5
  Hersden CT3 . . . . . 47 A1
Minerva Ave CT16. . . 149 C2
Minerva Rd **6** CT11 . . 52 D7
Minerva Rd ME2 . . . . 9 A8
Minnis Field CT4. . . . 126 E2
Minnis Gn CT4. . . . . 126 E2
Minnis La CT15, CT17 . . 148 C2
Minnis Rd CT7. . . . . 26 E7
Minnis Terr CT17. . . . 149 A2
Minnis Way CT14 . . . 94 B5
MINSTER
  Sheppey. 4 B7
  Thanet. 50 A4
Minster Abbey*
  Minster (Sheppey). . . 4 D6
  Minster (Thanet) CT12. . 4 B8
Minster CE Prim Sch
  CT12. . . . . 50 B5
Minster Cl CT10 . . . 30 A2
Minster Coll ME12 . . . 3 F6
Minster Dr
  Herne Bay CT6. . . . 22 D4
  Minster (Sheppey) ME12. . 4 B8
Minster Gatehouse Mus*
  ME12. . . . . 4 D6
Minster Lodge **4** CT11. . 52 C6
Minster Rd
  Acol CT12, CT7 . . . 27 C2
  Faversham ME13. . . 62 E1
  Gillingham ME8 . . . 11 C3
  Minster (Sheppey) ME12. . 4 B6
  Ramsgate CT11. . . . 52 B5
  Westgate on Sea CT8 . . 27 F7
Minster Sheppey Prim Sch
  ME12. . . . . 4 D6
Minster Sta CT12 . . . 50 C5
Mintching Wood La ME9 . 58 F2
Minter Ave CT18 . . . 162 F7
Minter Cl CT18 . . . . 162 F7
Minterne Ave ME10 . . 36 D2
Minterne Way **1** ME10 . 36 D2
Minters Ind Est CT14. . 117 B6
Mint The CT2 . . . . 66 C1
Miranda Ct ME12 . . . 1 C1
Misling La CT4 . . . . 143 C7
Missenden Ct **8** CT20. . 178 C5
Mitcham Rd CT14 . . . 195 C8
Mitchell Ave
  Chatham ME4. . . . 9 F2
  Hawkinge CT18 . . . 163 B5
Mitchell Cl ME17. . . . 101 C5
Mitchell St CT19 . . . 177 D6
Mitre Rd ME1 . . . . 9 B4
Mittell Ct TN29 . . . 205 B6
Moat Farm Rd CT19 . . 178 C7
Moat Farm Rd CT19 . . 178 C7
Moatfield Mdw TN23. . 156 B4
Moat Ho
  Canterbury CT1 . . . 87 F7
  Charing TN27 . . . 120 C7
Moat La
  Ash CT3 . . . . 71 E1
  Fordwich CT2. . . . 68 A3
  Rough Common CT2 . . 66 B4
Moat Pk TN23 . . . 120 C6
Moat Sole CT13. . . . 72 F1
Moat The TN27 . . . 120 C7
Moat Way ME11 . . . 3 A5
MOCKBEGGAR . . . 39 B1
Mockett Ct **4** ME10. . 36 E4
Mockett Dr CT10. . . . 29 F7
Mock La TN23 . . . . 155 B6
MOLASH. 105 F4
Molehill Cnr CT5 . . . 44 D8
Molehill Copse Prim Sch
  ME15. . . . . 97 D7
Molehill Rd
  Herne Bay CT6. . . . 22 A1
  Whitstable CT5 . . . 44 E8
Molineux Rd CT12 . . . 50 B6
Molland Cl CT3 . . . . 71 C2
Molland La
  Ash, Guilton CT3 . . . 71 C3
  Ash, Paramour Street CT3. . 71 D6
Molland Lea CT3 . . . 71 C2
Molloy Rd TN26. . . . 155 B1
Monarch Cl ME5. . . . 32 C2
Monarch Dr ME10. . . 14 F1
Monastery Ave CT16 . . 149 E1
Monastery St CT1 . . . 88 A8
Monckton's Ave ME14. . 74 F7
Monckton's Dr ME14 . . 74 F7
Monckton's La ME14 . . 74 F7
Moncrif Cl CT14 . . . 76 B4
Mongeham Church Cl
  CT14. . . . . 116 D3
Mongeham Rd CT14 . . 116 E3
Mongeham View CT14. . 116 E4
Monica Ct ME13 . . . 84 E8
Monins Rd
  Dover CT17. . . . 166 B7
  Iwade ME9 . . . . 14 D3
Monkdown ME15 . . . 76 A1
Monkery La TN25, TN27. . 104 D2
Monks Cl
  Canterbury CT2. . . 67 A2
  Faversham ME13. . . 62 B8
Monks Hill Cotts TN26. . 182 C6
Monkshill Rd ME13 . . 42 B2
Monks Way CT16 . . . 149 A3
Monk's Way CT13. . . 72 F3
Monks Wlk TN27 . . . 120 C7
MONKTON. 49 D7

Monkton CE Prim Sch
  CT12. . . . . 49 D7
Monkton Cl **2** TN23 . . 155 F6
Monkton Court La CT15. 131 D7
Monkton Ct CT5. . . . 44 D8
Monkton Gdns CT9 . . 8 E3
Monkton Manor CT12 . . 49 C7
Monkton Nature Reserve*
  CT12. . . . . 49 C8
Monkton Pl CT11 . . . 52 D7
Monkton Rd CT12. . . 50 A6
Monkton Rdbt CT12. . 49 D8
Monkton St CT12 . . . 49 D7
Monkwood Cl ME1. . . 31 C6
Monmouth Cl ME8 . . 11 D2
Mons Ct ME10 . . . . 14 F1
Montacue Ct CT20 . . 178 B4
Montague Cl ME14 . . 1 C1
Montague Rd CT11. . . 52 E8
Montague St CT5 . . . 22 D5
Montefiore Ave
  Broadstairs CT10. . . 30 A1
  Ramsgate CT11. . . 29 F1
Montefiore Cotts CT11. . 52 F8
Montfort Cl
  Ashford TN23. . . . 155 F7
  Canterbury CT2 . . . 67 A4
Montfort Rd
  Chatham ME5. . . . 31 F2
  Rochester ME2 . . . 9 A8
Montgomery Ave ME5. . 32 A7
Montgomery Rd ME7. . 10 C3
Montgomery Way CT19. 178 E8
Montpelier Ave CT5. . . 43 D6
Montpelier Bsns Pk
  TN23. . . . . 138 F1
Montpelier Gate ME16. . 74 B5
Montreal Cl **8** CT16 . . 149 B3
Montrose Ave ME5. . . 10 C2
Monument Way TN24 . . 156 F5
Moon Cl ME13 . . . . 15 A1
Moon Hill CT15 . . . . 130 E4
MOON'S GREEN . . . 188 A3
Moonstone Dr ME5 . . 32 B2
Moonstone Sq **1** ME10. 36 D6
Moore Cl TN29 . . . . 192 A3
Moore St ME2 . . . . 9 A8
Moorfield CT2. . . . . 66 F4
Moorings The ME9. . . 38 E6
Moor La
  Ivychurch TN29 . . . 192 D4
  Woodchurch TN26. . 180 E6
Moorland Rd CT15 . . 130 E4
Moor Park Cl ME8 . . . 34 A8
Moor St ME8 . . . . 34 A8
MOORSTOCK . . . 159 C2
Moorstock La TN25 . . 159 C2
MOOR STREET . . . 34 B7
Moorwell Dr CT15 . . . 130 D5
Moray Ave CT7 . . . . 26 F8
Mordaunt Ave CT8 . . 27 E8
Morden St ME1. . . . 9 C4
MOREHALL. 177 F6
Morehall Ave CT19. . . 177 F6
Morehall Prim Sch CT19 . 177 F6
Morella Wlk ME17 . . . 101 C5
Morello Cl ME9 . . . . 38 C2
Moreton Ct CT14. . . . 117 C2
Moreton Terr TN26 . . 171 A5
Morgan Kirby's Gdn ME13 83 D5
Morgan Rd ME2 . . . 9 A8
Morris Ave CT6 . . . . 21 F4
Morris Ct CT6 . . . . 21 F4
Morris Court Cl ME9 . . 37 D2
Morrison Rd CT20 . . . 178 E6
Morry La ME17 . . . . 99 D1
Mortimer Cl TN23 . . . 156 B7
Mortimer Rd CT16 . . 166 F8
Mortimer St CT5. . . . 22 F5
Morton Cl ME15. . . . 97 D6
Mossbank ME5 . . . . 32 A3
Moss End Mews CT11. . 52 E8
Mossy Glade ME8 . . . 33 E6
Mostyn Rd ME14 . . . 75 C4
Mote Ave ME15 . . . . 75 B3
Mote Hall Villas ME14 . . 76 C4
Mote Pk ME15 . . . . 75 D2
Motney Hill Rd ME8. . . 12 A4
Motorway Ind Est **6** ME8 12 C8
Mouat Ct ME5. . . . . 9 C4
Mountain St CT4. . . . 107 B6
MOUNTAIN STREET. . 107 B6
Mountbatten Ave ME5. . 32 A7
Mountbatten Ho CT14. . 117 D3
Mountbatten Way TN25. 158 E6
Mount Castle La ME17. . 101 F1
Mount Charles Wlk CT4. . 88 F1
Mount Dr ME14 . . . . 76 B4
Mount Ephraim Gdns*
  ME13. . . . . 64 A4
Mount Field
  Faversham ME13. . . 62 B6
  Queenborough ME11. . 3 A5
Mountfield Mews CT6 . . 27 D7
Mountfield Way CT8 . . 27 D6
Mount Green Ave CT21. . 51 D5
Mount La
  Hartlip ME9 . . . . 34 D4
  Maidstone ME14 . . 76 B4
Mount Lodge ME1 . . . 9 B2
Mount Pleasant
  Aldington TN25 . . . 173 A6
  Blean CT2 . . . . 66 A6
  Chatham ME5. . . . 10 B3
  Faversham ME13. . . 40 B2

Mount Pleasant *continued*
  Forstal ME20. . . . 53 A3
  Kingsdown CT14 . . . 134 D5
  Minster (Thanet) CT12. . 50 A4
  Tenterden TN30 . . . 179 C8
Mount Pleasant Dr CT18 . 161 C7
Mount Pleasant Dr ME14. . 76 A5
Mount Pleasant Rd **4**
  CT20. . . . . 178 D5
Mount Pleasant Terr
  ME17. . . . . 100 E2
Mount Rd
  Canterbury CT1 . . . 88 C6
  Chatham ME4. . . . 9 F3
  Dover CT17 . . . . 166 A6
  Rochester ME1 . . . 9 B2
Mounts Cl CT14. . . . 117 A5
Mountsfield Cl ME16. . . 74 D5
Mount St CT20 . . . . 176 C2
Mounts View TN23 . . 138 F4
Mountview ME9 . . . . 36 B2
Mount View Ct **8** ME4 . 9 F3
Mount View Rd CT6 . . 23 A2
Moyes Cl ME12 . . . . 51 D5
Moyle Cl ME8. . . . . 33 D4
Mozart Ct ME4. . . . 9 E3
Muddy Bush Cnr CT3 . . 90 F2
Muddy La ME10 . . . . 37 B2
Mudie Cl CT18. . . . . 163 A5
Muir Rd
  Maidstone ME15 . . 75 A2
  Ramsgate CT11. . . . 52 F8
Mulberry Cl
  Gillingham ME7 . . . 33 A4
  Ramsgate CT11. . . . 52 F8
  St Mary's Bay TN29. . 194 F4
Mulberry Ct
  Canterbury CT1 . . . 87 F8
  Hythe CT21 . . . . 176 D3
  Littlestone-on-Sea TN28. . 202 E5
  Maidstone ME14 . . 75 B5
Mulberry Field CT13 . . 72 F1
Mulberry Gdns TN30 . . 179 B8
Mulberry Hill CT4. . . . 85 D1
Mulberry Rd
  Ashford TN23. . . . 138 D3
  Sittingbourne ME10. . 37 C5
Mummery Cl ME13. . . 61 E2
MUNDAY BOIS . . . 135 F8
Munday Bois Cotts TN27 .135 F8
Munday Bois Rd TN27. . 118 C1
Mundella Prim Sch
  CT19. . . . . 178 D6
Mungeam Ho ME1 . . 9 C4
Munn's La ME9 . . . 35 E4
Munsgore La ME9 . . . 35 E3
Murrain Dr ME15 . . . 76 A1
Murray Rd ME2 . . . . 9 C8
MURSTON. 37 B5
Murston Inf Sch ME10. . 37 B4
Murston Jun Sch ME10. . 37 B5
Murston Rd ME10. . . 37 A4
Murthwaite Ct ME12 . . 4 A5
Murton Pl ME13 . . . 41 E1
Muscovy Rd TN25 . . . 139 C7
Muscovy Way CT16 . . 22 E3
Musgrave Cl CT12 . . . 27 F2
Musgrave Rd ME10 . . 36 F6
Musgrove TN23 . . . . 156 A8
Musket La
  Eythorne Street ME17. . 77 C2
  Leeds ME17 . . . . 77 A2
Mustards Rd ME12. . . 6 D2
Mutrix Gdns CT9 . . . 7 E1
Mutrix Rd CT9 . . . . 28 B8
Mutton La ME14 . . . 62 A6
Mymms Cl CT3. . . . 44 C8
Mynn Cres ME14 . . . 76 A4
Myrtle Cres ME5. . . . 31 F5
Myrtle Ct TN23 . . . . 156 A3
Myrtle Gn TN23 . . . . 138 D4
Myrtle Rd **5** CT19 . . 178 E6
Mystole Ho CT4. . . . 108 B8
Mystole La CT4 . . . . 108 B8

N

NACCOLT 140 E6
Nacholt Cl CT5 . . . . 21 A2
NACKINGTON . . . 88 A2
Nackington Pk CT4 . . 88 A4
Nackington Rd CT1, CT4. . 88 A3
Nagpur Ho **4** ME8 . . 33 C4
Nag's Head La ME1 . . 9 B4
Nailbourne Ct CT4 . . . 111 D3
Nailbourne Ct CT18 . . 161 C7
Naildown Cl CT21. . . . 177 A3
Naildown Rd CT21 . . . 177 A3
Nairne Cl TN26 . . . . 170 A8
Naldera Ct CT10 . . . . 30 C7
Namur Pl CT15 . . . . 149 F3
NAPCHESTER . . . 132 C3
Napchester Rd CT16 . . 149 A8
Napier Cl ME10 . . . . 36 C4
Napier Ct ME4 . . . . 9 E2
Napier Gdns CT21. . . 176 C1
Napier Prim Sch ME7. . 10 C4
Napier Rd
  Broadstairs CT10. . . 29 E6
  Dover CT16 . . . . 149 B2
  Gillingham ME7 . . . 10 C4
Napleton Ct **7** CT11 . . 52 C6

Napleton Rd
  Faversham ME13. . . 62 C7
  Ramsgate CT11. . . . 52 C6
Napoleon Wlk ME17 . . 100 E5
Napwood Cl ME8 . . . 33 D6
Nares Rd ME9 . . . . 33 D4
Nargate Cl CT3 . . . . 90 A8
Nargate St CT3 . . . . 90 A8
Narrabeen Rd CT19 . . 177 E6
Narrowbush La TN29 . . 200 E8
Naseby Ave CT20 . . . 177 D5
NASH. 70 F2
Nash Cl ME5. . . . . 32 C2
Nash Court Gdns CT9 . . 28 F8
Nash Court Rd CT9 . . 28 F8
Nashenden Farm La ME1. . 31 A8
Nashenden La ME1 . . 9 A2
Nash Gdns CT10 . . . 30 B4
Nash Hill CT18 . . . . 161 D6
Nash La CT9 . . . . 28 F7
Nash Rd
  Margate CT9, CT10 . . 28 F7
  Wingham CT3 . . . 70 D2
Nasmyth Rd CT7 . . . 27 A8
Natal Rd
  Chatham ME4. . . . 10 A3
  Dover CT16 . . . . 149 C4
Nativity Cl ME10 . . . 36 E4
Nat's La TN25 . . . . 141 A5
Nautilus Cl ME12 . . . 4 A6
Nautilus Dr ME12 . . . 4 A6
Naval Terr ME12 . . . 1 B3
Naylands CT7 . . . . 7 H1
Naylor's Cotts ME7 . . 33 B1
Neale St ME4 . . . . 9 F2
Neal's Place Rd CT2 . . 66 C3
Neame Ct CT7. . . . 27 A7
NEAMES FORSTAL . . 84 D7
Neason Way
  Folkestone CT19 . . . 178 F6
  Folkestone CT20 . . . 178 F6
Neath Rd TN29. . . . 204 C2
Neatscourt Cotts ME12. . 3 C4
Nelson Ave ME12 . . . 4 D5
Nelson Cl
  Ashford TN24. . . . 157 B8
  West Minster ME12 . . 3 A8
Nelson Cres CT11. . . . 52 E6
Nelson Ct
  Birchington CT7 . . . 26 E8
  Chatham ME5. . . . 10 C1
Nelson Gdns ME13 . . 62 C6
Nelson Ho **8** ME15 . . 97 F5
Nelson Mews TN28. . . 202 E5
Nelson Park Rd CT15 . . 150 E8
Nelson Pl CT10 . . . . 30 B5
Nelson Rd
  Gillingham ME7 . . . 10 D4
  Whitstable CT5 . . . 20 D1
Nelson St
  Deal CT14 . . . . 117 D7
  Faversham ME13. . . 62 C6
Nelson Terr ME5 . . . 10 C1
Nelson Wlk ME10 . . . 36 B5
Neptune Cl ME12 . . . 9 E7
Neptune Terr ME12 . . 1 E2
Neptune Way ME2 . . 9 E6
Nesbit Rd TN29 . . . . 194 F4
Ness Rd TN29 . . . . 205 C6
Ness The CT1. . . . . 88 B5
Nether Ave TN28 . . . 202 D6
NETHERCOURT . . . 52 A7
Nethercourt Cir CT12 . . 52 A6
Nethercourt Farm Rd
  CT11. . . . . 52 B7
Nethercourt Gdns CT11. . 52 B6
Nethercourt Hill CT11. . 52 B6
Nethergong Hill CT3 . . 47 B2
Netherhale Farm Rd CT7 . 26 B3
Nethersole Cl CT4 . . . 67 A4
Netherwood Rd CT4. . 112 F1
Netley Cl ME14 . . . . 75 D6
Nettlefield ME4 . . . . 9 E2
Nettlefield TN24 . . . . 139 E5
Nettlepole La TN27 . . 119 D1
Neville Cl ME14 . . . . 75 B8
Neville Ho CT14 . . . . 117 D6
Neville Rd
  Chatham ME4. . . . 9 E2
  Herne Bay CT6. . . . 23 F4
Nevine Ct CT14 . . . . 117 B1
Newark Cl **1** ME2 . . 9 B7
Newark Yd ME2 . . . 9 B7
NEWBARN. 161 B4
New Barns Rd ME13 . . 75 A8
New Beverley Ho CT2 . . 66 F2
New Bridge **6** CT16 . . 166 F7
Newbridge Ave ME10 . . 36 E7
Newbridge Way TN29. . 194 E3
New Brompton Coll ME7 . 10 B4
NEWBURY. 59 D4
Newbury Ave ME16 . . 74 C6
Newbury Cl
  Birchington CT7 . . . 27 B6
  Dover CT17 . . . . 165 F7
  Folkestone CT20 . . . 177 D5
Newcastle Hill **8** CT11. . 52 E7
NEWCHURCH . . . 184 E3
Newchurch La TN26 . . 193 A7
Newchurch Rd ME15 . . 75 A1
Newcomen Rd ME12 . . 1 D2
New Cotts
  Guston CT15 . . . . 149 E6
  Harbledown CT2 . . . 65 E1
  Teynham ME9 . . . . 38 A4
New Covenant Pl **4** ME1. . 9 D4
New Creek Rd ME12 . . 6 E8
New Cross St CT9. . . . 7 I2

New Cut ME15 . . . . 96 D7
New Cut Rd
  Chilham CT4, ME13 . . 85 A3
  Harbledown ME13 . . 65 A1
  Maidstone ME14 . . 75 D5
New Delhi Ho **5** ME15. . 97 F5
New Dover Rd
  Canterbury CT1, CT4 . . 88 C6
  Capel-le-Ferne CT18 . . 164 C2
Newenden Cl
  Ashford TN23. . . . 155 F6
  Maidstone ME14 . . 75 D6
New Forest La CT4. . . 85 B3
New Gardens Rd ME9 . . 38 C2
Newgate Gap CT9. . . 8 A3
Newgate Lower Prom CT9. .8 A3
Newgate Prom CT9 . . 8 A3
New Haine Rd CT12. . . 29 A3
New Hall Cl TN29 . . . 195 C8
New House Cl CT1 . . . 87 F7
Newhouse Cnr CT3 . . 48 D1
Newhouse Farm Cotts
  ME13. . . . . 83 E7
Newhouse La ME13 . . 83 D7
New House La CT4. . . 87 C2
Newing Cl CT3. . . . 89 E8
NEWINGREEN . . . 175 A5
NEWINGTON
  Folkestone. . . . 177 A8
  Ramsgate. 29 B1
  Sittingbourne. . . . 35 A6
Newington CE Prim Sch
  ME9 . . . . . 35 B4
Newington Com Prim Sch
  CT12. . . . . 52 A8
Newington Ent **7** CT12 . 29 B1
Newington Ent Ctr ME9. . 35 C8
Newington Ind Est ME9 . . 34 F6
Newington Rd
  Peene CT18 . . . . 177 A8
  Ramsgate CT12, CT11. . 29 B1
Newington Sta ME9. . . 35 B6
Newington Wlk ME14 . . 75 C6
New Inn Cotts ME15 . . 96 C7
New Kempes Ho ME5. . 123 E2
New La TN29 . . . . 205 C6
NEWLAND GREEN . . 135 D8
Newland Green La TN27 . 135 D8
Newland Rd ME12 . . . 2 F7
Newlands
  Ashford TN23. . . . 155 D6
  St Mary's Bay TN29 . . 194 F3
  Whitfield CT16. . . . 149 B6
Newlands Ave ME10 . . 36 B5
Newlands Dr CT14 . . . 134 B8
Newlands Farm Cotts
  ME13. . . . . 104 C4
Newlands Ho CT11. . . 29 E2
Newlands La CT12 . . . 29 D2
Newlands Prim Sch CT11. .29 E1
Newlands Rd
  Charing TN27 . . . 119 F5
  Ramsgate CT12. . . . 29 D1
New Lincoln Ho CT19 . . 178 D8
New Line Learning Academy
  ME15. . . . . 97 B6
Newlyn Ct **1** ME14 . . 75 A4
Newlyn's Mdw CT15 . . 147 D1
Newman Ct **3** CT21. . 176 B1
Newman Dr CT20. . . 37 A8
Newman Rd CT3 . . . 112 C5
Newmans Cl
  Broadstairs CT10. . . 30 A6
  7 Hythe CT21. . . . 176 B1
NEWNHAM. 81 C7
Newnham Cl ME8. . . . 11 C2
Newnham La ME9, ME13. . 81 D7
Newnham St ME4. . . 10 B3
Newport Ct CT1 . . . 88 B6
New Rd
  Chatham ME4. . . . 9 F4
  Egerton TN27 . . . 118 F3
  Egerton TN27 . . . 119 A2
  Elham CT4 . . . . 144 F4
  Eythorne CT15 . . . 131 C7
  Harbledown CT2 . . . 65 D3
  Herne CT2, CT6 . . . 45 C4
  Hythe CT21 . . . . 176 B1
  Hythe, Saltwood CT21. . 176 B4
  Langley ME17 . . . 98 C5
  Minster (Sheppey) ME12. . 4 C6
  Rochester ME1 . . . 9 D4
  Rough Common CT2 . . 66 B3
  Sheerness ME12 . . . 1 B1
New Rectory La TN23. . 156 B4
New Rents **5** TN23 . . 139 B2
New Road Ave ME4 . . 9 F4
New Road Cotts CT6. . 45 E5
New Road Hill TN25 . . 172 F4
New Road Ind Est ME12. . 1 B1
New Road Prim Sch **4**
  ME4. . . . . . 10 A3
NEW ROMNEY . . . 202 A5
New Romney Cl CT13 . . 93 F8
New Romney Sta* TN28. . 202 C6
New Romney Sta **11** CT21. . 67 A1
New St
  Ash CT3 . . . . 71 E1
  Ashford TN24. . . . 139 B2
  Canterbury CT1 . . . 87 E7
  Canterbury, St Dunstan's
    CT2. . . . . 66 E1
  Chatham ME4. . . . 9 E3
  Deal CT14 . . . . 117 D7
  12 Dover CT16, CT17. . 166 D8

New St continued
Folkestone CT20 . . . . **178** D5
Herne Bay CT6. . . . . **22** F5
Lydd TN29 . . . . **205** C6
Margate CT9 . . . . **7** I2
Sandwich CT13 . . . . **94** A8
Sheerness ME12 . . . . **1** C1
2 Whitstable CT5 . . . . **20** D2
New Strs ME4 . . . . **9** F6
Newton Cl
Chatham ME5. . . . . **32** C2
1 Maidstone ME16 . . . . . . **74** E3
Newton Rd
Faversham ME13 . . . . **62** D7
Whitstable CT5 . . . . **21** B2
NEW TOWN **156** D7
New Town La CT15 . . . . . . **156** D8
Newtown Rd TN23, TN24 . . **156** D7
New Town St
Canterbury CT1. . . . . **67** B2
Chartham CT4 . . . . **86** C5
New Villas ME15 . . . . **96** C7
Nicholas Cl ME10 . . . . **74** A3
Nicholas Dr CT12 . . . . **51** D5
Nicholas Rd TN24 . . . . **139** B6
Nicholls Ave CT10 . . . . **29** F2
Nicklaus Dr ME5. . . . . **31** F3
Nickleby Cl ME1 . . . . **9** C2
Nickle Cotts CT4. . . . . **86** A4
Nickley Wood Rd TN26 . . **170** C6
Nightingale Ave
Hythe CT21 . . . . **187** D8
Whitstable CT5 . . . . **43** B6
Nightingale Cl
Ashford TN24 . . . . **157** B7
Chartham CT4 . . . . **86** C6
Gillingham ME8 . . . . **13** C2
Nightingale La CT15 . . . . . **113** E2
Nightingale Pl CT9. . . . . **8** A2
Nightingale Rd
Dover CT16 . . . . **149** C2
Faversham ME13 . . . . **62** C7
Herne CT6 . . . . **45** F7
Nightingales The CT9 . . . . . **28** F8
Nile Rd ME7 . . . . **10** C4
Nine Acres TN24 . . . . **139** C5
Nine Ash La ME13 . . . . **63** D3
Ninn La TN23 . . . . **138** B2
Niwrim Way ME12 . . . . **1** H1
Nixon Ave CT12 . . . . **29** C1
Noah's Ark Rd CT17. . . . . . **166** A8
Noah's Ark Terr CT17. . . . **166** B8
Noakes Mdw TN23 . . . . . . **156** A8
Nobel Cl ME9. . . . . **38** C2
Nobel Ct ME13. . . . . **62** C7
Noble Ct CT9 . . . . **28** A8
Noble Gdns CT9 . . . . **28** A8
No Man's Orch Nature
Reserve* CT4. . . . . **86** D7
No Name St 3 CT13 . . . . **73** A1
NONINGTON **113** D5
Nonington CE Prim Sch
CT15. . . . . **113** C5
Nonington Ct CT15. . . . . . . **113** E5
Nonsuch Cl CT1 . . . . **88** C8
Nore Cl
Gillingham ME7 . . . . **10** E1
Sheerness ME12 . . . . **1** D1
Noreen Ave ME12 . . . . **4** A6
Norfolk Cl
Chatham ME5. . . . . **32** C3
Gillingham ME8 . . . . **11** D2
Norfolk Dr TN23 . . . . **139** A2
Norfolk Rd
Canterbury CT1. . . . . **87** E6
Maidstone ME15 . . . . **97** C8
Margate CT9 . . . . **8** B3
Margate, Lydden CT9. . . . . . . **28** D5
Norfolk Sq CT12 . . . . **29** B2
Norfolk St 3 CT5 . . . . **43** D8
Norman Castle* CT1. . . . . . **87** F7
Norman Cl
Gillingham ME8 . . . . **33** B5
Maidstone ME14. . . . . **75** B6
Norman Rd
Ashford TN23, TN24. . . . . . **156** B7
Broadstairs CT10. . . . . **29** F6
Canterbury CT1. . . . . **88** A7
Faversham ME13 . . . . **62** C7
Ramsgate CT11. . . . . **52** B6
St Margaret's at Cliffe
CT15. . . . . **151** B6
Warden ME12 . . . . **6** A6
Westgate on Sea CT8 . . . . **7** D1
Whitstable CT5 . . . . **43** E8
Norman St 3 CT17 . . . . **166** D8
Norman Tailyour Ho
CT14. . . . . **117** D5
Norreys Rd ME8 . . . . **33** E7
Norrie Rd CT27 . . . . **27** A6
Norrington Mead 3
CT19. . . . . **178** A7
Norrington Rd ME15 . . . . . . **97** B6
North Aux Boiler House Rd
TN29 . . . . **209** C2
North Ave CT11. . . . . **52** D6
North Barrack Rd CT14 . . . **117** B5
North Borough Jun Sch
ME14. . . . . **75** A6
NORTHBOURNE **116** A4
Northbourne Ave CT12 . . . **166** B8
Northbourne CE Prim Sch
CT14. . . . . **115** F5
Northbourne Park Pre Prep
Sch CT14. . . . . **115** D6

Northbourne Park Sch
CT14. . . . . **115** C6
Northbourne Rd
East Studdal CT15. . . . . **115** E1
Gillingham ME8 . . . . **11** B4
Great Mongeham CT14 . . . . **116** C4
Northbourne Way CT9 . . . . . **8** E2
Northbrooke TN24 . . . . **139** C3
Northbrooke La TN24 . . . . **139** C3
North Camber Way CT16 . **150** B3
North Cl CT20 . . . . **177** D8
Northcliffe Gdns CT10. . . . . **30** A7
North Close Bsns Ctr
CT20. . . . . **177** D4
North Contractor's Rd
TN29 . . . . **209** B3
Northcote Rd
Deal CT14 . . . . **117** D5
Kingsdown CT14 . . . . **134** D4
Rochester ME2 . . . . **9** A7
North Court Cl CT3 . . . . **91** A8
North Court La CT14 . . . . . **115** A4
North Court Rd CT3. . . . . . . **91** A8
North Cres ME17. . . . . **96** D4
North Ct CT14 . . . . **117** C7
North Ct 2 ME15 . . . . **75** A1
North Ct CT12 . . . . **29** B2
North Dane Way ME5 . . . . . . **32** C4
NORTHDOWN **8** D1
Northdown
Ashford TN24. . . . . **139** C4
Doddington ME9 . . . . **80** F7
Stockbury ME9 . . . . **56** D8
Northdown Ave CT9. . . . . **8** B2
Northdown Bsns Pk
ME7 . . . . **101** F6
Northdown Cl
Lenham ME17 . . . . **101** F6
Maidstone ME14 . . . . **75** B7
Northdown Hill CT10. . . . . . **29** D7
Northdown Park Rd CT9 . . . **8** C1
Northdown Prim Sch CT9 . . **8** C1
Northdown Rd
Broadstairs CT10. . . . . **29** E6
Margate CT9 . . . . **8** B2
Northdowns Cl CT15. . . . . . **132** B6
North Downs Ct CT14 . . . . . **85** C2
Northdown Trad Est CT10 . **29** E7
North Down View ME17 . . **100** F6
Northdown Way CT9 . . . . **8** C1
North Eastling Rd ME13 . . . **61** B7
NORTH ELHAM. **145** A6
Northern By-Pass TN27 . . **120** C8
North Exit Rd CT16 . . . . . . **166** H8
Northfleet Cl ME14. . . . . **75** C5
North Foreland Ave CT10. . **30** B7
North Foreland Hill CT10. . **30** B8
North Foreland Rd CT10. . . **30** B7
NORTHGATE. **67** A1
Northgate
Canterbury CT1. . . . . **67** A1
Rochester ME1 . . . . **9** C6
North Holmes Rd CT1. . . . . . **88** B8
North La
Canterbury CT2 . . . . **66** F1
Faversham ME13 . . . . **62** F1
7 Folkestone CT20. . . . . . . **177** E3
Selling ME13 . . . . **84** F8
North Lea CT14 . . . . **117** C7
Northleigh Cl ME15 . . . . **97** A6
North Lockside Rd ME4 . . . **10** D8
NORTH LYMINGE **161** C7
North Lyminge La CT18 . . **161** C7
North Military Rd CT17 . . **166** C7
North Pends TN24 . . . . **139** E5
Northpoint Bsns Est ME2 . . **9** D8
North Pondside Rd ME4. . . **10** A8
North Quay ME9 . . . . **38** E6
North Quay ME13 . . . . **40** D1
North Rd
Chatham, Brompton ME4,
ME7. . . . . **10** A7
Chatham ME4. . . . . **10** A7
Cliffs End CT13 . . . . **51** A1
Deal CT14 . . . . **134** D6
Dover CT17 . . . . **166** C8
Folkestone CT20 . . . . **177** D4
Hythe CT21. . . . . **176** B2
Queenborough ME11. . . . . **2** F5
Sandwich CT13 . . . . **95** H7
North Return Rd CT16. . . . **166** G8
North Road W CT21. . . . . . . **176** A3
North Sch The TN24. . . . . . **139** D1
North Side Three Rd ME4 . **10** C8
North Side
Ashford TN23. . . . . **139** C2
Deal CT14 . . . . **117** D7
Dover CT17 . . . . **166** B7
Folkestone CT19 . . . . **178** E5
Herne Bay CT6. . . . . **23** A5
New Romney TN28. . . . . **202** A6
Rochester ME2 . . . . **9** B7
Sheldwich ME13 . . . . **83** C8
Sittingbourne ME10. . . . . **36** F7
Warmlake ME17 . . . . **98** E1
NORTH STONAR **73** B6
NORTH STREET. **62** C1
Northumberland Ave
Ashford TN24. . . . . **139** D5
Gillingham ME8 . . . . **11** E1
Margate CT9 . . . . **8** C2
Northumberland Ct
Maidstone ME15 . . . . **97** D7
Margate CT9 . . . . **8** C3
Northumberland Rd ME15 **97** D8
North View
Hersden CT3 . . . . **46** F1
Maidstone ME15 . . . . **75** B1

North View Cotts ME15 . . . **96** C7
Northwall CT14 . . . . **117** C7
Northwall Mews CT14 . . . . **117** C7
Northwall Rd CT14. . . . . . . **117** B8
North Way
Finglesham CT14 . . . . **116** A7
Maidstone ME14 . . . . **75** B7
NORTHWOOD **29** C3
Northwood Dr ME10 . . . . . . **36** F1
Northwood Rd
Broadstairs, Ramsgate CT10,
CT12 . . . . **29** C3
Whitstable CT5 . . . . **20** F2
NORTON ASH **60** F8
Norton Ave CT6. . . . . **46** A8
Norton Dr CT12 . . . . **50** B6
Norton Gr ME5 . . . . **31** E3
Norton Knatchbull Sch The
TN24 . . . . **139** E2
Norton La TN26 . . . . **153** D5
Norton Rd
Five Wents ME17 . . . . **98** D1
Lewson Street ME13, ME9.. . **60** C5
Norview Rd CT5 . . . . **43** B7
Norway Dro CT15 . . . . **151** A8
Norway Terr 4 ME4 . . . . **75** A7
Norwood Gdns TN23 . . . . . **139** B2
Norwood La TN29 . . . . **193** E8
Norwood Rise ME10 . . . . **4** C7
Norwood Rd TN23. . . . . **139** B2
Norwood Walk E ME10 . . . . **36** B5
Norwood Walk W ME10 . . . **36** B5
Notley St CT1. . . . . **67** A1
Notley Terr 3 CT1 . . . . **67** A1
Nottingham Ave ME15. . . . . **97** D7
Nottingham Rd CT7 . . . . **26** F5
Nouds La ME9 . . . . **60** D6
Nouds Rd ME9 . . . . **60** D7
Nunnery Fields CT1. . . . . . . **88** A7
Nunnery Rd CT1 . . . . **87** F7
Nursery Ave
Maidstone, Bearsted
ME14. . . . . **76** B3
Maidstone ME16 . . . . **74** B6
Nursery Cl
Densole CT15 . . . . **163** A7
Ramsgate CT11 . . . . **52** C7
Sheerness ME12 . . . . **1** E1
Whitstable CT5 . . . . **21** A1
Nursery Fields
Acol CT7. . . . . **27** B3
Hythe CT21 . . . . **176** A2
Nursery Gdns CT10 . . . . **8** E1
Nursery La
Densole CT15 . . . . **163** A7
Sheldwich ME13 . . . . **83** D5
Whitfield CT16 . . . . **148** F7
Nurserylands CT6. . . . . **22** F3
Nursery Rd ME8 . . . . **33** D8
Nursery Wlk CT2. . . . . **66** E2
Nutberry Cl ME9 . . . . **38** D2
Nutfield Cl ME5 . . . . **32** B8
Nutfields ME10 . . . . **37** B3
Nutley La TN24. . . . . **139** C3
Nutts Ave ME2 . . . . **6** G2
Nutwood Cl ME14. . . . . **75** E4

O

OAD STREET **35** E1
Oakapple Ho 10 ME16. . . . . **74** A3
Oakapple La ME16 . . . . **74** A3
Oak Ave
Eythorne CT15 . . . . **131** D5
Gillingham ME7 . . . . **10** E6
Minster (Sheppey) ME12. . . . . **4** F1
Oak Bglws TN29 . . . . **205** C6
Oak Cotts
Barrowhill TN25. . . . . **174** D7
East Studdal CT15 . . . . **132** E8
Selling ME13 . . . . **84** D4
Oak Croft ME14. . . . . **76** B4
Oakdale Rd CT6 . . . . **23** A4
Oakdene Rd CT12. . . . . **29** C1
Oak Dr
Boughton Street ME13. . . . . . **64** A3
Hawkinge CT18. . . . . **163** B5
St Mary's Bay TN29 . . . . **194** F3
Oakenpole TN23 . . . . **138** E1
Oakfield Cl CT12. . . . . **52** B8
Oakfield Rd TN24 . . . . **139** D5
Oakfields ME10 . . . . **36** C3
Oak Gr CT15 . . . . **114** B2
Oak Hall Pass CT21 . . . . . . **176** C2
Oakham Dr TN29 . . . . **205** D7
Oak Hill CT13 . . . . **93** B6
Oak Ho 6 ME5. . . . . **31** F4
Oakhurst Cl ME5. . . . . **31** F4
Oak La
Lydd TN29 . . . . **205** B6
Minster (Sheppey) ME12. . . . . **4** F7
Upchurch ME9 . . . . **12** D2
Oakland Cl ME5. . . . . **31** F3
Oakland Ct
Cliffs End CT12 . . . . **51** C5
Herne Bay CT6. . . . . **22** E5
Oaklands
Ashford TN23. . . . . **138** F1
Loose ME15. . . . . **97** A8
Mersham TN25. . . . . **157** E4
Oaklands Ave CT10 . . . . **29** E5
Oaklands Inf & Jun Sch
ME5 . . . . **31** F4
Oaklands Way CT2 . . . . **68** B7
Oakleigh Cl ME15 . . . . **31** E2
Oakleigh Ho TN23. . . . . **155** E8

Oakleigh La CT4 . . . . **89** B5
Oakleys The CT15 . . . . **130** D5
Oak Lodge Rd TN28 . . . . . . **202** B7
Oak Rd ME10 . . . . **37** C5
Oak Ridge TN26. . . . . **183** F8
Oaks Ave CT6 . . . . **22** D2
Oaks Bsns Village The
CT5 . . . . **32** C1
Oaks Dene ME5. . . . . **31** F1
Oakside Rd CT3 . . . . **112** C5
Oaks Inf Sch The ME10. . . . **36** D2
Oaks Pk CT2 . . . . **66** B3
Oaks Rd
Folkestone CT20 . . . . **177** D6
Tenterden TN30 . . . . **179** B8
Oak St CT14 . . . . **117** D6
Oaks The
Broadstairs CT10. . . . . **29** F7
Hawkinge CT18 . . . . **163** B3
Hersden CT3 . . . . **46** F1
St Nicholas at Wade CT7 . . . . **25** F2
Whitstable CT5 . . . . **43** B6
Oaks View CT21 . . . . **187** C8
Oak Tree Ave ME15. . . . . **97** C7
Oak Tree Cl ME12 . . . . **5** A5
Oak Tree Gr CT9 . . . . **28** A8
Oaktree Ho ME10 . . . . **37** B3
Oak Tree Rd TN23 . . . . **155** F8
Oak Trees 10 ME15 . . . . **97** E5
Oak Trees Com Sch ME15 . **97** C7
Oakum Cl ME4. . . . . **10** B2
Oakvale Cl CT17 . . . . **166** B7
Oak Wlk CT21 . . . . **176** C2
Oakwood 2 CT14. . . . . **29** C8
Oakwood Ct ME16 . . . . **74** D3
Oakwood Dr CT5. . . . . **21** A1
Oakwood Ind Est CT10 . . . . **29** E6
Oakwood Park Gram Sch
ME16 . . . . **74** C3
Oakwood Rd
Maidstone ME16 . . . . **74** D3
Sturry CT2. . . . . **68** A7
Oakwood St CT19 . . . . **178** E7
Oakwood Terr ME10. . . . . . . **37** C4
Oakwood Villas CT11. . . . . . **29** E1
OARE **40** A3
Oare Gunpowder Works Ctry
Pk* ME13. . . . . **40** A1
Oare Marshes Nature
Reserve* ME13 . . . . **40** B6
Oast Cotts
Dargate ME13 . . . . **64** D8
Sheldwich ME13 . . . . **83** C8
Wormshill ME9 . . . . **79** C5
Oast Ct
Margate CT9 . . . . **28** F8
Sittingbourne ME10. . . . . **36** E2
Oast Ho CT4 . . . . **85** C2
Oast Ho The
Canterbury CT3 . . . . **88** F8
3 Gillingham ME8 . . . . **33** F8
Oasthouse Field TN29. . . . **192** F4
Oast La ME13 . . . . **104** E6
Oast Mdw TN24 . . . . **139** F1
Oast Paddock The CT3 . . . . **92** A6
Oasts The ME14. . . . . **76** C4
Oast The
Canterbury CT1. . . . . **88** B6
Staple CT3 . . . . **92** A6
Oastview ME8 . . . . **34** A8
Oaten Hill CT1 . . . . **88** A7
Oaten Hill Pl CT1 . . . . **88** A7
Oaze The CT5 . . . . **43** C6
Occupation Rd TN25 . . . . . **123** F2
Ocean Cl CT7 . . . . **27** B8
Ocean View
Broadstairs CT10. . . . . **30** A1
Herne Bay CT6. . . . . **23** F6
Ocelot Ct 6 ME4 . . . . **10** B3
Octavia Cl ME5 . . . . **32** B3
Octavian Dr CT21 . . . . **175** A3
Octavian Way TN23 . . . . . . **155** E5
Odd Rise ME7 . . . . **11** A5
Odiham Dr ME16. . . . . **74** C7
Odo Rd CT17 . . . . **166** C8
Officers' Rd ME4. . . . . **10** B8
Officers Terr ME4 . . . . **9** F7
Offley Cl CT9 . . . . **8** C1
Ogilvy Ct CT10 . . . . **29** E7
Okehampton Cl TN24. . . . . **139** F7
Olantigh Ct CT7 . . . . **27** A7
Olantigh Rd TN25, CT4 . . **123** F3
Olawe Rd CT9. . . . . **8** B1
Old Ash Cl TN24. . . . . **139** C5
Old Ashford Rd
Charing TN27 . . . . **120** C7
Lenham ME17 . . . . **101** E5
Old Badgins Rd ME13 . . . . . **83** B6
Old Bailey The ME17 . . . . . **100** E6
Old Bakery Cl TN29 . . . . . . **194** F3
Old Bakery Mews ME13 . . . **63** F4
Old Barn Cl ME7 . . . . **32** F6
Old Billet La ME12 . . . . **5** C6
Old Boundary Rd CT8. . . . . . **7** D1
Old Bridge Rd CT5. . . . . **20** E1
Old Carriageway The ME7 **32** F4
Old Charlton Rd CT16. . . . . **149** D2
Old Chatham Rd
Kit's Coty ME20. . . . . **53** D6
Sandling ME14. . . . . **53** F1
Oldchurch Ct 8 ME16. . . . . **74** E3
Old Church Rd CT4 . . . . **86** E1
Old Coachworks The 10
CT13. . . . . **72** F1
Old Coal Yd The 7 CT5 . . . . **20** D1

Old Coastgaurd Cotts
TN29 . . . . **209** D3
Old Corn Stores The
ME14. . . . . **76** C4
Old Court Hill CT15, CT3 . **113** C6
Old Crossing Rd 1 CT9 . . . . **28** B8
Old Dairy Cl 2 CT11. . . . . . . **52** F7
Old Dairy Yd CT12 . . . . **52** C7
Old Diary Mews The ME12. . . **3** D7
Old Dover Rd
Barham CT4. . . . . **112** B1
5 Canterbury CT1 . . . . **88** B6
Capel-le-Ferne CT18 . . . . . . **164** C1
Old Dr ME15. . . . . **96** F6
Old Dungeness Lighthouse*
TN29 . . . . **209** D2
Old Farm Cl CT5 . . . . **43** C6
Old Farm Rd CT7 . . . . **26** D7
Old Ferry Rd ME9. . . . . **14** E7
Oldfield Cl
Gillingham ME8 . . . . **33** D8
Maidstone ME15 . . . . **96** C7
Old Flour Mill The CT17 . **149** B2
Old Forstal Cl CT5 . . . . **44** C8
Old Folkestone Rd CT17. **166** A4
Old Forge La ME9. . . . . **56** F3
Old Garden Ct CT4. . . . . **86** E1
Old Gate Rd ME13 . . . . **62** B8
Old Green Rd
Broadstairs CT10. . . . . **29** F7
Margate CT9 . . . . **8** C1
Old Hall Dr CT12. . . . . **51** C5
Old Halls The 3 CT5 . . . . **20** D2
Old Ham La ME17 . . . . **101** A4
Oldhave Hill CT3, CT6 . . . . . **46** D7
Old High St The CT20 . . . . **178** E5
Old Hockley Rd ME13 . . . . . **82** C2
Old Hook Rd ME12. . . . . **4** F2
Old Hop Gdn The TN31 . . . **196** C2
Oldhouse La TN29. . . . . **191** E1
Old House La ME9 . . . . **34** E4
Old Kingsdown Cl CT10 . . . **29** E3
Old Lain ME17 . . . . **100** F6
Old Lenham Rd ME9 . . . . **80** C4
Old London Rd CT21 . . . . . **175** F2
Old Loose Cl ME15 . . . . **96** F5
Old Loose Hill ME15 . . . . . . **96** F4
Old Maidstone Rd ME9. . . . **33** F5
Old Mead CT19 . . . . **178** A7
Old Mill La ME20. . . . . **53** C3
Old Mill Mews CT19. . . . . . **177** F7
Old Mill Rd ME17. . . . . **76** F1
Old Oast Bsns Ctr The
ME20 . . . . **53** A1
Old Orch TN23 . . . . **155** D8
Old Orchard The ME8 . . . . . **34** A8
Old Palace Rd CT4 . . . . **89** C3
Old Park Ave
Canterbury CT1. . . . . **67** C2
Dover CT16. . . . . **149** A3
Old Park Cl CT16 . . . . **149** A4
Old Park Rd CT11 . . . . **67** A2
Old Park Hill CT16. . . . . . . **149** B4
Old Park Rd CT16. . . . . **149** B2
Old Pattens La ME4 . . . . **9** D2
Old Pk Hill CT15 . . . . **149** A5
Old Police Sta The 4
CT16. . . . . **25** D2
Old Pond Rd TN23 . . . . **155** F8
Old Print Ho 4 CT16. . . . . . **166** F1
Old Printworks Cl 5 CT5 . **43** D8
Old Priory Sch The CT11 . . **52** D6
Old Railway Works (Ind Est)
TN24 . . . . **156** D8
Old Rd
Chatham ME4. . . . . **9** F4
Elham CT4 . . . . **144** F4
Sarre CT7. . . . . **48** C6
Old Rectory Cl
Hawkinge CT18. . . . . **163** B4
Mersham TN25. . . . . **157** E5
Old Rectory The TN25 . . . . **122** E2
Old Roman Rd CT15. . . . . . **133** C1
OLD ROMNEY **201** B7
Old Ruttington La CT1 . . . . **67** A1
Old Saltwood La CT21. . . . **176** B4
Old Saw Mill The TN26 . . . **153** E6
Old School Cl
Lenham ME17 . . . . **101** D4
Sturry CT2. . . . . **67** F6
Old School Ct
Egerton TN27. . . . . **118** F3
Folkestone CT20. . . . . **178** B4
Old School Gdns CT9 . . . . . . **8** A1
Old School Mews CT4. . . . . . **86** C2
Old School Pl ME14. . . . . **75** A5
Old School Rd TN24. . . . . . **156** D8
Old School Yd 2 CT10 . . . . . **29** E5
Old Sch The
Capel-le-Ferne CT18 . . . . . . **164** C4
St Margaret's at Cliffe
CT15. . . . . **150** F7
Old Stables The CT11 . . . . . . **52** C5
Oldstairs Rd CT14 . . . . **134** D4
Old Surrenden Manor
TN26 . . . . **154** C5
Old Surrenden Manor Rd
TN26 . . . . **154** C5
Old Timber Yard E CT12 . . . **52** A8
Old Timber Yard Ind Est
CT11. . . . . **52** A7
Old Tovil Rd ME15. . . . . **75** A2
Old Town Gaol Mus* 18
CT17. . . . . **166** D8
Old Trafford CT16 ME16 . . . **74** B6
Old Tree La ME17 . . . . **97** D3
Old Tree Rd CT3 . . . . **47** B7
Old Valley Rd CT4. . . . . **128** F7

Old Vicarage Gdn CT2.......67 F6
Old Vicarage Gdns TN25...123 E2
Old Vicarage The CT13...93 C7
Old Walting St 21 CT1....87 F8
Old Way TN26...........190 D7
OLD WIVES LEES.........85 C3
Olive Gr 12 CT11.........52 F7
Oliver Cl ME4............10 B2
Olivers Row ME4.........76 C4
Oliver Twist Cl ME1......9 B4
Olivine Cl
  Chatham ME5............54 A8
  Sittingbourne ME10.....36 C7
Olliffe Cl ME5...........31 F2
Omer Ave CT9............8 E2
Onslow Rd ME1...........9 D3
Ontario Way CT16.......149 B3
Onyx Dr ME10............36 D6
Opal Gn ME5.............32 B2
Opie Wlk CT18..........162 F3
Orache Dr ME14..........75 E5
Orange St CT1............9 P5
Orange Terr ME1..........9 D5
Orbital Pk TN24..........156 F6
Orbit Cl ME5.............54 A8
Orchard Ave CT14.......117 B5
Orchard Bank
  East Farleigh ME16.....96 A8
  Faversham ME13........62 E5
Orchard Cl
  Canterbury CT2.........66 F4
  Coxheath ME17.........96 C3
  Langley Heath ME17.....98 E4
  Littlebourne CT3........89 F7
  Mersham TN25..........157 A4
  Minster (Thanet) CT12...50 B7
  Ramsgate CT12..........29 B3
  Whitfield CT16.........148 F8
  Whitstable CT5..........20 F3
  Wingham CT3............91 A7
Orchard Cotts
  East Farleigh ME16......96 A8
  Faversham ME13.........62 E5
Orchard Gr
  Crabble CT17...........148 E3
  Hythe CT21............176 B1
  Littlebourne-on-Sea TN28..202 E6
  Maidstone ME14.........75 E4
  Newington ME9..........35 A5
  Wye TN25..............123 F1
Orchard End CT11........52 A5
Orchard Field TN26.....153 D4
Orchard Fields CT11....160 E2
Orchard Flats CT11.......88 D7
Orchard Gdns CT9........28 A8
Orchard Gr
  Minster (Sheppey) ME12...4 C6
  Whitstable CT5..........43 D8
Orchard Ho 9 ME4........9 F3
Orchard Hts TN23........43 B3
Orchard Ind Est ME15....97 F3
Orchard La
  Ashford TN24...........139 F6
  Challock TN25..........105 B2
  Monkton CT7, CT12......49 A4
  St Nicholas at Wade CT7..25 F1
Orchard Mews CT14......117 D5
Orchard Pk CT6...........23 D4
Orchard Pl
  Coxheath ME17..........96 C3
  Faversham ME13.........62 D7
  2 Maidstone ME16......74 E3
  Sittingbourne ME10......37 A3
Orchard Rd
  Eastry CT13............93 B3
  Herne Bay CT6..........22 F3
  Margate CT9............28 A8
  St Mary's Bay TN29....195 A5
  Tenterden TN30.........167 A3
Orchard Residences The
  CT1....................9 B6
Orchard Row CT5.........23 A1
Orchard Sch The CT1.....87 F6
Orchard St
  Canterbury CT1.........87 F7
  Gillingham ME8.........33 E8
  Maidstone ME15.........75 A3
Orchards The CT4........144 F4
Orchard The
  Maidstone ME14.........76 B4
  Monkton CT12...........49 D6
ORCHARD VALLEY........176 B3
Orchard Valley CT21....176 A2
Orchard View
  Ash CT3.................71 F1
  Detling ME14............76 A8
  Tenterden TN30.........179 C8
  Teynham ME9............38 C3
Orchard Villas
  1 Chatham ME4...........9 F3
  Kearsney CT17.........148 E4
Orchard Way
  Eastchurch ME12.........5 D1
  Peasmarsh TN31........196 C1
Orchid Cl ME12...........4 A4
Orchid Ct TN23..........156 D2
Orchids The
  Etchinghill CT18.......161 D4
  Mersham TN25..........157 E4
Ordinance Way TN23....138 F4
Ordnance St ME4..........9 E4
Ordnance Terr 9 ME4.....9 E4
Orgarswick Ave TN29...195 C2
Orgarswick Way TN29...195 C2
Orient Pl CT2............66 F1

Orion Rd ME1............31 C7
Orion Way TN24.........156 E8
Orlestone View TN26....182 F7
Orlestone Villas TN26...183 A8
Ormonde Ct CT21........176 C1
Ormonde Rd
  10 Folkestone CT20....178 E6
  Hythe CT21............176 C1
Ormsby Gn ME8...........33 E3
Orpins Cl TN25.........158 D6
Orr Cl CT18............162 F4
Osborne Gdns CT6........23 D4
Osborne Rd
  Ashford TN24..........156 F8
  Gillingham ME7.........10 C5
  Kingsdown CT14........134 C6
Osborne Terr CT9.........7 J1
Osbourn Ave CT18........4 D8
Osbourne Rd CT10........29 F4
Oscar Rd CT10...........30 B4
Osier Field TN24........139 E7
Osier Rd ME9............38 E3
Osprey Ave ME9..........38 E3
Osprey Ct CT5...........43 C7
Osprey Ct
  2 Dover CT16.........149 B2
  Hawkinge CT18........162 F3
  Sittingbourne ME10.....37 A3
OSPRINGE...............62 B6
Ospringe CE Prim Sch
  ME13..................62 A6
Ospringe Pl ME13........62 B6
Ospringe Rd ME13........62 B7
Ospringe St ME13........62 A6
Ostend Ct ME10..........14 F1
Ostlers La CT7...........48 D6
Oswald Pl CT17.........149 B2
Oswald Rd CT17.........149 B2
OTHAM.................98 B7
Otham Cl CT2............98 B7
OTHAM HOLE............98 B6
Otham La ME15...........76 C2
Otham St
  Maidstone ME15.........76 C2
  Otham ME15............98 B7
Ottawa Cres CT16.......149 C3
Ottawa Way CT16.......149 B3
Otterpool La ME15.......75 C1
Otterden Cl
  Ashford TN23..........155 F6
  Ashford TN23..........155 F6
Otterden Rd ME13........81 D3
OTTERHAM QUAY.........12 C3
Otterham Quay La ME8...12 B2
Otteridge Rd ME14.......76 A3
Otterpool La CT21, TN25..174 D4
OTTINGE..............144 D1
Otway St
  Chatham ME4............10 A3
  Gillingham ME7.........10 D6
Otway Terr 1 ME4........10 A3
OUT ELMSTEAD..........111 C7
Out Elmstead La CT4.....111 F2
Outfall Ave TN29.......209 C2
Oval The TN29..........186 D1
Overland La CT3..........71 A3
OVERLAND..............84 F7
Overton Ho ME12..........1 D2
Owen's Cl CT21.........177 B3
Owens Court Cotts ME13..83 F8
Owen Sq CT1............117 B2
Owens Way ME7..........11 A6
Owletts Cl ME15.........97 D8
Owl's Hatch Rd CT6......22 C2
Oxenden Cnr CT3.........23 F1
Oxenden Cres CT3........91 A8
Oxenden Park Dr CT6....22 E4
Oxenden St CT5..........22 E5
Oxenden Way CT4.......128 F8
Oxen Lease TN23........155 E8
Oxenturn Rd TN25......140 E8
Oxford Cl 6 ME5........20 D1
Oxford Ct CT11..........87 F7
Oxford Mans 6 CT5......20 D1
Oxford Rd
  Canterbury CT1.........87 F7
  Gillingham ME7.........10 D3
  Maidstone ME15.........97 D8
Oxford St
  4 Margate CT9...........7 J1
  Whitstable CT5.........20 D1
Oxford Terr CT20.......178 D4
Oxney Cl CT7............26 F7
Oxney Cotts TN30.......190 A4
Oyster Cl
  Herne Bay CT6..........22 B3
  Sittingbourne ME10.....36 E6
Oyster Mews 4 CT5......20 D1
Ozengell Pl CT12.........29 A2

P

Packer Pl ME5...........32 A8
Packer's La 5 CT11.......52 E2
Padbrook La CT3.........70 D6
PADDLESWORTH..........162 C4
PADDOCK...............104 E1
Paddock Cl
  Deal CT14.............116 F5
  Folkestone CT20.......177 F5
  Lydd TN29.............205 B6
Paddock The
  Ashford TN23..........155 E7
  2 Birchington CT7......27 A7

Paddocks The
  Ashford TN23..........138 C1
  Broadstairs CT10........29 F7
  Densole CT18..........163 A8
  Gillingham ME7.........33 A5
  Herne Bay CT6..........23 F5
  Margate CT9.............8 C1
Paddock The
  Canterbury CT1.........88 B8
  Chatham ME4............9 F4
  Dover CT16............166 D8
  Old Wives Lees CT4.....85 C2
  Woodchurch TN26......169 A1
Paddock View CT5........43 E7
Pad's Hill ME15..........75 A4
Padsole La ME15.........75 A4
Padstow Manor 1 ME7...10 C6
Padwell La TN23........155 C8
Paffard Cl CT2...........67 F6
Paffard Ct CT2...........67 F6
Page Pl CT19...........178 D8
Page Rd CT13..........162 F3
Paget Row ME7..........10 C5
Paget St ME7...........10 C5
Pagitt St ME4...........66 E6
Paine Ave TN29.........205 C6
Painesfield Ct TN29....186 C4
PAINTER'S FORSTAL......61 E3
Painter's Forstal Rd ME13..61 A4
Palace Ave ME15.........75 A4
Palace Cl CT5...........21 B2
Palace Cotts ME9........80 F8
Palace Ct
  Gillingham ME5.........10 D2
  Hythe CT21............176 C2
Palace Ind Est ME15.....97 F4
Palace St 10 CT1........67 A1
Palace Wood Prim Sch
  ME16..................74 C6
Pal Cres CT17...........27 E5
Palmar Rd ME16.........74 D6
Palmars Cross Hill CT2..66 A1
Palmarsh CT21..........187 D7
PALMARSH..............187 D7
Palmarsh Cres CT21....187 D7
Palmarsh Prim Sch
  CT21.................187 D8
Palm Bay Ave CT9........8 D3
Palm Bay CP Sch CT9.....8 D3
Palm Bay Gdns CT9.......8 D3
Palmbeach Ave CT21....187 D8
Palm Ct CT18...........7 C1
Palmer Cl CT6...........46 B8
Palmer Cres CT3.........29 C8
Palmer Rd CT3..........91 A8
Palmerston Ave
  Broadstairs CT10........30 B3
  Deal CT14............117 D2
Palmerston Rd
  Chatham ME4............9 F1
  Dover CT16............148 F4
Palmerston St 4 CT19...178 D6
Palmerston Wlk ME10....97 A4
PALMSTEAD.............127 D5
Palm Tree Cl CT11......131 D7
Palm Tree Way CT18....161 B7
Palting Way CT20.......178 B4
Pamela Ct ME7..........10 D5
Pannell Dr CT18.........162 F4
Pantheon Gdns TN23....155 F5
Panton Cl ME5...........32 C4
Paper La TN24..........156 F6
Papion Gr ME5...........31 E2
Papworth Cl 1 CT19....178 A7
Parade CT1..............87 F8
Parade Rd CT20.........177 F5
Parade The
  Ashford TN24..........156 F6
  Birchington CT7........26 D8
  Eastry CT13............93 B2
  Folkestone CT20.......178 F7
  Greatstone-on-Sea TN28,
    TN29.................206 E7
  Margate CT9.............7 I3
  Sittingbourne ME10.....36 F2
Paradise CT11...........52 D7
Paradise Cotts ME9......34 E5
Paradise Row CT13.......72 F1
Paragon CT11............52 E5
Paragon St CT11........52 D5
Paraker Way CT18......177 B4
PARAMOUR STREET.......71 D7
Pardoner Cl CT2.........87 C7
Pardoners Way CT16....149 A3
Parfitt Way CT16.......149 B2
Parham Cl CT11.........67 B2
Parham Ct CT11.........67 B2
Parham Rd
  Canterbury CT1.........67 B2
  Chatham ME4............9 F1
Paris Cnr TN26.........153 F6
Parish Cl CT10..........29 E6
Parish Rd
  Chartham CT4, ME4.....86 C3
  Minster (Sheppey) ME12...4 A5
Park Ave
  Birchington CT7........27 A6
  Broadstairs CT10........29 E2
  Deal CT14.............117 C5
  Dover CT16............149 D1
  Gillingham ME7.........10 D3
  Leysdown-on-Sea ME12...6 G1
  Maidstone ME17.........96 E2
  Minster, Penenden Heath
    ME14.................4 A4
  Queenborough ME11......3 B4

Park Ave continued
  Sittingbourne ME10.....36 E1
  Whitstable CT5.........20 F3
Park Barn Rd ME17......99 C5
Park Chase CT10.........29 E2
Park Cl
  Hawkinge CT18........163 A4
  Margate CT9.............8 D1
Park Cotts
  Preston CT3............70 B6
  Ramsgate CT11.........29 E2
Park Cres ME4...........31 F8
Park Crescent Rd CT9....8 A1
Park Ct ME13............62 E7
Park Dr
  Hothfield TN26........138 A6
  Sittingbourne ME10.....36 D1
Parker Cl
  Gillingham ME8.........33 E5
  Hamstreet TN26........183 A7
Parker Pl CT18.........163 C5
Park Farm Cl
  Folkestone CT19......178 C8
  Shadoxhurst TN26.....155 A1
  Tyler Hill CT2..........66 E6
Park Farm Prim Sch
  CT19.................178 C6
Park Farm Rd CT19.....178 C6
Park Farm Ret Pk CT19..178 B8
Parkfield Rd
  Folkestone CT19.......178 C6
  Gillingham ME8.........11 F1
Park Gate CT10..........29 F2
Park Ho
  Dover CT16............149 D1
  Maidstone ME14.........75 B6
Park La
  Bethersden TN26.......154 C8
  Birchington CT7........27 A6
  Bishopsbourne CT4....111 C5
  Elham CT4............144 F5
  Maidstone, Cock Stone
    ME17.................97 D2
  Maidstone, Ringleston
    ME14.................74 C7
  Margate CT9.............8 A2
Parkland Ct CT10........29 F6
Park Lea CT14..........117 C5
Park Mall Sh Ctr 2
  TN24.................139 B2
Park Manor ME7.........10 B5
Park Mews 6 CT16......166 D8
Park Par CT9...........195 C7
Park Pl
  Ashford, Beaver TN23..156 B7
  Ashford, Willesborough
    TN24.................156 F8
  Dover CT16............166 D8
  Herne CT6..............46 A8
  Margate CT9.............7 I1
Park Rd
  Ashford TN24..........156 F8
  Birchington CT7........27 C7
  Broadstairs CT10........30 B6
  Dover CT16............149 B2
  Faversham ME13........62 D7
  Folkestone CT19......177 E6
  Herne Bay CT6..........22 F4
  Hythe CT21............176 B1
  Littlebourne-on-Sea TN28..202 E5
  Maidstone ME15.........75 C1
  Margate CT9.............8 A2
  Preston CT3............70 D7
  Queenborough ME11......2 F5
  Ramsgate CT11.........52 C7
  Sheerness ME12.........14 B1
  Sittingbourne ME10.....36 E3
  Temple Ewell CT16....148 D5
  Westgate on Sea CT7...27 D6
Park Road N TN24.......139 B3
PARK SIDE.............146 D7
Park Side CT14.........117 C5
Parkside Com Prim Sch
  CT1....................67 D2
Parkside Ct
  Herne Bay CT6..........22 F5
  Ramsgate CT11.........52 C7
Parkside Pl CT1.........67 D3
Park St
  Ashford TN24..........139 C2
  Deal CT14.............117 D6
  Dover CT16............166 D8
  Lydd TN29.............205 C6
Park Terr
  Throwley ME13..........82 C7
  Woodnesborough CT13...93 D7
Park Vale TN24.........139 D6
Park View
  Folkestone CT19......178 E7
  Margate CT9.............8 A2
Park View Cl CT3........91 D2
Park View Ct CT5........22 A8
Park View Rd CT5.......113 D4
Park View Rise CT15...113 D4
Park View Rd 2 TN30...179 C7
Park Villas ME14........75 C4
Park Way
  Coxheath ME17.........96 D3
  Maidstone ME15.........75 B1
Park Way Prim Sch ME15..75 B1
Parkway The CT7.........27 D2
PARK WOOD
  Gillingham.............33 D4
  Maidstone..............97 E4
Parkwood TN31.........197 B4
Parkwood Cl CT10.......29 F2
Park Wood Cl TN23.....156 B5

Park Wood Forest Wlks*
  TN26.................181 C4
Park Wood Gn ME8.......33 D5
Park Wood Ind Est ME8...98 A4
Parkwood Jun Sch ME8...33 E5
Parkwood Par 13 ME15...97 F5
Park Wood Rd CT2.......66 C4
Park Wood St CT18......33 D5
Park Wood Trad Est
  ME8..................98 A4
Parr Ave ME7............10 D6
Parrs Head Mews ME1....9 C6
Parsley Way ME16........74 A3
Parsonage Chase ME12...3 A5
Parsonage Cotts Mews...58 A5
Parsonage Farm ME13....82 A4
Parsonage Fields CT12...49 C7
Parsonage La
  Rochester ME2...........9 C8
  Sittingbourne ME9......36 A8
Parsonage Oast CT12....49 C7
Parsonage Rd CT6........23 A3
Parsonage Stocks Rd
  ME13..................82 F5
Parsonage Villas CT15..165 C5
Parsons Way CT11.......149 A3
Partridge Cl CT6........23 C3
Partridge La CT13........62 D7
Pasley Rd ME4, ME7......10 B7
Pasley Road E ME7.......10 B7
Pasley Road N ME4......10 B7
Pasley Road W ME7......10 A7
Passmore Way ME15......74 E1
Pastime Cl ME10.........36 E8
Pasture The
  Ashford TN24..........139 D6
  Hawkinge CT18........163 B4
Patchways TN29........184 E3
Path Field Cotts CT15..164 E5
Pathway The 22 CT10....30 B4
Patricia Way CT10.......29 D3
PATRIXBOURNE..........89 B2
Patrixbourne Ave ME8...11 C2
Patrixbourne Rd CT4....89 B2
Pattens Gdns ME7........9 E2
Pattens La ME4, ME5.....9 E1
Pattens Pl ME1..........9 D2
Patterson Cl CT14......117 A4
Pattison Farm Cl TN25..172 F4
Paul's Pl 8 CT16.......149 C1
Paviour The TN30.......167 B3
Pavilion Cl CT14.......117 C8
Pavilion Ct 4 CT20....178 E4
Pavilion Dr ME10........14 F1
Pavilion Mdw CT17.....148 E4
Pavilion Rd CT19.......178 D6
Pavings The ME7.........77 C2
Paxton Ave CT18.......162 F3
Payden St ME17........102 D8
PAYDEN STREET.........80 B1
Payne's Pk CT20........178 D5
Payne's La ME15.........97 B7
Pay St CT18............162 F7
Payton Cl CT9...........29 A7
Payton Mews 4 CT7.......67 B1
Peacock Mews 7 ME16...74 E4
Peacock Pl ME14........84 A6
Peacock Rd ME5.........32 A4
Peafield Wood Rd CT7...127 E4
Peak Dr CT13............93 B3
Pean Court Rd CT5......43 D3
Pean Hill CT5...........43 D2
Pearmain Wlk CT11......88 C7
Pearman Cl ME8.........12 A1
Pearson's Way CT10.....29 E7
Pear Tree Alley 2 ME10..36 E5
Pear Tree Cl CT10.......29 C4
Peartree Cotts ME8.....34 B8
Pear Tree La
  Dymchurch TN29.......186 D1
  Gillingham ME7.........32 E2
  Loose ME15.............97 B6
Peartree Rd CT6.........23 C3
Pear Tree Row ME7......98 B5
Pear Tree Wlk ME9.......35 A5
PEASMARSH.............196 B4
Peasmarsh CE Prim Sch
  TN31.................196 B1
Peckham Ct ME2..........9 C8
Pedding Hill CT3.........71 A1
Pedding La CT3..........92 A8
PEDLINGE..............175 D4
Peel Dr ME10............37 C4
Peelers Ct CT2..........66 F1
Peel St ME14............75 A3
PEENE.................177 B8
Peene Cotts CT18.......162 B1
PEENING QUARTER......188 B6
PEGWELL...............52 B5
Pegwell Ave CT11........52 B5
Pegwell Bay Ctry Pk*
  CT12..................51 C2
Pegwell Bay Nature
  Reserve* CT11.........51 C3
Pegwell Cl CT11.........52 A5
Pegwell Ct CT11.........52 B5
Pegwell Rd CT11.........52 B5
Pelham Gdns CT20......178 A4
Pelwood Rd TN31.......203 A2
Pemberton Ct CT21.....177 B3
Pemberton Rd TN24....139 D2
Pemberton Sq 4 ME2.....9 C8
Pembroke Ave ME4......10 B8
Pembroke Ave CT9........7 F1

Pembroke Ct
　Chatham ME4 . . . . .10 A4
　Folkestone CT19 . . . . . .178 E6
　1 Ramsgate CT11 . . . .52 E7
Pembroke Gdns ME8 . . . . .33 E4
Pembroke Ho TN28 . . . .202 E5
Pembroke Mews TN28. .202 C8
Pembroke Rd ME17 . . . . . .96 C3
Pembroke Rise ME4 . . . . . .10 A7
Pembury Ct **6** ME10 . . . .36 E4
Pembury Gdns ME16 . . . .74 D3
Pembury Pl TN25 . . . . . . .138 F4
Pembury St ME8. . . . . .36 E4
Pembury Way ME8. . . . . . .11 E2
Penbury CT14 . . . . .117 C1
Pencester Ct **3** CT16 . . .166 E8
Pencester Rd CT16. . . . . .166 D8
Penderel Mews TN30. . . .179 B8
Penenden ST ME14 . . . . . .75 D5
PENENDEN HEATH 75 B7
Penenden Heath Rd ME14 .75 C7
Penenden St ME14. . . . . . .75 A6
Penfield La ME9. . . . . .59 A4
Penfold Cl
　Chatham ME5. . . . . .32 B7
　Maidstone ME15 . . . . . .97 E5
Penfold Gdns
　Maidstone ME15 . . . . . .97 E4
　Shepherdswell CT15 . .130 E5
Penfold Hill ME17. . . . . . . .99 B8
Penfold Rd CT19 . . . . . . .178 F6
Penfold Way ME16 . . . . . .96 F6
Pengelly Cl CT2 . . . . .66 F2
Penhurst CI ME14 . . . . . . .75 F5
Penlee Point TN24 . . . . . .139 D5
Pennant Rd ME1. . . . . .31 C7
Penn CI ME10 . . . . .37 B2
Penn Hill TN23. . . . . .155 C6
Pennine Way
　Ashford TN24. . . . . .139 B4
　Maidstone ME15 . . . . . .76 A1
Pennington Cl CT2. . . . . . .68 C7
Penny Cress Gdns ME16..74 C3
Penny Cress Rd ME12 . . . .4 A4
PENNYPOT. 175 F3
Pennypot Ind Est CT21..175 F1
Penny Pot La CT21 . . . . .108 B4
Penrith CT ME7 . . . . .11 A5
Penrose Ct CT21 . . . . . . .176 C1
Penryn Manor **4** ME7 . .10 C6
Pensand Ho CT21 . . . . . .176 D1
Penshurst CI
　Canterbury CT2 . . . . .67 A3
　Gillingham ME8 . . . . .11 E2
Penshurst Gdns CT9 . . . . .8 F2
Penshurst Rd CT11 . . . . . .52 F7
Penshurst Rise ME13. . . .62 B8
Penstocks The ME15 . . . .74 D2
Pentagon Sh Ctr ME4 . . . .9 F4
Pent Vale Cl CT19. . . . . . .177 F7
Pepys Ave ME12 . . . . .1 C2
Pepy's Way ME2 . . . . .9 A8
Percival Terr CT17 . . . . . .166 B7
Percy Cl CT10 . . . . .8 F2
Percy Rd
　Broadstairs CT10. . . . . . .29 F5
　Margate CT9 . . . . .8 A3
　Ramsgate CT11 . . . . .52 D8
Peregrine Cl CT21 . . . . . .187 D8
Peregrine Dr ME10 . . . . . .37 A2
Peri Ct CT1. . . . . .87 E6
Peridot Ct ME15 . . . . .97 E5
Perie Row **9** ME7 . . . . . .10 A6
Perimeter Rd CT16. . . . . .166 G8
Periwinkle Cl CT3 . . . . . . .48 E3
Periwinkle Ct **8** ME10 . .36 E5
Perkins Ave CT9 . . . . .28 F8
Perrins Mead CT19. . . . . .177 B7
Perrot Way CT18. . . . . . . .163 B5
PERRY 70 C3
Perryfield St ME14 . . . . . .74 F6
Perry La CT3 . . . . .70 C3
Perry's CI ME13. . . . . .62 D8
Perry St
　Chatham ME4. . . . . .9 E5
　Maidstone ME14 . . . . . .74 F6
PERRYWOOD. 84 C4
Perth Gdns ME10 . . . . .36 C4
Perth Way CT18. . . . . . . .149 C3
PESTED. 105 B4
Pested Bars Rd ME17 . . . .97 D5
Pested La TN25 . . . . .105 C4
Petchell Mews **11** CT1 . .67 B2
Peter Candler Way TN24 .139 E4
Petfield Cl ME12. . . . . .4 A3
PETHAM. 109 B3
Petham Gn ME8 . . . . .11 C2
Petham Prim Sch CT4. . .109 C3
Petlands ME17. . . . . .97 D5
Petrel Cl CT6 . . . . .23 F4
Petrel Way CT18 . . . . .163 A3
PETT BOTTOM 110 B5
Pett Bottom Rd CT4. . . . .110 C5
Pettfield Hill Rd ME13. . . .82 B1
Pett Hill CT4. . . . . .88 F1
Pett La
　Charing TN27 . . . . .120 D7
　Silver Street ME9. . . . . . .57 B7
Pettman Cl CT6. . . . . .22 F3

Pettman Ct **5** CT10. . . . .29 E5
Pettmans Mews CT5 . . . .20 C2
Pett's Cres CT12. . . . . .50 B5
Petts La CT3. . . . . .91 A8
Pevenset Ct ME16. . . . . . .74 F4
Peverel Dr ME14 . . . . .76 A5
Peverel Gn ME8 . . . . .33 D4
Peverell Rd CT16 . . . . . . .149 B4
Pewter Ct CT13. . . . . .87 F7
Pfizer Monk's Wall Nature
　Reserve* CT13. . . . . .72 E3
Pharos Dr CT16. . . . . .149 E1
Pheasant La ME11. . . . . . . .3 E5
Pheasant Rd ME4 . . . . . . .10 C2
Pheasants' Hall Rd CT4 ..110 F2
Philip Corby Cl CT9 . . . . . .8 B2
Philippa Ho CT19 . . . . . . .178 F6
Philippa Cl ME10. . . . . . . .36 E8
Phillip Rd CT19 . . . . .177 E6
Phillips Cl ME8 . . . . .11 B2
Phillips Rd CT7 . . . . .27 A6
Phoenix Com Prim Sch
　CT24. . . . . .139 D5
Phoenix Cl **11** ME12. . . .10 C6
Phoenix Ind Est ME9 . . . . .9 D7
Phoenix Pk ME15 . . . . . . .97 F4
Phoenix Rd ME15. . . . . . . .32 B2
Piccadilly Apartments **4**
　ME5 . . . . .10 B3
Pickelden La CT4 . . . . . . .107 F8
Pickering St ME15 . . . . . . .97 B6
Pickhill Oast TN30 . . . . . .179 B4
Pickneybush La TN29 . . .194 A7
Pickwick Cres ME1 . . . . . . .9 C3
Picton Rd CT11 . . . . .52 C7
Pie Factory Rd CT15 . . . .113 C2
Pier Approach Rd ME7. . . .10 D7
Pier Ave
　Herne Bay CT6. . . . . .22 E4
　Whitstable CT5 . . . . .21 A2
Pierpoint Rd CT5 . . . . .43 D7
Pier Rd ME7 . . . . .10 E7
Pierremont Ave CT10 . . . .30 A4
Pier Road Ind Est ME7 ...10 D7
Pier Sports Ctr The CT6....22 E5
Pier The CT16 . . . . .148 F8
Pigeon La CT6 . . . . .23 A2
Pigtail Cnr ME12. . . . . .4 E6
Pike Cl CT19 . . . . .178 A7
Pikefields ME8 . . . . .11 C2
Pike Rd CT14. . . . . .114 C4
Pike Rd Ind Est CT15 . . .114 D1
Pilar Ct CT8 . . . . .7 I1
Pilckem Cl CT17. . . . . .67 D1
Pilgrims Cl ME17 . . . . .79 A3
Pilgrims Ct TN27. . . . . . . .120 C7
Pilgrims La
　Chilham CT4. . . . . .85 E1
　Whitstable CT5 . . . . .43 B4
Pilgrims Lakes ME17. . . .100 E6
Pilgrim Spring CT19 . . . .178 D8
Pilgrims Way CT1. . . . . . . .88 C7
Pilgrims View ME14. . . . . .76 C1
Pilgrims' Way TN25 . . . . .159 E8
Pilgrims' Way Prim Sch
　CT1. . . . . .88 C7
Pilot Rd ME1 . . . . .31 C8
Pilots Ave CT14 . . . . .117 A4
Pilot's Farm Rd CT4 . . . .110 A4
Pimpernel Ct ME14 . . . . . .76 B4
Pimpernel Way ME5. . . . . .31 E4
Pimp's Court Cotts ME15..96 E6
Pincus Ho ME10 . . . . .36 D5
Pine Cotts ME14 . . . . .74 E8
Pine Gr
　Gillingham ME7 . . . . .33 A5
　Maidstone ME14 . . . . . .75 B6
PINEHAM 149 D8
Pineham Rd CT15 . . . . . .149 D6
Pine Ho
　3 Chatham ME5. . . . . .31 F5
　5 Chatham ME5. . . . . .31 B4
Pine Lodge ME16 . . . . .74 B4
Pine Lodge Ct CT14 . . . .117 B5
Pine Pl ME15 . . . . .74 E1
Pines Calyx* CT15 . . . . . .151 B5
Pines Garden The*
　CT15. . . . . .151 B5
Pineside Rd CT3 . . . . .89 E8
Pines The
　Broadstairs CT10. . . . . . .29 D4
　Canterbury CT1 . . . . .88 A6
Pine Tree Ave CT2 . . . . . . .66 E2
Pinetree Cl CT5. . . . . .20 F3
Pine Tree Cl CT7 . . . . .27 B7
Pine Way CT19 . . . . .177 D7
Pine Wlk CT6. . . . . .23 E5
Pinewood Cl CT2 . . . . .29 C1
Pinewood Dr ME5 . . . . . . .54 D8
Pin Hill CT1 . . . . .87 F7
Pinks Cnr CT12. . . . . .50 D6
Pinners Hill CT15, CT3 ..113 C6
Pinners La CT3 . . . . .113 C5
Pinnock Wall CT14. . . . . . .94 D5
Pintail Dr ME9. . . . . .14 E3

Pintail Way CT6. . . . . .23 C2
Pioneer Bsns Pk CT11. . . .52 C8
Pioneer Rd CT16. . . . . . . .149 A3
Pippin Ave CT4 . . . . .111 B8
Pippin CI
　Ash CT3. . . . . .71 E1
　Coxheath ME17 . . . . .96 B2
　8 Sittingbourne ME10 . .36 B6
Pippin Croft ME7. . . . . .33 A6
Pitstock Rd ME9 . . . . .59 B5
Pittlesden TN30 . . . . .179 A7
Pittlesden Pl **1** TN30 . .179 A7
Pittock Ho CT14 . . . . .117 B3
Pitt Rd
　Chartway Street ME17. . .99 A2
　Maidstone ME16 . . . . . .74 B1
Pivington La TN27 . . . . . .119 C2
Pixwell La CT14. . . . . .116 D3
Place La
　Hartlip ME9 . . . . .34 D4
　Woodchurch TN26 . . . .169 B3
Place The CT4 . . . . .112 F1
Plain Cotts CT20 . . . . . . .178 A4
Plain Rd
　Brabourne Lees TN25 . .158 F5
　Folkestone CT20 . . . . . .178 B4
Plains Ave ME15 . . . . .75 C1
Plains of Waterloo CT11 ..52 F7
Plaistow Sq ME14. . . . . . . .75 C6
Plantation Dr TN26 . . . . .138 A7
Plantation Ct ME9 . . . . . . .14 E4
Plantation La ME14 . . . . . .76 A3
Plantation Rd
　Faversham ME13 . . . . . . .62 C7
　Gillingham ME7 . . . . .11 A6
　Whitstable CT5 . . . . .21 D2
Platters The ME8 . . . . .33 C7
PLATT'S HEATH 100 E1
Platts Heath Prim Sch
　ME17 . . . . .100 F2
Playdell Ct **2** CT20 . . . .178 D4
Playden La TN31 . . . . .197 C3
Playhouse Theatre* **15**
　CT5 . . . . .20 D1
Playing Fields CT13. . . . . .93 E7
Playstool Cl ME9. . . . . .35 B6
Playstool Rd ME9. . . . . . . .35 A6
Plaza Ct **7** ME10 . . . . . . .37 A4
Pleasance Road Central
　TN29. . . . . .209 D7
Pleasance Road N TN29..206 E5
Pleasant Row **10** ME7. . .10 A6
Pleasant Valley La ME15...96 B4
Pleasent Pl ME12 . . . . .4 A4
Plenty Brook Dr CT6 . . . . .22 F3
Plewis Ho ME17 . . . . .96 E2
Pleydell Cres CT7. . . . . . . .27 B7
Pleydell Gdns CT20 . . . . .178 D4
Plimsoll Ave CT19 . . . . . .178 E8
Plomley Cl ME8. . . . . .33 D4
Plough Cotts ME17. . . . . . .98 C2
Plough Ct CT6. . . . . .23 D2
Plough Hill CT15 . . . . .165 C4
Plough La CT15 . . . . .21 D3
Ploughmans Way
　Ashford TN23. . . . . .155 D5
　Chatham ME5. . . . . .32 A1
　Gillingham ME8 . . . . .33 E6
Plough Rd ME12 . . . . .5 C5
Plough Wents Rd ME17 . .98 B2
Plover Cl
　Chatham ME5. . . . . .32 D1
　Herne Bay CT6. . . . . .23 F5
Plover Rd
　Hawkinge CT18 . . . . . . .162 F3
　Minster (Sheppey) ME12....4 A5
PLUCKLEY. 136 D7
Pluckley CE Prim Sch
　TN27. . . . . .136 D7
Pluckley Cl ME8 . . . . .11 C3
Pluckley Gdns CT9. . . . . . . .8 E2
Pluckley Rd
　Bethersden TN26. . . . . .153 D7
　Charing TN27. . . . . .120 B5
　Hothfield TN26, TN27. .137 B4
　Smarden TN27 . . . . .135 D2
Pluckley Sta TN27 . . . . . .136 C3
PLUCKLEY THORNE 136 B6
PLUCKS GUTTER 48 F3
Plumford Rd ME13. . . . . . .62 A2
Plumpton Wlk
　5 Canterbury CT1 . . . .67 B1
　4 Maidstone ME15 . .97 F6
Plumpudding La ME13 . . .42 E1
Plumstone Rd CT7. . . . . . .26 F1
Plum Tree Gdns TN26 . . .169 B1
Plumtree Gr ME7 . . . . .33 A4
Plumtrees ME14 . . . . .76 A4
Plurenden Manor Farm Cotts
　TN26. . . . . .168 D7
Plurenden Rd TN26. . . . . .168 E7
Poachers Cl ME5 . . . . .32 C5
Poachers End CT3 . . . . . . .24 B1
Pochard Cres CT6 . . . . . . .22 E3
Podkin Wood ME5 . . . . . . .53 F8
Poets Cnr CT3 . . . . .24 B1
Poets Wlk CT14. . . . . .117 C1
Poison Cross CT13. . . . . . .93 B4
Poldark Ct **22** CT11 . . . .52 F7
Poles The ME9 . . . . .12 E4
Polhill Dr ME5 . . . . .31 F2
Pollard Cl TN23. . . . . .155 F8
Pollard Ct ME7 . . . . .10 C5
Pollard Pl **3** CT5 . . . . . . .43 C6

Polo Way CT5 . . . . .21 D1
Pomfret Ho CT4 . . . . .86 D1
Pomfret Rd CT4 . . . . .86 D1
Pommeus La CT14 . . . . . .133 D7
Poncia Rd TN23. . . . . .156 A7
Pond Cotts
　Herne Bay CT6. . . . . .23 D2
　Sittingbourne ME10 . . . .58 D8
Pond Dr ME10 . . . . .37 A2
Pond Farm Rd
　Hucking ME17. . . . . .56 D1
　Oad Street ME9 . . . . .35 F1
Pond Hill CT3 . . . . .90 D1
Pond Hill Rd CT20 . . . . . .177 C5
Pond La
　St Margaret's at Cliffe
　　CT15. . . . . .150 D7
　Womenswold CT4, CT3 ..112 D3
Pondmore Way TN25. . . .138 F4
Ponycart La CT4 . . . . .126 E3
Poorhole La CT10 . . . . .29 B5
Poot La ME9 . . . . .12 E5
Pope House La TN30 . . . .167 B4
Popes La CT2 . . . . .67 F7
Pope St
　Godmersham CT4 . . . . .107 E4
　Maidstone ME16 . . . . . .74 C2
Popes Wood ME14 . . . . . . .75 F6
Popjack Rd ME9 . . . . .58 E6
Poplar Cl CT14 . . . . .117 B3
Poplar Dr
　Elvington CT15. . . . . . . .114 B2
　Herne Bay CT6. . . . . .22 D2
Poplar Field TN30. . . . . . .188 D4
Poplar Gr ME16 . . . . .74 C5
Poplar La TN29 . . . . .205 D7
Poplar Rd
　Broadstairs CT10. . . . . . .29 E6
　Ramsgate CT11 . . . . .52 D7
　Wittersham TN30. . . . . .188 D4
Poplar Row CT17 . . . . .27 E5
Poplars TN26 . . . . .182 A7
Poplars The
　Ashford TN23. . . . . .156 A7
　Bethersden TN26. . . . . .153 E5
　Hersden CT3 . . . . .46 F1
Poplar View ME13. . . . . . .63 E3
Poppy Cl
　Gillingham ME7 . . . . .10 E5
　Maidstone ME16 . . . . . .74 D3
Poppy Cres ME12 . . . . .4 A4
Poppyfield TN31 . . . . .197 C1
Poppy Mead TN23. . . . . .156 C2
Popsal La CT3 . . . . .91 B6
Porchester CI ME15. . . . . .97 A6
Portal House Sch CT15.. 151 A6
Port CI
　Chatham ME5. . . . . .32 B3
　Maidstone ME14 . . . . . .76 A5
Portobello Ct CT14 . . . . . .117 D7
Porter Cl ME12 . . . . .4 A6
Porter's La ME13 . . . . .62 B2
Porters Wlk ME17 . . . . . . .98 E4
Portery The CT14 . . . . . . .117 D6
Portland Ave ME10 . . . . . .37 C4
Portland Cl
　Ashford TN24. . . . . .139 C7
　Hythe CT21. . . . . .176 B2
Portland Ct **3**
　3 Hythe CT21. . . . . . .176 B2
　Ramsgate CT11 . . . . .52 E7
Portland Rd
　Gillingham ME7 . . . . .10 E6
　Hythe CT21. . . . . .176 B2
Portland Sq CT1. . . . . .88 B7
Portland St **1** ME4 . . . . .10 B2
Portland Terr
　Ripple CT14 . . . . .133 D8
　Sheerness ME12 . . . . .1 D2
Portlight Pl CT5 . . . . .43 A6
Port Lympne Wild Animal
　Pk* CT21. . . . . .174 D2
Portree Mews CT1 . . . . . . .67 B2
Port Richborough Bsns Pk
　CT13. . . . . .73 A7
Port Rise ME4 . . . . .9 F3
Portsdown CI ME16 . . . . . .74 B2
Portway CT5. . . . . .43 C8
Post Barn Rd ME4 . . . . .9 F2
Postley Ind Ctr ME15. . . . .75 A2
Postley Rd ME15 . . . . .75 A1
POSTLING 160 F2
Postling TN23 . . . . .138 E1
Postling Rd CT19 . . . . . . .177 E7
Postling Wents CT21 . . . .175 F8
Postmill Dr ME15 . . . . .74 F1
Post Office Row CT14. . . . .84 D1
Pot Kiln La TN26 . . . . .152 E4
POTTEN STREET 25 D3
Potten Street Rd CT7 . . . .25 E3
Potteries The ME9 . . . . . . .12 C3
Potters CT TN24 . . . . .138 E6
Potters Cnr TN24 . . . . . . .138 E6
POTTERS CORNER. 138 F6
POTTER'S FORSTAL 118 B2
Potter St CT13. . . . . .73 A1
Pottery Cotts TN25 . . . . .140 E5
Potyn Ho ME1 . . . . .9 C4
Pouces Cotts CT12. . . . . . .27 F1
Poulders Gdns CT13 . . . . .93 E8
Poulders Rd CT13 . . . . . . .93 E8
Poulsen Ct **8** ME7 . . . . . .37 B4
Poulton CI CT17 . . . . .165 F8
Poulton Close Bsns Pk
　CT17. . . . . .148 E1
Poulton La CT3 . . . . .92 C8
Pound Ct TN23. . . . . .156 A3
Pound Farm Cotts CT18. 177 A7

Pound Ho TN23. . . . . .156 B8
Poundhurst Rd TN26. . . .171 C3
Pound La
　Ashford TN23. . . . . .155 F4
　Brabourne Lees TN25 . .158 F5
　Canterbury CT1 . . . . .66 F1
　Elham CT4 . . . . .144 F4
　Molash CT4 . . . . .105 F4
Pound Way CT10. . . . . . . .178 Q8
Powell Rd ME20 . . . . .53 A3
Powell Cotton Dr CT7 . . . .27 B5
Powell Cotton Mus* CT7..27 B5
Powerhub Bsns Ctr ME16..74 F7
Power Station Rd ME12....3 E7
Pragma Rd ME20 . . . . .53 A3
PRATLING STREET. 53 C4
Precincts The CT1 . . . . . . .88 A8
Premier Bsns Ctr ME4 . . .10 C1
Premier Way ME10. . . . . . .36 C5
Prentis Cl ME13 . . . . .36 C5
Prentis Quay ME10. . . . . . .36 F5
Prescott Cl CT15. . . . . . . .149 E6
Prescott Ho TN28 . . . . . .202 A7
Prestedge Ave CT11. . . . . .29 E7
PRESTON
　Ash 70 B6
　Faversham. 62 D6
Preston Ave
　Faversham ME13 . . . . . . .62 E5
　Gillingham ME7 . . . . .10 E1
Preston Ct ME13. . . . . .62 D6
Preston Gr ME13. . . . . .62 D6
Preston Hall Gdns ME12....6 E4
Preston Hill CT3 . . . . .70 B5
Preston La
　Faversham ME13 . . . . . . .62 D6
　Preston CT3. . . . . .70 B5
Preston Malt Ho ME13 . . .62 D6
Preston Pk ME13 . . . . .62 E5
Preston PK Mews CT3 . . .70 C6
Preston Prim Sch CT3 . . .70 C6
Preston Rd
　Manston CT12 . . . . .28 E2
　Stourmouth CT3. . . . . . . .48 D1
　Wingham CT3 . . . . .70 B3
Preston St ME13 . . . . .62 D7
Preston Way ME8 . . . . .11 E2
Pretoria Ho **8** ME15 . . . .97 E5
Pretoria Rd
　Canterbury CT1 . . . . .88 B8
　Chatham ME4. . . . . .9 F2
　Gillingham ME7 . . . . .10 D3
Price's Ave
　Margate CT9 . . . . .8 B2
　Ramsgate CT11 . . . . .52 C6
Prices Ct **5** ME10 . . . . . .37 B4
Priest Ave CT2 . . . . .87 C7
Priestdale Ct ME4 . . . . .9 E3
Priestfield Rd ME7 . . . . . . .10 E5
Priestfields ME1 . . . . .9 C1
Priest Fields CT6 . . . . .23 F5
Priestfield Stad (Gillingham
　FC) ME7 . . . . .10 E5
Priest & Sow Cnr CT5. . . .21 B3
Priest Wlk CT5 . . . . .21 C3
Primrose Ave ME8 . . . . . . .33 B5
Primrose Cl ME4. . . . . .31 E7
Primrose Dr TN23. . . . . . .156 B4
Primrose Gr ME9 . . . . .58 A6
Primrose Hill CT4 . . . . .86 B7
Primrose Ho **10** ME15 . .97 E7
Primrose La ME9 . . . . .58 A6
Primrose Pl CT17 . . . . . . .149 A1
Primrose Rd CT17 . . . . . .149 A1
Primrose Way
　Cliffs End CT12 . . . . .51 C5
　Whitstable CT5 . . . . .21 C1
Prince Andrew Rd CT10. . .29 E7
Prince Arthur Rd ME7. . . .10 B6
Prince Charles Ave
　Chatham ME5. . . . . .32 B4
　Minster (Sheppey) ME12....4 C6
　Sittingbourne ME10 . . . .37 C3
Prince Charles Rd CT10 . .29 E7
Prince of Wales Rdbt
　CT17. . . . . .166 D6
Prince of Wales Residential
　Pk CT21. . . . . .187 E8
Prince of Wales Terr
　CT14. . . . . .117 D5
Princes Ave
　Chatham ME5. . . . . .32 B5
　Minster (Sheppey) ME12....4 D7
Prince's Ave CT12 . . . . . . .29 B1
Princes Cl CT7 . . . . .26 D7
Princes Cres **10** CT9 . . . .7 J2
Princes Dr CT13 . . . . .95 A8
Princes Gate **18** CT20 . .178 E5
Prince's Gdns CT9 . . . . .8 C2
Princes Par CT21 . . . . . . .176 E2
PRINCES PARK 32 B6
Princes Rd CT11. . . . . .52 D8
Princess Anne Rd CT10 . .29 E7
Princess Cl CT5. . . . . .21 C3
Princess Margaret Ave
　Margate CT9 . . . . .7 J1
　Ramsgate CT12 . . . . .29 A1
Princess Mary Ave ME4 . .10 B7
Princess Rd CT5 . . . . .21 D3
Princess St CT19 . . . . . . .178 E6
Princes St
　Deal CT14 . . . . .117 D7
　11 Dover CT16. . . . . .166 D7
　Maidstone ME14 . . . . . .75 A5
Prince's St
　Margate CT9 . . . . .7 J2
　9 Ramsgate CT11 . . . .52 C6
　Rochester ME1 . . . . .9 C4

Princes Terr CT21 . . . . .175 F1
Princes Way
Canterbury CT2 . . . . .66 E1
Detling ME14 . . . . .55 A1
Prince's Wlk CT9 . . . . .8 D3
Prince William Ct CT14 . .117 D2
Prinys Dr ME8 . . . . .33 C4
Prioress Rd CT12 . . . . .87 D8
Prioress Wlk CT16 . . . . . . .149 A3
Prior Pl ME1 . . . . .9 B1
Prior Rd TN28 . . . . .206 E8
Prior's Lees ◨ CT20 . . . . .178 D4
Priory Rd
Broadstairs CT10 . . . . .29 F3
East Farleigh ME15 . . . . . . .96 B8
New Romney TN28 . . . . . .201 F6
Priory Ct
Gillingham ME8 . . . . .11 A2
Leysdown-on-Sea ME12 . . .6 G1
Rochester ME1 . . . . .9 D5
Priory Ctyd CT11 . . . . .52 D6
Priory Fields Sch CT11 . . .166 B8
Priory Gate ◪ ME14 . . . . .75 A5
Priory Gate Rd CT17 . . . . .166 C8
Priory Gdns
Canterbury CT1 . . . . .88 A6
Folkestone CT20 . . . . .178 D4
Priory Gr CT17 . . . . .166 C8
Priory Hill CT17 . . . . .166 C8
Priory Ho CT17 . . . . .166 C7
Priory Inf Sch CT11 . . . . . .52 D7
Priory La
Herne Bay CT6 . . . . .23 A3
Sellindge TN25 . . . . .159 D3
Pk of St Jacob CT1 . . . . . .87 E6
Priory Pl ME13 . . . . .40 C1
Priory Rd
Aldington TN25 . . . . .172 C4
Dover CT16, CT17 . . . . . . .166 C8
Faversham ME13 . . . . .62 C8
Gillingham ME8 . . . . .11 A2
Maidstone ME15 . . . . .75 A3
Ramsgate CT11 . . . . .52 D6
Rochester ME2 . . . . .9 A6
Priory Row ME13 . . . . .62 C8
Priory St ◪ CT16 . . . . .166 D8
Priory Station Approach Rd
CT17 . . . . .166 C8
Priory The TN29 . . . . .205 C6
Priory Way TN30 . . . . .179 C7
Pritchard Ct CT18 . . . . . . .163 A4
Probyn Mews CT18 . . . . . .162 F3
Proctor ME4 . . . . .162 F4
Progress Est The ME15 . . .198 A4
Promenade
Birchington CT7 . . . . .26 F8
Deal CT14 . . . . .117 D3
Promenade The ME12 . . . . .6 G2
Prospect Ave ◪ ME2 . . . . .9 B8
Prospect Cl CT18 . . . . .27 E7
Prospect Cotts
Boughton Lees TN25 . . . . .122 E3
Harbledown CT2 . . . . .65 E1
Shepherdswell CT15 . . . . .130 D4
Prospect Ct ◨ CT11 . . . . .52 E6
Prospect Gdns CT12 . . . . . .50 B7
Prospect Hill CT6 . . . . .23 A5
Prospect Mews CT11 . . . . .176 C2
Prospect Pl
◨ Broadstairs CT10 . . . . .30 B4
Canterbury CT1 . . . . .88 A7
Dover CT17 . . . . .149 B1
Eastling ME13 . . . . .81 E6
Hamstreet TN26 . . . . .182 F7
Maidstone ME14 . . . . .74 E3
St Nicholas at Wade CT7 . .25 E1
Prospect Rd
Birchington CT7 . . . . .26 F7
Broadstairs CT10 . . . . .30 B4
Folkestone CT20 . . . . .177 D3
Hythe CT21 . . . . .176 C2
Minster (Thanet) CT12 . . . .50 B6
Prospect Terr
Elham CT4 . . . . .144 F4
◪ Ramsgate CT11 . . . . . . .52 E6
Prospect Way TN25 . . . . . .158 E5
Provender La ME13, ME9 . . .61 A6
Provender Way ME14 . . . . .75 E5
Providence St TN23 . . . . . .156 C4
Puckle La CT1 . . . . .88 A6
Pudding La
Ash CT3 . . . . .71 D1
Maidstone ME14 . . . . .74 F4
Pudding Rd ME8 . . . . .33 F8
Puffin Ct CT18 . . . . .163 A3
Puffin Rd CT6 . . . . .23 F4
Pullman Cl CT12 . . . . .52 A8
Pump La
Gillingham ME7, ME8 . . . .11 D3
◨ Margate CT9 . . . . .7 J2
Purbeck Rd ME4 . . . . .9 E2
Purchas Ct CT2 . . . . .66 C4
Purchase La TN26 . . . . . . .154 E8
Purr Wood CT4 . . . . .107 B2
Purser Way ME7 . . . . .10 C2
Puttney Dr ME10 . . . . .37 A8
Pye Alley La CT5 . . . . .43 C3
Pymps Court Farm Ctr*
ME15 . . . . .96 E6
Pynson's Ind Est CT10 . . . .29 D4
Pyott Mews ◪ CT1 . . . . . . .67 B1
Pyrus Cl ME5 . . . . .54 A8
Pyson's Road Ind Est
CT10 . . . . .29 D3

Q

Quain Ct CT20 . . . . .178 C4
Quantock Dr TN24 . . . . . . .139 B4
Quantock Gdns CT12 . . . . .29 B3
Quarries The ME17 . . . . .97 C4
Quarrington La TN25 . . . . .158 B8
Quarry Cotts TN30 . . . . . .189 C3
Quarry Rd
Hythe CT21 . . . . .176 B3
Maidstone ME15 . . . . .75 A2
Quarry Sq ME14 . . . . .75 A2
Quarry View TN23 . . . . . . .155 D7
Quarry Wlk CT21 . . . . .177 A3
Quarry Wood TN25 . . . . . .173 A6
Quay Cotts ME9 . . . . .38 E6
Quay Ct CT5 . . . . .20 E2
Quay La
Faversham ME13 . . . . .62 D8
Sandwich CT13 . . . . .73 A1
Quayside ME4 . . . . .10 B8
Quay The ME9 . . . . .38 E6
Queen Anne Rd ME14 . . . . .74 E5
Queen Bertha Rd CT11 . . . .52 C6
Queen Bertha's Ave CT7 . .27 C8
QUEENBOROUGH 3 A5
Queenborough Dr ME12 . . .4 B7
Queenborough Fst Sch
ME11 . . . . .3 B5
Queenborough Rd
Halfway Houses ME12 . . . . .4 A6
Queenborough ME11 . . . . . .3 C4
Queenborough Sta ME11 . . .3 A4
Queendown Ave ME8 . . . . .33 D5
Queendown Rd CT7 . . . . . .28 A8
Queendown Warren Nature
Reserve* ME9 . . . . .34 B3
Queen Elizabeth Ave CT9 . .8 D1
Queen Elizabeth Rd
CT16 . . . . .166 F8
Queen Elizabeth's Gram Sch
ME13 . . . . .62 D8
Queen Elizabeth Sq ME15 .97 D6
Queen Elizabeth the Queen
Mother Hospl CT9 . . . . . .28 F8
Queen Mother Ct CT14 . .117 D2
Queen Mother Ct The ME1 . .9 B4
Queens Ave
Canterbury CT2 . . . . .66 E1
Dover CT17 . . . . .166 A7
Folkestone CT20 . . . . .177 B6
Herne Bay CT6 . . . . .23 D5
Queen's Ave
Birchington CT7 . . . . .26 D7
Broadstairs CT10 . . . . .30 B6
Maidstone ME16 . . . . .74 D5
Margate CT9 . . . . .8 A3
Ramsgate CT12 . . . . .29 B1
Queensbridge Dr CT6 . . . . .22 C4
Queens Ct
Ashford TN24 . . . . .139 C3
Gillingham ME8 . . . . .34 A8
◪ Hythe CT21 . . . . .176 B1
Margate CT9 . . . . .7 J3
Queen's Ct CT5 . . . . .23 A4
Queensdown Rd CT14 . . . .134 D4
Queensgate ME16 . . . . .74 D5
Queens Gate Rd CT11 . . . . .52 C8
Queens Gdns
Broadstairs CT10 . . . . .30 B3
Herne Bay CT6 . . . . .22 F5
Queen's Gdns CT16, CT17 .166 D8
Queens Ho ME14 . . . . .74 B3
Queen's Lea CT15 . . . . . . .164 E5
Queens Lodge CT9 . . . . .8 A3
Queens Mews CT14 . . . . .117 D6
Queens Par
◪ Faversham ME13 . . . . . .62 D7
Margate CT9 . . . . .8 A3
Queen's Prom CT9 . . . . .8 B3
Queens Rd
Aylesham CT3 . . . . .112 F5
Minster (Sheppey) ME12 . . .4 D7
Whitstable CT5 . . . . .21 A2
Queen's Rd
Ash CT3 . . . . .71 D2
Ashford TN24 . . . . .140 A1
Broadstairs CT10 . . . . .30 B4
Chatham ME5 . . . . .10 D1
Faversham ME13 . . . . .62 D7
Gillingham ME7 . . . . .10 C7
Littlestone-on-Sea TN28 . .202 D6
Lydd TN29 . . . . .205 C6
Maidstone ME16 . . . . .74 C4
Ramsgate CT11 . . . . .52 F7
Westgate on Sea CT8 . . . . .27 F8
Queen's Rise CT14 . . . . . . .133 F5
Queens Rd
◪ Canterbury CT1 . . . . . .67 B1
Maidstone ME15 . . . . .75 A2
Queens St
Ashford TN24 . . . . .139 B2
Chatham ME4 . . . . .10 A4
Deal CT14 . . . . .117 D6
Dover CT16, CT17 . . . . . .166 D7
Folkestone CT20 . . . . .178 E5
Herne Bay CT6 . . . . .22 F5
Margate CT9 . . . . .7 I2
Ramsgate CT11 . . . . .52 E6
Rochester ME1 . . . . .9 C4
Queens The CT14 . . . . .117 D5
Queensway
Dymchurch TN29 . . . . . . .186 E2
Lydd TN29 . . . . .205 C6
Queens Way ME14 . . . . . . .55 A1
Queen's Way ME12 . . . . .3 A8
Queenswood Rd ME20 . . . . .53 D7

R

Rabbit Hole CT4 . . . . .129 A7
Radcliffe Ct CT21 . . . . . . .176 B2
RADFALL 44 C5
Radfall Cnr CT5 . . . . .44 C6
Radfall Gate CT5 . . . . .44 C6
Radfall Hill CT5 . . . . .44 C5
Radfall Rd CT5 . . . . .44 D4
Radfall Ride CT5 . . . . .44 C5
RADFIELD 38 A2
Radleigh Gdns ME1 . . . . . . .9 E1
Radley Cl CT10 . . . . .30 A6
Radnor Bridge Rd CT19,
CT20 . . . . .178 E5
Radnor Chambers ◨
CT20 . . . . .178 D4
Radnor Cl
Herne Bay CT6 . . . . .23 B1
Maidstone ME14 . . . . .74 E7
Radnor Cliff CT20 . . . . .178 A3
Radnor Cliff Cres CT20 . . .178 A3
Radnor Park Ave CT19 . . . .178 C6
Radnor Park Cres CT19 . . .178 C5
Radnor Park Gdns CT19 . . .178 C5
Radnor Park Ho CT19 . . . . .178 C6
Radnor Park Rd CT19 . . . . .178 C6
Radnor Park W CT19 . . . . .178 B5
Radnor St ◪ CT19 . . . . . . .178 E5
RAF Manston Spitfire &
Hurricane Meml Mus*
CT12 . . . . .28 A2
Raggatt Pl ME15 . . . . .75 B2
Raglan Pl ◪ CT10 . . . . .30 B4
Ragstone Fields ME15 . . . . .97 E4
Ragstone Hollow TN25 . . . .173 A6
Ragstone Rd ME15 . . . . . . .76 A2
Railway Ave CT5 . . . . .20 E1
Railway Cotts ME9 . . . . . . .38 D3
Railway Hill CT4 . . . . .128 E8
Railway Rd ME12 . . . . .1 C2
Railway St
Chatham ME4 . . . . .9 F4
Gillingham ME7 . . . . .10 D6
Railway Street Ind Pk
ME7 . . . . .10 D6
Railway Terr
Margate CT9 . . . . .7 H1
Queenborough ME11 . . . . . .3 A5
RAINHAM 33 E8
Rainham Cl ME15 . . . . .75 A1
Rainham Mark Gram Sch
ME8 . . . . .11 D2
Rainham Rd ME5 . . . . .10 C3
Rainham Sch for Girls
ME8 . . . . .33 C8
Rainham Sta ME8 . . . . .11 F1
Raite Gn ◪ ME10 . . . . .36 D6
Raleigh Cl
Ashford TN24 . . . . .157 A8
Chatham ME5 . . . . .32 A6
Raleigh Ct ◪ CT1 . . . . .67 B5
Raleigh Way ME12 . . . . .3 E6
Ramillies Cl ME5 . . . . .32 A6
Ram La TN25, TN27 . . . . . .137 C8
RAM LANE 120 E2
Ramp A CT16 . . . . .166 H8
Ramp B CT16 . . . . .166 G8
Ramp C CT16 . . . . .166 G8
Ramp D CT16 . . . . .166 H8
Rampion Cl ME14 . . . . .75 E5
Ramsey Cl
Canterbury CT2 . . . . .66 E1
Maidstone ME15 . . . . .75 A2
Ramsey Ho
◪ Canterbury CT1 . . . . . .87 F7
Deal CT14 . . . . .117 C3
RAMSGATE 52 C4
Ramsgate Holy Trinity Prim
Sch CT12 . . . . .30 A1
Ramsgate Maritime Mus*
CT12 . . . . .52 E6
Ramsgate Rd
Broadstairs CT10 . . . . .30 B4
Broadstairs, Dumpton CT10,
CT11 . . . . .29 F2
Margate CT10, CT9 . . . . . .29 A6
Sandwich CT13 . . . . .73 A7
Ramsgate Sports Ctr
CT11 . . . . .52 D7
Ramsgate Sta CT12 . . . . . . .52 C8
Ramstone Cl TN25 . . . . . . .158 E5

R (continued)

Rancorn Rd CT9 . . . . .7 G1
Randall Rd ME4 . . . . .9 F3
Randalls Row ME15 . . . . . . .96 F5
Randall St ME15 . . . . .74 F6
Randle Way ME9 . . . . .37 E2
Randolph Cl CT1 . . . . .88 A7
Randolph Ct CT8 . . . . .7 C1
Randolph Gdns TN25 . . . . .156 E3
Randolph Ho
◩ Folkestone CT20 . . . . .178 E5
Gillingham ME7 . . . . .10 C5
Randolph La TN31 . . . . . . .197 B3
Randolph Rd
Dover CT17 . . . . .149 B1
Gillingham ME7 . . . . .10 C5
Randolph Sq CT9 . . . . .7 J3
Ranelagh Gdns ◧ CT10 . . .29 E5
Ranelagh Gr CT10 . . . . .29 E5
Ranelagh Rd
Deal CT14 . . . . .117 D5
Sheerness ME12 . . . . .1 D2
Range Rd
Eastchurch ME12 . . . . .5 D1
Hythe CT21 . . . . .176 B1
Range Road Ind Est
CT21 . . . . .176 B1
Ransley Gn TN26 . . . . .183 F8
Ransome Way CT7 . . . . .26 F6
Rare Species Conservation
Area* CT13 . . . . .93 E6
Raspberry Hill La ME9 . . . .14 D6
RATLING 113 A8
Ratling Rd CT3 . . . . .112 F7
Rattington St CT4 . . . . .86 E2
Ravelin Ho ME12 . . . . .1 D2
Ravenlea Rd CT20 . . . . . . .178 A5
Ravensbourne Ave CT6 . . . .23 B3
Ravenscourt Rd
Deal CT14 . . . . .117 C5
Rough Common CT2 . . . . .66 B3
Ravens Dane Cl ME15 . . . . .76 A1
Ravenswood Ave ◧ ME2 . . .9 B8
Rawdon Rd
Maidstone ME15 . . . . .75 A3
Ramsgate CT11 . . . . .52 C6
Rawling St ME9 . . . . .58 F3
Rayham Rd CT5 . . . . .44 A8
Rayleigh Cl ME16 . . . . .74 D7
Rayleigh Ho ◪ ME15 . . . . .97 D8
Raymer Rd ME14 . . . . .75 B8
Raymond Ave CT1 . . . . .88 A8
Raymond Fuller Way
TN24 . . . . .139 E4
Raymoor Ave TN29 . . . . . .195 A4
Rayner Hill Cotts ME17 . . .102 C5
Rayners Hill ME17 . . . . . . .102 C5
Raywood Office Complex
TN27 . . . . .120 B4
Reach Cl CT15 . . . . .150 F5
Reachfields CT21 . . . . .176 A1
Reach Mdw CT15 . . . . .151 A6
Reach Rd
Lympne CT21 . . . . .174 D2
St Margaret's at Cliffe
CT15 . . . . .150 F5
Reactor One Rd TN29 . . . .209 C3
Reactor Two Rd TN29 . . . .209 C2
Readers La TN31 . . . . .196 F5
Reading Cl CT4 . . . . .117 B1
Reading Ho ◪ ME15 . . . . . .97 F5
Reading Rd CT17 . . . . .165 F7
Reading St
Broadstairs CT10 . . . . .29 F8
Tenterden TN30 . . . . .180 C2
READING STREET
Broadstairs 29 F7
Tenterden 180 C2
Reading Street Rd CT10,
CT9 . . . . .29 F7
Readscroft Rd ME8 . . . . . . .33 D5
Realgar Ct ◪ ME10 . . . . . . .36 D6
Reams Way ME10 . . . . .15 A1
Rebecca Ct ◪ CT19 . . . . . . .8 B2
Recca La CT5, CT18 . . . . . .146 A4
Recreation Cl ME14 . . . . . .75 B6
Recreation Ground Rd
TN30 . . . . .179 B7
Recreation Way ME10 . . . . .15 A1
Rectory Bglws TN26 . . . . . .169 F8
Rectory Cl TN26 . . . . .169 A2
Rectory Gdns CT5 . . . . .21 D2
Rectory Grange ME1 . . . . . . .9 C2
Rectory La
Barham CT4 . . . . .112 A2
Harrietsham ME17 . . . . . .100 E5
Hythe CT21 . . . . .176 B5
Lyminge CT18 . . . . .161 C6
Maidstone ME16 . . . . .74 A1
Rectory Rd
Broadstairs CT10 . . . . .30 B5
Deal CT14 . . . . .116 F4
Sittingbourne ME10 . . . . . .37 B3
St Mary in the Marsh TN29 .194 B4
Rectory Way TN24 . . . . . . .139 C5
Rectory Wlk TN26 . . . . . . .183 A7
RECULVER 24 D7
Reculver CE Prim Sch
CT6 . . . . .24 A4
Reculver Ct CT6 . . . . .24 B5
Reculver Ctry Pk* CT6 . . . .24 B6
Reculver La CT6 . . . . .24 B5
Reculver Rd CT6 . . . . .24 B6
Reculvers Rd CT8 . . . . .27 F7
Reculver Towers and Roman
Fort* CT6 . . . . .24 D7
Reculver Wlk ME15 . . . . . . .97 F7

Redan Pl ME12 . . . . .1 E2
Red Barn La CT15 . . . . . . .147 E3
Redberry Rd TN23 . . . . . . .156 B5
Red Brick Cotts ME13 . . . . .85 A6
Redbridge Cl ME5 . . . . .32 C4
Redbrook St TN26 . . . . . . .168 D5
Redbrooks Way CT21 . . . . .175 F2
Redcliffe La ME14 . . . . .75 B7
Redcot La CT2 . . . . .68 B7
Redfern Ave ME7 . . . . .10 E5
Redhill Rd CT8 . . . . .27 E8
Red Ho The TN28 . . . . .202 E6
Redhouse Farm CT14 . . . . .95 B1
Redhouse La CT4 . . . . .109 D6
Redhouse Wall CT14 . . . . . .95 B1
Redington TN24 . . . . .139 C3
Redlands Ct CT17 . . . . .148 E4
Redland Shaw ME4 . . . . .9 E1
Red Lion Ct ◧ CT21 . . . . . .176 B2
Red Lion Ct ◨ CT15 . . . . . .130 D2
Red Lion Sq ◪ CT14 . . . . . .176 B2
Redmill Ct CT20 . . . . .177 E5
Redoubt Way TN29 . . . . . . .187 B4
Red Rd CT2 . . . . .66 B4
Red Robin Cotts ME9 . . . . .35 B6
Redruth Manor ◪ ME7 . . . .10 C6
Redsells ME15 . . . . .76 A1
Redsull Ave CT14 . . . . .117 A3
Red Tree Orch TN23 . . . . . .155 E7
Redvers Cotts CT16 . . . . . .148 E5
Redvers Rd ME4 . . . . .10 A2
Redwing Cl CT18 . . . . .163 A3
Redwing Rd ME5 . . . . .32 B7
Redwood Cl
Canterbury CT2 . . . . .66 E2
Chartham CT4 . . . . .86 E1
Chatham ME5 . . . . .32 B2
Redwood Ct TN24 . . . . .140 A1
Redyear Cotts TN24 . . . . . .140 A1
Redyear Ct CT9 . . . . .7 J1
Reece Adams Ho CT18 . . . .164 B3
Reed Ave CT1 . . . . .67 D3
Reed Cres TN23 . . . . .156 C3
Reedland Cres CT14 . . . . . .62 C8
Reedmace Cl TN23 . . . . . . .155 D8
Reeds Cl CT6 . . . . .23 C4
Reeves Alley ◧ CT5 . . . . . .20 D1
Reeves Cl CT2 . . . . .87 C8
Reeves Pas ◪ CT9 . . . . .62 C7
Reeves Way CT5 . . . . .21 C2
Reeves Yd CT5 . . . . .20 D2
Reform Rd ME4 . . . . .10 B2

Regency Cl
Gillingham ME8 . . . . .33 C3
Sheerness ME12 . . . . .1 B3
Whitstable CT5 . . . . .43 F7
Regency Ct ME10 . . . . .36 D4
Regency Pl CT1 . . . . .67 B2
Regency Sch of English
CT11 . . . . .52 D5
Regency Villas CT4 . . . . . .129 C5
Regent Dr ME15 . . . . .97 A8
Regent Rd ME7 . . . . .10 C4
Regents Ct ◪ TN23 . . . . . . .139 B2
Regents Pl TN23 . . . . .139 B2
Regent St CT5 . . . . .20 D2
Regents Wlk CT9 . . . . .23 D5
Reginald Rd ME14 . . . . .74 E3
Regis Bsns Pk ME12 . . . . . . .1 B1
Regis Cres ME10 . . . . .36 F7
Regis Ind Est ME12 . . . . . . .3 A8
Regis Manor Com Prim Sch
ME10 . . . . .36 E7
Reinden Gr ME15 . . . . .75 F1
Remston Mews ◪ CT7 . . . .67 B2
Remus Cl TN23 . . . . .155 F4
Renault Cl CT16 . . . . .22 A4
Rendezvous St CT20 . . . . .178 D5
Rendezvous The CT9 . . . . . .7 I3
Renown Rd ME5 . . . . .32 C2
Rentain Rd CT4 . . . . .86 D2
Repton Cl CT10 . . . . .29 F6
Repton Manor Rd TN23 . . .139 A3
Repton Way ME5 . . . . .31 F4
Reservoir Ave TN29 . . . . . .209 D2
Reservoir Rd CT5 . . . . .20 E2
Resolution Cl ME5 . . . . .32 A6
Rest Harrow ME13 . . . . .83 C5
Restharrow Rd ME14 . . . . . .75 E4
Retreat The
Birchington CT7 . . . . .27 B8
Doddington ME9 . . . . .80 D7
Ramsgate CT12 . . . . .52 B8
Rettenden Dr ME10 . . . . . . .36 F8
Revenge Rd ME5 . . . . .54 C8
Reynolds Cl CT6 . . . . .23 B4
Reynolds La CT3 . . . . .24 D3
Rhee Wall TN26 . . . . .190 C7
Rheims Ct CT2 . . . . .66 D1
Rheims Way CT1, CT2 . . . . .87 C8
Rhodaus Cl CT1 . . . . .87 F7
Rhodaus Ho CT1 . . . . .87 F7
Rhodaus Town CT1 . . . . . . .87 F7
RHODE COMMON 85 A6
Rhodes Gdns CT10 . . . . . . .30 A6
Rhodes Ho ◪ ME5 . . . . . . .10 C2
RHODES MINNIS 144 A3
Rhode St ME14 . . . . .74 A4
Rhodewood Cl ME14 . . . . . .16 A1
Ribston Way TN23 . . . . . . .155 B8
Richard Ct ◪ CT1 . . . . .88 B2
Richardson Way CT12 . . . . .51 D5
Richard St
Chatham ME4 . . . . .9 F4
Rochester ME1 . . . . .9 C3
Richborough Rd CT8 . . . . . .27 F7

Richborough Roman Fort★
CT13. . . . . .72 E5
Richborough Way TN23 . .155 E5
Richburgh Rd CT13 . . . . .72 E3
Richdore Rd CT4 . . . . . . .125 C6
Richmond Ave CT9 . . . . . . .8 B1
Richmond Cl ME5 . . . . . . .32 B4
Richmond Ct CT16 . . . . . .149 D1
Richmond Dr
  Herne Bay CT6 . . . . .23 E5
  New Romney TN28 . . . . .202 C8
  Sittingbourne ME10 . . . . .36 E7
Richmond First Sch ME12 . .1 E2
Richmond Gdns CT2 . . . . .66 C2
Richmond Ho 20 CT20. . .178 E5
Richmond Meech Dr
  TN24 . . . . .139 E4
Richmond Rd
  Gillingham ME7 . . . . .10 C2
  Ramsgate CT11 . . . . .52 D6
  Whitstable CT5 . . . . .21 B1
Richmond St
  Folkestone CT19 . . . . . . .177 D6
  Herne Bay CT6 . . . . .22 F5
  Sheerness ME12 . . . . .1 E2
Richmond Way ME7 . . . . .97 A8
Riddles Rd ME10, ME9 . . .36 C3
Ridge Meadow Prim Sch
  ME5 . . . . .31 F6
RIDGE ROW 145 E1
Ridge The TN24 . . . . .139 E6
Ridgeway CT21 . . . . .175 D3
Ridgeway Cliff CT6 . . . . . .22 C5
Ridgeway Rd CT6 . . . . . . .46 A7
Ridgeway Terr TN25 . . . . .158 C5
Ridgeway The
  Boughton Street ME13 . . .64 A3
  Broadstairs CT10 . . . . . . .29 F3
  Chatham ME4 . . . . .31 E7
  Crabble CT17 . . . . .148 E2
  Gillingham ME7 . . . . .10 C7
  Margate CT9 . . . . .8 B1
  Smeeth TN25 . . . . .158 A5
  Whitstable CT5 . . . . .21 B1
Ridgeway Wlk CT6 . . . . . .46 A7
Ridgway ME16 . . . . .74 B2
Ridham Ave ME10 . . . . . . .15 A1
Ridham Dock ME9 . . . . . .15 B6
Riding Hill TN24 . . . . . . .139 C6
Ridings The
  ☑ Canterbury CT1 . . . . . .67 B1
  Margate CT9 . . . . .8 F3
  Whitstable CT5 . . . . .21 D1
Ridlands CT1 . . . . .88 A5
Ridley Cl CT6 . . . . .46 A8
Ridley Rd ME1 . . . . .9 B4
Rigden Rd TN23. . . . . . . .156 B7
Rigden's Ct ☑ ME10 . . . . .36 E5
Rigshill Rd ME13 . . . . . . .103 B6
Riley Ave CT6 . . . . .21 F4
Rimpton Ct CT10 . . . . .29 F7
Ringlemere La CT13 . . . . .92 F6
RINGLESTONE
  Harrietsham 78 F4
  Maidstone 74 E7
Ringlestone Cres ME14 . . .74 F8
Ringlestone Rd ME17 . . . . .78 D4
Ringold Ave CT12 . . . . . . .52 A8
Ringsloe Ct CT7 . . . . .26 D8
Ringwood Cl
  Canterbury CT2 . . . . .66 E3
  Gillingham ME8 . . . . .33 D8
Ringwood Rd ME15 . . . . . .97 C8
RINGWOULD 133 F5
Ringwould Rd
  Kingsdown CT14 . . . . . . .134 B5
  Ringwould CT14, CT15 . .133 C8
Ripley Rd TN24 . . . . .157 A8
Ripon Cl ME8 . . . . .11 D3
Ripper's Cross TN26 . . . .137 D4
RIPPLE 133 D8
Ripple Cross CT14 . . . . . .133 E8
Ripple Rd CT14 . . . . .133 F7
Ripplevale Sch CT14 . . . .133 E8
Risborough La CT19,
  CT20. . . . . .177 D5
Risborough Way CT20. . . .177 E6
Risdon Cl CT2 . . . . .67 F6
Rise The
  Ashford TN23. . . . . .155 E2
  Borden ME9 . . . . .36 B2
  Chatham ME4. . . . . .10 A7
  Gillingham ME7 . . . . .33 A3
  Halfway Houses ME12. . . . .3 C5
  Kingsdown CT14 . . . . . . .134 D5
  Rochester ME1 . . . . .9 A1
  St Margaret's at Cliffe
    CT15. . . . . .151 B6
Rising Rd TN23 . . . . .139 A1
RIVER 148 E3
River Bank Cl ☑ ME15 . . .75 B4
Riverbank Way TN24 . . . .156 D6
Riverbourne Ct ☑ ME10 . .36 F4
River Cl ME15 . . . . .96 A7
River Ct
  Chartham CT4 . . . . .86 D3
  Crabble CT17 . . . . .148 F2
River Dale CT17 . . . . .148 F3
Riverdale Rd CT1 . . . . .67 B2
River Dr TN17 . . . . .148 F2
Riverhead Cl
  Maidstone ME16 . . . . . . .74 D6
  Margate CT9 . . . . .8 B1
  Sittingbourne ME10 . . . . .36 C3
River Mdw CT17 . . . . . . .148 F3

Rivermead Sch ME7 . . . . .10 E6
River Prim Sch CT17 . . . .148 E3
River Rd CT13 . . . . .73 B4
Riversdale Rd
  Ashford TN23. . . . . .156 C8
  Ramsgate CT12 . . . . .29 B1
Riverside
  Chartham CT4 . . . . .86 C3
  Crabble CT17 . . . . .148 F3
  Temple Ewell CT16 . . . . .148 C5
Riverside Bsns Pk TN24 . .139 D2
Riverside Cl
  Bridge CT4 . . . . .89 A1
  Kingsnorth TN23 . . . . . .156 A4
Riverside Ct ☑ CT17 . . . .148 F2
Riverside Ctry Pk & Visitor
  Ctr★ ME7 . . . . .11 D5
Riverside Ind Est CT21 . . .175 B1
Riverside Mews CT4 . . . . .89 A1
Riverside Pk ME1 . . . . . . .96 A8
Riverside Prim Sch ME8. . .12 A1
Riverside Rd CT13 . . . . . . .51 A1
Riverside Ret Pk ME7 . . . .87 D6
Rivers Rd ME4 . . . . .38 D2
River St
  ☑ Chatham ME7. . . . . . . .10 A6
  River CT17. . . . . .148 E3
Rivers Wlk ME17 . . . . . . .101 C5
Riverview TN23 . . . . .138 E1
River View
  Gillingham ME8 . . . . .11 D3
  Maidstone ME15 . . . . . . .74 F2
  Sturry CT2 . . . . .67 F7
River View Cl ☑ ME4 . . . . .9 F3
Riviera Ct ☑ CT20 . . . . . .177 E3
Riviera Rd CT20 . . . . .178 A3
Riviera The CT20 . . . . . . .177 F3
Roach St ME2 . . . . .9 A7
Road of Remembrance
  CT20. . . . . .178 D4
Robert Brundett Cl TN24 .139 E5
Robert Napier Sch The
  ME7 . . . . .10 E3
Roberts Cl ME10 . . . . .36 D7
Roberts Rd
  Gillingham ME8 . . . . .11 D3
  Greatstone-on-Sea TN28 . .202 E1
  Whitstable CT5 . . . . .42 F6
Robert St CT14 . . . . .117 D7
Robeshaw ME9 . . . . .58 E2
ROBHURST 168 C2
Robina Ct ☑ CT3 . . . . .8 D3
Robin Cl
  ☑ Rochester ME1. . . . . . . .9 D4
  Whitstable CT5 . . . . .21 A3
Robin Ho ☑ ME16 . . . . . .74 E4
Robin Hood La
  Chatham ME5. . . . . .31 D1
  Lydd TN29 . . . . .205 C5
Robin Hood Lane (Lower)
  ME5 . . . . .31 F2
Robin Hood Lane (Upper)
  ME5 . . . . .31 E1
Robin St ME14 . . . . .205 C6
Robins Ave ME17 . . . . . . .101 C5
Robins Cl ME17 . . . . .101 C4
Robin's Ct CT21 . . . . .187 C8
Robins Cse ME14 . . . . . . .75 B7
Robson's Yd CT17 . . . . . .166 C8
Robus Ct CT18 . . . . .161 C7
Robus Terr CT18 . . . . . . .161 C7
Roby Cotts TN26 . . . . . . .167 E8
ROCHESTER 9 A4
Rochester Airport ME1,
  ME5 . . . . .31 C6
Rochester Airport Ind Est
  ME1 . . . . .31 C5
Rochester Ave
  Canterbury CT1 . . . . .88 B7
  Rochester ME1 . . . . .9 C4
Rochester Castle★ ME1. . . .9 C4
Rochester Cath★ ME1. . . . .9 C4
Rochester Ct
  Canterbury CT1 . . . . .88 B6
  Rochester ME2 . . . . .9 B7
Rochester Gate ME1 . . . . . .9 D5
Rochester Ho ☑ ME15 . . .97 D7
Rochester Ind Coll ME1 . . .9 C5
Rochester St
  Burham ME1. . . . . .53 A8
  Chatham ME5, ME1 . . . . .31 C4
  Pratling Street ME20. . . . .53 B4
Rochester Stn ME1 . . . . . . .9 C5
Rock Ave ME7 . . . . .10 C3
Rock Hill Rd TN27 . . . . . .118 E2
Rockingham Pl CT16. . . . . .23 B2
Rock Rd
  Maidstone ME14 . . . . .75 A4
  Sittingbourne ME10. . . . . .36 E4
Rockstone Way CT12 . . . . .29 A1
Rockwell Ct ME15 . . . . . . .74 E1
Rocky Bourne Rd TN25 . .172 D5
Rocky Hill ME16 . . . . .74 E3
Rocky Hill Terr ☑ ME16 . .74 E4
Rodmer Rd ME20 . . . . .4 C8
RODMERSHAM 59 C8
Rodmersham Gn ME9 . . . .59 B7
RODMERSHAM GREEN . . .59 B7
Rodmersham Prim Sch
  ME9 . . . . .59 B7
Rodney St CT11. . . . . .52 D6
Roebuck Bsns Pk ME17 . .100 C5
Roebuck Ho ME1 . . . . .9 E5

Roebuck Rd
  Faversham ME13. . . . . . . .62 A7
  Rochester ME1 . . . . .9 C5
Roentgen Ho ME10 . . . . . .36 D5
Roethorne Gdns TN30. . . .179 B8
Roffen Rd ME1 . . . . .9 C2
Rogersmead ☑ TN30. . . .179 A7
Rokesley Rd CT16 . . . . . .149 B5
Rolfe La TN28. . . . . .202 B7
Roll's Ave CT5 . . . . .5 C1
Rolvenden Ave ME8 . . . . . .11 C3
Rolvenden Dr ME10 . . . . . .36 B5
Roly Eckhoff Ho CT16 . . .149 B3
Roman Amphitheatre★
  CT1. . . . . .72 E4
Roman Cl
  Chatham ME5. . . . . .31 D1
  Deal CT14 . . . . .117 B6
Roman Hts ME14 . . . . . . .75 C6
Roman Painted House★
  CT17. . . . . .166 D8
Roman Rd
  Canterbury CT4 . . . . .88 D4
  Dover CT16 . . . . .149 D2
  East Studdal CT15 . . . . . .132 C5
  Faversham ME13 . . . . . . .62 D7
  Ramsgate CT12 . . . . .29 C2
  Whitfield CT15 . . . . .149 D8
Roman Sq ME15 . . . . .36 F3
Roman Way
  Elvington CT15 . . . . .114 B2
  Folkestone CT19 . . . . . . .177 C6
  Maidstone ME15 . . . . . . .156 C4
  St Margaret's at Cliffe
    CT15. . . . . .150 F5
Romany Ct ME5 . . . . .10 D1
Romany Rd ME8 . . . . .11 C2
ROMDEN 135 C1
Romden Rd
  Smarden, Haffenden Quarter
    TN27 . . . . .152 B8
  Smarden, Romden TN27 . .135 D1
Rome House Cnr TN28 . . .202 A6
Rome Rd TN28 . . . . .202 A6
Rome Terr ME4 . . . . .9 F4
Romilly Gdns CT12 . . . . . .29 C2
Romney Ct CT20 . . . . . . .177 F5
Romney Cl
  ☑ Birchington CT7 . . . . . .27 A7
  Maidstone ME14 . . . . . . .76 A3
Romney Ct ME10. . . . . . . .36 E5
Romney, Hythe & Dymchurch
  Rly★ CT21 . . . . .176 A2
Romney Marsh Ho 195 C7
Romney Marsh Rd TN23,
  TN24 . . . . .156 B6
Romney Marsh Visitor Ctr★
  TN28 . . . . .194 D1
Romney Pl ME15. . . . . . . .75 A4
Romney Point TN25 . . . . .138 F4
Romney Rd
  Ashford TN24. . . . . .139 E1
  Chatham ME5. . . . . .32 B5
  Hamstreet TN26. . . . . . . .183 A7
  New Romney TN29 . . . . .201 E3
Romney Sands Sta★
  TN28 . . . . .206 E8
Romney Warren Ctry Pk★
  TN28 . . . . .194 D1
Romney Way CT21 . . . . . .175 F1
Romsey Cl TN24 . . . . .140 A2
Romulus Gdns TN23 . . . . .155 F4
Ronalds St ☑ ME10 . . . . . .37 A4
Rookery Cl
  Ashford TN24. . . . . .138 D3
  Breadgar ME9 . . . . .58 A6
Rookery View ME9 . . . . . . .14 D4
Rook La ME9 . . . . .35 F6
Rookston Cnr CT3 . . . . . . .48 D1
Rooks View ME9 . . . . .35 E6
Roonagh Ct ME10 . . . . . . .36 E2
Roosevelt Ave ME5. . . . . . .32 A8
Roosevelt Rd CT16 . . . . . .149 B3
Ropemakers Ct ME4 . . . . . .10 A1
Roper Cl
  Canterbury CT2 . . . . .66 C1
  Gillingham ME8 . . . . .33 C3
Roper Rd
  Canterbury CT2 . . . . .66 C1
  Teynham ME9. . . . . .38 D3
Rope Walk Mews CT13. . . .93 F8
Rope Wlk ME4 . . . . .9 F5
Rosamund Ct CT19. . . . . .178 C6
ROSEACRE 76 A4
Roseacre Cl CT2 . . . . .66 E3
Roseacre Ct CT9 . . . . .8 E2
Roseacre Gdns ME14 . . . . .76 A3
Roseacre Jun Sch ME14. . .76 A4
Roseacre La ME14 . . . . . . .76 A4
Rose Acre Rd CT3 . . . . . . .89 F7
Rosebery Ave
  Herne Bay CT6 . . . . .23 E5
  Ramsgate CT11 . . . . .29 F1
Rosebery Cl ME10 . . . . . . .37 D4
Rosebery Rd
  Chatham ME5. . . . . .9 E2
  Gillingham ME7 . . . . .10 D7
Rose Cotts
  Hythe CT21 . . . . .176 B4
  Lenham Heath ME17 . . . .119 B8
Rose Ct ME17 . . . . .96 D1
Rose Farm La TN27 . . . . .136 A5
Rose Gdns
  Birchington CT7 . . . . .26 F6
  Eythorne CT15 . . . . .131 D7

Rose Gdns continued
  Herne Bay CT6 . . . . .23 C4
  Minster (Thanet) CT12. . . .50 B6
Rose Hill
  ☑ Ramsgate CT11 . . . . . .52 E6
  Wittersham TN30. . . . . . .189 B5
Roseholme ME16 . . . . .74 D2
Rose La
  Bishopsbourne CT4 . . . . .111 C6
  Canterbury CT1 . . . . .87 F8
  Lenham Heath ME17 . . . .119 B8
Roselands CT14. . . . . .117 C1
Roselands Gdns CT2 . . . . .66 D2
Roselawn Gdns ☑ CT9. . . .28 B8
Roselea Ave CT6. . . . . .22 F3
Roseleigh Ave ME16 . . . . .74 C5
Roseleigh Rd ME10 . . . . . .36 D2
Rosemary Ave
  Broadstairs CT10. . . . . . . .30 A3
  Halfway Houses ME12. . . . .3 A4
Rosemary Cl ☑ ME5 . . . . .31 F4
Rosemary Cnr CT20 . . . . .199 D8
Rosemary Ct ☑ ME1 . . . . . .9 D4
Rosemary Gdns
  Broadstairs CT10. . . . . . . .29 F2
  Whitstable CT5 . . . . .44 A8
Rosemary La ☑ CT1 . . . . .87 F8
Rosemary Rd ME15 . . . . . .76 A3
Rosemount Cl ME15. . . . . .96 F4
Rose St
  Rochester ME1 . . . . .9 D3
  Sheerness ME12 . . . . .1 C2
Rose Street Sch ME12. . . . .1 C2
Rose Terr ME13 . . . . .62 D5
Rosetower Ct CT10 . . . . . .29 F8
Rose Wlk CT18 . . . . .163 A4
Rosewood Dr TN25. . . . . .138 F4
Rosewood Way CT7 . . . . . .27 B7
Rose Yd ME14 . . . . .75 A4
Rosiers Ct ☑ CT2. . . . . . . .66 E1
Rossendale Ct ☑ CT20. . .178 E6
Rossendale Gdns ☑
  CT20. . . . . .178 E6
Rossendale Rd CT20 . . . .178 E6
Rossetti Ct CT7. . . . . .26 F7
Rossetti Rd CT7 . . . . .26 F8
Ross Gdns CT2 . . . . .66 B3
Rossland Rd CT12. . . . . . .52 A8
Rosslyn Gn ME16 . . . . . . .74 B5
Ross St ME1 . . . . .9 D4
Ross Way CT20 . . . . .177 E5
Rotary Gdns ME7 . . . . . . .10 F2
Rothbrook Dr TN24 . . . . .139 C7
Rother Vale ME5. . . . . .32 C2
Rothley Ct CT11 . . . . .29 F1
Rothsay Ct CT11 . . . . .29 E1
ROUGH COMMON 66 B3
Rough Common Rd CT2. . .66 B3
Roundel Cl ME9 . . . . .38 D2
Roundel The ME10 . . . . . . .36 F2
Roundwell ME14 . . . . .76 D3
Round Wood Cl ME5 . . . . .32 A1
Rover Rd ME5 . . . . .32 B2
Rowan Cl
  Ashford TN23. . . . . .138 D2
  Staple CT3 . . . . .92 A6
  Sturry CT2 . . . . .67 F6
Rowan Ct
  Ashford TN24. . . . . .156 E8
  Broadstairs CT10. . . . . . . .30 A5
Rowan Ho
  ☑ Chatham ME5. . . . . . . .31 F5
  ☑ Maidstone ME16 . . . . .74 A3
Rowan Lea ME5 . . . . .10 B1
Rowans The ME12. . . . . . . .4 B7
Rowan Tree Pk CT5 . . . . . .43 B6
Rowan Wlk ME4 . . . . .9 E8
Rowbrocke Cl ME8. . . . . . .33 D3
Rowe Cl CT9 . . . . .28 F7
Rowena Rd CT8. . . . . .7 C1
Rowetts Way ME12. . . . . . .5 D3
Rowland Ave ME7. . . . . . . .10 E2
Rowland Cl
  Gillingham ME7 . . . . .10 E1
  Maidstone ME16 . . . . . . .74 E3
Rowland Cotts CT21 . . . . .174 F3
Rowland Cres CT6 . . . . . . .23 E5
Rowland Dr CT6 . . . . .22 C2
ROWLING 92 A2
Rowling St ME14 . . . . . . .171 E6
ROWLING STREET. 171 E6
Row The
  Ash CT3 . . . . .71 E5
  Chillenden CT3. . . . . . . .113 F8
  Elham CT4 . . . . .144 F5
  Ruckinge TN26. . . . . . . .183 F8
Roxburgh Rd CT8 . . . . .7 D1
Royal Ave CT5 . . . . .43 C5
Royal Cl CT10. . . . . .29 F4
Royal Cres
  Margate CT9 . . . . .7 H2
  Ramsgate CT11 . . . . .52 D5
Royal Dr CT5 . . . . .21 A3
Royal Eagle Cl ME2 . . . . . .9 E7
Royal Engineers Mus★
  ME7 . . . . .10 B6
Royal Espl
  Margate CT9 . . . . .7 F1
  Ramsgate CT11 . . . . .52 C5
Royal Fountain Mews
  ME12 . . . . .1 B2
Royal Harbour App CT11 . .52 C5
Royal Mews 10 CT11 . . . . .52 F7
Royal Military Ave CT14 . .119 B8
Royal Military Canal (dis)★
  CT21. . . . . .176 D2
Royal Military Rd CT21 . .175 E1

Royal Mus & Free Liby★ 25
  CT1 . . . . .87 F8
Royal Navy Way 2 CT5 . . .43 A6
Royal Par CT11 . . . . .52 E6
Royal Rd
  Ramsgate CT11 . . . . .52 D6
  Sheerness ME12 . . . . .1 C2
Royal St George's Golf
  Links★ CT13 . . . . .73 E2
Royal School for Deaf
  Children The CT9 . . . . .7 J2
Royal Sovereign Ave ME4 .10 B7
Royal Star Arc ☑ ME14 . . .74 F4
Royal Victoria Hospl
  CT19. . . . . .178 C6
Royal Victoria Pl ☑
  CT16. . . . . .166 D8
Royds Rd TN24 . . . . .156 D6
Royston Gdns CT15 . . . . .150 F6
Royston Rd ME15 . . . . . . .76 A3
Roystons Cl ME8 . . . . .11 F2
Royton Ave ME17 . . . . . . .101 D5
Rubery Dro CT3 . . . . .72 C6
Ruby Cl ☑ ME10 . . . . .36 D6
RUCKINGE 183 F8
Ruckinge Cnr TN26 . . . . .183 F6
Ruckinge Rd TN26 . . . . . .183 A7
Ruckinge Way ME8 . . . . . .11 C3
Rudge Cl ME5 . . . . .32 D2
Ruffets Wood TN23 . . . . .156 C3
Rugby Cl
  Broadstairs CT10. . . . . . . .29 F5
  Chatham ME5. . . . . .31 F4
Rugby Gdns TN23 . . . . . . .156 C3
Rugby Rd CT17 . . . . .166 A6
Rugby Way TN27 . . . . . . .120 B7
Ruins Barn Rd ME9. . . . . . .58 D6
Rule Ct ME12 . . . . .3 B8
Rumfields Rd CT10 . . . . . .29 D4
Rumstead La ME17, ME9 . .56 D4
Rumstead Rd ME9 . . . . . . .56 E4
Rumwood Ct ME17 . . . . . .98 B5
Runcie Ho ☑ CT1 . . . . . . .87 F7
Runcie Pl CT2 . . . . .66 D1
Runham La ME17 . . . . . . .100 E3
Running Foxes La TN23 . .155 D7
Running Horse Rdbt The
  ME14 . . . . .53 E1
Runnymede Gdns ME15 . .97 A8
Runnymede Mews ME13 . .62 C7
Rusham Rd CT3. . . . . .70 C1
Rush Ct
  Chatham ME5. . . . . .32 A3
  Dymchurch TN29 . . . . . .195 B6
RUSHENDEN 2 F3
Rushenden Ct ME11. . . . . . .2 F3
Rushenden Rd ME11 . . . . . .3 A4
Rushett La ME13. . . . . .60 F4
Rushmead Cl CT2 . . . . . . .66 D2
Rushmead Dr ME15 . . . . . .97 A7
Ruskins View CT6 . . . . . . .23 C1
Russell Cl ME10 . . . . .36 C3
Russell Ct ME4 . . . . .10 B3
Russell Dr CT5 . . . . .21 D3
Russell Pl ME13. . . . . .40 B3
Russell Rd
  ☑ Folkestone CT19. . . . . .178 D6
  Kit's Coty ME20 . . . . .53 D7
Russells Ave ME8 . . . . .34 A8
Russell St
  Dover CT16 . . . . .166 E7
  Sheerness ME12 . . . . .1 C2
Russet Ave ME13 . . . . .62 E5
Russet Ct ME17 . . . . .96 C3
Russets The
  Maidstone ME16 . . . . .74 B5
  Whitstable CT5 . . . . .21 D1
Russett Cl CT3 . . . . .73 F1
Russett Rd CT1. . . . . .88 C8
Rutherford Coll CT2. . . . . .66 E4
Rutherford Rd TN24. . . . .139 B5
Ruth Ho ☑ ME16 . . . . . . .74 E5
Ruth St ME4 . . . . .10 A2
Rutland Ave CT9 . . . . .8 C2
Rutland Ct CT11 . . . . .88 D7
Rutland Gdns
  Birchington CT7 . . . . .26 F7
  Margate CT9 . . . . .8 C2
Rutland Ho ☑ CT9. . . . . . .8 C2
Rutland Pl ME8 . . . . .33 C3
Rutland Rd CT16 . . . . . . .149 B3
Rutland Sch of English
  CT9. . . . . .7 G1
Rutland Way ME15 . . . . . .97 E8
Ruxley Cl CT10 . . . . .76 A2
Rycault Cl ☑ ME5 . . . . . . .31 F4
Rycaut Ct ME8 . . . . .33 D3
Rydal Ave CT11 . . . . .52 B7
Rydal Ho ME15 . . . . .97 E7
Ryde Cl ME5 . . . . .32 B8
Ryder's Ave CT8 . . . . .27 D8
Ryde St CT2 . . . . .66 E1
Rye Ct TN23 . . . . .155 D7
RYE FOREIGN 196 E1
Ryegrass Cl ME5. . . . . .32 C6
Rye Rd
  Brookland TN29 . . . . . . .199 D8
  Peasmarsh TN31 . . . . . . .196 E2
  Wittersham TN30. . . . . . .189 A2
Rye Wlk CT6 . . . . .23 C2
Ryland St ☑ CT20 . . . . . .178 E5
Ryland Pl ☑ CT20 . . . . . .178 E5
Rylands Rd TN24. . . . . . . .139 D5
Ryland St TN29 . . . . .205 C5
Ryswick Mews TN28. . . . .202 C8

S

Sabre Ct ME7 . . . . .11 A1
Sackett's Gap CT9 . . . . .8 C3
Sacketts Hill CT14 . . . . .29 C6
Sackville Cl TN26 . . . . .138 A4
Sackville Cres TN23 . . . . . .139 A2
Saddlers Cl ME14 . . . . .75 E5
Saddlers Hill CT3 . . . . .91 D2
Saddlers Mews
Ramsgate CT12 . . . . .28 F1
Whitstable CT5 . . . . .20 D1
Saddler's Wall La TN29 . .191 B1
Saddlers Way TN23 . . . . . .156 B5
Saddleton Gr ⬛ CT5 . . . . . .43 D8
Saddleton Rd CT5 . . . . .43 D8
Sadlers Cl ME5 . . . . .31 D2
Saffron Cl ME16 . . . . .74 B3
Saffron's Pl ⬛ CT20 . . . . .178 E5
Saffron Way
⬛ Chatham ME5 . . . . .31 F5
Sittingbourne ME10 . . . . . .36 F7
Sage Rd ME1 . . . . .9 B3
Sailfield Ct ME4 . . . . .9 F7
Sailmakers Ct ⬛ ME4 . . . . .10 B2
St Agnes Gdns ME12 . . . . . .1 D1
St Albans Cl ME7 . . . . .10 E7
St Alban's Ct CT3 . . . . .46 E1
St Alpheage CE Inf Sch ⬛
CT5 . . . . .20 D1
St Alphege CE Jun Sch
CT5 . . . . .20 D1
St Alphege Ct ⬛ CT1 . . . . .66 F1
St Alphege Rd ⬛ CT16 . .149 C1
St Ambrose Gn TN25 . . . .123 E2
St Andrews CT19 . . . . .178 E5
St Andrews Cl
Canterbury CT1 . . . . .87 E7
Folkestone CT19 . . . . .178 B7
Herne Bay CT6 . . . . .23 A4
Margate CT9 . . . . .28 F7
St Andrew's Cl
Maidstone ME16 . . . . .74 A2
Whitstable CT5 . . . . .43 E7
St Andrew's Gdns CT15 . .130 E5
St Andrew's Lees CT13 . . . .94 A8
St Andrews Pk ME16 . . . . .74 A3
St Andrews Rd
Gillingham ME7 . . . . .10 D7
Ramsgate CT11 . . . . .52 F8
St Andrew's Rd
Deal CT14 . . . . .117 C6
Littlebourne-on-Sea TN28 . .202 E6
Maidstone ME16 . . . . .74 A3
St Andrews Sch ME1 . . . . . .9 C4
St Andrews Way CT14 . . . .115 A4
St Andrew Terr CT17 . . . . .149 A2
St Angela's Jun Sch CT8 . .27 D7
St Annes Ct ME16 . . . . .74 F4
St Anne's Ct
⬛ Dover CT16 . . . . .149 B2
Herne Bay CT6 . . . . .22 E5
St Anne's Dr CT6 . . . . .22 D4
St Anne's Gdns CT9 . . . . . .28 F8
St Ann's Rd
Dymchurch TN29 . . . . .195 B7
Faversham ME13 . . . . .62 B7
St Anselms RC Sch CT1 . . .88 C5
St Anthonys Cl CT9 . . . . . . .8 C1
St Anthony's Way CT19 . . . .8 C1
St Augustine of Canterbury
RC Prim Sch ME8 . . . . . . .33 D3
St Augustine's* CT1 . . . . . .27 E8
St Augustine's Abbey
CT11 . . . . .52 D5
St Augustine's Abbey (rems
of)* CT1 . . . . .88 A8
St Augustine's Ave CT9 . . .28 F8
St Augustines Bsns Pk
CT5 . . . . .21 E3
St Augustines Cath Prim Sch
CT21 . . . . .176 A3
St Augustines Cres CT5 . . .21 D3
St Augustines Ct ⬛ CT1 . .88 B8
St Augustines Pk CT8 . . . . .27 E8
St Augustines Pk CT11 . . . .52 C6
St Augustine's Rd
Canterbury CT1 . . . . .88 B7
Deal CT14 . . . . .116 F4
Ramsgate CT11 . . . . .52 D5
St Augustine's Sch CT8 . . .27 E8
St Barnabas Cl
Ashford TN23 . . . . .155 F7
Gillingham ME7 . . . . .10 D3
Maidstone ME16 . . . . .74 C4
St Bartholemews Ct ⬛
CT17 . . . . .166 C8
St Bartholomew's Hospl
ME1 . . . . .9 E4
St Bartholomew's Hospl
CT13 . . . . .94 A7
St Bartholomew's La ⬛
ME1 . . . . .9 E4
St Bartholomew's Terr ⬛
ME1 . . . . .9 E4
St Bart's Cl ⬛ CT17 . . . . .166 C8
St Bart's Rd CT13 . . . . .93 F8
St Benedict's Lawn CT11 . .52 D5
St Benedicts Prim Sch
ME5 . . . . .32 C2
St Benet's Ct TN30 . . . . . .179 B8
St Benet's Rd CT8 . . . . .27 E7
St Benets Way TN30 . . . . .179 B8

St Catherines TN29 . . . . . .201 A7
St Catherines Ct
Ramsgate CT11 . . . . .29 F1
Rochester ME1 . . . . .9 D5
St Catherine's Dr ME13 . . .62 D6
St Catherine's Gr CT12 . . . .28 D1
St Cecelia Ho CT14 . . . . . .117 B1
St Christopher Cl CT9 . . . . .29 D8
St Christophers Gn CT10 . .29 F5
St Christophers Mews
CT11 . . . . .52 D8
St Christophers Sch ⬛
CT1 . . . . .88 B6
St Clare Rd CT14 . . . . .117 C1
St Clements Cl ⬛ CT13 . . .73 A1
St Clements Cl ME12 . . . . . .6 D2
St Clement's Ct
Broadstairs CT10 . . . . .29 E6
Folkestone CT20 . . . . .178 F5
Ramsgate CT11 . . . . .52 D8
St Clement's Ct CT6 . . . . . .23 A3
St Clement's Ho ME1 . . . . . .9 D5
St Clements Rd ME12 . . . . .6 E3
St Clement's Rd CT16 . . . . .7 C1
St Cosmus CT TN25 . . . . .105 B1
St Crispin's Inf Sch CT8 . . .27 E7
St Crispin's Rd CT8 . . . . . . .27 E7
St Cuby CT10 . . . . .30 C7
St Davids Ct CT17 . . . . . . .166 A5
St David's Cl
Birchington CT7 . . . . .27 B8
Whitstable CT5 . . . . .43 E8
St Davids Gate ME16 . . . . .74 A2
St Davids Rd ⬛ CT11 . . . .52 F8
St David's Rd
Deal CT14 . . . . .117 C6
Ramsgate CT11 . . . . .29 F1
St Denys Rd CT18 . . . . . . .163 B5
St Dunstan's CT2 . . . . .66 D1
St Dunstan's Cl ⬛ CT2 . . .66 E1
St Dunstans Rd CT9 . . . . . . .8 A2
St Dunstan's St CT2 . . . . . .66 E1
St Dunstan's Terr CT2 . . . . .66 E1
St Eanswythe CE Prim Sch
⬛ CT20 . . . . .178 E4
St Eanswythe Way ⬛
CT20 . . . . .178 D5
St Edmund's Ct ⬛ CT16 . .149 D2
St Edmund's RC Sch
CT16 . . . . .149 D2
St Edmunds Rd ⬛ CT11 . . .29 F1
St Edmund's Rd CT14 . . . .116 E4
St Edmund's Sch CT2 . . . . .66 A1
St Edmunds Way ME8 . . . .12 B1
St Edward's RC Prim Sch
ME12 . . . . .1 C1
St Elisabeth Ho CT11 . . . . . .67 A1
St Ethelberts RC Prim Sch
CT11 . . . . .52 F8
St Faith's at Ash Sch CT3 . .71 C1
St Faiths Cl ME14 . . . . .76 B4
St Faith's La ME14 . . . . . . .76 B4
St Faith St ME14 . . . . .74 F4
St Francis Cl
Deal CT14 . . . . .116 F4
Maidstone ME14 . . . . .75 B7
Margate CT9 . . . . .29 D8
St Francis Cl TN23 . . . . . .155 F7
St Francis' RC Prim Sch
ME15 . . . . .74 C4
St Francis Rd CT14 . . . . . .177 F6
St Gabriel's Ct ⬛ CT20 . .178 E6
St Georges Ave ME12 . . . . . .5 D2
St George's Ave
Herne Bay CT6 . . . . .22 D4
Sheerness ME12 . . . . .1 C1
St George's Bsns Ctr
TN23 . . . . .156 A8
St Georges Bsns Pk ME10 .37 B4
St Georges CE Foundation
Sch CT10 . . . . .29 C5
St Georges CE Prim Sch
ME12 . . . . .4 E6
St Georges Cl CT5 . . . . .43 E7
St Georges Cres CT17 . . . .166 B5
St Georges Ct CT17 . . . . . .149 A2
St George's Ct ME12 . . . . . .3 B8
St George's La CT1 . . . . . . .88 A8
St George's Lees CT13 . . . .94 A8
St George's Pas CT14 . . . .117 D6
St Georges Pl
Sandwich CT13 . . . . .94 B8
St Margaret's at Cliffe
CT15 . . . . .150 F6
St George's Pl
Canterbury CT1 . . . . .88 A8
Hythe CT21 . . . . .187 D8
St Georges Rd CT11 . . . . . .52 F8
St George's Rd
Broadstairs CT10 . . . . .30 A4
Deal CT14 . . . . .117 D6
Folkestone CT19 . . . . .177 F6
Gillingham ME7 . . . . .10 C6
Sandwich CT13 . . . . .94 A8
St Georges Sq
⬛ Ashford TN24 . . . . . .139 B2
Maidstone ME16 . . . . .74 E3
St Georges St CT1 . . . . .88 A8
St George's Terr CT6 . . . . . .22 E5
St Giles Cl CT17 . . . . .166 B5
St Giles Rd CT17 . . . . .166 B5
St Giles Wlk CT17 . . . . . . .166 B5
St Gregory's Cl CT14 . . . . .116 F4
St Gregory's Ct ⬛ CT11 . .67 B1
St Margarets Dr
Deal CT14 . . . . .134 B8

St Gregory's Rd CT1 . . . . . .67 B1
St Helen's Rd ME12 . . . . . . .1 E1
St Helier's Cl ME16 . . . . . . .74 B2
St Hilda Rd CT19 . . . . .177 E6
St Hilda's Rd CT21 . . . . . . .176 B1
St Jacob's Pl CT1 . . . . .87 D6
St James Ave CT12 . . . . . . .52 C8
St James' Ave
Broadstairs CT10 . . . . .29 C5
Ramsgate CT12 . . . . .29 B1
St James Cl ME12 . . . . .6 E4
St James' Gdns CT5 . . . . . .43 D8
St James La ⬛ CT16 . . . . .166 E7
St James' Park Rd CT5 . . . .43 D8
St James St CT16 . . . . .166 E7
St James' Terr CT7 . . . . .27 B8
St Jean's Rd CT8 . . . . .27 B8
St John Fisher RC Sch (Main
Site) ME4 . . . . .9 E3
St John Fisher RC Sch (Sixth
Form Site) ME4 . . . . .9 F2
St Johns Ave
Ramsgate CT12 . . . . .29 A1
Sittingbourne ME10 . . . . . .37 B3
St John's CE Inf Sch ME4 . . .9 B3
St John's CE Prim Sch
ME14 . . . . .75 E4
St John's Church Rd
CT19 . . . . .178 C6
St John's Cl CT18 . . . . .163 A7
St John's Commandery (rems
of)* CT15 . . . . .146 E4
St John's Cotts
Bethersden TN26 . . . . .153 D5
⬛ Sandwich CT13 . . . . . .72 F1
St Johns Cres CT24 . . . . . .157 A6
St John's Ct CT24 . . . . .66 D6
St John's Hospl ⬛ CT1 . . .67 A1
St John's La
Ashford TN23, TN24 . . . . . .139 C2
Canterbury CT1 . . . . .87 F8
St John's Pl CT1 . . . . .67 A1
St Johns Rd
Elvington CT15 . . . . .114 B2
Hythe CT21 . . . . .176 A3
St John's Rd
Dover CT17 . . . . .166 C7
Faversham ME13 . . . . .62 D7
Gillingham ME7 . . . . .10 C5
Margate CT9 . . . . .7 J2
New Romney TN28 . . . . . . .202 A6
Whitstable CT5 . . . . .21 D3
St John's St
Folkestone CT20 . . . . .178 D5
⬛ Margate CT9 . . . . .9 A2
St John's Way CT18 . . . . . .163 A7
St Joseph's RC Prim Sch
Aylesham CT3 . . . . .113 A5
⬛ Broadstairs CT10 . . . . .29 F5
St Julien Ave CT1 . . . . .67 D1
St Katherine Rd ME12 . . . . . .3 E7
St Laurence Ave ME14 . . . .74 C8
St Laurence CE Jun Sch
CT11 . . . . .52 B8
St Laurence Cl ME9 . . . . . . .37 D2
St Laurence Cl CT11 . . . . . .52 C7
St LAWRENCE 52 B8
St Lawrence Ave CT11 . . . .52 B5
St Lawrence Chase CT11 . .52 B7
St Lawrence Cl CT11 . . . . . .88 B6
St Lawrence Coll CT11 . . . .52 B6
St Lawrence Coll Jun Sch
CT11 . . . . .52 B8
St Lawrence Ct TN28 . . . . .202 A6
St Lawrence Forstal CT1 . . .88 B6
St Lawrence Gd The (Kent
Cty Cricket Club) CT11 . .88 B6
St Lawrence Ind Est CT11 . .52 B7
St Lawrence Rd CT11 . . . . .88 B6
St Leonards Ave ME1 . . . . . .9 F2
St Leonards Cl ⬛ CT21 . .176 B1
St Leonards News ⬛
CT21 . . . . .176 B1
St Leonards Rd
Hythe CT21 . . . . .176 B1
Maidstone ME16 . . . . .74 A6
St Leonard's Rd CT14 . . . .117 B4
St Louis Gr CT6 . . . . .22 C4
St Luke's Ave ME14 . . . . . . .75 B8
St Luke's Cl CT5 . . . . .43 E7
St Lukes Cl CT8 . . . . .27 E8
St Lukes Cl
Ashford TN23 . . . . .155 F7
Maidstone ME14 . . . . .75 A6
St Luke's Rd
Maidstone ME14 . . . . .75 B5
Ramsgate CT11 . . . . .52 E8
St Luke's Wlk CT18 . . . . . .162 F4
St Magnus Cl CT7 . . . . .27 A8
St Magnus St CT7 . . . . .27 A8
St Malo Ct ⬛ CT20 . . . . .178 C4
St MARGARET'S AT
CLIFFE 151 A6
St Margaret's at Cliffe Prim
Sch CT15 . . . . .151 A6
St Margaret's at Troy Town
Prim Sch ME1 . . . . .9 C4
St Margarets Banks ME1 . .9 C5
St Margarets Cl CT5 . . . . . .43 A6
St Margarets Cl ⬛ CT5 . . .43 A6
St Margaret's Ct ⬛ ME8 . .33 F8
St Margarets
Deal CT14 . . . . .134 B8

St Margarets Dr continued
Gillingham ME8 . . . . .33 C5
St Margaret's Inf Sch ME8 33 E8
St Margaret's Jun Sch
ME8 . . . . .33 E8
St Margaret's Mews ME1 . . .9 C5
St Margarets Rd
St Margaret's at Cliffe
CT15 . . . . .134 A1
Westgate on Sea CT7 . . . . .27 F3
St Margaret's Rd
St Margaret's at Cliffe
CT15 . . . . .151 A5
Westgate on Sea CT8 . . . . .27 E7
St Margaret's St
Canterbury CT1 . . . . .87 F8
Rochester ME1 . . . . .9 C5
St Marks Cl CT5 . . . . .43 E8
St Mark's Cl CT20 . . . . . . .177 D5
St Marks Rd ME7 . . . . .10 C5
St MARTIN'S 88 B8
St Martins Ave CT1 . . . . . . .88 B8
St Martin's Church* CT1 . .88 B8
St Martins Cl
Canterbury CT1 . . . . .87 F8
Newington ME9 . . . . .35 C7
St Martin's Ct ⬛ CT11 . . .88 C8
St Martin's Hill CT1 . . . . . . .88 C8
St Martins Ho CT17 . . . . . .166 D5
St Martins Hospl CT1 . . . . . .88 B8
St Martin's Pl CT1 . . . . .88 B8
St Martins Rd
Folkestone CT20 . . . . .177 D6
New Romney TN28 . . . . . . .202 B6
St Martin's Rd
Canterbury CT1 . . . . .67 B1
Deal CT14 . . . . .116 F4
Dover CT15 . . . . .149 E4
St Martins Sch CT17 . . . . .166 A7
St Martin's Terr CT1 . . . . . .88 B8
St Martin's View CT6 . . . . .46 A8
St Mary Cl ⬛ ME13 . . . . . .62 D7
St MARY IN THE
MARSH 194 B4
St Mary of Charity CE Prim
Sch ME13 . . . . .62 D7
St Mary's Ave CT19 . . . . . .177 F6
St MARY'S BAY 195 A4
St Mary's Bay Sta* TN29 194 F4
St Marys CE Prim Sch
⬛ Dover CT16 . . . . .166 E8
Folkestone CT19 . . . . .178 F6
St Mary's Church* CT14 . .24 C7
St Mary's Cl CT18 . . . . . . .161 D3
St Mary's Ct
Eastry CT13 . . . . .93 C2
Hamstreet TN26 . . . . .183 A8
Nonington CT15 . . . . .113 C5
Woodnesborough CT13 . . . .93 B6
St Mary's Gdns
Chatham ME4 . . . . .10 B7
St Mary's Bay TN29 . . . . . .195 A5
Upstreet CT3 . . . . .47 E3
St Marys Gn TN24 . . . . . . .139 C2
St Mary's Gr
Tilmanstone CT14 . . . . . . .115 A4
Whitstable CT5 . . . . .21 B8
St Marys Mdw CT3 . . . . . . .91 A8
St Marys Mews TN24 . . . .156 F8
St Mary's Pl ME9 . . . . .35 C7
St Mary's RC Prim Sch
CT5 . . . . .20 F2
St Mary's Rd
Tilmanstone CT14 . . . . . . .115 A4
Whitstable CT5 . . . . .21 B8
St Marys Row TN24 . . . . . .156 F8
West Hythe CT21 . . . . .175 B1
St Mary's RC Prim Sch
TN29 . . . . .194 C5
West Hythe CT21 . . . . .175 B1
St Mary's Row ME12 . . . . . .4 A6
St Mary's St CT1 . . . . .87 F8
St Mary's Terr ⬛ CT20 . .178 E5
St Mary's View ME9 . . . . . .35 C7
St Matthew's Dr ME1 . . . . .9 A2
St Matthews Dr ME1 . . . . . .7 C1
St Mawes CT8 . . . . .27 E8
St Michael & All Angels
Church CT14 . . . . .117 C4
St MICHAELS 167 B4
St Michael's Alley ⬛
CT11 . . . . .52 D8
St Michaels Ave CT9 . . . . . .29 D8
St Michael's CE Inf Sch
ME16 . . . . .74 E3
St Michael's CE Jun Sch
ME16 . . . . .74 E3
St Michael's CE Prim Sch
Houghton Green TN31 . . . .197 C2
Tenterden TN30 . . . . .167 A3
St Michaels Cl
Canterbury CT2 . . . . .66 A1
Pratling Street ME20 . . . . . .53 C3

St Michael's Cl
Chatham ME4 . . . . .9 F3
⬛ Sittingbourne ME10 . . .36 F4
St Michael's Ct
⬛ Folkestone CT20 . . . .178 E5
⬛ Rochester ME2 . . . . . . .9 B8
St Michael's Pl CT12 . . . . . .66 E2
St Michael's RC Prim Sch ⬛
ME4 . . . . .9 F3
St Michael's Rd
Canterbury CT2 . . . . .66 E2
Maidstone ME16 . . . . .74 D3
Sittingbourne ME10 . . . . . .36 F4
St Michael's St CT20 . . . . .178 E5
St Michael's Terr TN30 . . .167 A3
St Michael's Wlk CT18 . . . .162 F4
St Mildred's Ave
Birchington CT7 . . . . .26 E8
Broadstairs CT10 . . . . .30 A4
Ramsgate CT11 . . . . .52 B5
St Mildred's Cl ⬛ TN30 . .179 A7
St Mildreds Ct
Canterbury CT1 . . . . .87 E8
Deal CT14 . . . . .117 C1
Westgate on Sea CT8 . . . . . .7 D1
St Mildred's Gdns CT8 . . . . .7 D1
St Mildred's Pl CT1 . . . . . . .87 E7
St Mildreds Prim Inf Sch ⬛
CT10 . . . . .30 A4
St Mildred's Rd
Margate CT9 . . . . .8 A2
Minster (Thanet) CT12 . . . .50 B5
Ramsgate CT11 . . . . .52 C6
Westgate on Sea CT7 . . . . . .7 C1
St Monicas
Deal CT14 . . . . .134 D6
Dover CT17 . . . . .166 C7
St Monicas Rd CT14 . . . . . .134 D6
St NICHOLAS AT WADE . . .25 E1
St Nicholas at Wade CE Prim
Sch CT7 . . . . .25 E2
St Nicholas CE Inf Sch
ME2 . . . . .9 A7
St Nicholas CE Prim Sch
TN28 . . . . .202 B7
St Nicholas Cl
Deal CT14 . . . . .116 F4
Sturry CT2 . . . . .67 F7
St Nicholas Cnr CT7 . . . . . .25 F1
St Nicholas Ho CT3 . . . . . . .71 D2
St Nicholas Hospl CT2 . . . . .66 C1
St Nicholas Lodge CT10 . . .29 F4
St Nicholas Rd
Canterbury CT1 . . . . .87 D6
Faversham ME13 . . . . .62 A7
Hythe CT21 . . . . .176 A2
Littlebourne-on-Sea TN28 . .202 E6
St Nicholas Rdbt CT7 . . . . .26 B2
St Nicholas Sch CT1 . . . . . .87 F6
St Nicholas Terr ⬛ CT21 .176 B2
St Patrick's Cl
Deal CT14 . . . . .117 C6
Whitstable CT5 . . . . .43 E7
St Patricks Rd
Dover CT17 . . . . .166 A4
Ramsgate CT11 . . . . .52 F8
St Patrick's Rd CT14 . . . . .117 C6
St Patrick's Row ME9 . . . . .59 B7
St Paul's Ave ME13 . . . . . . .62 A7
St Pauls Cres ME13 . . . . . . .64 A3
St Pauls Ct ME9 . . . . .60 A6
St Pauls Ct CT20 . . . . .177 E4
St Pauls Inf Sch ME14 . . . .75 A7
St Paul's Rd ME13 . . . . .64 A3
St Paul's St ME10 . . . . .36 E5
St Pauls Terr ME1 . . . . .88 B8
St Paul's Way CT20 . . . . . .177 F4
St Peter in Thanet CE Jun
Sch CT10 . . . . .29 F7
St PETER'S 29 E5
St Peter's Bridge ME14 . . . .74 F4
St Peters CE Prim Sch
Folkestone CT19 . . . . .178 A5
Forstal ME20 . . . . .53 A3
St Peter's Cl ME12 . . . . .3 D6
St Peters Cotts ⬛ CT5 . . . .20 D2
St Peter's Ct
Broadstairs CT10 . . . . .29 F5
Faversham ME13 . . . . .62 A7
St Peters Footpath ⬛ CT9 .8 A1
St Peter's Footpath
Margate CT9 . . . . .7 J1
Margate, Drapers Mill CT9 . .29 A8
St Peter's Gr CT1 . . . . .87 F8
St Peters Inf Sch ME1 . . . . . .9 D5
St Peter's La CT1 . . . . .66 F1
St Peters Meth Prim Sch
CT2 . . . . .87 F8
St Peter's Park Rd CT10 . . .29 F5
St Peter's Path ME1 . . . . . . .9 D5
St Peters Pl CT1, CT2 . . . . .87 F8
St Peter's RC Prim Sch
ME10 . . . . .36 D2
St Peter's Rd
Boughton Street ME13 . . . .64 A3
Broadstairs CT10 . . . . .29 F5
Margate CT10, CT9 . . . . . . .29 A7
Whitstable CT5 . . . . .20 D2
St Peter's Row TN26 . . . . .153 D5
St Peters Sch of English ⬛
CT1 . . . . .66 F1
St Peters St ⬛ CT1 . . . . . .66 F1

St Peter's St
Canterbury CT1, CT2 . . . . . . .87 F6
Maidstone ME16 . . . . .74 F4
Sandwich CT13 . . . . .73 A1
St Peter St ME1 . . . . .9 D4
St Peter's Way TN26 . . . .170 A8
St Peters Wharf Ret Pk
ME16 .74 F4
St Philip Howard RC Prim
Sch CT6 . . . . .22 E5
St Philip's Ave ME15 . . . . .75 B2
St Pierre CT14 . . . . .117 D5
ST RADIGUND'S 149 A2
St Radigund's Ct CT17 . .149 A1
St Radigund's Pl CT1 . . . . .67 A1
St Radigund's Rd CT17 . .149 A1
St Radigunds St CT1 . . . . .66 F1
St Richards RC Prim Sch
CT16 . . . . .149 D1
St Richard's Rd CT14 . . . .116 F3
St Richard's Wlk CT17 . . .166 A4
St Ronan's Cl ME15 . . . . . .97 C7
St Saviour's CE Jun Sch
CT8 . . . . .27 E8
St Saviours Cl CT19 . . . . .178 D7
St Saviour's Cl ME13 . . . .62 E7
St Saviours Ct CT8 . . . . . . .27 E8
St Saviours Rd ME15 . . . . .97 D6
St Simon of England RC Prim
Sch TN23 . . . . .156 A8
St Simon Stock RC Sch
ME16 . . . . .74 C4
ST STEPHEN'S 66 F2
St Stephen's Cl
Canterbury CT2 . . . . .66 F2
Newington ME9 . . . . .35 D2
St Stephens Ct CT2 . . . . . .66 F1
St Stephens Fields 5 CT2 66 F1
St Stephen's Fields CT2 . .66 F1
St Stephen's Gn CT2 . . . . .66 F3
St Stephen's Hill CT2 . . . .66 E4
St Stephens Ho 1 CT2 . . .66 F1
St Stephen's Inf & Jun Sch
CT2 . . . . .66 F3
St Stephen's Lodge CT2 . .66 F2
St Stephen's Manor CT10 30 B7
St Stephens Mews ME1 . .31 E8
St Stephens Mews TN23 156 A6
St Stephens Pathway 4
CT2 . . . . .66 F2
St Stephen's Rd CT2 . . . . .66 F2
St Stephen's Sq ME15 . . . .74 E2
St Stephen's Way CT20 . .177 F4
St Stephen's Wlk TN23 . .155 F7
St Swithin's Rd CT5 . . . . . .21 B3
St Teresas RC Prim Sch
TN24 . . . . .139 B4
St Theresas CT14 . . . . . . .139 B3
St Thomas' Cross CT14 . .170 D3
St Thomas Hill CT2 . . . . . .66 D3
St Thomas More RC Prim
Sch ME5 . . . . .32 A5
St Thomas of Canterbury RC
Prim Sch ME8 . . . . .11 B2
St Thomas' RC Prim Sch 2
CT1 . . . . .67 A1
St Thomas's Hospl CT13 . .72 F1
St Vincent Rd CT14 . . . . .150 F7
St Vincent's Cl
Littlebourne CT3 . . . . .68 F1
Whitstable CT5 . . . . .5 D4
St Welcume's Way ME17 100 E6
St William of Perth Prim Sch
ME1 . . . . .9 B2
St William's Way ME1 . . . . .9 D2
St Winifred Rd CT17 . . . . .177 F6
Salbris Cl TN29 . . . . .195 D8
Salem St ME15 . . . . .75 A3
Salisbury Ave
Broadstairs CT10 . . . . .29 F2
Gillingham ME8 . . . . .33 D8
Ramsgate CT11 . . . . .52 F8
Salisbury Cl ME10 . . . . . . .37 C4
Salisbury Ho
Canterbury CT2 . . . . .66 D2
4 Maidstone ME15 . . . . .97 D7
Salisbury Rd
Canterbury CT2 . . . . .66 E2
Chatham ME4 . . . . .10 A3
Deal CT14 . . . . .117 B2
Dover CT16 . . . . .149 D1
Folkestone CT19 . . . . .177 E7
Herne Bay CT6 . . . . .23 C5
Kit's Coty ME20 . . . . .53 B4
Maidstone ME14 . . . . .75 A6
St Margaret's at Cliffe
CT15 . . . . .151 B6
Whitstable CT5 . . . . .43 D8
Sally Port ME7 . . . . .10 A6
Sally Port Gdns ME7 . . . . .10 B6
Salmestone Grange CT9 . .28 E8
Salmestone Prim Sch CT9 . .28 E8
Salmestone Rd CT9 . . . . . .28 F8
Salmestone Rise CT9 . . . . .28 E8
Salmon Cres ME12 . . . . .3 F6
Salters La ME13 . . . . .62 D4
Salter's La TN29 . . . . .199 C8
Salthouse Cl TN29 . . . . . .199 D8
Saltings The
Iwade ME9 . . . . .14 D4
Littlestone-on-Sea TN28 . . .202 E5
10 Whitstable CT5 . . . . .20 D2
Salt Marsh La 21 CT5 . . . . .20 D2
Salt's Ave ME15 . . . . .96 F3
Salts Cl CT5 . . . . .20 D1

Salt's Dr CT10 . . . . .29 E5
Salts La ME15 . . . . .97 A4
SALTWOOD 176 C4
Saltwood CE Prim Sch
CT21 . . . . .176 B4
Saltwood Gdns CT9 . . . . . . .8 E2
Saltwood Rd ME15 . . . . . . .74 F1
Samara Cl ME1 . . . . .32 A1
Samian Cres CT19 . . . . . .177 C6
Samphire Cl ME14 . . . . . . .75 E4
Samphire Ct CT16 . . . . . . .166 E8
Samphire Hoe Ctry Pk*
CT15 . . . . .165 E2
Samuel Cl CT9 . . . . .8 A3
Samuel Dr ME10 . . . . .15 A1
Samuel Mews TN29 . . . . .205 D7
Samuels Twr ME4 . . . . .10 B4
Sancroft Ave CT2 . . . . .66 C1
Sanctuary Cl
Broadstairs CT10 . . . . .29 F2
Kearsney CT17 . . . . .148 D4
Sanctuary Rd ME8 . . . . . . .11 A3
Sanctuary The CT13 . . . . . .95 A7
Sandalwood Dr CT7 . . . . . .25 F1
Sandbach Ho CT7 . . . . .8 B3
Sandbanks Rd ME13 . . . . . .41 C2
Sandbourne Dr ME14 . . . . .53 F1
Sandcroft TN28 . . . . .202 F7
Sandcroft Way ME15 . . . . .75 A2
Sand Ct ME14 . . . . .6 G2
Sand End CT5 . . . . .43 C6
Sanderling Rd CT6 . . . . . . .23 F5
Sanderling Way ME9 . . . . .14 D5
Sanders Cl ME12 . . . . .4 C5
Sandford Rd ME10 . . . . . . .36 B5
SANDGATE 177 E3
Sandgate Ct ME8 . . . . .33 C4
Sandgate Espl CT20,
CT21 . . . . .177 D2
Sandgate High St CT20 . .177 E3
Sandgate Hill CT20 . . . . . .178 A4
Sandgate Prim Sch CT20 177 F4
Sandgate Rd
Folkestone CT20 . . . . .178 C4
Folkestone CT20 . . . . .178 D4
Sandgates CT4 . . . . .143 E7
Sandhurst Cl
Canterbury CT2 . . . . .67 A4
Gillingham ME8 . . . . .11 C3
Sandhurst Rd CT9 . . . . .8 F2
Sandilands TN24 . . . . .139 E2
Sandle's Rd CT7 . . . . .26 F7
SANDLING 53 F1
Sandling Cl TN23 . . . . . . .155 F6
Sandling Ct ME14 . . . . .75 B7
Sandling La ME14 . . . . .75 A8
Sandling Park Woodland
Gdn* TN25 . . . . .175 G6
Sandling Prim Sch ME14 . .75 A8
Sandling Rd
Hythe CT21 . . . . .175 F6
Maidstone ME14 . . . . .74 F6
Maidstone, Ringleston
ME14 . . . . .74 F7
Sandling Sta CT21 . . . . . . .175 F6
Sandown Cotts
Margate CT9 . . . . .8 A3
Teynham ME9 . . . . .38 E1
Sandown Ct CT14 . . . . . . .117 C7
Sandown Dr
Gillingham ME8 . . . . .33 D7
Herne Bay CT6 . . . . .22 D4
Sandown Lees CT13 . . . . . .94 D8
Sandown Pl CT14 . . . . .117 C7
Sandown Prim Sch CT14 117 C7
Sandown Rd
Deal CT14 . . . . .117 D8
Sandwich CT13 . . . . .94 B8
Sandpiper Ct 3 CT7 . . . . . .26 E8
Sandpiper La ME9 . . . . . . .14 E3
Sandpiper Rd
Chatham ME5 . . . . .32 D2
Hawkinge CT18 . . . . .163 A3
Whitstable CT5 . . . . .43 B7
Sandpit Hill CT3 . . . . .47 C4
Sandra Ct 5 ME2 . . . . .9 B4
Sandringham Ho ME1 . . . . .9 B4
Sandringham Rd ME8 . . . .33 E3
Sandstone Dr CT20 . . . . . .178 A3
Sandstone Rise ME5 . . . . .54 C8
SANDWAY 101 A3
Sandway Rd ME17 . . . . . . .100 F4
SANDWICH 73 B1
Sandwich Bay Bird Obsy*
CT13 . . . . .94 E2
Sandwich Cl CT20 . . . . . . .177 F5
Sandwich Guildhall Mus*
CT13 . . . . .73 A1
Sandwich Ind Est CT13 . . . .73 B1
Sandwich Inf Sch CT13 . . . .72 F1
Sandwich Jun Sch CT13 . . .93 F7
Sandwich Rd
Ash CT3 . . . . .71 F1
Cliffs End CT12 . . . . .51 D4
Eastry CT13 . . . . .93 C3
Eythorne CT15 . . . . .131 C8
Nonington CT15, CT3 . . . . .113 F6
Sandwich CT13, CT14 . . . . .93 D5
Whitfield CT15, CT16 . . . . .149 A7
Woodnesborough CT13 . . . .93 D7
Sandwich Sta CT13 . . . . . . .94 A8
Sandwich Tech Sch CT13 . .93 F6
Sandwood Rd
Ramsgate CT9 . . . . .29 F1
Sandwich CT13 . . . . .93 F8
Sandy Cnr TN26 . . . . .154 F5

Sandy Dell ME7 . . . . .33 A3
Sandyhurst La TN25 . . . . .139 B8
Sandy La
Ashford TN24 . . . . .140 B1
Daniel's Water TN26 . . . . . .154 E6
Hythe CT20, CT21 . . . . .177 B3
Maidstone, Harbourland
ME14 . . . . .75 C8
Maidstone, Penenden Heath
ME14 . . . . .75 C7
Maidstone, Ware Street
ME14 . . . . .76 B5
Tenterden TN30 . . . . .179 B7
Sandy Mount ME14 . . . . . .76 B5
Sandy Pl TN25 . . . . .158 D5
Sanger Cl CT9 . . . . .7 I1
Sangro Pl CT1 . . . . .67 D1
San Remo CT8 . . . . .7 C1
Sanspareil Ave ME12 . . . . . .4 A6
Santon La CT3 . . . . .70 E8
Sapphire Cl ME10 . . . . .36 C7
Sapphire Cl ME7 . . . . .11 A1
Saracen Fields ME5 . . . . . .54 C8
Sarafand Ho ME4 . . . . .9 B4
Saracen Cl ME7 . . . . .11 A1
Sarre Cl CT7 . . . . .48 D7
Sarre Pl CT13 . . . . .93 F8
Sarre Windmill* CT7 . . . . .48 D7
Sarsen Hts ME5 . . . . .31 F1
Sassoon Cl CT18 . . . . .163 A4
Satis Ave ME10 . . . . .36 E7
SATMAR 164 D3
Satmar La CT15, CT18 . . .164 E4
Satmore La CT18 . . . . .164 C4
Saunders La CT3 . . . . .71 F1
Saunders St
7 Chatham ME4 . . . . .9 F3
Gillingham ME7 . . . . .10 C6
Savage Rd ME5 . . . . .32 B2
Savernake Dr CT6 . . . . . . .23 B2
Savoy The 3 CT11 . . . . .52 C6
Saw Lodge Field TN23 . .156 C4
Sawpit Rd ME9 . . . . .59 B2
Sawyers Ct ME4 . . . . .10 B2
Saxon Ave ME12 . . . . .4 B6
Saxon Cl CT21 . . . . .176 E2
Saxon Rd
Bridge CT4 . . . . .89 A1
Faversham ME13 . . . . .62 C7
Ramsgate CT11 . . . . .52 B6
Westgate on Sea CT8 . . . . . . .7 D1
Saxons Cl CT14 . . . . .117 C8
Saxons Dr ME14 . . . . .75 B7
Saxon Shore
Sittingbourne ME10 . . . . . . .15 A1
Whitstable CT5 . . . . .43 C8
Saxon St 9 CT17 . . . . .166 D8
Saxon Way Prim Sch ME7 10 E6
Saxon Wlk ME9 . . . . .14 D4
Saxton Rd TN29 . . . . .206 E5
Saxton St ME7 . . . . .10 C8
Sayer Rd TN27 . . . . .120 C8
Sayers La 6 TN30 . . . . . . .179 A7
Scaffold St 6 TN29 . . . . . .209 D2
Scanlons Bridge Rd
Folkestone CT21 . . . . .177 C2
Hythe CT21 . . . . .176 A2
Scarborough Dr ME12 . . . . .4 C8
Scarlett Cl ME5 . . . . .32 C5
Sceales Dr CT12 . . . . .51 D6
Sceptre Way CT5 . . . . .43 B7
School Ave ME7 . . . . .10 E4
School Cl The CT8 . . . . .7 C1
School Hill CT14 . . . . .107 B8
School Ho ME10 . . . . .36 E3
School La
Bekesbourne CT4 . . . . .89 C4
Blean CT2 . . . . .66 A6
Borden ME9 . . . . .35 F4
Boughton Street ME13 . . . . .63 F3
Herne Bay CT6 . . . . .23 B1
Fordwich CT2 . . . . .68 A4
Goodnestone CT3 . . . . .91 D2
Herne Bay CT6 . . . . .23 B1
Hoath CT3 . . . . .46 E6
Ickham CT3 . . . . .90 C8
Iwade ME9 . . . . .14 C4
Lower Halstow ME9 . . . . . . .13 B2
Lower Hardres CT4 . . . . . . .110 B6
Maidstone ME15 . . . . .75 E1
Newington ME9 . . . . .35 B7
Peasmarsh TN31 . . . . .196 B2
Platt's Heath ME17 . . . . . . .100 F2
Ramsgate CT11 . . . . .52 E7
Sittingbourne ME9 . . . . .37 D2
Stalisfield Green ME13 . . . .103 D6
Staple CT3 . . . . .92 A6
Stourmouth CT3 . . . . .48 E2
Wingham CT3 . . . . .91 A7
School News ME9 . . . . .14 E4
School Path CT3 . . . . .89 F7
School Rd
Appledore Heath TN26 . . . .181 C1
Ash CT3 . . . . .71 C2
Bethersden TN26 . . . . .153 D4
Charing TN27 . . . . .120 C8
Densole CT18 . . . . .162 E7
Faversham ME13 . . . . .62 C6
Hothfield TN26 . . . . .138 A7
Hythe CT21 . . . . .176 B4
Sandwich CT13 . . . . .72 F1
Sittingbourne ME10 . . . . . . .37 B3
Tilmanstone CT14 . . . . .114 F4
School View ME9 . . . . .58 C8
Schrieber Mews ME7 . . . . .10 D5

Scimitar Cl ME7 . . . . .11 A1
Scocles Cotts ME12 . . . . . . .4 C5
Scocles Rd ME12 . . . . .4 C5
Scoggers Hill ME13 . . . . . . .85 A7
Scoones Cl ME9 . . . . .37 E2
Scotby Ave ME5 . . . . .32 B4
Scotchmen Cl ME12 . . . . . . .3 E7
Scotland Comm CT16 . . . .148 D4
Scot's La TN25 . . . . .159 F8
Scott Ave
Canterbury CT1 . . . . .87 E5
Gillingham ME8 . . . . .12 A1
Scotteswood Ave ME4 . . . . .9 F2
Scotton St TN25 . . . . .123 F2
Scott St ME14 . . . . .74 F6
Scott's Terr ME4 . . . . .9 F3
Scragged Oak Rd
Detling ME14 . . . . .55 C5
Hucking ME17 . . . . .56 C1
Scrapsgate Rd ME12 . . . . . . .4 A5
Scraps Hill ME9 . . . . .37 F4
Scrubbs La ME16 . . . . .74 D4
Sea App ME12 . . . . .6 E4
Seabourne Cl TN29 . . . . . .195 B6
Seabourne Way TN29 . . .195 B7
Seabrook CE Prim Sch
CT21 . . . . .177 B3
Seabrook Ct CT21 . . . . . . .177 B3
Seabrook Gdns CT21 . . . .177 B2
Seabrook Gr CT21 . . . . . . .177 A2
Seabrook Rd CT21 . . . . . . .176 E2
Seabrook Vale CT21 . . . . .177 B4
Seacroft Rd CT10 . . . . .30 A1
Seadown Cl CT21 . . . . .177 A4
Seafield Rd
Broadstairs CT10 . . . . .30 A4
Ramsgate CT11 . . . . .52 C6
Whitstable CT5 . . . . .21 B3
Seaford Ct ME1 . . . . .9 B5
Seagar Rd ME13 . . . . .40 B1
Seager Rd ME12 . . . . .1 F2
Seagrave Cres CT19 . . . . .178 F6
Sealand Ct ME1 . . . . .9 B5
Seamark Cl CT12 . . . . .117 A7
Seamark Rd CT12, CT7 . . . .26 E2
Sea Meadows Sch CT10 . .29 F2
Seapoint Rd CT10 . . . . .30 B3
Sea Rd
Deal CT14 . . . . .134 D6
Hythe CT21 . . . . .177 A2
Westgate on Sea CT8 . . . . . . .7 C1
SEASALTER 43 A7
Seasalter Beach CT5 . . . . .43 A7
Seasalter Cl ME12 . . . . .6 E4
Seasalter Cross CT5 . . . . .43 A6
Seasalter La CT5 . . . . .43 A5
Seasalter Rd ME13 . . . . . . .41 E3
Seascape 10 CT20 . . . . . . .177 E3
Seaside Ave ME12 . . . . .4 C5
Sea St
Herne Bay CT6 . . . . .22 C3
St Margaret's at Cliffe
CT15 . . . . .151 A6
Whitstable CT5 . . . . .20 D2
Seathorpe Ave ME12 . . . . . .4 C8
Seaths Cnr CT3 . . . . .91 A7
SEATON 69 D2
Seaton Ave CT21 . . . . .176 B3
Seaton Cotts TN25 . . . . . .122 E3
Seaton Rd
Gillingham ME7 . . . . .10 E3
Wickhambreaux CT3 . . . . . . .69 D2
Seaview Ave ME15 . . . . .6 H1
Sea View Ave CT5 . . . . .26 E8
Sea View Cl CT18 . . . . .164 B1
Sea View Cotts ME10 . . . . .30 B4
Seaview Ct CT10 . . . . .30 B3
Sea View Ho CT19 . . . . . . .178 D8
Seaview Hts TN29 . . . . . . .195 C2
Sea View Hts CT7 . . . . .26 D8
Seaview Rd
Gillingham ME7 . . . . .10 C4
Greatstone-on-Sea TN28 . .202 E1
Sea View Rd
Birchington CT7 . . . . .26 A6
Broadstairs CT10 . . . . .30 A6
Cliffs End CT12 . . . . .51 D6
Herne Bay CT6 . . . . .23 C5
St Margaret's at Cliffe
CT15 . . . . .150 F4
Sea View Sq CT6 . . . . .22 F5
Sea View Terr
Folkestone CT20 . . . . .177 D3
Margate CT9 . . . . .7 A2
Minster (Sheppey) ME12 . . . .5 A5
Seaville Dr CT6 . . . . .23 E5
Sea Wall
Dymchurch TN29 . . . . .195 D8
Whitstable CT5 . . . . .20 D2
Seaway Cotts CT5 . . . . . . .20 C1
Seaway Cres TN29 . . . . . .194 F4
Seaway Gdns TN29 . . . . .194 F4
Seaway Rd TN29 . . . . .195 A4
Second Ave
Broadstairs CT10 . . . . .8 G3
Chatham ME4 . . . . .10 C1
Eastchurch ME12 . . . . .5 E1
Gillingham ME7 . . . . .10 E3
Margate CT9 . . . . .8 F4
Sheerness ME11 . . . . .2 F1
Secret Gdns of Sandwich
The* CT13 . . . . .73 A1
Sedge Cres ME5 . . . . .31 E4
Sedgemoor Ho ME1 . . . . . . .9 E5

Sedley Cl ME8 . . . . .33 C3
SEED 81 A6
Seeshill Cl CT5 . . . . .43 E8
Segrave Rd CT19 . . . . .178 F5
Seibey Cl CT6 . . . . .23 C4
Selborne Ho CT17 . . . . . . .166 C7
Selborne Rd CT9 . . . . .29 B8
Selborne Rd ME7 . . . . .10 D7
Selbourne Terr CT17 . . . .166 C7
Selbourne Wlk ME15 . . . . .97 F6
Selby Ct ME9 . . . . .38 D2
Selby Rd ME15 . . . . .97 F4
Selkirk Rd CT16 . . . . .149 B3
SELLINDGE 159 D1
Sellindge Prim Sch
TN25 . . . . .159 C1
SELLING 84 C6
Selling CE Prim Sch ME13 84 B6
Selling Cl ME13 . . . . .84 C5
Selling Gn ME8 . . . . .11 C3
Selling Rd
Chilham CT4 . . . . .85 B3
Faversham ME13 . . . . .62 F3
Selling ME13 . . . . .84 E6
Selling St ME13 . . . . .84 B6
Selling Sta ME13 . . . . .84 E7
Selsea Ave CT6 . . . . .22 F5
SELSON 93 A3
Selstead Cl ME13 . . . . .11 C2
SELSTED 146 B5
Selsted CE Prim Sch
CT15 . . . . .146 C6
Selway Ct CT14 . . . . .117 B3
Selwood Cl CT14 . . . . .3 E6
Selwyn Ct CT10 . . . . .29 F5
Selwyn Dr CT10 . . . . .29 F5
Semaphore Rd CT7 . . . . . . .26 F8
Semple Cl CT12 . . . . .50 C7
Semple Gdns ME4 . . . . .9 E3
Senacre La ME15 . . . . .97 E6
Senacre Sq ME15 . . . . .97 F7
Senacre Wood Prim Sch
ME15 . . . . .97 F7
Sene Pk CT21 . . . . .176 D3
Senlac Cl CT11 . . . . .52 B6
Serene Ct 12 CT10 . . . . . . .30 B4
Serene Pl 9 CT10 . . . . .30 B4
Sessions House Sq ME14 74 F5
Setford Rd ME5 . . . . .32 C6
Setterfield Ho CT21 . . . . . .176 D2
Setterfield Rd CT9 . . . . .7 J1
Settington Ave ME5 . . . . . .10 C1
Sevastopol Pl CT1 . . . . .67 D1
Sevenacre Rd ME13 . . . . . .62 C8
Sevenscore CT12 . . . . .51 A5
Sevenscore Farm Cotts
CT12 . . . . .51 A5
Seven Stones Dr CT10 . . . .30 A1
Severn Rd ME5 . . . . .32 C5
SEVINGTON 157 B6
Sevington La TN24 . . . . . . .157 A7
Seville Rd ME15 . . . . .96 F6
Sewell Cl CT17 . . . . .27 A6
Sextant Pk ME2 . . . . .9 E6
Seymour Ave
Westgate on Sea CT9 . . . . . . .7 D1
Whitstable CT5 . . . . .20 E1
Seymour Cl CT6 . . . . .23 B1
Seymour Pl CT1 . . . . .87 E7
Seymour Rd
1 Chatham ME5 . . . . .10 B3
Gillingham ME8 . . . . .12 C1
St Margaret's at Cliffe
CT15 . . . . .150 F8
Seymour Villas 10 CT20 . .177 F3
Shackleton Cl ME5 . . . . . . .32 B6
SHADOXHURST 170 A8
Shadoxhurst Rd TN26 . . .169 C7
Shaftesbury Ave CT19 . . .177 E7
Shaftesbury Ct CT14 . . . . .117 D2
Shaftesbury Dr ME16 . . . . .74 C4
Shaftesbury Rd
Canterbury CT2 . . . . .66 F3
Hersden CT3 . . . . .46 E1
Whitstable CT5 . . . . .20 D1
Shaftsbury St CT11 . . . . . . .52 F7
Shah Pl CT11 . . . . .52 D7
Shakespeare Ct CT17 . . . .166 B7
Shakespeare Pas CT7 . . . . .7 H2
Shakespeare Rd
Birchington CT7 . . . . .27 A8
Dover CT17 . . . . .166 B6
Gillingham ME7 . . . . .10 C3
Margate CT9 . . . . .7 J1
Sittingbourne ME10 . . . . . . .37 A4
Shakespeare Terr 12
CT20 . . . . .178 C4
Shalder Ho ME7 . . . . .10 D7
Shalfleet Cl 1 ME5 . . . . . . .32 A7
Shalloak Rd CT2 . . . . .67 D6
Shallows Rd CT10 . . . . .29 D6
Shalmsford Ct CT4 . . . . . . .86 C2
Shalmsford Rd CT4 . . . . . . .85 E2
Shalmsford St CT4 . . . . . . .86 B2
SHALMSFORD STREET . . .86 B1
Shamel Bsns Ctr CT2 . . . . . .9 A5
Shamley Rd ME5 . . . . .32 D2
Shamrock Ave CT5 . . . . . . .43 B7
Shanklin Cl ME5 . . . . .32 C8
Shapland Cl CT6 . . . . .23 C3
Share & Coulter Rd CT5 . .21 D1
Sharfleet Cres ME11 . . . . . .14 D4
Sharon Cres ME5 . . . . .31 F4
Sharps Gn ME8 . . . . .11 D5
Sharsted Hill ME9 . . . . .81 C8
Sharsted Way
Gillingham ME7 . . . . .33 A3

Sharsted Way continued
Maidstone ME14 . . . . .76 B5
SHATTERLING 70 E1
Shatterlocks Inf Sch 7
CT16. . . . . .149 B2
Shaw CI ME14 . . . . .75 C7
Shaw Cross TW24 . . . . . .139 D5
Shawdon Ave CT13. . . . . . .95 A3
Shawstead Rd ME7, ME7. .32 D5
Shaws Way ME1 . . . . .9 C3
Sheal's Cres ME15 . . . . . . .75 A2
Sheals CI ME15 . . . . .75 A2
Shearers CI ME14 . . . . . . .75 A2
Shearwater ME16. . . . . . . .74 B5
Shearwater Ave CT5 . . . . .43 C7
Shearwater CI ME12 . . . . . .3 B8
Shearwater Ho TN29 . . . .195 A3
Shear Way TN29 . . . . .186 C5
Shearway Bsns Pk CT19 . .177 F7
Shearway Rd CT19 . . . . . .177 F7
Sheen Ct CT9. . . . . .7 I2
Sheep Ct La CT4. . . . . .126 A3
Sheepfold La TN23 . . . . . .156 C4
SHEERNESS 1 D3
Sheerness Harbour Est
ME12. . . . . .1 B3
Sheerness Heritage Ctr*
ME12. . . . . .1 D2
Sheerness-on-Sea Sta
ME12. . . . . .1 C1
Sheerness Swim Pool
ME12. . . . . .1 C3
Sheerstone ME9 . . . . .14 D4
SHEERWATER 70 F6
Sheerwater Rd CT3 . . . . . .70 F5
Sheerways ME11 . . . . .62 A6
Sheet Glass Rd ME11 . . . . .3 A3
Sheffield Gdns CT14 . . . .117 C4
Shelden Dr ME8 . . . . .33 F8
Shelden Bsns Ctr ME2 . . . .9 D8
Sheldon CI CT3 . . . . .113 A6
Shelduck CI ME9 . . . . .14 E4
SHELDWICH. 83 C6
Sheldwich CI
3 Ashford TN23 . . . . .155 F6
Ashford TN23. . . . . .156 A6
SHELDWICH LEES 83 C5
Sheldwich Prim Sch
ME13. . . . . .83 C6
Shellbeach ME12 . . . . .4 C5
Shelley Ave CT1 . . . . .67 C2
Shelley Rd ME16 . . . . .74 C2
Shelley Rise ME1 . . . . .9 A3
Shell Grotto* 15 CT9 . . . . .7 J2
Shellness Rd ME12. . . . . . .19 D7
Shellons St CT20. . . . . . . .178 D5
SHELVIN 129 C3
Shelvin La CT4 . . . . .129 C3
Shenley Gr ME14. . . . . .53 F2
Shepherd Dr TN23 . . . . . . .155 F5
Shepherd Dr TN29 . . . . . . .57 A8
Shepherd Neame Brewery*
16 ME13 . . . . .62 D4
Shepherds Close Rd CT4 . .89 C1
Shepperds CI Rd CT4 . . . . .89 E1
Shepperton CI ME5 . . . . . .32 C4
Sheppey CI 8 CT7 . . . . . . .27 A7
Sheppey Coll ME12 . . . . . .1 C3
Sheppey Community Hospl
ME12. . . . . .4 A5
Sheppey Cotts ME12 . . . . . .1 E2
Sheppey Leisure Complex
The ME12 . . . . .1 D3
Sheppey Little Theatre*
ME12. . . . . .1 D1
Sheppey Rd ME15 . . . . .97 A7
Sheppey St ME12 . . . . .1 B2
Sheppey Terr ME12. . . . . . . .4 F5
Sheppey View CT5. . . . . . .43 C6
Sheppey Way
Iwade ME9 . . . . .14 F2
Queenborough ME12, ME9 . .3 D2
Sittingbourne ME9. . . . . . . .14 F4
SHEPWAY 97 D8
Shepway TN24 . . . . .139 E5
Shepway CI CT19 . . . . . . .178 D6
Shepway Cross CT21 . . . .185 B3
Shepway St ME12 . . . . . . .97 C8
Sheraton CI ME1 . . . . .31 F1
Sherbourne Dr ME16 . . . . .74 B2
Sheridale Bsns Ctr ME2 . .9 A6
Sheridan CI
Chatham ME5. . . . . .32 C4
Maidstone ME14 . . . . .74 E8
Sheridan CI ME1. . . . . .9 C3
Sheridan Rd TN16 . . . . . . .149 B3
Sheriff Dr ME5 . . . . .32 A2
Sheringham CI ME16 . . . . .74 A2
Sheringham Ho 5 ME15 . .97 B8
Sherman CI ME7 . . . . .11 B1
Shernolds ME15 . . . . .97 B7

Shernold Sch ME16 . . . . . .74 D5
Sheron CI CT14 . . . . .117 A5
Sherriffs Court La CT12 . . .49 E6
Sherwood Ave ME5 . . . . . .32 A2
Sherwood CI
Ashford TN24. . . . . .139 D7
Faversham ME13. . . . . .40 B1
Herne Bay CT6. . . . . .23 C2
Whitstable CT5 . . . . .43 C6
Sherwood Ct CT8 . . . . .7 C1
Sherwood Dr CT5. . . . . . . .43 C6
Sherwood Gdns CT11 . . . . .29 E1
Sherwood Ho ME5 . . . . . . .32 A3
Sherwood Rd CT7. . . . . . . .26 F5
Shillingheld CT14 . . . . .75 F5
Shimmin Rd ME9 . . . . .58 D5
Ship CI TN29. . . . . .195 C8
Ship La ME1 . . . . .9 E4
SHIPLAND 136 D8
Shipland Rd TN27 . . . . . . .136 D8
Shipley CT ME14 . . . . .75 A4
Shipley Mill CL TN23 . . . .156 C4
Shipman Ave CT2 . . . . .87 C8
Shipmans Way CT12 . . . .149 A3
Ship St CT5 . . . . .178 D6
Shipway Ho CT21 . . . . . . .176 D1
Shipwrights Ave ME12 . . .10 B2
Shipwrights Lee CT5 . . . . .20 C2
Shipyard Area ME13 . . . . .40 D1
Shire La CT13 . . . . .103 C6
Shireway CT CT19 . . . . . . .178 A7
SHIRKOAK 169 A5
Shirkoak Pk TN26 . . . . . . .169 A5
Shirley Ave
Chatham ME5. . . . . .31 D5
Ramsgate CT11 . . . . .29 E1
Shirley Ct ME15 . . . . .97 E5
Shirley Way ME15. . . . . . . .76 A3
Shoebury Terr ME12. . . . . . .5 A5
SHOLDEN. 116 F5
Sholden Bank CT14 . . . . .116 E4
Sholden CE Prim Sch
CT14. . . . . .116 F5
Sholden New Rd CT14 . . .116 F6
Shooters Chase ME9 . . . . .14 D4
Shooters Hill CT15 . . . . . .131 C8
Shooter's Hill 6 CT17 . . .149 C1
Shore CI
Birchington CT7. . . . . .26 D8
Herne Bay CT6. . . . . .22 B3
Shorefields ME8 . . . . .12 B2
Shoregate La CT6. . . . . . . .12 F6
Shoreham La TN30 . . . . . .167 A3
Shoreham Wlk ME15 . . . . .97 F7
Shorland Ct ME1. . . . . .9 B5
Shorncliffe Cres CT20 . . .177 E6
Shorncliffe Ind Est CT20 .177 D6
Shorncliffe Rd CT20. . . . . .177 F5
Short La
Alkham CT15 . . . . .147 D1
Snargate TN29 . . . . .191 D6
Short St
3 Chatham ME4. . . . . . . .10 B3
Chillenden CT3. . . . . .114 A8
5 Sandwich CT13 . . . . . . .73 A1
Sheerness ME12 . . . . .1 C2
Shorts Way ME1 . . . . .9 A3
Shotfield CI CT3 . . . . .70 C6
Shottendane Rd CT9, CT8 . .28 C7
Shottenden La CT4 . . . . . .106 A7
Shottenden Rd
Gillingham ME7. . . . . .10 D7
Shottenden CT4, CT3 . . . .105 D8
Shrimpton CI CT4. . . . . . . .85 B3
Shropshire Terr 1 ME15 . .97 F2
Shrubbery The CT14 . . . . .117 C1
Shrubcote CT14 . . . . .117 C1
Shrub Hill Rd CT5 . . . . . . .44 D7
Shrubsole Ave ME12 . . . . . .1 D1
Shrubsole Dr ME14 . . . . . .53 F3
Shuart La CT7 . . . . .25 F4
Shunters CT ME13 . . . . . . .62 E6
Shurland Ave
Leysdown-on-Sea ME12. . . .6 H1
Minster (Sheppey) ME12 . . .4 B6
Sittingbourne ME10. . . . . .36 F1
Shutler Rd CT21 . . . . .176 B2
SHUTTLESFIELD. 162 A6
Shuttlesfield La CT4 . . . . .144 D1
Sibert's CI CT13. . . . . .130 F5
Sibertswold CE Prim Sch
CT15. . . . . .130 E4
Sidings CI ME13 . . . . .62 E6
Sidings The
Dymchurch TN29 . . . . . . .195 B3
Lyminge CT18 . . . . .161 C7
Whitstable CT5 . . . . .20 C2
Sidney Cooper Gall* CT1 . .66 F1
Sidney Rd
Gillingham ME7. . . . . .10 C7
Rochester ME1 . . . . .9 A2
Signal Ct 6 ME8 . . . . .11 F1
Silchester CI ME14. . . . . . .75 C7
Silecroft St TN23 . . . . . . .138 E1
Silvanus Ho 5 CT11 . . . . .52 D7
Silver Ave CT7 . . . . .27 B6
Silver Bank ME5 . . . . .32 A6
Silverbirch Ct TN26 . . . . .155 A1
Silver Birch Ct TN26 . . . . .155 A1

Silver Birches
Chatham ME5. . . . . .32 A3
Sheerness ME12 . . . . .1 H1
Silver Birches Mobile Homes
Pk TN26. . . . . .171 A4
Silver Birch Gr TN23 . . . . .156 B4
Silverdale ME10 . . . . .74 A2
Silverdale Ave ME12 . . . . . .4 A6
Silverdale Dr
Gillingham ME8. . . . . .33 F7
Herne Bay CT6. . . . . .23 D2
Silverdale Gr ME10. . . . . . .36 D3
Silverdale Rd CT11. . . . . . .52 A5
Silver Hill
Chatham ME4. . . . . .9 F3
Rochester ME1 . . . . .9 A2
Tenterden TN30 . . . . .167 B1
Silver Hill Gdns
Ashford TN24. . . . . .140 A1
4 Chatham ME4. . . . . .9 F3
Silver Hill Rd TN24. . . . . . .140 A1
Silverlands Rd CT18. . . . . .161 C7
Silverspot CT14 . . . . .33 F7
Silver St
Deal CT14 . . . . .117 D7
Silver Street ME9 . . . . . . .57 F5
Silvers The CT10 . . . . .29 C4
SILVER STREET 57 F5
Silver Tree ME5 . . . . .32 B1
Silverweed Rd ME5 . . . . . .31 F4
Simmonds La ME15 . . . . . .98 B6
Simmonds Rd CT1 . . . . . . .87 E7
Simon Ave CT9 . . . . .8 D2
Simone Weil Ave TN24 . . .139 B4
Simon Langton Girls Gram
Sch CT1. . . . . .88 C3
Simon Langton Gram Sch for
Boys CT1. . . . . .88 A4
Simon's Ave TN23. . . . . . . .155 F7
Simon's Rd TN23 . . . . .155 F7
Sinclair CI ME4 . . . . .33 E5
Sindal Shaw Ho ME5. . . . . .31 E4
Singapore Dr ME7 . . . . . . .10 B5
Singer Ave CT6 . . . . .22 B4
Singledge Ave CT16. . . . . .148 F6
Singledge La CT15 . . . . . .131 C2
SINGLETON 155 E7
Singleton Ct CT12 . . . . .52 A3
Singleton Ctr The TN23. . .155 D8
Singleton Hill TN23 . . . . .155 D8
Singleton Rd TN23 . . . . . .138 C1
Sion Hill CT11 . . . . .52 E6
Sion Pass 12 CT11 . . . . . . .52 E6
Sir Evelyn Rd ME1 . . . . .9 B1
Sir John Fogge Ave
TN23 . . . . .138 F4
Sir John Hawkins Hospl
ME4 . . . . .9 E4
Sir John Hawkins Way ME4 .9 F4
Sir John Moore Ave
CT21. . . . . .176 B2
Sir John Moore Ct 5
CT20. . . . . .177 E3
Sir Joseph Williamson's
Mathematical Sch ME1 . .9 C1
Sir Roger Manwoods Sch
CT13. . . . . .94 B8
Sir Thomas Longley Rd
ME2 . . . . .9 E6
Siskin CI
Ashford TN25. . . . . .139 B7
Hawkinge CT18 . . . . .162 F4
Sissinghurst Dr ME16 . . . . .74 B4
SITTINGBOURNE 36 D8
Sittingbourne Com Coll
ME10. . . . . .37 C2
Sittingbourne Ind Pk
ME10. . . . . .36 F5
Sittingbourne & Kemsley
Light Rly* ME10 . . . . .37 A7
Sittingbourne Meml Hospl
ME10. . . . . .36 F3
Sittingbourne Rd
Maidstone, Detling ME14 . .75 E8
Maidstone, Penenden Heath
ME14. . . . . .75 B6
Sittingbourne Retail Pk
ME10. . . . . .36 F5
Sittingbourne Sta* ME10 . .36 E5
Sittingbourne Sta ME10 . .36 F4
Six Bells Pk TN26 . . . . . . .169 A3
Six Fields Path TN30 . . . . .179 A7
SIXMILE 143 D5
SKEETE 160 D7
Skeete Rd CT18 . . . . .160 D7
Skene CI ME8. . . . . .12 A1
Skinner Rd TN29 . . . . .205 C6
Skinner's Alley 3 CT5 . . . .20 D1
Skinners CI ME10 . . . . .53 A6
Skinner St
Chatham ME4. . . . . .9 F3
Gillingham ME7 . . . . .10 C5
Skinner Street Prim Sch 13
ME7 . . . . .10 C6
Skinner's Way ME17 . . . . . .98 E4
Skye CI ME15 . . . . .97 A7
Skylark Way TN23 . . . . . . .156 D3
SLADE 80 E1
Slade Rd ME17 . . . . .102 D8
Slades CI CT5 . . . . .44 C8
Slatin Rd ME2 . . . . .9 B8
Sleigh Rd CT2 . . . . .67 F6
Slicketts Hill ME4. . . . . . . .10 A4
Slip La CT15 . . . . .147 C2
Slipway Rd ME12 . . . . .1 A3
Sloe La CT10, CT9 . . . . . . .29 B6
Slough Rd ME9 . . . . .59 A3

SLUTSHOLE. 64 A5
SLY CORNER 181 F5
SMALL HYTHE 179 B4
Small Hythe CI ME15 . . . . .76 B2
Smallhythe Place (Mus)*
TN30 . . . . .179 C1
Small Hythe Rd TN30. . . . .179 B4
Smarden Prim Sch TN27 .135 A1
Smarden ME8 . . . . .12 B1
Smarden Rd TN27. . . . . . . .136 B6
Smarden Wlk ME8 . . . . . . .76 C4
Smeed CI 4 ME11 . . . . .76 C4
Smeed-Dean Ctr The
ME10. . . . . .37 A4
SMEETH. 158 D5
Smeeth Prim Sch TN25. . .158 D5
Smith Rd ME5 . . . . .32 B3
Smiths Orch ME9 . . . . .57 F1
Smith St ME2 . . . . .9 A6
Smithy Dr TN23 . . . . .156 C4
Smugglers Leap Cvn Pk
CT12. . . . . .50 C8
Smuggler's Way CT7 . . . . .27 A8
Snakes Hill CT3. . . . . .91 A5
SNARGATE 191 E6
Snargate La TN29 . . . . . . .191 C5
Snargate St CT17 . . . . . . .166 D6
Snelgrove Rd 14 CT16. . . .166 D6
Snell Gdns CT16 . . . . .22 B2
Snipe CI TN25 . . . . .139 C7
SNIPESHILL. 37 D4
Snodhurst Ave ME5 . . . . . .31 E5
Snodhurst Ho 2 ME5 . . . . .32 A7
Snowball CI TN24 . . . . . . .156 B4
Snowdon Ave ME14 . . . . . .75 B5
Snowdon Cl ME5 . . . . .32 B7
Snowdon Par ME14 . . . . . .75 C5
SNOWDOWN 113 A3
Snowdown CI CT3 . . . . . . .112 F5
Snowdown Sta CT15 . . . . .113 B3
Snowdrop CI CT19 . . . . . . .178 C6
Snow No ME7 . . . . .10 C1
Sobraan Way CT1 . . . . .67 D1
Solar Ct CT12 . . . . .52 C7
Solent Gdns ME14 . . . . . . .32 B8
Soleshill Rd CT4 . . . . .84 E1
SOLE STREET 125 B7
Sole Street Cotts CT4 . . . .125 A7
Solomon Ho CT14 . . . . . . .117 A3
Solomon Rd ME8 . . . . .12 A1
Solomons La ME13 . . . . . . .62 D7
Solomons Rd ME4 . . . . .9 F4
Somerfield Barn Ct
TN25 . . . . .174 C8
Somerfield La ME16 . . . . . .74 D5
Somerfield Hospl The
ME16. . . . . .74 E5
Somerfield La ME16. . . . . . .74 D5
Somerfield Rd ME16 . . . . . .74 D4
Somerset CI
Chatham ME5. . . . . .32 C4
Sittingbourne ME10. . . . . .36 C4
Whitstable CT5 . . . . .43 D7
Somerset Ct
7 Broadstairs CT10 . . . . . .30 A4
Deal CT14 . . . . .117 C3
Ramsgate CT12 . . . . .29 B2
Somerset Rd
Ashford TN24. . . . . .139 B3
Canterbury CT1 . . . . .88 D3
Deal CT14 . . . . .117 C3
Folkestone CT19 . . . . .177 E6
Maidstone ME15 . . . . .97 C8
Somme Ct CT1 . . . . .67 D1
Sommerville CI ME13 . . . . .62 E7
Somner Ct CT21 . . . . .66 D1
Somner Wlk ME15 . . . . .97 F4
Sondes Ct CT14 . . . . .23 A2
Sondes Rd CT14 . . . . .117 D5
Sonora Way ME10. . . . . . . .36 C7
Sorrell Rd ME5 . . . . .31 F4
Sotherton TN24 . . . . .156 F7
Souberg CI CT14 . . . . .117 C8
SOUTH ALKHAM 164 D3
Southall CI CT14 . . . . .50 C7
SOUTH ASHFORD 156 E6
South Ave
Aylesham CT15 . . . . .113 A3
Gillingham ME8 . . . . .12 B2
Sittingbourne ME10. . . . . .37 A3
South Avenue Jun & Inf Schs
ME10. . . . . .37 A3
South Bank of the Swale
Nature Reserve* ME13 . .41 A6
South Barham Rd CT4 . . . .128 C3
South Borough Prim Sch
ME15. . . . . .75 A2
Southbourne TN23 . . . . . . .155 E5
Southbourne Gr ME5. . . . . .32 A4
Southbourne Rd CT19 . . . .178 E5
South Brooks Rd TN29 . . .207 H6
South Bush La ME5 . . . . . . .31 F4
South Camber Way CT10 .150 B3
South CI CT11. . . . . .88 A8
South Court Dr CT3. . . . . . .91 A7
South Cres ME17 . . . . .96 A4
South Ct
Deal CT14 . . . . .117 D6
Ramsgate CT12 . . . . .29 B2
Southdown Rd ME13 . . . . . .3 E6
South Eastern Rd
Ramsgate CT11 . . . . .52 D7
Rochester ME2 . . . . .9 C7
Southenay La TN25 . . . . . .159 C4
Southern Way CT19 . . . . . .178 E6

Southernwood Rise
CT20 . . . . .177 F4
South Exit Rd CT16 . . . . . .166 G8
Southfields ME1 . . . . .9 C3
South Foreland Lighthouse*
CT15. . . . . .150 F3
Southgate Rd TN30 . . . . . .179 C7
South Goodwin Ct CT14. .117 D8
SOUTH GREEN 57 A5
South Green La ME4 . . . . . .56 F6
Southhill Rd ME4 . . . . .9 F3
South Kent Coll (Ashford
Campus) TN23. . . . . .156 A8
South Kent Coll (Dover
Campus) 10 CT16. . . . . .166 D8
South Kent Coll (Folkestone
Campus) CT20. . . . . .178 B5
South Kent Coll (South
Ashford Campus) TN23 .155 F6
South Lea TN23 . . . . .156 A3
Southlees La ME9 . . . . .56 F3
South Lodge CT5 . . . . .20 E3
South Lodge CI CT5. . . . . . .20 E3
Southmead CI CT19 . . . . . .178 A6
South Military Rd CT17. . .166 C5
South Rd TN23. . . . . .138 F1
South of England Rare
Breeds Ctr* TN26 . . . . . .169 D1
Southover Ct 2 CT20 . . . . .177 E3
South Park Bsns Village
ME15 . . . . .75 A1
South Pondside Rd ME4. . .10 A8
South Quay ME13 . . . . .40 D1
South Rd
Chatham, Brompton ME4,
ME7 . . . . .10 A7
Chatham ME4. . . . . .10 B7
Dover CT17 . . . . .166 B8
Faversham ME13. . . . . .62 C7
Herne Bay CT6. . . . . .23 A5
Hythe CT21 . . . . .176 D1
Kingsdown CT14 . . . . .134 D5
Sandwich CT13 . . . . .73 A8
Southsea Ave ME12 . . . . . . .4 C8
Southsea Dr CT6. . . . . .22 D4
South Side Three Rd ME4 .10 D8
South St
Canterbury CT1 . . . . .67 C2
Deal CT14 . . . . .117 D6
3 Folkestone CT20. . . . . .178 E4
Lydd TN29 . . . . .205 C6
Queenborough ME11. . . . . . .2 F5
Selling ME13 . . . . .84 F8
Whitstable CT5 . . . . .44 A7
Southstone Ct CT21 . . . . . .176 C1
SOUTH STOUR 157 B1
South Stour Ave TN23 . . . .156 C8
SOUTH STREET
Selling 84 F8
Stockbury. 56 C7
Whitstable 44 A7
Southstreet Crossing CT5 .44 A7
South Street Rd ME9 . . . . . .56 C7
South Tankerton 21 A7
South Turbine Hall Rd
TN29 . . . . .209 C2
South View CT3 . . . . .46 F1
Southview Gdns CT3. . . . . .92 B8
South View Gdns ME12 . . . .1 D1
South Wall CT5. . . . . .43 D6
Southwall Ind Est CT14 . .117 B8
Southwall Rd CT14. . . . . . .117 B6
SOUTH
WILLESBOROUGH 156 E6
Southwold PI CT8. . . . . .27 E7
Southwood Gdns CT11 . . . .52 C6
Southwood Rd CT11 . . . . . .52 C6
Southwood Rd
Ramsgate CT11 . . . . .52 C6
Whitstable CT5 . . . . .21 B2
Sovereign Bvd ME7, ME8. .33 E7
Sovereigns The ME16 . . . . .74 D4
Sowell St CT10 . . . . .29 F5
Spade La ME9 . . . . .34 C6
Spanton Cres CT21. . . . . . .176 A3
Sparrow Castle 3 CT9 . . . . .7 J1
Sparrow Way CT3 . . . . .47 A1
Spartan Rd TN23 . . . . .155 C8
Speakman Ct 5 CT11. . . . . .52 C6
Spearhead Rd TN24 . . . . . .74 F7
Spearpoint Cnr TN24 . . . . .139 F5
Spectrum Bsns Ctr ME2 . .9 E8
Spectrum Bsns Est ME15 .97 F4
Speedwell Ave ME5 . . . . . . .31 F4
Speedwell CI
Gillingham ME7. . . . . .10 E5
Maidstone ME14 . . . . .75 E5
Speedwell Rd CT5 . . . . .43 B6
Speke Rd CT10 . . . . .29 E6
Spekes Rd ME7 . . . . .33 B6
Spelders Hill TN25 . . . . . .141 A5
Speldhurst CI TN23 . . . . . .155 E5
Speldhurst CI ME16 . . . . . .74 D4
Speldhurst Gdns CT9 . . . . . .8 E3
Spembley Ct ME4 . . . . .9 E4
Spence CI CT18. . . . . .163 A4
Spencer CI ME5 . . . . .32 A5
Spencer Flats ME5 . . . . . . .32 B8
Spencer Ho 3 CT20 . . . . . .177 F5
Spencer Rd ME2 . . . . .27 A8
Spencer Sq CT11 . . . . .52 D6
Spencer St 6 CT11 . . . . . . .52 D6
Spencer Way ME15 . . . . . . .97 F2
Spenlow Dr ME5 . . . . .54 A8

Spenser Rd CT6 . . . . .22 F4
Spicer Homes ME10. . . . . . .36 F2
Spicers Ct CT21. . . . . .175 C6
Spicers Field CT6. . . . . .23 D2
Spicer's Pl CT3 . . . . .69 C2
Spiers The ME7 . . . . .11 C5
Spillett Cl ME13 . . . . .62 B6
Spillway The ME15. . . . . . . .74 F8
Spindle Glade ME14. . . . . . .75 C5
Spindlewood Cl ME5. . . . . .32 B3
Spindlewood End TN23. . .138 D4
Spinnaker Ct ◀ ME1. . . . . . .9 C1
Spinners Acre Jun Sch
ME5 . . . . .32 C1
Spinney La CT3 . . . . .112 E4
Spinney The
Ashford TN23. . . . . .138 E3
Chatham ME5. . . . . .32 B1
Crabble CT17. . . . . .148 E2
Maidstone ME15 . . . . .75 B2
Margate CT9 . . . . .8 E1
Spire Alexandra Hospl
ME5 . . . . .54 A8
Spire Ave CT5 . . . . .44 A8
Spires Acad CT5. . . . . .68 C8
Spire St Saviour's Hospl
CT21. . . . . .176 F2
Spires The
Canterbury CT2 . . . . .66 F2
Maidstone ME16 . . . . .74 D4
Spitalfield La TN28. . . . . . .201 F6
Spitalfield Terr TN28 . . . . .201 F6
Spitfire Cl ME5 . . . . .32 B6
Spitfire Way CT18. . . . . . . .163 B3
Splashes L Ctr ME8 . . . . . .11 D1
Split Ho CT17. . . . . .149 A1
Split La CT14 . . . . .127 A5
Spong Wood Nature
Reserve* TN25. . . . . . . .143 A8
Sportsfield ME14 . . . . .75 B5
Spot La ME15. . . . . .76 A2
Spratling La CT12. . . . . .28 E1
Spratling St CT12. . . . . .28 E1
Sprig The ME14 . . . . .76 A4
Springett Way ME17. . . . . .96 D3
Spring Farm TN29 . . . . . . .192 D5
Springfarm Rd TN29 . . . . .192 C5
Springfield Ave
Maidstone ME14 . . . . .74 F7
Tenterden TN30 . . . . .167 C2
Springfield Cl CT11. . . . . . .29 E2
Springfield Pass CT21. . . .176 B2
Springfield Rd
Dover CT16 . . . . .149 B2
Gillingham ME7. . . . . .10 E6
Margate CT9 . . . . .8 E3
Sittingbourne ME10. . . . . .36 D5
Springfield Terr ▣ ME4. . . .9 F4
Springfield Way CT21 . . .177 B3
Spring Grove Sch TN25. . .123 C2
Springhead Rd ME13. . . . . .40 D1
Spring Ho CT21. . . . . .176 C2
Spring Hollow TN29 . . . . .195 A4
Spring La
Canterbury CT1 . . . . .88 C7
Fordwich CT2. . . . . .68 A4
Hythe CT21 . . . . .175 E6
Springside Terr CT18. . . . .161 C6
Spring Terr ▣ CT20 . . . . . .178 D5
Springvale
Gillingham ME8 . . . . .33 C6
Iwade ME9 . . . . .14 D4
Spring Vale ME16 . . . . .74 E4
Spring Wlk CT5. . . . . .43 C7
Springwood Cl
Ashford TN23. . . . . .138 E3
▣ Maidstone ME14. . . . . . .74 A3
Springwood Ct TN20 . . . .202 B6
Springwood Dr TN23. . . . .138 E3
Springwood Rd ME10 . . . . .36 E6
Sprotlands Ave TN24 . . . .139 F1
Sprotshill Cl ME10 . . . . . . .36 E6
Spurgeons Cotts ME17. . . .96 E2
Spurway ME14. . . . . .76 A4
Square Hill ME15 . . . . .75 B4
Square Hill Rd ME15. . . . . .75 B4
Square The
Birchington CT7 . . . . .27 A7
Chilham CT4. . . . . .107 B8
Lenham ME17 . . . . .101 D5
Selling ME13 . . . . .84 A6
Sittingbourne ME10. . . . . .14 F1
Squeeze Gut Alley ◀ CT15 20 D2
Squire Ave CT2 . . . . .87 C8
Squires Ct ME12 . . . . .5 E3
Squires Way CT16. . . . . . .149 A3
Squirrel La TN25. . . . . .138 F5
Stable Cl ME5 . . . . .32 C5
Stable Ct
Chilham CT4. . . . . .107 B7
Faversham ME13. . . . . . . .62 D6
Stablemead CT19 . . . . .178 A2
Stace Cl TN30. . . . . .179 C8
Staceys St ME14 . . . . .74 F5
Stade St CT21 . . . . .176 C1
Stade The CT19 . . . . .178 E5
Stadium Way ME10 . . . . . . .37 C6
Stadler Cl ME16 . . . . .74 D7
Staffa Rd ME15 . . . . .97 A7
Stafford Cl TN23 . . . . .138 F2
Stafford House Sch of
English ▣ CT16. . . . . . .149 A8
Staffordshire St ◀ CT11 . .52 E7
Stafford St ME7. . . . . .10 C5
Stag Rd ME5. . . . . .32 B5

Stagshaw Cl ME15 . . . . . . .75 A2
Staines Hill CT2 . . . . .68 B7
Staines Pl CT10. . . . . .30 B5
Stalham Bsns Ctr ME11 . . .3 A3
Stalham Ct ME7 . . . . .33 B4
Stalin Ave ME5 . . . . .32 B8
STALISFIELD GREEN 103 D6
Stalisfield Rd
Charing TN27 . . . . .103 E3
Stalisfield Green ME13,
TN27. . . . . .103 C5
Throwley ME13. . . . . .82 C6
Stamford Villas ME12. . . . . .5 C2
Stampers The ME15. . . . . . .74 D2
Stanbury Cres CT19 . . . . .178 F7
Stancomb Ave CT11. . . . . . .52 C5
Standard Ave CT6. . . . . .22 A4
Standen Ct ME8 . . . . .33 E4
Standen La CT18. . . . . .163 E5
Staner Ct CT12 . . . . .52 A8
Staner Hill CT12 . . . . .51 F8
STANFORD. 160 B1
Stanford Dr ME16. . . . . .74 C3
Stangate Dr ME9 . . . . .14 D4
STANHOPE. 155 F6
Stanhope Ave ME10. . . . . . .37 A3
Stanhope Ct ME14 . . . . .74 E7
Stanhope Rd
Ashford TN23. . . . . .155 C6
Deal CT14 . . . . .117 D6
Dover CT16 . . . . .149 C2
Rochester ME2 . . . . .9 A7
Stanhope Sq TN23 . . . . . . .155 F6
Stanley Ave
Minster (Sheppey) ME12. . .4 D7
Queenborough ME11. . . . . .3 A4
Stanley Cl CT19 . . . . .187 B4
Stanley Gdns CT6. . . . . .22 F3
Stanley Pl
Broadstairs CT10. . . . . . . .30 A4
Ramsgate CT11. . . . . .52 E7
Stanley Rd
Broadstairs CT10. . . . . . . .30 A6
Chatham ME5. . . . . .32 C6
Deal CT14 . . . . .117 D5
Folkestone CT19 . . . . . . .177 E6
Gillingham ME7 . . . . .10 C6
Herne Bay CT6. . . . . .22 F4
Margate CT9 . . . . .8 A3
Ramsgate CT11. . . . . .52 D8
Whitstable CT5 . . . . .43 D7
Stanmore Ct CT1. . . . . .88 B7
Stansfeld Ave CT18 . . . . . .163 A4
Stansted Cl ME16 . . . . .74 D7
STAPLE. 92 A5
Staple Cl ME10 . . . . .36 E5
Staplehurst Ave CT10 . . . . .30 A2
Staplehurst Gdns CT9. . . . . .8 E2
Staplehurst Lodge Ind Est
ME10 . . . . .36 D5
Staplehurst Rd
Gillingham ME8 . . . . .11 B3
Sittingbourne ME10. . . . . .36 D5
Staple Rd CT3 . . . . .91 C6
Staplers Ct ME14 . . . . .75 B8
Staple St ME13 . . . . .63 F5
STAPLESTREET. 64 A5
Staplestreet Rd ME13 . . . . .64 A4
Star Hill ME1 . . . . .9 D5
Star La
Folkestone CT19 . . . . . . .177 D7
Gillingham ME7 . . . . .33 A7
Margate CT9 . . . . .29 A5
Starle Cl CT1 . . . . .67 B1
Star Mill Ct ME5 . . . . .10 D2
Star Mill La ME5 . . . . .10 D2
Starnes Ct ▣ ME14 . . . . . . .75 A5
Star Rd TN24 . . . . .139 D2
Starvation Cnr ◀ CT5. . . . .20 D2
Starveacre La ME9. . . . . . . .36 B1
STATENBOROUGH. 93 C4
Station App
Adisham CT3 . . . . .112 E8
Birchington CT7. . . . . .27 A7
Maidstone ME16 . . . . .74 F3
Martin Mill CT15 . . . . . . .133 C2
Minster (Thanet) CT12. . . .50 C5
New Romney TN28. . . . . .202 C6
Station App Rd CT11. . . . . .52 C8
Station Approach Rd
CT11. . . . . .52 D8
Station Chine CT6 . . . . .22 F5
Station Cotts ME13 . . . . . . .84 F7
Station Dr CT14 . . . . .117 A1
Station Hill Cotts ME15 . . .96 A7
Station Mews
Elham CT4 . . . . .144 F4
▣ Ramsgate CT12 . . . . . . .29 C1
▣ Tenterden TN30 . . . . . .179 A7
Station Rd
Adisham CT3 . . . . .90 E1
Ashford TN23. . . . . .139 C2
Bekesbourne CT4 . . . . . . .89 C4
Birchington CT7. . . . . .27 A7
Bridge CT4. . . . . .88 F2
Charing TN27 . . . . .120 C7
Chartham ME4 . . . . .86 D3
Deal CT14 . . . . .117 B1
Dymchurch TN29 . . . . . . .195 B7
East Farleigh ME15. . . . . .96 A7
Faversham ME13. . . . . . . .62 D6
Folkestone CT19 . . . . . . .177 F5
Gillingham ME8 . . . . .12 A2
Harrietsham ME17. . . . . .100 D6
Herne Bay CT6. . . . . .22 E4
Hythe CT21 . . . . .176 D3
Lydd TN29 . . . . .205 D7
Lyminge CT18 . . . . .161 C6

Station Rd continued
Maidstone ME14 . . . . .74 F5
Margate CT9 . . . . .7 H2
Martin Mill CT15 . . . . . . .133 D1
Minster (Thanet) CT12. . . .50 C5
Newington ME9 . . . . .35 B6
New Romney TN28. . . . . .202 C6
Pluckley TN27 . . . . .136 C5
Rochester ME2 . . . . .9 C7
Shepherdswell CT15 . . . .130 D5
Smeeth TN25 . . . . .158 B3
St Margaret's at Cliffe
CT15 . . . . .150 E8
Tenterden TN30 . . . . .179 A7
Teynham ME9. . . . . .38 D2
Westgate on Sea CT8 . . . .27 A1
Whitstable CT5 . . . . .20 E2
Station Road E CT1 . . . . . . .87 F7
Station Road W CT2 . . . . . .66 F1
Station Row ME9 . . . . .38 D3
Station St ME10 . . . . .36 F4
Station Terr TN28 . . . . . . .202 C6
Steddy Cl ◀ TN23 . . . . . . .155 F6
Steed Cl CT16 . . . . .146 B8
Steeds Cl TN23 . . . . .156 A1
Steeds La TN23, TN26. . . .156 B1
Steele St ME2 . . . . .9 A8
Steerforth Cl ME1. . . . . .9 C2
Stella Maris RC Prim Sch
CT19. . . . . .178 C6
STELLING MINNIS 126 F2
Stelling Minnis CE Prim Sch
CT4. . . . . .126 F6
Stembrook CT16 . . . . .166 D8
Stembrook Ct ◀ CT16 . . . .166 D7
Stempe CT17. . . . . .163 B3
Stephen Cl CT10 . . . . .30 A4
Stephen Ct ▣ CT20 . . . . . .178 D5
Stephens Cl
Faversham ME13. . . . . . . .62 B8
Ramsgate CT11. . . . . .52 C8
Stephen's Cl CT9 . . . . .28 B7
Stephenson Rd CT2. . . . . . .66 F3
Steps Hill Rd ME9 . . . . .56 D6
Step Style ME10 . . . . .37 B2
Sterling Ave ME14 . . . . .74 C5
Sterling Cl CT10 . . . . .29 E5
Sterling Ct ▣ CT21 . . . . . . .66 F1
Sterling Rd
Queenborough ME11. . . . . .3 A5
Sittingbourne ME10. . . . . .36 D1
Sterry Gdns ME15. . . . . . . .97 E7
Steven Cl ME4. . . . . .10 A3
Stevens Cl TN30 . . . . .179 A7
Stevens Cotts TN30 . . . . . .179 A7
Stevens Ho CT17 . . . . .166 C8
Stevenson Cl ME15 . . . . . . .74 F3
Stickfast La ME9. . . . . .14 A1
STIFF STREET. 57 E7
Stiles Cl
Folkestone CT19 . . . . . . .178 A2
Minster (Sheppey) ME12. . .4 A6
Stirling Cl
Gillingham ME8 . . . . .33 E4
◀ Rochester ME1 . . . . .9 A3
Stirling Way CT12. . . . . .29 A2
Stirlng Rd TN24. . . . . .156 D7
Stisted Way TN27 . . . . .118 F3
STOCKBURY. 56 E8
Stockbury Dr ME16 . . . . . . .74 D7
Stockbury Gdns CT9 . . . . . . .8 E2
Stockbury Hill Wood Nature
Reserve* ME9. . . . . .56 D6
Stockdale Gdns CT14 . . . .117 C4
Stockers Brow ME9 . . . . . . .59 A7
STOCKER'S HEAD 103 F1
Stocker's Hill ME13 . . . . . . .63 E4
Stockett La ME15 . . . . .96 D6
Stockham Ct CT17 . . . . . . .177 E2
Stock La TN25 . . . . .158 A4
Stocks Mill Windmill*
TN30 . . . . .189 A3
Stocks Rd TN30. . . . . .188 F3
Stocks The ME13. . . . . .83 C6
Stockton Cl ME9 . . . . .75 B8
Stockwood Chase CT2 . . . .66 A2
Stoddart Rd CT14. . . . . . . .177 E6
STODMARSH. 69 B6
Stodmarsh National Nature
Reserve* CT3. . . . . .68 C3
Stodmarsh Rd CT3. . . . . . . .68 C3
Stombers La CT18 . . . . . . .163 C6
Stonar Cl
Ramsgate CT11. . . . . .29 E1
Sandwich CT13 . . . . .73 A1
Stonar Gdns CT13. . . . . . . .73 A2
Stoneacre* ME9. . . . . .98 B7
Stoneacre Ct ME8 . . . . .33 D3
Stoneacre Ct ◀ ME15. . . . .75 A1
Stoneacre La ME15 . . . . . . .95 B7
Stone Barn Ave CT7. . . . . . .27 A6
Stone Bay Sch CT10. . . . . . .30 B6
Stonebridge TN25. . . . . . . .141 A5
Stonebridge Cotts TN23. .156 B8
STONEBRIDGE GREEN . . .119 A4
Stonebridge Green Rd
TN27 . . . . .118 F4
Stonebridge Rd CT2 . . . . . .67 A2
Stonebridge Way ME13. . . .62 B7
Stone Cnr TN30. . . . . .189 A6
STONE CROSS
Aldington Frith. 171 F6
Sandwich. 93 E7
Stonecross Lea ME5 . . . . . .10 C1

Stone Cross Lees CT13 . . . .93 F7
Stone Cross Rd TN25. . . . .171 E5
Stonedane Ct ME13 . . . . . . .62 C8
Stonegate TN25. . . . . .123 E2
Stone Gdns CT10 . . . . .30 B5
Stone Gn TN30 . . . . .189 F4
STONEHALL. 147 F8
Stonehall Rd CT15 . . . . . . .147 F8
Stonehead Rd CT14, CT15 115 E1
STONE HILL. 159 A2
Stone Hill TN25 . . . . .159 F2
Stone Hill Rd TN27 . . . . . .118 F2
Stone Ho CT10. . . . . .30 B7
Stone House Mews
CT10 . . . . .30 B7
STONE-IN-OXNEY 189 F4
Stonerock Cl CT2 . . . . .66 B7
Stone St
Faversham ME13 . . . . .62 C7
Lympne CT21 . . . . .175 A4
Stanford CT21 . . . . .160 C3
Stelling Minnis CT4 . . . . .126 D4
Westenhanger TN25, CT21 175 B6
Stonestile Farm Rd
CT7 . . . . .103 A3
Stone Stile La CT4 . . . . .84 D1
STONESTREET GREEN . . .173 A7
Stoneway Rd CT4. . . . . . . .126 D2
Stoney Bank ME7 . . . . .10 F1
Stoney Rd ME13 . . . . .64 B3
Stony La ME1 . . . . .31 C5
Stonyway La CT15 . . . . . . .165 C5
Stopford Rd ME7 . . . . .10 D4
Storehouse Wharf ME12. . . .1 A3
Stores Rd TN29 . . . . .209 C2
Storey Cres CT18. . . . . . . .163 A5
Stour Cl
Ashford TN23. . . . . .138 E1
Chartham CT4 . . . . .86 D2
Stour Cres CT1 . . . . .67 B3
Stour Ct
◀ Canterbury CT1. . . . . . .87 F8
◀ Sandwich CT13 . . . . . . .72 F1
Stour Ctr TN24. . . . . .139 C1
Stourfields TN24 . . . . .139 D4
Stourmouth Rd CT3. . . . . . .70 C8
Stour Rd CT4. . . . . .86 D2
Stour Retail Pk CT1. . . . . . .67 D3
Stourside Studios ▣ CT1 .66 F1
Stour St CT1. . . . . .87 F8
Stour Valley Cl CT3 . . . . . . .47 D3
Stour Valley Ind Est CT4. . .86 E4
Stourville ▣ CT1 . . . . .87 F8
Stowell Cl TN23. . . . . .155 C8
STOWTING. 160 A8
Stowting CE Prim Sch
TN25. . . . . .160 B8
STOWTING COMMON . . .143 A4
Stowting Hill TN25 . . . . . .143 A1
Straight La TN26 . . . . .191 F1
Strakers Hill
East Studdal CT15 . . . . . .132 D8
Tilmanstone CT15 . . . . . .115 C1
Strand Approach Rd ME7 .10 E7
Strand L Pool & Pk ME7 . .10 E7
Strand Rdbt The ME7 . . . . .10 E7
Strand St CT13 . . . . .72 F1
Strand The CT14 . . . . .117 D4
Stranger's Cl CT1. . . . . .87 C6
Stranger's La CT1. . . . . .87 C6
Strangford Pl CT6 . . . . .23 B2
Strangford Rd CT5. . . . . . . .20 D2
Strasbourg St CT9 . . . . .29 A6
Stratford Ave ME8 . . . . .33 D8
Stratford Dr ME15 . . . . .97 D6
Stratford La ▣ ME8. . . . . . .33 F8
Straw Mill Hill ME15. . . . . .74 E1
Stream Wlk CT5 . . . . .20 D2
Street E TN29. . . . . .209 D2
Streete Court Rd CT8 . . . . .27 F8
Streete Ct CT8. . . . . .27 F8
STREET END. 109 F7
Street End CT3 . . . . .71 E1
Street End Rd ME5. . . . . . . .10 B1
Streetfield CT6 . . . . .46 B8
Streetfield Rd ME8 . . . . .11 F1
Street The
Acol CT7. . . . . .27 B3
Adisham CT3 . . . . .112 D8
Appledore TN26 . . . . .190 D8
Ash CT3 . . . . .71 D1
Ashford, Great Chart TN23 138 C1
Ashford, Kennington TN24 .139 C4
Ashford, Willesborough Lees
TN24. . . . . .157 B8
Barham CT4. . . . . .111 F1
Bethersden TN26. . . . . . .153 D5
Bishopsbourne CT4 . . . . .111 C6
Borden ME9. . . . . .36 B2
Bossingham CT4. . . . . . . .127 A7
Boughton Street ME13 . . .64 A3
Boxley ME14 . . . . .54 C3
Brabourne TN25. . . . . . . .159 C8
Bredgar ME9 . . . . .58 A5
Bredhurst ME7. . . . . .33 B1
Brook TN25 . . . . .141 B6
Chilham CT4. . . . . .107 B8
Deal CT14 . . . . .116 F6
Denton CT4. . . . . .129 B3
Detling ME14 . . . . .55 A1
Doddington ME9 . . . . .80 E7
East Langdon CT15 . . . . .133 A1
Eastling ME13 . . . . .81 E6
Egerton TN27 . . . . .118 F3
Eythorne CT15 . . . . .131 D7
Faversham ME13 . . . . .40 B2
Finglesham CT14 . . . . . . .116 B8
Godmersham CT4 . . . . . .107 B2

Street The continued
Goodnestone CT3 . . . . . . .91 D2
Guston CT15 . . . . .149 E6
Hamstreet TN26. . . . . . . .183 A7
Hartlip ME9 . . . . .34 D5
Hastingleigh TN25 . . . . . .142 B6
Hawkinge CT18 . . . . .163 B5
Hernhill ME13 . . . . .138 A6
Ickham CT3. . . . . .90 E2
Iwade ME9 . . . . .14 E4
Kingston CT14 . . . . .111 D3
Lower Halstow ME9. . . . . .13 B3
Lympne CT21 . . . . .174 F2
Lynsted ME9 . . . . .60 A6
Maidstone ME14 . . . . .76 C4
Martin Mill CT15 . . . . . . .133 E3
Mersham TN25. . . . . .157 E4
Molash CT4. . . . . .105 F4
Newnham ME9 . . . . .81 C8
Nonington CT15. . . . . . . .113 D1
Northbourne CT14 . . . . . .116 A5
Patrixbourne CT4. . . . . . . .89 B3
Peene CT18 . . . . .177 A7
Petham CT4 . . . . .109 B3
Pluckley TN27 . . . . .136 D7
Postling CT21. . . . . .160 F2
Preston CT3. . . . . .70 C6
Selling ME13 . . . . .84 B6
Shadoxhurst TN26 . . . . . .170 A8
Sittingbourne ME9. . . . . . .37 E3
Smarden TN27 . . . . .135 A1
Staple CT3. . . . . .91 F6
St Nicholas at Wade CT7. .25 F2
Stourmouth CT3. . . . . .70 C6
Stone in Oxney TN30 . . .190 A5
Stourmouth CT3. . . . . .48 E1
Upchurch ME9. . . . . .12 F4
West Hougham CT15. . . .164 F5
Wickhambreaux CT3 . . . . .69 C2
Wittersham TN30. . . . . . .188 D3
Womenswold CT4 . . . . . .112 D2
Woodnesborough CT13 . . .93 C7
Wormshill ME9 . . . . .79 A7
Worth CT14. . . . . .94 B5
Street W TN29 . . . . .209 C2
Stretton Ct CT14 . . . . .117 D5
Stringer Dr CT7. . . . . .27 A6
Strode Cres ME12. . . . . .1 D2
Strode Park Rd CT6. . . . . . .23 A2
Strond St CT17 . . . . .166 D6
STROOD 9 A6
Strood Ret Pk ME2. . . . . .9 B7
Strood Sta ME2 . . . . .9 C7
Strouts Rd TN23 . . . . .155 D7
Strover St ME7 . . . . .10 C7
Stuart Cl ME14 . . . . .75 C6
Stuart Ct
Canterbury CT1 . . . . .88 A6
Dover CT17. . . . . .166 C8
Stuart Ho CT14 . . . . .117 A5
Stuart Rd
Folkestone CT19 . . . . . . .178 E6
Gillingham ME7 . . . . .10 D3
STUBB'S CROSS. 155 C2
STUDDAL. 132 C7
STUDD HILL. 22 A3
Studds Cotts CT6. . . . . .22 A3
Studfall Cl CT21 . . . . .160 F2
Studio Cl TN24 . . . . .139 E6
Stumble La TN23 . . . . .156 B1
Stuppington Court Farm
CT1. . . . . .87 E4
Stuppington La CT1. . . . . . .87 F5
Sturdee Ave ME7 . . . . .10 E4
Sturdy Cl CT21. . . . . .176 D2
Sturges Rd TN24 . . . . .139 B3
Sturla Rd ME4 . . . . .10 A3
Sturmer Cl CT1. . . . . .88 C7
STURRY 67 F7
Sturry CE Prim Sch CT2. . .68 A7
Sturry Court Mews CT2 . . .67 F6
Sturry Hill CT2 . . . . .67 F6
Sturry Rd CT1, CT2 . . . . . . .67 C3
Sturry Sta CT2 . . . . .67 F5
Sturry Way ME8 . . . . .11 C2
Style Cl ME8. . . . . .33 F8
Styles La ME14 . . . . .54 C3
Subdown Cotts TN25 . . . .159 C8
Sudbury Pl CT8 . . . . .27 E7
Suffolk Ave
Gillingham ME8 . . . . .11 F1
Westgate on Sea CT8 . . . .27 D7
Suffolk Ct ◀ ME8. . . . . .11 F1
Suffolk Dr TN23. . . . . .139 A2
Suffolk Gdns CT17 . . . . . . .165 F7
Suffolk Rd
Canterbury CT1 . . . . .88 D8
Maidstone ME15 . . . . .97 D8
Suffolk St CT5 . . . . .43 D8
Sugarloaf Wlk CT19. . . . . .178 D8
Sullivan Cl CT1. . . . . .87 D6
Sultan Mews ME5. . . . . .32 C2
Sultan Rd ME5. . . . . .32 C2
Summer Cl
Hythe CT21 . . . . .175 F2
Tenterden TN30 . . . . .167 C1
Summer Ct
Canterbury CT1 . . . . .66 C1
Whitstable CT5 . . . . .21 C2
SUMMERFIELD. 92 B4
Summerfield Ave CT5 . . . . .20 F1
Summerfield Rd CT9. . . . . . .8 E2
Summerhill TN23. . . . . . . .155 E6
Summer Hill CT1 . . . . .66 C1
Summer Hill Pk TN24 . . . .157 C7
Summer La CT4. . . . . .66 E6
Summer Leeze TN24 . . . . .156 B8

Summer Leeze Gdns
TN24 ....156 E8
Summer Rd CT7 ....25 E1
Summerson Cl ME1 ....9 C1
Summerville Ave ME12 .....4 A5
Sumpter Way ME10 .....61 F7
Sunbeam Ave CT6 .....21 H4
Sunderland Cl ME1 ......9 A3
Sunderland Dr ME8 ....34 A8
Sunderland Ho 3 ME7 .10 C7
Sundew Gr CT11 ....52 E8
Sundridge Cl CT2 ......67 A4
Sundridge Dr ME5 .....32 A4
Sun La
  Hythe CT21 ....176 C2
  St Nicholas at Wade CT7 ..25 F2
Sunningdale Ave 4
CT19 ....178 A7
Sunningdale Cl ME8 ....33 D6
Sunningdale Cl ME15 ..75 B4
Sunningdale Dr ME8 ...33 D6
Sunningdale Wlk CT6 ..22 D1
Sunny Bank
  Hythe CT15 ....131 B8
  Hythe CT21 ....175 F2
  Sittingbourne ME10 ....37 B5
Sunny Cnr CT17 ......166 B5
Sunnyfields Cl ME8 ...33 E8
Sunnyfields Dr ME12 ...3 C6
Sunnyhill Rd CT6 .....22 C4
Sunnymead CT2 ......66 D7
Sunnymead Ave ME7 ..10 E5
Sunnyside
  Doddington ME9 ....80 E7
  Littlebourne-on-Sea TN28 .202 D6
  Lydd TN29 ....205 B6
Sunnyside Ave ME12 ....4 A6
Sunnyside Cl CT14 ...116 D1
Sunnyside Cotts CT14 .117 A6
Sunnyside Gdns CT13 ..93 E8
Sunnyside Rd
  Whitstable CT20 .....177 D3
  Whitstable CT5 ......43 D5
Sunray Ave CT5 ....43 B7
Sun Rise TN25 ......138 F5
Sunset Cl
  Eastchurch ME12 ....6 C6
  Whitstable CT5 ....43 C6
Sunshine Ct 1 ME8 ....33 E7
Sun St CT1 ....87 F8
Sunstone Dr ME10 .....36 C7
Sun Terr ME5 ....32 B4
Sun Valley Way CT15 ..131 C8
Superabbey Est ME20 ..53 B2
Surf Cres ME12 ....5 F6
Surrenden Rd CT19 ...177 F6
Surrey Cl 4 CT12 .....29 B1
Surrey Gdns CT7 ......26 F7
Surrey Rd
  Canterbury CT1 ....88 D7
  Maidstone ME15 ......97 D8
  Margate CT9 ....8 B3
Surtees Cl ME12 ......156 E6
Susan's Hill TN26 ....168 A3
Sussex Ave
  Ashford TN24 ....139 B3
  Canterbury CT1 ......88 D7
  Margate CT9 ....7 J1
Sussex Cl CT6 ....22 B4
Sussex Dr ME5 ....32 A4
Sussex Gdns
  Birchington CT7 ......26 F7
  Herne Bay CT6 ......22 B4
  Westgate on Sea CT8 ..7 D1
Sussex Mans CT5 ......7 D1
Sussex Rd
  5 Folkestone CT19 ...178 D6
  Maidstone ME15 ......97 D8
  New Romney TN28 ....202 A6
Sussex St CT11 ....88 D7
Sussex Wlk CT1 ....88 D7
Sutherland Cl CT21 ..176 A2
Sutherland Dr CT7 ....27 B6
Sutherland Gdns ME8 .33 E6
Sutherland Ho CT21 ..176 C1
Sutherland Dr CT14 ..117 D5
SUTTON 133 A7
Sutton Baron Rd ME9 .58 A8
Sutton Cl
  Folkestone CT19 ....178 A7
  Gillingham ME8 ......34 A8
Sutton Cotts ME13 ...84 C3
Sutton Hts ME15 .....97 F6
Sutton La
  Ringwould CT14 .....133 F5
  Ripple CT14 ....133 C8
Sutton Rd
  Hersden CT3 ....46 E1
  Langley ME17 ....98 C5
  Maidstone ME15 ......97 D6
Sutton Row CT14 ....117 B5
Sutton St ME14 ....76 D4
Suttons The TN31 ....203 A1
Swadelands Cl ME17 .101 C5
Swadelands Sch ME17 101 C5
Swaffer Way TN23 ...155 C2
Swain Rd
  Gillingham ME8 ....33 B6
  Tenterden TN30 ......167 D3
Swakeley Wlk CT5 ....21 D3
Swale Ave
  Rushenden ME11 ......2 F3
  Sheerness ME12 ....1 C1
Swale Cl CT6 ....23 A3
SWALECLIFFE 21 E3
Swalecliffe Ave CT6 ..22 B4
Swalecliffe Com Prim Sch
CT5 ....21 B2

Swalecliffe Court Dr CT5 .21 D3
Swalecliffe Rd CT5 ...21 B2
Swale Ho ME1 ....2 F5
Swale National Nature
Reserve* ME12 ......19 E4
Swale Sta ME9 ....15 A7
Swale View ME13 .....64 B6
Swale Way
  Sittingbourne ME10 ...14 F2
  Sittingbourne ME10 ...37 D5
Swallow Ave CT5 .....43 B6
Swallow Cl CT9 ....28 C8
Swallow Cl CT6 ....45 F7
Swallowfield TN24 ...156 E7
Swallow Ho
  Dover CT17 ....166 A6
  4 Maidstone ME16 ...74 E4
Swallow Rise ME5 ....32 A5
Swallows L Ctr ME10 ..36 F3
Swallows The CT13 ...94 A8
Swamp Rd TN29 .....201 B4
Swan Apartments 12
ME15 ....10 E8
Swan Cl ME10 ....37 B4
Swan Cotts TN30 ....188 D3
Swanfield Rd CT5 ....43 D8
Swan La ME13 ....159 D1
Swan La TN25 ....159 E2
Swann Way CT18 ....163 A4
Swan St TN30 ....188 C3
Swanstree Ave ME10 .37 B2
Swanton La
  Littlebourne CT3 .....68 D2
  Lydden CT15 ....147 C6
SWANTON STREET ...57 F3
Swarling Hall CT4 ...109 C7
Swaynes Way CT13 ...93 B2
Sweechbridge Rd CT6 .23 F3
Sweechgate CT2 .....67 E7
Sweet Bay Cres TN23 .138 D3
Sweet Briar Cl ME15 .74 D5
Sweetbriar La CT15 ..114 B2
Sweetlove Pl CT3 .....91 A8
Sweyn Rd CT9 ....8 A3
Swift Cres ME5 ......32 C6
Swift Ho 6 ME16 ....74 E4
Swinburne Ave CT10 ..30 A3
Swinford Gdns CT9 ...29 C8
Swingate Cl ME1 .....32 B2
Swingate Inf Sch ME5 .32 C1
SWINGFIELD MINNIS .146 B3
SWINGFIELD STREET .146 E4
Swiss Way CT13 .....178 F7
Switch House Ave TN29 .209 C2
Sycamore Ave CT3 ...112 C5
Sycamore Cl
  Broadstairs CT10 .....29 C4
  Chartham CT4 ....86 F1
  Dymchurch TN29 ....195 C8
  Herne Bay CT6 ....23 C5
  Hythe CT21 ....175 E1
  Lydd TN29 ....205 D7
  Margate CT9 ....28 E7
Sycamore Cres ME16 .74 C5
Sycamore Dr CT14 ...117 B4
Sycamore Gdns TN29 .195 D8
Sycamore Grange CT1 .29 E1
Sycamore La TN23 ...138 E4
Sycamores The 68 E8
Sydcot Dr CT14 .....117 D8
Sydenham Rd CT14 ..117 D7
Sydenham St CT5 ....20 D2
Sydney Ave ME10 ....36 C4
Sydney Cooper Ct CT1 .66 E3
Sydney Cooper Gallery* 22
CT1 ....66 F1
Sydney Rd
  Chatham ME4 ....10 A3
  Deal CT14 ....117 A1
  Ramsgate CT11 ......52 F8
  Whitstable CT5 ......43 E8
Sydney St TN23 ....156 C8
Sylewood Cl ME1 ....31 B8
Sylvan Glade ME5 ...54 A8
Sylvan Rd ME8 ......33 C8
Symmonds Rd ME11 ..37 A6
Symons Ave ME4 .....10 A2
Syndale Pl 5 CT11 ...52 F7

Tabret Cl TN24 .....139 C4
Tadburn Gn ME5 .....32 B4
Taddington Wood La ME5 .31 E2
Taddy Gdns CT9 .....29 C8
Tadley Ct
  Gillingham ME7 ....10 F6
  Rochester ME1 ......31 C8
Tadworth Rd TN24 ..139 D8
Tailour Cl ME10 ......36 F7
Tail Race The ME15 ..74 E2
Talavera Rd CT1 .....88 D8
Talbot Ave CT1 ......22 B3
Talbot Rd
  Maidstone ME16 ....74 C6
  Margate CT9 ....8 B2
Tall Trees Cl ME17 ..99 D2
Tally Ho Rd TN26 ...155 E7
Tamarind Cl ME7 ....33 A4
Tamarisk ME12 ....19 E5
Tame La CT3 ....185 F6
Tamley La TN25 ....142 B6
Tams Gdns ME12 ......4 D6
Tangier CT5 ....149 E3
Tanglewood Cl ME8 ..33 C6
Tangmere Cl ME7 ....10 F5

Tanhouse La TN31 ...196 A2
Tanker Hill ME8 .....33 D6
TANKERTON 21 A3
Tankerton Cir CT5 ...20 F3
Tankerton Ct CT5 ....21 B3
Tankerton Hts CT5 ..20 E3
Tankerton Mews CT5 .20 E3
Tankerton Rd CT5 ...20 F3
Tanners CT21 ....176 B4
Tanner's Hill CT21 ..176 C3
Tanner's Hill Gdns CT21 .176 C3
Tanners St ME13 .....62 C7
Tannery Ct 5 ME10 ..36 E5
Tannery La
  Ashford TN23 ....139 C2
  1 Sandwich CT13 ...72 F1
Tapleys Hill CT4 ...110 B5
Taplin Ct 5 CT7 .....27 A7
Target Bsns Ctr ME15 .97 F4
Target Firs CT15 ....148 E5
Tariff Reform Cotts ME13 .62 D5
Tar Pot La TN25, TN26 .184 B6
Tarragon Rd ME16 ...74 A3
Tartane La TN29 ....195 C8
Taryes Ho 2 CT11 ...52 C6
Tasker Cl CT5 ....76 B3
Tassell's Wlk CT5 ...21 D3
Taswell Ct CT16 ....166 E8
Taswell Rd ME8 .....12 A1
Taswell St CT16 ....166 E8
Tatchell Dr TN27 ...122 D7
Tatler Cl ME5 ....32 D2
Tatsfield Cl ME8 .....11 A2
Tattershall Rd ME15 ..75 A1
Taunton Cl ME15 ....97 F6
Taverners Rd ME8 ...33 E7
Tavistock Cl
  Chatham ME5 ....31 F1
  Gillingham ME8 ......33 E7
Tavistock Rd CT11 ...36 D4
Tay Cl ME5 ....32 B5
Taylers Yd CT15 ....123 E2
Taylor Rd
  Folkestone CT19 ....177 E6
  Lydd-on-Sea TN29 ..206 E6
  Minster (Thanet) CT12 ..50 B6
Taylors Hill CT4 ....107 B8
Taylors La TN29 ....194 F3
Taylor's La ME2 ......9 B7
Taymouth Rd 1 CT16 .166 E8
Taywood CT14 ......139 F1
Teal Cl CT18 ....162 F3
Teal Dr CT6 ....22 E2
Teal Way ME9 ......194 C8
Teasaucer Hill ME15 .96 F8
Teasel Cl ME14 ......74 F4
Teasel Rd ME5 ......31 F4
Teddars Leas Rd CT18 .161 E4
Tedder Ave CT7 ......32 A2
Teddington Cl CT1 ...67 B2
Teelin Cl CT11 .....195 A4
Telegraph Hill Ind Pk
CT12 ....50 D7
Telegraph Rd CT14 ..117 B3
Telescope Alley ME12 .1 E2
Telford Ct
  Folkestone CT19 ....178 E6
  Herne Bay CT6 ....22 C2
Telford Ho 1 ME14 ..75 A4
Telford St CT5 ......22 E5
Telham Ave CT12 ....52 B8
Temeraire Hts CT20 .177 C3
Temeraire Manor 2 ME7 .10 A6
Templar Ct
  9 Canterbury CT1 ..66 F1
  11 Dover CT17 .....149 C1
Templar Rd TN16 ...148 D5
Templar St CT17 ...166 C8
Temple Cl
  Ashford TN23 ......155 F5
  Temple Ewell CT16 ..148 D6
Temple Ct CT1 ....66 D1
TEMPLE EWELL 148 D4
Temple Ewell CE Prim Sch
CT16 ....148 D5
Temple Gdns
  Rochester ME1 ....9 A6
  Sittingbourne ME10 ..37 B3
Templeman Liby CT2 .66 E4
Temple Manor* ME2 ..9 A6
Temple Mews 10 CT1 .87 F8
Temple Rd CT2 ......66 D1
Temple Side CT16 ..148 D6
Temple Way CT14 ...94 A4
Ten Acre Way ME8 ..12 B1
Tennison Way ME15 .97 D6
Tennyson Ave CT1 ...67 D3
Tennyson Gdns CT13 .112 F6
Tennyson Pl
  Canterbury CT1 ......67 D3
  Folkestone CT19 ...178 E7
Tennyson Rd
  Ashford TN23 ......156 A6
  Gillingham ME7 ......10 C3
Ten Perch Rd CT7 ...87 D6
TENTERDEN 179 C6
Tenterden CE Jun Sch
TN30 ....179 B7
Tenterden Dr CT2 ...67 C6
Tenterden Inf Sch TN30 .179 B7
Tenterden L Ctr TN30 .179 B7

Tenterden Rd
  Appledore Heath TN26 ..181 B1
  Chatham ME5 ....32 B5
Tenterden Station Est
TN30 ....179 A8
Tenterden Town Sta*
TN30 ....179 A8
Tenterden Vineyard*
TN30 ....179 C1
Terance Butler Ave ME2 ..9 E8
Terence Cl ME4 ......10 A2
Terlingham La CT18 ..163 A2
Terminus Dr CT6 .....23 D5
Terminus Rd ME16 ...74 A2
Terminus Wlk 3 CT20 .178 E5
Terrace Apartments The
CT21 ....176 C1
Terrace Rd
  Elvington CT15 .....114 B1
  Maidstone ME16 ....74 E3
  Sittingbourne ME10 ..37 B3
Terrace The
  Canterbury CT1 ......66 F3
  Chatham ME4 ....9 F7
  Faversham ME13 .....62 A1
  Pluckley TN27 ......120 A1
  Rochester ME1 ....9 A5
  Shepherdswell CT15 .130 D5
Teynham Cl CT19 ....9 E8
Teynham Dr CT5 ....20 F2
Teynham Gn ME8 ...21 A4
Teynham Parochial CE Prim
Sch ME9 ....38 C2
Teynham Rd CT5 .....99 D2
Teynham St ME9 ....38 F4
Teynham Sta ME9 ...38 D3
TEYNHAM STREET ..38 E4
Thames Ave
  Gillingham ME8 ......33 E8
  Sheerness ME12 ....1 C1
Thames Ct ME2 ....6 G2
Thames View Inf Sch
ME8 ....11 D2
Thames View Jun Sch
ME8 ....11 D2
Thanet Cl CT10 ......30 B5
Thanet Coll
  Broadstairs CT10 .....30 A3
  Margate CT9 ....7 J2
Thanet Ent Ctr CT10 ..29 D7
Thanet Gdns CT19 ...178 E6
Thanet Ho 7 ME15 ..97 F5
Thanet Place Gdns CT10 .30 B6
Thanet Rd
  Broadstairs CT10 .....30 B4
  Gillingham ME8 ......33 C4
  Margate CT9 ....7 J2
  Ramsgate CT11 ......52 F7
  Westgate on Sea CT8 .27 D8
Thanet Reach Bsns Pk
CT10 ....29 C4
Thanet Stars Sch of Dance &
Drama CT9 ....7 H1
Thanet Terr TN26 ...138 A6
Thanet View
  Eythorne CT15 .....131 B8
  St Nicholas at Wade CT7 .25 F2
Thanet Way
  Boughton Street ME13 .63 D6
  Herne Bay CT6 ......22 C3
  Whitstable CT5 ......21 C2
  Yorkletts CT5, TN23 ..42 E2
THANINGTON 87 B6
Thanington Court Farm
CT1 ....87 C6
Thanington Rd CT1 ..87 C6
Thatchers The ME16 .74 B5
Theatre Royal*
Theatre Sq 7 TN30 .179 C7
Theatre St CT1 .....176 C2
THE BRENTS 40 D1
The Cut ME4 ....9 F4
The Davenport Ctr CT12 .52 A8
THE FORSTAL 157 D3
THE LEACON 182 D7
THE LEES 105 A1
The Marlowe Acad CT12 .29 A2
Theodore Pl ME7 .....10 C5
THE QUARRIES 97 C4
THE QUARTER
  Headcorn 135 B5
  Tenterden 179 A6
Theresa Rd CT21 ...176 B1
THE STOCKS 189 A3
THE VALLEY 103 D8
Third Ave
  Chatham ME5 ....10 C1
  Eastchurch ME12 .....5 F6
  Gillingham ME7 ......10 F4
  Margate CT9 ....8 B3
Thirlmere Cl ME16 ..74 D8
Thirlmere TN24 ....139 D6
Thirlmere Ave CT11 ..52 A7
Thirlmere Cl ME7 ...11 A5
Thirlmere Gdns CT13 .112 D8
Thirsk Ho 8 ME15 ..97 F6
Thistlebank ME5 ....32 A4
Thistledown
  Deal CT14 ....134 B8
  Maidstone ME14 .....75 F4
Thistledown Cl ME7 .33 A4
Thistle Dr CT5 ......43 B6
Thistle Hill Way
  Minster (Sheppey) ME12 ..4 A4

Thistle Hill Way continued
  Minster (Sheppey) ME12 ..4 C5
Thistle Wlk ME10 .....4 D8
Thomas Aveling Sch The
ME1 ....31 C8
Thomas Ct TN23 ....156 A6
Thomas Ct 9 ME10 ..37 B4
Thomas Rd
  Faversham ME13 ....62 D7
  Sittingbourne ME10 ..37 B4
Thomas Rider Way ME15 .97 E4
Thomas Smith Rds
ME1 ....3 A3
Thomas St ME1 ......9 C3
Thomas Way CT3 ....47 A1
Thompson Cl
  Deal CT14 ....134 B8
  Folkestone CT19 ...178 B7
  Margate CT9 ....34 A8
Thomson Rd TN25 ..139 B5
Thornbridge Rd CT14 .117 B2
Thorn Cl ME5 ....31 D1
Thorndale ME5 ....31 D4
Thornden Cl CT2 ....22 B2
Thornden Ct CT2 ....66 C4
Thornden Wood Rd
  Herne Bay CT6 ......22 C6
  Whitstable CT6 ......44 E4
Thorndike Cl ME4 ...31 F8
Thorndike Ho ME4 ..31 F8
Thorndike Rd TN29 .186 C4
Thorne Hill CT12 ....51 A6
Thorne Rd CT12 .....50 B6
Thorn Est The TN27 .136 B6
Thorneycroft Cl ME17 .99 D2
Thorneycroft Rd ME13 .103 D5
Thorn Gdns CT15 ....29 E1
Thornham Rd ME1 ..11 C3
Thornhill Pl ME14 ...75 A6
Thorn Ndll Rd ME12 ..6 D4
Thornhurst CT6 .....23 D4
Thorn La CT4 ....126 C2
Thornlea TN23 .....138 E2
Thornton Cl TN24 ..140 A1
Thornton La CT13, CT14 .166 F7
Thornton's La 8 CT16 .166 E7
Thorn Wlk ME10 .....37 C5
Thorold Rd ME5 .....10 B3
Thorpe Wlk ME4 ....33 D3
Thrale Way ME8 .....33 E4
Thread La ME13 .....64 B4
Three Acres Site CT19 .178 B8
Three King's Yd CT13 .73 A1
Threshers Dr ME14 .75 E5
THROWLEY 82 E4
Throwley Dr CT6 ....22 C4
THROWLEY FORSTAL .82 B5
Throwley Rd ME13 ..82 D5
Thrupp Paddock CT10 .8 G1
Thrush Cl ME5 ....32 B7
Thruxted La CT4 .....86 B1
Thundersland Rd CT6 .23 B4
Thurlow Ave CT6 ....23 C5
THURNHAM 76 A4
Thurnham CE Inf Sch
ME14 ....76 A4
Thurnham La ME14 ..76 C7
Thurstone Ct ME14 ..74 F6
THURSTON PK 20 E1
Thurston Pk CT5 ....20 E1
Thyme Wlk ME14 ....74 B3
Tiber Cl CT19 ......177 C6
Tichborne Ct ME16 ..74 C6
TICKENHURST 92 D1
TICKHAM 60 D6
Tickham La ME9 .....60 C5
Ticker's La TN29 ...192 B1
Tideway The ME1 ...31 C8
Tilbury Rd ME8 .....12 A2
Tilden Cl TN26 .....167 D7
Tilden Ct TN26 .....167 E7
Tilden Gill Rd TN30 .179 C7
Tile Fields ME17 ....77 D2
Tile Fields CT16 ....77 D2
Tile Ho The CT21 ..176 C2
Tile Kiln Hill CT2 ...66 B5
Tile Kiln La CT19 ..177 F7
Tile Kiln Rd TN24 ..139 C7
Tile Lodge Cotts TN27 .119 E8
Tile Lodge Rd TN27 .119 E8
Tillard Ct CT4 ......109 B3
Tillery La TN29 ....200 A8
Timberbank ME5 ....32 A6
Timber Tops ME5 ...54 D8
Timeball Tower Mus*
CT14 ....117 D5
Timperley Cl CT14 ..117 B6
Tina Gdns CT10 .....30 A6
Tinbridge Pk ME13 ..63 A5
Tinker's Alley ME12 ..9 F7
Tintagel Manor 6 ME7 ..10 C6
Tintern Rd ME15 ....74 D8
Titchfield Cl 5 ME15 .97 F6
Titchfield Rd ME15 ..97 F6
Tithe Barn La TN23 .155 D8
Tithe Yd ME17 .....101 D5
Tivoli Brooks CT9 ....7 I1
Tivoli Park Ave CT9 ..7 H1
Tivoli Rd CT9 ....28 E8
Tobruk Way ME5 ....31 F6
Toby Rd TN29 .....206 E6
Todd Cres ME10 .....37 A8
Toddington Cres ME5 .31 F6
Toke Cl TN23 ......138 C1

Tolgate La ME2 . . . 9 B7
Tolgate Way ME14 . . . 53 E4
Tollemache CI CT12 . . . 27 F2
Toll Gate CT14 . . . 117 A4
Tolgate CI CT15 . . . 43 C8
Toll La TN27 . . . 120 C7
Tolputt Ct CT19 . . . 178 E6
Tolsford CI
  Etchinghill CT18 . . . 161 D3
  Folkestone CT19 . . . 177 D6
Tomay Cotts CT6 . . . 24 A3
Tomlin Dr CT9 . . . 29 C8
Tonbridge Ct ME16 . . . 74 D3
Tonbridge Rd ME16 . . . 74 C3
Tonford La
  Canterbury CT1 . . . 87 B6
  Harbledown CT2 . . . 87 A7
TONGE CORNER . . . 37 F7
Tonge Rd ME10 . . . 37 C4
TONG GREEN . . . 82 B1
Tontine St CT20 . . . 178 E5
Tonkey Rd TN28 . . . 202 B6
Topaz Dr ME10 . . . 36 C6
Top Rd TN30 . . . 189 E3
Tormore Mews CT14 . . . 117 A4
Tormore Pk CT14 . . . 117 A4
Toronto Ct **6** CT16 . . . 149 B3
Toronto Rd ME7 . . . 10 E4
Torrington Cotts CT12 . . . 50 D7
Torrington Rd TN23 . . . 156 C8
Tothill St CT12 . . . 50 C7
Tourmaline Dr ME10 . . . 36 C6
Tournay CI TN23 . . . 155 F8
Tourney CI CT21 . . . 174 F3
Tourney Rd TN29 . . . 205 C5
Tourtel Rd CT1 . . . 67 A1
Tovey Sq ME7 . . . 10 F6
TOVIL . . . 74 E1
Tovil Gn ME15 . . . 74 E1
Tovil Green Bsns Pk ME15 . . . 74 E1
Tovil Hill ME15 . . . 74 E2
Tovil Rd ME15 . . . 74 E2
Tovil Sch ME15 . . . 74 D2
Tower Bglws CT7 . . . 27 A8
Tower Ct **4** CT20 . . . 177 E3
Tower Est TN29 . . . 186 E2
Tower Gdns
  Hythe CT21 . . . 176 C1
  Maidstone ME14 . . . 76 B4
TOWER HAMLETS . . . 166 B8
Tower Hamlets Rd CT17 . . . 166 C8
Tower Hamlets St **1** CT17 . . . 166 C8
Tower Hill
  Dover CT17 . . . 166 C8
  Whitstable CT5 . . . 20 E3
Tower La ME14 . . . 76 B4
Tower Par CT5 . . . 20 E3
Tower Rd CT5 . . . 20 E3
Towers Point ME1 . . . 9 B4
Towers Sch The TN24 . . . 139 D8
Tower St CT17 . . . 166 C8
Towers The TN21 . . . 103 E1
Towers View TN24 . . . 139 C7
Tower View CT4 . . . 86 F1
Tower Way **1** CT1 . . . 87 F1
Town Hill CT4 . . . 88 F2
Town La CT4 . . . 86 C6
TOWNLAND GREEN . . . 169 A1
Townley St CT11 . . . 52 D6
Town Rd CT4 . . . 109 C5
Townsend Farm Rd CT15 . . . 150 F6
Townsend Terr CT17 . . . 166 B5
Townwall St CT16 . . . 166 E7
Town Wlk CT20 . . . 178 D4
Tracies The ME9 . . . 35 C6
Tradewinds CT5 . . . 43 B6
Trafalgar Dr CT14 . . . 117 D4
Trafalgar Par ME12 . . . 4 A6
Trafalgar Rd CT7 . . . 27 F3
Trafalgar St ME7 . . . 10 C5
Tram Rd The CT20 . . . 178 E5
Tramways ME5 . . . 10 C2
Transformer Ave TN29 . . . 209 C2
Transom Ho **3** ME1 . . . 9 C1
Trapfield CI ME14 . . . 76 C4
Trapfield La ME14 . . . 76 C4
Trapham Rd ME14 . . . 74 D5
Travers Gdns ME9 . . . 57 F5
Travers Rd CT14 . . . 117 A5
Travertine Rd ME1 . . . 31 B3
Treasury View CT3 . . . 90 C8
Trefoil The ME9, ME10 . . . 60 E6
Trefor Jones Ct CT16 . . . 149 B2
Trelawn Ceres ME5 . . . 32 B2
Trenley Dr CT3 . . . 67 F1
Trenton CI ME16 . . . 74 B5
Trent Rd ME5 . . . 32 B5
Trevale Rd ME1 . . . 9 B1
Trevino Dr ME5 . . . 31 F2
Trevor Dr ME16 . . . 74 C5
Tribune CI ME12 . . . 3 B8
Tribune Dr ME10 . . . 36 F6
Trident CI ME2 . . . 9 E7
Triggs Cotts ME9 . . . 38 D2
Trigg's Row ME9 . . . 38 D2
Trilby Way CT5 . . . 43 B6
Trimworth Rd CT19 . . . 177 F6
Trinity Crees CT20 . . . 178 B4
Trinity Ct
  Deal CT14 . . . 117 A4
  Forstal ME20 . . . 53 A3
  Margate CT9 . . . 7 J3
Trinity Gdns CT20 . . . 178 C4

Trinity Hill CT9 . . . 7 J3
Trinity Homes CT14 . . . 117 C1
Trinity Pl
  Deal CT14 . . . 117 A4
  Ramsgate CT11 . . . 52 F7
Trinity Rd
  Ashford TN24 . . . 139 B7
  Folkestone CT20 . . . 178 B4
  Gillingham ME7 . . . 10 C6
  Sheerness ME12 . . . 1 D2
  Sittingbourne ME10 . . . 36 F7
Trinity Sch ME1 . . . 9 D4
Trinity Sq
  Broadstairs CT10 . . . 29 F7
  Margate CT9 . . . 7 J3
Trinity Trad Est ME10 . . . 36 F6
Trinity Way ME12 . . . 1 D2
Tristram Way CT1 . . . 149 B5
Tritton CI TN24 . . . 139 F7
Tritton Fields TN24 . . . 139 F7
Tritton Gdns TN29 . . . 186 D1
Tritton La TN28 . . . 202 B6
Trona Ct **7** ME10 . . . 36 D6
Troodos Hill ME14 . . . 74 F8
Trotts Hall Gdns ME10 . . . 58 C3
Trotwood Ct ME5 . . . 54 A8
Trotwood Pl TN23 . . . 156 D8
Troubridge CI TN24 . . . 157 B2
Troughton Mews CT9 . . . 7 H1
Trove Ct **7** CT11 . . . 52 F7
TROY TOWN
  Brook . . . 141 B5
  Rochester . . . 9 C5
Troy Town La TN25 . . . 141 B5
Trueman CI CT2 . . . 66 A7
Trumpet Ho TN23 . . . 156 B8
Trunley Way CT18 . . . 162 F3
Truro CI ME8 . . . 11 D3
Truro Rd CT11 . . . 52 F7
Tudor Ave
  Dymchurch TN29 . . . 186 D1
  Maidstone ME14 . . . 75 B6
Tudor Byway TN24 . . . 139 D6
Tudor CI CT7 . . . 27 B8
Tudor Ct
  Canterbury CT2 . . . 66 C4
  Whitstable CT5 . . . 21 A3
Tudor End TN24 . . . 139 D5
Tudor Farm Ct TN23 . . . 156 A3
Tudor Gdns ME3 . . . 33 F8
Tudor Ho CT14 . . . 117 A5
Tudor Ho* CT9 . . . 7 J3
Tudor Mews CT14 . . . 117 B4
Tudor Rd
  Ashford TN24 . . . 139 D5
  Canterbury CT1 . . . 87 E7
  Folkestone CT19 . . . 177 D6
Tufa CI ME1 . . . 32 B1
Tufton Rd
  Ashford TN24 . . . 139 D2
  Gillingham ME8 . . . 11 F1
  Hothfield TN26 . . . 138 A7
Tufton St
  Ashford TN23 . . . 139 B2
  Maidstone ME14 . . . 75 A4
Tufton Wlk TN23 . . . 139 B2
Tumbledown Hill TN25 . . . 121 F3
Tunbridge Way CT21 . . . 155 C8
Tunbury Ave ME5 . . . 31 F1
Tunbury Avenue ME5 . . . 31 F1
Tunbury Prim Sch ME5 . . . 31 F1
Tunis Ct CT1 . . . 67 D1
Tunis Row CT10 . . . 30 B5
TUNSTALL . . . 58 D8
Tunstall CE Prim Sch ME9 . . . 58 C8
Tunstall Rd
  Canterbury CT1 . . . 67 A4
  Sittingbourne ME10, ME9 . . . 58 D8
Tupman CI ME1 . . . 9 B4
Turbine Hall Ave TN29 . . . 209 C2
Turgis Ct ME17 . . . 98 E4
Turketel Rd CT20 . . . 178 A4
Turmine Ct ME12 . . . 4 A5
Turnagain La **3** CT1 . . . 87 F8
Turnden Gdns CT9 . . . 8 E2
Turner CI
  Ashford TN24 . . . 156 E7
  Sittingbourne ME10 . . . 37 A7
Turner Ct
  5 Folkestone CT20 . . . 177 F5
  Margate CT9 . . . 8 A2
Turners Ave TN30 . . . 179 B8
Turners CI ME12 . . . 1 E1
Turnpike CI CT21 . . . 52 E7
Turnpike Hill CT21 . . . 176 A3
Turnstone CI ME9 . . . 14 E4
Turnstone Ct TN29 . . . 194 F3
Turnstone Rd ME5 . . . 32 C1
Turrets The
  Deal CT14 . . . 117 C1
  5 Sittingbourne ME10 . . . 37 A4
Tuscan Dr ME5 . . . 32 C1
TUTT HILL . . . 121 A1
Tweed Terr CT21 . . . 176 A1
Twelve Acres TN24 . . . 156 F8
Twiss Ave CT21 . . . 176 D2
Twiss Gr CT21 . . . 176 D2
Twiss Rd CT21 . . . 176 D2
TWITHAM . . . 91 E6
TWYDALL . . . 11 B2
Twydall Ent Ctr ME8 . . . 11 C4
Twydall Gn ME8 . . . 11 B3
Twydall Inf Sch ME8 . . . 11 B2
Twydall Jun Sch ME8 . . . 11 B2

Twydall La ME8 . . . 11 B2
Twyford Ct ME8 . . . 12 A2
Twyford St CT14 . . . 75 D6
Twymans Mill ME13 . . . 62 C7
Twyne Ct CT2 . . . 68 A6
Twysden Ct TN25 . . . 123 E2
Tydeman Rd ME15 . . . 75 F2
Tydeman's Ave CT5 . . . 21 C2
Tye La CT18 . . . 163 A5
Tyland Barn Wildlife Park* . . . 53 E3
Tyland La ME14 . . . 53 F3
Tyler CI CT2 . . . 66 F3
Tyler Dr ME8 . . . 33 E4
TYLER HILL . . . 66 E6
Tyler Hill Rd CT2 . . . 66 C6
Tyler Way CT5 . . . 21 E3
Tyndale Pk CT6 . . . 23 B5
Tyne CI ME5 . . . 32 C5
Tyrwhitt-Drake Mus of
  Carriages* **9** ME15 . . . 75 A3
Tysoe Ct ME14 . . . 4 A5
Tyson Ave CT9 . . . 7 E1
Tyson Rd CT19 . . . 178 E7

U

Uden Rd TN29 . . . 187 B4
Uffington Ct CT3 . . . 91 A2
Ufton CI ME15 . . . 75 E1
Ufton La ME10 . . . 36 E3
Ulcombe Gdns CT2 . . . 67 A3
Ulcombe Hill ME17 . . . 99 F1
Ulcombe Rd ME17 . . . 98 E3
Ulley Rd TN24 . . . 139 D7
Ullswater Gdns CT3 . . . 112 F6
Ullswater Ho **6** ME15 . . . 97 E7
Ulster Rd CT9 . . . 28 F8
Undercliff CT20 . . . 177 E3
Undercliffe Rd CT14 . . . 134 D5
UNDERDOWN . . . 108 B8
Underdown Ave ME4 . . . 9 F1
Underdown La CT6 . . . 22 F2
Underdown Rd
  Dover CT17 . . . 166 B7
  Herne Bay CT6 . . . 22 F5
Underhill Cotts CT18 . . . 177 B8
Underhill Rd CT20 . . . 177 B5
Underwood CT18 . . . 163 C6
Underwood CI
  Ashford TN24 . . . 139 D6
  Canterbury CT1 . . . 88 B5
  Maidstone ME15 . . . 74 F2
Underwood Ct **1** ME15 . . . 88 B6
Unicorn Cotts CT14 . . . 89 B5
Unicumes La ME16 . . . 74 C2
Union Cres CT9 . . . 7 J2
Union Pk ME15 . . . 97 F4
Union Pl
  4 Canterbury CT1 . . . 67 A1
  Chatham ME4 . . . 10 A4
Union Rd
  Bridge CT4 . . . 88 F1
  Deal CT14 . . . 117 D6
  Minster (Sheppey) ME12 . . . 4 C7
  Ramsgate CT11 . . . 52 F8
Union Row CT9 . . . 7 J2
Union Sq **3** CT10 . . . 30 B4
Union St
  Canterbury CT1 . . . 67 A1
  Chatham ME4 . . . 10 A3
  Dover CT17 . . . 166 D6
  Faversham ME13 . . . 62 C7
  Maidstone ME14 . . . 75 A5
  12 Ramsgate CT11 . . . 52 E7
  Rochester ME1 . . . 9 C5
Unity Ct ME12 . . . 1 E2
Unity Pl **3** CT11 . . . 52 F7
Unity St
  Sheerness ME12 . . . 1 E2
  Sittingbourne ME10 . . . 36 E3
Univ Centre Folkestone **28** CT20 . . . 178 D5
University Rd CT2 . . . 66 D3
Univ for the Creative Arts at Canterbury CT1 . . . 87 B7
Univ for the Creative Arts at Maidstone ME16 . . . 74 C3
Univ for the Creative Arts at Rochester ME1 . . . 9 E4
Univ of Greenwich The ME4 . . . 10 B8
Univ of Kent (Canterbury) CT2 . . . 66 D4
Univ of Kent (Universities at Medway Campus) ME4 . . . 10 B8
Unwin CI ME3 . . . 53 A3
Upbury Way ME4 . . . 10 A4
UPCHURCH . . . 12 F4
Upchurch Wlk CT9 . . . 8 E2
Updown Way CT14 . . . 86 F1
Uphill CT18 . . . 163 B4
Uplands CT21 . . . 84 A8
Uplands Way ME12 . . . 3 C5
Uplees Cotts ME13 . . . 39 F5
Uplees Rd ME13 . . . 40 A3
Upnor Ho ME15 . . . 97 E8
Upper Approach Rd CT10 . . . 30 A3
Upper Brents ME13 . . . 62 D8
Upper Bridge St
  Canterbury CT1 . . . 88 A8
  Wye TN25 . . . 123 F2
Upper Britton Pl ME7 . . . 10 B5
Upper Chantry La CT1 . . . 88 A7

Upper Corniche CT20 . . . 177 C3
Upper Dane Ct CT9 . . . 8 B1
Upper Dane Rd CT9 . . . 8 B1
UPPER DEAL . . . 117 B4
Upper Denmark Rd TN23 . . . 156 B8
Upper Dumpton Park Rd CT11 . . . 52 E8
Upper East Rd ME4 . . . 10 B8
UPPER EYTHORNE . . . 131 C7
Upper Fans La ME9 . . . 14 C4
UPPER FANT . . . 74 D3
Upper Fant Rd ME16 . . . 74 D2
Upper Field Rd ME10 . . . 37 B5
Upper Free Down CT6 . . . 23 B2
UPPER GOLDSTONE . . . 71 E5
Upper Gore La CT13 . . . 93 A2
UPPER HARBLEDOWN . . . 65 F1
Upper Hunton Hill ME15 . . . 96 A3
Upper Luton Rd ME5 . . . 10 C2
Upper Malthouse Hill CT21 . . . 176 B2
Upper Maltings Pl CT2 . . . 26 F7
Upper Queens Rd TN24 . . . 139 B3
Upper St
  Hollingbourne ME17 . . . 77 E3
  Kingsdown CT14 . . . 134 D5
  Leeds ME17 . . . 98 F5
  Tilmanstone CT14 . . . 115 A3
Upper Stone St ME15 . . . 75 A3
Upper Strand St CT13 . . . 73 A1
Upper Tickham Cotts ME9 . . . 60 B2
Upper Vicarage Rd TN24 . . . 139 D7
UPPER WALMER . . . 117 B1
UPSTREET . . . 47 D3
Upstreet CT18 . . . 161 D3
UPTON . . . 29 F4
Upton CI CT19 . . . 178 A4
Upton Jun Sch CT10 . . . 29 F4
Upton Rd CT10 . . . 29 F5
UPTON WOOD . . . 130 E2
Upton St CT13 . . . 93 D8
Ursuline Coll CT8 . . . 27 D8
Ursuline Ct CT8 . . . 27 D7

V

Valebrook CI CT20 . . . 177 C5
Vale Cotts ME9 . . . 57 A8
Vale CI **10** CT11 . . . 52 D6
Vale Dr ME5 . . . 31 E6
Valence Ho ME15 . . . 97 C7
Valenciennes Ho ME4 . . . 10 A4
Valenciennes Rd ME10 . . . 36 E3
Valentine CI ME7 . . . 11 A1
Valentine Rd ME15 . . . 97 E7
Vale Pl CT11 . . . 52 D6
Vale Rd
  Broadstairs CT10 . . . 29 F4
  Maidstone ME15 . . . 96 F4
  Ramsgate CT11 . . . 52 D6
  Ripple CT14, CT15 . . . 133 B8
  Whitstable CT5 . . . 43 D8
Valerian CI ME5 . . . 31 E4
Vale Sq CT11 . . . 52 D6
Valestone CI CT21 . . . 177 B4
Vale View
  Chatham ME4 . . . 10 A4
  Valetta Way ME4 . . . 9 B4
Vale View Com Sch CT17 . . . 166 B7
Vale View Rd
  Aylesham CT3 . . . 112 E5
  Dover CT17 . . . 166 B7
Valiant Rd ME5 . . . 32 C2
Valkyrie Ave CT5 . . . 43 C7
Vallance The ME9 . . . 60 A6
Valley Cotts
  Alkham CT15 . . . 147 C5
  Stalisfield Green ME13 . . . 103 B8
Valley L Ctm CT19 . . . 177 B6
Valley Park Com Sch ME14 . . . 75 C4
Valley Rd
  Barham CT4 . . . 111 E2
  Canterbury CT1 . . . 87 E6
  Crabble CT17 . . . 148 E3
  Folkestone CT20 . . . 177 E4
  Gillingham ME7 . . . 10 E4
  Margate CT9 . . . 28 E4
Valley Rise ME5 . . . 31 F1
Valley View CT15 . . . 131 C8
Valley View Rd ME1 . . . 9 B1
Valley Wlk CT21 . . . 176 C1
Vancouver Dr ME8 . . . 11 C1
Vancouver Rd CT14 . . . 149 C3
Vange Cottage Mews ME1 . . . 9 B4
Vanguard Way ME2 . . . 9 E8
Vanity La ME17 . . . 96 E1
Vanners La CT14 . . . 84 A5
Varne CI CT20 . . . 177 F3
Varne La CT20 . . . 177 E3
Varne Pl CT19 . . . 178 F5
Varne Rd CT19 . . . 178 F5
Vaughan Dr ME10 . . . 36 F4

Vauxhall Ave
  Canterbury CT1 . . . 67 A5
  Herne Bay CT6 . . . 22 A3
Vauxhall Cres CT1 . . . 67 C3
Vauxhall Industrial Rd CT1 . . . 67 D4
Vectis Dr ME10 . . . 36 F8
Ventnor Ct ME15 . . . 32 C8
Venture La **12** CT9 . . . 7 J2
Venture CI TN29 . . . 186 D1
Vere Rd CT6 . . . 30 A4
Vereth Rd **2** CT11 . . . 52 D6
Vernon Pl
  Canterbury CT1 . . . 88 A7
  Deal CT14 . . . 117 D8
Verwood CI CT2 . . . 66 E2
Vespasian Way TN23 . . . 155 F4
Vesper Ct TN27 . . . 135 A1
Vestey Ct CT8 . . . 7 A1
Viaduct CI CT12 . . . 52 C8
Viaduct Terr CT16 . . . 182 F7
Viaduct The CT14 . . . 166 C5
Viburnum CI TN23 . . . 138 E2
Vicarage Cotts ME9 . . . 13 C3
Vicarage Cres **8** CT9 . . . 7 J1
Vicarage Ct ME7 . . . 11 A1
Vicarage Gdn CT12 . . . 49 C7
Vicarage Gdns CT3 . . . 91 A7
Vicarage Hill CT4 . . . 109 B4
Vicarage La
  Ashford TN24 . . . 139 C2
  Blean CT7 . . . 66 A6
  Charing Heath TN27 . . . 119 C7
  Deal CT14 . . . 116 F5
  East Farleigh ME15 . . . 96 B6
  Elham CT4 . . . 144 F4
  Faversham ME13 . . . 62 A4
  Lower Halstow ME9 . . . 13 C3
  Nonington CT15 . . . 113 C5
  4 Sandwich CT13 . . . 72 F1
  Selling ME13 . . . 84 C6
  St Margaret's at Cliffe CT15 . . . 150 F6
  Tilmanstone CT14 . . . 115 A3
Vicarage Pl CT9 . . . 7 J1
Vicarage Rd
  Gillingham ME7 . . . 10 C5
  Minster (Sheppey) ME12 . . . 4 D7
  Rochester ME2 . . . 9 B8
  Sittingbourne ME10 . . . 36 E6
Vicarage St
  Broadstairs CT10 . . . 29 E5
  Tenterden ME13 . . . 62 D8
Vicary Way ME16 . . . 74 D5
Vickers Ct CT18 . . . 163 A4
Victor Ave CT9 . . . 8 E1
Victoria Ave
  Broadstairs CT10 . . . 29 E8
  Hythe CT21 . . . 176 B2
  Margate CT9 . . . 8 B1
  St Margaret's at Cliffe CT15 . . . 151 B6
  Westgate on Sea CT8 . . . 27 F8
Victoria CI ME5 . . . 31 D2
Victoria Cres
  Ashford TN23 . . . 139 B1
  Dover CT16 . . . 166 D8
Victoria Ct
  Hythe CT21 . . . 176 C1
  6 Maidstone ME16 . . . 74 E3
Victoria Dr CT6 . . . 22 C5
Victoria Gr
  12 Folkestone CT20 . . . 178 D5
  Hythe CT21 . . . 177 B2
Victoria Ho **7** CT5 . . . 20 D2
Victoria Hospl CT14 . . . 117 B5
Victoria Mews
  Deal CT14 . . . 117 C6
  Westgate on Sea CT8 . . . 7 D1
Victoria Orch CT16 . . . 74 B3
Victoria Par
  Broadstairs CT10 . . . 30 B4
  Ramsgate CT11 . . . 52 F7
Victoria Park Mews **2** CT16 . . . 166 C8
Victoria Pk
  Dover CT16 . . . 166 E8
  Herne Bay CT6 . . . 23 A5
Victoria Pl
  Faversham ME13 . . . 62 C7
  Hythe CT21 . . . 176 B4
Victoria Rd
  Ashford TN23 . . . 139 B1
  Broadstairs CT10 . . . 29 E6
  Canterbury CT1 . . . 87 E7
  Capel-le-Ferne CT18 . . . 164 B2
  Chatham, Kit Hill ME5 . . . 31 E3
  Chatham, Luton ME4 . . . 10 B2
  Deal CT14 . . . 117 D5
  Folkestone CT20 . . . 178 C5
  Hythe CT21 . . . 176 C1
  Kingsdown CT14 . . . 134 C4
  Littlestone-on-Sea TN28 . . . 202 E5
  Margate CT9 . . . 7 J2
  Margate, Lydden CT9 . . . 28 D4
  Ramsgate CT11 . . . 52 F7
  Sittingbourne ME10 . . . 36 D4
Victoria Road Ind Pk TN23 . . . 139 B1
Victoria Road Prim Sch TN23 . . . 139 B1
Victoria Row
  Canterbury CT1 . . . 67 A1
  Ramsgate CT11 . . . 52 C5
Victoria St
  Dover CT17 . . . 149 B1

Victoria St continued
Gillingham ME7 . . . . .10 D6
Maidstone ME16 . . . . .74 E3
New Romney TN28 . . . . .202 A6
Rochester ME1 . . . . .9 D5
Rochester, Strood ME2 . . . . .9 B7
Sheerness ME12 . . . . .1 D1
Whitstable CT5 . . . . .20 D2
Victoria Terr
Hythe CT21 . . . . .177 B2
Minster (Sheppey) ME12 . . . .5 A5
Rochester ME1 . . . . .9 A2
Sittingbourne ME10 . . . . . .36 D4
Victoria Yd **21** CT1 . . . . . . .67 A1
Victory Pk ME2 . . . . .9 E7
Victory Rd CT5 . . . . .133 F1
Victory St ME11 . . . . .1 C2
Vidal Manor ME7 . . . . .10 C5
Viewlands ME5 . . . . .10 C3
Vigo Terr ME9 . . . . .38 C1
Viking Cl CT7 . . . . .26 D8
Viking Ct
Broadstairs CT10 . . . . .30 B3
Canterbury CT2 . . . . .66 F2
Margate CT9 . . . . .8 A2
Viking Ship 'Hugin'*
CT12 . . . . .51 E5
Village View ME5 . . . . .10 E5
Village Way TN26 . . . . . . .183 A7
Villas The CT3 . . . . .47 A1
Villiers Cl CT17 . . . . .166 C7
Villiers Ho CT10 . . . . .30 B7
Villiers Rd CT17 . . . . .67 C5
Vincent Cl
Broadstairs CT10 . . . . .29 C3
Folkestone CT19 . . . . .177 D5
Vincent Ct ME12 . . . . .1 D1
Vincent Gdns ME12 . . . . . .1 D1
Vincent Pl TN24 . . . . .139 F4
Vincent Rd
Kit's Coty ME20 . . . . .53 C7
Margate CT9 . . . . .28 C4
Sittingbourne ME10 . . . . . .37 C3
Vine Cl CT11 . . . . .29 E5
Vine End CT11 . . . . .29 E2
Vine Lands TN29 . . . . .205 B6
Vine Lo CT11 . . . . .29 E2
Vineries The ME7 . . . . .10 E5
Viners Cl ME10 . . . . .36 F1
Vines La ME1 . . . . .9 C5
Vineyard Cres ME8 . . . . . .12 B1
Viney's Gdns TN30 . . . . . .167 C1
Vinson Cl ME13 . . . . .41 D1
Vinten Cl CT6 . . . . .46 B8
Vinters Rd ME14 . . . . .75 B4
**Vinters Valley Nature
Reserve*** ME14 . . . . .75 D5
Vinters Way ME14 . . . . . . .75 E4
Violet Ave CT12 . . . . .29 C2
Violet Cl ME5 . . . . .54 A8
Violet Ct ME10 . . . . .36 F2
Violet Way TN23 . . . . .156 C2
Virginia Rd
Gillingham ME7 . . . . .10 C7
Whitstable CT5 . . . . .44 A8
Vixen Cl ME5 . . . . .32 C6
Vlissingen Dr CT14 . . . . . .117 C8
Volante Dr ME10 . . . . .36 E7
Vulcan Cl
Chatham ME5 . . . . .32 B7
Whitstable CT5 . . . . .43 C7

W

Wacher Cl CT2 . . . . .66 F2
Waddenhall Barns CT4 . . .126 B5
Waddington Dr CT18 . . . .163 A4
Waddle Cnr TN30 . . . . . . .189 D3
Wades Cl TN29 . . . . .194 E3
Wadham Pl ME10 . . . . .37 B2
Waghorn St ME4 . . . . .10 B2
Wagoners Cl ME17 . . . . . . .75 E4
Wain Cl ME12 . . . . .4 A5
Wainwright Ct CT10 . . . . . .30 B6
Wainwright Pl TN24 . . . . .156 D8
Wakefield Way CT21 . . . . .176 B3
Wakefield Wlk CT21 . . . . .176 D1
Wakehurst Cl ME17 . . . . . .96 B3
Wakeley Rd ME8 . . . . .12 A1
Wakeleys Cotts ME8 . . . . .34 B8
Wake Rd ME1 . . . . .31 C8
Walcheren Cl CT14 . . . . . .117 C8
Walcot Pl CT6 . . . . .23 B3
Walden Ct CT2 . . . . .67 A3
Waldens The ME17 . . . . . . .99 E2
Waldershare Ho CT15 . . . .95 A7
Waldershare La CT15 . . . .132 E2
Waldershare Rd CT15 . . . .132 A5
WALDERSLADE 31 F1
WALDERSLADE BOTTOM . .32 A2
Walderslade Ctr ME23 . . . .32 A3
Walderslade Girls Sch **2**
ME5 . . . . .31 F5
Walderslade Prim Sch
ME5 . . . . .32 A3
Walderslade Rd ME5 . . . . .31 F6
Walderslade Village By-pass
ME5 . . . . .31 F3
Walderslade Woods ME5 . .31 E2
Waldron Dr ME5 . . . . .96 F6
Waldron Rd CT10 . . . . .30 B2
Walker La CT7 . . . . .26 D8
Walk The ME17 . . . . .99 E2
Wallace Mews CT19 . . . . .178 D7

Wallace Rd ME1 . . . . .31 E8
Wallace Way CT10 . . . . . . .29 E4
Wallbridge La ME8 . . . . . . .12 D3
WALL END 47 F4
Waller Rd TN28 . . . . .206 E2
Wallers Rd ME13 . . . . .62 A7
Wallis Ave ME15 . . . . .97 E5
Wallis Ct CT6 . . . . .23 F5
Wallis Oak Ave **12** ME15 . . .97 F5
Wallis Rd TN24 . . . . .139 D2
Wall Rd TN24 . . . . .139 B3
Wall The ME10 . . . . .36 E5
Wallwood Rd CT11 . . . . . . .52 F8
WALMER 117 C2
Walmer Castle* CT14 . . . .117 C1
Walmer Castle Rd CT14 . .117 C1
Walmer Ct **5** ME14 . . . . . .75 A5
Walmer Gdns
Cliffs End CT12 . . . . .51 D5
Deal CT14 . . . . .117 A2
Sittingbourne ME10 . . . . . .36 D5
Walmer Rd CT5 . . . . .43 E8
Walmer Science Coll
CT14 . . . . .117 B2
Walmer Sta CT14 . . . . . . .117 A1
Walmer Way
Deal CT14 . . . . .117 A2
Margate CT9 . . . . .8 B2
Whitstable CT5 . . . . .20 C5
WALMESTONE 70 D3
Walmsley Ho **4** CT19 . . . .178 E6
Walmsley Rd CT10 . . . . . . .29 F5
Walmer Gdns TN28 . . . . . .202 B7
Walner La TN28 . . . . .202 B7
Walnut Cl
Ashford TN24 . . . . .139 D6
Broadstairs CT10 . . . . .29 F2
Chatham ME5 . . . . .32 B8
Walnut Mews CT7 . . . . .26 F7
Walnut Ridge TN25 . . . . . .173 A6
Walnut Tree Ave ME15 . . . .97 A5
Walnut Tree Cl **6** CT7 . . . .27 A7
Walnut Tree Cotts ME13 . .84 E8
Walnut Tree La
Loose ME15 . . . . .97 A5
Westbere CT2 . . . . .68 D7
Walpole Rd CT9 . . . . .7 J3
Walsby Dr ME10 . . . . .37 A8
Walsham Rd ME5 . . . . .31 F1
Walshaw Ho **2** ME14 . . . . .75 A5
Walsingham Cl ME8 . . . . . .33 D3
Walsingham Ho **3** ME14 . .74 F6
Walter Burke Ave ME4 . . . .10 A8
WALTHAM 125 E6
Waltham Cl
Ashford TN24 . . . . .140 A2
Margate CT9 . . . . .8 E2
Waltham Rd
Gillingham ME8 . . . . .11 C3
Petham CT4 . . . . .109 B3
Waltham CT4 . . . . .108 F1
Walton Gdns CT19 . . . . . .178 D7
Walton Manor Cl CT19 . . .178 D7
Walton Rd CT19 . . . . .178 D6
Waltons The CT19 . . . . . . .178 C8
WANDEN 135 B7
Wanden La TN27 . . . . .135 C8
Wanstall Ct CT7 . . . . .27 A7
Wantsum Cl CT6 . . . . .23 F5
Wantsume Lees CT13 . . . . .72 E2
Wantsum Mews **7** CT13 . .72 F1
Wantsum Way CT7 . . . . . . .25 E3
Warblers Cl **3** ME2 . . . . . . .9 A7
WARDEN 6 D4
Warden Bay Rd ME12 . . . . .6 E3
Warden Cl ME16 . . . . .74 C4
Warden Ct **10** CT17 . . . . .149 C1
Warden House Mews
CT14 . . . . .117 A4
Warden House Prim Sch
CT14 . . . . .117 A4
Warden Point Way 2
CT5 . . . . .43 C6
Warden Rd
Rochester ME1 . . . . .9 C2
Warden ME12 . . . . .6 B5
Warden Terr ME12 . . . . .5 A6
Warden View Gdns ME12 . . .6 D1
Warden Way ME12 . . . . .6 B5
Wardour Cl CT10 . . . . .30 B4
Wards Hill Rd ME12 . . . . . . .4 C8
Wardwell La ME9 . . . . .13 C1
WARE 71 B6
WAREHORNE 182 D6
Warehorne Rd TN26 . . . . .183 A7
Ware St ME14 . . . . .76 A5
WARE STREET 76 B5
Warlingham Cl ME8 . . . . . .12 A1
WARMLAKE 98 D1
Warmlake Rd ME17 . . . . . .98 F1
Warmlake Bsns Est ME17 . .98 E1
Warmlake Rd ME17 . . . . . .98 C1
Warner St ME4 . . . . .9 F3
Warnford Gdns ME15 . . . . .97 A8
Warnford Pl ME15 . . . . . . .97 A8
Warre Ave CT11 . . . . .52 C5
Warren Cl
Folkestone CT19 . . . . .178 F6
Sittingbourne ME10 . . . . . .37 B2
Warren Ct CT11 . . . . .29 E5
Warren Dr The CT8 . . . . . . .27 D7
Warren Hos TN27 . . . . . . .119 E8
Warren Hts TN25 . . . . . . .158 E5
Warren La
Ashford TN24 . . . . .139 A4
Lydden CT15 . . . . .147 D6
Yelsted ME9 . . . . .34 C3
Warren Lo CT1 . . . . .87 B6

Warren Rd
Folkestone CT19 . . . . .178 F6
Kit's Coty ME5 . . . . .53 D7
Littlestone-on-Sea TN28 . .202 D6
Warren Ret Pk TN24 . . . . .139 B4
Warren St
Stalisfield Green ME13 . . .103 A3
Warren Street ME17 . . . . .102 D7
WARREN STREET 102 D7
Warren The
Brabourne Lees TN25 . . . .158 E5
Selling ME13 . . . . .84 E7
Whitstable CT5 . . . . .43 C6
Warren View TN23 . . . . . . .155 E8
Warren Way CT19 . . . . . . .178 F6
Warren Wood Com Prim Sch
ME1 . . . . .31 C8
Warren Wood Rd ME1 . . . .31 C7
Warten Rd CT11 . . . . .29 F1
Warwick Cres ME10 . . . . . .36 C5
Warwick Dr CT11 . . . . .52 B5
Warwick Pl ME16 . . . . .74 E3
Warwick Rd
Ashford TN24 . . . . .139 E5
Canterbury CT1 . . . . .88 C8
Deal CT14 . . . . .117 D2
Margate CT9 . . . . .8 B2
Whitstable CT5 . . . . .20 C5
Washford Farm Rd TN23 .155 E5
Washington Cl **4** CT16 . . .149 B3
Washington Ho ME15 . . . . .97 E5
Washington La TN29 . . . . .200 C6
Wass Dro CT3 . . . . .71 B7
Watchester Ave CT11 . . . . .52 C5
Watchester La CT12 . . . . . .50 B5
Watchmans Terr **6** ME5 . .10 C2
Watercress Ho ME5 . . . . . .54 A7
Watercress La
Ashford TN23 . . . . .155 F8
Wingham CT3 . . . . .90 F6
Waterditch La ME17,
TN27 . . . . .102 E5
Weddington La CT3 . . . . . .71 E2
Wedgewood Cl ME16 . . . . .74 B5
Wedgewood Dr ME5 . . . . .32 A7
Weeds Wood Rd ME5 . . . . .31 F4
Weekes Cl ME11 . . . . .3 A5
Week St ME14 . . . . .75 A4
Weigall Pl CT11 . . . . .52 C7
Weighbridge Way CT16 . .166 H8
Welcombe Cl ME15 . . . . . .33 D8
Well Cl CT2 . . . . .68 A6
Weller Ave ME1 . . . . .9 D2
Wellesley Ave CT14 . . . . .117 C3
Wellesley Rd
Broadstairs CT10 . . . . .29 C3
Westgate on Sea CT8 . . . . .27 E7
Wellesley Ct **15** CT11 . . . .52 E7
Wellesley Ho CT11 . . . . . .117 C1
Wellesley House Sch
CT10 . . . . .29 F3
Wellesley Rd
Ashford TN23 . . . . .139 C2
Dover CT16 . . . . .166 C2
Margate CT9 . . . . .8 C4
Sheerness ME12 . . . . .1 E2
Westgate on Sea CT8 . . . . .27 E7
Wellesley Terr CT13 . . . . . .94 A8
Wellesley Villas TN24 . . . .139 C3
Wellfield Rd CT20 . . . . . . .178 A5
Wellington Cl
Gillingham ME7 . . . . .10 C4
Whitstable CT5 . . . . .20 D2
Waterloo St ME15 . . . . .75 A3
Waterloo Terr ME12 . . . . . .5 A5
Waterlow Rd ME14 . . . . . . .75 A6
Waterman Ho TN23 . . . . .156 B8
Watermead Cl ME17 . . . . .32 F6
Watermill Cl
Maidstone ME16 . . . . .74 B5
Rochester ME2 . . . . .9 C8
Waters Edge ME15 . . . . . . .74 F2
Watersend CT16 . . . . .148 D5
Waterside
Ashford TN24 . . . . .139 F1
Maidstone ME14 . . . . .74 F4
Waterside Cl ME13 . . . . . . .40 D1
Waterside Ct **5** CT21 . . . .176 B2
Waterside Ct ME2 . . . . .9 E6
Waterside Dr CT8 . . . . .7 D1
Waterside Gate ME16 . . . . .74 F5
Waterside La ME10 . . . . . .14 F7
Waterside Terr TN23 . . . . .138 C1
Waterside View ME15 . . . . .6 E4
Watersmeet ME15 . . . . . . .75 A1
Waters Pl ME7 . . . . .33 A6
Water St CT14 . . . . .117 D7
Waterstone Pl ME13 . . . . . .62 A6
Waterworks Hill CT15 . . . .133 B3
Waterworks Rd CT15 . . . . .133 B3
Watery La CT4 . . . . .109 C5
Watkin Rd CT19 . . . . .178 C6
Watling Ave ME5 . . . . .10 D2
Watling Pl ME10 . . . . .37 A3
Watling St
Canterbury CT1 . . . . .87 F8
Gillingham ME5 . . . . .10 D2
Watson Ave ME5 . . . . .31 D5
Watsons Cl TN25 . . . . .139 C8
Watsons Hill ME10 . . . . . . .36 E5
Wattle Cnr TN30 . . . . .189 D3
Watts' Ave ME4 . . . . .9 C4
Watts Cotts TN24 . . . . . . .139 C7
Watts' St ME4 . . . . .9 E3
Watts Yd **5** CT13 . . . . . . .72 F1
Wat Tyler Way ME15 . . . . .75 A4
Wauchope Rd
Whitstable CT5 . . . . .42 F6
1 Whitstable CT5 . . . . . . .43 A6
Wave Crest CT5 . . . . .20 C1
Waverley Ave ME12 . . . . . . .4 B7

Waverley Cl
Chatham ME5 . . . . .32 D2
Coxheath ME17 . . . . .96 C3
Waverley Rd CT9 . . . . .28 C8
WAY .50 E7
Wayborough Hill CT12 . . . .50 D7
Way Farm Cotts CT12 . . . .50 E7
WAYFIELD 32 A8
Wayfield Com Prim Sch
ME5 . . . . .32 A7
Wayfield Rd ME5 . . . . .32 A7
Way Hill CT12 . . . . .50 E7
Wayne Cl CT10 . . . . .29 E5
Wayside TN30 . . . . .167 B2
Wayside Ave TN30 . . . . . .167 B3
Wayside Flats TN30 . . . . .167 B3
Weald Cl ME15 . . . . .97 C6
Weald Ct
Charing TN27 . . . . .103 E1
Sittingbourne ME10 . . . . . .36 D5
Wealden Ave TN30 . . . . . .167 B1
Wealdhurst Pk CT10 . . . . .29 D5
Weald The TN24 . . . . .139 C3
Wear Bay Cres CT19 . . . . .178 F6
Wear Bay Rd
Folkestone CT19 . . . . .178 F5
Folkestone CT19 . . . . .178 F5
Weatherall Cl ME13 . . . . . .64 B2
Weatherly Cl ME1 . . . . .9 C4
Weatherly Dr CT10 . . . . . . .29 F2
Weavering Lodge ME14 . . .75 E3
Weavering St ME14 . . . . . .75 F4
WEAVERING STREET 75 F5
Weavers The ME16 . . . . . . .74 B5
Weavers Way
Ashford TN23 . . . . .155 E7
Dover CT16 . . . . .149 A3
Webb Cl CT19 . . . . .178 A7
Webster Rd ME8 . . . . .11 F1
Webster Way CT18 . . . . . .163 B4
WEDDINGTON 71 E3
Weddington La CT3 . . . . . .71 E2
Wedgewood Cl ME16 . . . . .74 B5
Wedgewood Dr ME5 . . . . .32 A7
Weeds Wood Rd ME5 . . . . .31 F4
Weekes Cl ME11 . . . . .3 A5
Week St ME14 . . . . .75 A4
Weigall Pl CT11 . . . . .52 C7
Weighbridge Way CT16 . .166 H8
Welcombe Cl ME15 . . . . . .33 D8
Well Cl CT2 . . . . .68 A6
Weller Ave ME1 . . . . .9 D2
Wellesley Ave CT14 . . . . .117 C3
Wellesley Rd
Ashford TN23 . . . . .139 C2
Dover CT16 . . . . .166 C2
Margate CT9 . . . . .8 C4
Sheerness ME12 . . . . .1 E2
Westgate on Sea CT8 . . . . .27 E7
Wellesley Terr CT13 . . . . . .94 A8
Wellesley Villas TN24 . . . .139 C3
Wellfield Rd CT20 . . . . . . .178 A5
Wellington Cl
Gillingham ME7 . . . . .10 C4
Whitstable CT5 . . . . .20 D2
Wellington Cres CT11 . . . . .52 E6
Wellington Ct CT14 . . . . . .117 D3
Wellington Gdns
2 Dover CT16 . . . . .149 B3
Margate CT9 . . . . .7 J3
Wellington Ho
6 Maidstone ME15 . . . . . .97 E5
Margate CT9 . . . . .8 C3
Wellington Par
Deal CT14 . . . . .134 D7
Kingsdown CT14 . . . . .134 E6
Wellington Pl
Folkestone CT20 . . . . .177 D3
Maidstone ME14 . . . . .74 F6
Wellington Rd
Deal CT14 . . . . .117 D5
Folkestone CT20 . . . . .177 D5
Gillingham ME7 . . . . .10 C4
Margate CT9 . . . . .28 D4
Sittingbourne ME10 . . . . . .36 B6
Temple Ewell CT16 . . . . . .148 D5
Westgate on Sea CT8 . . . . .27 E7
Wellington St CT5 . . . . .43 C6
Wellington Terr CT20 . . . .177 D3
Wellis Gdns CT9 . . . . .7 G1
Well La
Fordwich CT2, CT3 . . . . . . .68 A3
Painters Forstal ME13 . . . .61 B3
St Margaret's at Cliffe
CT15 . . . . .150 A2
Well Rd
Lyminge CT18 . . . . .161 C6
Maidstone ME14 . . . . .75 A5
Queenborough ME11 . . . . . .3 A5
Rushenden ME11 . . . . .2 F3
Wells Ave CT1 . . . . .88 C7
Wells Cl
New Romney TN28 . . . . . .202 C6
Tenterden TN30 . . . . .179 B8
Wells Ho ME10 . . . . .37 B4
Wells Rd CT19 . . . . .177 F6
Well St ME15, ME17 . . . . . .96 E1
Wells Way ME13 . . . . .40 B1
Well Winch Rd ME10 . . . . .36 D5
Welsdene Rd CT9 . . . . .28 B8
Welson Rd CT20 . . . . .178 A5
Wemmick Cl ME1 . . . . .31 D7

Wemyss Ct **13** CT1 . . . . . . .67 B2
Wemyss Ho **14** CT1 . . . . . .67 B2
Wemyss Way CT1 . . . . .67 C1
Wenderton La CT3 . . . . . . .70 A2
Wenham's La CT1 . . . . . . .192 E3
Wents Wood ME14 . . . . . . .75 F5
Wentworth Ave CT9 . . . . . . .7 E1
Wentworth Cl CT18 . . . . . .161 C6
Wentworth Dr
Gillingham ME8 . . . . .33 E7
Ramsgate CT12 . . . . .29 A1
Sittingbourne ME10 . . . . . .36 C5
Wentworth Gdns CT6 . . . . .22 D2
Wentworth Ho ME10 . . . . .36 C5
Wesley Sch Rd TN23 . . . . .155 D7
Wesley Terr CT18 . . . . .161 C7
West Beach CT5 . . . . .20 C1
WESTBERE 68 C7
Westbere La CT2 . . . . .68 C7
**West Blean Wood Nature
Reserve*** CT6 . . . . .45 D5
West Borough Prim Sch
ME16 . . . . .74 B3
Westbourne TN23 . . . . . . .155 D6
Westbourne Ct CT10 . . . . .178 A4
Westbourne St ME10 . . . . .36 E4
WESTBROOK 7 E1
Westbourne Ave CT9 . . . . . .7 F1
Westbrook Cotts CT9 . . . . .7 G1
Westbrook Ct ME4 . . . . . . .10 A2
Westbrook Gdns CT9 . . . . . .7 G1
Westbrook La CT6 . . . . . . .22 B3
Westbrook Prom CT9 . . . . . .7 G2
Westbrook Rd CT9 . . . . .7 G2
Westbury Ct CT17 . . . . . . .166 B6
Westbury Hts CT17 . . . . . .166 B6
Westbury Rd
Dover CT17 . . . . .166 B6
Westgate on Sea CT8 . . . . .27 E8
West Cliff CT5 . . . . .20 C6
West Cliff Arc **10** CT11 . . .52 E6
West Cliff Ave CT10 . . . . . .30 B3
West Cliff Cl CT10 . . . . .30 B3
Westcliff Dr ME12 . . . . .4 D8
West Cliff Dr CT10 . . . . . . .52 F8
WEST CLIFFE 150 D6
Westcliff Gdns CT9 . . . . . . .7 F1
West Cliff Gdns
Folkestone CT20 . . . . .178 D4
Herne Bay CT6 . . . . .22 B4
Westcliff Ho **4** CT20 . . . . .178 D4
West Cliff Prom CT11 . . . . .52 C5
West Cliff Rd CT9 . . . . .7 G1
West Cliff Rd
Broadstairs CT10 . . . . .30 B3
Ramsgate CT11 . . . . .52 D6
West Cliff Terr CT11 . . . . . .52 B5
Westcourt La CT15 . . . . . .130 C5
West Ct CT14 . . . . .10 A6
West Ct **3** ME15 . . . . .75 A1
Westdean Ct CT17 . . . . . . .148 E2
West Dr ME1 . . . . .31 D5
WEST DUMPTON 29 D2
West Dumpton La CT11 . . .29 C1
WEST END
Doddington 80 D7
Herne Bay 45 B8
West End TN26 . . . . .168 F3
West End Cotts ME17 . . . . .96 C7
Westenhanger Castle*
CT21 . . . . .175 A7
WESTENHANGER 175 B6
Westenhanger Sta TN25 . .175 B7
Westerham Cl
Canterbury CT1 . . . . .67 A4
Gillingham ME8 . . . . .11 B3
Margate CT9 . . . . .8 F1
Westerham Rd ME10 . . . . .36 C3
Westerhill Rd ME17 . . . . . .96 C1
Westerhout Cl CT14 . . . . .117 C8
Westerly Mews **5** CT2 . . . .66 E1
Western Ave
Ashford TN23 . . . . .139 A3
Bridge CT4 . . . . .89 A1
Chatham ME4 . . . . .10 A8
Halfway Houses ME12 . . . . .3 D6
Herne Bay CT6 . . . . .22 E4
Western Ct CT17 . . . . .166 C6
Western Espl
Broadstairs CT10 . . . . .30 B2
Herne Bay CT6 . . . . .22 C5
Western Gdns TN24 . . . . .156 E8
WESTERN HEIGHTS 166 C6
Western Heights Rdbt
CT17 . . . . .166 C5
Western Ho CT14 . . . . .117 C7
Western Mts* CT17 . . . . . .166 C6
Western Link ME13 . . . . . .62 A8
Western Rd
Deal CT14 . . . . .117 C7
Maidstone ME16 . . . . .74 C2
Margate CT9 . . . . .29 C8
Western Service Rd
CT16 . . . . .166 G8
Western Undercliff CT11 . .52 C5
Westfield CT2 . . . . .66 A6
Westfield Bsns Ctr ME2 . . .9 C7
Westfield Cotts ME8 . . . . . .13 A2
Westfield Gdns ME9 . . . . . .35 C3
Westfield La CT18 . . . . . . .161 C3
Westfield Rd
Birchington CT7 . . . . .27 A7
Margate CT9 . . . . .28 C8
Westfields TN27 . . . . .136 D8
WESTFIELD SOLE 54 C7

Westfield Sole Rd ME5,
ME14 . . . . 54 D8
Westgate Ave CT7 . . . . 28 A4
Westgate Bay Ave CT8 . . . . 7 C1
Westgate Cl CT2 . . . . 66 C1
Westgate College for Deaf
People CT9 . . . . 7 J2
Westgate Court Ave CT2 . . 66 D1
Westgate Ct 8 CT2 . . . . 66 E1
Westgate Garden Flats
CT2 . . . . 87 E8
Westgate Gr CT2 . . . . 66 C1
Westgate Hall Rd 14 CT1 . . 66 F1
WESTGATE-ON-SEA 7 B2
WESTGATE ON SEA 27 E7
Westgate-on-Sea Sta
CT8 . . . . 27 E8
Westgate Rd ME13 . . . . 62 E7
Westgate Terr CT5 . . . . 20 E2
Westgate Tower Mus*
CT1 . . . . 66 F1
West Gn ME10 . . . . 14 F1
West Hill Rd CT6 . . . . 22 C5
WEST HOUGHAM 164 F5
West Hythe Rd CT21 . . . . . 187 A8
West La
Sheerness ME12 . . . . 1 B2
Sittingbourne ME10 . . . . . . 37 A4
Westlands Ave ME10 . . . . . . 36 B4
Westlands Rd CT6 . . . . 22 C3
Westlands Sch The ME10 . . 36 B4
Westland Way CT18 . . . . . . 163 B3
West Lane Trad Est ME10 . . 37 A4
WEST LANGDON 132 D3
West Lawn Gdns CT20 . . . . 177 D3
West Lea CT14 . . . . 117 C7
Westlea CT CT20 . . . . 178 A3
Westleigh Rd CT8 . . . . 27 D8
WESTMARSH 71 B7
Westmarsh Dr CT9 . . . . 8 E2
Westmarsh Dro CT3 . . . . 71 A8
Westmeads Com Inf Sch
CT5 . . . . 20 D1
Westmeads Rd CT5 . . . . 20 E2
WEST MINSTER 3 A7
West Minster Prim Sch
ME12 . . . . 3 B8
Westminster Rd CT1 . . . . . . 67 C4
Westminster Sq ME16 . . . . 74 B4
Westminster Wlk CT1 . . . . . 29 C1
Westmoors CT3 . . . . 155 C6
Westmoreland Dr ME9 . . . . 13 C3
Westmorland Cl ME15 . . . . . 97 E7
Westmorland Gn ME15 . . . . 97 E7
Westmorland Rd ME15 . . . . 97 E7
West Motney Way ME8 . . . . 12 A3
Westmount Ave ME4 . . . . . . 9 F3
Westmount Ho 4 CT9 . . . . . 8 B2
West Norman Rd CT16 . . . 166 C8
Weston Rd ME2 . . . . 9 A8
Westonville Ave CT9 . . . . . . 7 F1
Westover Gdns CT10 . . . . . 29 E7
Westover Rd CT10 . . . . 29 E6
West Par CT21 . . . . 176 B1
West Park Ave CT5 . . . . 8 D1
West Park Rd ME15 . . . . 75 B2
West Pas ME12 . . . . 1 D8
West Pl TN29 . . . . 199 D4
West Ramp CT16 . . . . 166 G8
West Rd
Chatham ME4 . . . . 10 A7
Cliffs End CT13 . . . . 51 A1
Folkestone CT20 . . . . 177 C4
Westree Ct 7 ME16 . . . . 74 E3
Westree Rd ME16 . . . . 74 E3
West Ridge ME10 . . . . 36 D3
West Side CT15 . . . . 133 A1
Westside Apartments 10
CT2 . . . . 66 F1
West St
Ashford TN23 . . . . 139 B2
Deal CT14 . . . . 117 D6
Dover CT17 . . . . 166 C8
Faversham ME13 . . . . 62 C7
Gillingham ME7 . . . . 10 C6
Harrietsham ME17 . . . . . . 100 C6
Hothfield TN26 . . . . 137 F7
Lenham ME17 . . . . 79 E1
New Romney TN28 . . . . . . 202 A6
Queenborough ME11 . . . . . . 2 F5
Sheerness ME12 . . . . 1 B2
Sittingbourne ME10 . . . . . . 36 E4
Woodside Green ME17 . . . 101 B8
WEST STOURMOUTH 48 D2
WEST STREET
101 E8
Eastry 93 F1
Lenham 79 E1
West Street Cotts CT14 . . . 94 A1
West Tank Farm Rd
TN29 . . . . 209 C2
West Terr CT20 . . . . 178 D4
West View CT19 . . . . 178 D8
West View Cl CT6 . . . . 22 C2
West View Rd ME15 . . . . . . 96 C3
WESTWELL 121 E3
Westwell Ct TN25 . . . . 121 E3
Westwell La
Charing TN25, TN27 . . . . . 120 F5
Potters Corner TN24,
TN25 . . . . 138 E7
Westwell TN25, TN26 . . . . 121 B4
WESTWELL LEACON 120 D4

West Wlk ME16 . . . . 74 B3
WESTWOOD
Barham 127 E8
Broadstairs 29 B5
Westwood Ct ME13 . . . . . . 62 E3
Westwood Ind Est CT9 . . . . 29 A6
Westwood Pl ME13 . . . . 62 D5
Westwood Rd
Broadstairs CT10 . . . . 29 C4
Kingston CT4 . . . . 110 F1
Loose ME15 . . . . 97 A7
West Wood Rd ME9 . . . . 56 B8
Westwood Ret Pk CT10 . . . 29 A5
Westwood Wlk ME9 . . . . . . 35 B7
WETHAM GREEN 12 F5
Wetheral Dr ME5 . . . . 10 A3
Wexford Pl ME15 . . . . 97 D6
Weybridge Cl ME5 . . . . 32 C4
Weyburn Dr CT12 . . . . 29 A1
Wey Cl ME5 . . . . 32 C5
Weyhill ME14 . . . . 75 C6
Weymouth Cl CT19 . . . . . . 177 D7
Weymouth Rd CT19 . . . . . 177 D6
Weymouth Rd CT19 . . . . . 177 D7
Wey St TN26 . . . . 183 D3
Wharfdale Sq ME15 . . . . . . 74 E1
Wharfedale Rd CT9 . . . . 8 A1
Wharf Rd
Gillingham ME7 . . . . 10 C7
Maidstone ME15 . . . . 74 E2
Sandwich CT13 . . . . 73 B4
Wharton Gdns TN24 . . . . . 156 E8
Whatman Cl ME14 . . . . 75 C6
Whatman Ho ME13 . . . . 63 F4
Whatmer Cl CT3 . . . . 68 A6
WHATSOLE STREET 142 F5
Wheatcroft Cl ME10 . . . . . . 37 A4
Wheatcroft Gr ME8 . . . . 33 F7
Wheatear Way CT12 . . . . . . 32 B7
Wheatfields
Chatham ME5 . . . . 32 C2
Maidstone ME14 . . . . 75 D4
Wheatley Rd
Ramsgate CT12 . . . . 29 C1
Whitstable CT5 . . . . 20 E2
Wheatsheaf Cl
Boughton Street ME13 . . . . 64 A3
Loose ME15 . . . . 97 B8
Wheatsheafe La CT15 . . . . 133 B2
Wheatsheaf Way CT13 . . . . 73 A6
WHEELBARROW TOWN . . . 143 F8
Wheeler St ME14 . . . . 75 A5
Wheelers The ME8 . . . . 33 B6
Wheelwrights The ME17 . . 100 D6
Wheelwrights Way CT13 . . 93 B2
Wheler Ct ME13 . . . . 62 A7
Wheler Rd TN27 . . . . 120 C8
Wherry Cl CT9 . . . . 29 A5
Whewell Terr 1 CT20 . . . . 178 E5
Whiffen's Ave ME4 . . . . 9 F5
Whiffen's Ave W ME4 . . . . . . 9 F5
Whigham Cl TN23 . . . . 155 D7
Whimbrel Cl ME10 . . . . 36 F8
Whimbrel Wlk ME5 . . . . 32 C1
Whinfell Ave CT12 . . . . 51 F7
Whinless Rd CT17 . . . . 166 A8
Whiston Ave TN26 . . . . 153 C4
Whitbourne Ct 4 CT5 . . . . . 43 E8
Whitby Rd CT20 . . . . 177 D6
Whitchurch Cl ME16 . . . . . . 74 E4
Whitcombe Cl ME5 . . . . 32 C3
White Acre Dr CT14 . . . . . 134 B8
Whiteacre La CT4 . . . . 125 E4
Whitebeam Ct TN23 . . . . . 138 D4
Whitebeam Dr ME17 . . . . . . 96 B3
White Cl ME15 . . . . 149 B5
White Cliffs 11 CT20 . . . . . 178 D4
White Cliffs Bsns Ctr
CT16 . . . . 149 A6
White Cliffs Bsns Pk
CT16 . . . . 149 A6
White Cliffs of Dover Visitor
Ctr* CT17 . . . . 150 A1
White Cliffs Prim Coll for the
Arts CT17 . . . . 149 A1
Whitecliff Way CT19 . . . . . 178 F6
White Ct 8 CT20 . . . . 177 E3
Whitefriars Mdw 15 CT13 . . 72 F1
Whitefriars Way CT13 . . . . . 72 F1
Whitegate Ct ME8 . . . . 33 D5
WHITEHALL 29 C1
Whitehall
Brookland TN29 . . . . 199 E8
Sandwich CT13 . . . . 95 A7
Whitehall Bridge Rd CT2 . . 87 E8
Whitehall Cl CT2 . . . . 87 E8
Whitehall Dr ME17 . . . . 99 D3
Whitehall Gdns CT2 . . . . . . 66 E1
Whitehall Rd
Broad Street ME14 . . . . 77 A6
Canterbury CT2 . . . . 87 E8
Canterbury, Harbledown
CT2 . . . . 87 D7
Ramsgate CT12 . . . . 29 C1
Sittingbourne ME10 . . . . . . 36 E2
Whitehall Way TN25 . . . . . 159 D1
White Hart Mans ME7 . . . . . 7 I3
Whiteheads La ME14 . . . . . . 76 B4
WHITEHILL 61 F3
White Hill
Boughton Aluph TN25 . . . 123 B6
Chalock TN25 . . . . 105 E1
Chilham CT4 . . . . 85 E1
White Hill Cl CT4 . . . . 110 A8
White Hill Rd ME9, ME14 . . 33 D1
Whitehorse Mdws ME15 . . . 10 B3
White Horse Hill CT18 . . . 163 C3

White Horse La
6 Canterbury CT1 . . . . 87 F8
Otham Hole ME15 . . . . 98 A6
Rhodes Minnis CT4 . . . . . 144 A3
White Horse Wood Cntry
Park* ME14 . . . . 55 D2
Whitehouse Cres ME1 . . . . . 53 A8
Whitehouse Dro CT13,
CT3 . . . . 72 D7
White House Farm CT
CT15 . . . . 113 E5
Whitelocks Cl CT4 . . . . 111 D3
White Marsh Ct CT5 . . . . . . 20 E2
White Mill Rural Her Ctr*
CT13 . . . . 72 E2
Whitenbrook CT21 . . . . . . 177 A2
Whitenbrook Dell CT21 . . . 177 A3
Whiteness Gn CT10 . . . . 8 F1
Whiteness Rd CT10 . . . . 8 G1
Whitepost 12 CT5 . . . . 20 D2
White Post ME17 . . . . 78 B5
White Post Gdns CT3 . . . . . 71 E1
White Rd ME4 . . . . 10 A2
White Rock Pl ME2 . . . . 9 D7
White Rock Pl 8 ME16 . . . . 74 E3
Whites Hill CT14 . . . . 115 B2
Whitewall Ctr ME2 . . . . 9 D8
Whitewall Way ME2 . . . . 9 D7
Whiteway Rd ME11, ME12 . . 2 F7
White Willow Cl TN24 . . . . 156 D6
White Wood Rd CT13 . . . . . 93 B1
Whitfeld Rd TN23 . . . . 156 B8
WHITFIELD 149 A7
Whitfield Ave
Broadstairs CT10 . . . . 29 E7
Dover CT16 . . . . 149 B2
Whitfield Cotts TN23 . . . . 156 B8
Whitfield Ct CT16 . . . . 149 A6
Whitfield Hill
Dover CT16 . . . . 148 F4
Temple Ewell CT16 . . . . . 148 E4
Whitfield Lodge CT16 . . . . 149 A8
Whitfield Rdbt CT16 . . . . . 149 A6
Whitfield Sch & Aspen Prim
Sch CT16 . . . . 149 A7
Whitgift Ct CT2 . . . . 66 D1
Whiting Cres ME13 . . . . 62 A8
Whiting Ho TN29 . . . . 205 C5
Whitmore St ME16 . . . . 74 D2
WHITSTABLE 20 D2
Whitstable Jun Sch 12
CT5 . . . . 20 D1
Whitstable Mus & Art
Gallery* 14 CT5 . . . . 20 D1
Whitstable Rd
Canterbury CT2 . . . . 66 D2
Faversham, Goodnestone
ME13 . . . . 63 B6
Faversham ME13 . . . . 62 E7
Herne Bay CT5, CT6 . . . . . 22 B3
Rough Common CT2 . . . . . 66 B4
Whitstable & Seasalter
Endowed CE Jun Sch 16
CT5 . . . . 20 D1
Whitstable Sports Ctr CT5 43 F8
Whitstable Sta CT5 . . . . 20 E1
Whitstable & Tankerton
Hospl CT5 . . . . 21 A2
Whittaker St ME4 . . . . 10 A4
Whittington Terr CT15 . . . 130 D4
Whybornes Chase ME12 . . . . 4 C2
Whyman Ave ME4 . . . . 10 A1
Whytecliffs CT10 . . . . 30 A2
WICHLING 80 C5
Wichling Cl CT2 . . . . 67 A3
Wickenden Cres TN24 . . . . 157 A8
Wicken Ho ME16 . . . . 74 E4
Wicken La TN25, TN27 . . . 120 E6
Wickets The CT4 . . . . 156 F7
Wicketts End
9 Whitstable CT5 . . . . 20 D1
Whitstable CT5 . . . . 43 D8
Wickham Ave CT11 . . . . 52 G8
WICKHAMBREAUX 69 C2
Wickhambreaux CE Prim Sch
CT3 . . . . 69 C2
Wickham Cl ME9 . . . . 35 B6
Wickham Court La CT3 . . . . 69 B3
Wickham La CT3 . . . . 69 B1
Wickham Mill CT3 . . . . 69 C2
Wickham Pl ME17 . . . . 101 D5
Wickham Rd CT3 . . . . 69 B2
Wickham Rise ME16 . . . . . . 74 E4
Wickham Terr ME11 . . . . 2 F5
Wick La CT4 . . . . 129 F7
Widgeon Wlk CT18 . . . . . . 163 B3
Widred Rd CT17 . . . . 166 C8
Wierton La ME17 . . . . 97 E1
Wife of Bath Hill CT4 . . . . . 87 C8
Wigeon Rd ME9 . . . . 14 E3
WIGMORE 33 B4
Wigmore Cotts CT15 . . . . . 131 C8
Wigmore Gdns ME8 . . . . . . 33 B4
Wigmore La CT15 . . . . 131 C8
Wigmore Rd ME8 . . . . 33 B4
Wigmore Wood CT15 . . . . . 131 C8
Wigwam Paddocks CT7 . . . . 27 A8
Wihtred Rd ME9 . . . . 37 D2
Wilberforce Rd
Coxheath ME17 . . . . 96 D3
Folkestone CT20 . . . . 177 E3
Wilbrough Rd CT7 . . . . 27 A7
Wilcox Cl CT13 . . . . 112 D5
Wild Air CT7 . . . . 26 F8
Wilderness Hill CT9 . . . . 8 A2
Wildfell Cl ME5 . . . . 54 C8
Wildish Rd ME13 . . . . 62 A8

Wildman Cl ME8 . . . . 33 D3
Wildwood Cl ME17 . . . . 99 E2
Wildwood Glade ME7 . . . . . 33 B4
Wildwood Rd CT2 . . . . 67 F6
Wildwood Wealden Forest
Pk* CT2, CT6 . . . . 45 E4
Wiles Ave TN28 . . . . 202 B6
Wiles Ho TN28 . . . . 202 B6
Wilfred Rd CT11 . . . . 52 C8
WILGATE GREEN 82 F6
Wilgate Green Rd ME13 . . . 82 F6
Wilkes Rd CT10 . . . . 29 E4
Wilkie Rd CT7 . . . . 27 A8
Wilkinson Dr CT14 . . . . 117 D3
Wilks Cl ME8 . . . . 12 B2
Will Adams Ct 8 ME7 . . . . . 10 C6
Will Adams Rdbt ME8 . . . . . 10 F2
Will Adams Way ME8 . . . . . 10 F1
Willement Rd ME13 . . . . . . 62 B7
WILLESBOROUGH 156 F8
Willesborough Ind Pk
TN24 . . . . 140 A1
Willesborough Inf & Jun
Schs TN24 . . . . 157 A8
WILLESBOROUGH LEES . . 140 B1
Willesborough Rd TN24 . . 139 F4
Willesborough Windmill*
TN24 . . . . 140 A1
Willetts Hill CT12 . . . . 49 D7
William Ave
Folkestone CT19 . . . . 178 B7
Margate CT9 . . . . 29 C8
William Gibbs Ct 14 ME13 62 D7
William Harvey Hospl
TN24 . . . . 140 C1
William Judge Dr TN30 . . . 179 D7
William Muge Ho 15
CT16 . . . . 166 D8
William Pitt Ave CT16 . . . . 117 B6
William Pitt Cl CT21 . . . . . 176 D2
William Pitt Rd TN23 . . . . 156 B8
William Rigby Dr ME12 . . . . 3 E7
Williams Cl ME9 . . . . 58 E5
Williamson Rd TN29 . . . . . 206 E5
William St
Faversham ME13 . . . . 62 D7
Gillingham ME8 . . . . 12 A1
Herne Bay CT6 . . . . 22 F5
Sittingbourne ME10 . . . . . . 36 E4
Whitstable CT5 . . . . 20 D2
Willington Terr TN23 . . . . 155 E5
Willingdon Pl CT14 . . . . . . 117 C1
Willingdon Rd CT16 . . . . . 149 A5
WILLINGTON 75 E1
Willington Gn ME15 . . . . . . 97 E7
Willington St ME15 . . . . . . 75 F2
Willis Ct ME12 . . . . 3 F5
Willis Ho ME1 . . . . 9 C4
Willop Cl TN29 . . . . 186 F3
Willop Way TN29 . . . . 186 F3
Willoughby Ct 13 CT1 . . . . 87 F8
Willow Ave
Broadstairs CT10 . . . . 29 D4
Faversham ME13 . . . . 62 A7
Willow Bank TN24 . . . . 140 A1
Willowbank CT19 . . . . 195 A4
Willow Bank Ct 12 ME15 . . 75 B4
Willow Bank Ind Est ME9 . . 14 E6
Willowby Gdns ME8 . . . . . . 33 E4
Willow Cl
Canterbury CT2 . . . . 67 A2
Harrietsham ME17 . . . . . . 100 D6
Hythe CT21 . . . . 175 E1
Margate CT9 . . . . 8 C2
Willow Ct
Broadstairs CT10 . . . . 30 A5
Folkestone CT20 . . . . 177 E4
Loose ME15 . . . . 97 A6
Whitstable CT5 . . . . 43 E8
Willow Dr
Hamstreet TN26 . . . . 183 A7
St Mary's Bay TN29 . . . . . 194 F3
Willow Farm Way CT6 . . . . . 23 C2
Willow Ho
Ashford TN23 . . . . 138 F1
8 Chatham ME5 . . . . 31 F5
8 Maidstone ME16 . . . . . . 74 A3
Sheerness ME12 . . . . 1 C2
Sittingbourne ME10 . . . . . . 37 B3
Willow Lodge CT19 . . . . . . 178 D3
Willow Rd
Great Mongeham CT14 . . . 116 C3
Willow Rise ME15 . . . . 75 F1
Willows Ct CT4 . . . . 86 C3
Willows Prim Sch The
CT6 . . . . 23 B4
Willows The
Ashford TN24 . . . . 139 D6
Gillingham ME8 . . . . 11 E2
Newington ME9 . . . . 35 B6
Sittingbourne ME10 . . . . . . 14 F1
Willow Tree Cl
Ashford TN24 . . . . 139 F1
Herne Bay CT6 . . . . 23 D5
Willow Way
Maidstone ME15 . . . . 75 B3
Margate CT9 . . . . 28 C8
Whitstable CT5 . . . . 44 C8
Willow Wood CT5 . . . . 131 D7
Willowwood 8 ME15 . . . . . . 97 E5
Wills La TN29 . . . . 184 C4
Wilson's Rd CT11 . . . . 52 D6
Wilmecote Ct ME8 . . . . 33 D8
Wilmington Way ME8 . . . . . 11 B2
Wilmott Pl CT13 . . . . 93 B2

Wilson Ave
Deal CT14 . . . . 116 F4
Rochester ME1 . . . . 31 E7
Wilson Cl
Ashford TN24 . . . . 140 A1
Maidstone ME15 . . . . 97 E7
Wilsons La ME15 . . . . 96 A5
Wiltie Ct CT19 . . . . 178 C5
Wiltie Gdns CT19 . . . . 178 C5
Wilton Cl CT14 . . . . 117 C5
Wilton Rd
Folkestone CT19 . . . . 178 B6
Ramsgate CT12 . . . . 28 F1
Wilton Terr ME10 . . . . 36 B5
Wiltshire Cl ME5 . . . . 32 C8
Wiltshire Way 4 ME8 . . . . . 11 C2
Wimborne Pl CT12 . . . . 52 B8
Wimbourne Dr ME8 . . . . . . 33 D6
Winant Way CT18 . . . . 149 B3
Winch Dr ME9 . . . . 58 E6
Wincheap CT1 . . . . 87 E7
Wincheap Gn 4 CT1 . . . . . . 87 F7
Wincheap Ind Est CT1 . . . . 87 D7
Wincheap Prim Sch CT1 . . 87 E6
Winchelsea Ct 4 CT17 . . . 166 C7
Winchelsea Rd
Chatham ME5 . . . . 32 B5
Dover CT17 . . . . 166 B7
Winchelsea St CT17 . . . . . 166 B7
Winchelsea Terr CT17 . . . . 166 B7
Winchester Ave ME5 . . . . . . 31 F4
Winchester Gdns CT1 . . . . . 88 A6
Winchester Ho 3 ME5 . . . . . 97 C7
Winchester Mews CT14 . . 117 B3
Winchester Pl 9 ME14 . . . . 75 A5
Winchester Way ME8 . . . . . 34 A8
Winch Rd ME9 . . . . 58 D6
Windermere ME13 . . . . 62 G6
Windermere Ave CT11 . . . . 52 A7
Windermere Cres TN24 . . . 139 C4
Windermere Dr ME8 . . . . . . 33 D7
Windermere Gdns CT13 . . 112 F6
Windermere Gr ME10 . . . . . 36 D3
Windermere Ho 4 ME15 . . . 97 E7
Windermere Rd ME5 . . . . . . 31 F4
Wind Hill TN27 . . . . 119 E7
Wind Hill La TN27 . . . . 119 E7
Winding Hill ME13 . . . . 83 F6
Windmill Ave CT12 . . . . 29 B3
Windmill Cl
Ashford TN24 . . . . 140 A1
Bridge CT4 . . . . 89 A1
Canterbury CT1 . . . . 88 C8
Herne Bay CT6 . . . . 23 A2
Windmill Ct ME17 . . . . 97 B3
Windmill Hill ME17 . . . . . . 100 B1
Windmill Hts ME14 . . . . 76 B4
Windmill La ME13 . . . . 40 B1
Windmill Manor ME7 . . . . . 10 C4
Windmill Quay Rd ME12 . . . 4 E2
Windmill Rd
Canterbury CT1 . . . . 88 C8
Gillingham ME7 . . . . 10 C4
Herne Bay CT6 . . . . 23 A2
Sittingbourne ME10 . . . . . . 36 D6
Whitstable CT5 . . . . 43 D7
Windmill Rise ME12 . . . . 4 A6
Windmill Row ME17 . . . . . . 98 D2
Windmill St CT21 . . . . 176 B1
Windmill View CT9 . . . . 29 A8
Windmill Wlk CT12 . . . . 29 B1
Windsor Ave
Chatham ME4 . . . . 9 F2
Margate CT9 . . . . 8 B1
Windsor Cl
Broadstairs CT10 . . . . 29 E5
Maidstone ME14 . . . . 75 B6
Windsor Ct
Deal CT14 . . . . 117 C2
Gillingham ME7 . . . . 10 D5
Margate CT9 . . . . 8 B1
Windsor Dr ME10 . . . . 36 D2
Windsor Gdns
Herne Bay CT6 . . . . 22 B3
Warden ME12 . . . . 6 D4
Windsor Ho
Deal CT14 . . . . 117 A5
6 Dover CT17 . . . . 166 D7
Whitstable CT5 . . . . 20 D1
Windsor Mews
9 Margate CT9 . . . . 7 J2
New Romney TN28 . . . . . . 202 C8
Windsor Rd
Canterbury CT1 . . . . 87 C6
Cliffs End CT12 . . . . 51 D7
Gillingham ME7 . . . . 10 D5
Windward Rd ME1 . . . . 9 C1
Windyridge ME7 . . . . 10 E1
Winehouse La CT18 . . . . . . 164 D3
Wineycock ME9 . . . . 81 C8
Winford Mews ME1 . . . . 9 A2
Wingate Ct 7 ME10 . . . . 36 E4
Wingate Rd CT19 . . . . 178 D7
WINGHAM 91 B7
Wingham Cl
Gillingham ME8 . . . . 11 C3
Maidstone ME15 . . . . 97 F7
WINGHAM GREEN 90 F7
Wingham Ind Est CT3 . . . . . 91 B6
Wingham Prim Sch CT3 . . . 91 A7
Wingham Rd CT3 . . . . 90 D8
WINGHAM WELL 90 F6
Wingham Well La CT3 . . . . . 90 F5
Wingham Wildlife Pk*
CT3 . . . . 70 C1
Wing Ho ME12 . . . . 6 H1
WINGMORE 128 B2
Wing Rd ME12 . . . . 6 H1

Wingrove Dr
  Maidstone ME14 . . . . .75 E5
  Rochester ME2 . . . . .9 C7
Wingrove Hill CT17 . . . .148 E2
Wings Cl CT10 . . . . .30 B5
Winifred Ave CT12 . . . . . . .29 C2
Winifred Rd ME15 . . . . .75 F3
Winkle Cl CT6 . . . . .22 B3
Winnipeg Cl CT16 . . . . . . .149 C3
Win Pine Ho CT21 . . . . . . .176 A1
Winstanley Cres CT11 . . .52 D8
Winstanley Rd ME12 . . . . . . .1 D2
Winston Cl CT1 . . . . .88 C7
Winston Ct CT17 . . . . .27 A8
Winston Gdns CT6 . . . . . . .23 D4
Winston Ho **4** CT20 . . . .177 F5
WINTERBOURNE 85 A8
Winter Dr CT18 . . . . .163 B5
Winter Gdns & Queens Mus
  CT9 . . . . .7 J3
Winterstoke Cres CT11 . . .52 G8
Winterstoke Way CT11 . . .52 F8
Winton Way TN29 . . . . . .195 A5
Wirrals The ME5 . . . . .32 A4
Wises La ME10, ME9 . . . . . .36 A4
Wish The TN26 . . . . .181 F6
WISSENDEN 152 F7
Wissenden La
  Bethersden TN26 . . . . . . .153 B6
  Smarden, Romden TN27 . . .135 D1
Wisteria Ho **11** ME15 . . . .97 E7
WITHERSDANE 140 F8
Withersdane Cotts TN25 . 124 A2
Witley Wlk CT16 . . . . .149 B7
WITTERSHAM 188 D3
Wittersham CE Prim Sch
  TN30 . . . . .188 D2
Wittersham Cl ME5 . . . . . .32 B5
Wittersham La TN31 . . . . .197 B5
Wittersham Rd
  Iden TN31 . . . . .197 B2
  Stone in Oxney TN30 . . . .189 C3
  Wittersham TN30 . . . . . . .188 C5
Wivenhoe TN23 . . . . .155 E5
Wivenhoe Cl ME8 . . . . . . .12 A2
Wolfe Ct CT14 . . . . .117 D3
Wolfe Rd ME16 . . . . .74 B2
Wolf Ho ME4 . . . . .10 B8
Wollaston Cl ME8 . . . . .33 D3
Wollaston Rd CT14 . . . . . .117 D4
Wolseley Ave CT6 . . . . . . .22 A4
Wolseley Pl **2** TN24 . . . .139 B3
Wolseley Terr TN29 . . . . .205 C5
WOLVERTON 147 F2
Women's Land Army Mus
  The* CT15 . . . . .165 E5
WOMENSWOLD 112 D2
Woodberry Dr ME15 . . . . . .37 C3
Woodberry Flats CT10 . . . .30 A3
Woodbridge Dr ME15 . . . . .74 F1
Woodbrook TN27 . . . . . . .120 D7
Woodbury La TN30 . . . . . .179 A7
Woodbury Rd ME5 . . . . . . .31 F1
WOODCHURCH
  Margate 27 F3
  Tenterden 169 A2
Woodchurch CE Prim Sch
  TN26 . . . . .169 A2
Woodchurch Cl ME5 . . . . . .32 B5
Woodchurch Cotts CT7 . . . .27 F4
Woodchurch Cres ME8 . . . .11 C2
Woodchurch Ho ME8 . . . . . .11 C2
Woodchurch Rd
  Appledore Heath TN26 . . .181 C4
  Margate CT7, CT9 . . . . . . .28 A5
  Shadoxhurst TN26 . . . . . .155 A1
  Tenterden TN30 . . . . .179 D8
  Westgate on Sea CT7 . . . . .27 F3

Woodchurch Windmill*
  TN26 . . . . .169 A3
Woodcock Gdns CT18 . . . .163 A4
Woodcote CT5 . . . . .21 D1
Wood Cottage La CT19 . . .177 D7
Woodcourt CT10 . . . . .36 E2
Woodcut ME14 . . . . .75 A8
Woodfield Ave CT19 . . . . .177 E7
Woodfield Cl CT19 . . . . . .177 E7
Woodford Ave CT11, CT12 . .29 D1
Woodford Ct CT7 . . . . .27 A7
Woodford Rd ME16 . . . . . .74 B2
Woodgate CT4 . . . . .110 E3
Woodgate Cl ME13 . . . . . . .62 C8
Woodgate Ct ME13 . . . . . . .84 E7
Woodgate La ME9 . . . . .35 C2
Woodgates Cl TN26 . . . . . .167 D7
Woodgrove Prim Sch
  ME10 . . . . .36 D3
Woodhall Terr ME11 . . . . . . .3 A5
Wood Hill CT2 . . . . .66 E6
Woodhurst ME5 . . . . .31 D4
Wood La TN23 . . . . .156 D3
WOODLAND 160 F8
Woodland Ave
  Aylesham CT3 . . . . .112 C5
  Birchington CT7 . . . . .27 B6
Woodland Cl CT17 . . . . . .148 C2
Woodland Cotts CT18 . . . .161 B7
Woodland Dr ME12 . . . . .4 B7
Woodland Rd
  Herne Bay CT6 . . . . .22 B2
  Lyminge CT18 . . . . .160 E8
Woodlands
  Blean CT2 . . . . .65 F7
  Chatham ME5 . . . . .32 A2
  Coxheath ME17 . . . . .96 B3
  Hernhill ME13 . . . . .64 C7
Woodlands Cl
  Maidstone ME14 . . . . .75 B7
  Peasmarsh TN31 . . . . .196 C2
Woodlands Ct ME5 . . . . . . .31 F3
Woodlands Dr CT21 . . . . .177 A4
Woodlands Prim Sch ME7 10 F4
Woodlands Rd
  Adisham CT3 . . . . .112 C8
  Ashford TN24 . . . . .139 F2
  Gillingham ME7 . . . . .10 F4
  Sittingbourne ME10 . . . . . .37 B3
Woodlands Terr ME7 . . . . .10 F3
Woodland View TN30 . . . .188 E4
Woodland Way
  Broadstairs CT10 . . . . .8 G1
  Canterbury CT2 . . . . .66 D4
  Dymchurch TN29 . . . . . . .187 A5
  Maidstone ME14 . . . . .75 B7
  Woodnesborough CT13 . . . .93 C6
Woodlawn St CT5 . . . . .20 D2
Woodlea TN24 . . . . .139 C3
Woodman Ave CT5 . . . . . . .21 E3
WOODNESBOROUGH 93 C6
Woodnesborough La
  CT13 . . . . .93 B3
Woodnesborough Rd
  CT13 . . . . .93 E7
Woodpecker Dr ME9 . . . . .14 E4
Woodpecker Glade ME8 . . .33 D6
Wood Rd CT21 . . . . .176 B1
Woodrow Chase CT6 . . . . .23 A1
Woodruff Cl ME8 . . . . .12 D4
Woods Hill CT4 . . . . .125 C5
Woodshole Cotts ME9 . . . .14 D1
Woodside
  Ashford TN23 . . . . .155 E6
  Boughton Street ME13 . . . .64 B2
  Gillingham ME8 . . . . .33 C6
Woodside Ave CT4 . . . . . . .86 D2
Woodside Cl CT16 . . . . . . .148 E4
Woodside Cotts ME13 . . . . .64 B2
Woodside Gdns ME10 . . . . .36 D2

WOODSIDE GREEN 101 F8
Woodside Rd
  Maidstone ME15 . . . . .97 C7
  Sturry CT2 . . . . .67 F7
Woods Ley CT3 . . . . .71 D2
Wood's Pl CT17 . . . . .149 B2
Wood St
  Chatham ME7 . . . . .10 A6
  Dover CT16 . . . . .166 D8
  Lynsted ME9 . . . . .59 F8
  Sheerness ME12 . . . . .1 D2
WOODSTOCK 58 E6
Woodstock Rd
  Deal CT14 . . . . .117 C4
  Rochester ME2 . . . . .9 B7
  Sittingbourne ME10 . . . . . .36 E1
Woodstock Way TN24 . . . .139 C6
Woodvale Ave CT5 . . . . . . .44 C8
Wood View CT3 . . . . .46 E5
Woodville Cl CT1 . . . . .87 D6
Woodville Rd
  Maidstone ME15 . . . . .75 A2
  Ramsgate CT12 . . . . .29 C1
Wood Yd CT14 . . . . .117 D6
WOOLAGE GREEN 129 F8
WOOLAGE VILLAGE 112 F1
Woolaston Cl ME5 . . . . . . .74 F1
Woolbrook Cl ME8 . . . . . . .12 B2
Woolcomber St CT16 . . . . .166 E7
Wooldeys Rd ME5 . . . . .11 F2
Woolett Rd ME10 . . . . .36 C5
Woollatt Cl CT6 . . . . .22 C3
Woollett St ME14 . . . . .75 A5
Woolley Rd ME15 . . . . .97 F7
Woolmer Dr TN24 . . . . . . .157 A7
Woolpack Hill TN25 . . . . . .158 D5
Woolreeds Rd TN23 . . . . .156 A7
Woolwich Cl ME5 . . . . .32 A7
WOOTON 129 C1
Wootton Cl CT4 . . . . .109 A4
Wootton Dr CT4 . . . . .109 A4
Wootton La CT15, CT4 . . . .146 C7
Wopsle Cl ME1 . . . . .31 D7
Worcester Cl
  Faversham ME13 . . . . .62 E6
  Minster (Sheppey) ME12 . . . .4 C6
Worcester Dr ME10 . . . . . .36 D6
Worcester Gr CT10 . . . . . . .29 F6
Worcester La CT3 . . . . .88 E7
Worcester Rd ME15 . . . . . .97 D7
Wordsworth Cl ME5 . . . . . .32 C7
Wordsworth Cl ME13 . . . .112 F6
Wordsworth Rd ME14 . . . . .75 B7
Workhouse La
  Chartway Street ME17 . . . . .99 A1
  Coxheath ME15 . . . . .96 C4
Workhouse Rd ME13 . . . . .82 F1
World's End ME9 . . . . .60 E7
Wormdale Hill ME9 . . . . . .35 B3
Wormdale Rd ME9 . . . . . . .35 B4
WORMSHILL 79 A7
Worsfold Ct **5** ME15 . . . . .75 A1
WORTEN 137 F3
WORTH 94 B4
Worthgate Pl **2** CT1 . . . .87 F7
Worthington St **11** CT16,
  CT17 . . . . .166 D8
Worth La CT20 . . . . .177 E3
Worth Prim Sch CT14 . . . . .94 B5
Wotton Cl ME15 . . . . .97 E5
Wotton Rd TN23 . . . . .156 B6
Wotton Trad Est TN23 . . . .156 B6
Wraightsfield Ave TN29 . 195 D8
Wraik Hill CT5 . . . . .43 C5
Wrangleden Cl ME15 . . . . .97 E5
Wrangleden Rd ME15 . . . . .97 E5
Wreight Ct ME13 . . . . .40 B1
Wren Ind Est ME15 . . . . . . .97 F4

Wren's Cross ME15 . . . . . . .75 A3
Wrens Ct ME9 . . . . .58 A8
Wrens Rd ME9 . . . . .58 A7
Wrentham Ave CT6 . . . . . . .22 B2
Wren Way ME5 . . . . .32 B6
Wright Cl ME8 . . . . .11 C2
Wrights Cl TN30 . . . . .179 A8
Wright's Way ME12 . . . . . . .17 C8
Wrotham Ave **20** CT10 . . .30 B4
Wrotham Rd CT10 . . . . .30 B4
Wyatt Ho **1** ME2 . . . . .9 A7
Wyatt Pl ME2 . . . . .9 A7
Wyatt St ME14 . . . . .75 A4
Wych Elm Way CT21 . . . . .187 E8
Wycherley Cres CT16 . . . .149 B7
WYE 123 F1
Wye Bsns Pk TN25 . . . . . .123 E3
Wye Gdns CT9 . . . . .8 F2
Wye Gn CT6 . . . . .22 F3
Wye National Nature
  Reserve* TN25 . . . . .141 D7
Wye Rd TN25 . . . . .122 F3
Wye Sta TN25 . . . . .123 D2
Wykeham Cl ME11 . . . . .2 F3
Wykeham Cotts ME17 . . . . .96 F2
Wykeham Rd ME17 . . . . . . .99 A7
Wykeham Rd ME10 . . . . . . .37 B4
Wykeham St ME2 . . . . .9 B8
Wyke Manor Rd ME14 . . . .75 A4
Wyles Rd ME4 . . . . .9 E2
Wyles St ME7 . . . . .10 C7
Wyllie Ct ME10 . . . . .36 E7
Wyndham Ave CT9 . . . . .8 B2
Wyndham Rd
  Chatham ME4 . . . . .9 E2
  Dover CT17 . . . . .166 B8
Wynd The TN27 . . . . .103 D1
Wyndy La TN25 . . . . .138 F4
Wynn Ellis Ho CT5 . . . . . . .20 E3
Wynn Rd CT5 . . . . .21 A2
Wytchlings The ME17 . . . . .99 D2
Wytherling Cl ME14 . . . . . .75 F5
Wyvern Cl ME10 . . . . .36 E7
Wyvern Sch The TN23 . . . .138 E1
Wyvern Way TN24 . . . . . .139 C3
Wyvill Cl ME8 . . . . .33 E5

Y

Yardhurst Gdns CT9 . . . . . . .8 F3
Yardley Ho CT10 . . . . .30 B7
Yard The
  Barham CT4 . . . . .111 F1
  Chatham ME5 . . . . .32 B3
Yarrow Cl CT10 . . . . .30 A3
Yarrow Ct ME14 . . . . .75 F5
Yarrow Dr ME12 . . . . .4 A5
Yarrow Rd ME5 . . . . .31 F4
Yates Cl TN31 . . . . .203 A2
Yaugher La ME9 . . . . .34 C3
Yeates Dr ME10 . . . . .37 A8
Yellow Sands ME12 . . . . . .19 E5
YELSTED 34 A1
Yelsted La
  Chatham ME14 . . . . .54 D7
  Yelsted ME5 . . . . .34 A1
Yelsted Rd ME9 . . . . .56 A7
Yeoman Ct ME14 . . . . .76 B3
Yeoman Dr ME7 . . . . .10 F1
Yeoman Gdns TN24 . . . . . .157 B8
Yeoman Ho ME1 . . . . .9 D4
Yeoman La ME14 . . . . .76 B4
Yeoman Pk ME15 . . . . .76 A2
Yeomans Dr CT2 . . . . .87 C8
Yeomans Sq TN23 . . . . . . .155 D8
Yeoman Way ME15 . . . . . . .76 A2
Yevele Cl ME11 . . . . .3 A5
Yew Cl TN23 . . . . .138 E2
Yew Hedges ME13 . . . . . . .81 E4

Win−Zio 245

Yew Tree Cl
  Broadstairs CT10 . . . . .29 D4
  Chatham ME5 . . . . .32 D1
  Deal CT14 . . . . .117 A4
  Stanford TN25 . . . . .160 B1
Yew Tree Cotts ME14 . . . . .53 F1
Yewtree Cross CT18 . . . . .161 C8
Yew Tree Farm CT3 . . . . . .114 A8
Yew Tree Gdns
  Birchington CT7 . . . . .27 A7
  Fordwich CT2 . . . . .68 A4
Yewtree Ho **2** ME1 . . . . . . .9 D4
Yew Tree Mews CT14 . . . .117 A3
Yew Tree Pk ME7 . . . . . . .102 F1
Yew Tree Pl ME7 . . . . .83 E8
Yew Tree Rd TN29 . . . . . .194 F3
Yoakes La TN29 . . . . .192 F1
Yoakley Sq CT9 . . . . .28 F8
Yoke Cl ME2 . . . . .9 B8
Yokosuka Way ME7 . . . . . . .11 A7
York Ave
  18 Broadstairs CT10 . . . . .30 B4
  Chatham ME5 . . . . .31 F3
  Gillingham ME7 . . . . .10 C4
York Cl CT6 . . . . .22 D4
York Hill ME5 . . . . .10 C3
York Ho **10** CT17 . . . . . . .166 D7
YORKLETTS 42 F2
York Mews CT19 . . . . .177 E7
York Rd
  Ashford TN24 . . . . .139 D5
  Canterbury CT1 . . . . .87 E7
  Deal CT14 . . . . .117 D4
  Herne Bay CT6 . . . . .22 D5
  Maidstone ME15 . . . . .75 C2
  Rochester ME1 . . . . .9 C3
York St
  Broadstairs CT10 . . . . .30 B4
  Dover CT16, CT17 . . . . . .166 D7
  Ramsgate CT11 . . . . .52 E6
York Street Rdbt CT16,
  CT17 . . . . .166 D7
York Terr CT7 . . . . .27 B7
Young Cl CT14 . . . . .117 B6
Young's Pl CT15 . . . . .164 F5
Ypres Ct CT1 . . . . .67 D1
Ypres Dr ME10 . . . . .14 F1

Z

Zarena Ct **8** CT20 . . . . . .177 F3
Zealand Rd CT1 . . . . .87 F6
Zetland Ave ME7 . . . . .10 E2
Zillah Gdns ME8 . . . . .33 C6
Zion Pl CT9 . . . . .7 J3